MySQL

Building
User Interfaces

Contents at a Glance

MySQL
Building User Interfaces

Matthew Stucky

New Riders

www.newriders.com

201 West 103rd Street, Indianapolis, Indiana 46290
An Imprint of Pearson Education
Boston • Indianapolis • London • Munich • New York • San Francisco

MySQL: Building User Interfaces

Trademarks

Warning and Disclaimer

Publisher
David Dwyer

Associate Publisher
Al Valvano

Executive Editor
Stephanie Wall

Managing Editor
Gina Kanouse

Acquisitions Editor
Ann Quinn

Development Editor
Laura Loveall

Product Marketing Manager
Stephanie Layton

Publicity Manager
Susan Nixon

Project Editors
Kristy Knoop
Caroline Wise
Todd Zellers

Copy Editors
Audra McFarland
Gayle Johnson

Indexer
Lisa Stumpf

Manufacturing Coordinator
Jim Conway

Book Designer
Louisa Klucznik

Cover Designer
Brainstorm Design, Inc.

Cover Production
Aren Howell

Proofreader
Debra Neel

❖

To Mom and Dad, of course, for getting me off on the right foot, and Jena, for all the blessings I now enjoy.

❖

Table of Contents

About the Author

Matthew Stucky was born and raised in Colorado. He graduated from the University of Colorado in 1990 and served four years in the U.S. Navy as an officer. Soon after release from active duty, he enrolled at the University of West Florida to obtain a master's degree in software engineering, graduating in the summer of 1998. By that time he had worked as a Novell LAN administrator and an Access, VB, and SQL Server developer. Since then he has worked for Dimensional Insight (www.dimins.com) as a consultant, utilizing a wide variety of tools, including all manner of databases, operating systems, and software. He still maintains that the best thing about UWF was the football team—go War Snails!

About the Technical Reviewers

These reviewers contributed their considerable hands-on expertise to the entire development process for *MySQL: Building User Interfaces*. As the book was being written, these dedicated professionals reviewed all the material for technical content, organization, and flow. Their feedback was critical to ensuring that *MySQL: Building User Interfaces* fits our readers' needs for the highest quality technical information.

John Dean received a BSc(Hons) from the University of Sheffield in 1974 in Pure Science. It was as an undergraduate at Sheffield that John developed his interest in computing. In 1986, John received an MSc from Cranfield Institute of Science and Technology in Control Engineering. While working for Roll Royce and Associates, John became involved in developing control software for computer-aided inspection equipment of a nuclear steam raising plant. Since leaving RR&A in 1978, he has worked in the Petrochemical Industry developing and maintaining process control software. From 1996, John worked as a volunteer software developer for MySQL until May 2000 when he joined MySQL as a full-time employee. John's area of responsibility is MySQL on MS Windows and developing a new MySQL GUI client using Trolltech's Qt GUI application toolkit on both Windows and platforms that run X-11.

Hang T. Lau is an adjunct professor of the Computer Science Department at Concordia University in Montreal, Canada. He has worked as a systems engineer for Nortel Networks for the past twenty years in areas including network planning, speech recognition applications in telecommunication, and transport access radio network systems.

Acknowledgments

First off, I would like to thank New Riders Publishing for taking a chance on a new author, and immeasurable thanks to my Development Editor, Laura Loveall, for her patience and guidance throughout the entire process. I would also like to thank Ann Quinn and Stephanie Wall for their help and guidance.

An equal heaping helping of thanks goes out to my tech editors, John Dean and Hang Lau, who kept me from making some really inexcusable errors in front of the whole world. Any other errors or omissions are my responsibility, and mine alone.

Additionally, there are a number of "point problem solvers" who stepped in and helped me with some very thorny issues as this book was in development. Special thanks go out to: Havoc Pennington at Red Hat, Monty Widenius at MySQL, Tor Lilqvist for his work to port GTK+ and Gimp to Windows, and Jan Dvorak who provided the `libmysqlclient.a` file to finish out Chapter 13, "Compiling the Key Business Indicators Application." Also thanks to Paul DuBois, author of *MySQL* (the seminal work on the subject), for his help in the early stages of this book.

I would also like to acknowledge everyone who has contributed to Linux, any open source project, and especially the tools used in this book.

Tell Us What You Think

As the reader of this book, you are the most important critic and commentator. We value your opinion and want to know what we're doing right, what we could do better, what areas you'd like to see us publish in, and any other words of wisdom you're willing to pass our way.

As the Executive Editor for the Web Development team at New Riders Publishing, I welcome your comments. You can fax, email, or write me directly to let me know what you did or didn't like about this book—as well as what we can do to make our books stronger.

Please note that I cannot help you with technical problems related to the topic of this book, and that due to the high volume of mail I receive, I might not be able to reply to every message. When you write, please be sure to include this book's title and author as well as your name and phone or fax number. I will carefully review your comments and share them with the author and editors who worked on the book.

Fax: 317-581-4663
Email: stephanie.wall@newriders.com
Mail: Stephanie Wall
         Executive Editor
         New Riders Publishing
         201 West 103rd Street
         Indianapolis, IN 46290 USA

Introduction

What brought the database to the small business? I believe it was Microsoft Access and its $119 price tag, which at the time undercut the competition by orders of magnitude. Running on the relatively recent technology of Windows 3.x, it provided a very powerful tool for businesses that had previously only wished for such technology. Many businesses today are shelling out a lot of money for software for their employees. If you have 200 employees all of whom need an operating system and office suite, it can run to more than $1,000 per employee in licensed software. That's $200,000 to outfit a business with new or upgraded software. Businesses pay it because it is a necessary cost of doing business in today's economy, and that is just for the software. Additional costs include the system administrators, database administrators, and programmers. If your organization is viewing the potential cost savings of a Linux desktop and you are wondering about databases and custom database applications and how to write them, this book is for you.

I believe the time is ripe for businesses to discover the cost savings—without loss of functionality—that Linux offers. This book attempts to show that existing client/server skills can be transferred to the Linux arena, and that Linux and Windows can coexist. This book attempts to show that "it can be done, and it's not that difficult." There are other books on the market that discuss Star Office and other cross-platform office suites; this work is directed at the Information Systems department that has done some type of client/server programming, such as SQL Server and Visual Basic, and is interested to see how those skills can be leveraged in the Windows environment.

I also believe that "every business problem is a database problem" and that the cost of capturing, cleaning, and reporting on "data" is no longer an optional part of doing business. Linux is making great inroads to the desktop market in an attempt to show that custom software applications can be ported to the Linux desktop.

Who Should Read This Book

This book is primarily aimed at corporate developers who are either using or considering using Linux in their organizations and who have some Windows client/server experience such as VB and SQL Server. Secondarily, it is intended to serve as a guide to assist businesses in converting to Linux and to answer questions for software project managers regarding the feasibility of such projects.

Skills Expected of the Reader

This is not a beginner level text. The author has made the following assumptions about the reader's technical expertise:

- *C.* The code in this book is in C, but no C tutorial is given.

- *"Visual" development.* A very basic understanding of GUI development will be helpful; Visual Basic or Visual C++ will be more than adequate. This book makes the assumption that the reader has done some (or is at least familiar) with custom database programming; Visual Basic is assumed to be the starting point for most readers. In Chapters 2, 3, and 4, for example, there are a number of comparisons between GTK+ "widgets" and VB "controls." If you don't know what a "VB control" is, you may have a tough time following along.

- *Database administration experience.* The sections in the book that set up and fill database tables for the application make the assumption that the reader is familiar with relational data and their structures. Access, SQL Server, or similar experience should be sufficient.

- *Basic Linux expertise.* You should know the basics of the Linux operating system, for example, how to move around the file system, launch programs, and so on.

- *SQL and relational database theory and practice.* The SQL in the examples makes no attempt to explain how or why database tables are joined.

- A very basic understanding of XML will be helpful, although I have included a simple explanation in Chapter 5.

Organization of This Book

Part I, "Quick and Dirty," deals with the main tools used throughout the book. MySQL is covered in Chapter 1, "MySQL for Access and SQL Server Developers and DBAs." MySQL is the database that will be used in all examples throughout this book; it will be the "backend database" for the example applications. GTK+ is covered in Chapter 2, "GTK+ for VB Developers," Chapter 3, "More GTK+ Widgets," and Chapter 4, "Advanced GTK+ Layout Widgets." GTK+ is the toolkit that will be used to create the user interfaces (UI's) in the example projects. Glade is covered in Chapter 5, "Glade for VB Developers." Glade is the integrated development environment (IDE) that will be used to point-and-click the UI into place "visually" so that the creation of the UI becomes much simpler.

Part II, "Real World Implementations," presents the following three "demo projects" taken from my personal experience working in the industry:

- *Project 1: Order Entry, A Simple Transactional Application* is covered in Chapter 6, "Order Entry Abstract and Design," and Chapter 7, "Construction of the SESI Order Entry Application."

- *Project 2: Worldwide Commissions Application* is a simple data processing system, and it is covered in Chapter 8, "Commission Calculations Abstract and Design," Chapter 9, "Constructing the Commissions Application," and Chapter 10, "Commission Calculations Deployment."

- *Project 3: Management Reporting, Key Business Indicators* is a simple reporting/graphing system. It is covered in Chapter 11, "Management Reporting Abstract and Design," Chapter 12, "Management Reporting Construction," and Chapter 13, "Compiling the Key Business Indicators Application."

Chapter 14, "Dynamic User Interface Control with XML," gives a couple of quick demonstrations on how to use `glade.h` to build user interfaces at runtime versus compile time.

The appendixes contain files relevant to the projects but that are not directly covered in the main chapters; in general, this means the `interface.c` file and the `*.glade` file as generated by Glade. Appendix A, "Glade-Generated Files from the SESI Order Application," has some supporting code listings from Project 1 (Chapters 6 and 7). Appendix B, "Glade-Generated Files from the Worldwide Commissions Application," has those same files for Project 2 (Chapters 8, 9, 10). Appendix C, "Glade-Generated Files from the Key Business Indicators Application," has the support files for Project 3 (Chapters 11, 12, and 13).

Conventions Used in This Book

This book follows a few typographical conventions:

- A new term is set in *italics* the first time it is introduced.

- Program text, functions, variables, and other "computer language" are set in a fixed-pitch font, for example, `printf ("Hello, world!\bksl n")`.

- Names of commands, files, and directories are also set in a fixed-pitch font, for example, `cd /`.

- When I show interactions with a command shell, I use `%` as the shell prompt (your shell is probably configured to use a different prompt). Everything after the prompt is what you type, while other lines of text are the system's response.

For example, in this interaction,

```
% uname
Linux
```

the system prompted you with %. You entered the uname command. The system responded by printing Linux.

- Where it is useful, line numbers have been added to the code listing, but that is not the case in every code listing. Where a code listing shows line numbers to the left of the code, like this

```
001  #include <stdio.h>
002  #include <gtk/gtk.h>
003  /* This program ....
```

the reader should remember that these line numbers are not part of the program.

I wrote this book and developed the programs listed in it using the Red Hat 6.2 distribution of GNU/Linux. This distribution incorporates release 2.2.14 of the Linux kernel, release 2.1.3 of the GNU C library, and the EGCS 1.1.2 release of the GNU C compiler. The information and programs in this book should generally be applicable to other versions and distributions of GNU/Linux as well, including 2.4 releases of the Linux kernel and 2.2 releases of the GNU C library.

I

Quick and Dirty

MySQL for Access and SQL Server Developers and DBAs

THIS CHAPTER PRESENTS MYSQL PRIMARILY AS IT DIFFERS FROM Microsoft's databases (Access and MS SQL Server). Those two are the most common in the marketplace, and database administrators range from the complete newbie to the seasoned veteran.

This chapter assumes that you are somewhat familiar with at least one of those products or something similar. Because this book is targeted at those who are converting to MySQL from another database, it presents differences, omissions, and additions.

Specifically, you should meet these basic requirements:

- Have some experience with a relational database; MS Access and SQL Server are as good as any.

- Have some experience with SQL.

- Have an understanding of two- and three-tier client/server application development, even if only from a theoretical standpoint.

- Be familiar with the basics of the Linux system, such as how to move around the directory tree, use basic commands, and so on.

Why You Should Use MySQL

What are some advantages of using MySQL? Why is it a good choice? Can it stand up to enterprise-level work? MySQL is a highly capable database that can compete with anything on the market for these reasons:

- *Speed.* MySQL is very lean. The MySQL Web site maintains data on how MySQL stacks up against several other database products. See for yourself at http://www.mysql.com/information/crash-me.php.

- *Scalability.* MySQL can handle an unlimited number of simultaneous users and 50 million records. Most likely, you won't outgrow it anytime soon.

- *Simplicity.* MySQL is for those who know what they're doing so that they can work around or program their own advanced functions, such as stored procedures or subselects. MySQL is at its core a small, fast database, and keeping it this way means that certain resource-intensive features are kept out by design.

- *Cost.* Is MySQL free? Yes. (See the next section.) If you do purchase a license, your cost will be around $200—not bad for a world-class database that stands shoulder-to-shoulder with the best.

- *Portability.* If MySQL hasn't been ported to your platform, it probably will be soon, and if it isn't, you can do the port yourself. Because you can compile from source, you can at least compile it to run on whatever machine you use. MySQL already works on all major platforms: MS Windows, Linux, Sun, and so on.

Licensing Issues

To those who are unfamiliar with the "Open Source" software movement, it often means "free." The term "free software" scares a lot of people, especially those used to paying for software that doesn't function as advertised. Yes, you can get a lot of software off the Net for no cost (other than electricity and phone time), but you will probably "pay for it" one way or another. The normal mode of payment is in the form of a steep learning curve—as in, "there is no GUI." So if your time is limited, you should seriously consider using software with an easier learning curve.

Most "professional database administrators," however, appreciate power features more than your typical manager or others who might be interested in a database product. Plus, once you learn the fundamentals of what makes up a good database, that knowledge transfers to other products readily because MySQL is ANSI 92-compliant.

As of June 2000, MySQL is General Public License (GPL). What does that mean? To most people, it means you can download the software and use it, even to run your business. However, because I do not officially or unofficially speak for anyone at MySQL, I will take the liberty of reprinting the following paragraph from their Web site (http://www.mysql.com/information/index.html):

"MySQL is Open Source Software. Open source means that it is possible for anyone to use and modify. Anybody can download MySQL from the Internet and use it without paying anything. Anybody so inclined can study the source code and change it to fit their needs. MySQL uses the GPL (GNU General Public License) http://www.gnu.org, to define what you may and may not do with the software in different situations. If you feel uncomfortable with the GPL or need to embed MySQL into a commercial application you can buy a commercially licensed version from us."

You will have to decide if that fits your needs. For a full text of the GPL, go to www.gnu.org. In practice, MySQL is free for all uses, except when you embed MySQL into a not-open-source program, in which case you can buy a license to get the MySQL source under another copyright. MySQL AB makes most of their money not on license revenue but by providing many different kinds of support for MySQL. This strategy ensures that they stay close to their users and also that they get money so they can continue developing MySQL.

Datatypes: MySQL Compared to Access 2000 and SQL Server 7

Table 1.1 lists data types (column types) for MySQL as they are compared to Access 2000 and SQL Server 7. Note that some types have no corresponding type; those entries are blank.

If you are converting a database or wondering whether your data will fit into one of MySQL's types, Table 1.1 might be of help. Additionally, although two data (or column) types might have the same name, their storage requirements might be different.

Table 1.1   Datatype Conversion Matrix, MySQL, Access2000, and SQL Server 7

Datatype	Storage in Bytes	Access2000	SQL Server 7	Notes
tinyint	1	byte	tinyint	
smallint	2	integer	smallint	
mediumint	3			
int	4	Long Integer	int or integer	
bigint	8			
float	4	single	float[1] or real	
double	8	double		
decimal	1 per digit + 2		decimal, numeric[2]	
char	1 per character	text, memo	char	
varchar	length + 1		varchar[3]	
tinyblob	length + 1			
blob	length + 2			
mediumblob	length + 3			

continues

Table 1.1   **Continued**

Datatype	Storage in Bytes	Access2000	SQL Server 7	Notes
longblob	length + 4		binary, varbinary	
tinytext	length + 1			255 max
text	length + 2			65,535 max
mediumtext	length + 3			16,777,215 max
longtext	length + 4			
enum	1 for 1–255 members 2 for 256–65,535 members			
set	1 for 1–8 members 2 for 9–16 3 for 17–24 4 for 25–32 8 for 33–64			
date	3			
time	3			
datetime	8	date/time	datetime, timestamp	
timestamp	4		smalldatetime	0 is midnight, 1/1/1970
year	1			1900–2155
	16 for a pointer		image, text	
format()[4]	8	currency	money	
	2 × number of chars		nchar	Fixed length Unicode
	16 + 2 × number of chars		ntext	Variable length Unicode
	2 × number of chars		nvarchar	Unicode
	4		smallmoney	
	16		Uniqueidentifier	
	12	decimal		

1. *For float, 4–8 bytes, depending on the precision specified*

2. *5–17 bytes*

3. *Length, not length + 1*

4. *Although it's not a "data type," the MySQL* **FORMAT ( )** *function yields the same results.*

As you can see, MySQL offers many more choices. MySQL is far more flexible in the integer and text types, but it lacks the dedicated currency types. In essence, MySQL requires you to somewhat know and understand your data—more than Access or SQL Server do, anyway. MySQL is strongest in the text, numeric, and date types, but it lacks defined money types.

What MySQL Lacks

The following section is not short, nor are some of the missing things trivial, such as a stored procedure language, triggers, and enforced referential integrity. MySQL is GPL; it is open source. The same hacker community that built the Internet is working on and improving MySQL; any image it has to protect is one based on competence, not marketing. Personally, I would rather hear the downside up front than find out when I am hip-deep in code that "you can't do that."

Therefore, the following sections present some of the shortcomings of MySQL. Table 1.2 summarizes what MySQL lacks, and the following sections provide pertinent information about each feature that was available at the time this book was written.

Table 1.2   **Quick Guide to Functionality Missing from MySQL**

Functionality	Notes
GUI	In progress when this book was written.
Stored procedures	Scheduled for version 4.1; Zend scripting engine. Possibly Python and others, too.
Referential integrity	Reported to be in alpha testing.
Transactions	New table-type BDB supports transactions, but MyISAM is still considered the "default" table type.
Cursors	Reported to be implemented in 4.1.
Triggers	Scheduled for version 4.1; Zend scripting engine.
Record-level locking	Scheduled for version 4.
Subselects	Scheduled for version 4.1.
Named views	Single-table views should be in 4.0 or 4.1. Multi-table views should be in 4.1.

GUI: "Houston, We Have Command Line Only"

Get used to it: MySQL is designed to be used from the command line. Owing to Linux's UNIX heritage, that should come as no surprise. It's just an observation, but my experience is that the "power db admins" use and prefer command-line functionality over GUI. Why? Well, the learning curve is steeper, but after that's conquered, productivity goes up. (Specifically, being able to write complex shell scripts to perform advanced functionality can be an extremely powerful tool.) Think of the difference between vi and Notepad (if you are familiar with vi). Yes, it is harder to learn, but in the end, the more difficult tool is more productive.

Actually, as this was being written, a GUI was in beta. Figure 1.1 shows the main form.

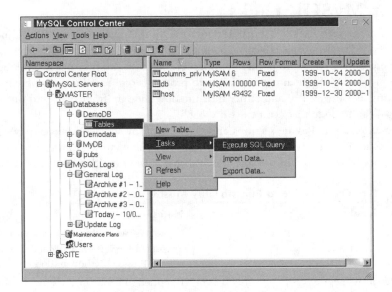

Figure 1.1   Beta stages of the MySQL client GUI interface.

As you can see, not all the functionality was available, but like everything else in the Open Source universe, that will continue to change rapidly. If this is of interest to you, by the time this book is in print, a fully developed product might be worth investigating.

Transactions

When you need to conform to business rules and maintain data integrity, you can use a *transaction* to ensure that multiple operations against a database are all complete or that they are all incomplete and the data is in its original state. The most common example of this is when a bank transfers money between two accounts. The bank doesn't want to credit one account and then find that the debit from the originating account failed. That would leave the money in both accounts. The idea of transactions is that before any changes are *committed* to the database, all actions have been completed successfully. If not, all pending changes must be "rolled back," and the data is reset to original values.

Actually, as this book was being written, MySQL posted a press release claiming that the program supports transactions (of sorts). In a press release dated May 9, 2000, MySQL announced "experimental support" in version 3.23.15 for Berkely DB from

SleepyCat Software (www.sleepycat.com), "a transaction-safe database handler." Version 3.23.25 fully implemented this, but it is not enabled by default. The press release is at http://www.mysql.com/news/index.html. From there you can follow the link to see if this will suit your needs.

It appears that MySQL is introducing a new table type ("BDB"), with which you can use a Begin/Commit/Rollback syntax and mechanism. (I did not have a chance to play with this before finishing this book.) By the time you have this book, there should be available a MySQL binary with BDB support. With BDB tables, it appears you can do all the standard stuff you expect from transactions: BEGIN, COMMIT, ROLLBACK, and also working in AUTOCOMMIT mode. As always, check the MySQL Web site for the latest, and subscribe to the announcements mailing list.

You can partially emulate transactions (in other table types) by locking the tables in question, but you must supply your own rollback mechanism. See http://www.mysql.com for a discussion of COMMIT/ROLLBACK, paying particular attention to the section "How to Cope Without Commit/Rollback."

Stored Procedures and Cursors

A *stored procedure* is a series of statements grouped into a single "program" that can be executed in the database. The advantage of stored procedures is that they can be optimized by the database for maximum performance. Also, the database can have a "stored procedure language" that normally resembles a hybrid of SQL and a "programming language." This pseudo-language allows you to manipulate data in ways that are not standard to SQL—specifically, iterating row-by-row through the data in order to manipulate individual fields or maintain variables. Such row-by-row iterations are called *cursors*.

Because MySQL lacks a stored procedure mechanism, specialized language, and cursors, you must supply your own mechanism.

A stored procedure mechanism is on the MySQL developers' "to do" list; it's reported that it will be included in version 4.

How to Emulate Stored Procedures and Cursors

Now that you know stored procedures and cursors are not part of MySQL, here are a few hints on how to emulate them.

For standard SQL-compliant statements, you can create a text file that contains the SQL statements, including select statements. You separate SQL statements with semicolons. The text file can then be fed to mysql to perform the queries, as follows:

```
% mysql test_db < day_check.sql
```

mysql is the program name of the MySQL client, and test_db is the database to which it should connect. day_check.sql is the text file that contains the SQL statements. Multiple SQL statements are separated by semicolons. Note that this is the short syntax using the defaults; your installation might require something along these lines:

```
%mysql --host=localhost --user=yourname --password=your_pword test_db <
day_check.sql
```

If you need more advanced capabilities, such as the ability to iterate by row and make changes, you will probably have to create a program that connects to your MySQL database and that does the processing in another language, such as C, PHP, or Perl. To emulate cursors, you must encapsulate row-by-row processing in your C programs outside the database. You will see many examples of this throughout the book.

Triggers

A *trigger* is a procedure, usually in the database's stored procedure language (an embedded scripting language such as Zend or Python), that can be set to "fire" when an event happens, such as when a table is deleted, updated, or added to. For example, if you wanted auditing on a database to know who changed, added, or deleted what data and when, you might set triggers for all three events for all tables. That way, if some data was found to be incorrect, you could follow the audit trail to find out when the data was changed and possibly by whom.

If an audit trail is high on your list, look carefully into the logging capabilities already built into MySQL. The `--log` option to `safe_mysqld` produces a detailed log file. If really detailed logging is necessary, consider starting `safe_mysqld` with the `--debug` option. If you only want to record what's happening, you should use the `--log-bin` option.

If you have triggers in your C programs, you must supply your own triggers in your C code, as you will see in examples later in this book. In short, you must know what you want to happen and then program your own mechanism for doing it.

As a final note, this is scheduled to be implemented in version 4 using the Zend scripting engine. Word has it that it will be a general API that will work with any scripting engine, but it will initially work with Zend and Python.

Enforced Foreign Key Referential Integrity

Foreign key referential integrity requires you to have an entry in one table in order to make an entry in another table. For example, suppose you have two tables: an invoice header table and an invoice line item table. It makes no sense to enter rows into the line item table unless you have matching rows in the invoice header table first. If you go to join the two tables on `InvoiceNumber`, the rows from the line item table that do not have corresponding entries in the header table will be left out of the result set. In this case, referential integrity would require that an entry exist in the invoice header table before one could be created in the invoice line items table.

Although MySQL supports the FOREIGN KEY keywords in the CREATE TABLE statement, that's for portability to other databases. MySQL doesn't enforce referential integrity. Of course, if you can't do this in your application, you have probably made some mistakes already. (That is, if you understand the concept of referential integrity, you can add and delete records correctly without a mechanism to enforce it.)

To do this, you must know what you're doing: You must understand your data and your application, and you must program both to support your requirements. (As this book goes to press, this is in alpha testing.)

Record-Level Locking

Normally, you don't want any two persons or applications connected to a database to be able to overwrite the same data in the same record in the same table. Therefore, some databases allow you to lock the data at the "row" level. This means that the first person to start making changes has the data "locked," and when he is finished, the data is unlocked, and the next person can make changes.

MySQL doesn't support record-level locking, although you can use table-level locking. (BDB tables, mentioned previously, do support page-level locking.) When designing your database and application, you might have to take this into consideration, but there are ways to get around it if you anticipate it will be a problem. For example, you could set up an area to handle table additions and have a separate set of tables for updates and deletions. Or you could create a table of "pending changes" that anyone can append to and then use an automated mechanism to execute the changes on a regular basis, such as every 5 minutes or every night, depending on the requirements.

So, what happens when there is a conflict, such as when two separate processes try to update the same table? In such a case, one of the processes has to wait until the other is finished. Updates are considered to have priority over selects, but that can be changed. For more information and a discussion of how to change priorities, see the section titled "Table Locking Issues" at http://www.mysql.com/documentation/mysql/ bychapter/manual_Performance.html.

Finally, this is reported to be included in the version 4 release.

Subselects

In SQL, you could use the following command to select when the amount is less than the average order amount, even if you don't know the average order amount ahead of time:

```
select * from tbl_orders where order_amount < (select avg(order_amount) from
tbl_orders);
```

The second select statement (the one in parentheses) is called a *subselect*.

MySQL does not support subselects, but workarounds are often possible. Obviously, one very easy way around using subselects in the previous example is to query first for the average order amount and then work that result into your SQL statement for the "main" query. Clearly, to do this, you need some mechanism for storing the first result for use; this is straightforward when you use C or other procedural languages.

Another workaround is to store the result in a server-side variable:

```
select @a:=avg(order_amount) from tbl_orders);
select * from tbl_orders where order_amount < @a;
```

Still another way to get around this is through the use of temporary tables. In the preceding example, you could create a table of one row to hold the average order amount, join that table with the orders table (not using any join criteria, thus appending a column with the average order repeated for each row), and then use a calculation to compare the order amount to the average order amount on a row-by-row basis. The advantage of this approach is that it uses all SQL, and with MySQL, the temporary tables are dropped automatically when the connection that created them is closed.

Again, this is reportedly to be included in the version 4 release.

Named Views

These are "logical tables" or defined views, normally of multiple tables. For example, if you had an Invoice Header table and an Invoice Line Item table (in a one-to-many relationship), you could define an "Invoice View" that would show all columns for both tables in which the invoice number was the same. Views are normally defined within the database, where the database engine can optimize the view and maintain it.

MySQL does not support views, but it is on the to-do list. You can emulate this by putting the SQL statement defining the view into a text file in your project directory and then feeding the contents of the text file to the MySQL server. (The people at MySQL tell me that single-table views should be in 4.0 or 4.1. Multi-table views should be in 4.1.)

MySQL, MYSQL, and mysql—They're Not the Same Thing

MySQL, MYSQL, and mysql are three very different things. When each one is used, it references something different from the others. Throughout this chapter and the entire book, when you see one of these terms, remember that it refers to something very specific:

- MySQL is the overall database—the entire package.
- MYSQL is a C API structure for managing a connection to a database.
- mysql is the client package—the tool you use to communicate with a MySQL database server from the command line. It is also the name of the database that stores system information (what you might expect to be called "sysobjects" or "systables" in other databases).

mysql: The Command-Line Interface

The program *mysql* is really one of a suite of utilities for accessing and managing MySQL. The mysql program has been the standard way to access data in a MySQL implementation. It is roughly equivalent to MS SQL Server's `isql` or `osql` utility.

mysql is normally used as described here. From the command prompt, type `mysql`. This causes the command prompt to change to `mysql>`. Type in your SQL statement, and terminate it with a semicolon:

```
% mysql
mysql> select * from tbl_sales_people;
```

Usage:

```
% mysql [OPTIONS] [database_name]
```

The mysql program takes several command-line flags that are of interest. They are listed in Table 1.3.

Table 1.3 **The More Common mysql Command Flags**

Option Short	Option Long	Description
-B	--batch	Runs in batch; results are output in tab-delimited format with column headers in the first row. To suppress column headers, use the --skip-column-names option.
-T	--debug-info	Outputs debug info at program end. The information includes such things as user time, page faults, and so on.
-e qry	--execute=qry	Executes the query specified, and then quits. Enclose qry in quotation marks; separate multiple queries with semicolons.
-f	--force	Continues processing when an error occurs; the default behavior is to exit when an error occurs.
-H	--html	Outputs in HTML. Specifically, inserts table tags into the data output.
-I	--ignore-space	Ignores spaces between function names and the parentheses that hold the argument list. The default behavior requires that the first parenthesis immediately follow the function name.
-q	--quick	Displays each row as it is retrieved; the default is to wait for all rows from the server before displaying.
-N	--skip-column-names	Does not display column headers in results.
-t	--table	Outputs in table format, with columns lined up and separated by vertical bars (the | character). This is the default.

continues

Table 1.3 **Continued**

Option Short	Option Long	Description
-E	--vertical	Prints query results vertically, each line with a column name and value.
-w	--wait	Waits and attempts again to connect to the MySQL server if a connection cannot be made.

In addition, from the mysql> prompt, you can issue a number of commands. These are listed in Table 1.4.

Table 1.4 **Common Commands to Use at the *mysql>* Prompt**

Short Command	Long Command	Description
\c	clear	Cancels a command; *not* for queries that have been sent and are in the process of returning results.
\r	connect	Connects to a specified host. Usage: \r [database_name [host_name]] connect [database_name [host_name]]
\e	edit	Edits the current query; uses vi as the default. When you invoke this command, you are taken to the vi edit screen. When finished, you return to the mysql prompt, with your altered query in the buffer. Enter a semicolon to execute the query you edited in vi.
	exit	
	quit	Terminates the mysql program.
\g or ;	go	Sends the current query to the server.
\h	help	Displays the available mysql commands and flags.
\p	print	Prints the current query, not the query results.
\#	rehash	Completes the database, table, and column. Actually, this command orders a refresh of the information needed for the completion functionality.
\s	status	Displays the server version and current database, connection id, server version, uptime, and such.

Short Command	Long Command	Description
\u	use	Selects a certain database as the current database. Usage: mysql> use database_name mysql> \u database_name

For Access Converts Only: Daemons and Services

MS SQL Server administrators will be familiar with the concept of a *service,* because MS SQL Server runs as a service under Windows (and so does the Windows version of MySQL). However, if you have used only Access, a bit of explanation will help you better understand MySQL. Use MS SQL Server as an example. In Access, you directly open the *.mdb file, which is where the data (among other things) is stored. Call that "shared file mode," because multiple users can open and read data simultaneously from the same *.mdb file. Unlike in Access, when you use MS SQL Server, you don't directly access the file that holds the data. In MS SQL Server, the data files have the .mdf extension, but when you request the data that is in the file—whether through an ODBC data source, a bound VB control, or whatever—the "SQL Server service" handles the request, including any necessary security or login information. This service, which is a background process running under the operating system, is what actually looks into the file where the data is stored and retrieves the requested data. It then passes the data back to the requesting resource—you (probably on another machine, although the client and server processes can both be on the same machine running at the same time).

In the Linux world, such services are called *daemons,* but they are the same thing, at least by the nature of their function. MySQL runs as a service, but not in "shared-file" mode like Access.

Safely Launching the mysql Daemon (mysqld)—and Why You Should Care

The biggest reason to launch mysqld from the safe_mysqld script is that the script starts mysqld and then continuously verifies that mysqld is still running. If for any reason the daemon has died, safe_mysqld restarts it.

safe_mysqld understands the same options as mysqld.

Table 1.5 lists some of the more common or useful options for mysqld/safe_mysqld.

Table 1.5 **Common Options for mysqld and** *safe_mysqld*

Short Option	Long Option	Description
`-b path`	`--basedir=path`	Indicates the path to the MySQL installation directory.
`-h path`	`--datadir=path`	Indicates the path to the MySQL data directory.
	`--default-table-type=tbl_type`	The default is `MyISAM`, but `tbl_type` can also be `heap` or `isam`.
	`--init-file=file.sql`	Specifies a file of SQL statements to be executed at startup.
`-l path`	`--log[=path]`	Initiates logging regarding queries and connections to clients.
	`--log-isam[=file]`	Index file logging for debugging ISAM or MyISAM operations.
	`--log-update[=path]`	The update log contains the text of any action query.
`-Sg`	`--skip-grant-tables`	When verifying user connections, skips the grant tables. This gives any client full access to everything. Reset to using the grant tables by sending `mysqladmin` flush-privileges.
	`--skip-networking`	Locks out all connections except local host.
	`--skip-thread-priority`	Action queries by default are given higher priority than select queries. This option sets all to equal priority.

Where to Get MySQL

The MySQL Web site (`http://www.mysql.com/downloads/index.html`) is, of course, the primary place to get MySQL, and it also has a list of mirror sites. Versions are available for Linux and MS Windows, as well as other operating systems. This Web site also has information that is not apparent at the FTP site, so it is considered a better source for beginners.

You will probably need FTP software so you don't have to use your browser. After your Internet connection is open, start a program such as Gftp. (If you are using Linux and Xwindows, check the "Internet" programs on your start bar, or check under "Gnome and X Apps" if you are using KDE.) Type in the host as `ftp.mysql.com`. Alternatively, `ftp://ftp.mysql.com/` might work from your browser.

Change directories to get the most current release, which in this case is the
/MySQL-3.23 directory. You should see a list of files available for download.

Mysql is also hosted on SourceForge. You might want to check the MySQL Web
site for the latest information or version, because things might have changed since this
book was published.

Deciding On an Installation Method: Pros and Cons

For starters and demo projects, I recommend the Red Hat Package Manager (RPM)
method. It is quick and works well. Defaults are preset so that you can see how the
databases are structured after they are installed. Installing from binaries and from source
are the other options. You might install from binaries if you have a predefined need to
put MySQL somewhere in a location other than the default. Install from source if you
have a very advanced need or you just like the pain.

RPM: The Quickest and Easiest

This section explains what RPM is and why you should care about it. The RPM is
the closest thing the Linux world has to an installer/uninstaller, which everyone in the
Windows world is familiar with. Obviously, it can be used on Red Hat systems, but it
can also be used on Caldera and SuSE (and Mandrake, which is built on Red Hat).
For other distributions, check the vendor's system documentation.

In addition to installing and uninstalling, RPM can be used to verify a package,
query it, or identify dependencies. It is more flexible and powerful than most of the
installer programs for Windows, but it is still very easy for the beginner to use. More
software needs to be built this way: powerful enough for the power user, but simple
enough for the newbie.

RPM maintains an embedded database as part of the package (not of the MySQL
variety, though) that lists which packages are installed, where, and so on. You can query
this database to see information on your system, use RPM to help update a new software package, and perform other related functions.

Just as in the Windows world, it is not absolutely necessary that you use an installer.
You can copy files, make Registry entries, and so on. In Linux, this is called installing
from binaries. See the next section for more information on that type of installation.

Binaries

For systems that don't support RPM or require more installation customization, you
can install from binaries. This means you will be installing the precompiled application
and support files, which are normally downloaded in a *.tar.gz file. Because this is a
"quick and dirty" section, I won't cover this installation method. Simply be aware that
if you need more customization in areas such as the location in the directory tree of

certain files, this method is available to you. For instructions, go to the MySQL Web site or pick up full-blown book on MySQL, such as Paul DuBois' *MySQL* (New Riders Publishing, 2000).

However, for 99% of all installations, the following command sequence should work:

```
% gunzip < mysql-distribution.tar.gz | tar xf -
% cd mysql-distribution
% scripts/mysql_install_db
% bin/safe_mysqld &
```

If this fails you, check the documentation that came with MySQL or the Web site for help.

Source—For Experts Only

Although it is possible to recompile the application from the source code, this is not something a Linux newbie should tackle. Although it is possible to install MySQL from the source code, I am also not going to cover this. First, the need to do so is very rare, and second, I have never had any reason to do it. The only reasons I have heard of others doing this was for something like a single-purpose machine, in which case performance is the driving parameter and they probably have recompiled their kernel also to support that end. If you have a reason to tweak the source code to MySQL, you have moved way beyond the scope of this book. Just know that it is possible if you want to do it.

What to Get for RPM Installation

To get the right files, go to the MySQL Web site and find the RPM files for Linux. The following list outlines the files you will need to develop the applications in this book. If you are transferring files in a Windows environment, you will probably want to use an FTP program or the ftp client that comes with Windows to avoid corrupting the files in transfer, which can happen if you download them with your browser.

> **Getting the Latest and Greatest**
>
> In this section, you'll see full filenames. You will *probably* want to get the newest version when you go to download the rpm files. I am using the full filenames as examples of what was current when this book was written, but that might not be current when you are reading it.

To install via RPM, you need to get the following three files (or their most recent equivalents):

- MySQL-3.23.25-1.i386.rpm. This is the "server" piece. It contains the actual database server that receives requests and returns results.

- `MySQL-client-3.23.25-1.i386.rpm`. This is the client piece, most notably the mysql program that gets you to the `mysql>` prompt, which in turn allows you to send queries to the database.
- `MySQL-devel-3.23.25-1.i386.rpm`. From this file, you need the C API header files.

Place these files anywhere you're comfortable; for this example, they're in the /usr/tmp/ directory.

Installation

Installation using the Red Hat Package Manager is extremely easy and painless, not to mention nearly trouble-free. A few commands, and you will be on your way…

Installing from the RPM

This is the easiest and, in my opinion, the best way to install MySQL if you are interested in immediate results. Because Red Hat is one of the most common Linux distributions, you can usually expect the RPM to get the job done. If your distribution supports this installation method, I highly recommend that you use it. It does, however, decide the default location for files, which makes you do some searching to know how your MySQL server is configured.

Installing the RPM

The RPM installation for MySQL presented in this book proceeds as follows: First, the server portion is installed (the process that serves up the requests from the mysql client), and then the client is installed (the normal way to query a MySQL database). This assumes that both will be loaded on the same machine. You will then test the installation, and finally, you will install the files needed for C program development.

Install the Server

You should note the location of certain files that the RPM will install for you. To do so, send the following command:

```
% rpm -qpl /usr/tmp/MySQL-3.23.21-1.i386.rpm | more
```

Use the space bar to view one screen at a time, and note the location of the `safe_mysqld` program. The `| more` part of the command allows you to view one screen at a time using the space bar. Find the `safe_mysqld` program, and note its location in the directory tree. In my case, it was /usr/bin.

To install, type the following command:

```
% rpm -i /usr/tmp/MySQL-3.23.21-1.i386.rpm
```

If you're running Linux-Mandrake, you can simply double-click on the file from the KDExplorer or whatever file manager you're using.

Install the Client

To install the client, type the following command, this time noting the location of the mysqladmin program and its location in the directory tree. The following command queries the package so that I can see the location of the mysqladmin utility:

```
% rpm -qpl /usr/tmp/MySQL-client-3.23.21-1.i386.rpm
```

In my case, the mysqladmin program was located in the /usr/bin directory. To actually install the package, use this code:

```
% rpm -i /usr/tmp/MySQL-client-3.23.21-1.i386.rpm
```

Test the Installation

These steps require that both the server and the client portions be installed. Type the following commands:

```
% cd /usr/bin

% mysqladmin version
```

If you get a response, the MySQL server daemon is running on your machine. The response should be something like the following (note that it will probably change with a different version that you will install after this book is published):

```
mysqladmin  Ver 8.13 Distrib 3.23.29a-gamma, for linux on i586
Copyright (C) 2000 MySQL AB & MySQL Finland AB & TCX DataKonsult AB
This software comes with ABSOLUTELY NO WARRANTY. This is free software, .
and you are welcome to modify and redistribute it under the GPL license

Server version          3.23.29a-gamma
Protocol version        10
Connection              Localhost via UNIX socket
UNIX socket             /tmp/mysql.sock
Uptime:                 6 hours 23 min 45 sec

Threads: 2  Questions: 938581  Slow queries: 0  Opens: 30
Flush tables: 1  Open tables: 2 Queries per second avg: 40.764

mysqladmin  Ver 8.7 Distrib 3.23.21-beta, for pc-linux-gnu on i686
TCX Datakonsult AB, by Monty
Server version          3.23.21-beta-log
Protocol version     10
Connection           Localhost via UNIX socket
UNIX socket          /var/lib/mysql/mysql.sock
Uptime:              37 min 45 sec

Threads: 1  Questions: 3  Slow queries: 0  Opens: 6  Flush tables:
1  Open tables: 2 Queries per second avg: 0.001
```

Another way to verify that your database server is functioning is to enter

```
% mysql
```

This changes the prompt from % to mysql>. Type

```
mysql> select now();
```

This should give you a response like the following:

```
+---------------------+
| now ()              |
+---------------------+
| 2000-07-05 08:31:28 |
+---------------------+
row in set (0.01 sec)
```

Finally, you can use this command

```
% mysqladmin ping
```

which returns the following (if your MySQL server is functioning):

```
mysqld is alive
```

You now have a running—but unsecured!—MySQL database server on your computer.

Install the Files for C Development

If you will be doing any program development, you need to install the files for C development. First, type

```
% rpm -qpl /usr/tmp/MySQL-devel-3.23.25-1.i386.rpm
```

and note the location of mysql.h. In this case, it is /usr/include/mysql/. You should also note the location of libmysqlclient.a. To install, send the following command:

```
% rpm -i /usr/tmp/MySQL-devel-3.23.25-1.i386.rpm
```

You need to know the location of mysql.h and libmysqlclient.a for program development later in this book.

Uninstall the RPM

You may or may not need to do this, but I want to include it here for completeness. First, you need to shut down the server:

```
% mysqladmin shutdown
```

Then enter the following command to find out the package name in the RPM package database:

```
% rpm -qa
```

The MySQL package(s) will probably appear at the bottom of the list, because they were installed most recently. It is important for you to know that you cannot simply give the `rpm -e` command with the original filename that you used to install. You must find out what the Red Hat Package Manager calls the packages you want to remove. To uninstall the packages, type

```
% rpm -e -vv MySQL-3.23.21-1
```

followed by

```
% rpm -e -vv MySQL-client-3.23.21-1
```

The `-e` option is for uninstall ("erase"), and the `-vv` is for verbose mode. Otherwise, you will have no idea what is happening; you will only know the operation is complete when your command prompt reappears.

Installing the Account to Administer the MySQL Server

If you're installing from RPM, the mysql user account is created automatically. If, after installing MySQL from the RPM, you look at the "user accounts" on your system (for example, using the `linuxconf` utility), you will see that there is a user with the login name "mysql" (although previously it might have been "mysqladm" or something similar, and it might change again in the future). The full name will be something like "MySQL server," and the home directory will be something like /var/lib/mysql. This is a user that can be managed just like a real person who logs onto the machine; it can have administrator privileges as well as others.

Starting and Stopping the MySQL Server Daemon

When you install from an RPM, the MySQL server daemon is started and stopped automatically for you, and the daemon is added to the boot and shutdown sequence of the machine on which it is installed. If you don't know what a daemon or process is on a database server, refer to the earlier section "For Access Converts Only: Daemons and Services."

If for some reason you need to start up the MySQL daemon, enter this code:

```
% cd /usr/local/mysql/bin
% safe_mysqld -user=mysql &
```

The `&` specifies a background process.

To enable logging, send

```
% safe_mysqld -user=mysql -log &
```

or

```
% safe_mysqld -log &
```

You could also use the `--log-bin` option, which would make accidentally deleted data recoverable.

You should log as much as you can until you get comfortable with MySQL.

To shut down the MySQL server daemon, send the following command:

```
% mysqladmin shutdown
```

Changing the *mysqladmin* Password

For added security, you need to change the password for the root user of mysql. This is done with either of the following commands:

```
/usr/bin/mysqladmin -u root -p password 'new-pas'
```

or

```
/usr/bin/mysqladmin -u root -h servername - p password 'new-password'
```

In this case, you have to be root and know the root password to change the password. To remove a password, try this:

```
mysqladmin -p password ""
```

Also remember that you can use SQL statements to update the user table. (Issue the Show Databases command to see it; one of the databases listed will be named mysql—that is the system database.) Setting the Password field to a zero-length string effectively removes the password.

The Whirlwind Tour: Creating, Accessing, and Dropping a Database

Listing 1.1 is a very simple terminal session for creating a database and then a table, entering some rows, and then dropping the database.

Listing 1.1 also serves as an introduction to how code is presented in this book. In some of the code listings (like this one), you see the entire source code with line numbers to the left for reference. Don't type the line numbers in your source.

Listing 1.1   **Creating, Accessing, and Dropping a Database**

```
01 % mysql
02 mysql> show databases;
03 +----------+
04 | Database |
05 +----------+
06 | mysql    |
07 | test     |
08 +----------+
09 2 rows in set (0.00 sec)
10
11 mysql> create database test_db;
12 Query OK, 1 row affected (0.00 sec)
13
14 mysql> show databases;
15 +----------+
```

continues

Listing 1.1 **Continued**

```
16 | Database |
17 +----------+
18 | mysql    |
19 | test     |
20 | test_db  |
21 +----------+
22 3 rows in set (0.01 sec)
23
24 mysql> use test_db;
25 Database changed
26 mysql> show tables;
27 Empty set (0.00 sec)
28
29 create table tbl_books_1
30 (  name   varchar(30),
31    title varchar(30),
32    year  int
33 );
34 Query OK, 0 rows affected (0.00 sec)
35 mysql> describe tbl_books_1;
36 +-------+-------------+------+-----+---------+-------+---------------------+
37 | Field | Type        | Null | Key | Default | Extra | Privileges|
38 +-------+-------------+------+-----+---------+-------+---------------------+
39 | title | varchar(30) | yes  |     | Null    |       |
select,insert,update,references |
40 | title | varchar(30) | yes  |     | Null    |       |
select,insert,update,references |
41 | title | varchar(30) | yes  |     | Null    |       |
select,insert,update,references |
42 +-------+-------------+------+-----+---------+-------+---------------------+
43 3 rows in set (0.00 sec)
44
45 mysql> show tables;
46 +------------------+
47 | Tables_in_test_db |
48 +------------------+
49 | tbl_books_1      |
50 +------------------+
51 1 row in set (0.00 sec)
52
53 mysql> insert into tbl_books_1 values ('Jack Kerouac', 'On The Road', 1957);
54 Query OK, 1 row affected (0.00 sec)
55
56 mysql> insert into tbl_books_1 values ('Ayn Rand', 'Atlas Shrugged', 1934);
57 Query OK, 1 row affected (0.00 sec)
58
59 mysql> select * from tbl_books_1;
```

```
60 +--------------+------------------+------+
61 | name         | title            | year |
62 +--------------+------------------+------+
63 | Jack Kerouac | On The Road      | 1957 |
64 | Ayn Rand     | Atlas Shrugged   | 1934 |
65 +--------------+------------------+------+
66 2 rows in set (0.00 sec)
67
68 mysql> drop database test_db;
69 Query OK, 3 rows affected (0.00 sec)
70
71 mysql> show databases;
72 +----------+
73 | Database |
74 +----------+
75 | mysql    |
76 | test     |
77 +----------+
78 2 rows in set (0.00 sec)
79
80 mysql> select * from tbl_books_1;
81 ERROR 1146:  Table 'test_db.tbl_books_1' doesn't exist
82 mysql> quit
83 Bye
84 %
```

Nonstandard or Unique SQL Constructs in MySQL (Extensions to ANSI SQL92)

The following list was taken from the MySQL Web site; you might want to check there for updated information (www.mysql.com). I have removed some items that you are not likely to ever use, and I have expanded certain items for clarity.

- "The field attributes AUTO_INCREMENT, BINARY, NULL, UNSIGNED and ZEROFILL."[1]
    - The AUTO_INCREMENT attribute may be applied to any integer column. When you attempt to insert a 0 or null, it will be set to the next highest value for that column by +1. If you delete the row with the current maximum value, it will not be reused. There can be only one AUTO_INCREMENT column per table, and it must be indexed. MySQL will work correctly only if the AUTO_INCREMENT column has positive values; inserting a negative number causes it to "wrap" and is considered a large positive value.
- "All string comparisons are case insensitive by default, with sort ordering determined by the current character set…"[1]

- "MySQL maps each database to a directory under the MySQL data directory, and tables within a database to filenames in the database directory. This has a few implications:
    - "Database names and table names are case sensitive … on operating systems that have case sensitive filenames (like most [Linux] systems). …
    - "Database, table, index, column or alias names may begin with a digit (but may not consist solely of digits).
    - "You can use standard system commands to back up, rename, move, delete and copy tables. For example, to rename a table, rename the '.MYD', '.MYI' and '.frm' files to which the table corresponds."[1] (You should, of course, ensure that the MySQL server is not up when doing this.)
- "In SQL statements, you can access tables from different databases with the `db_name.tbl_name` syntax. …"[1]
- "`LIKE` is allowed on numeric columns."[1] For example, `10 LIKE '1%'` is acceptable.
- "Use of `INTO OUTFILE` and `STRAIGHT_JOIN` in a `SELECT` statement. …"[1]
    - The `INTO OUTFILE` statement is the complement to the `LOAD DATA INFILE` statement. Usage is as follows:

        `Select * from tbl_invoices INTO OUTFILE 'invoices.txt'`

        The file is created on the server, it cannot already exist, and the creator must have the "file" privilege on the server. By default, it creates a tab-delimited file with no headers. Also note that if the filename is given without a path, it is put in the database directory, not the directory you were in when you called mysql.
    - The `STRAIGHT_JOIN` statement forces the optimizer to join the tables in the order in which they appear in the `FROM` clause. This might improve performance if MySQL is joining the tables in a less-than-optimum way.
- "`EXPLAIN SELECT` to get a description on how tables are joined."[1] This is really a prepending of the `EXPLAIN` keyword to a `select` statement. MySQL returns information about how it would process the query, including how tables are joined and in what order. It does not return the rows described by the `select` statement, only the query processing information.
    - You can also use `EXPLAIN table_name`, which is the same as `DESCRIBE table_name` and `SHOW COLUMNS from table_name`.
- "Use of index names, indexes on a prefix of a field, and use of `INDEX` or `KEY` in a `CREATE TABLE` statement. …"[1]

- "Use of TEMPORARY or IF NOT EXISTS with CREATE TABLE."[1]

  - If you create a table using the TEMPORARY keyword, that table will automatically be deleted if the connection is terminated. Two different connections can use the same table name in this case without conflict.

  - The IF NOT EXISTS keywords allow you to check for the existence of a table during the create statement and avoid an error if the table already exists. Note that it does not check the table's structure, only the name. Usage is as follows:

    ```
    CREATE [TEMPORARY] TABLE [IF NOT EXISTS] ...
    ```

- "Use of COUNT(DISTINCT list) where 'list' is more than one element."[1] Usage is as follows:

  ```
  select count(distinct exp1, exp2, ...) from table_name.
  ```

  This returns a count of distinct rows for the expressions listed—in this case, distinct rows for exp1 + exp2.

- "Use of CHANGE col_name, DROP col_name or DROP INDEX in an ALTER TABLE statement. ..."[1] For example:

  ```
  ALTER TABLE tbl_main CHANGE COLUMN age, age_prev INTEGER
  ALTER TABLE tbl_main DROP COLUMN age
  ALTER TABLE tbl_main DROP INDEX idx_age
  ```

  Actually, in the first two examples, the COLUMN keyword is optional.

- "Use of multiple ADD, ALTER, DROP or CHANGE clauses in an ALTER TABLE statement."[1]

- "You can drop multiple tables with a single DROP TABLE statement."[1] Separate table names with commas.

- "The LIMIT clause of the DELETE statement."[1] Add a clause to the end of the DELETE statement with the number of rows to be deleted:

  ```
  DELETE from tbl_main where age > 55 LIMIT 10
  ```

- "The DELAYED clause of the INSERT and REPLACE statements."[1] This means the client will get an immediate response from the server indicating success, but the server will insert the row when the table is not in use by any other thread. This primarily improves response time. Additionally, inserts from many clients are written together for improved speed. However, the inserted data is stored in memory, so if mysqld dies unexpectedly, any queued rows are lost.

- "Use of `LOAD DATA INFILE`."[1] You can read either from the client or server machine, but you must use the `LOCAL` keyword if you're reading from the client. Loading from the client is slower, but loading from the server requires the "file" permission. Use of the `REPLACE` and `IGNORE` keywords causes insert rows that violate `KEY` constraints to either replace existing rows or be discarded, respectively. The defaults expect a tab-delimited file with rows separated by newline characters and no fields enclosed by quotes, but these defaults can be overridden. There is also an `IGNORE` *number* `LINES` clause that can be set to ignore a number of lines—column headers, for example. MySQL can read fixed-width files as long as the display width for the columns exactly matches the file to be read.

- "The ... `OPTIMIZE TABLE` ... statement."[1] This allows you to reclaim unused space after you have deleted a sizeable part of a table or if you have made changes to a table with variable-length columns (varchar, blob, or text). MySQL maintains deleted records as a linked list, and subsequent `INSERT` statements reuse old positions. The `OPTIMIZE TABLE` statement reclaims that space. While `OPTIMIZE TABLE` is executing, no access is allowed (which improves speed).

- "The `SHOW` statement."[1] `SHOW` displays information about databases, tables, or columns. It can also show information on indexes, status, variables, processes, and grants. In many cases, it can also use a `LIKE` clause with wildcards. For example:

```
SHOW DATABASES
SHOW TABLES LIKE 'invoic%';
```

The following are equivalent:

```
SHOW INDEX FROM tbl_main FROM db_main;
SHOW INDEX FROM db_main.tbl_main;
```

- "Strings may be enclosed by either " [double quotes] or ' [single quotes]..."[1]

- "The `SET OPTION` statement."[1] This allows you to set various options of your session with the server.

- "You don't need to name all selected columns in the `GROUP BY` part. This gives better performance for some very specific, but quite normal queries."[1] For example:

```
select cust_num, cust_id, max(order_amt)
from tbl_invoices
GROUP BY cust_num
```

In ANSI SQL, you would have to add cust_name to the `GROUP BY` clause. Be advised that this requires you not only to know your data but also to be sure of your data integrity. Don't use this feature if the columns you omit aren't unique in the group! In my tests where the data was not unique, it returned the value in the first row it came to, but I have been able to find nothing that states this is the default behavior.

- "…[A]ll string functions support both ANSI SQL syntax and ODBC syntax."[1]
- "MySQL understands the || and && operators to mean logical OR and AND, as in the C programming language. In MySQL, || and OR are synonyms, as are && and AND. Because of this nice syntax, MySQL doesn't support the ANSI SQL || operator for string concatenation; use CONCAT() instead. Because CONCAT() takes any number of arguments, it's easy to convert use of the || operator to MySQL."[1]
- The "CREATE DATABASE or DROP DATABASE"[1] statements.
- "The =, <>, <= , <, >=, >, <<, >>, <=>, AND, OR or LIKE operators may be used in column comparisons to the left of the FROM in SELECT statements. For example:
  mysql> SELECT col1=1 AND col2=2 FROM tbl_name;"[1]

This can be used as a true/false test, which makes the output columns of zeros or ones. In this example, the output would be two columns with the expressions as headers and zeros or ones for values (assuming the columns are named col1 and col2 and the types are integer, with values that include 1 or 2).

- "The LAST_INSERT_ID() function."[1] This returns the last automatically generated value that was inserted into an AUTO_INCREMENT column.
- "CONCAT() or CHAR() with one argument or more than two arguments. (In MySQL, these functions can take any number of arguments.)"[1]
- "Use of TRIM() to trim substrings. ANSI SQL only supports removal of single characters."[1]
- "Use of REPLACE instead of DELETE + INSERT."[1] REPLACE syntax is very similar to INSERT, except that if an old record in the table has the same value for a unique key, that record is deleted before the new record is inserted.
- "The FLUSH flush_option statement"[1] where the most common flush options are HOSTS, LOGS, PRIVILEGES, or TABLES. HOSTS causes the host cache tables to be emptied; this can help if you get a "Host … is blocked" message, which means that the IP address exceeded the max_connect_errors value and thus has been blocked from connecting again. LOGS closes and reopens the standard and update log files. PRIVILEGES reloads the privileges from the grant tables. TABLES closes all open tables.

1. "5 How standards-compatible is MySQL? / 5.1 MySQL extensions to ANSI SQL92." *MySQL Reference Manual for Version 3.23.25-beta* [online]. August 2000 [cited 1 September 2000]. Available from Internet: http://www.mysql.com/documentation/mysql/bychapter/manual_Compatibility.html

Running MySQL in "ANSI Mode"

You can start mysqld with the `--ansi` option. When you do, MySQL handles certain things differently. This might be of importance to you primarily if you have portability issues with code or if you have unusual connections to other databases.[2]

Among the changes in the way mysql behaves: `||` is used for string concatenation, "REAL" will mean "FLOAT" (not "DOUBLE"), and so on. There are other behaviors as well; check `http:\\www.mysql.com` for the latest.[2]

Utilities and Programs for MySQL

In addition to the MySQL database server (mysqld), the MySQL "suite" includes a number of programs for administering the databases and the database server. These programs were installed when you installed via the RPM. `isamchk` and `myisamchk` are utilities that verify and repair database tables and files. `mysqlaccess` is used to grant, modify, and revoke user permissions. `mysqladmin` is a utility for higher-level administration, such as creating databases and shutting down the myslqd server. `mysqldump` comes in handy for exporting data or backing up tables in a pinch; it outputs data in SQL `insert` statements in such a way that the output file can be fed back into a MySQL server (or other database) and the rows will be loaded. `mysqlimport` is the bulk loader utility, and `mysqlshow` displays information about database objects such as tables.

isamchk: Examining and Repairing Damaged Tables

If, for some unknown reason, a database table becomes corrupted, this utility can attempt a repair. The underlying data files that hold the data are called Indexed Sequential Access Method (ISAM) files.

Usage:

```
% isamchk [OPTIONS] tablename.ISM
```

It is important to note that if you are using 3.23 or greater, you are using the MyISAM file format as the default. Unless you specified your tables in the old format, you need to be using the `myisamchk` utility, not `isamchk`. The ISAM table structure is being replaced by MyISAM, and at some point in the future, ISAM will not be supported.

Keep in mind that the options listed in Tables 1.6 and 1.7 do not constitute a complete list! Give the command

```
% isamchk -h | more
```

for a full list of options applicable to your system.

The `[OPTIONS]` portion of the usage line represents the options listed in Tables 1.6 and 1.7.

2. "5 How standards-compatible is MySQL? / 5.2 Running MySQL in ANSI mode." *MySQL Reference Manual for Version 3.23.25-beta* [online]. August 2000 [cited 1 September 2000]. Available from Internet: `http://www.mysql.com/documentation/mysql/bychapter/ manual_Compatibility.html`

> ## A Quick Note Regarding the Options Listed for the Utilities
> I have only included commands and options that I think are useful, unique, and/or relatively common. I
> have excluded those that I have never had any use for and cannot see any actual use for, either to a DBA
> or developer. Please do not think that just because there is no option listed for a particular task that such
> an option does not exist. As a starting point, find the help option for the utility and see if it lists any-
> thing that interests you or lends itself to your situation.

Table 1.6   **Options to Use When Examining Tables**

Option Short	Option Long	Description
-a	--analyze	Analyzes the distribution of keys in the target table.
-d	--description	Reports information on the target table.
-e	--extended-check	Thoroughly checks the target table. (isamchk should report all problems even without this option.)
-I	--information	Reports table statistics.
-v	--verbose	Reports much more for all operations (a personal favorite).

Table 1.7   **Options to Use When Repairing Tables**

Option Short	Option Long	Description
-o	--safe-recover	A slower, older recovery method, but it can handle more cases than -r can.
-r	--recover	General fix; won't work to fix unique keys that are, in fact, not unique.
-q	--quick	Used with -r to get a faster repair; the data file isn't touched.

Data Files and Their Structure

If you are like me, you cannot help but wonder how the data exists down at the
lowest level. Well, the short answer is "not in text format." Feel free to create a small
database and table and look at the files; you will find information in this section on
how MySQL stores your data. If you want more than that, you will probably have to
go to the source code.

ISAM Files: The Older Structure

This section describes the older ISAM structure, which has been replaced by MyISAM in version 3.23 and newer. Under the new format, you still have the option to use this type of storage, or perhaps you inherited an older implementation of MySQL.

Each table in the database is actually a set of three files: the `*.ISD` files contain the data, the `*.ISM` file contains information about the structure of the data, such as keys and indexes, and the `*.frm` files contain the structure of the table.

The `isamchk` utility only checks the `*.ism` file. The functions it can perform are similar to the Repair and Compact Database options available under Access.

If you are using 3.23 or newer, by default you will use the MyISAM storage format, which means you will then in turn use the `myisamchk` utility.

MyISAM File Structures

These are the newer file structures that allow greater flexibility than the old (and are the default in version 3.23 and newer). If I give the same commands as in the previous "whirlwind" tour section (Listing 1.1), and then examine the tables, I find that (on my system, anyway) three files are located in the /var/lib/mysql/test_db/ directory:

tbl_books_1.frm	72 bytes
tbl_books_1.MYI	1024 bytes
tbl_books_1.MYD	8604 bytes

The `*.frm` is the same type as the old structure, but the `*.MYI` files correspond to the old `*.ISM` files, and the `*.MYD` files correspond to the older `*.ISD` files. In this case, none of the files is very large, with `tbl_books_1.frm` weighing in at 8604 bytes. You can view the files, but because they are not stored in a text-friendly format, they won't have much meaning.

Listing 1.2 contains lines from Listing 1.1 that are of particular relevance here.

Listing 1.2   **Code from the Whirlwind Tour Section**

```
11 mysql> create database test_db;
24 mysql> use test_db;
26 mysql> show tables;
29 mysql> create table tbl_books_1
30 ( name  varchar(30),
31   title char   (30),
32   year  int
33 );
53 mysql> insert into tbl_books_1 values ('Jack Kerouac', 'On The Road', 1957);
56 mysql> insert into tbl_books_1 values ('Ayn Rand', 'Atlas Shrugged', 1934);
```

myisamchk

This utility is the updated version of `isamchk` for the MyISAM storage format. Its usage is essentially the same:

```
myisamchk [OPTIONS] tables.MYI
```

The options listed for the `isamchk` utility also apply to `myisamchk`, so they aren't repeated here, but Table 1.8 lists additional flags that are of interest. These flags apply to `myisamchk` only.

Table 1.8   **Additional Flags for** *myisamchk* **(Not Applicable to** *isamchk***)**

Option Short	Option Long	Description
-c	--check	Checks the target table for errors.
-m	--medium-check	Runs faster than an extended check, but finds only "99.99% of all errors" (whatever that means).

mysqlaccess

Perhaps one of the most useful arguments to this utility is the `-howto` command-line argument. When you send the following command, you get examples of how this utility can be used:

```
%mysqlaccess -howto
```

Note that the `%mysqlaccess -howto` option is different from the `-?` option. This utility has few flags, and they are pretty straightforward, so I won't go over them here. Give the `-?` option a try for a full list that is applicable to your machine.

Usage is pretty simple for `mysqlaccess`:

```
mysqlaccess [host [user [db]]]  OPTIONS
```

The user and the db must be provided here if no options are specified. If no host is provided, it assumes the local server ('localhost').

For example, suppose you have installed a local, single-person-only db server and are logged in as root. If you send the command

```
% mysqlaccess root mysql
```

you get the following output:

```
mysqlaccess Version 2.05, 17 Feb 2000
By RUG-AIV, by Yves Carlier (Yves.Carlier@rug.ac.be)
Changes by Steve Harvey (sgh@vex.net)
This software comes with ABSOLUTELY NO WARRANTY.
+++USING FULL WHERE CLAUSE+++
+++USING FULL WHERE CLAUSE+++
+++USING FULL WHERE CLAUSE+++
```

continues

continued

```
Access-rights
for USER 'root', from HOST 'localhost', to DB 'mysql'
    +----------------+---+    +------------------+---+
    | Select_priv    | Y |    | Shutdown_priv    | Y |
    | Insert_priv    | Y |    | Process_priv     | Y |
    | Update_priv    | Y |    | File_priv        | Y |
    | Delete_priv    | Y |    | Grant_priv       | Y |
    | Create_priv    | Y |    | References_priv  | Y |
    | Drop_priv      | Y |    | Index_priv       | Y |
    | Reload_priv    | Y |    | Alter_priv       | Y |
    +----------------+---+    +------------------+---+
BEWARE: Everybody can access your DB as user 'root' from host 'localhost'
      : WITHOUT supplying a password.
      : Be very careful about it!!

The following rules are used:
db    : 'No matching rule'
host  : 'Not processed: host-field is not empty in db-table.'
user  :
'localhost','root','','Y','Y','Y','Y','Y','Y','Y','Y','Y','Y','Y','Y','Y','Y'
BUGs can be reported by email to Yves.Carlier@rug.ac.be
```

As you can see, this gives a warning that anyone logged in at the local machine can access mysql.

mysqladmin

The general usage of this command is as follows:

```
% mysqladmin [OPTIONS] command
```

The options are pretty standard: -v for verbose, -t=XX for timeout to connect to the server, and so on. To see the latest list on your machine, send this command:

```
% mysqladmin -? | more
```

The *command* part is of more use on a regular basis. Not all the commands are listed in Table 1.9, but the most common and more interesting ones are. Again, to get a full list, send the preceding command.

Table 1.9 **Parameters to the *mysqladmin* Utility**

Command	Description
create db_name	Creates a database of name db_name.
drop db_name	Drops the database named.
flush-logs	Clears out all logs.
flush-privileges or reload	Reloads grant tables; either command does the same thing.

Command	Description
ping	Reports if mysqld is alive.
shutdown	Takes the server down.
status	Reports status from the server.

mysqldump

If you have a database like the one described in the MyISAM file structure (that is, one table with two rows) and you send this command

```
% mysqldump test_db
```

you will get the following output:

```
# MySQL dump 8.7
#
# Host: localhost    Database: test_db
#--------------------------------------------------------
# Server version    3.23.21-beta-log


#
# Table structure for table 'tbl_books_1'
#

ONEATE TABLE tbl_books_1 (
  name varchar(30),
  title varchar(30),
  year int(11)
);


#
# Dumping data for table 'tbl_books_1'
#

INSERT INTO tbl_books_1 VALUES ('Ayn Rand','Atlas Shrugged',1934);
INSERT INTO tbl_books_1 VALUES ('Jack Kerouac','On The Road',1957);
```

As you can see, this could be very useful in backing up, porting, or reloading the database.

Usage can be either of the following:

```
% mysqldump [OPTIONS] database [tables]
```

or

```
% mysqldump [OPTIONS]
```

In the second case, you must supply either the –databases or the --all-databases option.

Table 1.10 lists the important or unexpected flags that go with the `mysqldump` command.

Table 1.10   *mysqldump* **Flags**

Option Short	Option Long	Description
`-A`	`--all-databases`	Dumps all databases; same as `–databases` with all databases listed.
`-B`	`--databases`	Dumps several listed databases, as listed after the option. `USE db_name` will be included in the output.
`-c`	`--complete-insert`	Uses complete `insert`. In other words, inserts column names before the `VALUES` keyword in the `insert` statement.
`-e`	`--extended-insert`	Allows use of the new `INSERT` syntax. This means multiple rows per `insert` statement (in fact, all rows). Rows are surrounded by parentheses and separated by commas.
	`--add-drop-table`	Adds a `drop table` statement before each `CREATE TABLE` statement.
	`--allow-keywords`	Allows creation of column names that are keywords.
`-f`	`--force`	Continues the operation if an sql-error is generated.
`-t`	`--no-create-info`	Doesn't write table creation info.
`-d`	`--no-data`	Provides no row information. Only dumps the table structure, not the `INSERT` statements needed to repopulate the table.
`-T`	`--tab=/path/`	Creates a tab-separated text file for each table to the given path (in other words, creates `.sql` and `.txt` files). This works only when `mysqldump` is run from the same machine that is running the mysqld daemon.
		When using this flag, you also get the following: `--fields-terminated-by=` `--fields-enclosed-by=` `--lines-terminated-by=`
`-v`	`--verbose`	Gives more detailed information on the action taken.
`-w`	`--where=cond`	Dumps only records meeting condition `cond`, such as the following: `--where=user='jimf'`

mysqlimport

This is the bulk import utility for MySQL; it is analogous to SQL Server's `bcp` utility. It is a command-line interface to the `LOAD DATA` statement.

Usage is as follows:

```
% mysqlimport [OPTIONS] db_name file_name
```

Some of the more interesting flags are listed in Table 1.11.

Table 1.11   *mysqlimport* **Common Flags**

Option Short	Option Long	Description
-d	--delete	Empties the target table before loading it.
-f	--force	Continues loading even if an error occurs.
-i	--ignore	If an input row violates the unique key constraint for a row that is already in the table, keep the row that was there first and discard the input row. Compare to --replace.
-l	--lock-tables	Locks a table while it is being loaded.
-r	--replace	If an input row violates the unique key constraint for a row that is already in the table, this discards the row that was there and inserts the new row. Compare to --ignore.

mysqlshow

`mysqlshow` gives information about databases, tables, or columns. It is a command-line interface to the `SHOW` statement.

Usage:

```
% mysqlshow [OPTIONS] [database_name [table_name [column]]]
```

The specific options of importance are listed in Table 1.12.

Table 1.12   **Common** *mysqlshow* **Flags**

Option Short	Option Long	Description
-i	--status (3.23 or newer)	Displays table information—the same information that's shown by SHOW TABLE STATUS.
-k	--keys	Shows table key information as well as column information; only applicable when a table name is specified.

myisampack

myisampack compacts a MyISAM table into a much smaller space. myisampack is like gzip, but it works on tables. It operates on the .MYD file and compresses it to be much smaller (typically 30–70% smaller than an OPTIMIZED table). After running myisampack, you can view the table normally, but you can't update it anymore. In other words, this is perfect for archiving old tables that you no longer want to update. You can unpack a table with 'optimize table'. This is *not* analogous to other database tools that clean up and compress data files, which can become bloated from numerous read/write operations if the dbms does not automatically reclaim unused space. In that case, you'll want to use OPTIMIZE TABLE.

Usage:

```
%myisampack [options] filename.MYI
```

and

```
%myisamchk -rq filename.MYI
```

Note that myisamchk must be run after myisampack. This is to update keys, which are not automatically updated. If you get an error 2 on open message when you run this utility, check to make sure you have given the correct filename and path (and remember that Linux is case-sensitive by default). Table 1.13 lists some of the options for myisampack.

Table 1.13 **Common *myisampack* Options**

Option Short	Option Long	Description
-b	--backup	Backs up the table first to tbl_name.old.
-f	--force	Packs the table even if it gets bigger or a tempfile exists.
-j	--join='tbl'	Joins all given tables into one, called tbl. All tables named must have the same structure.
-t	--test	Only tests packing the table.
-v	--verbose	Details output mode.
-w	--wait	Tells the command to wait and try again if the table is in use.
-#	--debug=file	Outputs debug info to a file.
-?	--help	Displays option info and exits.

MySQL's C API

This section outlines the creation of a very simple C application for accessing the small database created in the preceding "whirlwind tour" section.

Don't Try This at Work, Kids

The program in Listing 1.3 makes a very good, tight, small, simple program. It does not make good Software Engineering. There are many things wrong with it, such as the following:

- Main() is entirely too long.
- The SHOW statements could be abstracted to a single function, with the only parameter being the string defining it.
- It does not contain enough comments.
- The database it is hitting is unsecured.
- The database name and host name are hardcoded in the routine.

And on and on. My point is, Listing 1.3 is an example for *this* section of *this* book. It is not representative of how good C code—and good code in general—is written.

Listing 1.3   A Simple C Program to Demonstrate MySQL's C Interface

```
#include <stdio.h>
#include <mysql.h>

#define def_host_name    "localhost"
#define def_user_name    NULL
#define def_password     NULL
#define def_db_name      "test_db"

MYSQL *cnx_init;
MYSQL *cnx_db;

MYSQL_RES *result_set;
MYSQL_ROW  row;

unsigned int ctr;

/* Function Prototypes */
void show_result_set (MYSQL_RES *in_result_set);

int main (int argc, char *argv[])
{
     printf("starting\n");

     cnx_init = mysql_init (NULL);
     if (cnx_init == NULL)
```

continues

Listing 1.3   **Continued**

```
                        { printf("failure in mysql_init\n");
                          printf("Exit code 1\n");
                          exit(1);
                        }

        cnx_db = mysql_real_connect ( cnx_init,
                              def_host_name,
                              def_user_name,
                              def_password,
                              def_db_name,
                              0,
                              NULL,
                              0) ;

    if (cnx_db == NULL) {
                    printf("failure in mysql_real_connect\n");
                    printf("Exit code 2\n");
                    printf("Error %u -- %s\n",
                      mysql_errno (cnx_init),
                      mysql_error (cnx_init));
                    exit(2);
    }

  printf("Databases\n");
  printf("=========\n");

  if (mysql_query (cnx_init, "SHOW DATABASES") != 0)
        printf("Failure in show databases\n");
    else
       {
       result_set = mysql_store_result (cnx_init);
       if (result_set == NULL)
          printf("failure in mysql_store_result
                    for SHOW DATABASES\n");
       else
           {
                show_result_set (result_set);
           }
    }

  printf("Tables\n");
  printf("======\n");

  if (mysql_query (cnx_init, "SHOW TABLES") != 0)
                printf("Failure in show tables\n");
    else
       {
       result_set = mysql_store_result (cnx_init);
       if (result_set == NULL)
```

```
                         printf("failure in mysql_store_result
                                    for SHOW TABLES\n");
            else
                  {
                            show_result_set (result_set);
                  }
          }

      printf("Rows\n");
      printf("====\n");

      if (mysql_query(cnx_init, "Select * from tbl_books_1") != 0)
  printf("Failure in show tables\n");
        else
            {
            result_set = mysql_store_result (cnx_init);
            if (result_set == NULL)
              printf("failure in mysql_store_result
                            for Select statement\n");
            else
                {
                            show_result_set (result_set);
                }
        }

      printf("Action Query\n");
      printf("============\n");

      if (mysql_query (cnx_init, "Update tbl_books_1
                                    set year = 1940
                                    where name='Ayn Rand'") != 0)

                  {  printf ("failure in mysql_query,
                                    Update statement.\n");
                      printf ("Exit code 4\n");
                      printf("Error %u -- %s\n",
                              mysql_errno (cnx_init),
                              mysql_error (cnx_init));
                      exit (4);
                  }
      else
      {printf ("statement succeeded:  %lu row(s) affected\n",
            (unsigned long) mysql_affected_rows(cnx_init));
      }

      mysql_close(cnx_init);

      printf("terminating\n");
      exit(0);
  }
```

continues

Listing 1.3   **Continued**

```c
void show_result_set (MYSQL_RES *in_result_set)
{
     while ((row = mysql_fetch_row (in_result_set)) != NULL)
      {for (ctr=0;ctr < mysql_num_fields (in_result_set); ctr++)
           {if ( ctr > 0 )
                fputc ('\t', stdout);
                printf ("%s",row[ctr]!=NULL?row[ctr]:"Null-val");
           }
           fputc ('\n', stdout);

      }
      if (mysql_errno (cnx_init) != 0)
      { printf ("failure in mysql_fetch_row\n");
        printf ("Exit code 3\n");
        printf("Error %u -- %s\n",
                  mysql_errno (cnx_init),
                  mysql_error (cnx_init));
        exit (3);
      }

      mysql_free_result (in_result_set);


}
```

Compiling and Linking

In Linux, the best compiler to use is gcc. It ships with virtually every distribution, it is an excellent product, and nearly every system has one.

In this case, the compile and link task consists of two steps: first compile, and then link.

I suggest you put them in a file, such as `chap1.build`. Then go to the command line and send this command:

```
% ./chap1.build
```

The contents of `chap1.build` would then be:

```
gcc -c -I/usr/include/mysql ch1.c
gcc -o ch1 ch1.o -L/usr/include/mysql -L/usr/lib/mysql \
      lmysqlclient -lz
```

The first line compiles the source code (in this case, `ch1.c`), and the third line does the linking. The `-I` in the first line is for the include files—in this case, the location of `mysql.h`, because it is not in the default search path. In the second line, the `-L` specifies the path or paths to link the library files—in this case, searching for the file `libmysql client.a`. Notice that for the preceding syntax, the leading `lib` and the trailing `.a` are not needed; the `-l` flag automatically assumes them. The small `l` tells which library to link, and -lz indicates to link zlib also. The backslash character (\) is the command-line continuation character.

> **Note:**
>
> The -lz option is necessary if you get a message similar to the following:
>
> ```
> [root@delfin client1]# make
> gcc -o client1 client1.o -L/usr/lib/mysql -lmysqlclient -lm
> /usr/lib/mysql/libmysqlclient.a(my_compress.o): In function 'my_uncompress':
> my_compress.o(.text+0x97): undefined reference to 'uncompress'
> /usr/lib/mysql/libmysqlclient.a(my_compress.o): In function 'my_compress_alloc':
> my_compress.o(.text+0x12b): undefined reference to 'compress'
> collect2: ld returned 1 exit status
> make: *** [client1] Error 1
> ```

The compress and uncompress functions are in zlib. Also note that you might get an error message stating something about the floor() function. If that happens, you need to link in the math library using -lm. If you are on Solaris, you might need other libraries as well. The mysql mailing list, mailing list archive, and Web site are a great source of information.

Makefiles

This section offers a quick introduction to makefiles as they are used in Linux C application development. Makefiles do what the second line of the gcc file script (just shown) does, except better.

A *makefile* is a set of commands similar to those you just saw, except that it is more customizable and rebuilds the application by recompiling only those files that have changed since the last compile. Quite simply, although a makefile is not necessary, it is better software engineering.

The following code is the makefile for the small program in the previous code:

```
CC = gcc
INCLUDES = -I/usr/include/mysql
LIBS = -L/usr/include/mysql -L/usr/lib/mysql -lmysqlclient -lz
PROG = ch1
all:: $(PROG)
.c.o:

$(CC) -c $(INCLUDES) $<
$(PROG): $(PROG).o
$(CC) -o $@ $(PROG).o $(LIBS)
clean::
rm -f $(PROG).o $(PROG)
```

This file should be put into a file called Makefile.in (this is one of the filenames make looks for by default). To execute the makefile, type make at the command line. Then cd to the directory where Makefile.in is located, and issue this command:

```
%make
```

By default, make finds a file called Makefile. make is not an easy program to use, but for complicated programs that take a long time to compile, it might come in handy.

By way of quick explanation, the first four lines define variables (for lack of a better term). You can see them used throughout the file. After the space, the next three lines compile the source and then the object files. Finally, the program removes (rm) the intermediate files.

2

GTK+ for VB Developers

THIS CHAPTER INTRODUCES THE GTK+ WIDGET SET, PRIMARILY for the Linux platform. The widgets have also been ported to the Microsoft Windows environment. However, before you go switching all your Windows development efforts, you need to know that cross-compiling the same code on both Linux and Windows is far from a painless process. This book focuses on Linux and considers Windows an option. At the time of this writing, the Windows port of the GTK+ widget set is considered alpha release, but continued improvement is expected in the immediate future. Although I have created and used applications for both Windows and Linux from the same source code, I have to caution you to approach such a task very carefully for any "mission critical" application. Do your homework and be very thorough in your testing process. Also, you need to know that although you can use Visual C++ to compile GTK+ code, it requires a couple of hacks and is not a terribly elegant process—not anywhere near as "clean" as compiling for Linux. Plus, you'll need the appropriate dll's and other files, which you then have to distribute to your end users. Caveat emptor: "Let the buyer beware."

The GTK+ widget set is a GUI toolkit for building windowing applications. A "widget" is what the MS Windows world calls a "control." On Linux, the primary windowing environment is called "X-Windows" or "X" for short. It is important to know that unlike in Microsoft Windows, the GUI environment is not integrated with the operating system. You can run an entire Linux machine from the command line. Most distributions of Linux ship with the XFree86 "windowing system." XFree86 is another example of open source software power. It is a powerful windows environment that was built by hackers from around the globe. The GTK+ widget set operates under the windowing environment, providing a set of GUI controls that is easy to implement and use, such as command buttons and text boxes.

However, it is important to note that the GTK+ widget set has nothing inherently comparable to the VB "data control(s)." This book will show you how to combine MySQL (introduced in Chapter 1, "MySQL for Access and SQL Server Developers and DBAs") with the GTK+ widget set.

Why would VB developers be interested in GTK+? First, they are used to "rapid development," and the conversion from controls-events to widgets-callbacks is a natural one. C++ developers will have it a little easier because the syntax and the object oriented (OO) paradigms of inheritance, polymorphism, and encapsulation are already second nature to them. Some will say OO is a way of programming and, therefore, any language can be OO, whereas others will say that OO is part of the language, as in C++. In this case, I think it works to borrow the OO concepts as I have here because it allows you to make the jump to MySQL/GTK+ more easily, especially if you already understand the OO concepts.

Second, most VB developers are used to working with some kind of database, which is why MySQL was introduced in the early part of this book.

Why You Should Use GTK+

If you are looking for a "development environment" for the Linux platform, you will have several to choose from. GTK+ is one of the leaders for GUI development on the Linux platform mainly for the following reasons:

- *It is simple.* The complexity behind drawing widgets and handling events has been hidden from you, so you can focus on your application's functionality.
- *It is extensible.* You can create your own widgets.
- *It is "open source."* You can read and modify the code.
- *It is portable to other operating systems that support the X-Window system.* (Ports are also underway to MS Windows and BeOS, among others. However, as of this writing, they should still be considered in the early stages of development and used only with caution.)
- *The GNOME desktop was built with GTK+.*

Other GUI toolkits are available for the Linux operating system, but none are as suited to our purposes. You may have heard of Motif. It can do most of what you will do later in this book, but it is more complicated and is not "open source," so you have to purchase licenses. Another product, Qt, is as easy to implement as GTK+, but it is not free and is based on C++ instead of C.

You may be asking, "Why is GTK+ and MySQL a good combination?" The primary reason is C. GTK+ has bindings for other languages, but at its heart it is a C toolkit. The C API for MySQL is strong, flexible, and robust. C itself is an all-around good choice because of its ubiquity and portability. C has, without a doubt, withstood the test of time.

Where to Get GTK+ and How to Install It

Again, I have to recommend RPMs as the way to go (see the section titled "Deciding On an Installation Method-Pros and Cons" in Chapter 1). I recommend that you get the latest from the GTK+ Web site: `www.gtk.org`. (At least go there first to find a list of mirror sites.)

When you're connected, fire up your FTP software and point it to `ftp.gtk.org`. (You can use your browser, just put in `ftp://ftp.gtk.org/`. However, this may cause occasional problems with the download, so it's best to stick to FTP software if you can.) At the time this book was written, the full path was `ftp.gtk.org/pub/gtk/v1.2/binary/RPMS/RedHat-6.2/RPMS/i386/`.

Be sure to check for newer files at the time you download. When this book was written, the directory above contained four files:

glib-1.2.8.i386.rpm

glib-devel-1.2.8-1.i386.rpm

gtk+-1.2.8-i386.rpm

gtk+-devel-1.2.8-1.i386.rpm

Download and install these four files. GTK+ is dependent on GLib. So, in order to install GTK+, you must have GLib. The "devel" normally marks tools needed for development; so, obviously those are necessary too. See the instructions regarding installation from an RPM in the previous chapter; all the command flags will be the same, only the `*.rpm` filenames will be different.

Licensing Issues

GTK+ is released under the GNU Lesser General Public License (LGPL). To avoid any confusion or misinterpretation, I am going to quote directly from `http://www.gtk.org/`:

> GTK+ is an Open Source Free Software GUI Toolkit, primarily developed for use with the X Window System. Everything about GTK+ from the object-oriented design to the Free Software LGPL licensing allows you to code your project with

the most freedom possible. You can develop open software, free software, or even commercial non-free software without having to spend a dime for licenses or royalties.[1]

According to the GNU Web page on licensing, the GNU LGPL "is a free software license" that "permits linking with non-free modules."[2]

A Note on GNOME, KDE, and MS Windows

This book is going to focus on the GTK+ widget set, but developers who will be developing *only* for GNOME may want to investigate the use of the GNOME libraries. These libraries are built on GTK+ and add functionality and simplicity to the GTK+ widgets. If, for example, your corporation has settled on GNOME as the "standard" for your Linux desktops, that library may be of use to you.

This work, however, will only make use of the GTK+ widget set because of the desire to build applications that can work across both the KDE and GNOME desktops—and, with the port of GTK+ to Microsoft Windows, even to that environment.

Regarding the port of GTK+ to Windows... At the time of this writing, there is a "caveat emptor" warning on the GIMP for Windows Web page (`http://user.sgic.fi/~tml/gimp/win32/`). Tor Lilqvist, the site author, does not feel that GIMP and GTK+ for Win32 is "ready for prime time" (my description), and those libraries should not be used in production systems. You will have to consider that, but you should also consider that I have been using them for nearly a year and have never had any significant problems. (And I believe it can only improve in the future.) For those reasons, I do not hesitate to use and recommend them.

A Note About Using C

A lot of VB developers feel uncomfortable using C because they think it is too complicated and doesn't allow for fast enough development time. Although that may be true about C, it is not true about the GTK+ widget set. When you use the GTK+ widgets (and the GIMP Drawing Kit and GLib, the building blocks on which GTK+ is built), the amount of C needed is rather limited. First off, GLib provides a full set of type-safe datatypes and data manipulation functions that account for shortcomings in the C language. And those functions are much simpler to use than their "raw" C counterparts. When you add in an Integrated Development Environment or "code builder" like Glade, you further reduce the amount of code you have to write "from the ground up."

An in-depth review of pointers in C will help. Because many of the GTK+ constructs used later are objects referenced by pointers, knowing how C implements and uses pointers will be useful.

I am going to assume the reader has at least a passing knowledge of C; this book isn't going to present a C tutorial or review. We are going to "hop right in."

---

1. Amundson, Shawn T. "The Gimp Toolkit [online]." [cited Sept. 4, 2000]. Available from Internet: www.gtk.org

2. Free Software Foundation, Inc. "GPL-Compatible, Free Software Licenses [online]." [cited Nov. 26, 2000]. Available from Internet: www.gnu.org/philosophy/license-list.html

GTK+ Overview

GTK+ is built on the concept of inheritance (or, more correctly, sub-classing), although the toolkit itself is C-based. Widgets are the basis of other widgets, and some widgets are container widgets. Even the "form" or main window of a program is a widget. Widgets emit signals (*events*) that are caught and handled by the signal handler and passed to the correct "callback," or function.

The Phases of a GTK+ Program

GTK+ programs operate in several distinct phases. First, you must create the widgets and set them to display as needed. You must then tell the program what signal to look for from which widget, and what function to run when that signal is emitted. Then you must explicitly show the widget (or show its parent, which will then show the child widget). When the widget is no longer needed (such as when the application terminates), you need to explicitly destroy the widget.

Object Hierarchy

Every object in the GTK+ widget set is derived from another object, with the "root" object being the GtkObject object.

The following is the object hierarchy for quite possibly the most pedestrian of all GUI controls: the lowly command button:

```
GtkObject
   +-GtkWidget
        +-GtkContainer
             +-GtkBin
                  +-GtkButton
```

And so on. In fact, the GtkToggleButton, GtkCheckButton, and GtkRadioButton are all descendants of the GtkButton type. This is called *inheritance*, and it allows the programmer to use behaviors already defined for an object, to override default behaviors, or create entirely new ones.

The GTK Web site (`www.gtk.org`) maintains a full object hierarchy tree. Check there for the latest widgets and up-to-date information on their uses.

GLib and GDK

These are the building blocks on which GTK+ is built. GLib deals primarily with unglamorous but necessary things like memory, strings, and so on. GDK is the toolkit used for drawing—in this case, drawing of widgets.

GLib

GLib is a set of routines that work with more primitive types; it is actually closer to C than to a GUI toolkit. However, it is fundamentally stronger than C. Glib provides a standard set of macros, functions, and datatypes. For example, it can provide datatypes of certain length no matter what the underlying hardware is, thus solving some major portability issues.

For example, there is a GLib function called `g_malloc()`. It is a replacement for C's `malloc()`. The advantage is that you do not need to check the return value; that is done by the function itself. To take it a step further, consider `g_malloc0()`. It zeroes out the memory for you.

The function prototypes are:

```
gpointer g_malloc ( gulong size );
gpointer g_malloc0 ( gulong size);
```

Notice all those g's. Everything has been converted to GLib. The same is true of string handling functions. GLib defines a new type called GString. Unlike a "normal" C string, a GString can grow automatically, and it is null-terminated. This protects you from buffer overflow errors.

The entire GLib library has been written for such use; if you are new to C, making use of GLib's types instead of native C types will help you produce better and safer code.

GDK

GDK stands for the GNOME Drawing Kit. It is primarily used for drawing graphics. For example, every command button that appears on the screen has to be drawn; this is where GDK comes in. It provides the different looks: non-active, active, pushed, selected, and so on. It also provides widgets for drawing things such as pie graphs and charts. You will see these later as `gdk_`... functions instead of `gtk_`... functions.

Widgets, Not Controls

Widgets are the fundamental building blocks of GTK+. A widget can be any object, seen or unseen. It may or may not have events and properties. In VB, they are called "controls;" here they are called widgets.

Table 2.1 compares common VB controls to their (closest) GTK+ counterparts. A more detailed discussion of widgets follows later in this chapter.

Table 2.1 **VB Basic Controls and Their Corresponding GTK+ Widgets**

VB Control	GTK+ Widget	Comments
PictureBox	GtkImage, GtkPixmap	GtkPixmap is normally used to display icons.
Label	GtkLabel	Very similar in form and function.
TextBox	GtkEntry, GtkText	One for single line, the other for multiple line text.

VB Control	GTK+ Widget	Comments
Frame	GtkFrame, GtkAspectFrame	Does not automatically group radio buttons like VB does.
CommandButton	GtkButton	Very similar in form and function.
CheckBox	GtkCheckButton, GtkToggleButton	Toggle button is a separate widget rather than a property of the check box.
OptionButton	GtkRadioButton	Frames do not automatically group; must be explicitly set.
ComboBox	GtkCombo	An entry widget with a pull-down list.
ListBox	GtkCList, GtkList	Multi-column list (GtkCList) is a separate widget rather than a property of GtkList.
HScrollBar	GtkHScrollbar	Very similar to VB.
VScrollBar	GtkVScrollbar	Very similar to VB.
Timer	GTimer	Gtimer is a GLib object
DriveListBox	N/A	No direct correlation; the idea of a "named drive" does not exist in Linux.
DirListBox	GtkFileSelection	Can be used to select a directory.
FileListBox	GtkFileSelection	Can also be used to select a directory.
Shape	N/A	GDK methods provide for shapes and lines.
Line	N/A	Also see GDK library and methods.
Image	GtkImage	Displays a GdkImage widget.
Data	GtkCList	Has no integrated data connectivity.
OLE	N/A	No correlation in GTK+.
Tab Control (third party)	GtkNotebook	Tabs can be put on any edge: top, bottom, left, or right.
Form	GtkWindow plus GtkLayout	Fails to take advantage of the integrated "resize" capabilities of GTK+.

As you can see, some VB controls have no direct counterparts; that's okay, because some widgets have no corresponding controls. In all, GTK+ provides more than 60 widgets.

Signals and Callbacks

These are what VB developers call "events," although an event in VB includes what GTK+ separates into an event, a signal, and a callback (the function to be executed). An "event" is what you are used to: button clicked, mouse over, and so on. The event causes a *signal* to be emitted from the widget. That signal is tied to a *callback function*, which contains the code that's actually to be executed when the button is pushed (for example). The connection mechanism is the GTK+ "signal handler"—the function gtk_main(), which is usually the last step of a GTK+ program. In GTK+, you have to connect signals to callbacks yourself. This will be covered in depth later in the book.

GTK+ programs will always have a `gtk_main()` function. Its purpose is to monitor for emitted signals and then initiate the correct callback functions. For further demonstration, see Listings 2.1 and 2.2.

Hello World—The Program

For those new to the GTK+ widget set, this Hello World program may prove very instructive. The following program attempts to demonstrate the near-minimum for creating and running a GTK+ program.

Hello World, in Listing 2.1, instantiates a single window and a single command button. It connects the program-terminate function call to the "pushed" event of the command button. Note that you could have made this program even tighter by omitting the command button and the `gtk_main_quit()` call. In that case, the user would have had to click the window-close button in the upper-left corner of the window (the "X" button that is normally instantiated as part of the window, even in X-Windows). That action would close the window, but the user would still have to press Ctrl+C to end the GTK+ program (which you also might have to do if your GTK+ program hangs for any reason).

Listing 2.1   **Minimal GTK+ Program**

```
01 #include <gtk/gtk.h>
02
03 void cmd_button_clicked()
04 {
05    gtk_main_quit();
06 }
07
08 int main (int argc, char *argv[])
09 {
10    GtkWidget *frm_main, *cmd_button;
11
12    gtk_init(&argc, &argv);
13
14    frm_main = gtk_window_new(GTK_WINDOW_TOPLEVEL);
15
16    cmd_button = gtk_button_new_with_label("Hello World.\nClick to close.");
17
18    gtk_signal_connect(GTK_OBJECT(cmd_button),
19                       "clicked",
20                       GTK_SIGNAL_FUNC(cmd_button_clicked),
21                       NULL);
22
23    gtk_container_add(GTK_CONTAINER(frm_main), cmd_button);
24
25    gtk_widget_show_all(frm_main);
26
27    gtk_main();
28
29    return 0;
30 }
```

As you can see, this is a very small and rather useless program. The important parts are outlined here:

Line 01: Include the GTK+ widgets for compilation.

Line 03: The event handler for when the command button is clicked.

Line 08: The main body of the program.

Line 10: Declare the objects, in this case, one window and one command button.

Line 12: Initialize the GTK+ system.

Line 14: Create the form; however, it is still not visible!

Line 16: Create the command button; again, it is not visible.

Line 18: Connect the function on line 03 with the "clicked" event of the command button.

Line 23: Add the button to the window (the container object).

Line 25: Make all widgets visible. (Until now, all widgets have been invisible.) This action is known to substantially increase the usefulness of any GUI application.

Line 27: Start the GTK+ event loop, which monitors for signals emitted from the widgets and fires the correct event handlers.

Line 29: Exit status; required for every C program.

As you can see, this is not terribly difficult ("for C," some of you are saying).

Hello World—The Compile

From the command line, send the following:

```
% gcc -Wall -g listing.2.1.c -o HelloWorld `gtk-config --cflags`
➥`gtk-config --libs`
```

This should produce an executable called HelloWorld in your current directory. You could have just as easily made it HelloWorld.exe by changing the filename after the output flag (-o). (You can omit -o HelloWorld from the preceding command; if you do, it will create a file called a.out by default, as the executable.) The -Wall instructs the gcc compiler to display all warnings, and the -g option instructs the compiler to include debug information for use with a debugger. If you want to avoid retyping, you could put the preceding line into a shell script (the Linux equivalent of a batch file, but it's not as good as a makefile). For example, if the shell script is named build.2.1, you would execute it by sending this command:

```
% ./build.2.1
```

In this case, build.2.1 is the name of the file that has the gcc line in it. Then, to run the program, send:

```
% ./HelloWorld
```

The window should come up. The ./ at the beginning of the above commands tells Linux to look in the current directory, not to search your default path for the file. The `gtk-config...` part of the command line is covered in the next section.

gtk–config

You may have noticed and wondered about the `gtk-config…` on the command line above. gtk-config is a program that expands to fill in flags that gcc will use as part of the compile. You could also think of it as a macro because it stands for something else that will be expanded at the time the information is needed.

This is important: The gtk config program is surrounded by back ticks, not single quotation marks! If you search the GTK+ mailing list archives, you will see how many people are tripped up by this! The back tick character (`) is located in the upper-left corner of most keyboards and usually shares its key with the tilde character (~). The back ticks tell gcc to execute the enclosed program. You can see this for yourself from the following command line:

```
% gtk-config --cflags
```

You will see that this expands to the flags gcc needs to compile a GTK+ program.

VB's "Form" Reincarnated as GtkWindow Plus GtkFixed or GtkLayout

Until this section, when dealing with GTK+, you have not dealt with GTK+ as a "container" widget set, although that is the primary paradigm of GTK+. That is, a window is a *container*. You add child widgets to it, and those child widgets fill the space they are given and automatically resize and adjust when their parent widget resizes or otherwise changes shape. Notice that this happens in HelloWorld (see Listing 2.1). The window widget has one child widget. If you resize the window, the button widget changes shape as well. GTK+ is designed to work this way, and a number of child widgets are designed to take advantage of this behavior.

However, many VB developers who are new to GTK+ may initially be attracted to the GtkFixed or GtkLayout widget because of how closely they resemble the development environments from which they came. Unlike most other widgets in GTK+, these do not resize automatically, at least not for their child widgets. Both are grid widgets on which you can lay out other child widgets, but when the size of the window changes, the child widgets placed on the GtkFixed or GtkLayout widget will not change size or location. This will all be very familiar to developers coming from Visual Basic or C++. The primary difference between the GtkFixed widget and the GtkLayout widget is that the GtkLayout widget has scroll bars that allow you to move around within the window if the window size becomes smaller than the displayable child widgets. The GtkFixed widget will simply cut the child widgets out of view. For the user to see them (or even know they are there!), the user has to resize the window.

A Note of Caution

By using the GtkFixed or GtkLayout widget, you might have an easier start, but you will probably run into a problem getting your window widget to default to the right size to properly display all the child widgets correctly. Be sure to thoroughly study the functions for sizing windows.

In Figure 2.1, notice the grid of dots for placing widgets. This looks very familiar to VB developers; when this window size is changed, the child widgets placed on the grid will not change size. VB developers new to GTK+ should know that this type of application is the exception; the overriding paradigm of GTK+ is what a VB developer would call an automatic resizer control. By using the container paradigm of GTK+, you get this automatic resizer effect without the need for any special widget. GtkLayout certainly has its uses, but in the long run, I suspect you'll be happier with your GTK+ programs if you adapt to the container-resize paradigm. I mention this because when I was a VB developer learning about GTK+, that was my initial reaction. In the long run, though, I found that letting GTK+ resize for me was easier and better. Also note that this figure was created using Glade; see Chapter 5, "Glade for VB Developers," for more information.

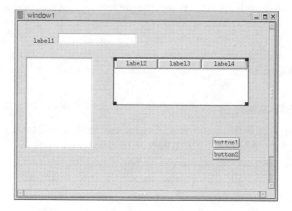

Figure 2.1   GtkWindow plus GtkLayout.

GTK+ Widgets Never Need "Tab Order" Adjustments

Actually, the fact that GTK+ Widgets never need "tab order" adjustments can be either a blessing or a curse. Anyone who has developed VB applications for long learns to hate setting the tab order (that is, the order the cursor follows from control to control when the user presses the Tab button). For industrial-strength application data-entry tasks, this can become a *very* important issue because users will quickly want to move from the mouse to the keyboard to navigate the form. This was one of the things the "old DOS screens" could do very well. Once the user got used to a certain set of keystrokes, he could enter massive amounts of data very quickly by keying ahead of the screen, and the buffer would hold the key strokes and process them in time.

The whole point of this, however, is that in GTK+, the tab order is set for you: right-to-left and top-to-bottom, just as you would "read" the controls on the screen if you were inclined to do so. Actually, GTK+ doesn't really have anything analogous to the tab order; it is handled for you. As I said at the start, though, this can be a blessing —but it can also be a curse. You decide. It can be a blessing because you do not have to code for tab order; it can be a curse because you cannot control the order.

GTK+ Containers as Resizer Controls

Certain widgets act like third-party resizer controls that are sold for VB development (including the GtkWindow widget, which also acts like a resizer control if you think about it). Among these widgets are the GtkButtonBox, the GtkVBox and GtkHBox, and the GtkTable. When resized, they automatically resize their child widgets. (A parent widget is one that contains children widgets.) The following sections describe the most common of these *packing widgets*.

The GtkVBox and GtkHBox Widgets

The GtkVBox widget creates a vertical box that will contain child widgets; the GtkHBox is horizontal. You can set policies, such as whether or not all children should remain the same size and how much spacing there should be between child widgets. See the sample program at the end of the chapter to get a feel for how to use and control these widgets.

Additionally, you can pack the boxes from either the start (top, or left) or the end (bottom, or right).

The GtkTable Widget

The GtkTable widget is what you would get if you crossed a GtkVBox widget with a GtkHBox widget: a widget with both rows and columns, into which you could place child widgets. You can set the same options you could for the preceding widgets, and you can specify that certain widgets should occupy more than one space in the grid.

GtkWindow

This is the main window widget; note that it is not a window into which you can add controls, but it is only a container (meaning that you can add one widget to it—for example, a command button as in HelloWorld). If you want to add more than one widget, you must add another container control to the window, such as a GtkTable widget, into which you can add multiple widgets. With the window widget, you have your basic window frame, with window handles around the edges of the window and the Close, Minimize, and Maximize buttons. That's it! In GTK+, you have to add your own child widgets. The types of windows are GTK_WINDOW_TOPLEVEL, GTK_WINDOW_POPUP, and GTK_WINDOW_DIALOG. The default size is 200 × 200 pixels. The usage is

```
my_window = gtk_window_new( GTK_WINDOW_TOPLEVEL);
```

where my_window has been declared as a GtkWidget type or GtkWindow. See Listing 2.2 at the end of the chapter for an example.

A Note About Instantiation

Generally, you can substitute the name of the widget type you want to instantiate as gtk_xxxxx_new—where xxxxx is the widget type, such as label, or vbox, or whatever.

A Note on Multiple Window Programs

If your program uses several windows and you need to pass data back and forth between the windows, you have a couple of choices. First, of course, you can make the necessary widgets (or all of them, for that matter) global in scope. This, of course, allows you the most and quickest flexibility, but it will also get you into trouble eventually with a program of any size or complexity. The other choice is to keep your global objects (in other words, the top-level windows) to a minimum and query them for the values in the child widgets they contain. This second option will be covered in more detail in Chapter 5. The first option is used in the "tour de widgets" program that follows because it is a rather simple program and its purpose is to demonstrate widget functionality, not give a lesson in variable scope. Although the global-variables option may seem easy and quick, the Glade paradigm of interrogating window widgets for child widgets is actually extremely simple and easy to implement, as you shall see. Actually, this makes sense from a software engineering standpoint: What could be more "global" than your top-level windows? This is explained in more detail in Chapter 5.

A Note About Multiple Document Interface (MDI)

GTK+ doesn't have an inherent way to create MDI applications, as you might be used to doing in Visual Basic. That is, it does not have one large container window in which the multiple windows of the application "float," or "dock," but still contains the multiple windows in one top-level window and shows one item on the taskbar. Instead, with GTK+, each window will show on the taskbar by default, and multiple windows will instantiate on the desktop as individual windows. Glade is a good example of this; see the figures in Chapter 5.

The Basic Widget Tour—As a Program

The program in Listing 2.2 is a short demonstration of what is required to build a GTK+ application. Listing 2.2 is a tour of the basic widgets: label, command button, toggle, check and radio buttons, List, and CList. The running program is designed to demonstrate the functionality of these widgets. It does nothing special, but it attempts to tie together some of the more common widgets to show how they work.

Listing 2.2   **Working Tour of Some Basic GTK+ Widgets**

```
#include <gtk/gtk.h>

/* These are the top-level windows. Normally, they would
 * be the only global variables, but in order to demonstrate
 * widget functionality, many widgets are declared global
 * that normally wouldn't be in a production
 * application.  */

GtkWidget *frm_main;
GtkWidget *frm_buttons;
GtkWidget *frm_text_entry;
```

continues

Listing 2.2   **Continued**

```c
GtkWidget *frm_list_widgets;

/* ================ Main Window ======================== */

void destroy_main(GtkWidget *frm_main, gpointer data);
void show_frm_buttons();
void show_frm_text_entry();
void show_frm_list_widgets();

void MsgBox(gpointer gdata);

gint main(gint argc, gchar * argv[])
{
   GtkWidget *vbox;
   GtkWidget *cmd_buttons;
   GtkWidget *cmd_text_entry;
   GtkWidget *cmd_list_widgets;

   gtk_init(&argc, &argv);
   frm_main = gtk_window_new(GTK_WINDOW_TOPLEVEL);

   /* The following line is where you could set the default window
    * size, in pixels. Without this, it will default to the smallest
    * size that can still completely hold all widgets.  */
   /* gtk_window_set_default_size(GTK_WINDOW(frm_main), 200, 300); */
   gtk_window_set_title(GTK_WINDOW(frm_main), "Widgets Demo");

   /* Instantiate a vertical packing box with three button widgets - the
    * main control box of the program.
    */
   vbox = gtk_vbox_new(TRUE, 0);
   cmd_buttons = gtk_button_new_with_label("Buttons Demo");
   cmd_text_entry = gtk_button_new_with_label("Text and Entry Demo");
   cmd_list_widgets = gtk_button_new_with_label("List and CList Demo");

   gtk_signal_connect(GTK_OBJECT(cmd_buttons),
         "clicked",
         GTK_SIGNAL_FUNC(show_frm_buttons),
         NULL);
   gtk_signal_connect(GTK_OBJECT(cmd_text_entry),
         "clicked",
         GTK_SIGNAL_FUNC(show_frm_text_entry),
         NULL);
   gtk_signal_connect(GTK_OBJECT(cmd_list_widgets),
         "clicked",
         GTK_SIGNAL_FUNC(show_frm_list_widgets),
         NULL);
   gtk_signal_connect(GTK_OBJECT(frm_main),
         "destroy",
```

```
            GTK_SIGNAL_FUNC (destroy_main),
            NULL);

        /* Now, pack the buttons into the vertical packing box… */
    gtk_box_pack_start(GTK_BOX(vbox), cmd_buttons, TRUE, TRUE, 0);
    gtk_box_pack_start(GTK_BOX(vbox), cmd_text_entry, TRUE, TRUE, 0);
    gtk_box_pack_start(GTK_BOX(vbox), cmd_list_widgets, TRUE, TRUE, 0);
    gtk_container_add(GTK_CONTAINER(frm_main), vbox);

        /* Finally, make the main window visible, and transfer control
         * to gtk_main();
         */
    gtk_widget_show_all (frm_main);
    gtk_main ();
    return 0;
}


void destroy_main(GtkWidget * frm_main, gpointer data)
{
        /* This function removes the necessity of hitting Ctrl+C to finally
         * terminate your program after the last window has been closed.
         */
    gtk_main_quit();
}

/*==================== Utility Functions ==================== */

void MsgBox(gpointer gdata)
{
        /* In this utility function, gdata is the message you want to show your
         * message box.
         */
    GtkWidget *msg_box_window;
    GtkWidget *vbox;
    GtkWidget *top_label;

        /* You could put an OK button in here if you wanted
         * to, but since this is a demo, I will just use the
         * Close window button in the upper-right of the window. */

    msg_box_window = gtk_window_new(GTK_WINDOW_DIALOG);
    gtk_window_set_default_size(GTK_WINDOW(msg_box_window), 150, 100);
    gtk_window_set_title(GTK_WINDOW(msg_box_window), "Message Box");
    gtk_window_set_modal(GTK_WINDOW(msg_box_window), TRUE);

    g_print("msgbox window created...\n");

        /* Actually, for this simple implementation, a packing box
         * is not technically necessary. However, having it will
         * make it easier to add other widgets later (such as
```

continues

Listing 2.2 **Continued**

```
    * an "OK" button).
    */

    vbox = gtk_vbox_new(TRUE, 0);

    /* The following line creates a label with a dummy message, and
     * then it fills in the correct message to display. It is done
     * this way to demonstrate the functions, not necessarily because
     * it has to be done this way.
     */
    top_label = gtk_label_new("this is the label");
    gtk_label_set_text(GTK_LABEL(top_label), gdata);

    g_print("child widgets created...\n");

    gtk_box_pack_start(GTK_BOX(vbox), top_label, TRUE, TRUE, 0);
    gtk_container_add( GTK_CONTAINER(msg_box_window), vbox);

    gtk_widget_show_all (msg_box_window);
}

/* ================= Buttons Demo Window ================= */

/* The following widgets are made global for ease of
 * demonstration, not good software engineering.
 * See the "lookup widget" function in support.c of the
 * Glade section for the proper way to handle this. */

GtkWidget *lbl_second;
GtkWidget *toggle_third;
GtkWidget *chk_button;

/* These are the command button events. */
void cmd_top_clicked();
void cmd_top_pressed();
void cmd_top_released();
void cmd_top_enter();
void cmd_top_leave();

/* These are the toggle button functions. */
void toggle_third_toggled();
void toggle_third_clicked();
void cmd_toggle_state_clicked();
void cmd_toggle_up_or_down_clicked();
void cmd_toggle_up_clicked();
void cmd_toggle_down_clicked();

/* These are the check button functions. */
void cmd_chk_button_state_clicked();
```

```
void show_frm_buttons() {

    /* This function creates and displays the window, with the title
     * "Buttons Demo Form," which is shown in Figure 2.2.
     */

    GtkWidget *button_vbox;
    GtkWidget *cmd_top;
    GtkWidget *cmd_toggle_state;
    GtkWidget *cmd_toggle_up_or_down;
    GtkWidget *cmd_toggle_up, *cmd_toggle_down;
    GtkWidget *cmd_chk_button_state;
    GtkWidget *rdo_grp1_btnA, *rdo_grp1_btnB, *rdo_grp1_btnC;
    GtkWidget *rdo_grp2_btnA, *rdo_grp2_btnB, *rdo_grp2_btnC;

    /* The following is for the group-1 radio buttons. */

    GSList *grp1 = NULL;

    /* Notice that the form isn't actually built until the
     * user clicks on the command button. */
    frm_buttons = gtk_window_new(GTK_WINDOW_TOPLEVEL);
    gtk_window_set_title(GTK_WINDOW(frm_buttons), "Buttons Demo Form");

    button_vbox = gtk_vbox_new(TRUE, 0);

    cmd_top = gtk_button_new_with_label("This button just shows events");

    /* Connect the signals to functions.
     * These are the five signals for a command button. */
    gtk_signal_connect(GTK_OBJECT(cmd_top),
         "clicked",
         GTK_SIGNAL_FUNC(cmd_top_clicked),
         NULL);
    gtk_signal_connect(GTK_OBJECT(cmd_top),
         "pressed",
         GTK_SIGNAL_FUNC(cmd_top_pressed),
         NULL);
    /* Be advised: When a command button is pressed, the clicked
     * event occurs before the release event. */
    gtk_signal_connect(GTK_OBJECT (cmd_top),
         "released",
         GTK_SIGNAL_FUNC(cmd_top_released),
         NULL);
    gtk_signal_connect(GTK_OBJECT(cmd_top),
         "enter",
         GTK_SIGNAL_FUNC(cmd_top_enter),
         NULL);
    gtk_signal_connect(GTK_OBJECT(cmd_top),
         "leave",
```

continues

Listing 2.2 **Continued**

```
            GTK_SIGNAL_FUNC(cmd_top_leave),
            NULL);
    /* The event sequence for the command button is: entered,
     * pressed, clicked, released, leave. */

    lbl_second = gtk_label_new("This is a label. The label has no events.");

    toggle_third = gtk_toggle_button_new_with_label("This is a toggle button.");

    /* Because the toggle button is derived from the standard
     * command button, it has all the same events, plus the
     * "toggled" event, below. However, only the clicked event is
     * demonstrated. */

    gtk_signal_connect(GTK_OBJECT(toggle_third),
            "toggled",
            GTK_SIGNAL_FUNC(toggle_third_toggled),
            NULL);
    gtk_signal_connect(GTK_OBJECT(toggle_third),
            "clicked",
            GTK_SIGNAL_FUNC(toggle_third_clicked),
            NULL);
    /* Be advised: The toggle event occurs before the clicked event.
     * Therefore, the event sequence is: entered, pressed, toggled, clicked,
     * released, and leave. */

    /* The following command button checks the state
     * of the toggle button when clicked. */

    cmd_toggle_state = gtk_button_new_with_label
            ("What is the state of the above toggle?");
    gtk_signal_connect(GTK_OBJECT(cmd_toggle_state),
            "clicked",
            GTK_SIGNAL_FUNC(cmd_toggle_state_clicked),
            NULL);

    /* This next command button is used to switch the
     * toggle button to the other state from
     * whatever state it is currently in. */

    cmd_toggle_up_or_down = gtk_button_new_with_label("Toggle to other position.");
    gtk_signal_connect(GTK_OBJECT(cmd_toggle_up_or_down),
            "clicked",
            GTK_SIGNAL_FUNC(cmd_toggle_up_or_down_clicked),
            NULL);

    /* These next two command buttons explicitly
     * place the toggle button in the up or down position. */
```

```
cmd_toggle_up = gtk_button_new_with_label("Toggle UP!");
cmd_toggle_down = gtk_button_new_with_label("Toggle DOWN!");
gtk_signal_connect(GTK_OBJECT(cmd_toggle_up),
      "clicked",
      GTK_SIGNAL_FUNC(cmd_toggle_up_clicked),
      NULL);
gtk_signal_connect(GTK_OBJECT(cmd_toggle_down),
      "clicked",
      GTK_SIGNAL_FUNC(cmd_toggle_down_clicked),
      NULL);

/* Moving on to the check button widget…
 * First, I will create it,
 * then I will demonstrate some of the functions for it.*/

chk_button = gtk_check_button_new_with_label("This is the Czech Button.");
cmd_chk_button_state = gtk_button_new_with_label
                          ("What is the state of the Czech Button?");
gtk_signal_connect(GTK_OBJECT(cmd_chk_button_state),
      "clicked",
      GTK_SIGNAL_FUNC(cmd_chk_button_state_clicked),
      NULL);

/* Finally, I will finish up with the radio buttons
 * widget. There will be two different groups of radio
 * buttons; one in which the group is created manually and
 * one in which the group is created automatically. First, the
 * hard (manual) way… Remember, the GtkFrame object does
 * not automatically group radio buttons for you.
 *
 * For each of the three following radio buttons, the first line
 * creates the radio button, and the second line adds it to grp1.
 * Remember, grp1 is of type GSList. */

rdo_grp1_btnA = gtk_radio_button_new_with_label(grp1, "Group 1, Choice A");
grp1 = gtk_radio_button_group(GTK_RADIO_BUTTON(rdo_grp1_btnA));

rdo_grp1_btnB = gtk_radio_button_new_with_label(grp1, "Group 1, Choice B");
grp1 = gtk_radio_button_group(GTK_RADIO_BUTTON(rdo_grp1_btnB));

rdo_grp1_btnC = gtk_radio_button_new_with_label(grp1, "Group 1, Choice C");
grp1 = gtk_radio_button_group(GTK_RADIO_BUTTON(rdo_grp1_btnC));

/* The above radio buttons will be added to the bottom of the packing
 * box later.
 *
 * Now, to add a radio button group the easy way… */

rdo_grp2_btnA = gtk_radio_button_new_with_label(NULL, "Group 2, Choice A");

/* When you create a new radio button with the "group" parameter
```

continues

Listing 2.2 **Continued**

```
 * set to NULL, GTK+ creates a default group for you. Then, to
 * add other radio buttons to the same group as another radio
 * button, you get the group of the first radio button and send
 * it as the parameter when you create the additional radio
 * buttons for the group, as shown below… */

rdo_grp2_btnB = gtk_radio_button_new_with_label
   (gtk_radio_button_group(GTK_RADIO_BUTTON(rdo_grp2_btnA)),
    "Group 2, Choice B");
rdo_grp2_btnC = gtk_radio_button_new_with_label
   (gtk_radio_button_group(GTK_RADIO_BUTTON(rdo_grp2_btnA)),
    "Group 2, Choice C");

/* Notice that the following lines pack the vbox from the top down.
 * Also, notice that I did not have to declare the number of spaces
 * for child widgets in the vbox; they are added dynamically. */

gtk_box_pack_start(GTK_BOX(button_vbox), cmd_top, TRUE, TRUE, 0);
gtk_box_pack_start(GTK_BOX(button_vbox), lbl_second, TRUE, TRUE, 0);
gtk_box_pack_start(GTK_BOX(button_vbox), toggle_third, TRUE, TRUE, 0);
gtk_box_pack_start(GTK_BOX(button_vbox), cmd_toggle_state, TRUE, TRUE, 0);
gtk_box_pack_start(GTK_BOX(button_vbox), cmd_toggle_up_or_down,TRUE,TRUE, 0);
gtk_box_pack_start(GTK_BOX(button_vbox), cmd_toggle_up, TRUE, TRUE, 0);
gtk_box_pack_start(GTK_BOX(button_vbox), cmd_toggle_down, TRUE, TRUE, 0);
gtk_box_pack_start(GTK_BOX(button_vbox), chk_button, TRUE, TRUE, 0);
gtk_box_pack_start(GTK_BOX(button_vbox), cmd_chk_button_state,TRUE, TRUE, 0);
gtk_box_pack_start(GTK_BOX(button_vbox), rdo_grp1_btnA, TRUE, TRUE, 0);
gtk_box_pack_start(GTK_BOX(button_vbox), rdo_grp1_btnB, TRUE, TRUE, 0);
gtk_box_pack_start(GTK_BOX(button_vbox), rdo_grp1_btnC, TRUE, TRUE, 0);
gtk_box_pack_start(GTK_BOX(button_vbox), rdo_grp2_btnA, TRUE, TRUE, 0);
gtk_box_pack_start(GTK_BOX(button_vbox), rdo_grp2_btnB, TRUE, TRUE, 0);
gtk_box_pack_start(GTK_BOX(button_vbox), rdo_grp2_btnC, TRUE, TRUE, 0);

gtk_container_add(GTK_CONTAINER(frm_buttons), button_vbox);

gtk_widget_show_all(frm_buttons);
}

/* The next five functions demonstrate the "event sequence" for the
 * button widget.
 */
void cmd_top_clicked()
{
   g_print("cmd_top was clicked\n");
}

void cmd_top_pressed()
{
   g_print("cmd_top was pressed\n");
```

```
}

void cmd_top_released()
{
    g_print("cmd_top was released\n");
}

void cmd_top_enter()
{
    g_print("cmd_top was entered\n");
}

void cmd_top_leave()
{
    g_print("cmd_top was left\n");
}

void toggle_third_toggled()
{
    g_print("toggle button toggled\n");
}

void toggle_third_clicked()
{
    gchar *str_toggles;
    static gint count_toggles = 0;

    count_toggles++;

    str_toggles = g_strdup_printf("%d", count_toggles);
    g_print("toggle button clicked, count_toggles is %d\n", count_toggles);
    /* In the following function call, note that the final argument in the
     * parameter list is NULL. This is required by the function.
     */
    gtk_label_set_text(GTK_LABEL(lbl_second),
                  g_strconcat("You toggled ", str_toggles, " time(s).", NULL));
}

void cmd_toggle_state_clicked()
{
    if (TRUE == gtk_toggle_button_get_active(GTK_TOGGLE_BUTTON(toggle_third)) )
        MsgBox("The toggle button is DOWN.");
    else
        MsgBox("The toggle button is UP.");
}

void cmd_toggle_up_or_down_clicked()
{
    g_print("toggling (is that a word??) toggle_third...\n");
    gtk_toggle_button_toggled(GTK_TOGGLE_BUTTON(toggle_third));
}
```

continues

Listing 2.2   **Continued**

```
/* Notice that the following two routines also trigger the "toggled" event. */
void cmd_toggle_up_clicked()
{
   /* In this case, "set_active" means "pushed down." */
   gtk_toggle_button_set_active(GTK_TOGGLE_BUTTON(toggle_third), FALSE);
}

void cmd_toggle_down_clicked()
{
   gtk_toggle_button_set_active(GTK_TOGGLE_BUTTON(toggle_third), TRUE);
}

void cmd_chk_button_state_clicked()
{
   /* Notice what is going on here. The check button widget does not have
    * a "get_active" function of its own. Therefore, in order to retrieve
    * this information, you use the toggle_button_get_active function. The
    * reason this works is that the check button is a first generation
    * descendant of the toggle button. If you think about it, the check
    * button is really nothing more than a different visual representation
    * of the toggle button concept. This also saves time and developer
    * resources because the developers don't have to create a
    * "check_button_get_active" function.
    *
    * The GTK_TOGGLE_BUTTON macro around chk_button, below, "promotes"
    * chk_button to a toggle button temporarily for the purposes of this
    * function. chk_button is still a check button, but this function
    * expects a toggle button. So, the macro takes care of this. */


   if (TRUE == gtk_toggle_button_get_active(GTK_TOGGLE_BUTTON(chk_button)) )
      MsgBox("The Czech button is DOWN.");
   else
      MsgBox("The Czech button is UP.");
}

/* ==================== Text and Entry Widgets Demo Form =================*/

GtkWidget *entry_1;
GtkWidget *text_1;
GtkWidget *opt_text, *opt_entry;
GtkWidget *target_widget;
GtkWidget *spin_start, *spin_end;

void cmd_vis_true_clicked();
void cmd_vis_false_clicked();
void cmd_line_wrap_true_clicked();
void cmd_line_wrap_false_clicked();
void cmd_word_wrap_true_clicked();
```

```
void cmd_word_wrap_false_clicked();
void cmd_editable_true_clicked();
void cmd_editable_false_clicked();
void cmd_editable_get_chars_clicked();

void show_frm_text_entry()
{
    /* This function creates and shows the window in Figure 2.2
     * that has the title, "Text and Entry Demo Form."
     */
    GtkWidget *main_hbox;
    GtkWidget *text_entry_vbox, *text_vbox;
    GtkWidget *lbl_entry, *lbl_text;
    GtkWidget *cmd_vis_true, *cmd_vis_false;
    GtkWidget *cmd_line_wrap_true, *cmd_line_wrap_false;
    GtkWidget *cmd_word_wrap_true, *cmd_word_wrap_false;
    GtkWidget *cmd_editable_true, *cmd_editable_false;
    GtkWidget *cmd_editable_get_chars;
    GtkWidget *get_chars_hbox;
    GtkWidget *lbl_get_chars, *lbl_to;

    /* Notice that the adjustment objects below are of
     * type GtkObject — not GtkWidget. The definition of the
     * adjustment is as an object. So, declaring it here as
     * an object prevents "cast-from-incorrect-type" errors
     * when the program is compiled. If you declared it
     * as type GtkWidget, the program would compile and run,
     * but the results might not be what you expect. */

    GtkObject *spin_start_adjustment, *spin_end_adjustment;

    frm_text_entry = gtk_window_new(GTK_WINDOW_TOPLEVEL);
    gtk_window_set_title(GTK_WINDOW(frm_text_entry),
            "Text and Entry Demo Form");

    /* The following three packing boxes fit together as follows:
     * main_hbox divides the screen into left and right halves,
     * text_entry_vbox then allows a vertical column of widgets
     * on the left half, and text_vbox holds a GtkText widget
     * on the right half of the form. */

    main_hbox = gtk_hbox_new(TRUE, 0);
    text_entry_vbox = gtk_vbox_new(TRUE, 0);
    text_vbox = gtk_vbox_new(TRUE, 0);

    lbl_text = gtk_label_new("To the right is a GtkText widget.");
    lbl_entry = gtk_label_new("Below is a GtkEntry widget.");

    /* The primary difference between the GtkEntry widget and
     * the GtkText widget is that the entry widget is restricted to a
     * single line, whereas the text widget can handle multiple lines.
```

continues

Listing 2.2 **Continued**

```
 *
 * First, the GtkEntry widget… */

entry_1 = gtk_entry_new();

/* You can set the initial string to be displayed… */

gtk_entry_set_text(GTK_ENTRY(entry_1), "This is the initial text.");

cmd_vis_true = gtk_button_new_with_label("Set Entry Visibility = True");
cmd_vis_false = gtk_button_new_with_label("Set Entry Visibility = False");

/* These are the signal callbacks for the two previously created buttons. */
gtk_signal_connect(GTK_OBJECT(cmd_vis_true),
     "clicked",
     GTK_SIGNAL_FUNC(cmd_vis_true_clicked),
     NULL);
gtk_signal_connect(GTK_OBJECT(cmd_vis_false),
     "clicked",
     GTK_SIGNAL_FUNC(cmd_vis_false_clicked),
     NULL);

/* Now, move on to the GtkText widget. */

text_1 = gtk_text_new(NULL, NULL);
gtk_text_insert(GTK_TEXT(text_1), NULL, NULL, NULL,
     "This is the initial text for the text widget. As you can see if you
resize the form, the GtkText widget will simply wrap lines at each letter, not
each word.", -1);

/* For the GtkText widget, the default is for line wrap to be ON. */
cmd_line_wrap_true = gtk_button_new_with_label("Set Text Line Wrap = True");
cmd_line_wrap_false = gtk_button_new_with_label("Set Text Line Wrap = False");

gtk_signal_connect(GTK_OBJECT(cmd_line_wrap_true),
     "clicked",
     GTK_SIGNAL_FUNC(cmd_line_wrap_true_clicked),
     NULL);
gtk_signal_connect(GTK_OBJECT(cmd_line_wrap_false),
     "clicked",
     GTK_SIGNAL_FUNC(cmd_line_wrap_false_clicked),
     NULL);

/* For the GtkText widget, the default is for word wrap to be OFF. */
cmd_word_wrap_true = gtk_button_new_with_label("Set Text Word Wrap = True");
cmd_word_wrap_false = gtk_button_new_with_label("Set Text Word Wrap = False");

gtk_signal_connect(GTK_OBJECT(cmd_word_wrap_true),
     "clicked",
```

```
        GTK_SIGNAL_FUNC(cmd_word_wrap_true_clicked),
        NULL);
gtk_signal_connect(GTK_OBJECT(cmd_word_wrap_false),
    "clicked",
    GTK_SIGNAL_FUNC(cmd_word_wrap_false_clicked),
    NULL);

opt_entry = gtk_radio_button_new_with_label(NULL, "Target is Entry Widget.");
opt_text  = gtk_radio_button_new_with_label
    (gtk_radio_button_group(GTK_RADIO_BUTTON(opt_entry)),
    "Target is Text Widget.");

cmd_editable_true = gtk_button_new_with_label("Set Editable = True");
gtk_signal_connect(GTK_OBJECT(cmd_editable_true),
        "clicked",
        GTK_SIGNAL_FUNC(cmd_editable_true_clicked),
        NULL);

cmd_editable_false = gtk_button_new_with_label("Set Editable = False");
gtk_signal_connect(GTK_OBJECT(cmd_editable_false),
        "clicked",
        GTK_SIGNAL_FUNC(cmd_editable_false_clicked),
        NULL);

/* Below are the spin button controls used to demonstrate the
 * extraction of a portion of text from a gtk_editable
 * widget.
 *
 * First, you need a small horizontal box to contain the widgets. */

get_chars_hbox = gtk_hbox_new(FALSE, 0);

/* The best way to use a spin button widget is to use it with an
 * adjustment object (see the object declarations at the top of this
 * function). An adjustment object abstracts the behavior out of
 * the spin button, allowing you to set the min, max, default, etc.,
 * independent of the spin widget. Note that the parameters to the
 * gtk_adjustment_new function below are of type gfloat, but using
 * integers also works without error or warning.
 *
 * Another note: You can use the same adjustment object for multiple
 * spin buttons, but then they will behave as if they are tied
 * to one another, which means that when you adjust one, the other will
 * mirror that action. */

spin_start_adjustment = gtk_adjustment_new(1.0, 1.0, 99.0, 1.0, 1.0, 1.0);
spin_end_adjustment = gtk_adjustment_new(1, 2, 99, 1, 1, 1);

lbl_get_chars = gtk_label_new("Get chars");
spin_start = gtk_spin_button_new(GTK_ADJUSTMENT(spin_start_adjustment),
                                  1.0, 0);
```

continues

Listing 2.2 **Continued**

```c
lbl_to = gtk_label_new(" to ");
spin_end = gtk_spin_button_new(GTK_ADJUSTMENT(spin_end_adjustment), 1.0, 0);

cmd_editable_get_chars = gtk_button_new_with_label("Get selected chars");
gtk_signal_connect(GTK_OBJECT(cmd_editable_get_chars),
     "clicked",
     GTK_SIGNAL_FUNC(cmd_editable_get_chars_clicked),
     NULL);

/* Now to build the form and then display it. */
gtk_box_pack_start(GTK_BOX(get_chars_hbox), lbl_get_chars, TRUE, TRUE, 0);
gtk_box_pack_start(GTK_BOX(get_chars_hbox), spin_start, FALSE, TRUE, 0);
gtk_box_pack_start(GTK_BOX(get_chars_hbox), lbl_to, TRUE, TRUE, 0);
gtk_box_pack_start(GTK_BOX(get_chars_hbox), spin_end, FALSE, TRUE, 0);

gtk_box_pack_start(GTK_BOX(text_entry_vbox),lbl_text,TRUE,TRUE,0);
gtk_box_pack_start(GTK_BOX(text_entry_vbox),lbl_entry,TRUE,TRUE,0);
gtk_box_pack_start(GTK_BOX(text_entry_vbox),entry_1,TRUE,TRUE,0);
gtk_box_pack_start(GTK_BOX(text_entry_vbox),cmd_vis_true,TRUE,TRUE,0);
gtk_box_pack_start(GTK_BOX(text_entry_vbox),cmd_vis_false,TRUE,TRUE,0);
gtk_box_pack_start(GTK_BOX(text_entry_vbox),cmd_line_wrap_true,TRUE,TRUE,0);
gtk_box_pack_start(GTK_BOX(text_entry_vbox),cmd_line_wrap_false,TRUE,TRUE,0);
gtk_box_pack_start(GTK_BOX(text_entry_vbox),cmd_word_wrap_true,TRUE,TRUE,0);
gtk_box_pack_start(GTK_BOX(text_entry_vbox),cmd_word_wrap_false,TRUE,TRUE,0);
gtk_box_pack_start(GTK_BOX(text_entry_vbox),opt_entry,TRUE,TRUE,0);
gtk_box_pack_start(GTK_BOX(text_entry_vbox),opt_text,TRUE,TRUE,0);
gtk_box_pack_start(GTK_BOX(text_entry_vbox),cmd_editable_true,TRUE,TRUE,0);
gtk_box_pack_start(GTK_BOX(text_entry_vbox),cmd_editable_false,TRUE,TRUE,0);
gtk_box_pack_start(GTK_BOX(text_entry_vbox),get_chars_hbox,FALSE,TRUE,0);
gtk_box_pack_start(GTK_BOX(text_entry_vbox),cmd_editable_get_chars,
                    TRUE, TRUE, 0);

gtk_box_pack_start(GTK_BOX(text_vbox), text_1, TRUE, TRUE, 0);

gtk_box_pack_start(GTK_BOX(main_hbox), text_entry_vbox, TRUE, TRUE, 0);
gtk_box_pack_start(GTK_BOX(main_hbox), text_vbox, TRUE, TRUE, 0);
gtk_container_add(GTK_CONTAINER(frm_text_entry), main_hbox);

gtk_widget_show_all(frm_text_entry);
}

void cmd_vis_true_clicked()
{
   gtk_entry_set_visibility(GTK_ENTRY(entry_1), TRUE);
   g_print("Visibility for entry_1 has been set True.\n");
}

void cmd_vis_false_clicked()
{
```

```
    gtk_entry_set_visibility(GTK_ENTRY(entry_1), FALSE);
    g_print("Visibility for entry_1 has been set False.\n");
}


void cmd_line_wrap_true_clicked()
{
    gtk_text_set_line_wrap(GTK_TEXT(text_1), TRUE);
}

void cmd_line_wrap_false_clicked()
{
    gtk_text_set_line_wrap(GTK_TEXT(text_1), FALSE);
}

void cmd_word_wrap_true_clicked()
{
    gtk_text_set_word_wrap(GTK_TEXT(text_1), TRUE);
}

void cmd_word_wrap_false_clicked()
{
    gtk_text_set_word_wrap(GTK_TEXT(text_1), FALSE);
}

void cmd_editable_true_clicked()
{
    if (TRUE == gtk_toggle_button_get_active(GTK_TOGGLE_BUTTON(opt_entry)) )
    {
        gtk_editable_set_editable(GTK_EDITABLE(entry_1), TRUE);
        MsgBox("The entry widget\nat top left\nis now editable.");
    }
    else
    {
        gtk_editable_set_editable(GTK_EDITABLE(text_1), TRUE);
        MsgBox("The text widget\nis now editable.");
    }
}

void cmd_editable_false_clicked()
{
    if (TRUE == gtk_toggle_button_get_active(GTK_TOGGLE_BUTTON(opt_entry)) )
    {
        gtk_editable_set_editable(GTK_EDITABLE(entry_1), FALSE);
        MsgBox("The entry widget\nat top left\nis now\nNOT\neditable.");
    }
    else
    {
        gtk_editable_set_editable(GTK_EDITABLE(text_1), FALSE);
        MsgBox("The text widget\nis now\nNOT\neditable.");
    }
```

continues

Listing 2.2 **Continued**

```c
}

void cmd_editable_get_chars_clicked()
{
  if (TRUE == gtk_toggle_button_get_active(GTK_TOGGLE_BUTTON(opt_entry)) )
  {
  /* Note: Because the gtk_editable_get_chars does not include
   * the character in the second parameter, you have to move it
   * back one space so as to be inclusive. For example, if the
   * user has selected characters 1 through 4, he expects to see
   * character 1, but the default behavior of the call below is
   * to show only characters 2 through 4.
   * One of the advantages to using the spin button controls here
   * is that they already have functions that return integers.
   * If you were to use an Entry or Text widget, you would have
   * to do the conversions yourself./*

    MsgBox(g_strconcat("The chars from the\nentry widget are: ",
            gtk_editable_get_chars(GTK_EDITABLE(entry_1),
            gtk_spin_button_get_value_as_int(GTK_SPIN_BUTTON(spin_start)) - 1,
            gtk_spin_button_get_value_as_int(GTK_SPIN_BUTTON(spin_end))),
            NULL)
        );
  }
  else
  {
  MsgBox(g_strconcat("The chars from the\ntext widget are: ",
            gtk_editable_get_chars(GTK_EDITABLE(text_1),
            gtk_spin_button_get_value_as_int(GTK_SPIN_BUTTON(spin_start)) - 1,
            gtk_spin_button_get_value_as_int(GTK_SPIN_BUTTON(spin_end))),
            NULL)
        );
  }
}

/* ====================== List Widgets Demo ==========================*/

void cmd_add_checkbox_clicked();
void cmd_add_pixmap_clicked();
void cmd_SINGLE_clicked();
void cmd_BROWSE_clicked();
void cmd_MULTIPLE_clicked();
void cmd_EXTENDED_clicked();

void cmd_prepend_clicked();
void cmd_append_clicked();
void cmd_insert_row_2_clicked();
void cmd_set_text_clicked();
void cmd_set_pixmap_clicked();
```

```
void cmd_set_pixtext_clicked();
void cmd_sort_clicked();

GtkWidget *list_left;
GtkWidget *clist_right;

/* These arrays are your data for the CList.
 * Note that the number of elements
 * must match that of the CList widget.
 */

gchar *a_row[3] = {"blank", "", ""};

void show_frm_list_widgets()
{
    /* This function creates and displays the
     * window titled "List and CList Demo Form"
     * that's shown in Figure 2.2.
     */

    GtkWidget *lists_hbox;
/* The List widget is on the left, and the CList widget is on the right. */
    GtkWidget *lbl_list_box, *lbl_clist_box;
    GtkWidget *vbox_left, *vbox_right;
    GtkWidget *cmd_SINGLE, *cmd_BROWSE, *cmd_MULTIPLE, *cmd_EXTENDED;
    GtkWidget *cmd_add_checkbox;
    GtkWidget *cmd_add_pixmap;
    GtkWidget *cmd_append, *cmd_prepend, *cmd_insert_row_2;
    GtkWidget *cmd_set_text, *cmd_set_pixmap, *cmd_set_pixtext;
    GtkWidget *cmd_sort;

    /* Next is an array of column headers for the CList widget. */
    gchar *col_heads[3] = {"Author", "Title", "Year"};

    GList *list_box_items = NULL;

    frm_list_widgets = gtk_window_new(GTK_WINDOW_TOPLEVEL);
    gtk_window_set_title(GTK_WINDOW(frm_list_widgets),
                         "List and CList Demo Form");

    /* These are the main widgets on the form. */

    lists_hbox = gtk_hbox_new(TRUE, 0);

    lbl_list_box = gtk_label_new("Below is a List Box.");
    lbl_clist_box = gtk_label_new("... and this is a CList Box.");

    vbox_left = gtk_vbox_new(FALSE, 0);
    vbox_right = gtk_vbox_new(FALSE, 0);

    list_left = gtk_list_new();
```

continues

Listing 2.2   **Continued**

```
/* Now, concentrate on the List widget.
 *
 * The great thing about the List widget is that you can
 * have any widget as a child widget. "ANY widget?" Well,
 * that's what they claim. Normally, this will be used
 * with label widgets, pixmaps (Linux' version of icons), and
 * check boxes. Those are the things you expect to see
 * in a list box. "But ANY widget? What about a window?
 * How about a List widget filled with CList widgets?"
 * I have never tried to do anything like that before,
 * and I cannot think of any kind of business application
 * where that would make a good user interface, but you
 * never know. If you get a chance to try something
 * nutso like that, be sure to drop me a line and let
 * me know how it turned out!
 *
 * Okay, here is the deal with list boxes. The list of
 * items in the list box is actually a separate object
 * (a linked list) from the list box itself.
 * At the top of this function, you defined a GList object named
 * list_box_items. This GList is filled with "list
 * items." Now, because a "list of labels" is so
 * common, GTK+ has a designated function just for adding
 * "list item" objects: gtk_list_item_new_with_label().
 * So you can create a GList and fill it with GtkListItem
 * widgets…
 */

list_box_items = g_list_append(list_box_items,
        gtk_list_item_new_with_label("list item 1"));
list_box_items = g_list_append(list_box_items,
        gtk_list_item_new_with_label("list item 2"));
list_box_items = g_list_append(list_box_items,
        gtk_list_item_new_with_label("list item 3"));

/* Once you have the GList of GtkListItem widgets, you take
 * that whole list and smack it into the GtkListBox widget
 * that you created:
 */

g_print("starting initial list append...\n");

gtk_list_append_items(GTK_LIST(list_left), list_box_items);

/* So, that's the easy case – all label widgets. Now let's see
 * if you can get a few other things in there too…
 *
 * Add a checkbox, too.
 */
```

```
cmd_add_checkbox = gtk_button_new_with_label("Add a checkbox.");
gtk_signal_connect(GTK_OBJECT(cmd_add_checkbox),
      "clicked",
      GTK_SIGNAL_FUNC(cmd_add_checkbox_clicked),
      NULL);


/* And how about a pixmap? */
cmd_add_pixmap = gtk_button_new_with_label("Add a pixmap.");
gtk_signal_connect(GTK_OBJECT(cmd_add_pixmap),
      "clicked",
      GTK_SIGNAL_FUNC(cmd_add_pixmap_clicked),
      NULL);


/* And how about some command buttons for setting the
 * selection mode of the List widget? */

cmd_SINGLE = gtk_button_new_with_label("Set selection mode SINGLE");
cmd_BROWSE = gtk_button_new_with_label("Set selection mode BROWSE");
cmd_MULTIPLE = gtk_button_new_with_label("Set selection mode MULTIPLE");
cmd_EXTENDED = gtk_button_new_with_label("Set selection mode EXTENDED");

gtk_signal_connect(GTK_OBJECT(cmd_SINGLE),
      "clicked",
      GTK_SIGNAL_FUNC(cmd_SINGLE_clicked),
      NULL);
gtk_signal_connect(GTK_OBJECT(cmd_BROWSE),
      "clicked",
      GTK_SIGNAL_FUNC(cmd_BROWSE_clicked),
      NULL);
gtk_signal_connect(GTK_OBJECT(cmd_MULTIPLE),
      "clicked",
      GTK_SIGNAL_FUNC(cmd_MULTIPLE_clicked),
      NULL);
gtk_signal_connect(GTK_OBJECT(cmd_EXTENDED),
      "clicked",
      GTK_SIGNAL_FUNC(cmd_EXTENDED_clicked),
      NULL);

/* Finally, add the CList widget.
 *
 * The CList widget is the closest GTK+ comes to a "data
 * control"; the problem is that you have to supply your own
 * database connectivity.
 *
 * Unlike the List widget, which can accept almost any
 * child widget to populate the list box, the CList
 * widget is limited to text and pixmaps.
 *
 * Also note that the CList widget has the same
 * selection modes as the List widget.
 */
```

continues

Listing 2.2   **Continued**

```
clist_right = gtk_clist_new_with_titles(3, col_heads);

/* Populating a CList widget is pretty simple, as you can see. */

gtk_clist_append(GTK_CLIST(clist_right), a_row);

cmd_append = gtk_button_new_with_label("Append Row");
gtk_signal_connect(GTK_OBJECT(cmd_append),
        "clicked",
        GTK_SIGNAL_FUNC(cmd_append_clicked),
        NULL);
cmd_prepend = gtk_button_new_with_label("Prepend Row");
gtk_signal_connect(GTK_OBJECT(cmd_prepend),
        "clicked",
        GTK_SIGNAL_FUNC(cmd_prepend_clicked),
        NULL);
cmd_insert_row_2 = gtk_button_new_with_label("Insert to Row 2");
gtk_signal_connect(GTK_OBJECT(cmd_insert_row_2),
        "clicked",
        GTK_SIGNAL_FUNC(cmd_insert_row_2_clicked),
        NULL);

cmd_set_text = gtk_button_new_with_label("Set Row 3 Col 1 to Text");
gtk_signal_connect(GTK_OBJECT(cmd_set_text),
        "clicked",
        GTK_SIGNAL_FUNC(cmd_set_text_clicked),
        NULL);
cmd_set_pixmap = gtk_button_new_with_label("Set Row 3 Col 2 to Pixmap");
gtk_signal_connect(GTK_OBJECT(cmd_set_pixmap),
        "clicked",
        GTK_SIGNAL_FUNC(cmd_set_pixmap_clicked),
        NULL);
cmd_set_pixtext = gtk_button_new_with_label("Set Row 3 Col 3 to PixText");
gtk_signal_connect(GTK_OBJECT(cmd_set_pixtext),
        "clicked",
        GTK_SIGNAL_FUNC(cmd_set_pixtext_clicked),
        NULL);

cmd_sort = gtk_button_new_with_label("Sort on Column 1");
gtk_signal_connect(GTK_OBJECT(cmd_sort),
        "clicked",
        GTK_SIGNAL_FUNC(cmd_sort_clicked),
        NULL);

/* Finally, add the interface. As before, you are going to pack the
 * widgets "from the inside out." */

gtk_box_pack_start(GTK_BOX(vbox_left), lbl_list_box, TRUE, TRUE, 0);
```

```
    gtk_box_pack_start(GTK_BOX(vbox_left), list_left, TRUE, TRUE, 0);
    gtk_box_pack_start(GTK_BOX(vbox_left), cmd_add_checkbox, TRUE, TRUE, 0);
    gtk_box_pack_start(GTK_BOX(vbox_left), cmd_add_pixmap, TRUE, TRUE, 0);
    gtk_box_pack_start(GTK_BOX(vbox_left), cmd_SINGLE, TRUE, TRUE, 0);
    gtk_box_pack_start(GTK_BOX(vbox_left), cmd_BROWSE, TRUE, TRUE, 0);
    gtk_box_pack_start(GTK_BOX(vbox_left), cmd_MULTIPLE, TRUE, TRUE, 0);
    gtk_box_pack_start(GTK_BOX(vbox_left), cmd_EXTENDED, TRUE, TRUE, 0);

    gtk_box_pack_start(GTK_BOX(vbox_right), lbl_clist_box, TRUE, TRUE, 0);
    gtk_box_pack_start(GTK_BOX(vbox_right), clist_right, TRUE, TRUE, 0);
    gtk_box_pack_start(GTK_BOX(vbox_right), cmd_append, TRUE, TRUE, 0);
    gtk_box_pack_start(GTK_BOX(vbox_right), cmd_prepend, TRUE, TRUE, 0);
    gtk_box_pack_start(GTK_BOX(vbox_right), cmd_insert_row_2, TRUE, TRUE, 0);
    gtk_box_pack_start(GTK_BOX(vbox_right), cmd_set_text, TRUE, TRUE, 0);
    gtk_box_pack_start(GTK_BOX(vbox_right), cmd_set_pixmap, TRUE, TRUE, 0);
    gtk_box_pack_start(GTK_BOX(vbox_right), cmd_set_pixtext, TRUE, TRUE, 0);
    gtk_box_pack_start(GTK_BOX(vbox_right), cmd_sort, TRUE, TRUE, 0);

    gtk_box_pack_start(GTK_BOX(lists_hbox), vbox_left, TRUE, TRUE, 0);
    gtk_box_pack_start(GTK_BOX(lists_hbox), vbox_right, TRUE, TRUE, 0);

    gtk_container_add(GTK_CONTAINER(frm_list_widgets), lists_hbox);

    gtk_widget_show_all(frm_list_widgets);
}

void cmd_add_checkbox_clicked()
{
    GtkWidget *chk_box_item;
    GtkWidget *list_item;

    chk_box_item = gtk_check_button_new_with_label("Check box item");
    list_item = gtk_list_item_new();
    gtk_container_add(GTK_CONTAINER(list_item), chk_box_item);

    gtk_container_add(GTK_CONTAINER(list_left), list_item);

    /* In essence, the line below "refreshes" the form. */
    gtk_widget_show_all(frm_list_widgets);
}

/* Looks like it is time to introduce pixmaps because one will be needed
 * for the next function call.
 *
 * Note that the pixmap could just as easily have been put in a
 * separate file and included with an #include statement.
 *
 * Here is how to read a pixmap file:
 *
 * The first line ("26 7 2 1") gives the dimensions of the pixmap.
 * In this case, that means 26 columns by 7 rows, 2 color values,
```

continues

Listing 2.2   **Continued**

```
* and 1 character is needed to display a color.
*
* The next two lines define the color values. "None" is for
* transparency, and the other is in hex.
*
* After that, the rows are laid out with parentheses around them,
* and the values within the parentheses must correspond to one
* of the colors listed.
*/

static const gchar *pixmap_xpm[] = {
   "26 7 2 1",
   "    c None",
   ".   c #AA8800",
  /*123456789.123456789.123456 <-- for spacing */
   "                          ",
   " ..   .  .   .  .    .. ",
   " . . . . .. .. .. . . .",
   " ..   .   .  . . ... .. ",
   " .    . . . .    . . . ",
   " .   .. . . .    . . . ",
   "                          "
};

/* Important Safety Tip: The semicolon on the preceding
 * line is necessary because the entire pixmap structure
 * above is a single variable. If you don't include the
 * pixmap, you will get a "parse error before…" message
 * when you compile.
 *
 * The pixmap above draws out the word "PIXMAP".
 */

void cmd_add_pixmap_clicked()
{
   GtkWidget *my_pixmap;
   GtkWidget *list_item;

   /* The following objects are needed for drawing a pixmap */

   GdkBitmap *a_bitmap;
   GdkPixmap *a_pixmap;

   a_pixmap = gdk_pixmap_colormap_create_from_xpm_d
      (NULL,
      gdk_colormap_get_system(),
      &a_bitmap,
      NULL,
      (gchar **) pixmap_xpm);
```

```
    my_pixmap = gtk_pixmap_new(a_pixmap, a_bitmap);

    list_item = gtk_list_item_new();
    gtk_container_add(GTK_CONTAINER(list_item), my_pixmap);

    gtk_container_add(GTK_CONTAINER(list_left), list_item);

    gtk_widget_show_all(frm_list_widgets);
}

void cmd_SINGLE_clicked()
{
    /* SINGLE mode allows one selection only. You must click and release
     * on the same item to select it. Click, hold, and drag changes the
     * focus, not the selection. The item is selected on the mouse up event.
     * Ctrl and Shift modifiers have no effect.
     */

    gtk_list_set_selection_mode(GTK_LIST(list_left), GTK_SELECTION_SINGLE);
}

void cmd_BROWSE_clicked()
{
    /* Only one selection is allowed. The item is selected on mouse down
     * event. Click, hold, and drag changes the selection. Ctrl and Shift
     * modifiers have no effect.
     */

    gtk_list_set_selection_mode(GTK_LIST(list_left), GTK_SELECTION_BROWSE);
}

void cmd_MULTIPLE_clicked()
{
    /* Multiple selections are allowed; other behaviors are similar to SINGLE
     * mode. Mouse up event selects, and you must click and release on the
     * same item to select. Click, hold, and drag changes focus, not
     * selection. Ctrl and Shift modifiers have no effect.
     */

    gtk_list_set_selection_mode(GTK_LIST(list_left), GTK_SELECTION_MULTIPLE);
}

void cmd_EXTENDED_clicked()
{
    /* Multiple selection; selection is on the mouse down event. Click,
     * hold, and drag selects all list items that come under the mouse.
     * Ctrl and Shift modifiers behave as expected: Shift selects all between
     * previous mouse click and current mouse click, Ctrl selects item that is
     * currently under the mouse in addition to previously selected items.
     */
```

continues

Listing 2.2 **Continued**

```c
   gtk_list_set_selection_mode(GTK_LIST(list_left), GTK_SELECTION_EXTENDED);
}

void cmd_prepend_clicked()
{
   a_row[0] = "Ayn Rand";
   a_row[1] = "Atlas Shrugged";
   a_row[2] = "1957";

   gtk_clist_prepend(GTK_CLIST(clist_right), a_row);
   gtk_clist_columns_autosize(GTK_CLIST(clist_right));
}

void cmd_append_clicked()
{
   a_row[0] = "Hermann Hesse";
   a_row[1] = "Steppenwolf";
   a_row[2] = "1898";

   gtk_clist_append(GTK_CLIST(clist_right), a_row);
   gtk_clist_columns_autosize(GTK_CLIST(clist_right));
}

void cmd_insert_row_2_clicked()
{
   a_row[0] = "Jack Kerouac";
   a_row[1] = "On The Road";
   a_row[2] = "1958";

   /* The 1 in the insert below is really "row 2";
    * the second parameter is zero-based.
    */
   gtk_clist_insert(GTK_CLIST(clist_right), 1, a_row);
   gtk_clist_columns_autosize(GTK_CLIST(clist_right));
}

/* For the next three function calls, which have to do with
 * setting text or pixmaps in a CList widget, the following is true:
 *
 * The row and column referenced need to already exist
 * (at least in this example) because you are not checking
 * return values for errors.
 *
 * Also note that a "2" referencing a row is actually
 * "row 3" because the CList widget's row and column
 * references are zero-based.
 */

void cmd_set_text_clicked()
{
   gtk_clist_set_text(GTK_CLIST(clist_right), 2, 0, "Text");
   gtk_clist_columns_autosize(GTK_CLIST(clist_right));
```

```
}

void cmd_set_pixmap_clicked()
{
    GtkWidget *my_pixmap;

    GdkBitmap *a_bitmap;
    GdkPixmap *a_pixmap;

    a_pixmap = gdk_pixmap_colormap_create_from_xpm_d
        (NULL,
        gdk_colormap_get_system(),
        &a_bitmap,
        NULL,
        (gchar **) pixmap_xpm);

    my_pixmap = gtk_pixmap_new(a_pixmap, a_bitmap);

    gtk_clist_set_pixmap(GTK_CLIST(clist_right), 2, 1, a_pixmap, a_bitmap);
    gtk_clist_columns_autosize(GTK_CLIST(clist_right));
}

void cmd_set_pixtext_clicked()
{
    GtkWidget *my_pixmap;

    GdkBitmap *a_bitmap;
    GdkPixmap *a_pixmap;

    a_pixmap = gdk_pixmap_colormap_create_from_xpm_d
        (NULL,
        gdk_colormap_get_system(),
        &a_bitmap,
        NULL,
        (gchar **) pixmap_xpm);

    my_pixmap = gtk_pixmap_new(a_pixmap, a_bitmap);

    gtk_clist_set_pixtext(GTK_CLIST(clist_right), 2, 2, "Text",
        10, a_pixmap, a_bitmap);
    gtk_clist_columns_autosize(GTK_CLIST(clist_right));
}

void cmd_sort_clicked()
{
    gtk_clist_set_sort_column(GTK_CLIST(clist_right), 0);
    gtk_clist_sort(GTK_CLIST(clist_right));

    /* Note that if the CList is to be sorted automatically each time
     * the data changes, there is a gtk_clist_set_auto_sort() function.
     */
}
```

> **Compiling with gcc**
>
> As with the C program demonstrating MySQL connectivity in Chapter 1 (Listing 1.3) and the HelloWorld program (Listing 2.1), you can compile from the command line, from a shell script, or from a Makefile. The choice is yours. This compile is not different from the compile done for HelloWorld, except for the *.c filename, of course. From the command line, send:
>
> ```
> %gcc -Wall -g listing.2.2.c `gtk-config --cflags --libs`
> ```

Figure 2.2 shows Listing 2.2 running, with all the window widgets visible. Notice the Text widget in the Text and Entry Demo Form window; the "curly arrows" at the end of the lines indicate that the text widget is wrapping the text, so the user doesn't have to enter hard returns as part of the text he or she is entering. If you compile and run the program, you will see other things, such as the List widget showing pixmaps.

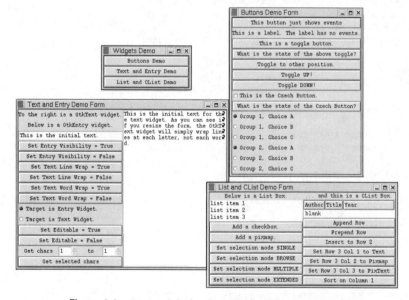

Figure 2.2 Listing 2.2, the Basic Widget Tour, running.

3

More GTK+ Widgets

This chapter continues the widget tour that started in the previous chapter. Each of the items listed below will have its own program. This chapter presents several short programs that demonstrate the functionality of the following widgets:

- GtkCombo
- GtkProgressBar and GtkStatusBar
- GtkFrame and GtkAspectFrame
- GtkDialog, GtkFileSelection, GtkColorSelectionDialog, and GtkFontSelectionDialog
- Menu Widget, ItemFactory, and Popup Menu widgets

The GtkCombo Widget

The GtkCombo widget is the GTK+ answer to the combo box. It has an entry widget with a drop-down list of values. The user can enter values directly into the entry widget, and if the entered value matches a value already in the list, the widget can be set to automatically fill in the value. One of the interesting things about the GtkCombo widget is that the list of values is actually maintained separately from the widget itself. Figure 3.1 shows the running program compiled from Listing 3.1. Note that the comments in the code in Listing 3.1 tell what is coming up rather than what just happened.

Figure 3.1 Combo widget demo program.

Listing 3.1 **GtkCombo Widget Demo Program**

```
#include <gtk/gtk.h>

GtkWidget *frm_combo;
GtkWidget *cbo_first;

void destroy_main();
void cmd_set_use_arrows_false_clicked();
void cmd_set_use_arrows_true_clicked();
void cmd_set_use_arrows_always_false_clicked();
void cmd_set_use_arrows_always_true_clicked();
void cmd_set_case_sensitive_true_clicked();
void cmd_set_case_sensitive_false_clicked();
void cmd_get_text_clicked();

gint main(gint argc, gchar *argv[])
{

   GtkWidget *vbox_main;
   GtkWidget *cmd_set_use_arrows_false, *cmd_set_use_arrows_true;
   GtkWidget *cmd_set_use_arrows_always_false, *cmd_set_use_arrows_always_true;
   GtkWidget *cmd_set_case_sensitive_true, *cmd_set_case_sensitive_false;
   GtkWidget *cmd_get_text;

   /* Notice that the list for the combo box is maintained separately
    * from the combo box itself. GList is a GLib data type.
    */

   GList *list_of_months = NULL;


   gtk_init(&argc, &argv);

   frm_combo = gtk_window_new(GTK_WINDOW_TOPLEVEL);

   gtk_window_set_title(GTK_WINDOW(frm_combo), "Combo and Options Demo");
```

```
gtk_signal_connect(GTK_OBJECT(frm_combo),
    "destroy",
    GTK_SIGNAL_FUNC(destroy_main),
    NULL);

vbox_main = gtk_vbox_new(TRUE, 0);

/* For the combo box, when the cursor is in the entry part of
 * the widget, pressing the Enter key displays the list, and
 * pressing the Esc key collapses the list.
 */

cbo_first = gtk_combo_new();

list_of_months = g_list_append(list_of_months, "January");
list_of_months = g_list_append(list_of_months, "February");
list_of_months = g_list_append(list_of_months, "March");
list_of_months = g_list_append(list_of_months, "April");
list_of_months = g_list_append(list_of_months, "May");
list_of_months = g_list_append(list_of_months, "June");
list_of_months = g_list_append(list_of_months, "July");
list_of_months = g_list_append(list_of_months, "August");
list_of_months = g_list_append(list_of_months, "AUGUST");

gtk_combo_set_popdown_strings(GTK_COMBO(cbo_first), list_of_months);

/* If you wait until after the GList of values has
 * been set, you can explicitly set the displayed value.
 * Note that if the following line had been before the
 * gtk_combo_set_popdown_strings() call, the combo box
 * would have defaulted to the first item in the GList
 * ("January"), not to the value that you explicitly set.
 */

gtk_entry_set_text(GTK_ENTRY(GTK_COMBO(cbo_first)->entry), "October");

/* The previous call is the first example so far of accessing a
 * "sub-object." In this case, the combo box is a composite widget,
 * and one of the child widgets is an entry box. The -> is C
 * pointer syntax.
 *
 * If the current value shown in the combo widget is not
 * in the GList for that widget, the up and down arrows
 * are disabled. This is because the up and down arrows work
 * by comparing the current value against the values in the
 * list and then selecting the correct replacement value
 * each time the key is pushed.
 */
/* Here are some buttons to demonstrate the functionality: */
```

continues

Listing 3.1   **Continued**

```
cmd_set_use_arrows_true = gtk_button_new_with_label("Set Use Arrows TRUE");
gtk_signal_connect(GTK_OBJECT(cmd_set_use_arrows_true),
                   "clicked",
                   GTK_SIGNAL_FUNC(cmd_set_use_arrows_true_clicked),
                   NULL);
cmd_set_use_arrows_false = gtk_button_new_with_label("Set Use Arrows FALSE");
gtk_signal_connect(GTK_OBJECT(cmd_set_use_arrows_false),
                   "clicked",
                   GTK_SIGNAL_FUNC(cmd_set_use_arrows_false_clicked),
                   NULL);

cmd_set_use_arrows_always_true = gtk_button_new_with_label("Set Always TRUE");
gtk_signal_connect(GTK_OBJECT(cmd_set_use_arrows_always_true),
                   "clicked",
                   GTK_SIGNAL_FUNC(cmd_set_use_arrows_always_true_clicked),
                   NULL);
cmd_set_use_arrows_always_false = gtk_button_new_with_label("Set Always
➥FALSE");
gtk_signal_connect(GTK_OBJECT(cmd_set_use_arrows_always_false),
                   "clicked",
                   GTK_SIGNAL_FUNC(cmd_set_use_arrows_always_false_clicked),
                   NULL);

cmd_set_case_sensitive_true = gtk_button_new_with_label("Case Sensitive TRUE");
gtk_signal_connect(GTK_OBJECT(cmd_set_case_sensitive_true),
                   "clicked",
                   GTK_SIGNAL_FUNC(cmd_set_case_sensitive_true_clicked),
                   NULL);
cmd_set_case_sensitive_false = gtk_button_new_with_label("Case Sensitive
➥FALSE");
gtk_signal_connect(GTK_OBJECT(cmd_set_case_sensitive_false),
                   "clicked",
                   GTK_SIGNAL_FUNC(cmd_set_case_sensitive_false_clicked),
                   NULL);

cmd_get_text = gtk_button_new_with_label("Get Text");
gtk_signal_connect(GTK_OBJECT(cmd_get_text),
                   "clicked",
                   GTK_SIGNAL_FUNC(cmd_get_text_clicked),
                   NULL);

/* Now assemble the interface… */

gtk_box_pack_start(GTK_BOX(vbox_main), cbo_first, TRUE, TRUE, 0);
gtk_box_pack_start(GTK_BOX(vbox_main), cmd_set_use_arrows_true,
                   TRUE, TRUE, 0);
gtk_box_pack_start(GTK_BOX(vbox_main), cmd_set_use_arrows_false,
                   TRUE, TRUE, 0);
gtk_box_pack_start(GTK_BOX(vbox_main), cmd_set_use_arrows_always_true,
                   TRUE, TRUE, 0);
```

```
    gtk_box_pack_start(GTK_BOX(vbox_main), cmd_set_use_arrows_always_false,
                       TRUE, TRUE, 0);
    gtk_box_pack_start(GTK_BOX(vbox_main), cmd_set_case_sensitive_true,
                       TRUE, TRUE, 0);
    gtk_box_pack_start(GTK_BOX(vbox_main), cmd_set_case_sensitive_false,
                       TRUE, TRUE, 0);
    gtk_box_pack_start(GTK_BOX(vbox_main), cmd_get_text, TRUE, TRUE, 0);

    gtk_container_add(GTK_CONTAINER(frm_combo), vbox_main);

    gtk_widget_show_all (frm_combo);
    gtk_main ();
    return 0;

}

void destroy_main()
{   gtk_main_quit();
}

void cmd_set_use_arrows_true_clicked()
{
    /* This is the default. */
    gtk_combo_set_use_arrows(GTK_COMBO(cbo_first), TRUE);
}

void omd_set_use_arrows_false_clicked()
{
    gtk_combo_set_use_arrows(GTK_COMBO(cbo_first), FALSE);
}

void cmd_set_use_arrows_always_true_clicked()
{
    /* This is the default. */
    gtk_combo_set_use_arrows_always(GTK_COMBO(cbo_first), TRUE);

    /* This function essentially sets the wrapping of the drop-down
     * list when the user presses the up and down keys. When
     * set to TRUE, the use of the up or down keys stops when
     * the value displayed is the first or last. From there,
     * pressing the up or down key moves the focus to
     * the next widget.
     */
}

void cmd_set_use_arrows_always_false_clicked()
{
    gtk_combo_set_use_arrows_always(GTK_COMBO(cbo_first), FALSE);

    /* When set to FALSE, pressing the up or down arrow in the
     * the combo box "wraps" the value shown. Try it.
     */
```

continues

Listing 3.1   **Continued**

```
}

void cmd_set_case_sensitive_true_clicked()
{
   gtk_combo_set_case_sensitive(GTK_COMBO(cbo_first), TRUE);
}

void cmd_set_case_sensitive_false_clicked()
{
   /* This is the default. */

   /* This option will select the first input in the list for
    * you that matches your input if you enter custom text in
    * the combo widget. For example, if you manually enter
    * "AuGuSt," it will be changed to "August".
    *
    * Also, note that if you bring up the drop-down box and
    * press the down arrow key to the bottom, the selection
    * will stop at "August" and not move down to
    * select "AUGUST."
    */

   gtk_combo_set_case_sensitive(GTK_COMBO(cbo_first), FALSE);
}

void cmd_get_text_clicked()
{
   g_print("Combo is: %s\n",
           gtk_entry_get_text(GTK_ENTRY(GTK_COMBO(cbo_first)->entry)));
}
```

The GtkProgressBar and GtkStatusBar Widgets

The GtkProgressBar and GtkStatusBar widgets are exactly what you'd expect: a
progress bar and a status bar. The GtkProgressBar widget indicates a sliding value from
0 to 100, normally. However, this can be customized in GTK+. Also, the progress can
be set to move visually from left to right, right to left, top to bottom, or bottom to
top. The GtkStatusBar widget allows the program to communicate short text messages
to the user. Normally, both would be found at the bottom of a user interface window.
Keeping with the previous listing, Figure 3.2 shows the program from Listing 3.2,
compiled and running.

A Note About the Status Bar Widget
The status bar widget is for handling text, and there doesn't appear to be an easy way to put other widgets into it (such as a progress bar). I am reluctant to say it *can't* be done, because about that time,
someone will do it. At this point, though, there are no built-in functions for doing that sort of thing.

Figure 3.2   The GtkProgressBar and GtkStatusBar demo program.

Listing 3.2   **GtkCombo GtkProgressBar and GtkStatusBar Demo Program**

```
#include <gtk/gtk.h>

GtkWidget *frm_bars;
GtkWidget *top_progress_bar, *bottom_status_bar;

/* The timeout variable below is like a timer object
 * or a timer control; every XXX milliseconds it will
 * call another function, which actually
 * updates the progress bar. Here it's at
 * the global level so that you can access it in
 * order to stop the motion of the progress bar.
 */

gint timeout_1 = 0;

void destroy_main();
void cmd_default_progress_clicked();
void cmd_zero_clicked();
void cmd_stop_clicked();
void cmd_lr_clicked();
void cmd_rl_clicked();
void cmd_bt_clicked();
void cmd_tb_clicked();
void cmd_activity_true_clicked();
void cmd_activity_false_clicked();
void cmd_string_clicked();

/* Below is the only status bar callback. */
void cmd_pop_clicked();

gint main(gint argc, gchar *argv[])
{

    GtkWidget *vbox_main;
    GtkWidget *cmd_zero;
```

continues

Listing 3.2 **Continued**

```
GtkWidget *cmd_default_progress;
GtkWidget *cmd_stop;
GtkWidget *cmd_lr, *cmd_rl, *cmd_bt, *cmd_tb;
GtkWidget *cmd_activity_true, *cmd_activity_false;
GtkWidget *cmd_string;
GtkWidget *cmd_pop;

gtk_init(&argc, &argv);

frm_bars = gtk_window_new(GTK_WINDOW_TOPLEVEL);

gtk_window_set_title(GTK_WINDOW(frm_bars),
                     "Progress and Status Bar(s) Demo");

gtk_signal_connect(GTK_OBJECT(frm_bars),
    "destroy",
    GTK_SIGNAL_FUNC(destroy_main),
    NULL);

vbox_main = gtk_vbox_new(FALSE, 0);

top_progress_bar = gtk_progress_bar_new();

/* You can also create a progress bar with an adjustment widget,
 * like you did for the spin buttons in Listing 2.2. In that case,
 * the instantiation call would be
 *
 * gtk_progress_bar_new_with_adjustment(GTK_ADJUSTMENT(adj_widget))
 *
 * This allows you to set the min, max, and so
 * on to be independent of the widget—in
 * this case, the progress bar. Because most applications will
 * use a 0-100 percent progress bar, you will accept the defaults
 * in this example.
 */

cmd_zero = gtk_button_new_with_label("Set Progress to 0");
gtk_signal_connect(GTK_OBJECT(cmd_zero),
                   "clicked",
                   GTK_SIGNAL_FUNC(cmd_zero_clicked),
                   NULL);

cmd_default_progress = gtk_button_new_with_label("Default Progress");
gtk_signal_connect(GTK_OBJECT(cmd_default_progress),
                   "released",
                   GTK_SIGNAL_FUNC(cmd_default_progress_clicked),
                   NULL);

cmd_stop = gtk_button_new_with_label("Stop Progress");
gtk_signal_connect(GTK_OBJECT(cmd_stop),
```

```
                            "clicked",
                            GTK_SIGNAL_FUNC(cmd_stop_clicked),
                            NULL);

/* The following command buttons control how the progress bar fills,
 * from the left, right, top, or bottom.
 */

cmd_lr = gtk_button_new_with_label("Progress L to R");
gtk_signal_connect(GTK_OBJECT(cmd_lr),
                            "clicked",
                            GTK_SIGNAL_FUNC(cmd_lr_clicked),
                            NULL);
cmd_rl = gtk_button_new_with_label("Progress R to L");
gtk_signal_connect(GTK_OBJECT(cmd_rl),
                            "clicked",
                            GTK_SIGNAL_FUNC(cmd_rl_clicked),
                            NULL);
cmd_bt = gtk_button_new_with_label("Progress B to T");
gtk_signal_connect(GTK_OBJECT(cmd_bt),
                            "clicked",
                            GTK_SIGNAL_FUNC(cmd_bt_clicked),
                            NULL);
cmd_tb = gtk_button_new_with_label("Progress T to B");
gtk_signal_connect(GTK_OBJECT(cmd_tb),
                            "clicked",
                            GTK_SIGNAL_FUNC(cmd_tb_clicked),
                            NULL);

cmd_activity_true = gtk_button_new_with_label("Activity Mode TRUE");
gtk_signal_connect(GTK_OBJECT(cmd_activity_true),
                            "clicked",
                            GTK_SIGNAL_FUNC(cmd_activity_true_clicked),
                            NULL);
cmd_activity_false = gtk_button_new_with_label("Activity Mode FALSE");
gtk_signal_connect(GTK_OBJECT(cmd_activity_false),
                            "clicked",
                            GTK_SIGNAL_FUNC(cmd_activity_false_clicked),
                            NULL);

cmd_string = gtk_button_new_with_label("Insert String");
gtk_signal_connect(GTK_OBJECT(cmd_string),
                            "clicked",
                            GTK_SIGNAL_FUNC(cmd_string_clicked),
                            NULL);

cmd_pop = gtk_button_new_with_label("Pop Last Status Msg");
gtk_signal_connect(GTK_OBJECT(cmd_pop),
                            "clicked",
                            GTK_SIGNAL_FUNC(cmd_pop_clicked),
                            NULL);
```

continues

Listing 3.2   **Continued**

```
bottom_status_bar = gtk_statusbar_new();

  /* Now assemble the interface… */

  gtk_box_pack_start(GTK_BOX(vbox_main), top_progress_bar, TRUE, TRUE, 0);
  gtk_box_pack_start(GTK_BOX(vbox_main), cmd_zero, TRUE, TRUE, 0);
  gtk_box_pack_start(GTK_BOX(vbox_main), cmd_default_progress, TRUE, TRUE, 0);
  gtk_box_pack_start(GTK_BOX(vbox_main), cmd_stop, TRUE, TRUE, 0);
  gtk_box_pack_start(GTK_BOX(vbox_main), cmd_lr, TRUE, TRUE, 0);
  gtk_box_pack_start(GTK_BOX(vbox_main), cmd_rl, TRUE, TRUE, 0);
  gtk_box_pack_start(GTK_BOX(vbox_main), cmd_bt, TRUE, TRUE, 0);
  gtk_box_pack_start(GTK_BOX(vbox_main), cmd_tb, TRUE, TRUE, 0);
  gtk_box_pack_start(GTK_BOX(vbox_main), cmd_activity_true, TRUE, TRUE, 0);
  gtk_box_pack_start(GTK_BOX(vbox_main), cmd_activity_false, TRUE, TRUE, 0);
  gtk_box_pack_start(GTK_BOX(vbox_main), cmd_string, TRUE, TRUE, 0);
  gtk_box_pack_start(GTK_BOX(vbox_main), cmd_pop, TRUE, TRUE, 0);

  gtk_box_pack_start(GTK_BOX(vbox_main), bottom_status_bar, TRUE, TRUE, 0);

  gtk_container_add(GTK_CONTAINER(frm_bars), vbox_main);

  gtk_widget_show_all (frm_bars);
  gtk_main ();
  return 0;

}

void destroy_main()
{   gtk_main_quit(); }

gint update_progress()
{

  /* Notice that in the *_get_value() call below, the number returned
   * is a whole number, not a float between 0 and 1. However, when
   * setting the progress bar, the *_set_value() function expects
   * a number between 0 and 1, which is declared as gfloat if
   * a variable is used. Thus, use the divide-by-100 calculation.
   */

  if (gtk_progress_get_value(GTK_PROGRESS(top_progress_bar)) <= 98)
  {
     gtk_progress_bar_update(GTK_PROGRESS_BAR(top_progress_bar),
                             gtk_progress_get_value
                                 (GTK_PROGRESS(top_progress_bar))/100 + .01
                          );
   return(TRUE);
  }
  else
  {
```

```c
        gtk_progress_bar_update(GTK_PROGRESS_BAR(top_progress_bar), 1);

        /* When a function called by the gtk_timeout_add function
         * returns false, the timeout is removed.
         */

        gtk_statusbar_push(GTK_STATUSBAR(bottom_status_bar),
                            1, "Done with progress bar update...");
        return(FALSE);
    }

}

void cmd_default_progress_clicked()
{
    /* This is the "basic" action of the progress bar—updating
     * from 0 to 100% in increments of one.
     *
     * If you press the "default progress" button multiple times,
     * the progress bar will speed up. The reason for this is that
     * each time, you create multiple timeout objects, each
     * of which operates on the same progress bar. This also
     * means you lose your tag to the previous timeout objects because
     * only one variable holds the most recent tag:
     * the timeout_1 variable.
     */

    g_print("Starting progress bar update...\n");
    gtk_statusbar_push(GTK_STATUSBAR(bottom_status_bar),
                        1, "Starting progress bar update...");

    /* The code above demonstrates the same thing in two ways.
     * (The corresponding "finished" message is in the update_progress()
     * function listed just prior to this one.)
     */

    timeout_1 = gtk_timeout_add(50, update_progress, NULL);
}

void cmd_stop_clicked()
{
    gtk_timeout_remove(timeout_1);
}

void cmd_zero_clicked()
{
    gtk_progress_bar_update(GTK_PROGRESS_BAR(top_progress_bar), 0);
}

void cmd_lr_clicked()
{
```

continues

Listing 3.2   **Continued**

```
        gtk_progress_bar_set_orientation(GTK_PROGRESS_BAR(top_progress_bar),
                                    GTK_PROGRESS_LEFT_TO_RIGHT);
}

void cmd_rl_clicked()
{
        gtk_progress_bar_set_orientation(GTK_PROGRESS_BAR(top_progress_bar),
                                    GTK_PROGRESS_RIGHT_TO_LEFT);
}

void cmd_bt_clicked()
{
        /* Notice that the shape of the progress bar changes when the
         * orientation is set to top-to-bottom or bottom-to-top.
         */

        gtk_progress_bar_set_orientation(GTK_PROGRESS_BAR(top_progress_bar),
                                    GTK_PROGRESS_BOTTOM_TO_TOP);
}

void cmd_tb_clicked()
{
        gtk_progress_bar_set_orientation(GTK_PROGRESS_BAR(top_progress_bar),
                                    GTK_PROGRESS_TOP_TO_BOTTOM);
}

void cmd_activity_true_clicked()
{
        /* In activity mode, the progress bar bounces a bar back and
         * forth inside the progress bar window. In this demo, this
         * must be used with the "Default Progress" button. The activity
         * mode also stops when the value of the progress exceeds 1. So,
         * to run in progress mode for as long as needed, keep the value
         * for the progress bar between 0 and 1.
         */

        gtk_progress_set_activity_mode(GTK_PROGRESS(top_progress_bar), TRUE);
        gtk_statusbar_push(GTK_STATUSBAR(bottom_status_bar),
                                    1, "Going into Activity Mode...");
}

void cmd_activity_false_clicked()
{
        gtk_progress_set_activity_mode(GTK_PROGRESS(top_progress_bar), FALSE);
        gtk_statusbar_push(GTK_STATUSBAR(bottom_status_bar),
                                    1, "Coming out of Activity Mode...");
}

void cmd_string_clicked()
{
```

```
    /* This places a formatted text string into the progress bar
     * window. This string is similar to a C printf string except
     * that the %-formatter can only be used with the following
     * values:
     *      %u - maximum of the progress bar
     *      %l - minimum
     *      %p - percentage of range
     *      %v - value of range
     * The example below shows all four, along with some
     * plain text.
     */

    gtk_progress_set_format_string(GTK_PROGRESS(top_progress_bar),
                         "Pct:%p Val:%v Min:%l Max:%u");
    gtk_progress_set_show_text(GTK_PROGRESS(top_progress_bar), TRUE);


    /* Setting and showing text in a progress bar is a two-step
     * process, as shown above. Note that when the progress bar
     * is in activity mode, text is not allowed in the progress
     * bar; it will disappear until the progress bar is taken
     * out of activity mode.
     *
     * The call below sets the position of the text. The last two
     * parameters can range between 0 and 1. 0, 0 is the upper-left
     * corner of the progress bar, and 1, 1 is the lower-right corner.
     * The first controls the horizontal positioning, and the second
     * controls the vertical. Thus, 0, 1 would be the lower-left corner,
     * and 1, 0 would be the upper-right corner. The values allowed for
     * each are floats between 0 and 1.
     */

    gtk_progress_set_text_alignment(GTK_PROGRESS(top_progress_bar), 0.5, 0.5);
}

void cmd_pop_clicked()
{
    /* The status bar object operates as a stack with corresponding
     * push/pop calls. When you want to display a message, you push it
     * onto the stack with the gtk_status_bar_push() call. It takes three
     * parameters: the first is the target status bar, the second is a
     * context identifier, and the third is the message to be displayed.
     * In this example, all the context identifiers are 1, but if you
     * need to access the advanced functionality of the status bar, you
     * may want to investigate this further. For example, you could remove
     * a message from the stack. For this example, a standard
     * last-in-first-out (LIFO) operation will suffice (and from my
     * experience, that would fit most business applications also).
     *
     * Note that the context identifier cannot be zero. In this case, "1"
     * is easy to remember because you are either pushing or popping
     * one message.
```

continues

Listing 3.2   **Continued**

```
 *
 * The gtk_status_bar_pop() function removes the message highest
 * in the stack with the given context identifier. In this example,
 * since all context identifiers are 1, the stack operates as pure
 * LIFO. However, you could have two or more classes of messages
 * and pop a message of either class. If you are not popping
 * the context identifier of the top message, though, you are not
 * going to see any change in the status bar.
 */

    gtk_statusbar_pop(GTK_STATUSBAR(bottom_status_bar), 1);
}
```

GtkFrame and GtkAspectFrame

The GtkFrame and GtkAspectFrame widgets are, like many other widgets, pretty much what you expect. The GtkFrame is a container object into which you can place other objects, and the GtkAspectFrame widget allows you to maintain the aspect of the child widget whenever the parent window is resized. Figure 3.3 shows Listing 3.3 in action.

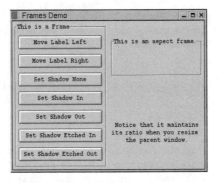

Figure 3.3   GtkFrame and GtkAspectFrame widgets demo program.

Listing 3.3   **Demo of the Frame and Aspect Frame Widgets: GtkFrame and GtkAspectFrame**

```
#include <gtk/gtk.h>

GtkWidget *frm_frames;
GtkWidget *left_frame;
GtkWidget *right_aspect_frame;

void destroy_main();
void cmd_left_clicked();
```

```
void cmd_right_clicked();
void cmd_shadow_none_clicked();
void cmd_shadow_in_clicked();
void cmd_shadow_out_clicked();
void cmd_shadow_etched_in_clicked();
void cmd_shadow_etched_out_clicked();

gint main(gint argc, gchar *argv[])
{
  GtkWidget *hbox_main;
  GtkWidget *vbox_left;
  GtkWidget *vbox_right;
  GtkWidget *vbtnbox_in_frame;
  GtkWidget *cmd_left, *cmd_right;
  GtkWidget *lbl;
  GtkWidget *cmd_shadow_none;
  GtkWidget *cmd_shadow_in;
  GtkWidget *cmd_shadow_out;
  GtkWidget *cmd_shadow_etched_in;
  GtkWidget *cmd_shadow_etched_out;
  GtkWidget *drawing_area_right;

  gtk_init(&argc, &argv);

  frm_frames = gtk_window_new(GTK_WINDOW_TOPLEVEL);

  gtk_window_set_title(GTK_WINDOW(frm_frames), "Frames Demo");

  gtk_signal_connect(GTK_OBJECT(frm_frames),
      "destroy",
      GTK_SIGNAL_FUNC(destroy_main),
      NULL);

  /* As before, this demo uses a layout where the frame demo
   * is on the left and the aspect frame is on the right. To do
   * this, this program uses a horizontal box that's separated into
   * left and right vertical boxes.
   */

  hbox_main = gtk_hbox_new(TRUE, 0);
  vbox_left = gtk_vbox_new(TRUE, 0);
  vbox_right = gtk_vbox_new(TRUE, 5);
  vbtnbox_in_frame = gtk_vbutton_box_new();
  gtk_vbutton_box_set_layout_default(GTK_BUTTONBOX_SPREAD);

  left_frame = gtk_frame_new("This is a Frame");
  gtk_frame_set_shadow_type(GTK_FRAME(left_frame), GTK_SHADOW_NONE);

  cmd_left = gtk_button_new_with_label("Move Label Left");
  gtk_signal_connect(GTK_OBJECT(cmd_left),
                    "clicked",
```

continues

Listing 3.3 **Continued**

```
                        GTK_SIGNAL_FUNC(cmd_left_clicked),
                        NULL);

    cmd_right = gtk_button_new_with_label("Move Label Right");
    gtk_signal_connect(GTK_OBJECT(cmd_right),
                        "clicked",
                        GTK_SIGNAL_FUNC(cmd_right_clicked),
                        NULL);

    cmd_shadow_none = gtk_button_new_with_label("Set Shadow None");
    gtk_signal_connect(GTK_OBJECT(cmd_shadow_none),
                        "clicked",
                        GTK_SIGNAL_FUNC(cmd_shadow_none_clicked),
                        NULL);
    cmd_shadow_in = gtk_button_new_with_label("Set Shadow In");
    gtk_signal_connect(GTK_OBJECT(cmd_shadow_in),
                        "clicked",
                        GTK_SIGNAL_FUNC(cmd_shadow_in_clicked),
                        NULL);
    cmd_shadow_out = gtk_button_new_with_label("Set Shadow Out");
    gtk_signal_connect(GTK_OBJECT(cmd_shadow_out),
                        "clicked",
                        GTK_SIGNAL_FUNC(cmd_shadow_out_clicked),
                        NULL);
    cmd_shadow_etched_in = gtk_button_new_with_label("Set Shadow Etched In");
    gtk_signal_connect(GTK_OBJECT(cmd_shadow_etched_in),
                        "clicked",
                        GTK_SIGNAL_FUNC(cmd_shadow_etched_in_clicked),
                        NULL);
    cmd_shadow_etched_out = gtk_button_new_with_label("Set Shadow Etched Out");
    gtk_signal_connect(GTK_OBJECT(cmd_shadow_etched_out),
                        "clicked",
                        GTK_SIGNAL_FUNC(cmd_shadow_etched_out_clicked),
                        NULL);

    gtk_box_pack_start(GTK_BOX(vbox_left), left_frame, TRUE, TRUE, 5);
    gtk_container_add(GTK_CONTAINER(left_frame), vbtnbox_in_frame);
    gtk_container_add(GTK_CONTAINER(vbtnbox_in_frame), cmd_left);
    gtk_container_add(GTK_CONTAINER(vbtnbox_in_frame), cmd_right);
    gtk_container_add(GTK_CONTAINER(vbtnbox_in_frame), cmd_shadow_none);
    gtk_container_add(GTK_CONTAINER(vbtnbox_in_frame), cmd_shadow_in);
    gtk_container_add(GTK_CONTAINER(vbtnbox_in_frame), cmd_shadow_out);
    gtk_container_add(GTK_CONTAINER(vbtnbox_in_frame), cmd_shadow_etched_in);
    gtk_container_add(GTK_CONTAINER(vbtnbox_in_frame), cmd_shadow_etched_out);

    /* Now set up the aspect frame on the right side.
     */

    right_aspect_frame = gtk_aspect_frame_new("This is an aspect frame.",
                                  0.5, 0.5, 3, FALSE);
```

```
    /* When running, the aspect frame keeps a ratio of 3 to 1.
     *
     * The parameters to this call are:
     *    label    (gchar)   - The label to go on the frame
     *    xalign   (gfloat)  - Alignment specification
     *    yalign   (gfloat)  - Alignment specification
     *    ratio    (gfloat)  - The ratio of the child widget
     *    obey_child (gint) - If true, override child widget aspect
     */

    lbl = gtk_label_new("Notice that it maintains\nit's ratio when you resize\nthe
parent window.");

    drawing_area_right = gtk_drawing_area_new();

    gtk_container_add(GTK_CONTAINER(right_aspect_frame), drawing_area_right);
    gtk_box_pack_start(GTK_BOX(vbox_right), right_aspect_frame, TRUE, TRUE, 5);
    gtk_box_pack_start(GTK_BOX(vbox_right), lbl, TRUE, TRUE, 5);

    /* Note that an aspect frame widget does not show until it has
     * a child widget to show.
     */

    gtk_box_pack_start(GTK_BOX(hbox_main), vbox_left, TRUE, TRUE, 5);
    gtk_box_pack_start(GTK_BOX(hbox_main), vbox_right, TRUE, TRUE, 5);

    gtk_container_add(GTK_CONTAINER(frm_frames), hbox_main);

    gtk_widget_show_all (frm_frames);

    gtk_main ();

    return 0;
}

void destroy_main()
{   gtk_main_quit(); }

void cmd_left_clicked()
{
    /* In the following *_set_label_* call, the parameters are
     *   -the target frame
     *   -the x-align value, from 0 to 1 as a gfloat
     *   -not used (it is listed as the y-align value in the prototype)
     */

    gtk_frame_set_label_align(GTK_FRAME(left_frame), 0, 0);
}

void cmd_right_clicked()
{
```

continues

Listing 3.3 **Continued**

```
    gtk_frame_set_label_align(GTK_FRAME(left_frame), 1, 0);
}

void cmd_shadow_none_clicked()
{
    gtk_frame_set_shadow_type(GTK_FRAME(left_frame), GTK_SHADOW_NONE);
}

void cmd_shadow_in_clicked()
{
    gtk_frame_set_shadow_type(GTK_FRAME(left_frame), GTK_SHADOW_IN);
}

void cmd_shadow_out_clicked()
{
    gtk_frame_set_shadow_type(GTK_FRAME(left_frame), GTK_SHADOW_OUT);
}

void cmd_shadow_etched_in_clicked()
{
    gtk_frame_set_shadow_type(GTK_FRAME(left_frame), GTK_SHADOW_ETCHED_IN);
}

void cmd_shadow_etched_out_clicked()
{
    gtk_frame_set_shadow_type(GTK_FRAME(left_frame), GTK_SHADOW_ETCHED_OUT);
}
```

GtkDialog, GtkFileSelection, GtkColorSelectionDialog, and GtkFontSelectionDialog

These are comparable to the "Windows Common Dialog Boxes." The GtkDialog widget is analogous to the start of a MessageBox form, and the rest are self-explanatory. The GtkFileSelection can also be used to select a directory. Figure 3.4 shows Listing 3.4 compiled and running. When you click the various buttons in that program, you access the dialog boxes represented in Figures 3.5, 3.6, and 3.7. The dialog box in Figure 3.5 is instantiated by the "File Selection" button in Figure 3.4, Figure 3.6 is instantiated by the "Color Selection" button, and Figure 3.7 is instantiated by the "Change My Font" button. Figures 3.5, 3.6, and 3.7 are placed in Listing 3.4 near the relevant code.

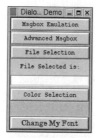

Figure 3.4 Selection widgets demo.

Listing 3.4 **Demo of the Dialog Widgets: GtkDialog, GtkFileSelection, GtkColorSelectionDialog, and GtkFontSelectionDialog**

```
#include <gtk/gtk.h>

GtkWidget *frm_dialogs;
GtkWidget *MsgBox;
GtkWidget *frm_quit;
GtkWidget *frm_file_sel;
GtkWidget *entry_filename;
GtkWidget *draw_area;
GtkWidget *frm_color_sel;
GtkWidget *frm_font_sel;
GtkWidget *cmd_font_sel;
GtkWidget *lbl_font_sel;

static GdkFont *font_sel;

void destroy_main();
void cmd_msgbox_clicked();
void cmd_advanced_msgbox_clicked();
void cmd_OK_clicked();
void cmd_save_clicked();
void cmd_quit_without_saving_clicked();
void cmd_file_sel_clicked();
void frm_file_sel_ok_clicked();
void frm_file_sel_cancel_clicked();
void cmd_color_sel_clicked();
void frm_color_sel_ok_clicked();
void frm_color_sel_cancel_clicked();
void cmd_font_sel_clicked();
void frm_font_sel_ok_clicked();
void frm_font_sel_cancel_clicked();

gint main(gint argc, gchar *argv[])
{

    GtkWidget *vbox_main;
    GtkWidget *cmd_msgbox;
```

continues

Listing 3.4 **Continued**

```
GtkWidget *cmd_advanced_msgbox;
GtkWidget *cmd_file_sel;
GtkWidget *lbl_file_sel;
GtkWidget *cmd_color_sel;

gtk_init(&argc, &argv);

frm_dialogs = gtk_window_new(GTK_WINDOW_TOPLEVEL);

gtk_window_set_title(GTK_WINDOW(frm_dialogs), "Dialogs Demo");

gtk_signal_connect(GTK_OBJECT(frm_dialogs),
    "destroy",
    GTK_SIGNAL_FUNC(destroy_main),
    NULL);

vbox_main = gtk_vbox_new(TRUE, 2);

cmd_msgbox = gtk_button_new_with_label("MsgBox Emulation");
gtk_signal_connect(GTK_OBJECT(cmd_msgbox),
    "clicked",
    GTK_SIGNAL_FUNC(cmd_msgbox_clicked),
    NULL);

cmd_advanced_msgbox = gtk_button_new_with_label("Advanced MsgBox");
gtk_signal_connect(GTK_OBJECT(cmd_advanced_msgbox),
    "clicked",
    GTK_SIGNAL_FUNC(cmd_advanced_msgbox_clicked),
    NULL);

cmd_file_sel = gtk_button_new_with_label("File Selection");
gtk_signal_connect(GTK_OBJECT(cmd_file_sel),
    "clicked",
    GTK_SIGNAL_FUNC(cmd_file_sel_clicked),
    NULL);

lbl_file_sel = gtk_label_new("File Selected is:");

entry_filename = gtk_entry_new();

cmd_color_sel = gtk_button_new_with_label("Color Selection");
gtk_signal_connect(GTK_OBJECT(cmd_color_sel),
    "clicked",
    GTK_SIGNAL_FUNC(cmd_color_sel_clicked),
    NULL);

draw_area = gtk_drawing_area_new();
```

```
    /* In the following command button, you will change the
     * font of the button. If the label of the command
     * button is a separate object, you can poke the style
     * directly into the label instead of going
     * through the button widget.
     */

    lbl_font_sel = gtk_label_new("Change My Font");
    cmd_font_sel = gtk_button_new();
    gtk_container_add(GTK_CONTAINER(cmd_font_sel), lbl_font_sel);
    gtk_signal_connect(GTK_OBJECT(cmd_font_sel),
        "clicked",
        GTK_SIGNAL_FUNC(cmd_font_sel_clicked),
        NULL);

    gtk_box_pack_start(GTK_BOX(vbox_main), cmd_msgbox, TRUE, TRUE, 0);
    gtk_box_pack_start(GTK_BOX(vbox_main), cmd_advanced_msgbox, TRUE, TRUE, 0);
    gtk_box_pack_start(GTK_BOX(vbox_main), cmd_file_sel, TRUE, TRUE, 0);
    gtk_box_pack_start(GTK_BOX(vbox_main), lbl_file_sel, TRUE, TRUE, 0);
    gtk_box_pack_start(GTK_BOX(vbox_main), entry_filename, TRUE, TRUE, 0);
    gtk_box_pack_start(GTK_BOX(vbox_main), cmd_color_sel, TRUE, TRUE, 0);
    gtk_box_pack_start(GTK_BOX(vbox_main), draw_area, TRUE, TRUE, 0);
    gtk_box_pack_start(GTK_BOX(vbox_main), cmd_font_sel, TRUE, TRUE, 0);
    gtk_container_add(GTK_CONTAINER(frm_dialogs), vbox_main);

    gtk_widget_show_all (frm_dialogs);

    gtk_main ();

    return 0;

}

void destroy_main()
{   gtk_main_quit(); }

void cmd_msgbox_clicked()
{
  GtkWidget *lbl_message;
  GtkWidget *cmd_OK;

  MsgBox = gtk_dialog_new();
  gtk_window_set_title(GTK_WINDOW(MsgBox), "Message Box");

  lbl_message = gtk_label_new(" This is the error message.");
  cmd_OK = gtk_button_new_with_label("OK");
  gtk_signal_connect(GTK_OBJECT(cmd_OK),
      "clicked",
      GTK_SIGNAL_FUNC(cmd_OK_clicked),
      NULL);
```

continues

Listing 3.4   **Continued**

```
    gtk_box_pack_start(GTK_BOX(GTK_DIALOG(MsgBox)->vbox), lbl_message,
                        TRUE, TRUE, 5);
    gtk_box_pack_start(GTK_BOX(GTK_DIALOG(MsgBox)->action_area), cmd_OK,
                        TRUE, TRUE, 0);

    gtk_widget_show_all(MsgBox);
}

void cmd_advanced_msgbox_clicked()
{
    GtkWidget *lbl_do_you_want_to;
    GtkWidget *cmd_save, *cmd_quit_without_saving;
    GtkWidget *chk_save_as_XML;
    GtkWidget *vbox;

    frm_quit = gtk_dialog_new();
    gtk_window_set_title(GTK_WINDOW(frm_quit), "Changes Not Saved");

    vbox = gtk_vbox_new(TRUE, 0);

    lbl_do_you_want_to = gtk_label_new(" Do you want to...");

    cmd_save = gtk_button_new_with_label("Save Changes?");
    gtk_signal_connect(GTK_OBJECT(cmd_save),
        "clicked",
        GTK_SIGNAL_FUNC(cmd_save_clicked),
        NULL);

    cmd_quit_without_saving = gtk_button_new_with_label("Quit without\nSaving
Changes?");
    gtk_signal_connect(GTK_OBJECT(cmd_quit_without_saving),
        "clicked",
        GTK_SIGNAL_FUNC(cmd_quit_without_saving_clicked),
        NULL);

    chk_save_as_XML = gtk_check_button_new_with_label("Save as XML");

    gtk_box_pack_start(GTK_BOX(GTK_DIALOG(frm_quit)->vbox),
                        lbl_do_you_want_to, TRUE, TRUE, 5);
    gtk_box_pack_start(GTK_BOX(vbox), cmd_save, TRUE, TRUE, 0);
    gtk_box_pack_start(GTK_BOX(vbox), chk_save_as_XML, TRUE, TRUE, 0);
    gtk_box_pack_start(GTK_BOX(vbox), cmd_quit_without_saving, TRUE, TRUE, 0);
    gtk_box_pack_start(GTK_BOX(GTK_DIALOG(frm_quit)->action_area), vbox,
                        TRUE, TRUE, 0);

    gtk_widget_show_all(frm_quit);
}

void cmd_OK_clicked()
{
```

```
      gtk_widget_destroy(GTK_WIDGET(MsgBox));
}

void cmd_save_clicked()
{
      gtk_widget_destroy(GTK_WIDGET(frm_quit));
}

void cmd_quit_without_saving_clicked()
{
      gtk_widget_destroy(GTK_WIDGET(frm_quit));
}

/* Figure 3.5 is inserted here because the code that is
 * relevant immediately follows. However, please keep in mind
 * that the code following the figure is a continuation of the
 * previous code listing.*/
```

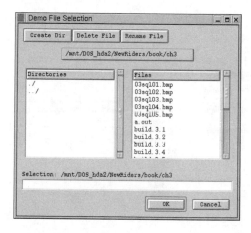

Figure 3.5   The File Selection Dialog widget.

```
void cmd_file_sel_clicked()
{

   frm_file_sel = gtk_file_selection_new("Demo File Selection");
   gtk_signal_connect(GTK_OBJECT(GTK_FILE_SELECTION(frm_file_sel)->ok_button),
                      "clicked",
                      GTK_SIGNAL_FUNC(frm_file_sel_ok_clicked),
                      NULL);
   gtk_signal_connect(GTK_OBJECT(GTK_FILE_SELECTION
                              (frm_file_sel)->cancel_button),
                      "clicked",
                      GTK_SIGNAL_FUNC(frm_file_sel_cancel_clicked),
                      NULL);
```

continues

Listing 3.4 **Continued**

```
    gtk_widget_show(frm_file_sel);
}

void frm_file_sel_ok_clicked()
{
    gtk_entry_set_text(GTK_ENTRY(entry_filename),
    gtk_file_selection_get_filename(GTK_FILE_SELECTION(frm_file_sel)));
    gtk_widget_destroy(frm_file_sel);
}

void frm_file_sel_cancel_clicked()
{
    gtk_widget_destroy(frm_file_sel);
    /* If you just wanted to hide the widget instead of destroying it,
     * you would use gtk_widget_hide(frm_file_sel);
     * and the next time you showed the widget, it would be as you
     * last left it.
     */
}

/* Again, Figure 3.6 is placed here because it is relevant to the
 * code that follows; this is still Listing 3.4.*/
```

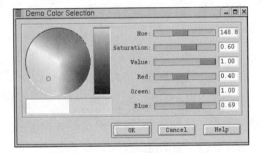

Figure 3.6 The Color Selection widget.

```
void cmd_color_sel_clicked()
{

    frm_color_sel = gtk_color_selection_dialog_new("Demo Color Selection");

    gtk_signal_connect(GTK_OBJECT(GTK_COLOR_SELECTION_DIALOG
                                (frm_color_sel)->ok_button),
                    "clicked",
                    GTK_SIGNAL_FUNC(frm_color_sel_ok_clicked),
                    NULL);
    gtk_signal_connect(GTK_OBJECT(GTK_COLOR_SELECTION_DIALOG
                                (frm_color_sel)->cancel_button),
```

```
                              "clicked",
                              GTK_SIGNAL_FUNC(frm_color_sel_cancel_clicked),
                              NULL);

    gtk_widget_show(frm_color_sel);
}

void frm_color_sel_ok_clicked()
{
    gdouble rgb[3];
    GdkColor gdk_color;
    GdkColormap *map;

    /* Note that there is a difference between GTK_COLOR_SELECTION and
     * GTK_COLOR_SELECTION_DIALOG. The former inherits from the GtkVBox
     * widget and is an orphan widget. The latter is the normal way to
     * create a color selection dialog box and inherits from the GtkDialog
     * widget. The ok_button, cancel_button, and help_button are only
     * available from GTK_COLOR_SELECTION_DIALOG.
     */

    gtk_color_selection_get_color(GTK_COLOR_SELECTION(
                                    GTK_COLOR_SELECTION_DIALOG
                                        (frm_color_sel)->colorsel),
                                    rgb);

    /* Initialize the colormap structure. */

    map = gdk_window_get_colormap(draw_area->window);

    gdk_color.red = (guint16)(rgb[0]*65535.0);
    gdk_color.green = (guint16)(rgb[1]*65535.0);
    gdk_color.blue = (guint16)(rgb[2]*65535.0);

    gdk_color_alloc (map, &gdk_color);

    gdk_window_set_background(draw_area->window, &gdk_color);

    /* The following command acts as a "refresh". */
    gdk_window_clear(draw_area->window);

    gtk_widget_destroy(frm_color_sel);
}

void frm_color_sel_cancel_clicked()
{
    gtk_widget_destroy(frm_color_sel);
}
```

continues

```
/* This is the last figure that goes with Listing 3.4. Figure 3.7
 * is called by the "Change My Font" button at the bottom of the
 * vertical packing box (as shown in Figure 3.4).*/
```

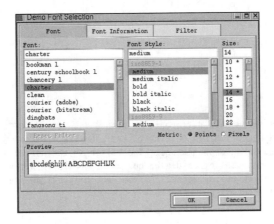

Figure 3.7   The Font Selection widget.

```
void cmd_font_sel_clicked()
{
   frm_font_sel = gtk_font_selection_dialog_new("Demo Font Selection");
   gtk_signal_connect(GTK_OBJECT(GTK_FONT_SELECTION_DIALOG
                                 (frm_font_sel)->ok_button),
                      "clicked",
                      GTK_SIGNAL_FUNC(frm_font_sel_ok_clicked),
                      NULL);
   gtk_signal_connect(GTK_OBJECT(GTK_FONT_SELECTION_DIALOG
                                 (frm_font_sel)->cancel_button),
                      "clicked",
                      GTK_SIGNAL_FUNC(frm_font_sel_cancel_clicked),
                      NULL);

   gtk_widget_show(frm_font_sel);
}

void frm_font_sel_ok_clicked()
{
   GtkStyle *style_sel;

   font_sel = gdk_font_load(gtk_font_selection_dialog_get_font_name(
                                GTK_FONT_SELECTION_DIALOG(frm_font_sel)));

   style_sel = gtk_style_copy(gtk_widget_get_style(GTK_WIDGET(cmd_font_sel)));
   style_sel->font = font_sel;
```

```
   /* In the following call, the font of the lbl_font_sel label
    * widget is set, which is the label for cmd_font_sel. For the following
    * call to work, it has to be sent a label; sending cmd_font_sel
    * in place of lbl_font_sel will not work.
    */

   gtk_widget_set_style(GTK_WIDGET(lbl_font_sel), style_sel);

   gtk_widget_destroy(frm_font_sel);
}

void frm_font_sel_cancel_clicked()
{
   gtk_widget_destroy(frm_font_sel);
}
```

Menu Widget, ItemFactory, and Popup Menu Widgets

Finally, I will cover the Menu widgets. In any part of a finished application, a menu at the top of the main application window is something users have come to expect, but somehow it also manages to be one of the things that gets left behind in the rush to deliver the application. Figure 3.8 shows the program compiled from Listing 3.5, which provides the menu options available in GTK+.

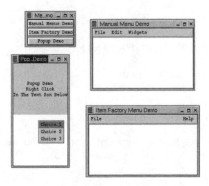

Figure 3.8   The Menu widgets demo.

Listing 3.5 **Demo of the Menu Widgets: Menu, ItemFactory, and Popup Menu Widgets**

```
#include <gtk/gtk.h>

GtkWidget *frm_menus;
GtkWidget *frm_item_factory;
GtkWidget *frm_popup;
GtkWidget *popup_menu;

void destroy_main();
void cmd_manual_menu_clicked();
void cmd_item_factory_clicked();
void item_factory_clicked();
void cmd_popup_clicked();

void popup_mnu_1_clicked();
void popup_mnu_2_clicked();
void popup_mnu_3_clicked();
void text_right_click_event();

gint main(gint argc, gchar *argv[])
{
   GtkWidget *vbox_main;
   GtkWidget *cmd_manual_menu;
   GtkWidget *cmd_item_factory;
   GtkWidget *cmd_popup;

   gtk_init(&argc, &argv);

   frm_menus = gtk_window_new(GTK_WINDOW_TOPLEVEL);

   gtk_window_set_title(GTK_WINDOW(frm_menus), "Menus Demo");

   gtk_signal_connect(GTK_OBJECT(frm_menus),
       "destroy",
       GTK_SIGNAL_FUNC(destroy_main),
       NULL);

   vbox_main = gtk_vbox_new(TRUE, 2);

   cmd_manual_menu = gtk_button_new_with_label("Manual Menus Demo");
   gtk_signal_connect(GTK_OBJECT(cmd_manual_menu),
     "clicked",
     GTK_SIGNAL_FUNC(cmd_manual_menu_clicked),
     NULL);

   cmd_item_factory = gtk_button_new_with_label("Item Factory Demo");
   gtk_signal_connect(GTK_OBJECT(cmd_item_factory),
       "clicked",
       GTK_SIGNAL_FUNC(cmd_item_factory_clicked),
```

```
        NULL);

    cmd_popup = gtk_button_new_with_label("Popup Demo");
    gtk_signal_connect(GTK_OBJECT(cmd_popup),
        "clicked",
        GTK_SIGNAL_FUNC(cmd_popup_clicked),
        NULL);

    gtk_box_pack_start(GTK_BOX(vbox_main), cmd_manual_menu, TRUE, TRUE, 0);
    gtk_box_pack_start(GTK_BOX(vbox_main), cmd_item_factory, TRUE, TRUE, 0);
    gtk_box_pack_start(GTK_BOX(vbox_main), cmd_popup, TRUE, TRUE, 0);
    gtk_container_add(GTK_CONTAINER(frm_menus), vbox_main);

    gtk_widget_show_all (frm_menus);

    gtk_main ();

    return 0;

}

void destroy_main()
{   gtk_main_quit(); }

/* ============= Creating a Menu the Hard Way =============== */

void cmd_manual_menu_clicked()
{
    GtkWidget *frm_manual;
    GtkWidget *vbox_manual;
    GtkWidget *menu_bar_manual;
    GtkWidget *menu_file, *menu_edit, *menu_widgets;
    GtkWidget *menu_item_tearoff1, *menu_item_separator1;
    GtkWidget *menu_item_file, *menu_item_open,
              *menu_item_exit, *menu_item_widgets;
    GtkWidget *menu_item_edit, *menu_item_cut, *menu_item_copy, *menu_item_paste;
    GtkWidget *hbox_cut;
    GtkWidget *icon_scissors;
    GdkPixmap *xpm_scissors;
    GdkBitmap *bmp;
    GtkWidget *lbl_cut, *lbl_ctrl_X;
    GtkAccelGroup *hot_keys;
    GtkWidget *menu_item_check, *chk_box_demo;
    GtkWidget *menu_item_cmd, *cmd_button_demo;
    GtkWidget *menu_item_check2;
    GtkWidget *text_manual;

    frm_manual = gtk_window_new(GTK_WINDOW_TOPLEVEL);
    gtk_window_set_title(GTK_WINDOW(frm_manual), "Manual Menu Demo");

    vbox_manual = gtk_vbox_new(FALSE, 0);
```

continues

Listing 3.5   **Continued**

```
menu_bar_manual = gtk_menu_bar_new();
menu_file = gtk_menu_new();
menu_edit = gtk_menu_new();
menu_widgets = gtk_menu_new();

/* File Menu */
menu_item_file = gtk_menu_item_new_with_label("File");
menu_item_tearoff1 = gtk_tearoff_menu_item_new();
menu_item_open = gtk_menu_item_new_with_label("Open");
menu_item_separator1 = gtk_menu_item_new();
menu_item_exit = gtk_menu_item_new_with_label("Exit - Not!");

/* Edit Menu */
menu_item_edit = gtk_menu_item_new_with_label("Edit");
menu_item_copy = gtk_menu_item_new_with_label("Copy");
menu_item_cut = gtk_menu_item_new();
hbox_cut = gtk_hbox_new(FALSE, 0);
gtk_container_add(GTK_CONTAINER(menu_item_cut), hbox_cut);
xpm_scissors = gdk_pixmap_colormap_create_from_xpm(
                    NULL,
                    gdk_colormap_get_system(),
                    &bmp,
                    NULL,
                    "/usr/share/icons/mini/mini.cut.xpm");
icon_scissors = gtk_pixmap_new(xpm_scissors, bmp);
gdk_pixmap_unref(xpm_scissors);
gtk_box_pack_start_defaults(GTK_BOX(hbox_cut), icon_scissors);
lbl_cut = gtk_label_new("Cut");
lbl_ctrl_X = gtk_label_new("Ctl+X");
gtk_label_set_justify(GTK_LABEL(lbl_ctrl_X), GTK_JUSTIFY_RIGHT);
gtk_box_pack_start(GTK_BOX(hbox_cut), lbl_cut, TRUE, FALSE, 0);
gtk_box_pack_start(GTK_BOX(hbox_cut), lbl_ctrl_X, FALSE, FALSE, 3);
menu_item_paste = gtk_menu_item_new_with_label("Paste");

/* As shown above, creating a menu item with an associated icon
 * is relatively straightforward. Because the menu item widget
 * is a descendant from GtkBin (which can hold only one child
 * widget), you have to put a horizontal packing box widget into
 * the menu item. Then put the pixmap on the left and
 * a label widget on the right.
 *
 * See Listing 2.2 for an example of how to place the pixmap
 * within the same program that uses it—specifically, the
 * list widget demo.
 *
 * If you are running this and an icon isn't showing,
 * it may be because the icon used above is not
 * on your system (the final parameter of the
 * gdk_pixmap_colormap_create_from_xpm() call).
```

```
 *
 * Either you can edit the line to use a pixmap on your system,
 * or you can copy a pixmap to the same directory as this program,
 * and then just put in the name—leaving off the path information.
 */

hot_keys = gtk_accel_group_new();
gtk_accel_group_attach(hot_keys, GTK_OBJECT(frm_manual));
gtk_widget_add_accelerator(menu_item_copy,
                           "activate",
                           hot_keys,
                           'C',
                           GDK_CONTROL_MASK,
                           GTK_ACCEL_VISIBLE);
gtk_widget_add_accelerator(menu_item_cut,
                           "activate",
                           hot_keys,
                           'X',
                           GDK_CONTROL_MASK,
                           GTK_ACCEL_VISIBLE);
gtk_widget_add_accelerator(menu_item_paste,
                           "activate",
                           hot_keys,
                           'V',
                           GDK_CONTROL_MASK,
                           GTK_ACCEL_VISIBLE);

/* Widgets Menu */

menu_item_widgets = gtk_menu_item_new_with_label("Widgets");

/* Because the menu item widget is a descendant of GtkBin, as
 * demonstrated above, you can (theoretically) put
 * any widget into a menu item.
 */

menu_item_check = gtk_menu_item_new();
chk_box_demo = gtk_check_button_new_with_label("Check me");
gtk_container_add(GTK_CONTAINER(menu_item_check), chk_box_demo);

/* Check boxes in menus are pretty standard for showing the
 * on/off setting of an attribute or such. But try
 * something a little different…
 */

menu_item_cmd = gtk_menu_item_new();
cmd_button_demo = gtk_button_new_with_label("Push me");
gtk_container_add(GTK_CONTAINER(menu_item_cmd), cmd_button_demo);

/* Because putting a check box into a menu is so common,
 * there is a widget specifically for that purpose.
```

continues

Listing 3.5   **Continued**

```
 * The primary difference between this one and the previous
 * check button is that *_check_menu_item_* will not
 * show the box part of the check box when the item is not checked.
 */

menu_item_check2 = gtk_check_menu_item_new_with_label("Check2");

/* Put it all together. */

gtk_menu_bar_append(GTK_MENU_BAR(menu_bar_manual), menu_item_file);
gtk_menu_item_set_submenu(GTK_MENU_ITEM(menu_item_file), menu_file);
gtk_menu_append(GTK_MENU(menu_file), menu_item_tearoff1);
gtk_menu_append(GTK_MENU(menu_file), menu_item_open);
gtk_menu_append(GTK_MENU(menu_file), menu_item_separator1);
gtk_menu_append(GTK_MENU(menu_file), menu_item_exit);

gtk_menu_bar_append(GTK_MENU_BAR(menu_bar_manual), menu_item_edit);
gtk_menu_item_set_submenu(GTK_MENU_ITEM(menu_item_edit), menu_edit);
gtk_menu_append(GTK_MENU(menu_edit), menu_item_cut);
gtk_menu_append(GTK_MENU(menu_edit), menu_item_copy);
gtk_menu_append(GTK_MENU(menu_edit), menu_item_paste);

gtk_menu_bar_append(GTK_MENU_BAR(menu_bar_manual), menu_item_widgets);
gtk_menu_item_set_submenu(GTK_MENU_ITEM(menu_item_widgets), menu_widgets);
gtk_menu_append(GTK_MENU(menu_widgets), menu_item_check);
gtk_menu_append(GTK_MENU(menu_widgets), menu_item_cmd);
gtk_menu_append(GTK_MENU(menu_widgets), menu_item_check2);

text_manual = gtk_text_new(NULL, NULL);

gtk_box_pack_start(GTK_BOX(vbox_manual), menu_bar_manual, FALSE, FALSE, 0);
gtk_box_pack_start(GTK_BOX(vbox_manual), text_manual, TRUE, TRUE, 0);
gtk_container_add(GTK_CONTAINER(frm_manual), vbox_manual);

gtk_widget_show_all(frm_manual);
}

/* ============= Creating a Menu the Easy Way =============== */

/* The following are notes regarding the GtkItemFactoryEntry structure:
 *
 * First, the parameters that are passed as strings are, of
 * course, case sensitive. "<separators>" will cause an
 * error—but at run time instead of compile time.
 * The same is true of checkitem or Checkitem instead of CheckItem.
 *
 * Second, when using underscores for names, it would probably
 * be best to avoid them for things like separators. However,
 * you could use sep_1 in the following instead of sep1. In
```

```
 * that case, you should avoid it because in this context, the
 * underscore has a meaning other than to separate words
 * for readability: It identifies accelerator characters
 * as well.
 */

static GtkItemFactoryEntry items[] = {
   {"/_File", NULL, 0, 0, "<Branch>"},
   {"/File/tear1", NULL, NULL, 0, "<Tearoff>"},
   {"/File/_Open", "<control>O", item_factory_clicked, 0},
   {"/File/sep1", NULL, NULL, 0, "<Separator>"},
   {"/File/_Exit", "<alt>E", item_factory_clicked, 0},
   {"/_Help", NULL, 0, 0, "<LastBranch>"},
   {"/Help/_CheckBox", NULL, NULL, 0, "<CheckItem>"},
   {"/Help/_About", "<shift>A", item_factory_clicked, 0}
};

/* As you might expect, there are tradeoffs to using an item
 * factory. With an Item Factory, you can't add images, the front slash
 * character '/', or other fancy widgets. Basically, you're limited
 * to a very standard text-based menu.
 */

void cmd_item_factory_clicked()
{
   GtkWidget *vbox_item_factory;
   GtkWidget *text_item_factory;
   GtkItemFactory *menu_item_factory;
   GtkWidget *menu_bar_item_factory;
   GtkAccelGroup *accel_group_item_factory;

   frm_item_factory = gtk_window_new(GTK_WINDOW_TOPLEVEL);
   gtk_window_set_title(GTK_WINDOW(frm_item_factory), "Item Factory Menu Demo");

   vbox_item_factory = gtk_vbox_new(FALSE, 0);

   accel_group_item_factory = gtk_accel_group_new();
   gtk_accel_group_attach(accel_group_item_factory,
                          GTK_OBJECT(frm_item_factory));

   /* Technically, an accelerator group is not absolutely necessary,
    * but without it, the underlined characters that should work with
    * ALT, such as ALT+F for "File", would not be active.
    */

   /* Hardware Note:
    * Be sure to try both ALT keys on your machine to test the
    * accelerators. On my laptop, only the left ALT key works to
    * bring up a menu. This is a limitation of the machine on
    * which I am running Linux, not of GTK+.
    */
```

continues

Listing 3.5   **Continued**

```
menu_item_factory = gtk_item_factory_new(GTK_TYPE_MENU_BAR,
                                     "<no_path>",
                                     accel_group_item_factory);
gtk_item_factory_create_items(menu_item_factory,
                              sizeof(items)/sizeof(items[0]),
                              items,
                              NULL);
menu_bar_item_factory = gtk_item_factory_get_widget(menu_item_factory,
                                              "<no_path>");

text_item_factory = gtk_text_new(NULL, NULL);

gtk_box_pack_start(GTK_BOX(vbox_item_factory), menu_bar_item_factory,
                   TRUE, TRUE, 0);
gtk_box_pack_start(GTK_BOX(vbox_item_factory), text_item_factory,
                   TRUE, TRUE, 0);
gtk_container_add(GTK_CONTAINER(frm_item_factory), vbox_item_factory);

gtk_widget_show_all(frm_item_factory);
}

/* As you can see, considerably less code is required with this
 * method than when you create the menu bar by hand.
 */

void item_factory_clicked()
{
    g_print("Item factory clicked...\n");
}

/* ============= Popup Menu on Right Click ==================== */

void cmd_popup_clicked()
{
    GtkWidget *vbox_popup;
    GtkWidget *lbl_right_click;
    GtkWidget *text_right_click;
    GtkWidget *mnu_1, *mnu_2, *mnu_3;

    frm_popup = gtk_window_new(GTK_WINDOW_TOPLEVEL);
    gtk_window_set_title(GTK_WINDOW(frm_popup), "Popup Menu Demo");

    vbox_popup = gtk_vbox_new(TRUE, 0);

    lbl_right_click = gtk_label_new("Popup Demo\nRight Click\nIn The Text Box
Below");
    text_right_click = gtk_text_new(NULL, NULL);

    /* Catch events that happen for the text box. The following
```

```
    * signal handler will catch all events; in the function,
    * it can be narrowed down to the desired events.
    */

   gtk_signal_connect(GTK_OBJECT(text_right_click),
                      "event",
                      GTK_SIGNAL_FUNC(text_right_click_event),
                      popup_menu);

   /* Now build the popup menu; it is very simple, with
    * three very non-descriptive choices.
    */

   popup_menu = gtk_menu_new();
   mnu_1 = gtk_menu_item_new_with_label("Choice 1");
   mnu_2 = gtk_menu_item_new_with_label("Choice 2");
   mnu_3 = gtk_menu_item_new_with_label("Choice 3");

   gtk_signal_connect(GTK_OBJECT(mnu_1),
                      "activate",
                      GTK_SIGNAL_FUNC(popup_mnu_1_clicked),
                      NULL);

   gtk_signal_connect(GTK_OBJECT(mnu_2),
                      "activate",
                      GTK_SIGNAL_FUNC(popup_mnu_2_clicked),
                      NULL);

   gtk_signal_connect(GTK_OBJECT(mnu_3),
                      "activate",
                      GTK_SIGNAL_FUNC(popup_mnu_3_clicked),
                      NULL);

   gtk_box_pack_start(GTK_BOX(vbox_popup), lbl_right_click, TRUE, TRUE, 0);
   gtk_box_pack_start(GTK_BOX(vbox_popup), text_right_click, TRUE, TRUE, 0);
   gtk_container_add(GTK_CONTAINER(frm_popup), vbox_popup);

   /* Add the menu items to the menu. */

   gtk_menu_append(GTK_MENU(popup_menu), mnu_1);
   gtk_menu_append(GTK_MENU(popup_menu), mnu_2);
   gtk_menu_append(GTK_MENU(popup_menu), mnu_3);

   gtk_widget_show_all(frm_popup);
}

void popup_mnu_1_clicked()
{
   g_print("popup menu item 1 clicked...\n");
}
```

continues

Listing 3.5 **Continued**

```
void popup_mnu_2_clicked()
{
   g_print("popup menu item 2 clicked...\n");
}

void popup_mnu_3_clicked()
{
   g_print("popup menu item 3 clicked...\n");
}

void text_right_click_event(GtkWidget *Widget, GdkEvent *event)
{
   /* g_print("inside text box event...\n"); */

   if (event->type == GDK_BUTTON_PRESS)
     {
        GdkEventButton *buttonevent = (GdkEventButton *) event;
        /* g_print("inside button press event...\n"); */

        if (buttonevent->button == 3)
          {
             /* g_print("inside right click event...\n"); */
             gtk_widget_show_all(popup_menu);
             gtk_menu_popup(GTK_MENU(popup_menu),
                            NULL, NULL, NULL, NULL,
                            buttonevent->button,
                            0);
          }
     }
}
```

4

Advanced GTK+
Layout Widgets

THIS CHAPTER COVERS SOME OF THE MORE advanced layout widgets. Specifically, it
covers the following:

- GtkTable
- GtkTree and GtkCTree
- GtkFixed
- GtkLayout
- GtkScrolledWindow
- GtkNotebook
- GtkPaned

GtkTable

The GtkTable widget is like a grid, or perhaps what you would get if you crossed a
horizontal packing box with a vertical packing box (see Figure 4.1). A tic-tac-toe
game would work well as a three-by-three GtkTable. In addition, you can tell the table
to span child widgets across more than one position in the table, either vertically or
horizontally.

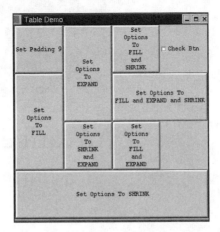

Figure 4.1   The GtkTable demo program running.

The GtkTable demo program shows the table widget in action (albeit in a slightly ugly implementation). It also shows a new paradigm for a program-in-action—that of destroying and re-creating a widget in response to events. Remember that if this were an application, you would have to find some way to preserve the data in order to restore it after the widgets were re-created. The compiled and running version of Listing 4.1 is shown in Figure 4.1.

Listing 4.1   **Demo of the GtkTable Widget**

```
#include <gtk/gtk.h>

GtkWidget *frm_table;
GtkWidget *tbl;

/* Each command button widget, below, will be specified by the location of
 * its top left corner. For example, the first one is row 1, column 1.
 * The second is row 2, column 1, and so on.
 */

GtkWidget *cmd_1_1;
GtkWidget *cmd_2_1;
GtkWidget *cmd_4_1;
GtkWidget *cmd_1_2;
GtkWidget *cmd_1_3;
GtkWidget *cmd_3_2;
GtkWidget *cmd_2_3;
GtkWidget *cmd_3_3;
GtkWidget *chk_1;

void destroy_main();
void make_table_buttons();
void attach_widgets();
void cmd_1_1_clicked();
```

```
void cmd_2_1_clicked();
void cmd_4_1_clicked();
void cmd_1_2_clicked();
void cmd_1_3_clicked();
void cmd_3_2_clicked();
void cmd_2_3_clicked();
void cmd_3_3_clicked();

gint main(gint argc, gchar *argv[])
{

    gtk_init(&argc, &argv);

    frm_table = gtk_window_new(GTK_WINDOW_TOPLEVEL);

    gtk_window_set_title(GTK_WINDOW(frm_table), "Table Demo");

    gtk_signal_connect(GTK_OBJECT(frm_table),
        "destroy",
        GTK_SIGNAL_FUNC(destroy_main),
        NULL);

    make_table_buttons();

     /* Initial setup of command buttons uses defaults.
      *
      * The only reason you use gtk_table_attach_defaults() here
      * instead of attach_widgets() is to demonstrate the
      * gtk_table_attach_defaults() function.
      */

    gtk_table_attach_defaults(GTK_TABLE(tbl), cmd_1_1, 0, 1, 0, 1);
    gtk_table_attach_defaults(GTK_TABLE(tbl), cmd_2_1, 0, 1, 1, 3);
    gtk_table_attach_defaults(GTK_TABLE(tbl), cmd_4_1, 0, 4, 3, 4);
    gtk_table_attach_defaults(GTK_TABLE(tbl), cmd_1_2, 1, 2, 0, 2);
    gtk_table_attach_defaults(GTK_TABLE(tbl), cmd_1_3, 2, 3, 0, 1);
    gtk_table_attach_defaults(GTK_TABLE(tbl), cmd_3_2, 1, 2, 2, 3);
    gtk_table_attach_defaults(GTK_TABLE(tbl), cmd_3_3, 2, 3, 2, 3);
    gtk_table_attach_defaults(GTK_TABLE(tbl), cmd_2_3, 2, 4, 1, 2);

    chk_1 = gtk_check_button_new_with_label("Check Btn");

    gtk_table_attach_defaults(GTK_TABLE(tbl), chk_1, 3, 4, 0, 1);

    gtk_container_add(GTK_CONTAINER(frm_table), tbl);

    gtk_widget_show_all (frm_table);
    gtk_main ();
    return 0;

}
```

continues

Listing 4.1 **Continued**

```
void destroy_main()
{   gtk_main_quit();
}

void attach_widgets(gint _OPTIONS, gint _PACKING)
{
    gtk_table_attach(GTK_TABLE(tbl), cmd_1_1, 0, 1, 0, 1, _OPTIONS, _OPTIONS,
_PACKING, _PACKING);
    gtk_table_attach(GTK_TABLE(tbl), cmd_2_1, 0, 1, 1, 3, _OPTIONS, _OPTIONS,
_PACKING, _PACKING);
    gtk_table_attach(GTK_TABLE(tbl), cmd_4_1, 0, 4, 3, 4, _OPTIONS, _OPTIONS,
_PACKING, _PACKING);
    gtk_table_attach(GTK_TABLE(tbl), cmd_1_2, 1, 2, 0, 2, _OPTIONS, _OPTIONS,
_PACKING, _PACKING);
    gtk_table_attach(GTK_TABLE(tbl), cmd_1_3, 2, 3, 0, 1, _OPTIONS, _OPTIONS,
_PACKING, _PACKING);
    gtk_table_attach(GTK_TABLE(tbl), cmd_3_2, 1, 2, 2, 3, _OPTIONS, _OPTIONS,
_PACKING, _PACKING);
    gtk_table_attach(GTK_TABLE(tbl), cmd_3_3, 2, 3, 2, 3, _OPTIONS, _OPTIONS,
_PACKING, _PACKING);
    gtk_table_attach(GTK_TABLE(tbl), cmd_2_3, 2, 4, 1, 2, _OPTIONS, _OPTIONS,
_PACKING, _PACKING);
    gtk_table_attach(GTK_TABLE(tbl), chk_1, 3, 4, 0, 1, _OPTIONS, _OPTIONS,
_PACKING, _PACKING);
}


void make_table_buttons()
{
    tbl = gtk_table_new(4, 4, TRUE);

    /* The parameters for the previous call are rows, columns, and homogenous.
     */

    cmd_1_1 = gtk_button_new_with_label("Set Padding 9");
    gtk_signal_connect(GTK_OBJECT(cmd_1_1),
        "clicked",
        GTK_SIGNAL_FUNC(cmd_1_1_clicked),
        NULL);
    cmd_2_1 = gtk_button_new_with_label("Set\nOptions\nTo\nFILL");
    gtk_signal_connect(GTK_OBJECT(cmd_2_1),
        "clicked",
        GTK_SIGNAL_FUNC(cmd_2_1_clicked),
        NULL);
    cmd_4_1 = gtk_button_new_with_label("Set Options To SHRINK");
    gtk_signal_connect(GTK_OBJECT(cmd_4_1),
        "clicked",
        GTK_SIGNAL_FUNC(cmd_4_1_clicked),
        NULL);
```

```
    cmd_1_2 = gtk_button_new_with_label("Set\nOptions\nTo\nEXPAND");
    gtk_signal_connect(GTK_OBJECT(cmd_1_2),
        "clicked",
        GTK_SIGNAL_FUNC(cmd_1_2_clicked),
        NULL);
    cmd_1_3 = gtk_button_new_with_label("Set\nOptions\nTo\nFILL\nand\nSHRINK");
    gtk_signal_connect(GTK_OBJECT(cmd_1_3),
        "clicked",
        GTK_SIGNAL_FUNC(cmd_1_3_clicked),
        NULL);
    cmd_3_2 = gtk_button_new_with_label("Set\nOptions\nTo\nSHRINK\nand\nEXPAND");
    gtk_signal_connect(GTK_OBJECT(cmd_3_2),
        "clicked",
        GTK_SIGNAL_FUNC(cmd_3_2_clicked),
        NULL);
    cmd_3_3 = gtk_button_new_with_label("Set\nOptions\nTo\nFILL\nand\nEXPAND");
    gtk_signal_connect(GTK_OBJECT(cmd_3_3),
        "clicked",
        GTK_SIGNAL_FUNC(cmd_3_3_clicked),
        NULL);
    cmd_2_3 = gtk_button_new_with_label("Set Options To\nFILL and EXPAND and
SHRINK");
    gtk_signal_connect(GTK_OBJECT(cmd_2_3),
        "clicked",
        GTK_SIGNAL_FUNC(cmd_2_3_clicked),
        NULL);
    chk_1 = gtk_check_button_new_with_label("Check Btn");
}

void cmd_1_1_clicked()
{
    /* This is something new that hasn't been covered yet. The table of
     * command buttons that the user presses will actually be destroyed
     * and then re-created, as will all the following
     * command button callbacks. This is because there is no *_set_*
     * command for the table widget.
     *
     * Even if there was, you could still do it this way if you wanted
     * to. Granted, this gets a little tedious, but if you change the
     * user interface, you know all the places to make changes in order
     * to maintain your layout.
     */

    gtk_widget_destroy(tbl);
    make_table_buttons();
    attach_widgets(0, 9);
    gtk_container_add(GTK_CONTAINER(frm_table), tbl);
    gtk_widget_show_all (frm_table);
}
```

continues

Listing 4.1 **Continued**

```
/* Clearly, the following could be better engineered as
 * a single function that reacted differently based on
 * the incoming parameters. However, it is
 * presented this way in order to show the different
 * values and their uses in an easy-to-compare format.
 */


void cmd_2_1_clicked()
{
   gtk_widget_destroy(tbl);
   make_table_buttons();
   attach_widgets(GTK_FILL, 0);
   gtk_container_add(GTK_CONTAINER(frm_table), tbl);
   gtk_widget_show_all (frm_table);
}

void cmd_4_1_clicked()
{
   gtk_widget_destroy(tbl);
   make_table_buttons();
   attach_widgets(GTK_SHRINK, 0);
   gtk_container_add(GTK_CONTAINER(frm_table), tbl);
   gtk_widget_show_all (frm_table);
}

void cmd_1_2_clicked()
{
   gtk_widget_destroy(tbl);
   make_table_buttons();
   attach_widgets(GTK_EXPAND, 0);
   gtk_container_add(GTK_CONTAINER(frm_table), tbl);
   gtk_widget_show_all (frm_table);
}

void cmd_1_3_clicked()
{
   gtk_widget_destroy(tbl);
   make_table_buttons();
   attach_widgets(GTK_FILL | GTK_SHRINK, 0);
   gtk_container_add(GTK_CONTAINER(frm_table), tbl);
   gtk_widget_show_all (frm_table);
}

void cmd_3_2_clicked()
{
   gtk_widget_destroy(tbl);
   make_table_buttons();
   attach_widgets(GTK_SHRINK | GTK_EXPAND, 0);
```

```
    gtk_container_add(GTK_CONTAINER(frm_table), tbl);
    gtk_widget_show_all (frm_table);
}

void cmd_3_3_clicked()
{
    gtk_widget_destroy(tbl);
    make_table_buttons();
    attach_widgets(GTK_FILL | GTK_EXPAND, 0);
    gtk_container_add(GTK_CONTAINER(frm_table), tbl);
    gtk_widget_show_all (frm_table);
}

void cmd_2_3_clicked()
{
    gtk_widget_destroy(tbl);
    make_table_buttons();
    attach_widgets(GTK_SHRINK | GTK_FILL | GTK_EXPAND, 0);
    gtk_container_add(GTK_CONTAINER(frm_table), tbl);
    gtk_widget_show_all (frm_table);
}
```

GtkTree and GtkCTree

The GtkTree and GtkCTree widgets are standard tree-type controls. The "C" in GtkCTree stands for "column(s)"; you could say it is a cross between a tree control and a data control (see Figure 4.2 and Listing 4.2). In terms of the GTK+ widget tree, GtkContainer is the parent widget of GtkList, GtkCList, and GtkTree. GtkCTree is the child of GtkCList. Although you can think of GtkCTree as being derived from GtkCList, the same does not necessarily apply to GtkTree and GtkList.

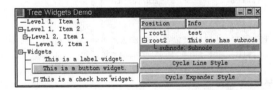

Figure 4.2   The Tree widgets demo program running.

In the following program, the GtkTree and GtkCTree widgets are presented side by side for comparison. The important difference between them is that the GtkCTree widget can accept only pixmaps and text as input, whereas the GtkTree widget can take any type of child widget.

Listing 4.2   **GtkTree and GtkCTree Demo**

```c
#include <gtk/gtk.h>

GtkWidget *frm_trees;
GtkWidget *tree_left, *ctree_right;
GtkWidget *subtree_item2;
GtkWidget *subtree_item3;
GtkWidget *subtree_widgets;

void destroy_main();
void cmd_cycle_line_style_clicked();
void cmd_cycle_expander_clicked();

gint main(gint argc, gchar *argv[])
{
    GtkWidget *hbox_main, *vbox_left, *vbox_right;
    GtkWidget *lvl1_item1, *lvl1_item2;
    GtkWidget *widgets_item;
    GtkWidget *label_widget, *button_widget, *check_box_widget;
    GtkWidget *item2_item1, *item2_item1_item1;
    GtkWidget *label_item, *button_item, *check_box_item;
    GtkWidget *cmd_cycle_line_style, *cmd_cycle_expander;

    GtkCTreeNode *root_node_1;
    GtkCTreeNode *root_node_2;
    GtkCTreeNode *root_node_3;

    /* The following sets the titles for the CTree widget.
     * The width of the columns will be determined by
     * the column headers, not the data in the columns.
     */

    gchar *column_titles[2] = {"Position", "Info"};

    gchar *root1_data[2] = {"root1", "test"};
    gchar *root2_data[2] = {"root2", "This one has subnodes."};
    gchar *root3_data[2] = {"subnode1", "Subnode."};

    gtk_init(&argc, &argv);

    frm_trees = gtk_window_new(GTK_WINDOW_TOPLEVEL);

    gtk_window_set_title(GTK_WINDOW(frm_trees), "Tree Widgets Demo");

    gtk_signal_connect(GTK_OBJECT(frm_trees),
        "destroy",
        GTK_SIGNAL_FUNC(destroy_main),
        NULL);
```

```
hbox_main = gtk_hbox_new(TRUE, 0);
vbox_left = gtk_vbox_new(TRUE, 0);
vbox_right = gtk_vbox_new(FALSE, 0);

/* The fundamental differences between GtkTree and GtkCTree
 * are similar to the differences between GtkList and GtkCList.
 * That is, GtkTree can accept any widget as a tree item,
 * whereas GtkCTree can accept only pixmaps or text.
 */

tree_left = gtk_tree_new();

/* A tree isn't much good if it doesn't have anything in it.
 * Fortunately, adding a "tree item" widget is quite simple…
 */

lvl1_item1 = gtk_tree_item_new_with_label("Level 1, Item 1");
lvl1_item2 = gtk_tree_item_new_with_label("Level 1, Item 2");

gtk_tree_append(GTK_TREE(tree_left), lvl1_item1);
gtk_tree_append(GTK_TREE(tree_left), lvl1_item2);

/* Unfortunately, this creates a tree that imitates a list
 * box. The tree widget is not useful unless (and until) you start
 * adding subtrees. Note that this is different from adding nodes
 * and pointers, which is taken care of for you by the subtree
 * structure.
 *
 * You don't add a tree to a tree; you add a tree to a "tree
 * item."
 */

subtree_item2 = gtk_tree_new();
item2_item1 = gtk_tree_item_new_with_label("Level 2, Item 1");
gtk_tree_append(GTK_TREE(subtree_item2), item2_item1);

gtk_tree_item_set_subtree(GTK_TREE_ITEM(lvl1_item2), subtree_item2);

/* You have to explicitly show the subtree tree items.
 *
 * Note that if the user has selected items in a subtree and then
 * collapses that branch of the tree, the items remain selected.
 */

gtk_widget_show(item2_item1);

subtree_item3 = gtk_tree_new();
item2_item1_item1 = gtk_tree_item_new_with_label("Level 3, Item 1");
gtk_tree_append(GTK_TREE(subtree_item3), item2_item1_item1);
```

continues

Listing 4.2   **Continued**

```
gtk_tree_item_set_subtree(GTK_TREE_ITEM(item2_item1), subtree_item3);

gtk_widget_show(item2_item1_item1);

widgets_item = gtk_tree_item_new_with_label("Widgets");
gtk_tree_append(GTK_TREE(tree_left), widgets_item);

subtree_widgets = gtk_tree_new();
gtk_tree_item_set_subtree(GTK_TREE_ITEM(widgets_item), subtree_widgets);

/* Add some widgets to the tree.
 *
 * First, construct a label widget and add it to the tree.
 */

label_item = gtk_tree_item_new();
label_widget = gtk_label_new("This is a label widget.");
gtk_container_add(GTK_CONTAINER(label_item), label_widget);
gtk_tree_append(GTK_TREE(subtree_widgets), label_item);
gtk_widget_show(label_widget);
gtk_widget_show(label_item);

/* Next, add a command button to the tree.
 */

button_item = gtk_tree_item_new();
button_widget = gtk_button_new_with_label("This is a button widget.");
gtk_container_add(GTK_CONTAINER(button_item), button_widget);
gtk_tree_append(GTK_TREE(subtree_widgets), button_item);
gtk_widget_show(button_widget);
gtk_widget_show(button_item);

/* And now a check box…
 */

check_box_item = gtk_tree_item_new();
check_box_widget = gtk_check_button_new_with_label("This is a check box
widget.");
gtk_container_add(GTK_CONTAINER(check_box_item), check_box_widget);
gtk_tree_append(GTK_TREE(subtree_widgets), check_box_item);
gtk_widget_show(check_box_widget);
gtk_widget_show(check_box_item);

/* Now look at the CTree widget for comparison.
 */

ctree_right = gtk_ctree_new_with_titles(2, 0, column_titles);

root_node_1 = gtk_ctree_insert_node(GTK_CTREE(ctree_right), NULL, NULL,
root1_data,
                0, NULL, NULL, NULL, NULL, FALSE, TRUE);
```

```
    root_node_2 = gtk_ctree_insert_node(GTK_CTREE(ctree_right), NULL, NULL,
root2_data,
                    0, NULL, NULL, NULL, NULL, FALSE, TRUE);
    root_node_3 = gtk_ctree_insert_node(GTK_CTREE(ctree_right), root_node_2, NULL,
root3_data,
                    0, NULL, NULL, NULL, NULL, FALSE, TRUE);

    /* As you can see, the construction of a CTree is much simpler.
     * Once you have the CTree widget instantiated, you essentially
     * create new nodes and attach them to existing nodes. The
     * parameters for the gtk_ctree_insert_node are as follows:
     *   ■ ctree—The ctree object in question.
     *   ■ parent—The parent node to attach to; NULL for root level.
     *   ■ sibling—The sibling node; NULL for end of branch.
     *   ■ text—A text array of values for the ctree columns; must
     *          contain the same number of values as the ctree
     *          contains columns.
     *   ■ spacing—Number of pixels between the tree-structure
     *             pixmap and the text.
     *   ■ pixmap_closed \
     *     bitmask_closed  \ Pixmap and bitmap pointers to display when
     *   ■ pixmap_opened   / the node is expanded or collapsed.
     *     bitmask_opened /
     *   ■ is_leaf—Boolean indicating whether or not this node is a
     *             leaf; if TRUE, it doesn't contain subnodes,
     *             and you won't be able to add subnodes.
     *   ■ expanded—Boolean indicating the default expanded/non-expanded
     *              state of the node.
     */

    cmd_cycle_line_style = gtk_button_new_with_label("Cycle Line Style");
    gtk_signal_connect(GTK_OBJECT(cmd_cycle_line_style),
        "clicked",
        GTK_SIGNAL_FUNC(cmd_cycle_line_style_clicked),
        NULL);

    cmd_cycle_expander = gtk_button_new_with_label("Cycle Expander Style");
    gtk_signal_connect(GTK_OBJECT(cmd_cycle_expander),
        "clicked",
        GTK_SIGNAL_FUNC(cmd_cycle_expander_clicked),
        NULL);

    gtk_box_pack_start(GTK_BOX(vbox_left), tree_left, TRUE, TRUE, 0);
    gtk_box_pack_start(GTK_BOX(vbox_right), ctree_right, TRUE, TRUE, 0);
    gtk_box_pack_start(GTK_BOX(vbox_right), cmd_cycle_line_style, TRUE, FALSE, 0);
    gtk_box_pack_start(GTK_BOX(vbox_right), cmd_cycle_expander, TRUE, FALSE, 0);

    gtk_box_pack_start(GTK_BOX(hbox_main), vbox_left, TRUE, TRUE, 0);
    gtk_box_pack_start(GTK_BOX(hbox_main), vbox_right, TRUE, TRUE, 0);
    gtk_container_add(GTK_CONTAINER(frm_trees), hbox_main);
```

continues

Listing 4.2 **Continued**

```
    gtk_widget_show_all (frm_trees);
    gtk_main ();
    return 0;

}

void destroy_main()
{   gtk_main_quit();
}

void cmd_cycle_line_style_clicked()
{
    static gint line_style = 1;

    if (line_style == 4)
        line_style = 1;
    else line_style++;

    switch (line_style)
     {
       case 1: gtk_ctree_set_line_style(GTK_CTREE(ctree_right),
                                     GTK_CTREE_LINES_NONE);
               break;
       case 2: gtk_ctree_set_line_style(GTK_CTREE(ctree_right),
                                     GTK_CTREE_LINES_SOLID);
               break;
       case 3: gtk_ctree_set_line_style(GTK_CTREE(ctree_right),
                                     GTK_CTREE_LINES_DOTTED);
               break;
       case 4: gtk_ctree_set_line_style(GTK_CTREE(ctree_right),
                                     GTK_CTREE_LINES_TABBED);
               break;
       default:  g_print("Should not see this line!!");
                 break;
     }

}

void cmd_cycle_expander_clicked()
{
    static gint expander_style = 1;

    if (expander_style == 4)
        expander_style = 1;
    else expander_style++;

    switch (expander_style)
     {
       case 1: gtk_ctree_set_expander_style(GTK_CTREE(ctree_right),
                                        GTK_CTREE_EXPANDER_NONE);
               break;
```

```
       case 2: gtk_ctree_set_expander_style(GTK_CTREE(ctree_right),
                                             GTK_CTREE_EXPANDER_SQUARE);
               break;
       case 3: gtk_ctree_set_expander_style(GTK_CTREE(ctree_right),
                                             GTK_CTREE_EXPANDER_TRIANGLE);
               break;
       case 4: gtk_ctree_set_expander_style(GTK_CTREE(ctree_right),
                                             GTK_CTREE_EXPANDER_CIRCULAR);
               break;
       default:  g_print("Should not see this line!!");
                 break;
   }

}
```

GtkFixed

The GtkFixed widget is initially attractive to developers coming from VB or VC++ because the paradigm is familiar to them. That is, unlike the GTK+ paradigm of packing widgets, the GtkFixed widget allows the developer to place widgets at certain points on a "grid" and to move the widgets around (see Figure 4.3). However, most developers will tend to gravitate toward the GtkLayout widget (see the following section, titled "GtkLayout") because it has slightly more advanced functionality.

Figure 4.3   The GtkFixed demo program running.

The program in Listing 4.3 is fairly simple: It has a GtkFixed widget and a single command button that jumps around within the GtkFixed widget when pushed. Compare this with the GtkLayout widget (covered in the next section) before you decide which one is best suited to your project.

Listing 4.3   **GtkFixed Demo**

```
#include <gtk/gtk.h>
#include <stdlib.h>
/* This is needed for the random number function in the callback
 * at the bottom of the listing. This random number function
 * is used to jump the command button (cmd1) around within the
```

continues

Listing 4.3   **Continued**

```
 * fixed widget.
 */

GtkWidget *frm_fixed;
GtkWidget *fixed_main;
GtkWidget *cmd1;

void destroy_main();
void cmd1_clicked();

gint main(gint argc, gchar *argv[])
{
    gtk_init(&argc, &argv);

    frm_fixed = gtk_window_new(GTK_WINDOW_TOPLEVEL);

    gtk_window_set_title(GTK_WINDOW(frm_fixed), "Fixed Widget Demo");

    gtk_signal_connect(GTK_OBJECT(frm_fixed),
        "destroy",
        GTK_SIGNAL_FUNC(destroy_main),
        NULL);

    fixed_main = gtk_fixed_new();

    /* The GtkFixed widget is very simple to use. As shown
     * below, you give it the coordinates at which to place
     * a child widget. The widget attributes of fill, expand,
     * padding, and so on, are irrelevant here; the child widgets
     * placed onto the fixed widget will default to the
     * minimum required to show correctly. This is the same
     * behavior of the GtkFixed widget; it will size itself
     * to the minimum required to show all its child
     * widgets. If a child widget is moved to an area outside
     * of the GtkFixed's current size, the fixed widget will
     * grow just enough to properly show the widget. If,
     * however, the child widgets are moved to a location
     * that would allow the window to shrink, the fixed
     * widget will not automatically shrink to the minimum
     * required size.
     *
     * This can lead to some unexpected behavior. For example,
     * suppose the initial position is 1, 1. Then the
     * position changes to 100, 100. If the position then
     * changes to 50, 50, the window size will not change.
     * If, however, the position changes to 150, 50, the
     * window will change size, to be just large enough to
     * properly show the widget. Another way to put it is
     * that the window will be redrawn whenever the child
     * widgets push an outside boundary of the window—
     * pushing either the right or the bottom boundary out. Then
```

```
 * the window will be resized. Thus, you could go from an
 * essentially square window to a long and thin one,
 * and vice-versa.
 *
 * Although the GtkFixed widget is simple to implement,
 * you will probably want to use the GtkLayout widget
 * in most instances. Examine it before deciding
 * which will best suit your project.
 */

cmd1 = gtk_button_new_with_label("Button 1");
gtk_signal_connect(GTK_OBJECT(cmd1),
    "clicked",
    GTK_SIGNAL_FUNC(cmd1_clicked),
    NULL);
gtk_fixed_put(GTK_FIXED(fixed_main), cmd1, 1, 100);

/* The third and fourth parameters of the previous call
 * are the distance from the left edge of the window in pixels,
 * and the distance from the top edge of the window in pixels,
 * respectively.
 */

gtk_container_add(GTK_CONTAINER(frm_fixed), fixed_main);

gtk_widget_show_all (frm fixed);
gtk_main ();
return 0;

}

void destroy_main()
{   gtk_main_quit();
}

void cmd1_clicked()
{
   gint x_pos, y_pos;

   x_pos = rand();
   y_pos = rand();

   /* The poor man's bounded random number generator. In
    * this case, the target is for a number between 1 and 200.
    */

   do{
      x_pos = x_pos - 200;
   } while (x_pos > 200);

   do{
```

continues

Listing 4.3   **Continued**

```
        y_pos = y_pos - 200;
    } while (y_pos > 200);

    gtk_fixed_move(GTK_FIXED(fixed_main), GTK_WIDGET(cmd1), x_pos, y_pos);
}
```

GtkLayout

The GtkLayout widget is very similar to the GtkFixed widget, but it allows a larger widget placement area. It also handles re-drawing of child widgets differently, necessitating the use of the *_freeze* and *_thaw* calls (see the end of Listing 4.4). Listing 4.4 is presented in Figure 4.4.

Figure 4.4   The GtkLayout demo program running.

Listing 4.4 and Figure 4.4 are intentionally very similar to Listing 4.3 and Figure 4.3. The purpose is to demonstrate the similarities and differences between these two very similar widgets; compile and run both to see which will best fit your needs.

Listing 4.4   **GtkLayout Demo**

```
#include <gtk/gtk.h>
#include <stdlib.h>

GtkWidget *frm_layout;
GtkWidget *layout_main;
GtkWidget *cmd1;

void destroy_main();
void cmd1_clicked();

gint main(gint argc, gchar *argv[])
{
    gtk_init(&argc, &argv);

    frm_layout = gtk_window_new(GTK_WINDOW_TOPLEVEL);
```

```
    gtk_window_set_title(GTK_WINDOW(frm_layout), "Layout Widget Demo");

    gtk_signal_connect(GTK_OBJECT(frm_layout),
         "destroy",
         GTK_SIGNAL_FUNC(destroy_main),
         NULL);

    layout_main = gtk_layout_new(NULL, NULL);

    /* Other than the call above to gtk_layout_new(),
     * which requires vertical and horizontal adjustment
     * objects as parameters, you could take the previous
     * listing and change every instance of "fixed" to
     * "layout," and the program should work.
     *
     * However, lines have also been added
     * to this program to demonstrate the Layout widget
     * functionality.
     */

    cmd1 = gtk_button_new_with_label("Button 1");
    gtk_signal_connect(GTK_OBJECT(cmd1),
         "clicked",
         GTK_SIGNAL_FUNC(cmd1_clicked),
         NULL);
    gtk_layout_put(GTK_LAYOUT(layout_main), cmd1, 1, 100);

    gtk_container_add(GTK_CONTAINER(frm_layout), layout_main);

    gtk_widget_show_all (frm_layout);
    gtk_main ();
    return 0;

}

void destroy_main()
{   gtk_main_quit();
}

void cmd1_clicked()
{
    gint x_pos, y_pos;

    x_pos = rand();
    y_pos = rand();

    /* The following is a poor man's bounded
     * random number generator. In this case,
     * the target is for a number between 1 and 200.
     */
```

continues

Listing 4.4 **Continued**

```
do{
    x_pos = x_pos - 200;
} while (x_pos > 200);

do{
    y_pos = y_pos - 200;
} while (y_pos > 200);

/* Here is one big difference between the Fixed and Layout widgets.
 * It is best to freeze and thaw the Layout widget, especially if you
 * have a lot of child widgets to move around and show simultaneously.
 * This prevents having to redraw the screen unnecessarily.
 */

gtk_layout_freeze(GTK_LAYOUT(layout_main));

gtk_layout_move(GTK_LAYOUT(layout_main), GTK_WIDGET(cmd1), x_pos, y_pos);

gtk_layout_thaw(GTK_LAYOUT(layout_main));
}
```

GtkScrolledWindow

The GtkScrolledWindow widget is a container widget that allows you to implement scroll bars on widgets that don't have them already integrated. This of course allows you to have multiple windows in your application and have the user scroll within each of those windows to view the widgets as needed. If you haven't guessed by now, Figure 4.5 is a screen shot of Listing 4.5.

Figure 4.5   The GtkScrolledWindow demo program running.

The scrolled window demo (Listing 4.5 and Figure 4.5) is a variation on the theme
used in Listing 4.3 and 4.4. In this case, there are two command buttons for setting the
relevant properties. Note that the policies do not always have to be the same for the
horizontal and vertical scroll bars; you can mix the "always" setting with the "automatic" setting. In Listing, 4.5, however, I have set both to the same setting instead of
mixing them.

Listing 4.5   **GtkScrolledWindow Demo**

```c
#include <gtk/gtk.h>

GtkWidget *frm_scrolled;
GtkWidget *scrolled_main;
GtkWidget *fixed_main;
GtkWidget *cmd_set_policy_auto, *cmd_set_policy_always;

void destroy_main();
void cmd_set_policy_auto_clicked();
void cmd_set_policy_always_clicked();

gint main(gint argc, gchar *argv[])
{
    gtk_init(&argc, &argv);

    frm_scrolled = gtk_window_new(GTK_WINDOW_TOPLEVEL);
    gtk_window_set_title(GTK_WINDOW(frm_scrolled), "Scrolled Window Demo");

    /* Notice that because you are not giving the window any
     * default sizing information, it will come up very small.
     * You will need to resize it to show the two command
     * buttons below and demonstrate the scroll button
     * policies they demonstrate.
     */

    gtk_signal_connect(GTK_OBJECT(frm_scrolled),
        "destroy",
        GTK_SIGNAL_FUNC(destroy_main),
        NULL);

    scrolled_main = gtk_scrolled_window_new(NULL, NULL);
    fixed_main = gtk_fixed_new();

    cmd_set_policy_auto = gtk_button_new_with_label("Set Policy Auto");
    gtk_signal_connect(GTK_OBJECT(cmd_set_policy_auto),
        "clicked",
        GTK_SIGNAL_FUNC(cmd_set_policy_auto_clicked),
        NULL);

    cmd_set_policy_always = gtk_button_new_with_label("Set Policy Always");
    gtk_signal_connect(GTK_OBJECT(cmd_set_policy_always),
```

continues

Listing 4.5 **Continued**

```
            "clicked",
            GTK_SIGNAL_FUNC(cmd_set_policy_always_clicked),
            NULL);

    gtk_fixed_put(GTK_FIXED(fixed_main), cmd_set_policy_auto, 200, 200);
    gtk_fixed_put(GTK_FIXED(fixed_main), cmd_set_policy_always, 50, 75);

    gtk_scrolled_window_add_with_viewport(GTK_SCROLLED_WINDOW(scrolled_main),
fixed_main);
    gtk_container_add(GTK_CONTAINER(frm_scrolled), scrolled_main);

    gtk_widget_show_all (frm_scrolled);
    gtk_main ();
    return 0;

}

void destroy_main()
{   gtk_main_quit();
}

void cmd_set_policy_auto_clicked()
{
    gtk_scrolled_window_set_policy(GTK_SCROLLED_WINDOW(scrolled_main),
                            GTK_POLICY_AUTOMATIC,
                            GTK_POLICY_AUTOMATIC);
}

void cmd_set_policy_always_clicked()
{
    /* This is the default behavior for the widget.
     */

    gtk_scrolled_window_set_policy(GTK_SCROLLED_WINDOW(scrolled_main),
                            GTK_POLICY_ALWAYS,
                            GTK_POLICY_ALWAYS);
}
```

GtkNotebook

The GtkNotebook widget is what VB developers might be used to calling a "tab control." It has a number of tabs that the user clicks on to allow controls to exist "in the same space;" it hides and shows groups of controls at the same time, which have been placed together on a page (meaning that "a tab shows a page," to use the terminology of some Windows tab controls).

The demo Notebook program is shown in Figure 4.6; its associated listing is of course Listing 4.6. In this program, note that you can add pages dynamically (as you can with all GTK+ widgets).

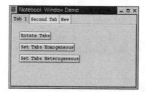

Figure 4.6 The GtkNotebook demo program running.

Listing 4.6 **GtkNotebook Demo**

```c
#include <gtk/gtk.h>

GtkWidget *frm_notebook;
GtkWidget *notebook_main;
GtkWidget *fixed_page1;
GtkWidget *vbox_page2;

void destroy_main();
void cmd_rotate_tabs_clicked();
void cmd_set_tabs_homogeneous_clicked();
void cmd_set_tabs_heterogeneous_clicked();
void cmd_add_page_clicked();
void cmd_get_page_index_clicked();
void notebook_switch_page();

gint main(gint argc, gchar *argv[])
{
   GtkWidget *cmd_rotate_tabs;
   GtkWidget *cmd_set_tabs_homogeneous, *cmd_set_tabs_heterogeneous;
   GtkWidget *cmd_add_page, *cmd_get_page_index;
   GtkWidget *lbl_tab1, *lbl_tab2;

   gtk_init(&argc, &argv);

   frm_notebook = gtk_window_new(GTK_WINDOW_TOPLEVEL);
   gtk_window_set_title(GTK_WINDOW(frm_notebook), "Notebook Window Demo");

   gtk_signal_connect(GTK_OBJECT(frm_notebook),
        "destroy",
        GTK_SIGNAL_FUNC(destroy_main),
        NULL);
```

continues

Listing 4.6 **Continued**

```
notebook_main = gtk_notebook_new();
gtk_signal_connect(GTK_OBJECT(notebook_main),
    "switch-page",
    GTK_SIGNAL_FUNC(notebook_switch_page),
    NULL);

/* Page 1 in the Notebook widget...
 */

fixed_page1 = gtk_fixed_new();
lbl_tab1 = gtk_label_new("Tab 1");

cmd_rotate_tabs = gtk_button_new_with_label("Rotate Tabs");
gtk_signal_connect(GTK_OBJECT(cmd_rotate_tabs),
    "clicked",
    GTK_SIGNAL_FUNC(cmd_rotate_tabs_clicked),
    NULL);

cmd_set_tabs_homogeneous = gtk_button_new_with_label("Set Tabs Homogeneous");
gtk_signal_connect(GTK_OBJECT(cmd_set_tabs_homogeneous),
    "clicked",
    GTK_SIGNAL_FUNC(cmd_set_tabs_homogeneous_clicked),
    NULL);

cmd_set_tabs_heterogeneous = gtk_button_new_with_label("Set Tabs
Heterogeneous");
gtk_signal_connect(GTK_OBJECT(cmd_set_tabs_heterogeneous),
    "clicked",
    GTK_SIGNAL_FUNC(cmd_set_tabs_heterogeneous_clicked),
    NULL);

gtk_fixed_put(GTK_FIXED(fixed_page1), cmd_rotate_tabs, 20, 20);
gtk_fixed_put(GTK_FIXED(fixed_page1), cmd_set_tabs_homogeneous, 20, 50);
gtk_fixed_put(GTK_FIXED(fixed_page1), cmd_set_tabs_heterogeneous, 20, 80);
gtk_notebook_append_page(GTK_NOTEBOOK(notebook_main), fixed_page1, lbl_tab1);

/* Now page 2...
 */
vbox_page2 = gtk_vbox_new(TRUE, 0);
cmd_add_page = gtk_button_new_with_label("Add a Page");
gtk_signal_connect(GTK_OBJECT(cmd_add_page),
    "clicked",
    GTK_SIGNAL_FUNC(cmd_add_page_clicked),
    NULL);

cmd_get_page_index = gtk_button_new_with_label("Get Page Index");
gtk_signal_connect(GTK_OBJECT(cmd_get_page_index),
    "clicked",
    GTK_SIGNAL_FUNC(cmd_get_page_index_clicked),
    NULL);
```

```
    gtk_box_pack_start_defaults(GTK_BOX(vbox_page2), cmd_add_page);
    gtk_box_pack_start_defaults(GTK_BOX(vbox_page2), cmd_get_page_index);

    lbl_tab2 = gtk_label_new("Second Tab");

    gtk_notebook_append_page(GTK_NOTEBOOK(notebook_main), vbox_page2, lbl_tab2);

    /* End of second tab. You're ready for the final assembly of the
     * main window.
     */

    gtk_container_add(GTK_CONTAINER(frm_notebook), notebook_main);

    gtk_widget_show_all (frm_notebook);
    gtk_main ();
    return 0;

}

void destroy_main()
{   gtk_main_quit();
}

void cmd_rotate_tabs_clicked()
{
    static gint tab_location = 1;

    if (tab_location == 4)
        tab_location - 1;
    else tab_location++;

    switch (tab_location)
    {
       case 1: gtk_notebook_set_tab_pos(GTK_NOTEBOOK(notebook_main), GTK_POS_TOP);
               break;
       case 2: gtk_notebook_set_tab_pos(GTK_NOTEBOOK(notebook_main), GTK_POS_RIGHT);
               break;
       case 3: gtk_notebook_set_tab_pos(GTK_NOTEBOOK(notebook_main), GTK_POS_BOTTOM);
               break;
       case 4: gtk_notebook_set_tab_pos(GTK_NOTEBOOK(notebook_main), GTK_POS_LEFT);
               break;
       default: g_print("Should never reach this line.\n");
    }
}

void cmd_set_tabs_homogeneous_clicked()
{
    gtk_notebook_set_homogeneous_tabs(GTK_NOTEBOOK(notebook_main), TRUE);
}

void cmd_set_tabs_heterogeneous_clicked()
```

continues

Listing 4.6   **Continued**

```
{
    /* You will notice that this has no effect when the location of the
     * tabs is left or right. The behavior is the same as that of the
     * cmd_set_tabs_homogeneous_clicked()
     * call in that case.
     */
    gtk_notebook_set_homogeneous_tabs(GTK_NOTEBOOK(notebook_main), FALSE);
}

void cmd_add_page_clicked()
{
    GtkWidget *fixed;
    GtkWidget *lbl;

    fixed = gtk_fixed_new();

    lbl = gtk_label_new("New");

    gtk_notebook_append_page(GTK_NOTEBOOK(notebook_main), fixed, lbl);

    /* Again, the following acts as a "refresh" command.
     */

    gtk_widget_show_all(notebook_main);
}

void cmd_get_page_index_clicked()
{
    /* Notebook page indices are zero-based. */
    g_print("Page index is %i.\n",
gtk_notebook_get_current_page(GTK_NOTEBOOK(notebook_main)));
}

void notebook_switch_page()
{
    g_print("page switched.\n");
}
```

GtkPaned

The GtkPaned widget allows the developer to split the desired space in two, either horizontally or vertically (see Figure 4.7). You split the space in half, but if you want thirds instead, you must then split one of the halves in half again (and again, and so on). The paned widget has a sizing handle that allows the user to grab and move the location of the pane, resizing the widgets in the two halves (if the options have been set correctly).

Figure 4.7   The GtkPaned widgets demo program running.

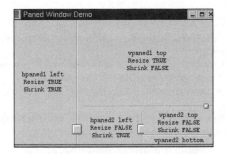

Finally, this chapter concludes with a demonstration of the Paned Widget demo—in Listing 4.7 and Figure 4.7. In Figure 4.7, notice the different sizes of the resizing handles and that one is "cut off" in its display. Such things can be handled by setting the "spacing" of your child widgets. If you do this, however, you must allow enough of a buffer that your child widgets don't display over things like sizing handles.

Listing 4.7 **GtkPaned Demo**

```
#include <gtk/gtk.h>

GtkWidget *frm_paned;

void destroy_main();

gint main(gint argc, gchar *argv[])
{
    GtkWidget *lbl_hpaned1_left;
    GtkWidget *lbl_vpaned1_top;
    GtkWidget *lbl_hpaned2_left;
    GtkWidget *lbl_vpaned2_top;
    GtkWidget *lbl_vpaned2_bottom;
    GtkWidget *hpaned1;
    GtkWidget *vpaned1;
    GtkWidget *hpaned2;
    GtkWidget *vpaned2;

    gtk_init(&argc, &argv);

    frm_paned = gtk_window_new(GTK_WINDOW_TOPLEVEL);
    gtk_window_set_title(GTK_WINDOW(frm_paned), "Paned Window Demo");

    gtk_signal_connect(GTK_OBJECT(frm_paned),
        "destroy",
        GTK_SIGNAL_FUNC(destroy_main),
        NULL);

    hpaned1 = gtk_hpaned_new();
    gtk_paned_gutter_size(GTK_PANED(hpaned1), 20);
    gtk_paned_handle_size(GTK_PANED(hpaned1), 20);
    lbl_hpaned1_left = gtk_label_new("hpaned1 left\nResize TRUE\nShrink TRUE");
```

continues

Listing 4.7 **Continued**

```
gtk_paned_pack1(GTK_PANED(hpaned1), lbl_hpaned1_left, TRUE, TRUE);

/* The gtk_paned_gutter_size() call sets the width between
 * the pane and the widgets next to it. As you can see,
 * a little space improves the aesthetics of the UI considerably.
 *
 * The gtk_paned_handle_size() call sets the box that the user
 * grabs with the mouse to resize the pane.
 *
 * The gtk_paned_pack1() call packs another widget into either the
 * left side of a horizontal paned widget or the top side of
 * a vertical pane. The gtk_paned_pack2() call (see the code below)
 * is inserted to the right or bottom of an hpaned or vpaned,
 * respectively.
 *
 * The parameters for gtk_paned_pack*() are listed here:
 * ■ pane – the target pane of the call
 * ■ child – the child widget to place left/right or top/bottom
 * ■ resize – if true, the child widget will resize to fit its
 *            new window proportionally when the window is resized
 * ■ shrink – if false, will not allow the pane to be resized
 *            smaller than the child widget
 */

vpaned1 = gtk_vpaned_new();
gtk_paned_gutter_size(GTK_PANED(vpaned1), 20);
lbl_vpaned1_top = gtk_label_new("vpaned1 top\nResize TRUE\nShrink FALSE");
gtk_paned_pack2(GTK_PANED(hpaned1), vpaned1, TRUE, FALSE);
gtk_paned_pack1(GTK_PANED(vpaned1), lbl_vpaned1_top, TRUE, FALSE);

hpaned2 = gtk_hpaned_new();
gtk_paned_handle_size(GTK_PANED(hpaned2), 20);
lbl_hpaned2_left = gtk_label_new("hpaned2 left\nResize FALSE\nShrink TRUE");
gtk_paned_pack2(GTK_PANED(vpaned1), hpaned2, FALSE, TRUE);
gtk_paned_pack1(GTK_PANED(hpaned2), lbl_hpaned2_left, FALSE, TRUE);

vpaned2 = gtk_vpaned_new();
gtk_paned_gutter_size(GTK_PANED(vpaned2), 5);
gtk_paned_handle_size(GTK_PANED(vpaned2), 5);
lbl_vpaned2_top = gtk_label_new("vpaned2 top\nResize FALSE\nShrink FALSE");
lbl_vpaned2_bottom = gtk_label_new("vpaned2 bottom");
gtk_paned_pack2(GTK_PANED(hpaned2), vpaned2, FALSE, FALSE);
gtk_paned_pack1(GTK_PANED(vpaned2), lbl_vpaned2_top, FALSE, FALSE);
gtk_paned_pack2(GTK_PANED(vpaned2), lbl_vpaned2_bottom, FALSE, FALSE);

gtk_container_add(GTK_CONTAINER(frm_paned), hpaned1);

gtk_widget_show_all (frm_paned);
gtk_main ();
return 0;
```

```
}

void destroy_main()
{   gtk_main_quit();
}
```

5

Glade for VB Developers

GLADE IS A DEVELOPMENT ENVIRONMENT FOR THE GTK+ widget set. Although it is not the only one available, it seems to be pulling into the lead as the Integrated Development Environment (IDE) of choice. It allows point-and-click user interface construction and then writes source code into an organized set of files for further development. Like Visual Basic (VB), it takes care of almost everything up to the point of writing the event handlers, leaving that to the developer.

About Glade

With a few exceptions, VB and VC++ developers will find it quite easy to adapt to Glade. In terms of parent-child widget relationships, the user interface behaves the way the developer intended.

Many VB and C++ developers may initially be attracted to the GtkFixed or GtkLayout widgets, which are similar to the behavior they are familiar with in "forms." Eventually, however (after much weeping and gnashing of teeth), they will move to the parent-child relationship where the window and its child controls resize and reposition automatically. Why? Because this automatic resizing is the default behavior of GTK+, the "static" widgets like GtkLayout are the exception. Thus, you may find that the static widgets require more attention in the long run, for example, getting them to size and display correctly upon opening. With widgets like GtkTable and the other packing box widgets, such behavior is not normally a concern.

"Visual" developers should make an extra effort to understand the parent-child widget mechanism wherein a widget may be placed inside of a widget, which then may be placed inside of another widget. This layering of widgets is the key to long-term effective development with Glade and GTK+.

Why You Should Use Glade

Glade is a code builder, that is, it allows you to point and click your way through the user interface (UI), and then it writes for you the code to instantiate your application. It organizes your application into separate files by function, such as interface and call-backs. It can write source code in several languages, but this book will stick with C. You should use Glade for the following reasons:

- As the GTK+ Web site says (or said when this book was written, anyway), "It is very cool."
- It is very easy to use.
- Like all good IDEs, it speeds up development time by abstracting the user inter-face design to a point-and-click operation.
- Unlike GTK+, it gives you some idea how your program will look without going through a compile and run cycle.

Where to Get Glade and How to Install

First, check to see if perhaps it was installed on your machine. From the command line, type

```
% glade
```

and see if anything comes up. If it does, you have a version on your machine, even if it is an older one. Check the About box to see what version you are running. You can also check the Glade Web site (http://glade.pn.org/) for the latest edition to see if you want to upgrade. If Glade is not installed on your machine, you will need to get it.

The RedHat FTP site (ftp://rawhide.redhat.com/pub/redhat/redhat-6.2/i386/RedHat/RPMS/) that's listed for GTK+ is also the place to get an RPM to install Glade. It is always up to date, and as of this writing, the Glade home page did not list RPM files among its downloads. The version listed there at the time of this writing is glade-0.5.5-4.i386.rpm. Remember, to install, you use the following command:

```
% rpm -i filename.rpm
```

To update, use this command:

```
% rpm -U filename.rpm
```

So be sure you know whether Glade is already on your system.

Licensing Issues

The Glade GUI builder is licensed under the GNU GPL. This same license is for MySQL; see Chapter 1, "MySQL for Access and SQL Server Developers and DBAs," for more information regarding the GPL.

Diving Right In: HelloWorld Done with Glade

This section repeats the HelloWorld non-application you used in Chapter 2, "GTK+ for VB Developers," but this time, it uses Glade.

One of the primary strengths—some would say the most important strength—of VB is that the IDE abstracted the user interface from the "work" code behind the scenes. It allowed the developer to click and drag the visual part of the application into place, without having to compile and run the application to see how it looks, only how it works. As you saw in Chapter 2, most of the code was concerned with setting up and configuring how the application would present itself visually when it first started. And that was a very simple screen.

HelloWorld Redux, Step by Step

The following steps take you through creating a new application using Glade. The result will be a new version of HelloWorld. Of course, if you normally run your Linux box from the command line, you will need to fire up your Xwindows system in order to use Glade.

1. First, create a directory. Go to the place you will want to keep your project and create a subdirectory for it. At the command line, enter this command:

   ```
   % mkdir HelloWorld
   ```

2. From the command line, type

   ```
   % glade
   ```

   or find it in the Start menu if it was installed with the operating system. On my system, it is under Development. If you are using KDE, it may be under the Gnome subdirectory.

   If you have Glade installed, three windows will pop up: "Glade: <untitled>," "Palette," and "Properties: <none>" (see Figure 5.1).

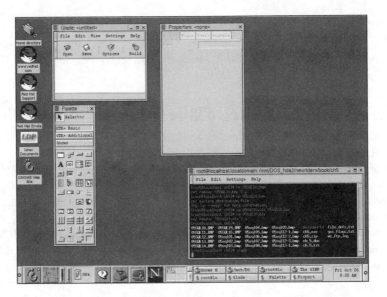

Figure 5.1 Glade IDE on GNOME.

If you type "glade" and don't get the windows shown, see the section "Where to Get Glade and How to Install."

3. In the Glade Project Window, select Options (see Figure 5.2).

Figure 5.2 The Glade Project Options button.

With the Options window open, set the Project Directory to the directory you created in Step 1. This is very important because otherwise it will set to a default, probably in your home directory. Set the Project Name to HelloWorld (and the program name—if it is different). See Figure 5.3 for an example.

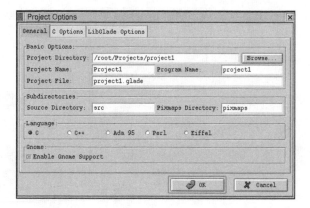

Figure 5.3 The Project Options for HelloWorld.

You can also set Enable Gnome Support to FALSE if you choose. (By default, it is set to TRUE on my version of Glade.) However, because this book is not Gnome-specific, it won't be necessary.

4. In the Palette window, under GTK+ Basic, click the top left window. Window1 appears (see Figure 5.4).

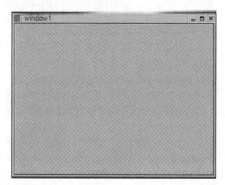

Figure 5.4 Window1 is an empty container widget.

5. In the Properties window, select the Widget tab and set the Name of the window to frm_main. For the title, enter HelloWorld (see Figure 5.5).

Figure 5.5　The Properties window with the name and title set.

6. Returning to the Palette, select "button" (it's the third one down on the left on my version). Then position the mouse over the center of the window area and click. A button should fill the space; after all, the window is a container widget, and GTK+ defaults to filling the container space (see Figure 5.6).

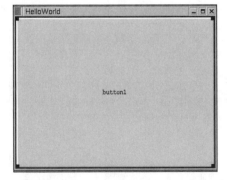

Figure 5.6　The Glade Command Button widget
inside a newly created form: Window1 with Button1.

7. Returning to the Properties window, make sure the properties displayed are for the command button you just created. Set the name to `cmd_main` and the label to `HelloWorld<ret>Click to Close`. (see Figure 5.7). (The `<ret>` is for the Return key. From Glade, you don't have to insert the `\n` newline character.)

Figure 5.7   Setting properties for the command button.

8. Select the Signals tab (make sure the widget that's selected is cmd_main). Then select the Signal... box (see Figure 5.8). See Chapter 2 for a discussion of Signals and Callbacks.

Figure 5.8   Use the Signals tab to set event actions.

9. In the Signals dialog box, select the clicked signal (see Figure 5.9).

Figure 5.9   Select the clicked signal.

10. Click OK, and then click Add. It is important for you to remember that the sig-
    nal is not added to the widget as a callback until you click the Add button. After
    you click Add, the clicked signal appears listed in the Signals tab for the com-
    mand button widget (see Figure 5.10).

Figure 5.10   The Clicked signal has been added.

11. Return to the Glade Project window. Click the Save button, and a "Project
    Saved" message should appear in the status bar. This saves your code in a *.glade
    file (unless you changed the settings from their default), which is an XML list of
    widgets, their properties, and the widget hierarchy tree. (This will be covered
    later in this chapter; see Listing 5.7.)

12. Next, click the Build button (on my version, it has interlocking gears for the
    icon). A message appears in the status bar saying "Source Code Written" (see
    Figure 5.11).

Figure 5.11 Use the Glade Build button to write source code.
Here, the Build button's tooltip is shown.

This writes code to four separate files and places them into a subdirectory of
your project directory called "src" (for "source"). The four files are named
`interface.c`, `support.c`, `main.c`, and `callbacks.c`. A full listing of each of these
files will be covered shortly, but each one is briefly described here:

File	Contents
`interface.c`	The windows and associated widgets, as functions to create and show
`support.c`	Functions that allow easier interaction with the way Glade operates
`main.c`	The program main
`callbacks.c`	Blank functions for signals specified in the Signals tab of the Properties window

13. Close Glade. At the Command line, move to the HelloWorld project directory
     and give the following command:

     `% ls -l -R`

This produces a listing of the files from this point down in the directory tree.
The `-l` flag tells the `ls` command to return information in the "long" format,
and the `-R` tells it to recursively display information for all subdirectories. Listing
5.1 shows the results of the `ls` command.

Listing 5.1 **Glade Output File Structure**

```
01 .:
02 total 288
03 -rwxr-xr-x   1 root     root          0 Sep  6 08:46 AUTHORS
04 -rwxr-xr-x   1 root     root          0 Sep  6 08:46 ChangeLog
05 -rwxr-xr-x   1 root     root        588 Sep  6 08:46 Makefile.am
06 -rwxr-xr-x   1 root     root          0 Sep  6 08:46 NEWS
07 -rwxr-xr-x   1 root     root          0 Sep  6 08:46 README
08 -rwxr-xr-x   1 root     root        195 Sep  6 08:46 acconfig.h
```

continues

Listing 5.1   **Continued**

```
09 -rwxr-xr-x   1 root      root        4499 Sep  6 08:46 autogen.sh
10 -rwxr-xr-x   1 root      root        1391 Sep  6 08:46 configure.in
11 -rwxr-xr-x   1 root      root        1635 Sep  6 08:46 helloworld.glade
12 -rwxr-xr-x   1 root      root        1635 Sep  6 08:43 helloworld.glade.bak
13 drwxr-xr-x   2 root      root       32768 Sep  6 08:46 po
14 drwxr-xr-x   2 root      root       32768 Sep  6 08:46 src
15 -rwxr-xr-x   1 root      root          10 Sep  6 08:46 stamp-h.in
16
17 ./po:
18 total 32
19 -rwxr-xr-x   1 root      root           0 Sep  6 08:46 ChangeLog
20 -rwxr-xr-x   1 root      root         114 Sep  6 08:46 POTFILES.in
21
22 ./src:
23 total 256
24 -rwxr-xr-x   1 root      root         290 Sep  6 08:46 Makefile.am
25 -rwxr-xr-x   1 root      root         286 Sep  6 08:46 callbacks.c
26 -rwxr-xr-x   1 root      root         162 Sep  6 08:46 callbacks.h
27 -rwxr-xr-x   1 root      root        1086 Sep  6 08:46 interface.c
28 -rwxr-xr-x   1 root      root          96 Sep  6 08:46 interface.h
29 -rwxr-xr-x   1 root      root         874 Sep  6 08:46 main.c
30 -rwxr-xr-x   1 root      root        4497 Sep  6 08:46 support.c
31 -rwxr-xr-x   1 root      root        1558 Sep  6 08:46 support.h
```

Glade created all the files and directories named in the listing when you pushed either the Save button or the Build button. Notice that Glade has created two directories: po and src. The directory po/potfiles.in contains a list of files with translatable strings. The src subdirectory contains the source code for the project.

In particular, we are interested in the following files:

Line 11	`helloworld.glade`
Line 09	`Autogen.sh`
Line 29	`main.c`
Line 27	`interface.c`
Line 25	`callbacks.c`
Line 30	`support.c`

These files are covered in detail later in this chapter, in the section titled "HelloWorld Files Dissected."

For now, you need to fill out a small portion of your application to make it work. You need to put some code behind the `cmd_main` clicked event. (`cmd_main` is the one button in the middle of the HelloWorld application window.) Change to the src directory so you can open `callbacks.c` with the text editor of your choice and insert some code.

When you open `callbacks.c`, you'll see a function called `on_cmd_main_clicked`. Within the braces of that function, enter the following line:

```
gtk_main_quit();
```

That's it! Save and exit. When the user clicks on `cmd_main`, it calls the `quit` function for the application. You have done everything needed to run the HelloWorld application. (Note that only clicking `cmd_main` will properly close the application; if you click the window's Close button—the one that normally has an "X" and sits in the top left corner of the window—, the window will disappear, but the program will still be running. This is because you did not attach the quit call to the window.)

Compile and Run

There are several ways to compile and run a Glade-created application. The first is to use the Autogen.sh file that Glade created for you when it wrote the source code for the application. That is not a foolproof way to compile though, and it can be a terrible hassle to sort out. The second way is to call it from the command line, or alternately, to put that command into a shell file of its own so you don't have to type the same command over and over.

Using the Generated *autogen.sh*

`autogen.sh` is a shell script (a Linux batch file) that should compile a Glade application. In my experience, it does not always work well. It should be as simple as entering these command lines of your project main directory type:

```
%./autogen.sh
% make
```

After that, go to the src subdirectory and type

```
% ./HelloWorld
```

or whatever your application is named, and off you go. As I said, it is supposed to be that simple, but very rarely is it. All I can tell you is if you have problems, try the following solutions:

- In the Project Options dialog box, remove Gettext support. This is a very common fix on the Glade mailing list.
- Verify that you have all the correct libraries installed with the most recent versions.
- Peruse the Glade mailing list archives for autogen problems, and see if someone else has had a similar one.

From the Command Line—A Hack

You can, of course, compile this (or any) C program from the command line. I say this is a hack because you are going to have to comment out some code that is not absolutely necessary but that does have a use (internationalization, to be exact). To compile from the command line, `cd` to the src subdirectory and type this line:

```
% gcc -Wall -g callbacks.c interface.c support.c main.c `gtk-config --cflags`
`gtk-config --libs`
```

The -Wall tells gcc to issue all warnings, and the -g option tells it to create debugging information for use with a debugger.

To run the program, type % ./a.out (or ./HelloWorld if you included a "-o HelloWorld" flag in the compile command).

Removing the add_pixmaps... Calls

When you compile from the command line, you will probably have to comment out two lines in main.c (in Listing 5.3, they are lines 28 and 29). Those two lines will cause compile errors if you use this method to compile. These lines refer to directories that are not needed for a command line compile, but they are used if the autogen.sh shell script is used instead.

From a Shell Script

If you put the compile command into a file, you can execute that command by calling the shell file. Listing 5.2 is a shell script that has two commands: The first clears the screen for readability, and the second starts the process of compiling the application. The backslash character (\) is the command line continuation character.

Listing 5.2 **Shell Script for Compiling a Glade Application**

```
clear

gcc -Wall -g callbacks.c interface.c \
        support.c main.c \
        `gtk-config --cflags --libs`
```

Notice that gtk-config has been abbreviated to have both options after the program command. Also, the clear command has been added. With the clear command, if the program encounters compile errors, they will be displayed on a clean screen for easier reading.

If you put the above commands in a file, call that file build.sh. Then you can just call ./build.sh to avoid all the retyping.

HelloWorld Files Dissected

Now you're going to take apart each of the files Glade created. First, start with the .c files to see how they fit together to make a complete program. After that, you will take a quick look at HelloWorld.glade to see how it is structured. Finally, you will get a quick word on autogen.sh.

main.c

Listing 5.3 shows the main.c file that's created by Glade when the Build button is clicked. If a main.c file already exists, Glade will not overwrite it (as stated in the initial comment). In this case, to allow for a clean and quick compile from the command line, lines 28 and 29 were commented out after Glade wrote the file.

Listing 5.3   **HelloWorld's** *main.c*

```
01 /*
02  * Initial main.c file generated by Glade. Edit as required.
03  * Glade will not overwrite this file.
04  */
05
06 #ifdef HAVE_CONFIG_H
07 #  include <config.h>
08 #endif
09
10 #include <gtk/gtk.h>
11
12 #include "interface.h"
13 #include "support.h"
14
15 int
16 main (int argc, char *argv[])
17 {
18   GtkWidget *frm_main;
19
20 #ifdef ENABLE_NLS
21   bindtextdomain (PACKAGE, PACKAGE_LOCALE_DIR);
22   textdomain (PACKAGE);
23 #endif
24
25   gtk_set_locale ();
26   gtk_init (&argc, &argv);
27
28 /*add_pixmap_directory (PACKAGE_DATA_DIR "/pixmaps");
29 add_pixmap_directory (PACKAGE_SOURCE_DIR "/pixmaps");
30 */
31 /*
32  * The following code was added by Glade to create one of each component
33  * (except popup menus), just so that you see something after building
34  * the project. Delete any components that you don't want shown initially.
35  */
36   frm_main = create_frm_main ();
37   gtk_widget_show (frm_main);
38
39   gtk_main ();
40   return 0;
```

As you can see, lines 1–4 are comments about how Glade uses this file. Note that if you add another form or other top-level widget, you will have to either remove this form and let Glade re-create it or manually edit the new parts.

On line 6, `config.h` has to do with library configuration information. Line 10 compiles in the GTK+ files, and lines 12 and 13 include the interface and support files for this project. Line 15 starts `main()`, and line 18 declares our main form. `ENABLE_NLS` has to do with internationalization of text strings, as docs `gtk_set_locale()`.

Line 26 initializes the GTK+ system, and lines 28 and 29 have to do with the project if compiled by `autogen.sh`. Lines 32–34 contain more comment code generated by Glade, and line 36 creates `frm_main` with a call to `create_frm_main`, which is in `interface.c`. Line 37 makes `frm_main` visible, and line 39 sends the application into the main gtk loop, waiting for signals emitted from the widgets. Lastly, line 40 returns 0, indicating the program terminated normally.

interface.c

`interface.c` is the file created by Glade that holds the code needed to instantiate the windows and widgets you've created using Glade. Its normal mode of operation is to have a `create_xxx()` function call to create the windows you specify, and then call those `create_xxx()` functions from `main.c` and return a pointer to the newly instantiated window.

Listing 5.4   **HelloWorld's** *interface.c*

```
01 /*
02  * DO NOT EDIT THIS FILE - it is generated by Glade.
03  */
04 #ifdef HAVE_CONFIG_H
05 #  include <config.h>
06 #endif
07
08 #include <sys/types.h>
09 #include <sys/stat.h>
10 #include <unistd.h>
11 #include <string.h>
12
13 #include <gdk/gdkkeysyms.h>
14 #include <gtk/gtk.h>
15
16 #include "callbacks.h"
17 #include "interface.h"
18 #include "support.h"
19
20 GtkWidget*
21 create_frm_main (void)
22 {
23   GtkWidget *frm_main;
24   GtkWidget *cmd_main;
```

```
25
26    frm_main = gtk_window_new (GTK_WINDOW_TOPLEVEL);
27    gtk_object_set_data (GTK_OBJECT (frm_main), "frm_main", frm_main);
28    gtk_window_set_title (GTK_WINDOW (frm_main), _("HelloWorld App"));
29
30    cmd_main = gtk_button_new_with_label (_("Hello World!\nClick to close."));
31    gtk_widget_ref (cmd_main);
32    gtk_object_set_data_full (GTK_OBJECT (frm_main), "cmd_main", cmd_main,
33                              (GtkDestroyNotify) gtk_widget_unref);
34    gtk_widget_show (cmd_main);
35    gtk_container_add (GTK_CONTAINER (frm_main), cmd_main);
36
37    gtk_signal_connect (GTK_OBJECT (cmd_main), "clicked",
38                        GTK_SIGNAL_FUNC (on_cmd_main_clicked),
39                        NULL);
40
41    return frm_main;
42 }
```

Lines 1–3 are generated by Glade. If you open HelloWorld.glade from Glade and click the Build button, this file will be overwritten.

have_config_h has already been covered (see Line 6 of Listing 5.3, as well as the commentary afterward). The include for sys/types.h has to do with primitive data type definitions, and stat.h deals with file characteristics, unistd.h has symbolic constants, and string.h deals with string handling functionality. gdkkeysyms.h contains key mapping definitions. gtk.h has already been covered also. Lines 16–18 get the functions necessary for create_frm_main to work.

Line 20 declares the return type from create_frm_main to be a GtkWidget type. Line 23 declares a second variable named frm_main. In spite of the fact that it is named the same, it will only be used within this function. The last line (line 42) returns this local frm_main, and main.c puts it into our global frm_main. As you can see from lines 23 and 24, you only need two widgets. Line 26's gtk_window_new has already been covered (see main.c in Listing 5.3).

Line 27 contains the gtk_object_set_data() function. This function allows GTK+ to associate any amount of information with an object. Line 28 sets the title that will appear in the title bar of frm_main. Line 30 instantiates a new command button into cmd_main, and the gtk_object_set_data_full() function associates the cmd_main widget with the frm_main widget and sets a notification when the frm_main object is destroyed.

Line 34 makes frm_main visible, and line 37 connects the clicked event of cmd_main to the function (in callbacks.c) on_cmd_main_clicked(). (This is the function to which you had to add gtk_main_quit() to properly close the application.)

support.c

Glade creates the file support.c to provide utility functions for use in your GTK+
program. The function lookup_widget() deserves special attention because it allows
you to give the window and the name of the child widget you are seeking, and it will
return a pointer to that child. This is very helpful when you are referencing widgets in
different windows.

Listing 5.5   **HelloWorld's** *support.c*

```
001 /*
002  * DO NOT EDIT THIS FILE - it is generated by Glade.
003  */
004
005 #ifdef HAVE_CONFIG_H
006 #   include <config.h>
007 #endif
008
009 #include <sys/types.h>
010 #include <sys/stat.h>
011 #include <unistd.h>
012 #include <string.h>
013
014 #include <gtk/gtk.h>
015
016 #include "support.h"
017
018 /* This is an internally used function to see whether a pixmap file exists. */
019 static gchar* check_file_exists          (const gchar      *directory,
020                                           const gchar      *filename);
021
022 /* This is an internally used function to create pixmaps. */
023 static GtkWidget* create_dummy_pixmap   (GtkWidget         *widget);
024
025 GtkWidget*
026 lookup_widget                           (GtkWidget         *widget,
027                                          const gchar       *widget_name)
028 {
029   GtkWidget *parent, *found_widget;
030
031   for (;;)
032     {
033       if (GTK_IS_MENU (widget))
034         parent = gtk_menu_get_attach_widget (GTK_MENU (widget));
035       else
036         parent = widget->parent;
037       if (parent == NULL)
038         break;
039       widget = parent;
040     }
041
042   found_widget = (GtkWidget*) gtk_object_get_data (GTK_OBJECT (widget),
043                                                      widget_name);
```

```
044   if (!found_widget)
045     g_warning ("Widget not found: %s", widget_name);
046   return found_widget;
047 }
048
049 /* This is a dummy pixmap you use when a pixmap can't be found. */
050 static char *dummy_pixmap_xpm[] = {
051 /* columns rows colors chars-per-pixel */
052 "1 1 1 1",
053 "  c None",
054 /* pixels */
055 " "
056 };
057
058 /* This is an internally used function to create pixmaps. */
059 static GtkWidget*
060 create_dummy_pixmap                    (GtkWidget       *widget)
061 {
062   GdkColormap *colormap;
063   GdkPixmap *gdkpixmap;
064   GdkBitmap *mask;
065   GtkWidget *pixmap;
066
067   colormap = gtk_widget_get_colormap (widget);
068   gdkpixmap = gdk_pixmap_colormap_create_from_xpm_d (NULL, colormap, &mask,
069                                              NULL, dummy_pixmap_xpm);
070   if (gdkpixmap == NULL)
071     g_error ("Couldn't create replacement pixmap.");
072   pixmap = gtk_pixmap_new (gdkpixmap, mask);
073   gdk_pixmap_unref (gdkpixmap);
074   gdk_bitmap_unref (mask);
075   return pixmap;
076 }
077
078 static GList *pixmaps_directories = NULL;
079
080 /* Use this function to set the directory containing installed pixmaps. */
081 void
082 add_pixmap_directory                  (const gchar     *directory)
083 {
084   pixmaps_directories = g_list_prepend (pixmaps_directories,
085                                  g_strdup (directory));
086 }
087
088 /* This is an internally used function to create pixmaps. */
089 GtkWidget*
090 create_pixmap                         (GtkWidget       *widget,
091                                        const gchar     *filename)
092 {
093   gchar *found_filename = NULL;
094   GdkColormap *colormap;
```

continues

Listing 5.5   **Continued**

```
095   GdkPixmap *gdkpixmap;
096   GdkBitmap *mask;
097   GtkWidget *pixmap;
098   GList *elem;
099
100   /* You first try any pixmap directories set by the application. */
101   elem = pixmaps_directories;
102   while (elem)
103     {
104        found_filename = check_file_exists ((gchar*)elem->data, filename);
105        if (found_filename)
106          break;
107        elem = elem->next;
108     }
109
110   /* If you haven't found the pixmap, try the source directory. */
111   if (!found_filename)
112     {
113        found_filename = check_file_exists ("../pixmaps", filename);
114     }
115
116   if (!found_filename)
117     {
118        g_warning (_("Couldn't find pixmap file: %s"), filename);
119        return create_dummy_pixmap (widget);
110     }
111
112   colormap = gtk_widget_get_colormap (widget);
113   gdkpixmap = gdk_pixmap_colormap_create_from_xpm (NULL, colormap, &mask,
114                                                    NULL, found_filename);
115   if (gdkpixmap == NULL)
116     {
117        g_warning (_("Error loading pixmap file: %s"), found_filename);
118        g_free (found_filename);
119        return create_dummy_pixmap (widget);
120     }
121   g_free (found_filename);
122   pixmap = gtk_pixmap_new (gdkpixmap, mask);
123   gdk_pixmap_unref (gdkpixmap);
124   gdk_bitmap_unref (mask);
125   return pixmap;
126 }
127
128 /* This is an internally used function to see whether a pixmap file exists. */
129 gchar*
130 check_file_exists                    (const gchar    *directory,
131                                       const gchar    *filename)
132 {
133   gchar *full_filename;
134   struct stat s;
135   gint status;
136
```

```
137    full_filename = (gchar*) g_malloc (strlen (directory) + 1
138                                 + strlen (filename) + 1);
139    strcpy (full_filename, directory);
140    strcat (full_filename, G_DIR_SEPARATOR_S);
141    strcat (full_filename, filename);
142
143    status = stat (full_filename, &s);
144    if (status == 0 && S_ISREG (s.st_mode))
145      return full_filename;
146    g_free (full_filename);
147    return NULL;
148 }
```

Lines 1 through 16 were covered previously in Listings 5.3 and 5.4 and their commentaries. Lines 18 through 23 are function prototypes for functions that come later in the file. Line 25 starts the `lookup_widget` function, which you will find to be extremely useful. It takes two parameters: The first is normally the top-level window, and the second is normally the name of a child widget within the top-level window parameter. Note that the child widget is passed in as a string, not a widget object. The purpose of this is to allow the project to have only the top-level windows as global variables, but to still allow access to any of the child widgets via the `lookup_widget` function. A full demonstration will follow at the end of this chapter. This file is smart, well-implemented, and solid from a software engineering standpoint.

The rest of the file contains some self-explanatory functions.

callbacks.c

Finally, you come to `callbacks.c`. Glade creates this file with empty functions relating to the signals you specified from the Properties window when you were using Glade. Glade will not overwrite the functions you create when or if you reopen Glade and edit your project. However, I have noticed that occasionally, it may create the same function twice after editing an existing project.

Listing 5.6 **HelloWorld's** *callbacks.c*

```
01 #ifdef HAVE_CONFIG_H
02 #  include <config.h>
03 #endif
04
05 #include <gtk/gtk.h>
06
07 #include "callbacks.h"
08 #include "interface.h"
09 #include "support.h"
10
11
12 void
```

continues

Listing 5.6   **Continued**

```
13 on_cmd_main_clicked                    (GtkButton      *button,
14                                         gpointer        user_data)
15 {
16    gtk_main_quit();
17 }
```

Line 16 was added as the last step for completing this program. Other than that, this is a straightforward file. It has one added callback on the clicked signal of cmd_main.

HelloWorld.glade

The file HelloWorld.glade is the Glade project file. It contains all the information needed to call up the project in Glade for editing. It stores the information in XML.

Listing 5.7   **HelloWorld.glade**

```
01 <?xml version="1.0"?>
02 <GTK-Interface>
03
04 <project>
05   <name>HelloWorld</name>
06   <program_name>helloworld</program_name>
07   <directory></directory>
08   <source_directory>src</source_directory>
09   <pixmaps_directory>pixmaps</pixmaps_directory>
10   <language>C</language>
11   <gnome_support>False</gnome_support>
12   <gettext_support>True</gettext_support>
13   <use_widget_names>False</use_widget_names>
14   <output_main_file>True</output_main_file>
15   <output_support_files>True</output_support_files>
16   <output_build_files>True</output_build_files>
17   <backup_source_files>True</backup_source_files>
18   <main_source_file>interface.c</main_source_file>
19   <main_header_file>interface.h</main_header_file>
20   <handler_source_file>callbacks.c</handler_source_file>
21   <handler_header_file>callbacks.h</handler_header_file>
22   <support_source_file>support.c</support_source_file>
23   <support_header_file>support.h</support_header_file>
24   <translatable_strings_file></translatable_strings_file>
25 </project>
26
27 <widget>
28   <class>GtkWindow</class>
29   <name>frm_main</name>
30   <title>HelloWorld</title>
31 <type>GTK_WINDOW_TOPLEVEL</type>
32 <position>GTK_WIN_POS_NONE</position>
33 <modal>False</modal>
34   <allow_shrink>False</allow_shrink>
```

```
35    <allow_grow>True</allow_grow>
36    <auto_shrink>False</auto_shrink>
37
38    <widget>
39      <class>GtkButton</class>
40      <name>cmd_main</name>
41      <can_focus>True</can_focus>
42      <signal>
43        <name>clicked</name>
44        <handler>on_cmd_main_clicked</handler>
45        <last_modification_time>Wed, 06 Sep 2000 15:41:32
GMT</last_modification_time>
46      </signal>
47      <label>HelloWorld
48 Click to Close.</label>
49    </widget>
50  </widget>
51
52 </GTK-Interface>
```

As you can see, this file is in XML. For those of you who don't know what XML is, here is a short explanation. By looking at the file, you can tell it is similar to HTML. (For those of you who don't know HTML, sorry, but I have to start somewhere... You still should be able to pick up the main points.) The difference is that in HTML, the tags are defined for you, whereas in XML you define not only the data, but the tags as well. Look at lines 27 through 29 in Listing 5.7. Line 27, <widget>, defines a widget object. Line 29 tells the name of the object defined on line 27; the tag <name> is followed by the data frm_main, followed by the closing tag </name>. Line 50 closes out the widget object started on line 27 with the </widget> tag. Notice that a sub-widget is defined between lines 38 and 49. In this manner, an entire tree of disparate object types can be defined; to read a file like this, all you need is an XML parser. You don't need to know anything about the data, what type it is, what structure it is in, and so on. That is the strength of XML.

As to Listing 5.7, once you understand XML, it is rather self-explanatory.

Glade by the Widgets

Now you'll take a closer look at each of the widgets and cover some of the rest of the features in Glade that have not received any attention up to this point. One of the most useful parts of Glade is the Widget Hierarchy tree.

Project Window

The Project Window is the main form of Glade; if you close it, you close your project too. It is pretty self-explanatory (see Figure 5.12). It contains standard components like Open, Close, Save a Project, Show the Palette or Properties Windows, and so on.

Figure 5.12 The Glade project window.

One very important dialog box accessible from within the main project window is the Project Options dialog box, which you can access from the File menu (see Figure 5.13). You already know how to set the project directory and project name. This screen also enables you to set the project language. Note that to use Ada95, Perl, or Eiffel, you must download and install additional files.

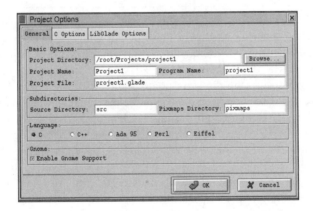

Figure 5.13 The Glade project window's Project Options dialog box.

The second tab in the Project Options dialog box is labeled C Options, and its options are self-explanatory (see Figure 5.14). Gettext Support has to do with the translation of text strings; the rest are obvious.

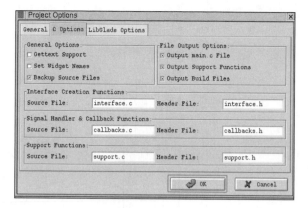

Figure 5.14   The C Options tab of the Project Options dialog box.

The third tab in the Project Options dialog box is the LibGlade Options tab (see Figure 5.15). As of this writing, the only option on this tab allows the development team to create a separate file for storage of translatable strings (again, this has to do with internationalization).

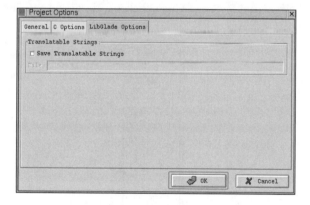

Figure 5.15   The LibGlade Options tab of the Project Options dialog box.

Palette Window

The Palette window is your widget toolbox (see Figure 5.16). It is divided into three bins (at least on my system, anyway, but by the time you read this, there may be more). The three bins are GTK+ Basic, GTK+ Additional, and Gnome. You have already read about most of the widgets in the GTK+ Basic selection; some of the widgets available in GTK+ Additional are rather narrow in use (such as the Gamma Curve widget), but this bin also offers things like a Calendar Widget and an Image Control.

Figure 5.16 The Palette window's Additional widgets.

The GNOME widgets are an extension to the GTK+ widget set, which will not be used in this book because I am not strictly targeting the GNOME desktop (see Figure 5.17). However, should your situation warrant it, I highly recommend that you use the GNOME widgets whenever possible. They include such things as a Dialog Box widget, an HREF Link widget, and Font and Color Picker widgets, and they are very handy.

Figure 5.17 The Palette window's list of GNOME widgets.

Properties Window

The Properties window is a context-sensitive window that contains different options depending on which widget is selected (see Figure 5.18). Except for the tab-control interface and the signals, its application is basically the same as the Properties window in VB. It allows you to set the initial properties of your widgets when the program initializes.

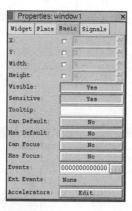

Figure 5.18   Properties for the selected widget.

Project Design: Knowing Your Object Hierarchy

Knowing and understanding the widget hierarchy in your project will make development of complex projects much more manageable. In addition, specifying the widget tree for your project in the design phase will help you avoid unnecessarily repeating work later in the project. The widget tree is key to understanding and creating effective user interfaces in GTK+.

The Widget Tree Window

As you can see in Figure 5.19, the widgets displayed are layered one inside the next. Understanding this paradigm will take you a long way toward understanding how best to use GTK+ widgets.

As you can see in Figure 5.20, if you right-click a displayed widget, a popup menu appears, displaying a list of widgets from the inside out. This allows you to select any widget in the tree, delete the widget, and add or insert widgets before or after other widgets in the selected "widget path." This is very helpful when you need to add a widget (for example, scrollbars to display a widget of some type) without deleting all widgets that will be the child of the widget you are adding and then having to re-create the widgets again and set their properties.

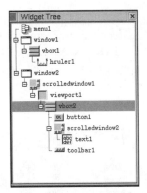

Figure 5.19   The widget hierarchy window.

Figure 5.20   Right-click a deeply embedded widget to access a popup menu of options.

Window-to-Window Communication in a Glade Project

One thing that will come up very quickly in a project of any size is the need to get data from one widget and move it to another widget. If both of the target widgets are in the same top-level window, this is easy to do with the standard call for the type of widget you are referencing. However, as you shall see, when the widgets containing the data are in two different top-level forms, getting and placing data can be more difficult. Fortunately, Glade includes a mechanism for handling situations such as these: the `lookup_widget()` function found in the `support.c` file.

Getting Cross-Window Widgets to Communicate

The problem is essentially one of scope. According to the way Glade creates functions, the `create_*` function to create the window and the `on_button1_clicked` callback (or whatever the callback function is called) are equal; they are both "global" in that they can be called from anywhere in the program. However, because Glade places the window variables inside of `main()`, those variables are not accessible from elsewhere in the program.

One answer is to make all variables global in nature, which means you must declare them at the top of `main.c`, before `main()`. This makes every widget visible from every calling program anywhere in the program. Occasionally, it makes sense to make a variable or widget global in nature. For example, if you have a widget that needs to be accessed from nearly every part of the program at some time or another, making it global is a simpler solution than constantly passing it around (at least to my way of thinking; however, such things tend to be issues of style).

This is the concept of *variable scope*, meaning that a variable should not be accessible from more places than necessary. It is possible—and certainly easy—to make all your variables global in scope, as in the "widget tour" examples you saw earlier in the book (in Chapters 2, 3, and 4). In fact, sometimes this even makes good programming and software engineering, but that is the exception and not the rule. As my 8th grade English teacher said, "It is okay to break the rule, but to do so, you have to first know the rule, and know it well." In software engineering, the rule is this: "Global variables are bad." And generally this is true. Glade still attempts to keep all variables local, but in order to facilitate inter-window communication, you will elevate the top-level windows to global scope. This makes sense from a software engineering perspective, too: What could be more "global" in scope than the top-level windows of a project? Doing so allows for access to all parts of the project, while at the same time preserving some level of variable scope protection, as you shall see.

The *lookup_widget()* Function

You already studied the `lookup_widget()` function in `support.c` (refer to Listing 5.5, lines 25 to 47). Forgive the oversimplification, but essentially the `lookup_widget()` function searches the widget tree to find the named widget and then returns a pointer to that widget. Thus, by assigning a temporary widget from the calling location that points to the found widget, you get access to the widget and its data.

A Simple Demonstration

Here you will create a simple two-window file that demonstrates inter-window communication. In each of the windows, there will be a vertical packing box with three widgets: a label, an entry widget, and a command button. When you click on the command button, it will either push or pull whatever data is in one entry widget to the other entry widget.

Follow these steps to create the application:

1. Create a subdirectory to hold the project if necessary.

2. Open Glade.

3. Set the project properties (options).

   - Make the project name CrossWindows.

   - Disable Gnome support because this application is designed to work on other desktops in addition to Gnome.

   - Set the project directory to the directory you created in step 1.

   - You will probably want to disable Gettext support as well. There is no need for internationalization on this application.

4. Click on the window widget to create a new window. It should be called window1 when it comes up. While you have it selected, go to the Properties window and select the Signals tab. Click the [...] button next to Signal:, and then scroll down to find the delete_event signal. (Note: This is NOT the destroy_event signal.) Select the delete_event signal, and then click OK. On returning to the Properties window, click Add. This event is where you will put the gtk_main_quit() call. The delete_event is called when the user terminates the application by closing the window; it is the signal that is emitted by the window when the close button in the upper-right corner of the window is pushed.

5. Click the vertical packing box widget on the palette. Return to window1 and click inside the main window area. When the New Vertical Box dialog box appears, make sure it indicates three rows, and then click OK. You should see the main area of window1 separated into three equal areas.

6. Click the label widget of the palette. Then click in the top of the three vertical boxes in window1. A new label should appear there, displaying the text "label1."

7. Click the entry widget in the palette, and then click in the middle of the three vertical packing boxes, just below the newly created label.

8. Finally, click the button widget on the palette, and then click inside the bottom of the three vertical packing boxes. The command button should appear just below the entry widget. Make sure the button you just created is selected, and click the Signals tab of the Properties window. Again, click on the [...] button next to the Signal box, and this time select the clicked signal. Click OK to return to the Properties window and be sure to click Add to add the signal.

9. At this point, you should have a window1 with one vertical packing box and a label, an entry widget, and a command button inside the vertical packing box.

10. Repeat steps 4 through 8, this time for window2, label2, and so on. In fact, everything should be exactly the same, except the names: *1 will now be *2. Other than that, no changes are necessary.

11. You should now have two windows: window1 and window2. Each should have a label, an entry widget, and a command button as visible widgets.

12. Back in the main project window box (which now says "Glade: CrossWindows" in the title bar), save the project and then build the project (write the source code).

13. Close the Glade IDE and with it the CrossWindows project.

14. Examine the project subdirectory to make sure the files are in place.

15. Use the `cd` command to change to the src subdirectory.

16. Open `callbacks.c` with your editor of choice.

17. You will notice that there are four functions, which correspond to the four signals you selected. The functions `on_window1_delete_event()` and `on_window2_delete_event()` contain one line: `return FALSE;`. Immediately prior to that line, add the following line:

    ```
    gtk_main_quit();
    ```

    Add this line to both functions so that they look identical. Both should look like the following:

    ```
    {
        gtk_main_quit();
        return FALSE;
    }
    ```

    With that line included, when either window is closed, the application terminates.

18. Now you'll do a quick compile just to make sure everything is okay up to this point. From the command line, send the following command:

    ```
    % gcc -Wall *.c `gtk-config --cflags --libs`
    ```

    This assumes you are in the src subdirectory.

    I have taken a couple of shortcuts here. First, I omitted the `-g` flag, which I normally would not do; having debugger information can be very useful if you need to track down bugs. Second, I used `*.c` instead of listing the files individually; that works in this case because I created a new subdirectory for this project, and I am sure that there are no other C files in this subdirectory.

    As before, I am going to put the `gcc` command into a shell script called "build." Thus, to compile, I actually will send

    ```
    % ./build
    ```

    The remaining steps assume that you have done the same.

Did it compile? No, not quite. On my system, I got the following errors:

```
main.c: In function 'main':
main.c:24: 'PACKAGE_DATA_DIR' undeclared (first use in this function)
main.c:24: (Each undeclared identifier is reported only once
main.c:24: for each function it appears in.)
main.c:24: parse error before string constant
main.c:25: 'PACKAGE_SOURCE_DIR' undeclared (first use in this function)
main.c:25: parse error before string constant
```

These are the same errors we encountered before (your line numbers may be different); they are used if autogen.sh is used to compile and make the application, for which there is no need or benefit here. Therefore, you can safely do without these lines in main.c. Open main.c and put comment characters around the offending lines so they look like this:

```
/*
add_pixmap_directory (PACKAGE_DATA_DIR "/pixmaps");
add_pixmap_directory (PACKAGE_SOURCE_DIR "/pixmaps");
*/
```

Now save main.c and attempt to compile again. If you do not get a clean compile at this point, retrace your steps until you do.

19. Run the program, in this case by sending the following command:

    ```
    % ./a.out
    ```

    because you did not specify a program name on the gcc command line with the -o prog_name option. Two windows should now appear: window1 and window2. These do absolutely nothing. The program should successfully return you to the command line after closing one of the windows.

20. Now you will add the functionality you want. When button1 in window1 is clicked, you want it to push data from entry1 to entry2. That is, anything typed into entry1 will overwrite anything in entry2. Second, when button2 in window2 is clicked, you want it to pull anything from entry1 to entry2. Thus, you always have entry1 feeding entry2, and you have button1 as a push mechanism and button2 as a pull mechanism.

21. Open callbacks.c for editing and go to the on_button1_clicked() function. Notice that it has no code in it. Enter the following code between the brackets that already exist:

    ```
    gtk_entry_set_text(GTK_ENTRY(entry2),
    gtk_editable_get_chars(GTK_EDITABLE(entry1), 0, -1));
    ```

    Then try to compile. You should get the following errors:

    ```
    callbacks.c: In function `on_button1_clicked':
    callbacks.c:26: 'entry2' undeclared (first use in this function)
    callbacks.c:26: (Each undeclared identifier is reported only once
    callbacks.c:26: for each function it appears in.)
    callbacks.c:27: 'entry1' undeclared (first use in this function)
    ```

Why can't it see entry1 and entry2? If you examine `main.c`, you will see that there are no global variables; window1 and window2 are the only GtkWidget variables declared, and they are declared inside of `main()`. Under the rules of C, they are not visible to the callback functions. Therefore, they need to be moved.

22. Open `main.c` for editing and change the following lines (you are simply moving two lines from inside `main()` to prior to it):

```
int
main (int argc, char* argv[])
{
GtkWidget *window1;
GtkWidget *window2;
```

The file should now read:

```
GtkWidget *window1;
GtkWidget *window2;

int
main (int argc, char* argv[])
{
```

Save and close `main.c`. (Note that you do need these at the global level, even though you are going to make some changes to `callbacks.c` in the next couple steps. If not, you will get a core dump error when you attempt to run the callback.)

23. Recompile and link. You should get the same error. Some people may wonder, " If window1 is available globally, why aren't its child widgets?" Well, C just doesn't work that way. However, your work was not in vain. You needed to elevate the top-level windows so that the `lookup_widget()` function could see them.

24. Again, return to `callbacks.c` in your favorite editor. Change the two lines you inserted in step 21 to the following:

```
gtk_entry_set_text(GTK_ENTRY(lookup_widget(window2, "entry2")),
gtk_editable_get_chars(GTK_EDITABLE(lookup_widget(
                                              window1,
                                              "entry1")
                    ), 1, -1));
```

The extra lines are created to improve readability. As you can see, the `lookup_widget()` function now fetches the target widgets for you—in this case, the entry widgets. Again, an attempt to compile gives the following errors:

```
callbacks.c: In function `on_button1_clicked':
callbacks.c:25: 'window2' undeclared (first use in this function)
callbacks.c:25: (Each undeclared identifier is reported only once
callbacks.c:25: for each function it appears in.)
callbacks.c:26: 'window1' undeclared (first use in this function)
```

Why isn't it seeing the window widgets? Under the rules of C, you have to re-declare the window widgets for the routines in `callbacks.c`.

25. Therefore, open `callbacks.c` and add the following anywhere before the first function:

    ```
    GtkWidget *window1;
    GtkWidget *window2;
    ```

    C will not confuse these as new widgets; the program will still reference the correct widget.

    Note that you could get yourself into a bit of trouble in a large, complicated program by declaring the same variable twice in two different files as I did above. If a variable is misspelled or accidentally declared to be of a different type, you could find yourself modifying several files to make all the correct changes. However, if you created a new include file where all global variables are stored and then included this file in `main.c`, `include.c`, and any other places, you could avoid those potential problems. I have done it here because I think it makes a better point regarding the discussion on variable scope.

26. Now rebuild the application. This time, it should compile and link without error. If it does not, retrace your steps to find the problem. Run the application to test it: You should be able to enter text into entry1 of window1, click button1, and see the same text appear in entry2 of window2.

27. Finally, you need to fill out the code for button2. Open `callbacks.c` and copy the code for button1 down to button2, and it should work correctly without change. (Remember, it is supposed to do exactly the same thing.) Compile and run, and it should work as required.

Global Variables and Good Software Engineering

Just a quick note on the method behind the madness here. Purists will deride my hack above (making the top-level window widgets global in scope), and technically speaking, they would be correct. It is probably more correct to tightly hide all widgets and pass them around as parameters to functions; however, I have my reasons for the method I have chosen, and it has to do with hard-learned lessons from several IT shops I have worked in.

First and foremost, I believe code should have longevity, which in my opinion means it will probably have to change in the future. Some of the studies on software development indicate that the sum total of work performed to get a version 1 product out the door will be dwarfed by the work needed to modify and maintain the code over its lifetime, which is normally much, MUCH longer than anybody anticipated. So I put ease of modification high on my list, but I also think "global variables are bad." Thus, I feel the mechanism used in the previous example strikes a balance.

So why do I care if it is easy to modify if I am going to modify it? "I know all about passing parameters in and out," you say. Well, mostly because the person who initially wrote the code probably will not be the one to modify it. Most likely, he or she will move on to other projects and probably other companies. Someone else will likely take ownership of that code and be responsible for maintaining it. In that case, if they understand the items in the following list, they completely understand the paradigm behind my application:

- The widget tree, in concept and application
- The principle that the top-level window widgets are the only global variables
- The principle that the `lookup_widget()` function gives them access to any widget in any window (they just have to know which window and the widget name)

This is much simpler than teaching a person who is new to C about passing around a list of parameters of pointers to widgets. Plus, it still keeps child widgets under wraps because they cannot be accessed directly.

As part of your overall project development strategy you will have to weigh the trade-offs and decide which widgets should be variable in scope and which should not. In this book, you will use the previous example as a template for your applications for the reasons just stated.

Real World Implementations

6

Order Entry Abstract and Design

THIS IS THE FIRST OF THE "REAL WORLD IMPLEMENTATION" examples that will comprise the remainder of the book. In this case, the client is looking to do a "proof of concept" project in order to evaluate the viability of Linux and MySQL. The client, Specialty Electrical Supply, Inc. (SESI), has chosen an application that needs to be done: entering orders phoned in by customers. They are interested in the low price point of the Linux operating system and would consider converting to an all-Linux shop if they could be reasonably certain they would not have to hire an expensive server administrator.

The main goal of this chapter is to set out a basic design for a simple GTK+ and MySQL application. The project in question is entering orders for the client, SESI. Although this chapter does not attempt to outline a "formal specification," it does set out to describe the problem in sufficient detail so you can understand what the application should do and why. Its purpose is to give you a "big picture" view of the application so that when the application is built (in Chapter 7, "Construction of the SESI Order Entry Applications"), you will be able to understand how things work together, and you will have a point of reference to understand the coding process. There is an appendix in this book that goes along with this chapter and Chapter 7. It is Appendix A, "Glade-Generated Files from the SESI Order Application."

Currently, SESI uses a system that's based on Excel spreadsheets and Word documents, and one of the managers, who has a strong technical background, manages the LAN as one of his part-time duties. Their customer and product master files are Excel spreadsheets, and they cut and paste orders to Word. They then send the order to the PC's printer for a quick walk down to the warehouse—a very tedious process. The goal is to replace this with a GTK+ windowing interface that can then output each order to a separate text file. Then these text files can be sent to the individual(s) responsible for filling them by FTP, email, or whatever other mechanism may be chosen. Further, the next obvious step will be to create an application that the worker on the shop floor who is filling the order can use to record what was shipped and when and what had to go on backorder. For those of you more on the business end, this will be the "bookings" part of "booking/billing/backlog."

Problem Definition and Design Issues

This section describes the problem in greater detail and works through some design decisions. Because this is a relatively simple problem and should be a straightforward implementation, this chapter does not go into much of the detailed design that a large multi-person project would need in order to ensure success.

Hardware Specifications

A PC will have Linux installed on it; the hard drive will be wiped, and a new Linux distribution will be installed: Red Hat 6.2 with the GNOME desktop (the version current when this book was written, Red Hat 7.x should work fine when it comes out). This is the out-of-the-box default configuration for Red Hat 6.2 (for a total cost of approximately $30 so far). The target machine will probably be a first-generation Pentium box with a 1- or 2-gigabyte hard drive; although you can put Linux on a hard drive as small as 300 megabytes, a 1-gigabyte hard drive is probably the minimum hard drive that should be used. There will be no need for modem/dialout, printing, and so on from this machine; initially, it will exist solely to run this application.

Network Information

The client already has a static IP LAN for file sharing and drive mapping under MS Windows. The existing LAN consists of 15 machines, all running either Windows 95 or Windows 98. There is no central server. No one else will need to access the Linux box except the data entry operator and the LAN administrator.

Existing Data Information

The "customer master file" and "product master file" are currently stored in Microsoft Excel spreadsheets. The data is relatively straightforward; no more information is kept than is needed. The client is confident of the data stored in the spreadsheets; only the data entry operator has touched or altered them in two years. Key values, such as "item number," are unique, addresses are complete and correct, and so on. These files will be output to text files, transferred to the Linux box, and then uploaded to the MySQL database using MySQL utilities (see Listing 6.1).

After that, the database will be considered the source of record for this information, and the spreadsheets will be retired.

The item master file currently has about 600 items in it, and it changes only once or twice a month, if at all. The customer master file currently has about 170 records in it and changes as needed. The user must be able to add a new customer quickly and easily while that customer is on the phone.

Existing Process Specification

The existing process works as described here:

- The data entry clerk receives a phone call (or retrieves the information from the answering machine) with the order information. He or she uses Notepad to enter the following information: customer information, the order, and any special instructions.

- The data entry clerk processing the order then opens three files: the customer and product master files in Excel, and a Word document (template) that will become the order form.

- Using cut and paste, he or she fills out the Word template with the necessary information until the Word document is complete. At that point, it is sent to the printer. The cut-and-paste operation is the single most tedious, time-consuming part of the whole operation because of the differences in format between Excel and Word; for example, you must put in carriage returns (vice tab characters) to separate address lines and so on.

- Several times a day, whatever orders come out of the printer are taken across the building to the warehouse and are given to the individual who will fill the order.

The Desired Process

In the "new improved" process, the data entry clerk will have access to two PCs—one with Windows and the other with Linux. He or she will be able to click an icon for a new order select from a pick list of existing customers, edit their customer information, or enter a new one if needed. The customer information will be filled in and displayed. From there, the data entry clerk can proceed to enter the items ordered by the customer. It is possible to directly type in the item number if it is available, select it from a list of all items, or search on a keyword of the character (not numeric) fields of the item master file.

When the order is complete, the application will write the order to the hard disk in the form of a text file (there will be a command button in the application for this, the data entry clerk will initiate it). The title of the text file will be the name of the customer and the date and time the file was created. Each order will be stored in a separate text file and formatted for quick printout on a printer in the order fulfillment office. Although the current Word document has some formatting, this is not necessary to the work flow and will be done away with.

At the desired time, as desired by either the person creating the order or the people in the order fulfillment section, the completed order text files will be transferred to the PC in the order fulfillment office. The mechanism for this could be any of the following:

- FTP. This method would be either a push operation instigated by the data clerk (i.e., sending the data from the Linux box to the PC in order fulfillment) or a pull operation instigated by the order fulfillment office staff (for example, someone in the order fulfillment office logs in to the Linux box and "pulls" the files over the network). The only potential problem with a "pull" operation is the possibility that a file will be pulled during its write operation.

- Email

- Mapped drives, via Samba

- Other similar mechanism

Whatever mechanism is used, it will be manually initiated by one of the concerned parties. From that point, the order fulfillment office will print each of the text files in turn. Once done, the files will be moved to an archive directory on the local PC. Again, this might be a batch file, or even a manual process. The users in order fulfillment will know how to do this, or they can be taught. From that point forward, the process will proceed as before.

Desired Characteristics of the Software

The following characteristics and other concepts should be included or excluded at the application level:

- The application should allow the user to keep his or her hands on the keyboard as much as possible, avoiding the mouse.

- There is no need for auditing or detailed logging. That is, the application doesn't need to record who changed what data and when. First, the data is not that sensitive, and second, because the data entry clerk is so familiar with the data, he or she can be relied on to understand and solve any problems that come up.

- There is no need for security at the application level beyond that which is standard for a PC (for example, a login). Again, the data is not that sensitive, and after it is processed into orders, it will be copied or transferred from the Linux machine anyway.

- The MySQL database server, client, and application will all be on the same machine.

- There won't be any need to save orders, read or edit existing orders; the process will proceed from start to finish, or else all order information will be lost. This is considered acceptable because an order rarely exceeds 20 items. So, if a customer gets halfway through an order and needs to call back later to finish, there will not be a significant penalty to start over from the beginning. Because of this, each instance of the application can be a different order and can remain open all day if necessary.

User Interface

This section outlines the design layout of the user interface. Going through this step saves a lot of work later on.

The Customer Data Form: frm_main

Figure 6.1 shows the design of the initial screen the user will see when the application opens. This form allows the data entry clerk to select and display customer information or enter the information for a new customer.

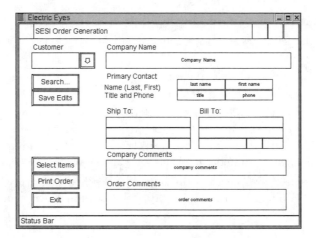

Figure 6.1   frm_main is the initial form the user sees when he starts the application.

Following are some of the features and functions of frm_main:

- The customer number drop-down box (Customer) contains all the customer numbers in the database, plus the word "New" as the first entry in the list. When the user selects New, all the text boxes are cleared, and the software generates a new customer number.

- The Save Edits button is active only if changes have been made to one of the database fields. To avoid disrupting the work flow, the application will not prompt the user if he or she attempts to close the application or change customers while edits are in progress. The Save Edits button provides a visual key to indicate that the data has changed and action must be taken to save the changes.

- There is no menu bar (this keeps the application simple).

The container layout for the form is shown in Figure 6.2. This is part of the GTK+ environment that must be planned for, and it is something that will be new to developers coming from the VB and VC++ environments. For a review of GTK+ and the concept of containers, refer to Chapter 2, specifically the sections titled "VB's 'Form' Reincarnated as GtkWindow Plus GtkFixed or GtkLayout" and "GTK+ Containers as Resizer Controls."

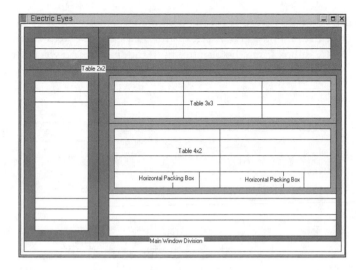

Figure 6.2   frm_main container layout.

As you can see from Figure 6.2, the first widget is a vertical packing box (vbox) with a space count of 2. Please note that in Figure 6.2 the shades of gray add to the visibility; they have nothing to do with the finished product. Initially, the window is a vertical packing box divided into two rows. The widget in the bottom half of that vbox widget is the status bar, and the top is for everything else. Inside the top half of that vbox widget, the first widget to be added is a 2-by-2 table. In the top left and right of that 2-by-2 table are vertical packing boxes, again with space for two widgets each. The bottom left of the 2-by-2 table contains a vertical button box because that vbox will have only command buttons. In the bottom right of the 2-by-2 table is a vertical packing box with space for six widgets. The first of these six widgets holds a 3-by-3 table, the second holds a 4-by-2 table, and the others have spaces for labels and text boxes. This fills out frm_main.

Selecting Items for the Order: frm_items_ordered

The other main form in the application is a window in which the user picks the individual items the caller has ordered and then tallies the totals. This makes up the line items on the invoice (see Figure 6.3).

Some of the functionality of frm_items_ordered is described here:

- The user should be able to add items quickly using the widgets in the upper-left corner. That is, when the user enters the item number and the quantity and clicks Add, the added item shows in the 4 Column CList box. This is intended to be the primary means of order entry because the customer should know the item number she wants to purchase when she calls.

- Alternatively, the user can select the item the customer wants to purchase and then click the Add button between the list boxes, and the item is added to the 4 Column CList box using the quantity from the spin box between the list boxes.
- The Remove button removes only the selected item from the 4 Column CList box.

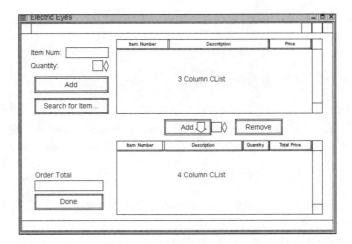

Figure 6.3 The frm_items_ordered layout diagram.

The Search Windows

Each of the windows covered previously has a Search for... button of some type. In frm_main, it is a search for customers. In frm_items_ordered, it is a search through the item master table. These buttons function very similarly: When the user clicks the Search button, a new modal window appears (see Figure 6.4). There, the user enters the search string and clicks the Find button, and the software returns a list of matching records. The search functions as a matching search with a wildcard both before and after the search string; that is, if the user searches for "eat", the list of returned items might include "treat," "eatery," and so on.

The application automatically searches all character columns. When doing a customer search, it attempts to find a match in all the character (non-numeric) fields: name, bill_to_addr1, bill_to_addr2, and so on. This minimizes the complexity presented to the user, and with this implementation (a small data set and all functions performed on the same machine), response time should be more than adequate.

In the Customer search form, the user types a text string into the text box and then clicks Find. The software searches all text fields and returns all records matching any part of the field text. If the desired customer record is found, the user can select it and close the search window, and the selected customer record data automatically appears in the widgets on frm_main.

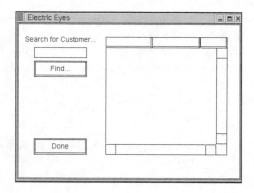

Figure 6.4   The Search for Customer modal window design.

The Item search form works the same as the Customer search form, except that it searches and returns items and fills in the "items ordered" Clist window on frm_items_ordered (refer to Figure 6.3).

In both of the search forms, when the user finds the customer or item they are searching for, they select it and click Done. The software automatically places the data into the correct place on the form. For frm_main, it displays the customer selected by the find operation, and for frm_items_ordered, it selects and displays that item in the 3 Column CList box that displays all the items in the database.

Creating the Database

In this section, you will create and fill the database with the initial data load. You will put all the statements except the `create database` into a file, which you can use to reload the database later if necessary.

Listing 6.1 assumes that a MySQL server is installed and running on the target machine.

First, start the MySQL command line tool by typing this line:

```
% mysql
```

This changes the prompt to `mysql>`.

Then create the database:

```
mysql> CREATE DATABASE sesi;
```

Listing 6.1 creates the SESI database for Chapters 6 and 7. It drops and refreshes the tables with the data being transferred in from the sample text files.

Usage (from the command prompt):

```
%mysql < listing.6.1
```

or

```
%mysql -t < listing.6.1
```

The -t option sends the output of the select statements to the screen in a table-like format (like you would get from the mysql> prompt).

As you can see, C-style comments will work (note the sections that start with /* and end with */). However, be careful not to use any semicolons, single quotation marks, or double quotation marks inside the comments! This can cause the parser to think there is something it should be handling, in which case it will issue an error and terminate.

Listing 6.1   **Create and Fill the Database For Specialty Electrical Supply, Inc.**

```
use sesi;

DROP TABLE if exists tbl_items;

CREATE TABLE tbl_items
(
    item            varchar(8)      NOT NULL    PRIMARY KEY,
    description     varchar(50)     NOT NULL,
    price           decimal(4,2)    NOT NULL
);

/* In the following statement and the second LOAD TABLE statement
 * further in the file, note that the fully qualified path name
 * has been put in for the file. This is necessary because MySQL
 * will look in the database directory by default, not in the current
 * local directory or your project directory.

 * Also note that the text files being imported are tab-delimited,
 * and they have the same number of fields as the table has columns.

 * In the following statement, the new_master_item.txt file has been
 * output from another application (probably a spreadsheet) and
 * copied into place so that the LOAD DATA INFILE statement will
 * work correctly. It contains the master list of items that the
 * company sells.
 *
 * Remember: the "/mnt/DOS_hda2..." path name is the one for the
 * test machine that was used to build this application.
 * Substitute the location you use on your machine.
 */

LOAD DATA INFILE "/mnt/DOS_hda2/newriders/book/ch6/new_item_master.txt"
    INTO TABLE tbl_items;


/* Check for the success of the import. It should be approximately
 * 600 records. Compare that to the text file in the statement for the
 * exact count. */

select count(*) from tbl_items;
```

```
DROP TABLE if exists tbl_customers;

CREATE TABLE tbl_customers
(
   num              smallint      NOT NULL   PRIMARY KEY,
   name             varchar(100)  NOT NULL,
   ship_to_addr1    varchar(100),
   ship_to_addr2    varchar(100),
   ship_to_city     varchar(35),
   ship_to_state    char(2),
   ship_to_zip      varchar(10),
   bill_to_addr1    varchar(100),
   bill_to_addr2    varchar(100),
   bill_to_city     varchar(35),
   bill_to_state    char(2),
   bill_to_zip      varchar(10),
   contact_first    varchar(50),
   contact_last     varchar(50),
   phone            varchar(12),
   title            varchar(50),
   comments         varchar(255)
);

/* In the following LOAD DATA INFILE statement, the cust_mast.txt
 * file has been exported from elsewhere and put into the location
 * stated. It contains the customer data. It is the customer master
 * file.
 */

LOAD DATA INFILE "/mnt/DOS_hda2/newriders/book/ch6/cust_mast.txt"
   INTO TABLE tbl_customers;

/* Again, check the success of the import operation. This time,
 * look for approximately 170 records. The best way to verify
 * that is to know the record count in the text file and to
 * compare it to the result returned by the next statement.
 */

select count(*) from tbl_customers;

/* Now alter tbl_customers to be auto-incremented on the first column.
 * See the Alter Table statement, which is next after this comment
 * block.

 * The following statement explains why you need to ALTER the
 * table that was just created and filled.

 * For the cust_mast.txt file data, the first data field is the
 * customer number, which is the primary key of the table. In the
 * MySQL database, this column should be an auto-incrementing field.
 * However, creating the table with the first field set to auto-
```

continues

Listing 6.1   **Continued**

```
 * increment may cause problems because the customer numbers are not
 * necessarily complete, nor do they start at 1. Therefore, in this
 * case, to avoid problems with the LOAD DATA INFILE statement,
 * you issue an ALTER TABLE statement to change the attributes
 * on the num field so it will auto-increment after the initial data load.

 * Also note that it is not necessary to restate PRIMARY KEY.
 * If you attempt to put it in the ALTER TABLE statement, MySQL
 * will issue a duplicate primary key error message.

 * One final comment: If you end one of these files with a comment,
 * it will produce an error when you attempt to feed it to MySQL.
 * Apparently, it expects a semicolon as the last character
 * in the file.
 */

ALTER TABLE tbl_customers
MODIFY num    SMALLINT
        NOT NULL
        AUTO_INCREMENT;
```

Deploying the Application

Because the application hasn't even been built yet, this might seem like we're jumping the gun. However, the deployment for this application is covered here because it is a rather simple exercise. Actually, for a small user base, this can be a very simple way to get the application out to the user. A word of caution, however: Don't try to use this manner of deployment for more than a handful of users; you'll likely find yourself making a lot of trips to the users' desks to install and upgrade your application. For a user base greater than 3–5, you will need something more scalable, such as an RPM, which is discussed in Chapter 8, "Commission Calculations Abstract and Design." Having said that, I will show you the simplest way to get the application in front of the user.

This is actually a very simple operation, primarily because of the small user base (for example, one). When the executable is built and working satisfactorily, the application can be dragged onto the desktop, the icon can be modified a bit, and it should be all set for the user. Remember, however, that in this case, the development and deployment machines are the same. This means the application was (obviously) run during development, and dependency libraries (such as GLib) are installed.

First, find the executable in the directory tree using the File Manager. Grab it with the mouse and drop it onto the desktop, as shown in Figure 6.5.

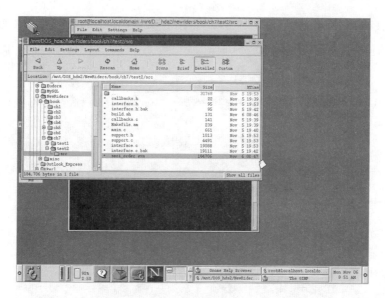

Figure 6.5   Dragging the application to the desktop.

In Figure 6.6, the executable is on the desktop. Notice the icon crossing the boundary from the file list to the desktop. That icon is for sesi_order.exe, which was the name of the application as stated in the compile command. You can double-click on the executable to launch the application. Also, note that drag and drop moves the actual file to the desktop, not just a copy of the file.

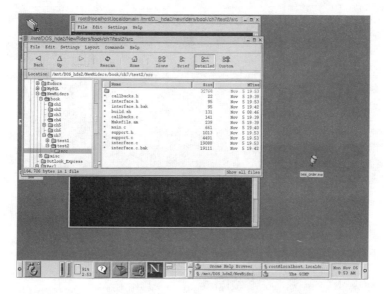

Figure 6.6   After the drag and drop, sesi_order.exe appears on the desktop.

Right-click the sesi_order.exe icon to display the pop-up menu (see Figure 6.7). Select the Properties item, and the Properties dialog box appears.

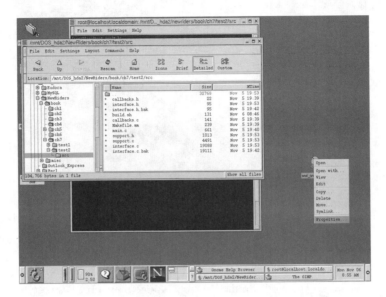

Figure 6.7 Customizing the icon.

In Figure 6.8, notice the entry widget that allows you to set the file name for the icon. In this case, change the name to New Order and leave off the .exe extension.

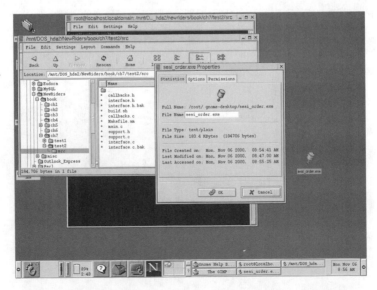

Figure 6.8 Change the file name from sesi_order.exe to New Order.

Next, select the Options tab and then click the icon button. As you can see, the system has selected a piston icon as the default for executables. Clicking the icon brings up the list of stock icons from which to choose. Scroll downward and find an icon for the application (see Figure 6.9).

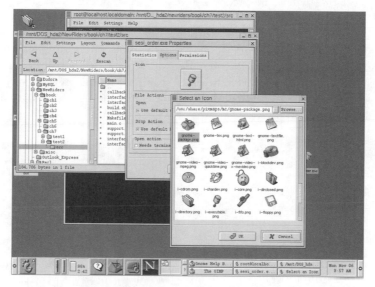

Figure 6.9   A list of stock Gnome icons.

Figure 6.10 shows the final result: an icon on the desktop for creating a new customer order.

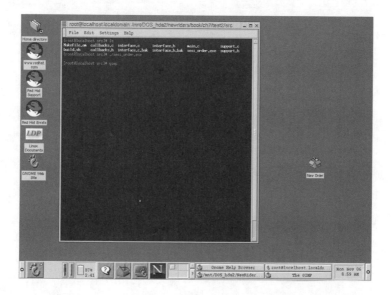

Figure 6.10   The final result: the application on the desktop.

Upgrading the Application

In this case, upgrading the application will be very simple because the client and server are the same machine and only one machine will be running the application. When the application needs to be updated, the developer works at the PC as time permits. Because the "actual" application is on the GNOME desktop (that is, the one the data entry clerk uses on a daily basis), the developer can work with the source code (refer to Chapter 7) and make new compiles down in the project directory without affecting the "production" executable on the user's desktop. When a new version is ready for daily use, the developer moves it to the desktop and deletes the previous version. This also gives some measure of protection in case the user somehow manages to delete the executable on the desktop.

Construction of the SESI Order Entry Application

THIS CHAPTER COVERS THE CONSTRUCTION OF THE Specialty Electrical Supply, Inc. (SESI) Order Entry application as specified and designed in Chapter 6, "Order Entry Abstract and Design." This chapter will move slower than is absolutely necessary and will cover some basic things in detail for readers who are new to this set of tools (MySQL, GTK+, and Glade); for example, certain things will be done step by step here that would be covered in a few sentences or paragraphs in the later sections of the book.

This chapter will proceed along the following lines. First, Glade will be used to construct the user interface. The user interface (UI) will be compiled to make sure that it operates correctly. Next will come the "utility" functions of the application. For example, the function that fills a drop-down combo box with values. These types of functions will be independent of the user interface to the greatest extent possible so that they can be used in other places easily. Another example would be a function that saves the values in the application's text or entry boxes to the database. At the initial project specification, there may be only one place where this function would be used, so it might seem more appropriate to put it in an event callback. However, it may come about at a later release that the "save" functionality is needed in several places. Making the "save" functionality modular from the beginning makes code maintenance that much easier down the road. In the third section, we will connect the two sections to make a functional application.

This chapter will proceed along the path of a "discovery;" that is, I am not going to present the finished final product with all the kinks and trip-ups solved. Instead, I will construct this project as you would. This means I might create or omit something in the UI that will not be discovered until I attempt to integrate the utility functions in the final section. In that case, I have not "gone back" to the UI built with Glade to correct the problem. I will handle it "as discovered, where discovered" to illustrate problems, bugs, and omissions in a realistic manner and hopefully emphasize them in a way that will enable you to learn more about the chosen tools (GTK+ and MySQL).

Finally, remember that the database was constructed in Chapter 6, including the initial fill of data from text files; recall that these text files were extracts from the "previous system" (whatever that may be) and that they have been already imported into the tables in the SESI database (which this application accesses). Appendix A, "Glade-Generated Files from the SESI Order Application," goes along with this chapter and Chapter 6. Appendix A contains the interface.c and sesi.glade files, as generated by Glade.

User Interface Construction with Glade

This section covers the construction of the user interface using Glade. Figures 6.1, 6.2, and 6.3 will be referenced extensively. So you may want to refresh your memory of them or dog-ear their pages.

Starting the frm_main Project

Launch glade from the command line. The UI should be constructed so it can be modified later, knowing that glade will overwrite `interface.c`, append to `callbacks.c`, and not touch `main.c`. Therefore, try not to make changes to files that will be overwritten unless you are willing to document those changes elsewhere so they can be re-created when necessary.

First, set the project options. The name of this application should be set to sesi, making the glade file sesi.glade. Disable Gnome support (tab 1) and gettext support (tab 2). Deselecting these two options will make this project simpler. Gnome support (recall that there is a set of `*_gnome_*` functions built on top of GTK+) is not needed in this or any project in this book, and gettext support is used in the internationalization of strings—again, something that is not needed for these projects because they are targeted at a small number of "in-house" users.

From the palette, select a new window (the top right icon). Name it frm_main in the Properties window and set the title of the window to SESI Customer Order. Then select a vertical packing box and drop it into the newly created window. Set the number of rows to 2 and in the Properties window, set its name to vbox_main. Select a status bar widget from the palette and drop it into the bottom half of the window; change its name to statusbar because this will be the only status bar widget you will use. Then, select a table from the palette and drop it into the top half of vbox_main. Set the number of rows and columns both to 2. Set the table name to table_2_by_2 in the Properties window.

Figure 7.1 shows your progress so far.

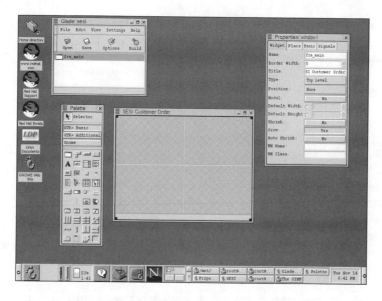

Figure 7.1 The starting structure of frm_main.

Filling Out the Left Side of frm_main

Select the vertical packing box from the palette and drop it into the top left section of table_2_by_2. Set the number of rows to 2. Now repeat this action for the top right section of table_2_by_2. For the names of these vertical packing boxes, enter vbox_customer_number and vbox_customer_name, respectively.

Select a vertical button box widget from the palette and drop it into the bottom left section of table_2_by_2. When prompted, set the number of rows to 5 in accordance with Figure 6.1. Name the vertical button box vbuttonbox since these will be the only command buttons on the form.

Now, within the vertical button box you just created, select the top button. Change its name from button2 to cmd_search and set its label to _Search.... Note the use of the underscore character (the _ in the label); this causes the S in Search to be underlined. Windows users will recognize this as the Alt+S combination, and indeed, there is no reason why your application can't conform to this convention.

With cmd_search still selected, click the Basic tab of the Properties window. Press the Accelerators button (the one marked "Edit...") at the bottom of the window. In modifiers, check the Alt box, type S in the Key text box, and click the ... button to the right of the Signal text box. Select the "clicked" signal and click OK. You should now have one Accelerator in CList box at the top of the Accelerators dialog box. Now the key combination of Alt+S should activate the cmd_search clicked event.

Repeat the procedure in the previous paragraph for the rest of the buttons. Change button2's name to cmd_save_edits and its label to read "Save _Edits", indicating that Alt+E should activate the clicked signal. button3 should similarly have its name changed to cmd_select_items with Alt+I as the accelerator, button4 changes to cmd_print_order (Alt+P), and button5 becomes cmd_exit (Alt+X).

Next, select a label widget and drop it into the upper-left section of the form, which is also the top of vbox_customer_number. Set the text of the label to Customer Number:. Set the label name to lbl_customer_number and the justification to Left. To finish out the left half of this form, select a combo box and drop it into the open section just below lbl_customer_number. Change the name to cbo_customer_number. At this point, you also need to select the combo-entry widget within cbo_customer_number; you can see the difference by clicking on the combo-entry part of the widget and the drop-down arrow on the right side of the widget. In addition to renaming the entire widget, you also need to change the name of the combo-entry part of the widget to combo-entry_customer_number (refer to Figure 7.6).

Figure 7.2 shows how the form should look at this point.

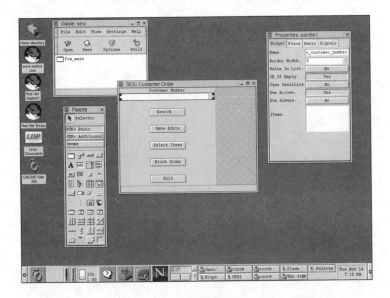

Figure 7.2 frm_main with the left half of the window filled out.

Filling out the Right Side of frm_main

Select another label widget and drop it into the open slot at the top on the right side. Change the name to lbl_customer_name and the label text to Customer Name; make it left justified. Now select a Text Entry widget and drop it into the open space immediately below lbl_customer_name. Name it entry_customer_name.

Select the vertical packing box again and drop it into the lower-right section of table_2_by_2, which at this point should be the only open section. Set the number of rows to 6 and the name to vbox_data. Select the table widget and drop it into the top slot of vbox_data. Set it to 3 rows and 3 columns if that is not the default. Then name it table_3_by_3. Select the table widget one more time, and this time drop it into the second slot of vbox_data, right below table_3_by_3. Set the rows to 4 and the columns to 4, and then name it table_4_by_2.

Select the label widget—twice—and put one each into vbox_data for lbl_order_comments and lbl_customer_comments. Here is your first change from your design of Figures 6.1 and 6.2. In those, Customer Comments were first, and Order Comments were underneath. As it turns out, the Customer Comments probably won't be changed every order, but the Order Comments could be different every time the customer places an order. So reverse the order of the Order and Customer comments labels and text widgets, making them the opposite of their order in Figure 6.2. This will allow the user to tab into the Order Comments—which is much more likely than the user changing or adding Customer Comments. When the label widgets are in place, enter the text widgets and change their names to txt_order_comments and txt_customer_comments. Be sure to set the editable property to Yes.

Figure 7.3 shows your application shaping up nicely.

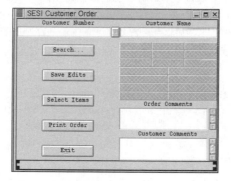

Figure 7.3   The construction of frm_main after you've filled in the right half of the form.

Finishing the frm_main User Interface

Now you'll move on to fill out table_3_by_3 and table_4_by_2. Select the label widget from the palette and drop it into the upper-left box of table_3_by_3. Change its name to lbl_primary_contact and its text to Primary Contact:. Set the justification to Left and under the Place tab of the Properties dialog box, set Col Span to 3. Place lbl_name_last_first in the second row in the leftmost box of table_3_by_3, and place lbl_title_and_phone in the bottom left box.

Next, you insert the text boxes for the contact's first and last name. Select the Text Entry widget from the palette and drop it into the center box of table_3_by_3; name it entry_last. On the Place tab of the Properties window, set the X Expand button to NO, and then go to the Basic tab and select the Width check box (to "true"). Finally, set the value in the Width text box to an even 100. This will make the text box a little narrower; only in the rare case that the person has a very long last name will part of the name be hidden from view. Again, select the Text Entry and repeat the process for entry_first, placing it in table_3_by_3 in the middle row, right box. To finish out table_3_by_3, repeat (again) the two previous steps for entry_title and entry_phone, putting them on the bottom row of table_3_by_3 in the center and far left spaces, respectively.

Fill out labels lbl_ship_to and lbl_bill_to (top row of table_4_by_2) and set their properties as you did for the previous label widgets. Into the middle two rows of table_4_by_2, drop four Text Entry widgets: entry_ship_to_addr1, entry_ship_to_addr2, entry_bill_to_addr1, and entry_bill_to_addr2 (see Figures 6.1 and 6.2 for clarification). Their default values of 158 are acceptable, and their X Expand buttons should be set to No.

The final part of this form's construction is nearly upon you—well, the visual part of it, anyway. Drop a horizontal packing box into each of the remaining bottom two spaces in table_4_by_2, where the City-State-ZIP fields will go for the Ship To and Bill To addresses. The widgets you are creating are entry_ship_to_city, entry_ship_to_st, and entry_ship_to_zip, followed by their equivalent *_bill_to_* widgets. Set the *_city widgets to a width of 100, 35, and 70 for city, state, and zip (for both sets of widgets).

At this point, the visible portion of frm_main is finished; you will add the events shortly. Be sure to hit the Save and Build buttons in Glade. Figure 7.4 shows frm_main as it appears from Glade. You can change the shape of the window (of frm_main) to get some idea of how it will be resized; however, you aren't guaranteed anything until you compile and resize the executable (see the following sidebar, "Compiling frm_main").

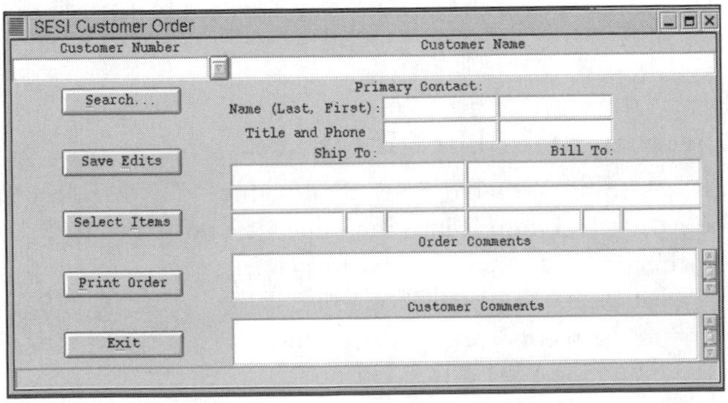

Figure 7.4 Completed frm_main.

Compiling frm_main

At this point, it might be a good idea to compile the application—which consists of only frm_main so far—just to see how it behaves. (For example, you want to see if a text box is resizing as desired.) To do that, you will have to do the following: Comment out the two lines in `main.c` that will cause problems (the lines that reference pixmaps, normally around line 23; these lines reference pixmaps, which won't be used in this application), cd to your project directory, cd to its src subdirectory, and then send the following from the command line (or put it into a shell script):

```
% gcc -Wall -g *.c `gtk-config --cflags --libs`
% ./a.out
```

After you do this, you will want to delete `main.c` and rebuild it from within Glade. If you don't delete it, Glade won't rebuild it, and because this is an intermediate build, you aren't to the point where you want to keep the changes to `main.c`.

Setting the Events for frm_main

As you might have noticed, you have not set any of the signal/callbacks or what you might be used to calling "events;" nor have you started frm_items_ordered (see Figure 6.3). Next, you will set the signals for frm_main, and later you will repeat all these steps for frm_items_ordered.

At this point—setting the events for frm_main—you are probably better off to err on the side of caution; that is, you should connect more signals than necessary. Because you are going to build most of your utility functions in a modular way, if it turns out that one signal is better than another for a certain function (by having that function already set), you will have to move only a small amount of code. You will not have to open Glade and search for signals.

Setting the Signals

To start with, connect the delete signal for frm_main; this will be your application shutdown code. Select the main window object of frm_main. You can do this by selecting frm_main in the window titled "Glade: sesi." You will know when you have selected the window object because the Properties window will say "Properties: frm_main" in the title bar.

With frm_main selected, click the Signals tab in the Properties window. Click the … button next to the Signal text box to bring up the Select Signal dialog box. Now the question becomes this: "Which signals will you use, or potentially use?" Remember, for an application this small, there is essentially no penalty for over-indulging and selecting too many signals. Figure 7.5 shows the Select Signal window.

Figure 7.5   The Select Signal dialog box.

Under GtkWindow signals, highlight set_focus and click OK. This returns values to the Signal and Handler text boxes of the Signals tab in the Properties window. The next step is very important: Click the Add button in the lower-left corner or your signal addition will be lost. This should put a `set_focus` signal into the list box at the top of the Signals tab. Repeat that procedure for all signals you think you'll use.

In this case, the following signals have been selected in addition to the `set_focus` event: `button_press_event`, `button_release_event`, `delete_event`, `event`, `hide`, `key_press_event`, `key_release_event`, and the `realize` event. The `delete` event will be the place to call the `gtk_main_quit()` call, and the others just might come in handy at some point in the future. As I said before, if it turns out not to be the case, the price is an empty function.

> ### Testing Event Sequences by Adding g_print Statements
>
> At this point, you might want to put a quick `g_print()` function call in all your callbacks, do a quick compile, and check to see that all the functions are firing when you think they are. To do this, you'll need to open `callbacks.c` for your project and add a `g_print()` call, changing the message to indicate which callback function is firing. Follow the compile instructions in the previous sidebar, "Compiling frm_main." If you have downloaded the source code from the companion Web site, you will notice that every callback has either a `g_print()` call or a commented-out `g_print()` call. I have left those in on purpose; in addition to helping with debugging, they make a good demonstration of event sequences.
>
> In fact, doing so confirms a couple of events in GTK+ that you will use to your advantage. When you get to the point that you have the clicked event for `cmd_search` with a statement in it like this
>
> ```
> g_print("cmd_search clicked...\n");
> ```
>
> you can confirm that Alt+S does indeed activate the `cmd_search` clicked event and that the keypress event for the window captures all keys. However, this now creates new problems: All keys means *all keys*, including the Tab key, which the user will probably use extensively.

Now select the `cmd_search` button and go to the Signals tab. Again select the
… button to view the possible signals for a command button. Select the `clicked`
signal under GtkButton Signals, click OK, and then click Add.

Repeat that same action for all the other command buttons on the form. You can
look through the list of events for the command button widget, but you won't be
using any events other than the `clicked` event. Also, go ahead and add
`gtk_main_quit()` to frm_main's delete event callback in `callbacks.c`.

Finally, turn to cbo_customer_number. Recall that when this widget was created,
you had to rename both the combo widget and its child combo-entry widget to
cbo_customer_number and combo-entry_customer_number, respectively. This
distinction will become very important shortly. Figure 7.6 shows the different
widgets selected.

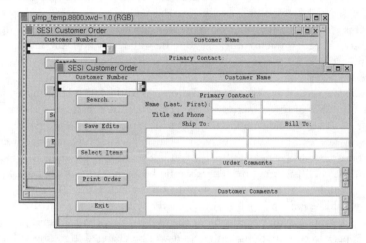

Figure 7.6   The difference between a combo widget and its child combo-entry widget.

With the combo widget selected, select the Properties window and then the Signals
tab. Using the … button, bring up the signals for the combo widget. Notice that you
have the signals for GtkContainer, GtkWidget, and GtkObject. Looking through the
list, none will be used in our application. However, if you go back and select combo-
entry_customer_number and then bring up the signals, you will see several that will
be needed.

Notice that the Select Signal window brings up the GtkEditable signals. Set the
signals for `activate`, `changed`, `delete_text`, and `insert_text`.

Making cmd_save_edits Inactive

Finally, you need to make cmd_save_edits inactive—or in GTK-speak, "insensitive."
Select the cmd_save_edits widget, and then open the Property Editor window if it is
not already open. Select the Basic tab and set the Sensitive toggle button to "No." This
sets the initial state of cmd_save_edits to be grayed-out.

At this point, the UI portion of frm_main using Glade is done. Again, it is probably advisable for you to open `callbacks.c`, enter a `g_print()` statement for each of the callbacks, and then compile and run the application just to see how everything fits together. Otherwise, it is time to move on to frm_items_ordered.

Creating frm_items_ordered

Chapter 6 did not present a container schematic for frm_items_ordered as it did for frm_main. It will be initially divided by a horizontal frame with the buttons, labels, and text widgets on the left, and the CList widgets on the right. The left side will be divided by vertical packing boxes into which the individual widgets will be added, and the right side will be divided by two more frame widgets.

From the Palette, select a window widget. Then, rather than selecting a horizontal packing widget with two columns, select and drop a horizontal pane widget into the window. This effectively allows the same division as a horizontal packing widget, but it allows the user to size the left and right sides. Be sure to set both the Gutter and Handle properties to 10 and deselect the Position check box; this allows the frame to size as needed instead of setting itself all the way to the left as a default.

Next, select a vertical packing box and drop it into the left side of the window; it asks for the number of rows to create. Referencing Figure 6.3, there is a chance to change the design a bit and simplify the UI at the same time. In Figure 6.3, the top leftmost widgets are in the same row of the vertical packing box, the label Item Num:, and its associated editable widget. What if you put each of these widgets into separate rows in your vertical packing box? There would be no need for a horizontal packing box, and it would not affect the vertical dimensions because the CList widgets on the right side would be longer (vertically) than all the widgets on the left side. While it doesn't give any immediate benefits other than simplifying the UI build process a bit, it doesn't appear to cost anything either. So it will be changed. Looking at Figure 6.3 again, you see a total of nine widgets on the left side. All of those will be placed into their own row within the left vertical packing box, which you will call vbox_left.

Select and drop into vbox_left the following items from top to bottom: a label widget, a text-entry widget, another label, a spin button widget, two command buttons, another label, a frame (and then inside the frame, insert label widget). Finally insert into the bottom row a command button. Rename the top label from label1 (or whatever the default name is) to lbl_item_number and set its text to Item Number:; set the justification and other properties as desired. Name the text-entry widget below it entry_item_number and set its max length to 12, which should be more than enough.

Next change the label in Row 3 to lbl_quantity, change the text to Quantity:, and change any other properties as needed. Name the spinbutton widget in row 4 spinbutton_quantity, and set the default Value: to 1 if it is not already set because this will be the most likely value for any given item.

For the next two command buttons down in the vertical packing box, change the names to cmd_add and cmd_search_for_item and set the label text according to Figure 6.3. For cmd_add, put an underscore before the "A" in the label to make it the hotkey and connect the Alt+A key combination to the `clicked` signal by going to the Basic tab in the Properties box and clicking the Accelerators: Edit... button. Check the Alt check box, set the Key to A and the Signal to clicked, and then click Add and Close. Repeat the steps for cmd_search_for_item, making F the hotkey. For both command buttons, set the Border Width property to 5; this improves readability of the UI a bit.

Finally, to fill out vbox_left, set lbl_order_total (the 7th row down) the same way you set the labels in rows 1 and 3. Row 8 now contains a frame widget (without a title), and inside the frame is a label widget. This label widget will be set with the amount of the order total, and because that number cannot be changed except by adding or deleting items, making it a label prevents the user from thinking he can edit it. Set this label to lbl_order_total_numeric and set its default text to 0.00. Also, select the frame surrounding it (probably named frame1, by default) and set its Expand and Fill properties to No.

In row 9, set the properties for cmd_done in the same way you set the command buttons in rows 5 and 6.

Figure 7.7 shows how frm_items_ordered should look after you finish the left side of the horizontal packing box.

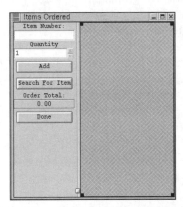

Figure 7.7   frm_items_ordered as it should look after you fill in the left half of the window.

Filling Out the Right Side of frm_items_ordered

Now it is time to fill out the right side of the main horizontal packing box. Again, instead of selecting a vertical packing box widget and dropping it onto the right side with the rows set to 3, you will use vertical pane widgets. As before, this gives the user room for greater customization, and in this case, it helps demonstrate the differences between using packing boxes and panes. Select the vertical pane widget (twice) and place it into the right side of the horizontal pane widget that divides frm_items_ordered. In the top row, select from the palette and drop a CList widget.

For the name of this CList widget, enter clist_items, and then select each of the column header labels in turn. Name them and set their text as shown in Figure 6.3. To avoid confusion, preface the column header label names with "clist_items_"; for example, the leftmost column label should be named clist_items_lbl_item_number. This prevents the possibility of confusing it with lbl_item_number, which is in the upper-left space of this same form. Although such a name is very long, because it's a widget, it will not change after it is created; it will be static for the life of the application, so you only have to set it once. Therefore, the three labels reading across the top of clist_items should be named clist_items_lbl_item_number, clist_items_lbl_description, and clist_items_lbl_price. Returning to clist_items, in the Property Editor under the Basic tab, select the Height and Width check boxes, which forces the CList to be displayed in the correct size. Otherwise the frame object that bounds it on the lower edge will push all the way to the top, effectively hiding clist_items.

Next, place another CList widget into the bottom space on the left side that's created by your two vertical frame widgets. Name it clist_items_ordered, in keeping with your overall naming convention. Change its properties and its column's properties the same way you did for clist_items, but also as depicted in Figure 6.3. That means the first label will be named clist_items_ordered_lbl_item_number, the second clist_items_ordered_lbl_description, and so on. Don't forget to select and set the Height and Width properties on the Basic tab.

Finally, resize both of the CList widgets to show proportionally: clist_items should show five or six lines of available items, whereas clist_items_ordered should show three or four items. Set the Height property of clist_items to 150 and the height of clist_items_selected to an even 100.

The only available space should now be the empty space between the two CList widgets. Into it, drop a horizontal packing box with three columns. I will refer to this as hbox3, the default name on my system; to follow along, you should set yours to the same. For hbox3, set the Border Width to 10, the Size to 3, Homogenous to Yes, and Spacing to 12. On the Place tab, set Shrink to Yes and Resize to No. The rest of the defaults should do fine.

Drop a command button object into the left available spot in hbox3. Set its name to cmd_add_down, and this time for its text, enter Add. At this point, you might be tempted to choose the stock button Down. That option shouldn't be used here because you have disabled Gnome support for this application, and the stock buttons are Gnome functions.

Next, drop another command button into the far right space in hbox3. Name this one cmd_remove, and because none of the stock buttons are what you're after, enter Remove for its label text. Both cmd_remove and cmd_add_down should have their Expand and Fill properties set to No.

Lastly, select a spin button widget and drop it into the center space of hbox3. Name it spinbutton_quantity_down to distinguish it from spinbutton_quantity in the upper-left corner of the form. In the Place tab of spinbutton_quantity_down, the Expand and Fill properties should be set to No.

Figure 7.8 shows frm_items_ordered with the UI filled in.

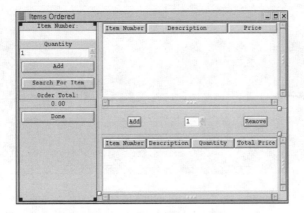

Figure 7.8   frm_itmes_ordered with all widgets added.

Setting the Events for frm_items_ordered

It is time to set the events. Set the same events as with frm_main for frm_items_ordered (at the window level), and set the same for the button widgets. See the Signals tab of frm_main for a list of signals to set. After that, you need to set the signals for the GtkEditable widgets (any text, entry, and in this case, spinbutton controls), as well as the CList widgets.

As you did with the GtkEditable objects on frm_main, set the `activate`, `changed`, `insert text`, and `delete text` signals for entry_item_number on frm_items_ordered. Although you could set the same signals for the spinbutton widgets, that won't be done because no actions are tied to the spinbutton widgets. They will be accessed to find out what integer they show, but nothing more will be done.

For the CList widgets, set the `select_row`, `unselect_row`, `button_press_event`, and `button_release_event` signals. Do so for both CList widgets.

Nearing the end of the UI building process with Glade, the last thing you need to do is build the "find customer" and "find item" search boxes. Figure 7.9 shows both windows built with Glade.

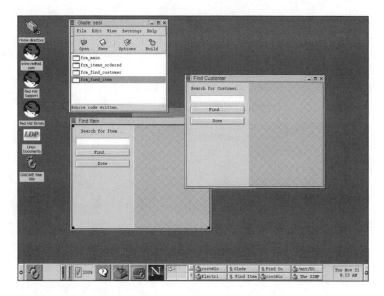

Figure 7.9   frm_find_item and frm_find_customer:
Note that each still needs a CList widget on the right half to be complete.

The detailed steps for creating these windows will not be covered here; all the widgets used are defined, and their properties are set along the same lines as were those of the previous widgets. Both are Modal, and their only trapped events are the clicked events of the command buttons and the delete event on the window. frm_find_item should have a CList widget on the right half with three columns, and frm_find_customer should have a CList widget on the right with 17 columns, each corresponding to its related database table. The application will fill in the rows, and if another Find operation occurs, the application will clear and refill the widget.

Utility Functions of the Application

In this section, you will construct the functions that will do the majority of the work for your application. You will construct these functions to make them as independent of any user interface as possible. This not only makes them easier to test during bug-tracking activities ("What is causing the bug: MySQL, the text box, or something else?"), but it forces a clarity of thought on the functions by forcing you to ask "What is this function really trying to do, what minimal inputs are needed, and what minimal outputs are required?" For example, when you're selecting a value (a customer number in this case), the input is the customer number, and for the output you would prefer to have a "record" rather than a number of "fields." So if you can build a function that will query your database and return a single database record, you have a better function than one that returns multiple values.

Creating *sesi_utils.c*

First, create a file called `sesi_utils.c`. This will be the file that contains the utility functions for the application. Refer to Listing 1.1 in Chapter 1, "MySQL for Access and SQL Server Developers and DBAs," if necessary. This section is going to present the file `sesi_utils.c` as a series of listings instead of one large listing so that the individual functions can be covered with a little more detail. It is important that all these utility functions reside in a single file: `sesi_utils.c` (and its companion, `sesi_utils.h`). Also remember that you can get all the files from this book at the book's companion Web site.

First, include the necessary files. Referring to Listing 1.1 (in Chapter 1), `stdio.h` and `mysql.h` were included, but only `mysql.h` needs to be included here. `stdio.h` was for the `printf` functions needed in Listing 1.1, but you will be using GLib functions in your application. `gtk.h` also needs to be declared here so that you have access to its functionality. Therefore, your heading should look like the following:

```
#include <mysql.h>
#include <gtk/gtk.h>
```

connect_to_db() function

The first thing the application must do is connect to the correct MySQL database. Because this application is meant to be opened, used, and closed in short cycles of a few minutes, it will be safe to make this connection to the database a global variable. This is one of those cases in which a global variable makes sense. Otherwise, the developer is faced with one of two choices: to create a non-global variable that gets passed into or out of nearly every function or to initiate a connection to the database for every query and then end that connection after every single operation is completed.

Listing 7.1 is the database connection routine. It has one purpose: to establish a connection to the MySQL database named "sesi."

Listing 7.1 is only one of the functions in the physical file `sesi_utils.c`. It will be much easier to cover each function on an individual basis than to present one long listing and try to cover it as a single topic. At the book's companion Web site, you can get all the code listings.

Listing 7.1   *connect_to_db()* **Function of** *sesi_utils.c*

```
void connect_to_db()
{
    /* Listing 7.1
     *
     * This function establishes a connection to database
     * "sesi." It establishes a value for the variable
     * conx, which is a (global) session connection
     * to the database.
     *
     * 0L is equal to NULL, but it is considered more portable.
```

continues

Listing 7.1 **Continued**

```
 * For a Linux-only program, NULL should work fine.
 */

g_print("Establishing db connection...\n");

conx = mysql_init ((MYSQL *)0L);

if (conx == 0L)
    {
      /* What should the software do if this error occurs?
       * Obviously, there is no reason to continue with
       * the application because it is of no use without a
       * MySQL database connection. In a larger application,
       * there would be some logging of the error that occurred
       * and various other pieces of information that would aid
       * in debugging. But for this application, those actions
       * weren't specified. So they will be left out.
       *
       * Therefore, when a fatal error occurs, the software will
       * communicate that to the user, and it will exit.
       */

      g_print("Failure in mysql_init...\n");
      gtk_statusbar_push(GTK_STATUSBAR(lookup_widget(frm_main, "statusbar")),
                  1,
                  "Database initialization failed,"
                  "contact administrator...");

      /* The fatal_msgbox() function is defined next.
       * Basically, it is used whenever an error occurs that
       * makes it useless to continue.
       */

      fatal_msgbox("Database initialization failed.\n"
                  "Contact the system administrator.");
    }

  /* In the following call, if the database parameter is misspelled
   * (in this case, "sesi"), it is important to note that the
   * function call will still return OK instead of an error. The reason
   * is that this function primarily connects to a server, not a
   * specific database. If you can't connect to the database
   * for some reason, you won't know until you attempt to query
   * the database for some information.
   */

conx = mysql_real_connect (conx, "localhost", "root", 0L, "sesi", 0, 0L, 0);
if (conx == 0L)
    {
      g_print("Failure in mysql_real_connect...\n");
```

```c
        /* The next two function calls are the first examples
         * of error handling in this application. In MySQL, these
         * are the error handling functions. Obviously, these
         * could be very helpful in debugging and error tracing.
         * So the software should attempt to report them.
         */

        g_print("Error Number is %i...\n", mysql_errno(conx));
        g_print("Error Description is %s...\n", mysql_error(conx));
        gtk_statusbar_push(GTK_STATUSBAR(lookup_widget(frm_main, "statusbar")),
                    1,
                    "Database connection failed, "
                    "contact administrator...");

        /* Again, if the mysql_real_connect call returns an error,
         * there is really no point in continuing.
         */

        fatal_msgbox(g_strconcat("The connection to the database could",
                            " not be established.\n\n",
                            "Error number: ",
                            g_strdup_printf("%d", mysql_errno(conx)),
                            "\nError description: \n",
                            g_strdup_printf("%s", mysql_error(conx)),
                            0L)
                );
    }

g_print("Connected to db...\n");

/* Hit the target database with a simple query as a final
 * confirmation that the connection to the database is open.
 */

if (mysql_query (conx, "select count(*) from tbl_customers") != 0)
    {
            fatal_msgbox(g_strconcat("Unable to connect to ",
                                "database SESI.\n\n",
                                "Error Number: ",
                                g_strdup_printf("%d",
                                        mysql_errno(conx)),
                                "\nError Description: ",
                                g_strdup_printf("%s",
                                        mysql_error(conx)),
                                0L)
                );

            g_print("Failure to connect to the correct database...\n");
    }
else g_print("Connected to database \"sesi\"...\n");
```

continues

Listing 7.1 **Continued**

```
/* Report to the user that everything to this point is okay.  */

gtk_statusbar_push(GTK_STATUSBAR(lookup_widget(frm_main, "statusbar")), 1,
                    "Connected to database SESI, ready for new order...");


}
```

fatal_msgbox() Function

In Listing 7.1, notice that in three places the `fatal_msgbox()` function is called. That function is shown in Listing 7.2.

Listing 7.2 **The *fatal_msgbox()* Function of *sesi_utils.c***

```
void fatal_msgbox(gchar *msg)
{
  /* Listing 7.2
   *
   * This function is called whenever a fatal but trapable application
   * error has occurred. Message boxes are a very poor way to
   * communciate to the user; however, when an error occurs that should
   * cause the application to terminate, it is nice to give the user
   * some form of feedback that attempts to tell him why and gives
   * him a chance to do something. In this case, basically all the user
   * can do is make a note of the problem and report it to the system
   * administrator.
   * This function uses the gtk_dialog_new() call to create a container
   * message box into which a label and an OK button are added.
   */

  GtkWidget *msgbox;
  GtkWidget *lbl;
  GtkWidget *cmd_ok;

  msgbox = gtk_dialog_new();
  lbl = gtk_label_new(g_strconcat("A fatal error has occurred.\n\n",
                                  msg,"\n\n",
                                  "You may want to make a ",
                                  "note of this information.\n\n",
                                  "The OK button below will terminate ",
                                  "this application",
                                  0L) );

  cmd_ok = gtk_button_new_with_label("Ok");

  gtk_box_pack_start(GTK_BOX(GTK_DIALOG(msgbox)->vbox),
                     lbl, FALSE, FALSE, FALSE);
  gtk_box_pack_start(GTK_BOX(GTK_DIALOG(msgbox)->action_area),
                     cmd_ok, FALSE, FALSE, FALSE);
```

```
/* Note the following two signal connection calls. The second one
 * should be very familiar to you by now, but notice that rather than
 * setting up a separate callback function in which gtk_main_quit()
 * would be called (as has been done in all examples
 * to this point), gtk_main_quit() is called directly.
 *
 * The first, gtk_signal_connect_object(), is used when the function
 * you are invoking has a single parameter of type GtkObject. Notice
 * that both produce the same effect. The first is needed because
 * there is no guarantee that the user will click the handy "OK"
 * button that has been created; he might hit the kill-window "X"
 * that is in the top right corner of all windows. Without a callback
 * on the delete_event signal, he would return to the application
 * but be unable to do anything.
 */
gtk_signal_connect_object(GTK_OBJECT(msgbox),
                          "delete_event",
                          GTK_SIGNAL_FUNC(gtk_main_quit),
                          GTK_OBJECT(msgbox) );

gtk_signal_connect(GTK_OBJECT(cmd_ok),
                   "clicked",
                   GTK_SIGNAL_FUNC(gtk_main_quit),
                   0L);

gtk_widget_show_all(msgbox);

}
```

connect_to_db() and *fatal_msgbox()* Functions

After you have created the two functions in Listing 7.1 and 7.2, you see that the
header area of file `sesi_utils.c` has changed, as shown in Listing 7.3.

Listing 7.3   **The Header of File** *sesi_utils.c* **After the Functions** *connect_to_db()* **and**
fatal_msgbox() **Are Created**

```
01  #include <mysql.h>
02  #include <gtk/gtk.h>
03
04  #include "support.h"
05
06  GtkWidget *frm_main;
07
08  /* conx is the connection to the database; it is global,
09   * and all functions in the application can use it to
10   * access database "sesi".
11   */
```

continues

Listing 7.3 **Continued**

```
12
13  MYSQL *conx;
14
15  /********** Function Prototypes **************/
16  void connect_to_db();
17  void fatal_msgbox(gchar *msg);
18
19  /********** Utility Functions **************/
20
```

Lines 4 and 6 are required because the function connect_to_db() references the lookup_widget() to place text into the status bar widget on frm_main. Line 13 is the global database connection variable. Lines 15 and 19 were added for readability, and line 17 is the function prototype for fatal_msgbox().

Next you'll look at the function that will fill combo box cbo_customer_number with the values for the drop-down box. This is one of the first things the application will have to do.

get_customer_numbers() Function

Listing 7.4 shows the get_customer_numbers() function. Notice that it returns a GList object; this is because it is easy to call the gtk_combo_set_popdown_strings() function, sending it a GList object as the second parameter.

Listing 7.4 **The *get_conx()* and *get_customer_numbers()* Functions of *sesi_utils.c***

```
void get_conx()
{
   /* This function refreshes the connection to the database as
    * needed. Note its lack of error handling; since that
    * was checked in detail when the application started, this
    * makes the assumption that things will still be OK - normally.
    */

   conx = mysql_init ((MYSQL*)0L);

   /* In the following function call, "root" is the user who was logged
    * in when MySQL was installed via the RPM. You might need to change
    * the user name for your system, depending on how it was installed.
    */

   mysql_real_connect (conx, "localhost", "root", 0L, "sesi", 0, 0L, 0);
}

GList *get_customer_numbers()
{
```

```
/* This function retrieves the list of customer numbers from
 * the database and fills cbo_customer_numbers on frm_main.
 */

GList       *list_of_customers = 0L;
MYSQL_RES   *result_set;
MYSQL_ROW   row;

get_conx();

/* When frm_main opens, it will default to the first item in the
 * drop-down list of the combo box.
 */

if (mysql_query (conx, "select distinct(num) from tbl_customers") != 0)
    {
            fatal_msgbox(g_strconcat("Unable to retrieve list",
                                     " of customer numbers.\n\n",
                                     "Error Number:   ",
                                     g_strdup_printf("%d",
                                            mysql_errno(conx)),
                                     "\nError Description:   ",
                                     g_strdup_printf("%s",
                                            mysql_error(conx)),
                                     0L)
                    );

            g_print("Failure to retreive list of customers..\n");
    }
else g_print("Retrieved customer numbers from db...\n");

/* Now iterate through the rows, get the values for customer
 * number, and add them to cbo_customer_number.
 */

result_set = mysql_store_result (conx);
while ((row = mysql_fetch_row (result_set)) != 0L)
    { list_of_customers = g_list_append(list_of_customers, row[0] );
    }

/* If you put the New customer number at the end of the list, the
 * user can use the up and down arrows to search through the customer
 * records without crossing the "New" value. Adding a new customer
 * will be a rather rare occurrance, and this way the user has to
 * purposefully go to "New" or type it in.
 */

list_of_customers = g_list_append(list_of_customers, "New");

return list_of_customers;
}
```

fill_customer_info(), *clear_frm_main()*, **and** *fill_frm_main()* **Functions**

Now that the combo box of customer numbers is filled, the user will normally pick one, in which case that customer's information should be entered into the text and entry widgets on frm_main. To perform that function, Listing 7.5 will fill in the customer data from the database; in addition, the functions for clearing the text and entry widgets on frm_main are listed.

Listing 7.5   **The** *fill_customer_info()*, *clear_frm_main()*, **and** *fill_frm_main()* **Functions**

```
void fill_customer_info()
{

    /* This function will retrieve a customer record from
     * the database and fill in the text boxes on frm_main by
     * calling fill_frm_main().
     */

    GtkCombo    *cbo;
    MYSQL_RES   *result_set;
    MYSQL_ROW   row;

    /* First, connect to the database, and then get the customer
     * number from the entry (child) widget of cbo_customer_number.
     */

    get_conx();

    cbo = GTK_COMBO(lookup_widget(frm_main, "cbo_customer_number"));
    g_print(gtk_entry_get_text(GTK_ENTRY(cbo->entry)));
    g_print("\n");

    /* Check to see if a new customer is being added rather than
     * querying for an existing customer. If so, clear frm_main
     * and call create_new_customer().
     */

    if (g_strcasecmp(gtk_entry_get_text (GTK_ENTRY(cbo->entry)), "New") == 0)
        {
            g_print("Creating new customer record...\n");
            clear_frm_main();

            create_new_customer();

            /* Exit this routine after setting up for a
             * new customer record. */

            return;
        }
```

```
/* What if cbo_customer_number is blank? Clear the form, because
 * there is no customer information associated with a "blank"
 * customer number.
 */

if (g_strcasecmp(gtk_entry_get_text (GTK_ENTRY(cbo->entry)), "") == 0)
    {
        g_print("No Data:  Blank Customer Record...\n");
        clear_frm_main();

        return;
    }

/* mysql_query() returns a result only indicating whether or not the
 * query sent was legal or not. In this case, sending a query
 * with a customer number that does not exist is legal, it just
 * returns zero rows.
 */

if (mysql_query (conx,
                 g_strconcat("select * ",
                             "from tbl_customers where num = ",
                             gtk_entry_get_text (GTK_ENTRY(cbo->entry)),
                             0L
                             )
                 ) != 0
    )
    {
      g_print("mysql_query failure in fill_customer_info()...\n");
      gtk_statusbar_push(GTK_STATUSBAR(lookup_widget(frm_main,
                                                "statusbar")), 1,
                    "Error retrieving customer data (illegal query)."
                    " Contact administrator.");
    }
else
    {
      g_print("Fetching customer data...\n");
      gtk_statusbar_push(GTK_STATUSBAR(lookup_widget(frm_main,
                                                "statusbar")), 1,
                              "Fetching Customer data...");

      result_set = mysql_store_result (conx);

      if (mysql_num_rows (result_set) == 0)
        {
          g_print("Invalid Customer Number...\n");
          gtk_statusbar_push(GTK_STATUSBAR(lookup_widget(frm_main,
                                                "statusbar")), 1,
                              "Invalid Customer Number...");

          /* Clear frm_main to avoid any confusion. */
          clear_frm_main();
```

continues

Listing 7.5 **Continued**

```
        }
        else
        {
            /* There could also be a check here to make sure not more than
             * one row returned, which would indicate that something is
             * wrong tbl_customers.num should be the table key.
             *
             * However, because that key has been specified
             * in the database structure (and to keep this routine a bit
             * simpler), that check will be skipped.
             */

            row = mysql_fetch_row (result_set);
            g_print("Preparing for widget fill...\n");

            /* Fill frm_main with customer data. The parameter being sent
             * is the row of data from the sesi database.
             */

            fill_frm_main(row);
            gtk_statusbar_push(GTK_STATUSBAR(lookup_widget(frm_main,
                                "statusbar")), 1,
                                "Customer data filled in...");
        }

    }
    return;

}

void clear_frm_main()
{

    /* This function clears all the text boxes on frm_main that
     * display customer information.
     */

    g_print("Clearing customer information...\n");

    gtk_entry_set_text(GTK_ENTRY(lookup_widget(frm_main,
                                        "entry_customer_name")), "");

    gtk_entry_set_text(GTK_ENTRY(lookup_widget(frm_main,
                                        "entry_ship_to_addr1")), "" );
    gtk_entry_set_text(GTK_ENTRY(lookup_widget(frm_main,
                                        "entry_ship_to_addr2")), "");
    gtk_entry_set_text(GTK_ENTRY(lookup_widget(frm_main,
                                        "entry_ship_to_city")), "");
    gtk_entry_set_text(GTK_ENTRY(lookup_widget(frm_main,
                                        "entry_ship_to_st")), "");
```

```
gtk_entry_set_text(GTK_ENTRY(lookup_widget(frm_main,
                              "entry_ship_to_zip")), "");

gtk_entry_set_text(GTK_ENTRY(lookup_widget(frm_main,
                              "entry_bill_to_addr1")), "");
gtk_entry_set_text(GTK_ENTRY(lookup_widget(frm_main,
                              "entry_bill_to_addr2")), "");
gtk_entry_set_text(GTK_ENTRY(lookup_widget(frm_main,
                              "entry_bill_to_city")), "");
gtk_entry_set_text(GTK_ENTRY(lookup_widget(frm_main,
                              "entry_bill_to_st")), "");
gtk_entry_set_text(GTK_ENTRY(lookup_widget(frm_main,
                              "entry_bill_to_zip")), "");

gtk_entry_set_text(GTK_ENTRY(lookup_widget(frm_main, "entry_first")), "");
gtk_entry_set_text(GTK_ENTRY(lookup_widget(frm_main, "entry_last")), "");
gtk_entry_set_text(GTK_ENTRY(lookup_widget(frm_main, "entry_title")), "");
gtk_entry_set_text(GTK_ENTRY(lookup_widget(frm_main, "entry_phone")), "");

/* Delete the text from the customer comments
 * text box. The order comments box should not
 * change no matter which customer is displayed
 * because the order comments go with the current
 * instantiation of this application.
 */

gtk_text_set_point(GTK_TEXT(lookup_widget(frm_main,
                              "txt_customer_comments")), 0);
g_print("current insertion point is %i\n...",
        gtk_text_get_point(GTK_TEXT(lookup_widget(frm_main,
                              "txt_customer_comments"))));

g_print("delete returned %i\n",
        gtk_text_forward_delete (GTK_TEXT(lookup_widget(frm_main,
                                    "txt_customer_comments")),
                    gtk_text_get_length(GTK_TEXT(lookup_widget(frm_main,
                                    "txt_customer_comments")))
        ));
}

void fill_frm_main(MYSQL_ROW in_row)
{
    /* This function will fill in the text boxes on frm_main
     * that display the customer information.
     *
     * Clear the form so that the fill operation starts from a known
     * state.
     */

    clear_frm_main();
```

continues

Listing 7.5 **Continued**

```
/* in_row is the parameter to this function. It contains one
 * row from tbl_customers, and that information is what is
 * to be displayed.
 */

gtk_entry_set_text(GTK_ENTRY(lookup_widget(frm_main,
                    "entry_customer_name")), in_row[1]);

if (in_row[2] != 0L ) {
   gtk_entry_set_text(GTK_ENTRY(lookup_widget(frm_main,
                    "entry_ship_to_addr1")), in_row[2]);
}
if (in_row[3] != 0L ) {
   gtk_entry_set_text(GTK_ENTRY(lookup_widget(frm_main,
                    "entry_ship_to_addr2")), in_row[3]);
}
if (in_row[4] != 0L ) {
   gtk_entry_set_text(GTK_ENTRY(lookup_widget(frm_main,
                    "entry_ship_to_city")), in_row[4]);
}
if (in_row[5] != 0L ) {
   gtk_entry_set_text(GTK_ENTRY(lookup_widget(frm_main,
                    "entry_ship_to_st")), in_row[5]);
}
if (in_row[6] != 0L ) {
   gtk_entry_set_text(GTK_ENTRY(lookup_widget(frm_main,
                    "entry_ship_to_zip")), in_row[6]);
}

if (in_row[7] != 0L ) {
   gtk_entry_set_text(GTK_ENTRY(lookup_widget(frm_main,
                    "entry_bill_to_addr1")), in_row[7]);
}
if (in_row[8] != 0L ) {
   gtk_entry_set_text(GTK_ENTRY(lookup_widget(frm_main,
                    "entry_bill_to_addr2")), in_row[8]);
}
if (in_row[9] != 0L ) {
   gtk_entry_set_text(GTK_ENTRY(lookup_widget(frm_main,
                    "entry_bill_to_city")), in_row[9]);
}
if (in_row[10] != 0L ) {
   gtk_entry_set_text(GTK_ENTRY(lookup_widget(frm_main,
                    "entry_bill_to_st")), in_row[10]);
}
if (in_row[11] != 0L ) {
   gtk_entry_set_text(GTK_ENTRY(lookup_widget(frm_main,
                    "entry_bill_to_zip")), in_row[11]);
}
```

```
        g_print("Filling contact information...\n");
        if (in_row[12] != 0L ) {
            gtk_entry_set_text(GTK_ENTRY(lookup_widget(frm_main,
                              "entry_first")), in_row[12]);
        }

        if (in_row[13] != 0L ) {
            gtk_entry_set_text(GTK_ENTRY(lookup_widget(frm_main,
                              "entry_last")), in_row[13]);
        }

        if (in_row[14] != 0L ) {
            gtk_entry_set_text(GTK_ENTRY(lookup_widget(frm_main,
                              "entry_phone")), in_row[14]);
        }

        if (in_row[15] != 0L ) {
            gtk_entry_set_text(GTK_ENTRY(lookup_widget(frm_main,
                              "entry_title")), in_row[15]);
        }

        if (in_row[16] != 0L ) {
            gtk_text_insert(GTK_TEXT(lookup_widget(frm_main,
                                "txt_customer_comments")),
                          0L, 0L, 0L,
                          in_row[16], -1
                          );
        }

        /* Because the data retrieved has not been edited,
         * set the need_to_save_edits flag to false and "gray-out"
         * cmd_save_edits to give the user a visual cue that the
         * data has not changed since it was pulled from the database.
         */

        need_to_save_edits = FALSE;
        gtk_widget_set_sensitive(lookup_widget(frm_main,
                                  "cmd_save_edits"), FALSE);
}
```

So far, this chapter has not addressed the code for entering a new customer. That code is shown in Listing 7.14.

fill_items_ordered() Function

When the user finds the desired customer, he will want to start entering items ordered. So that code is next. First, the "speed entry" method (which uses the widgets at the top left of frm_items_ordered) will be covered. Then, the slower method will be described using clist_items and cmd_add_down, which is meant to be a more mouse-intensive way of working. However, before any of that, the form has to fill in all the items and be prepared for use. Listing 7.6 does precisely that.

Listing 7.6 *fill_items_ordered()* **Function from** *sesi_utils.c*

```c
void fill_items_ordered()
{
    MYSQL_RES  *result_set;
    MYSQL_ROW  db_row;
    gchar      *clist_row[3] = {"", "", ""};

    /* This function does the initial fill of widgets in
     * frm_items_ordered, as needed. It is anticipated that it will
     * normally only be called from the realize or show events of
     * frm_items_ordered because the list of available items in the
     * database is not expected to change while the application is in
     * use.
     * The database access code will operate in a manner similar to other
     * functions previously listed.
     */

    get_conx();
    if (mysql_query (conx, "select * from tbl_items") != 0)
        {
            /* If this query is unable to return a list of items,
             * what should be done? Theoretically, if the user
             * knows the item number, the application should
             * be able to query the database for the desired information
             * (price). However, it is more likely that something
             * has gone wrong with the connection to the database and
             * any read operation against the database will fail. Still,
             * it should be given the benefit of the doubt…
             */

            g_print("Failure to retreive list of items...\n");

            /* …instead of a fatal_msgbox() call. If something
             * has really gone wrong, the calls to the database to
             * get the price of the item should produce the
             * fatal_msgbox() call.
             */
        }
    else g_print("Retrieved customer numbers from db...\n");

    /* Now iterate through the rows, get the values for customer number,
     * and add them to cbo_customer_number.
     */

    result_set = mysql_store_result (conx);
    while ((db_row = mysql_fetch_row (result_set)) != 0L)
        { clist_row[0] = db_row[0];
            clist_row[1] = db_row[1];
            clist_row[2] = db_row[2];
```

```
gtk_clist_append(GTK_CLIST(lookup_widget(frm_items_ordered,
                                      "clist_items")),
                      clist_row);
    }

}
```

speed_add() Function

Next, the normal course of events is that the user will use the widgets in the upper-left corner of frm_items_ordered to type in item numbers, tab to the Add button (cmd_add), and then repeat this cycle for the entire order. That is, when the customer is on the phone, they know what items they want and either the customer has those order numbers ready, or the person using the software knows the order numbers—at least the item numbers for the most common items. This will be called "speed add" and it is covered in Listing 7.7.

Listing 7.7   **Function** *speed_add()* **for Quickly Adding Items to the Order When the Item Number Is Known**

```
void speed_add()
{
    MYSQL_RES    *result_set;
    MYSQL_ROW    db_row;
    gchar        *sql;
    gchar        *clist_row[4] = {"", "", "", ""};
    gint         int_quantity;
    gchar        *str_quantity;
    gdouble      dbl_total_price;
    gchar        *str_total_price;
    gchar        *str_total_price_formatted;
    gchar        *str_order_total;
    gchar        *str_order_total_formatted;

    /* This function will be called whenever the user clicks on cmd_add,
     * which is in the upper-left corner of frm_items_ordered. This is
     * the "speedy" method of entering items, as opposed to the "slow"
     * method in function slow_add (the next function after this one).

     * First, get the item number and get that item's price from the
     * database.*/

    get_conx();
    sql = g_strconcat("select * from tbl_items where item = '",
                    gtk_editable_get_chars(
                        GTK_EDITABLE(lookup_widget(frm_items_ordered,
                                                  "entry_item_number"
                        )) , 0, -1), "'", 0L);
```

continues

Listing 7.7 **Continued**

```
g_print("sql is %s\n", sql);

if (mysql_query (conx, sql) != 0)
    {
      g_print("Failure to retreive item information from mysql_query...\n");
    }
else
    {
        result_set = mysql_store_result (conx);

        /* If the program gets to this point, it has issued a correct
         * SQL statement against the database; however, the item
         * number could be a non-existent item number. As with
         * fill_customer_info(), the software needs to check that the
         * number of rows is greater than 0.*/

        if (mysql_num_rows (result_set) == 0)
        {
            g_print("Invalid Item Number...\n");
            gtk_statusbar_push(GTK_STATUSBAR(lookup_widget(frm_main,
                                "statusbar")), 1,
                                "Invalid Item Number...");

            /* If the user gets to this point, they should see that
             * no line has been added to the lower CList box. This is
             * an assumption that you would not want to make on a
             * project any larger than this one, but the way
             * this project is defined makes it an acceptable tradeoff.
             */

        }
        else
        {
            g_print("Retreived item information...\n");

            /* Now that the item number has been verified,
             * get quantity, do the math,
             * and add to clist_items_ordered.
             */

            db_row = mysql_fetch_row (result_set);

            /* The next two calls demonstrate how to get the same
             * information from a spinbutton as two different
             * data types - int and gchar*.*/

            int_quantity = gtk_spin_button_get_value_as_int(GTK_SPIN_BUTTON(
                                lookup_widget(frm_items_ordered,
                                "spinbutton_quantity")));
```

```
str_quantity = gtk_editable_get_chars(
                 GTK_EDITABLE(
                   lookup_widget(frm_items_ordered,
                   "spinbutton_quantity")
                 ), 0, -1);

dbl_total_price =  int_quantity * atof(db_row[2]);
g_print("dbl_total_price is %f\n", dbl_total_price);

str_total_price = g_strdup_printf("%f", dbl_total_price);

clist_row[0] = db_row[0];
clist_row[1] = db_row[1];
clist_row[2] = str_quantity;

/* Next, format the output by finding the decimal and then
 * including the next three characters for output as in
 * ".xx".*/

str_total_price_formatted = g_strndup(str_total_price,
                            strcspn(str_total_price, ".") + 3);

clist_row[3] = str_total_price_formatted;

gtk_clist_append(GTK_CLIST
               (lookup_widget(frm_items_ordered,
                              "clist_items_ordered")),
                   clist_row);

/* Finally, recalculate the total and fill in that
 * label. It is easier to keep a running tally than to
 * try to access the contents of the CList widget.
 */

dbl_order_total = dbl_order_total + dbl_total_price;

str_order_total = g_strdup_printf("%f", dbl_order_total);
str_order_total_formatted = g_strndup(str_order_total,
                            strcspn(str_order_total, ".") +3);

gtk_label_set_text(GTK_LABEL(lookup_widget
                            (frm_items_ordered,
                             "lbl_order_total_numeric")),
                  str_order_total_formatted
                );

      }
   }
}
```

slow_add() Function

Listing 7.8 is the code for the user that is going to click his way through the order. Here, the user will select an item from clist_items, click cmd_add_down (the Add button between the CList widgets), and repeat that process.

Listing 7.8 **Function *slow_add()* for Adding Items to the Order Using the Mouse**

```
void slow_add()
{

    /* This function is the more mouse-intensive way to add
     * ordered items to the list, which tends to make it
     * a slower way to add items. It is called when the
     * user clicks the "Add" button between the two
     * list boxes on frm_items_ordered.
     */

    GtkCList      *clist_target;
    gint          row_target = -1;

    gchar         *cell_item_number;
    gchar         *cell_item_description;
    gchar         *cell_item_price;

    gchar         *clist_row[4] = {"", "", "", ""};
    gint          int_quantity;
    gchar         *str_quantity;
    gdouble       dbl_total_price;
    gchar         *str_total_price;
    gchar         *str_total_price_formatted;
    gchar         *str_order_total;
    gchar         *str_order_total_formatted;

    clist_target = GTK_CLIST(lookup_widget(frm_items_ordered, "clist_items"));

    /* The following call gets the row that is selected, not focused.
     * The 0 is for the "0th" item in the list of selected rows.
     */

    row_target = (gint)g_list_nth_data( (clist_target)->selection, 0 );

    g_print("Row to move down is %i...\n", row_target);

    if (row_target == -1)
        {
            gtk_statusbar_push(GTK_STATUSBAR(lookup_widget(frm_main,
                                                           "statusbar")), 1,
                            "No Item Selected...");

            g_print("No Item selected...\n");

            return;
        }
```

```
/* The next three calls get the information about the
 * item selected in CList_items, the list of available
 * items that a customer can order. They retrieve the
 * item number, the description, and the price for
 * use later in the function.
 */

gtk_clist_get_text(GTK_CLIST(lookup_widget(frm_items_ordered,
                    "clist_items")),
                    row_target, 0, &cell_item_number);
gtk_clist_get_text(GTK_CLIST(lookup_widget(frm_items_ordered,
                    "clist_items")),
                    row_target, 1, &cell_item_description);
gtk_clist_get_text(GTK_CLIST(lookup_widget(frm_items_ordered,
                    "clist_items")),
                    row_target, 2, &cell_item_price);


/* Spinbutton1 is the spinbutton next to cmd_add_down, between the
 * two CList boxes. Forgot to change the name on that one… :-|
 */

int_quantity = gtk_spin_button_get_value_as_int(GTK_SPIN_BUTTON(
                              lookup_widget(frm_items_ordered,
                              "spinbutton1")));
str_quantity = gtk_editable_get_chars(
                          GTK_EDITABLE(
                              lookup_widget(frm_items_ordered,
                              "spinbutton1")
                          ), 0, -1);

/* Compute the price by multiplying quantity with price,
 * then prepare the CList_row[] array by setting the
 * values that will be added to the CList widget of
 * items the customer has ordered, clist_items_ordered.
 */

dbl_total_price =  int_quantity * atof(cell_item_price);
g_print("dbl_total_price is %f\n", dbl_total_price);

str_total_price = g_strdup_printf("%f", dbl_total_price);

clist_row[0] = cell_item_number;
clist_row[1] = cell_item_description;
clist_row[2] = str_quantity;

str_total_price_formatted = g_strndup(str_total_price,
                              strcspn(str_total_price, ".") + 3);

/* The previous function call set formatted the price correctly
 * for display; the next sets the last field in the array to
```

continues

Listing 7.8 **Continued**

```
 * that formatted price. Immediately after that, the clist_row[]
 * array is added to clist_items_ordered.
 */

clist_row[3] = str_total_price_formatted;

gtk_clist_append(GTK_CLIST
                     (lookup_widget(frm_items_ordered,
                                    "clist_items_ordered")),
                 clist_row);

/* Recalculate the running total. */

dbl_order_total = dbl_order_total + dbl_total_price;
str_order_total = g_strdup_printf("%f", dbl_order_total);
str_order_total_formatted = g_strndup(str_order_total,
                                      strcspn(str_order_total, ".") +3);

gtk_label_set_text(GTK_LABEL(lookup_widget
                             (frm_items_ordered,
                              "lbl_order_total_numeric")),
                 str_order_total_formatted
                 );

}
```

remove_ordered_item() Function

Next follows the code to remove a line item that has been added. Listing 7.9 covers removing an item from clist_items_ordered, which also subtracts the appropriate amount from the order total.

Listing 7.9 **Function** *remove_ordered_item()* **from** *sesi_utils.c*

```
void remove_ordered_item()
{

   /* This function removes a line from clist_items_ordered,
    * most likely because the order entry clerk made a mistake
    * or the customer changed his mind. In either case,
    * the item needs to be removed and the order total price
    * must be recalculated.
    */

   GtkCList   *clist_target;
   gint       row_target = -1;
   gchar      *cell_line_item_price;
```

```
clist_target = GTK_CLIST(lookup_widget(frm_items_ordered,
                                  "clist_items_ordered"));

/* The following call gets the row that is selected, not focused.
 * The 0 is for the "0th" item in the list of selected rows.
 */

row_target = (gint)g_list_nth_data( (clist_target)->selection, 0 );

g_print("Row to delete is %i...\n", row_target);

if (row_target == -1)
    {
        gtk_statusbar_push(GTK_STATUSBAR(lookup_widget(frm_main,
                              "statusbar")), 1,
                              "Select an item to remove first...");

        g_print("No Item selected from clist_items_ordered...\n");

        return;
    }

/* …else continue with the remove operation… */

/* First, get the amount of this line item so that it can be
 * subtracted from the total before the line is deleted.
 */

gtk_clist_get_text(GTK_CLIST(lookup_widget(frm_items_ordered,
                        "clist_items_ordered")),
                        row_target, 3, &cell_line_item_price);

dbl_order_total = dbl_order_total - atof(cell_line_item_price);

gtk_label_set_text(GTK_LABEL(lookup_widget
                              (frm_items_ordered,
                               "lbl_order_total_numeric")),
                        g_strdup_printf("%f", dbl_order_total)
                        );

/* Finally, remove the line item that is selected. */

gtk_clist_remove(clist_target, row_target);
}
```

select_item() Function

The select_item() function is a utility function that is used in several places. It takes a
single input parameter, searches clist_items for the input parameter, and then selects
and shows the selected row in clist_items. The code is in Listing 7.10.

Listing 7.10 **Function** *select_item()* **from** *sesi_utils.c,* **Which Selects and Shows the Line in** *clist_items* **That Corresponds to Its Parameter**

```c
void select_item(gchar *target_item_num)
{
  /* This function is required for frm_items_ordered to
   * work - the find item widget will search the database for an
   * item number and then call this function to select that item in
   * clist_items. When given as an input for an item number (the
   * only parameter to this function), this function iterates
   * through all lines in clist_items and finds the one that
   * matches the input parameter.
   */

  GtkCList    *target_clist;
  gint        number_of_rows;
  gint        counter;
  gchar       *clist_item_number;

  g_print("Target item number is:  %s...\n", target_item_num);

  target_clist = GTK_CLIST(lookup_widget(frm_items_ordered, "clist_items"));

  /* First, find out how many rows are in the CList widget.
   */

  number_of_rows = ((target_clist)->rows);

  g_print("number_of_rows is:  %i", number_of_rows);

  /* Iterate through all the rows searching for the target row. */

  for(counter = 0; counter < number_of_rows; counter++)
    {
        gtk_clist_get_text(GTK_CLIST(lookup_widget(
                                    frm_items_ordered,
                                    "clist_items")),
                        counter, 0, &clist_item_number);

        if (g_strcasecmp(clist_item_number, target_item_num) == 0)
          {
            g_print("Found target line %i in clist_items..\n", counter);
            break;
          }
        else
          {
            /* continue searching... */
          }

    }
```

```
/* When you have found the desired line in clist_items, select and move it
 * into view in the window.
 */

gtk_clist_select_row(target_clist, counter, 0);
gtk_clist_moveto(target_clist, counter, 0, 0, 0);

}
```

enter_found_items() Function

If the user needs to search for an item, he will open up frm_find_item. There, the function enter_found_items() (shown in in Listing 7.11) will enable him to search the database for matches on the desired character string (the single parameter). With a list of matching items, enter_found_items() (see Listing 7.11) will populate the CList widget in frm_find_item. The user will then pick from that list a single row to return to frm_items_ordered.

Listing 7.11   Function *enter_found_items()* from *sesi_utils.c*; It Searches the Database for Matching Items and Populates the CList Widget in *frm_find_item*

```
void enter_found_items(gchar *str)
{

    /* This function will search the tbl_items table for possible
     * matches to the user's text (which is "str", the parameter passed
     * into this function). It will display those found records
     * in clist_found_items.
     *
     * First, connect to the database and get a result set of
     * the possible rows.
     *
     * Remember that the search will be on a string (the
     * input parameter), against
     * all possible columns that could match a string,
     * that is, all non-numeric fields.
     */

    MYSQL_RES    *result_set;
    MYSQL_ROW    db_row;
    gchar        *sql;
    gchar        *clist_row[3] = {"", "", ""};
    gint         counter;
    gint         number_of_rows;

    g_print("starting create_find_item_clist...\n");

    get_conx();
```

continues

Listing 7.11 **Continued**

```c
/* In MySQL, the percent character is the wildcard for all
 * possible matches.
 */

sql = g_strconcat("select * from tbl_items where item like '%",
                  str,
                  "%' or description like '%",
                  str,
                  "%'",
                  0L);

g_print("sql is :  %s\n", sql);

if (mysql_query (conx, sql) != 0)
   {
     g_print("Failure to retreive find item data from mysql_query...\n");
   }
else
   {

       /* Retrieve the results and clear clist_found_items. */

       result_set = mysql_store_result (conx);
       db_row = mysql_fetch_row (result_set);

       /* Clear the CList widget of all items. */
       gtk_clist_clear(GTK_CLIST(lookup_widget(frm_find_item,
                       "clist_found_items")));

       number_of_rows = mysql_num_rows(result_set);
       g_print("number_of_rows is:  %i", number_of_rows);

       /* Iterate through the result set and add each row to
        * clist_found_items.
        */

       for (counter = 0; counter < number_of_rows; counter++)
         {
             clist_row[0] = db_row[0];
             clist_row[1] = db_row[1];
             clist_row[2] = db_row[2];

             gtk_clist_append(GTK_CLIST(lookup_widget
                             (frm_find_item,
                              "clist_found_items")),
                              clist_row);

             /* Fetch the next row. */
```

```
                db_row = mysql_fetch_row (result_set);
            }
        }

    g_print("exiting create_find_item_clist...\n");

}
```

select_customer() and *enter_found_customers()* Functions

Function `enter_found_customers()` (see Listing 7.12) performs a similar function in frm_find_customer. Function `select_customer()` (also Listing 7.12) sets cbo_customer_number to a specified customer and refreshes the data displayed in frm_main. Both are called from the callback initiated by the Done button on frm_find_customer.

Listing 7.12 **Functions** *select_customer()* **and** *enter_found_customers()* **from** *sesi_utils.c*

```
void select_customer(gchar *target_customer_num)
{

    /* Set cbo_customer_number to target_customer_num, the
     * parameter passed in, and then call fill_customer_info.
     */

    GtkCombo *cbo;

    cbo = GTK_COMBO(lookup_widget(frm_main, "cbo_customer_number"));
    gtk_entry_set_text(GTK_ENTRY(cbo->entry), target_customer_num);

    /* Use the existing customer information fill routine. */

    fill_customer_info();
}

void enter_found_customers(gchar *str)
{

    /* This function searches for matches to str, the parameter
     * passed in, in tbl_customers, and then enters those
     * records to clist_found_customer.
     *
     * First, connect to the database and get a result_set of
     * the possible rows.
     *
     * Remember that the search will be on a string, against
     * all possible columns that could match a string.
     */

    MYSQL_RES    *result_set;
```

continues

Listing 7.12 **Continued**

```
MYSQL_ROW    db_row;
gchar        *sql;
gchar        *clist_row[17] = {"","","","","",
                               "","","","","",
                               "","","","","",
                               "",""};

gint         counter;
gint         number_of_rows;

g_print("starting enter_found_customer...\n");

get_conx();

/* In MySQL, the percent character is the wildcard for all
 * possible matches.
 */

sql = g_strconcat("select * from tbl_customers where name like '%",
                  str,
                  "%' or ship_to_addr1 like '%",
                  str,
                  "%' or ship_to_addr2 like '%",
                  str,
                  "%' or ship_to_city like '%",
                  str,
                  "%' or ship_to_state like '%",
                  str,
                  "%' or ship_to_zip like '%",
                  str,
                  "%' or bill_to_addr1 like '%",
                  str,
                  "%' or bill_to_addr2 like '%",
                  str,
                  "%' or bill_to_city like '%",
                  str,
                  "%' or bill_to_state like '%",
                  str,
                  "%' or bill_to_zip like '%",
                  str,
                  "%' or contact_first like '%",
                  str,
                  "%' or contact_last like '%",
                  str,
                  "%' or phone like '%",
                  str,
                  "%' or title like '%",
                  str,
                  "%' or comments like '%",
                  str,
                  "%'",
                  0L);
```

```
g_print("sql is :   %s\n", sql);

if (mysql_query (conx, sql) != 0)
   {
     g_print("Failure to retreive find item data from mysql_query...\n");
   }
else
   {

       /* The query succeeded, so store the result
        * and prepare the CList widget to display the
        * results.
        */

       result_set = mysql_store_result (conx);
       db_row = mysql_fetch_row (result_set);

       /* Clear the CList widget of all items. */
       gtk_clist_clear(GTK_CLIST(lookup_widget(frm_find_customer,
                                         "clist_found_customer")));

       number_of_rows = mysql_num_rows(result_set);
       g_print("number_of_rows is:  %i", number_of_rows);

       /* Fill the array, which will in turn fill
        * clist found customer.
        */

       for (counter = 0; counter < number_of_rows; counter++)
         {
               clist_row[0] = db_row[0];
               clist_row[1] = db_row[1];
               clist_row[2] = db_row[2];
               clist_row[3] = db_row[3];
               clist_row[4] = db_row[4];
               clist_row[5] = db_row[5];
               clist_row[6] = db_row[6];
               clist_row[7] = db_row[7];
               clist_row[8] = db_row[8];
               clist_row[9] = db_row[9];
               clist_row[10] = db_row[10];
               clist_row[11] = db_row[11];
               clist_row[12] = db_row[12];
               clist_row[13] = db_row[13];
               clist_row[14] = db_row[14];
               clist_row[15] = db_row[15];
               clist_row[16] = db_row[16];
               clist_row[17] = db_row[17];

               /* Finally, append the row to clist_found_customer. */
```

continues

Listing 7.12   **Continued**

```
                gtk_clist_append(GTK_CLIST(lookup_widget
                                 (frm_find_customer,
                                  "clist_found_customer")),
                                  clist_row);

            /* Fetch the next row. */

                db_row = mysql_fetch_row (result_set);
            }
        }
    }
```

---

write_order() Function

Function `write_order()` produces the final result of this application. Its purpose is to create a filename and then write the order to that disk file. In this case (lacking a better option), it writes to the current directory. It is rather long but fairly straightforward; see Listing 7.13

Listing 7.13   **Function *write_order()* from *sesi_utils.c.* At the End of the Listing are Functions *right_pad()* and *left_pad()*, Which are Only Used by *write_order()*.**

```
void write_order()
{
    /* This function computes an appropriate filename, gathers
     * data from the various forms in the application, and writes
     * an order to disk. It uses the current directory by default.
     */

    gchar       *str_now;
    time_t      now;
    GtkCList    *target_clist;
    gint        number_of_line_items;
    GtkCombo    *cbo;
    gchar       *cust_name_num;
    gchar       *file_name;
    FILE        *fp;
    gchar       *str_ship_to_csz, *str_bill_to_csz;
    gint        counter;
    gchar       *cell_item_number, *cell_description, *cell_quantity, *cell_price;
    gchar       *str_order_total, *str_order_total_formatted;

    /* First, some basic error checking.
     * Has a customer been selected?
     */

    cbo = GTK_COMBO(lookup_widget(frm_main, "cbo_customer_number"));
```

```
if (g_strcasecmp(gtk_entry_get_text (GTK_ENTRY(cbo->entry)), "New") == 0)
    {
        g_print("New customer record, not valid for writing an order...\n");
        gtk_statusbar_push(GTK_STATUSBAR(lookup_widget(frm_main,
                        "statusbar")), 1,
                        "New is not a valid customer number "
                        "for order generation...");
        return;
    }

if (g_strcasecmp(gtk_entry_get_text (GTK_ENTRY(cbo->entry)), "") == 0)
    {
        g_print("No customer record, not valid for writing an order...\n");
        gtk_statusbar_push(GTK_STATUSBAR(lookup_widget(frm_main,
                        "statusbar")), 1,
                        "Customer Number can not be blank...");
        return;
    }

/* Have items been ordered? */

target_clist = GTK_CLIST(lookup_widget(frm_items_ordered,
                        "clist_items_ordered"));
number_of_line_items = ((target_clist)->rows);

if (number_of_line items == 0)
  {
      gtk_statusbar_push(GTK_STATUSBAR(lookup_widget(frm_main,
                        "statusbar")), 1,
                        "No items have been selected for this invoice...");

      return;
  }

/* When the error checking is done, it is time to generate a
 * filename for this order.
 *
 * First come the customer name and number.
 */

cust_name_num = g_strconcat(gtk_entry_get_text(
                        GTK_ENTRY(lookup_widget(frm_main,
                                "entry_customer_name"))),
                        ".",
                        gtk_entry_get_text(GTK_ENTRY(cbo->entry)),
                        ".",
                        0L
                        );

g_print("cust_name_num is: %s\n", cust_name_num);
```

continues

Listing 7.13 **Continued**

```
/* Next are the date and time of the order.
 *
 * The g_strstrip() call is necessary because the ctime() call
 * returns a CR/LF character at the end of the string. g_strstrip()
 * removes all non-printable characters from the start and end
 * of the string that it is given as its parameter.
 */

time(&now);
str_now = g_strstrip((gchar *) ctime(&now));

g_print("ctime returns:  %s\n", str_now);

/* Now you'll put them all together to get the filename of the order.
 * Note that the spaces and colons will be replaced by dots.
 */

file_name = g_strconcat(cust_name_num, str_now, ".txt", 0L);
g_print("file_name is %s\n", file_name);

/* The g_strdelimit() function replaces all occurrences, any
 * member of the second parameter with the first. In this
 * case, any space, colon, OR comma will be replaced with
 * a period.
 *
 * Note that the second parameter is surrounded by double
 * quotes, and the third parameter is surrounded by single quotes.
 *
 * The idea here is to create a filename that is sufficiently
 * descriptive and will not cause problems on the largest
 * number of operating systems. This application was
 * built with the idea that the output file produced by this
 * function would be transferred to another machine – most
 * likely an FTP transfer to a Win32 machine.
 */

file_name = g_strdelimit(file_name, " :,", '.');

g_print("file_name is now %s\n", file_name);

/* Now to open a file handle for writing. */

if ((fp = fopen (file_name, "w")) == 0L)
    {
        /* Could not write to the file for some reason. */
        gtk_statusbar_push(GTK_STATUSBAR(lookup_widget(frm_main,
                            "statusbar")), 1,
                            "Unable to write to file, "
                            "contact system administrator...");
    }
else
    {
```

```
/* File handle is open for write operation. */
gtk_statusbar_push(GTK_STATUSBAR(lookup_widget(frm_main,
                   "statusbar")), 1,
                   "File is open for write operation...");

/* This file will be fixed width, and to be on the safe side,
 * it will be assumed that the "page" is 70 columns wide instead
 * of the normal 80.
 */

/* First, write the header information: date, time, customer name
 * and number, and so on.
 */

fprintf(fp, "Specialty Electrical Supply, Inc."); fprintf(fp, "\n");
fprintf(fp, "Shipping Order Form");               fprintf(fp, "\n");
fprintf(fp, "================================="); fprintf(fp, "\n");
                                                  fprintf(fp, "\n");

fprintf(fp, str_now);              fprintf(fp, "\n");
fprintf(fp, cust_name_num);        fprintf(fp, "\n");
                                   fprintf(fp, "\n");

/* Write the addresses to the file in a side-by-side format. */

fprintf(fp, right_pad("Ship to Address", " ", 35));
fprintf(fp, "Bill to Address"); fprintf(fp, "\n");

fprintf(fp, right_pad(gtk_entry_get_text(GTK_ENTRY(
                      lookup_widget(frm_main,
                      "entry_ship_to_addr1"))), " ", 35));
fprintf(fp, gtk_entry_get_text(GTK_ENTRY(lookup_widget(frm_main,
                      "entry_bill_to_addr1"))));
fprintf(fp, "\n");

fprintf(fp, right_pad(gtk_entry_get_text(GTK_ENTRY(
                      lookup_widget(frm_main,
                      "entry_ship_to_addr2"))), " ", 35));
fprintf(fp, gtk_entry_get_text(GTK_ENTRY(lookup_widget(frm_main,
                      "entry_bill_to_addr2"))));
fprintf(fp, "\n");

/* Gather the city, state, and ZIP info into one string, and then pad it.
 */

str_ship_to_csz = g_strconcat
                  (
                      gtk_entry_get_text(GTK_ENTRY(
                      lookup_widget(frm_main,
                      "entry_ship_to_city"))), " ",
                      gtk_entry_get_text(GTK_ENTRY(
```

continues

Listing 7.13 **Continued**

```
                                      lookup_widget(frm_main,
                                      "entry_ship_to_st"))), "   ",
                                gtk_entry_get_text(GTK_ENTRY(
                                      lookup_widget(frm_main,
                                      "entry_ship_to_zip"))),
                                0L
                        );

        str_bill_to_csz = g_strconcat
                        (
                                gtk_entry_get_text(GTK_ENTRY(
                                      lookup_widget(frm_main,
                                      "entry_bill_to_city"))), " ",
                                gtk_entry_get_text(GTK_ENTRY(
                                      lookup_widget(frm_main,
                                      "entry_bill_to_st"))), "   ",
                                gtk_entry_get_text(GTK_ENTRY(
                                      lookup_widget(frm_main,
                                      "entry_bill_to_zip"))),
                                0L
                        );

        fprintf(fp, right_pad(str_ship_to_csz, " ", 35));
        fprintf(fp, str_bill_to_csz);
        fprintf(fp, "\n");
        fprintf(fp, "\n");

        fprintf(fp, "Order Detail Information\n");
        fprintf(fp, "========================\n");
        fprintf(fp, "\n");

        fprintf(fp, right_pad("Item Num", "-", 12));
        fprintf(fp, right_pad("Item Description", "-", 37));
        fprintf(fp, left_pad("Quantity", "-", 8));
        fprintf(fp, left_pad("Price", "-", 13));
        fprintf(fp, "\n");

        /* Iterate through clist_items_ordered and write the
         * order information for each line.
         */

        for (counter = 0; counter < number_of_line_items; counter++)
          {
             gtk_clist_get_text(target_clist, counter, 0, &cell_item_number);
             gtk_clist_get_text(target_clist, counter, 1, &cell_description);
             gtk_clist_get_text(target_clist, counter, 2, &cell_quantity);
             gtk_clist_get_text(target_clist, counter, 3, &cell_price);
```

```
                    fprintf(fp, right_pad(cell_item_number, " ", 12));
                    fprintf(fp, right_pad(cell_description, " ", 40));
                    fprintf(fp, left_pad(cell_quantity, " ", 5));
                    fprintf(fp, left_pad(cell_price, " ", 13));

                    fprintf(fp, "\n");

                    str_order_total = g_strdup_printf("%f", dbl_order_total);
                    str_order_total_formatted = g_strndup(str_order_total,
                                      strcspn(str_order_total, ".") +3);

                }
            fprintf(fp, left_pad("=============", " ", 70)); fprintf(fp, "\n");
            fprintf(fp, left_pad(str_order_total_formatted, " ", 70));

            fprintf(fp, "\n");

            fprintf(fp, "Order Comments\n");
            fprintf(fp, "==============\n");

            fprintf(fp, gtk_editable_get_chars(GTK_EDITABLE(lookup_widget(frm_main,
                    "txt_order_comments")), 0, -1));

            fprintf(fp, "\n");

            fclose(fp);

            gtk_statusbar_push(GTK_STATUSBAR(lookup_widget(frm_main,
                            "statusbar")), 1,
                            "Order file has been created.  "
                            "Push exit to close...");
        }

}

gchar *right_pad(gchar *in_str, gchar *pad_char, gint final_length)
{

    /* This function pads characters to the right of in_str, to
     * a length of final_string.
     */

    while (strlen(in_str) < final_length)
      {
         in_str = g_strconcat(in_str, pad_char, 0L);
      }

    return in_str;
}
```

continues

Listing 7.13 **Continued**

```
gchar *left_pad(gchar *in_str, gchar *pad_char, gint final_length)
{
   /* This function pads characters to the left of in_str, to
    * a length of final_string.
    */



   while (strlen(in_str) < final_length)
     {
         in_str = g_strconcat(pad_char, in_str, 0L);
     }

   return in_str;
}
```

update_database() function

The update_database() function writes changes to the database. It takes the "don't force it, just get a bigger hammer" approach: It overwrites all available fields in the record based on the table key ("num," the customer number). See Listing 7.14.

Listing 7.14 **Function** *update_database()*, **Which Writes Updates to** *tbl_customers*

```
void update_database()
{
   /* This routine will update the sesi database when changes to a
    * customer record have been made.
    */

   gchar    *sql;
   GtkCombo *cbo;

   /* Update tbl_customers; don't try to figure out which text
    * box was edited, just update all fields.
    */

   get_conx();

   cbo = GTK_COMBO(lookup_widget(frm_main, "cbo_customer_number"));

   sql = g_strconcat("update tbl_customers set ",
                     "name = '",
gtk_entry_get_text(GTK_ENTRY(lookup_widget(frm_main,
                              "entry_customer_name"))), "', ",
                  "ship_to_addr1 = '", gtk_entry_get_text(GTK_ENTRY(
                                     lookup_widget(frm_main,
                                     "entry_ship_to_addr1"))), "', ",
```

```
              "ship_to_addr2 = '", gtk_entry_get_text(GTK_ENTRY(
                                   lookup_widget(frm_main,
                                   "entry_ship_to_addr2"))), "', ",
              "ship_to_city = '", gtk_entry_get_text(GTK_ENTRY(
                                   lookup_widget(frm_main,
                                   "entry_ship_to_city"))), "', ",
              "ship_to_state = '", gtk_entry_get_text(GTK_ENTRY(
                                   lookup_widget(frm_main,
                                   "entry_ship_to_st"))), "', ",
              "ship_to_zip = '", gtk_entry_get_text(GTK_ENTRY(
                                   lookup_widget(frm_main,
                                   "entry_ship_to_zip"))), "', ",
              "bill_to_addr1 = '", gtk_entry_get_text(GTK_ENTRY(
                                   lookup_widget(frm_main,
                                   "entry_bill_to_addr1"))), "', ",
              "bill_to_addr2 = '", gtk_entry_get_text(GTK_ENTRY(
                                   lookup_widget(frm_main,
                                   "entry_bill_to_addr2"))), "', ",
              "bill_to_city = '", gtk_entry_get_text(GTK_ENTRY(
                                   lookup_widget(frm_main,
                                   "entry_bill_to_city"))), "', ",
              "bill_to_state = '", gtk_entry_get_text(GTK_ENTRY(
                                   lookup_widget(frm_main,
                                   "entry_bill_to_st"))), "', ",
              "bill_to_zip = '", gtk_entry_get_text(GTK_ENTRY(
                                   lookup widget(frm_main,
                                   "entry_bill_to_zip"))), "', ",
              "contact_first = '", gtk_entry_get_text(GTK_ENTRY(
                                   lookup_widget(frm_main,
                                   "entry_first"))), "', ",
              "contact_last = '", gtk_entry_get_text(GTK_ENTRY(
                                   lookup_widget(frm_main,
                                   "entry_last"))), "', ",
              "phone = '", gtk_entry_get_text(GTK_ENTRY(
                                   lookup_widget(frm_main,
                                   "entry_phone"))), "', ",
              "title = '", gtk_entry_get_text(GTK_ENTRY(
                                   lookup_widget(frm_main,
                                   "entry_title"))), "', ",
              "comments = '", gtk_editable_get_chars(GTK_EDITABLE(
                                   lookup_widget(frm_main,
                                   "txt_customer_comments")),
                                   0, -1), "' ",
              "where num = ", gtk_entry_get_text(GTK_ENTRY(cbo->entry)),
              0L
              );

/* Finally, check for the success or failure of the update statment. */

if (mysql_query (conx, sql) != 0)
   {
```

continues

Listing 7.14   **Continued**

```
        g_print("Failure to update customer record,"
                " contact administrator...\n");
          gtk_statusbar_push(GTK_STATUSBAR(lookup_widget(frm_main,
                                             "statusbar")), 1,
               "Failure to update customer record, contact administrator.");
      }
    else
      {
       g_print("Customer record has been updated...\n");
         gtk_statusbar_push(GTK_STATUSBAR(lookup_widget(frm_main,
                          "statusbar")), 1,
                 "Customer record has been updated...");

      }

    g_print("sql is %s\n", sql);

  }
```

create_new_customer() Function

At the end of `sesi_utils.c` is the `create_new_customer()` function. The little piece of
magic it does is to insert a new record into the sesi database, inserting into the "name"
field. Recall that only the "num" and "name" fields are set to NOT NULL. By inserting a new record with only a "name," the autonumber feature of tbl_customers sets
the "num" field of the newly created record to max(num) +1. `create_new_customer()`
(shown in Listing 7.15) takes advantage of this behavior by creating the record and
then selecting the maximum number from the database, which should be the newly
created record (if that operation succeeded). It then sets frm_main to show the
newly created record. Note that the user can either select "New" from
cbo_customer_number or type it in. Either way, cbo_customer_number
changes to reflect the new customer number.

Listing 7.15   **The *create_new_customer()* Code from *sesi_utils.c***

```
void create_new_customer()
{
    /* This routine creates a new customer. It does this by inserting a
     * record where only the "num" and "name" fields are entered. The
     * autonumbering feature of MySQL automatically creates a new
     * customer number in the "num" field. The routine then returns the
     * maximum "num" from tbl_customers, which has to be the customer
     * just created.
     * With this customer number, frm_main is set to show the newly
     * created customer, which will have blank text and entry boxes.
     * The user then needs to enter the customer information, such as
```

```
 * phone, address, and so on.
 */

gchar       *sql;
MYSQL_RES   *result_set;
MYSQL_ROW   db_row;
get_conx();

sql = "insert into tbl_customers (name) values ('new customer')";

/* Send the query against the database. */

if (mysql_query (conx, sql) != 0)
    {
      g_print("Failure to create new customer record...\n");
       return;
    }
else
    {
        g_print("New customer record created...\n");
        gtk_statusbar_push(GTK_STATUSBAR(lookup_widget(frm_main,
                        "statusbar")), 1,
                        "New customer record has been created...");


    }

/* Refresh the combo box of customer numbers. */

gtk_combo_set_popdown_strings(GTK_COMBO(lookup_widget(frm_main,
                                "cbo_customer_number")),
                        get_customer_numbers());

/* Get the max(num) from tbl_customers, which should be the record
 * just created.
 */

sql = "select max(num) from tbl_customers";

if (mysql_query (conx, sql) != 0)
    {
      g_print("Failure to retrieve newly created customer record...\n");
       return;
    }
else
    {
        g_print("New customer record created...\n");

        result_set = mysql_store_result (conx);
        db_row = mysql_fetch_row (result_set);
```

continues

Listing 7.15   **Continued**

```
        /* Next set cbo_customer_number to the just-retrieved
         * customer number, which then displays all the fields
         * for that customer. In this case, those text and
         * entry boxes will be blank, all except for "name."
         */

        select_customer(db_row[0]);

        gtk_statusbar_push(GTK_STATUSBAR(lookup_widget(frm_main,
                        "statusbar")), 1,
                        "New customer record has been "
                        "created and retrieved, ready for edit...");


    }
}
```

Finishing *sesi_utils.c*

To finish up with sesi_utils.c, you'll start where you began. Listing 7.16 is the header section of sesi_utils.c after the code is finished.

Listing 7.16   **Final Header Configuration for** *sesi_utils.c*

```
#include <mysql.h>
#include <gtk/gtk.h>

/* stdlib.h is needed for atof function.
 * string.h is needed for the string search functions used
 *          when formatting numbers for output.
 * time.h   is needed for the write-to-file operation.
 * stdio.h  is also needed for the write-to-file operation.
 */

#include <stdlib.h>
#include <string.h>
#include <time.h>
#include <stdio.h>

#include "support.h"

/********** Global Variables *****************/

GtkWidget *frm_main;
GtkWidget *frm_items_ordered;
GtkWidget *frm_find_item;
GtkWidget *frm_find_customer;
```

```c
/* conx is the connection to the database; it is global,
 * and all functions in the application can use it to
 * access database "sesi".
 */

MYSQL      *conx;

/* dbl_order_total is a global variable that
 * can be calculated and accessed without
 * converting to and from gchar/gfloat/gdouble
 * and so on.
 */

gdouble    dbl_order_total = 0;

/* The variable need_to_save_edits tells whether
 * changes have been made to any of the text
 * widgets that display database fields from
 * tbl_customers. Because it needs to be checked
 * from many different places and at different times,
 * making it global saves time and effort.
 */

gboolean   need_to_save_edits;

/********** Function Prototypes **************/

void    connect_to_db();
void    fatal_msgbox(gchar *msg);
void    get_conx();
GList   *get_customer_numbers();
void    fill_customer_info();
void    clear_frm_main();
void    fill_frm_main(MYSQL_ROW in_row);
void    speed_add();
void    slow_add();
void    remove_ordered_item();
void    select_item(gchar *target_item_num);
void    enter_found_items(gchar *str);
void    select_customer(gchar *target_customer_num);
void    enter_found_customers(gchar *str);
void    write_order();
gchar   *right_pad(gchar *in_str, gchar *pad_char, gint final_length);
gchar   *left_pad(gchar *in_str, gchar *pad_char, gint final_length);
void    create_new_customer();
```

Connecting the Interface to the Utility Functions

The previous two sections concentrated on building the user interface and constructing the functions to do the majority of the work. Now put the two together to produce a final product.

callbacks.c

Listing 7.17 lists all the callbacks from `callbacks.c` that have any code in them other than what Glade produces. (If you download `callbacks.c` for this project from the companion Web site, you will see more functions than are in Listing 7.17.)

Listing 7.17 **Selected Functions from** *callbacks.c*

```
#ifdef HAVE_CONFIG_H
#  include <config.h>
#endif

#include <gtk/gtk.h>
#include <mysql.h>

#include "callbacks.h"
#include "interface.h"
#include "support.h"
#include "sesi_utils.h"

GtkWidget *frm_main;
GtkWidget *frm_items_ordered;
GtkWidget *frm_find_item;
GtkWidget *frm_find_customer;

MYSQL     *conx;
gboolean  need_to_save_edits;

gboolean
on_frm_main_delete_event                  (GtkWidget      *widget,
                                           GdkEvent       *event,
                                           gpointer        user_data)
{
    g_print("on_frm_main_delete_event...\n");
    gtk_main_quit();

    /* The "return FALSE;" call below interrupts the
     * delete event. Change it to true to "not delete"
     * the form. In this case, terminating the application is
     * the desired behavior. So it is left as FALSE (the
     * default by Glade).
     */
```

```
    return FALSE;
}


void
on_frm_main_realize                     (GtkWidget       *widget,
                                         gpointer         user_data)
{
   g_print("on_frm_main_realize event...\n");
   connect_to_db();

}


void
on_cmd_search_clicked                   (GtkButton       *button,
                                         gpointer         user_data)
{
   g_print("on_cmd_search_clicked event...\n");
   gtk_widget_show_all (frm_find_customer);

}


void
on_cmd_save_edits_clicked               (GtkButton       *button,
                                         gpointer         user_data)
{
   g_print("on_cmd_save_edits_clicked event...\n");
   update_database();

   need_to_save_edits = FALSE;
   gtk_widget_set_sensitive(lookup_widget(frm_main, "cmd_save_edits"), FALSE);
}


void
on_cmd_select_items_clicked             (GtkButton       *button,
                                         gpointer         user_data)
{
   g_print("on_cmd_select_items_clicked event...\n");
   gtk_widget_show_all(frm_items_ordered);

}


void
on_cmd_print_order_clicked              (GtkButton       *button,
                                         gpointer         user_data)
{
```

continues

Listing 7.17 **Continued**

```
    g_print("on_cmd_print_order_clicked event...\n");
    write_order();

}


void
on_cmd_exit_clicked                        (GtkButton       *button,
                                            gpointer        user_data)
{
    g_print("on_cmd_exit_clicked event...\n");
    gtk_widget_destroy(frm_main);
    gtk_main_quit();
}


void
on_combo_entry_customer_number_changed (GtkEditable      *editable,
                                        gpointer         user_data)
{
    g_print("on_combo_entry_customer_number_changed event...\n");
    fill_customer_info();

}


gboolean
on_frm_items_ordered_delete_event          (GtkWidget       *widget,
                                            GdkEvent        *event,
                                            gpointer        user_data)
{
    g_print("on_frm_items_ordered_delete_event...\n");

    /* If the user clicks the "X" (close window) button in the top
     * right of the window, GTK+ will proceed to delete the window.
     * This is not the desired behavior; it is preferred that the
     * user click the "Done" button, but since that cannot be
     * guaranteed, the software should still react correctly regardless
     * of which way the user attempts to close the window. Therefore,
     * the "return TRUE" call below halts the delete event for the
     * window. The next time the user opens the form, it will be
     * in the same state as it was when it was closed, which is
     * acceptable.
     *
     * Instead, hide the form first, then return the TRUE ("halt").
     */

    gtk_widget_hide(frm_items_ordered);
    return TRUE;
}
```

```
void
on_frm_items_ordered_realize             (GtkWidget      *widget,
                                          gpointer        user_data)
{
   g_print("on_frm_items_ordered_realize event...\n");
   fill_items_ordered();

}


void
on_frm_items_ordered_show                (GtkWidget      *widget,
                                          gpointer        user_data)
{
   g_print("on_frm_items_ordered_show event...\n");

   /* Here is a bit of an afterthought – the numeric
    * columns in the CList widgets should be right
    * justified. This can, of course, be set from Glade;
    * however, that portion of this project is considered
    * stable, and it shouldn't be messed with "after the
    * fact." Therefore, the justification can be set here,
    * and incorporated into the Glade project file for
    * the next version.
    */

   gtk_clist_set_column_justification(GTK_CLIST(
                             lookup_widget(frm_items_ordered,
                             "clist_items")),
                              2, GTK_JUSTIFY_RIGHT);
   gtk_clist_set_column_justification(GTK_CLIST(
                             lookup_widget(frm_items_ordered,
                             "clist_items_ordered")),
                              2, GTK_JUSTIFY_RIGHT);
   gtk_clist_set_column_justification(GTK_CLIST(
                             lookup_widget(frm_items_ordered,
                             "clist_items_ordered")),
                              3, GTK_JUSTIFY_RIGHT);
}


void
on_cmd_Add_clicked                       (GtkButton      *button,
                                          gpointer        user_data)
{
   g_print("on_cmd_Add_clicked event...\n");
   speed_add();

}
```

continues

Listing 7.17 **Continued**

```
void
on_cmd_search_for_item_clicked          (GtkButton      *button,
                                         gpointer       user_data)
{
   g_print("on_cmd_search_for_item_clicked event...\n");
   gtk_widget_show_all (frm_find_item);
}


void
on_cmd_done_clicked                      (GtkButton      *button,
                                         gpointer       user_data)
{
   g_print("on_cmd_done_clicked event...\n");
   gtk_widget_hide (frm_items_ordered);
}


void
on_cmd_add_down_clicked                  (GtkButton      *button,
                                         gpointer       user_data)
{
   g_print("on_cmd_add_down_clicked event...\n");
   slow_add();

}


void
on_cmd_remove_clicked                    (GtkButton      *button,
                                         gpointer       user_data)
{
   g_print("on_cmd_remove_clicked event...\n");
   remove_ordered_item();

}


void
on_clist_items_select_row                (GtkCList       *clist,
                                          gint           row,
                                          gint           column,
                                          GdkEvent       *event,
                                          gpointer       user_data)
{
   g_print("on_clist_items_select_row event...\n");
   g_print("row is %i...\n", row);

}
```

```
void
on_clist_items_ordered_select_row      (GtkCList    *clist,
                                         gint        row,
                                         gint        column,
                                         GdkEvent    *event,
                                         gpointer    user_data)
{
   g_print("on_clist_items_ordered_select_row event...\n");
   g_print("Row to remove is %i\n", row);
}



void
on_frm_main_show                        (GtkWidget   *widget,
                                         gpointer    user_data)
{
   g_print("on_frm_main_show event...\n");
   gtk_combo_set_popdown_strings(GTK_COMBO
                    (lookup_widget(frm_main, "cbo_customer_number")),
                    get_customer_numbers()
                    );

}



gboolean
on_frm_find_customer_delete_event       (GtkWidget   *widget,
                                         GdkEvent    *event,
                                         gpointer    user_data)
{
   g_print("on_frm_find_customer_delete_event...\n");

   /* Returning true halts the delete event. */

   gtk_widget_hide(frm_find_customer);
   return TRUE;
}



void
on_cmd_find_customer_clicked            (GtkButton   *button,
                                         gpointer    user_data)
{
   g_print("on_cmd_find_customer_clicked event...\n");
   enter_found_customers((gchar *) gtk_editable_get_chars(GTK_EDITABLE(
                    lookup_widget(frm_find_customer, "entry_find_customer")),
                    0, -1));
}
```

continues

Listing 7.17 **Continued**

```
void
on_cmd_find_customer_done_clicked        (GtkButton      *button,
                                          gpointer        user_data)

{
    gchar      *target_customer;
    GtkCList   *clist_target;
    gint       row_target;

    g_print("on_cmd_find_customer_done_clicked event...\n");

    /* Get the customer number of the selected row in
     * clist_found_customer, and send it to select_customer().
     */

    clist_target = GTK_CLIST(lookup_widget(frm_find_customer,
                             "clist_found_customer"));
    row_target = (gint) g_list_nth_data ( (clist_target)->selection, 0);
    gtk_clist_get_text(clist_target,
                       row_target, 0, &target_customer);

    g_print("Target customer is:  %s\n", target_customer);

    select_customer(target_customer);

    /* Hide the form. */

    gtk_widget_hide (frm_find_customer);
}



gboolean
on_frm_find_item_delete_event            (GtkWidget       *widget,
                                          GdkEvent        *event,
                                          gpointer        user_data)

{
    g_print("on_frm_find_item_delete_event...\n");

    /* Returning true halts the delete event. */

    gtk_widget_hide(frm_find_item);
    return TRUE;
}



void
on_cmd_find_item_clicked                 (GtkButton       *button,
                                          gpointer        user_data)

{
    g_print("on_cmd_find_item_clicked event...\n");
```

```
    enter_found_items((gchar *) gtk_editable_get_chars(GTK_EDITABLE(
                        lookup_widget(frm_find_item, "entry_find_item")),
                        0, -1));
}


void
on_cmd_find_item_done_clicked        (GtkButton      *button,
                                      gpointer       user_data)
{
   gchar       *target_item;
   GtkCList    *clist_target;
   gint        row_target;

   g_print("on_cmd_find_item_done_clicked event...\n");

   /* Get the item number of the selected row in clist_items_found,
    * and send it to select_item().
    */

   clist_target = GTK_CLIST(lookup_widget(frm_find_item, "clist_found_items"));
   row_target = (gint) g_list_nth_data ( (clist_target)->selection, 0);
   gtk_clist_get_text(clist_target,
                        row_target, 0, &target_item);

   select_item(target_item);

   /* Hide the form. */

   gtk_widget_hide (frm_find_item);
}


void
on_entry_customer_name_changed        (GtkEditable    *editable,
                                       gpointer       user_data)
{
   g_print("on_entry_customer_name_changed event...\n");
   gtk_widget_set_sensitive(lookup_widget(frm_main, "cmd_save_edits"), TRUE);
   need_to_save_edits = TRUE;
}


void
on_entry_last_changed        (GtkEditable    *editable,
                              gpointer       user_data)
{
   g_print("on_entry_last_changed event...\n");
   gtk_widget_set_sensitive(lookup_widget(frm_main, "cmd_save_edits"), TRUE);
   need_to_save_edits = TRUE;
}
```

continues

Listing 7.17 **Continued**

```
void
on_entry_first_changed                 (GtkEditable    *editable,
                                        gpointer        user_data)
{
   g_print("on_entry_first_changed event...\n");
   gtk_widget_set_sensitive(lookup_widget(frm_main, "cmd_save_edits"), TRUE);
   need_to_save_edits = TRUE;
}


void
on_entry_title_changed                 (GtkEditable    *editable,
                                        gpointer        user_data)
{
   g_print("on_entry_title_changed event...\n");
   gtk_widget_set_sensitive(lookup_widget(frm_main, "cmd_save_edits"), TRUE);
   need_to_save_edits = TRUE;
}


void
on_entry_phone_changed                 (GtkEditable    *editable,
                                        gpointer        user_data)
{
   g_print("on_entry_phone_changed event...\n");
   gtk_widget_set_sensitive(lookup_widget(frm_main, "cmd_save_edits"), TRUE);
   need_to_save_edits = TRUE;
}


void
on_entry_ship_to_addr1_changed         (GtkEditable    *editable,
                                        gpointer        user_data)
{
   g_print("on_entry_ship_to_addr1_changed event...\n");
   gtk_widget_set_sensitive(lookup_widget(frm_main, "cmd_save_edits"), TRUE);
   need_to_save_edits = TRUE;
}


void
on_entry_ship_to_addr2_changed         (GtkEditable    *editable,
                                        gpointer        user_data)
{
   g_print("on_entry_ship_to_addr2_changed event...\n");
   gtk_widget_set_sensitive(lookup_widget(frm_main, "cmd_save_edits"), TRUE);
   need_to_save_edits = TRUE;
}
```

```
void
on_entry_bill_to_addr2_changed             (GtkEditable      *editable,
                                            gpointer         user_data)
{
   g_print("on_entry_bill_to_addr2_changed event...\n");
   gtk_widget_set_sensitive(lookup_widget(frm_main, "cmd_save_edits"), TRUE);
   need_to_save_edits = TRUE;
}


void
on_entry_ship_to_city_changed              (GtkEditable      *editable,
                                            gpointer         user_data)
{
   g_print("on_entry_ship_to_city_changed event...\n");
   gtk_widget_set_sensitive(lookup_widget(frm_main, "cmd_save_edits"), TRUE);
   need_to_save_edits = TRUE;
}


void
on_entry_ship_to_st_changed                (GtkEditable      *editable,
                                            gpointer         user_data)
{
   g_print("on_entry_ship_to_st_changed event...\n");
   gtk_widget_set_sensitive(lookup_widget(frm_main, "cmd_save_edits"), TRUE);
   need_to_save_edits = TRUE;
}


void
on_entry_ship_to_zip_changed               (GtkEditable      *editable,
                                            gpointer         user_data)
{
   g_print("on_entry_ship_to_zip_changed event...\n");
   gtk_widget_set_sensitive(lookup_widget(frm_main, "cmd_save_edits"), TRUE);
   need_to_save_edits = TRUE;
}


void
on_entry_bill_to_city_changed              (GtkEditable      *editable,
                                            gpointer         user_data)
{
   g_print("on_entry_bill_to_city_changed event...\n");
   gtk_widget_set_sensitive(lookup_widget(frm_main, "cmd_save_edits"), TRUE);
   need_to_save_edits = TRUE;
}
```

continues

Listing 7.17   **Continued**

```
void
on_entry_bill_to_st_changed          (GtkEditable      *editable,
                                      gpointer         user_data)
{
   g_print("on_entry_bill_to_st_changed event...\n");
   gtk_widget_set_sensitive(lookup_widget(frm_main, "cmd_save_edits"), TRUE);
   need_to_save_edits = TRUE;
}


void
on_entry_bill_to_zip_changed         (GtkEditable      *editable,
                                      gpointer         user_data)
{
   g_print("on_entry_bill_to_zip_changed event...\n");
   gtk_widget_set_sensitive(lookup_widget(frm_main, "cmd_save_edits"), TRUE);
   need_to_save_edits = TRUE;
}


void
on_txt_customer_comments_changed     (GtkEditable      *editable,
                                      gpointer         user_data)
{
   g_print("on_txt_customer_comments_changed event...\n");
   gtk_widget_set_sensitive(lookup_widget(frm_main, "cmd_save_edits"), TRUE);
   need_to_save_edits = TRUE;
}
```

main.c

In closing, Listing 7.18 is `main.c` from this application. Once Glade has written this file, it will not overwrite it. That means you can change it, but if you need Glade to create a new one, you will have to delete or rename the existing one.

Listing 7.18   *main.c* **For the SESI Order Application**

```
/*
 * Initial main.c file generated by Glade. Edit as required.
 * Glade will not overwrite this file.
 */

#ifdef HAVE_CONFIG_H
#  include <config.h>
#endif

#include <gtk/gtk.h>
#include <mysql.h>
```

```
#include "interface.h"
#include "support.h"

GtkWidget *frm_main;
GtkWidget *frm_items_ordered;
GtkWidget *frm_find_item;
GtkWidget *frm_find_customer;

MYSQL *conx;

int
main (int argc, char *argv[])
{
  gtk_set_locale ();
  gtk_init (&argc, &argv);

  /*
   * The following code was added by Glade to create one of each
   * component (except popup menus), just so that you see something
   * after building the project. Delete any components you
   * don't want shown initially.
   */
  frm_main = create_frm_main ();
  gtk_widget_show (frm_main);

  frm_items_ordered = create_frm_items_ordered();

  frm_find_item = create_frm_find_item();

  frm_find_customer = create_frm_find_customer();

  gtk_main ();
  return 0;
}
```

Notice that all four of the windows are created, but only frm_main is shown at this point. The others are shown and hidden as needed.

Compiling the Program

Listing 7.19 is the file used to compile this program. If you get it from the companion Web site, it will be called build.sh. To compile, at the command line send

```
% ./build.sh
```

Listing 7.19   File *build.sh* contents: The Commands Used to Compile the SESI Order Application

```
01  clear
02
03  gcc -Wall -g -o sesi_order.exe callbacks.c interface.c \
04            support.c   main.c  sesi_utils.c \
05      `gtk-config --cflags --libs` \
06      -I/usr/include/mysql \
07      -L/usr/lib/mysql -lmysqlclient -lm -lz
```

Line 1 simply clears the screen; this makes it more readable if any compile errors occur. Lines 3 and 4 are the compile commands and the target files; the backslash character (\) is the line-continuation character.

Line 5 sets the GTK+ flags and libraries. (Don't forget that those are back-tick marks, not single quotation marks.) Line 6 "includes" the MySQL library, whereas line 7 "links" the MySQL, math, and zlib libraries.

Project Post-Mortem

Every project that was worth doing should have a post-project debrief. What went wrong? What could have been done better? While the ideas are still fresh, you have to ask yourself what things should go into the next version.

The application probably could have made all changes be automatically saved (to the customer record, frm_main) and the cmd_save_edits button could have been removed altogether. The times when edits won't be saved will be very rare. So such a change probably wouldn't impact usefulness and would save more keystrokes than it created. Instead, simply run the update database procedure every time frm_main is moved off the current record.

Regarding the changes made to frm_items_ordered, simple is best. If a set of widgets can be put into a vertical packing box as opposed to a vertical packing box with a number of child horizontal packing boxes, that is simpler and better to implement, assuming it doesn't affect usability.

Check the resize action of the window widgets early in the development cycle—as soon as possible after all the child widgets have been filled in—to see that the form is resizing correctly. As an example, see Figure 7.10. Notice the wasted space when this form is resized. Even though this form will rarely be used (due to the way it is used and its short life cycle), it would have been nice for it to look correct even when maximized.

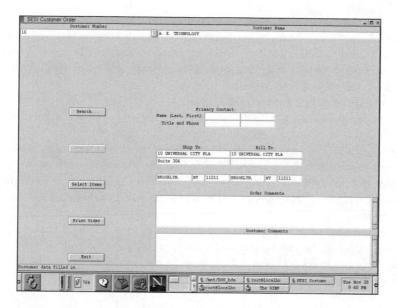

Figure 7.10   frm_main maximized; clearly this is not the desired result!

Figure 7.10 shows frm_main in its maximized state. Fortunately, there is no really good reason for the user to do this while using the application! Clearly, more time could have been taken to make sure that the resize action was a bit more, um, palatable. Compare Figure 7.10, however, with Figure 7.11.

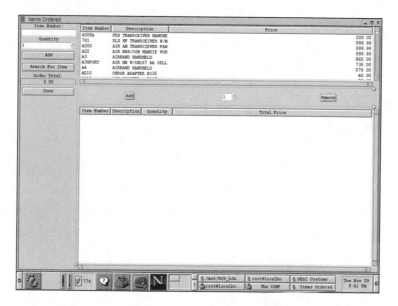

Figure 7.11   frm_items_ordered maximized; now that's more like it!

Figure 7.11 shows frm_items_ordered maximized, and although it was never intended to *be* maximized, it doesn't look too bad. The primary difference between them is that frm_main used all vertical and horizontal packing boxes, while frm_items_ordered used the horizontal and vertical paned widgets.

The add-quantity box between the CList boxes in frm_items_ordered probably could have been done away with. In fact, so could the other quantity spinbutton in the upper-left corner. Instead, the user could have just entered the same item twice to clist_items_ordered, and the result would have been the same. This only makes sense if it is far more normal to order only one of something; if quantities of two or more occur (for example, 40% of the time or more), then perhaps the way it was done is best. This is something that would need study in the actual environment in which it was being used.

A double-click event on the rows of the clist_widgets would have been useful; for example, to double-click clist_items and to have it run the same code as on_cmd_add_down_clicked() would have been an easy and functional addition using already existing code. Unfortunately, there is no double-click event in the GTK+ event model.

The desired functionality of being able to do nearly everything—at least the common things, anyway—all from the keyboard was achieved. Someone who takes time to learn the keystrokes and the various key shortcuts (like Shift-Tab to go back one widget in Tab order) will be able to enter orders extremely quickly.

8

Commission Calculations
Abstract and Design

I N THIS, THE SECOND OF THE BOOK'S "REAL WORLD IMPLEMENTATION" examples, the application relates to a much larger corporation. In this case, the client is an international corporation with salespeople scattered all over the world. Their Financial Analysis department is made up of a mix of Europeans and Americans, and most of the Europeans have come into the department as a result of the acquisition of a European competitor. Each department has its own Information Systems (IS) division whose sole purpose is to support the computing needs of the parent department. As far as "American" companies go, the Financial Analysis department is quite diverse technology-wise: In addition to a mix of servers (NT Server, Sun Solaris, Linux, and AS400), it also has a mix of Linux and Windows workstations including Windows95, Windows98, Red Hat, and SuSE Linux.

This "weird mix" of systems has led to no small number of integration problems, but it has also allowed them to choose the best tool for any given application. It has also meant that things tend to be brought down to the "lowest common denominator": text-based files, comma- or tab-delimited files, "chaining" of applications, heavy use of FTP and other cross-platform applications, and so on.

One of the Financial Analysts (FAs) has the monthly duty of computing and reporting to Accounts Payable the commissions for more than 100 salespeople, as well as producing reports for each of the managers for individual countries (such as the United States and France) in the Marketing Department. The FA with these duties is currently using a spreadsheet to perform this function, and it takes approximately two weeks out of each month to produce the required information. The desire is to reduce the process to one or two days.

Problem Definition

The first step in the process is for the Marketing Department to produce a list of invoices that were filled in the previous month; normally this happens by the 5th day of the new month. (For this example, this file is called `tbl_revenue.txt`, and it is available from the book's Web site, which is located at `www.newriders.com`). From that list, the FA processing the commissions applies a series of business rules against the data to generate the commissions for each salesperson.

The first two lines from `tbl_revenue.txt` are shown here:

```
customer_number,customer_name,salesperson,country,city,state,zipcode,ship_date,item_
number,order_quantity,unit_price,net_value,invoice_number,invoice_date,
invoice_quantity,invoice_value

250-700,ExecuData,4181,United States,Houston,TX,77001,2/24/2001
0:00:00,A1000050CZ,1,18.75,18.75,64-225904,3/27/2001 0:00:00,1,18.75
```

As you can see, the first line is the column headers, and the data starts on the second line. From this data file, the FA applies the "business rules" that determine how the data is processed, and he or she is responsible for producing the following in the form of ASCII text files:

- How much each salesperson is to be paid in commission.
- A report for each salesperson that details (as best as possible) which invoices they were paid on, what customers those invoices were for, and so on. Therefore, at the end of the processing steps, the FA should have a text file that can be emailed to each salesperson giving the individual a breakdown of his or her "activity" for the month (for example, "which customers bought which products on which invoices").
- A report for each "Country Manager" as to how much was paid to salespeople in his or her country, both in US dollars and the local currency. The commissions are paid out according to the following rules:

  The most common type of commission is paid on a geographic region such as state or country. Some people are paid on all invoices worldwide, and some are paid on everything in a particular country all the way down to a specific zip code (in the US) or an equivalent in another country (Post Code, Cedex, or Post Leitzahl, for example).

The revenue file (`tbl_revenue.txt`) that starts the entire process contains a "salesperson" field that is tied to the invoice number on that line. Obviously, that salesperson should be paid on the invoice on that line.

Some commissions are paid to managers based on the production of other salespeople. That is, a salesperson may get a commission based on an invoice, but that salesperson's manager may also get a commission based on that invoice.

Finally, a number of "one-off" rules have to be applied manually, such as "Salesperson X is paid on everything in country Y, except customer Z." These rules are not coded into the system; it is "cheaper" in terms of person-hours to have them entered manually. Additionally, these "one-off" rules are the business rules that are most likely to change. So keeping them out of the application reduces the likelihood of maintenance coding in the future.

End User Information

Essentially, there are only two kinds of users: those authorized to alter the data and "process" commissions, and those with read-only access to one or more tables. At any given time, exactly one person will primarily be assigned to processing the data. Once a month this person will open the application, archive the tables from the previous month, and then process the current month's data.

Only a handful of people at any given time will access the database—perhaps six to eight authorized users. All but one of them will be read-only users.

Security Concerns

Because this application will deal with the confidential subject of payroll and money, there are essentially three security choices for the application:

- *Server-level security.* Users have access to the Linux box via operating system security. After they are logged in, however, there is still the problem of keeping the read-only users in read-only mode.
- *Database-level security.* The users have logins to the MySQL database server.
- *Application-level security.* The application asks for a login and password (or uses the currently logged-on user) and authenticates it against an internal table of users and their permissions.

In the current setup, all the relevant spreadsheets are kept on one FA's desktop PC. His or her login is all the security on the current system.

For this application, the last option (application-level security) will be used. It allows all the login names and other information to be kept in one place and makes it easier for the application to check the validity of the person logging in.

Essentially, the MySQL server will have a new login—a generic *application login* that will have full rights within the database. The compiled application will connect to the database via this application login, and then the application itself will query the "commish" database to see what rights have been granted to the currently logged in user (the commish database will have tables that list access permissions for the users). The application will then control security for the users by presenting or not presenting options to the user. Given the previous security arrangements, this is considered a step up.

Additionally, this application will also need to do some basic logging: who logged in, when they logged in, from where (if possible), who modified which data, when it was modified, what information was viewed, and so on.

Existing Data Information

As with the previous example (the "SESI" project in Chapter 6 "Order Entry Abstract and Design," and Chapter 7 "Construction of the SESI Order Entry Application"), the existing data is kept in one or more spreadsheets. Again, these will be exported to delimited files, except that this time the files will be comma-separated, rather than tab-separated. These files are available at the Web site for this book; they follow the naming scheme *tbl_*.txt* where *tbl_** represents the matching table in the database. Their names match up with the tables used in the database for this example.

Work Flow Specification

The once-a-month processing of the commissions data should proceed along the following steps. Additionally, keep in mind that while the process is "normally" run once a month at the beginning of the month, there is no guarantee that it will be run only once a month or that it will be run at the beginning of the month. It could be run at any time during the month to make corrections or additions. However, once it has been run and the data has been sent off to the "country managers" and payroll (via email), no other changes can be entered until the next month's processing. Thus, the salespeople are paid once a month.

The specific steps in the work flow are outlined here:

1. Archive the previous month's data. This will involve moving it to a new table. Provide the user the opportunity to name the table dynamically from within the software. Also, clear out any intermediate tables that were used.

2. Import the "revenue" file. It tells what was sold to whom, for how much, and so on in the previous calendar month. This will be a comma-separated values (CSV) file that will be received via FTP each month.

3. Provide a way for the user to manually adjust any values in the revenue table before moving on.

4. Based on the revenue table, calculate commissions for people, not necessarily in the following order:

   - Pay salespeople based on the salesperson's numbers and invoice amounts that were contained in the "revenue file" (tbl_revenue.txt).
   - Pay those people who get paid a commission on everything worldwide.
   - Pay those people who get paid a commission based on which country the customer was from.
   - Pay those people who get paid for sales in a certain state (in the US) or an equivalent locator (in foreign countries).
   - Pay those who get a commission based on a certain ZIP code (in the US) or equivalent locator (in foreign countries).
   - Pay those who get paid based on what other people are getting paid.

5. Allow the user to manually adjust the payments calculated above as necessary (either at any time in the six processing steps above or after all payments have been produced).

6. Produce a comma-separated values file for each salesperson in the table, showing as much data as possible including a breakdown as to what they were paid on, how much, and so on.

7. Produce a report for each country showing who was paid and how much—in both dollars and the local currency.

It is important to remember that these steps will be performed by one person and that all others with access to the database will normally be authorized to view only a subset of the tables.

User Interface

This application will be called "Worldwide Commissions," and the MySQL database will be called "commish." The user will initially be presented with a login form (frm_login), followed by a table-view form (frm_table_view) in which she can view the tables she is authorized to see, along with some basic sorting capabilities. The one person authorized to alter the data and produce the commissions reports will also have access to the form that processes the data (frm_commissions); changes to the data can only be made from frm_commissions.

Login Screen: frm_login

First the user will be presented with the login screen. Figure 8.1 shows the schematic of the Login screen. The user will be able to log in and also be able to change his password for the commissions application. In order to change the password, a user will have to enter their login and password anyway. So if all checks pass, the "Change Password" button will also log them in.

Figure 8.1 frm_login, the Commissions login screen for design.

lbl_messages at the bottom of the screen will be used to communicate messages to the user such as "Could not connect to server..." or "Your new password must have at least four characters in it" and so on. Figure 8.2 shows the widget container schema for frm_login.

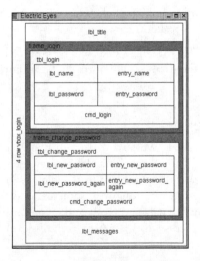

Figure 8.2 frm_login widget container schema.

frm_login will start with a four-row vertical packing box, into which will be placed the widgets as displayed. The login entry boxes will be placed inside three-by-three table widgets. Clearly, the widgets could be placed into a single vertical packing box, but in this case, users have an expectation of what a login screen "should look like." So it is probably best to try to meet that expectation.

Table Display Form: frm_table_display

When the user logs in, this will be the screen he will initially see. Figure 8.3 shows the form design. This window is dominated by the CList widget in the center; it will dynamically show the table selected in the combo box.

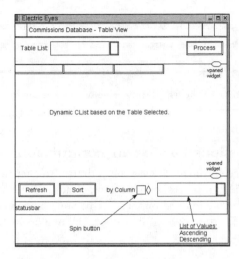

Figure 8.3   The frm_table_display design.

frm_table_display will display the following behaviors:

- The Table List combo box in the upper-left corner will list all tables the user has privileges to view. It will be filled from one of the database tables, based on the login name given. When the user changes it, the CList widget in the center of the form will change to the newly selected table. The combo box will have its "Limit to List" property set to Yes.

- The Process button in the upper-right corner will only be visible to the person currently listed as authorized to do the processing in the database security table(s). It will be a hide/show widget rather than active/inactive and set at login time.

- The Refresh button in the lower-left corner will refresh the CList widget.

- The Sort button will work in combination with the spinbutton widget and combo box at the bottom of the screen. Read from left to right, the widgets will be used like this: "sort column X ascending/descending." These will allow the user to sort the CList widget based on a designated column. For a long list of items, this will make searching for a certain row easier, without having to code a find routine.

Figure 8.4 shows the widget containment scheme for frm_display_table.

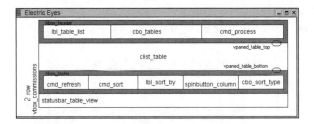

Figure 8.4 The frm_display_table widget container schema.

Process Commissions Form: frm_commissions

Only one FA at any given time will have the authority to alter the database. That is, only the designated FA can process commissions, or add, delete, or modify a data row. Since these permissions are granted only to one person, the controls to perform these functions can all be placed on frm_commissions. Figure 8.5 shows the design layout of frm_commissions.

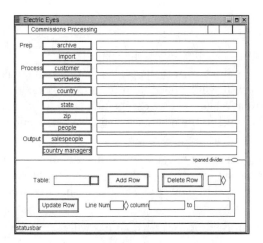

Figure 8.5 frm_commissions is used for processing commissions and editing tables.

frm_commissions will function according to the following points:

- The processing function can be broken into 10 steps: 2 prep, 6 processing, and 2 output or post-processing steps. The 10 command buttons in the top half of Figure 8.5 are for performing these steps. The FA needs to be able to process each step and then verify what was done. The boxes to the right of the command buttons are labels for communicating results to the user.

- The two preparation steps are (1) archive previous data and (2) import the revenue data into tbl_revenue.
- The six processing steps are outlined here:

  1. Calculate the commissions as indicated in the imported table.
  2. Calculate the commissions for those paid "worldwide."
  3. Calculate the commissions for those paid for all sales in a country.
  4. Calculate the commissions for those paid for all sales in a state.
  5. Calculate the commissions for those paid for all sales made within a ZIP code.
  6. Calculate the commissions for those paid based on other people's revenue.

- The two output or post-processing steps are (1) create an information file for each salesperson who was paid anything and (2) create a file for each country showing who was paid and how much.
- The three command buttons at the bottom of Figure 8.5 are for making changes to the data in the tables. They allow the authorized user to add, delete, or change the data in any of the tables.

Figures 8.6 and 8.7 show the container widget schema for frm_commissions. Note that Figure 8.7 shows the detail for the table that makes up the largest part of the form (table_10_by_3); this is done simply to make the diagrams more easily understandable. Figure 8.6 gets too cluttered when it also contains Figure 8.7.

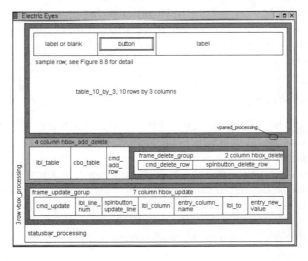

Figure 8.6   The frm_commissions widget container schema.

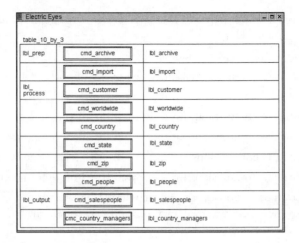

Figure 8.7 table_10_by_3 shows a detailed section from Figure 8.7.

Database and Login Setup

This application will maintain its own security tables. The table (or tables) will control who can see what and so on. Because of that, only one "application login" is, needed and no new logins are allowed at the operating system level. When this application launches, it (the application, not the individual user) logs in to the MySQL server. The login and password the user enters will be compared against application tables, to set the user interface correctly for the given user. The application login and password will be the following:

- Login: com_user
- Password: syL0U812

That's syL (case is important), zero, then U812. That is the login the compiled application will use to access the database. From there it will query the security tables for specifics about the user.

Next, the MySQL server on the server machine needs to know which machines on the network will be logging in via the application login (com_user). Specifically, access needs to be granted for those machines to connect to this MySQL server. In the following, "einstein" is the server machine, and for an example, "delfin" will be one of the desktop machines. Launch mysql as administrator, and from the `mysql>` prompt, send this command:

```
mysql>  Grant All on commish.* to com_user@delfin Identified by "syL0U812";
```

Remember that commish is the name of the database (see the "Security Concerns" section earlier in this chapter). Also, to test the application and develop it on the server, the same command needs to be sent regarding the server:

```
mysql>  Grant All on commish.* to com_user@einstein Identified by "syL0U812";
```

Now all the parameters of the `mysql_real_connect()` call can be filled out in the database connection code of the application. Note that this will have to be done for every machine that is going to access the commish database. To test the success of the `Grant` commands, either from the server or a workstation, send this command to see if the MySQL daemon on the server grants access:

```
%  mysql -h einstein -u com_user -p commish
```

The `-p` means it will request your password. If the previous command works and connects to the database from a remote (workstation) machine, permissions have been set correctly.

Creating the Database

As with Listing 6.1, this section will detail the initial construction of the commish database and the initial data load procedures. In this case, the data format will be slightly different. The tables to be loaded will be comma delimited with the first row containing the field names (as opposed to the tab-delimited files from the SESI Application in Chapters 6 and 7). It is important to note that the data tables being imported for this application have already been "scrubbed." For example, in a comma-delimited file, the customer name "Smak Moduler, Inc." will screw up a `MySQL LOAD DATA` statement because `LOAD DATA` will take the comma to mean that "Smak Moduler" is one field and "Inc." is another, when in fact they are one field in the data. Although the double quotation mark character can be used as the field delimiter, trouble can arise if someone has included a double quotation mark character in the data, either accidentally or on purpose. Data quality is everything, and in this case the data has already been cleansed (prior to its inclusion in this book) so that the import procedures go smoothly.

There will be two separate procedures: one to import the revenue table (tbl_revenue) which is the file to be imported monthly, and the other to load the tables that will determine how the data in tbl_revenue will be processed. Listing 8.1 is the data load procedure for loading tbl_revenue, and Listing 8.2 is for the initial load of the rest of the tables.

First, create the database by launching mysql as root (or equivalent). Then create the database:

```
mysql>  create database commish;
```

Exit mysql and run Listing 8.1 with this command:

```
%mysql -t < listing.8.1
```

Or run it with whatever the name of the file is. Refer to Listing 6.1 and its surrounding text for a detailed explanation of the -t option and the peculiarities of directing a file to mysql in this manner.

Listing 8.1 **Loading the Revenue Data to tbl_revenue**

```
use commish;

/* Listing 8.1
 *
 * This file loads the data from the tbl_revenue.txt file
 * into tbl_revenue in the commish database.
 *
 * usage:
 *
 * % mysql -t < listing.8.1
 */

drop table if exists tbl_revenue;

create table tbl_revenue
(
        line_number       INT   PRIMARY KEY    AUTO_INCREMENT,
        customer_number   varchar(50),
        customer_name     varchar(50),
        salesperson       varchar(50),
        country           varchar(50),
        city              varchar(50),
        state             char(2),
        zip               varchar(50),
        ship_date         varchar(50),
        item_number       varchar(50),
        order_quantity    smallint,
        unit_price        decimal(10,2),
        net_value         decimal(10,2),
        invoice_number    varchar(50),
        invoice_date      varchar(50),
        invoice_quantity  smallint,
        invoice_value     decimal(10,2)
);

LOAD DATA INFILE "/mnt/DOS_hda2/newriders/book/ch8/tbl_revenue.txt"
    INTO TABLE tbl_revenue
    FIELDS TERMINATED BY ','
    IGNORE 1 LINES
      (customer_number,
       customer_name,
       salesperson,
       country,
       city,
```

```
        state,
        zip,
        ship_date,
        item_number,
        order_quantity,
        unit_price,
        net_value,
        invoice_number,
        invoice_date,
        invoice_quantity ,
        invoice_value);

select count(*) from tbl_revenue;
```

Listing 8.2 creates and loads the rest of the database, including the security and event tables.

Listing 8.2   Loading the Remaining Data to the Commish Database

```
use commish;

/* This file loads all tables except tbl_revenue (which
 * is loaded by Listing 8.1).
 *
 * usage:
 *
 * % mysql -t < listing.8.2
 */

/* The following table lists the salespeople that are being paid
 * or have the potential to be paid a commission.
 */

drop table if exists tbl_people;

create table tbl_people
(
        line_number     SMALLINT     PRIMARY KEY     AUTO_INCREMENT,
        salesperson     char(4),
        last_name       varchar(50),
        first_name      varchar(35),
        country         varchar(50),
        commission      decimal(6,4)
);

/* In the LOAD DATA statement that follows, the last part
 * of the statement – the part in parentheses – is the
 * column-list. It tells MySQL which columns to put
 * the data in. In this case, it serves the purpose of
 * allowing the line_number field to be first in the table
```

continues

Listing 8.2 **Continued**

```
 * structure without trying to load a value
 * from the text file into it.
 */

LOAD DATA INFILE "/mnt/DOS_hda2/newriders/book/ch8/tbl_people.txt"
    INTO TABLE tbl_people
    FIELDS TERMINATED BY ','
    IGNORE 1 LINES
    (salesperson,
     last_name,
     first_name,
     country,
     commission);

/* tbl_people.txt should look something like the following (which
 * is actually the first three lines from the file):
 *     salesperson_num,last_name,first_name,country,commission
 *     3565,Regreb,Jenny,Germany,0.0028
 *     4101,Facile,Francis,South Africa,0.00513
 *
 * The following table holds the currency exchange rates
 * for various countries.
 */

drop table if exists tbl_exchange_rates;

create table tbl_exchange_rates
(
     line_number SMALLINT    PRIMARY KEY    AUTO_INCREMENT,
     country     varchar(50),
     rate        decimal(8,2)
);

LOAD DATA INFILE "/mnt/DOS_hda2/newriders/book/ch8/tbl_exchange_rates.txt"
    INTO TABLE tbl_exchange_rates
    FIELDS TERMINATED BY ','
    IGNORE 1 LINES
    (country,
     rate);

/* The following table lists those salespeople who are paid for sales
 * in a certain state and which state that is.
 */

drop table if exists tbl_people_paid_on_state;

create table tbl_people_paid_on_state
(
     line_number SMALLINT    PRIMARY KEY    AUTO_INCREMENT,
```

```
        salesperson varchar(50),
        state       varchar(20)
);

LOAD DATA INFILE "/mnt/DOS_hda2/newriders/book/ch8/tbl_people_paid_on_state.txt"
    INTO TABLE tbl_people_paid_on_state
    FIELDS TERMINATED BY ','
    IGNORE 1 LINES
    (salesperson,
     state);

/* The following table lists those salespeople who are paid for
 * sales in a certain ZIP code and which ZIP_code that is.
 */

drop table if exists tbl_people_paid_on_zipcode;

create table tbl_people_paid_on_zipcode
(
      line_number SMALLINT    PRIMARY KEY    AUTO_INCREMENT,
      salesperson varchar(50),
      zipcode     varchar(20)
);

LOAD DATA INFILE "/mnt/DOS_hda2/newriders/book/ch8/tbl_people_paid_on_zipcode.txt"
    INTO TABLE tbl_people_paid_on_zipcode
    FIELDS TERMINATED BY ','
    IGNORE 1 LINES
    (salesperson,
     zipcode);

/* That represents the last of the data files to be loaded.
 *
 * The remaining tables in the database are shown below.
 *
 * For those that have only a few rows of data, or where
 * no data file was available for import, individual
 * insert statements have been created.
 *
 * The next table to be created lists those people who
 * are paid for all sales worldwide.
 */

drop table if exists tbl_people_paid_on_worldwide;

create table tbl_people_paid_on_worldwide
(
      line_number   SMALLINT    PRIMARY KEY    AUTO_INCREMENT,
      salesperson   varchar(4)
);
```

continues

Listing 8.2 **Continued**

```
insert into tbl_people_paid_on_worldwide(salesperson)
           values('4838'), ('5383');

/* Next is the table of people who are paid on
 * everything sold in a certain country.
 */

drop table if exists tbl_people_paid_on_country;

create table tbl_people_paid_on_country
(
      line_number    SMALLINT     PRIMARY KEY     AUTO_INCREMENT,
      salesperson    varchar(4),
      country        varchar(50)
);

insert into tbl_people_paid_on_country(salesperson, country)
       values ('4070', 'United States'),
              ('4515', 'United States'),
              ('4191', 'United States'),
              ('5646', 'United States'),
              ('4333', 'China'),
              ('3686', 'Germany'),
              ('5151', 'Poland'),
              ('5919', 'Honduras');


/* Next is the commissions table. Each month,
 * the application fills this table
 * and the one that is archived at the
 * start of the monthly processing.
 *
 * The software will perform a series of steps to fill
 * this table each month. The data from this table
 * will be used for reporting to the salespeople and
 * the country managers.
 */

drop table if exists tbl_commissions;

/* Notice that the line number field in this table is
 * INT instead of SMALLINT. That is because
 * this table is expected to surpass 32767 within the first
 * month or two of use. Although the MEDIUMINT
 * data type could also be used, it has a maximum value of 8388607.
 * But the INT data type has a maximum value of over two billion.
 * That should be more than enough.
 */
```

```
create table tbl_commissions
(
    line_number    INT     PRIMARY KEY     AUTO_INCREMENT,
    salesperson    varchar(4),
    invoice_num    varchar(10),
    commission     decimal(8,2)
);

/* Finally, create the security and administration tables.
 *
 * You'll create three tables here. One will hold the access
 * permissions – that is, who can view which tables in the database.
 * Another will hold logins and passwords.
 * The third is the application log, which records events.
 */

drop table if exists tbl_permissions;

create table tbl_permissions
(
    login          varchar(35),
    form           varchar(35)
);

insert into tbl_permissions
       values ('processor', 'process'),
              ('processor', 'tbl_exchange_rates'),
              ('processor', 'tbl_people'),
              ('processor', 'tbl_people_paid_on_country'),
              ('processor', 'tbl_people_paid_on_worldwide'),
              ('processor', 'tbl_people_paid_on_state'),
              ('processor', 'tbl_people_paid_on_zipcode'),
              ('processor', 'tbl_revenue'),
              ('processor', 'tbl_commissions'),
              ('analyst1', 'tbl_people_paid_on_worldwide'),
              ('analyst1', 'tbl_revenue'),
              ('analyst1', 'tbl_commissions'),
              ('boss1', 'tbl_exchange_rates'),
              ('boss1', 'tbl_people'),
              ('boss1', 'tbl_people_paid_on_country'),
              ('boss1', 'tbl_people_paid_on_worldwide'),
              ('boss1', 'tbl_people_paid_on_state'),
              ('boss1', 'tbl_people_paid_on_zipcode'),
              ('boss1', 'tbl_revenue'),
              ('boss1', 'tbl_commissions');

drop table if exists tbl_security;

/* In the following table, rather than use "login"
 * and "password" as the field names, we have chosen to
 * use names that will prevent problems – even though
```

continues

Listing 8.2 **Continued**

```
 * mysql would accept "login" and "password" as
 * field names.
 */

create table tbl_security
(
      user_login      varchar(35),
      pass_word       varchar(35)
);

/* The password() function encrypts the given text
 * in a one-way operation.  In the application,
 * the password() function will be used on the value
 * entered in entry_password and then compared against
 * the database.
 */

insert into tbl_security
       values ('processor',  password('smile')),
              ('analyst1' ,  password('salsa')),
              ('boss1'    ,  password('sippycup')));


drop table if exists tbl_logged_events;

/* In the following create table statement, the TIMESTAMP
 * data type not only creates a date-time column, but
 * also sets the default value to the current date and time.
 */

create table tbl_logged_events
(
      time_stamp      TIMESTAMP   NOT NULL,
      user_login      varchar(35),
      event           varchar(255)
);

insert into tbl_logged_events (user_login, event)
       values ('administrator', 'database created and loaded');

select * from tbl_logged_events;
```

9

Constructing the Commissions Application

THIS CHAPTER DESCRIBES THE BUILD PROCESS AND LIST code for the project described in Chapter 8, "Commission Calculations Abstract and Design." The project will have one item separate from the rest of the project: a data display control (DDC). It is called this because it allows the display of a table, but it will not allow the user to update that table directly from the DDC. It is essentially nothing more than a replaceable dynamically generated CList widget.

User Interface (UI) Construction with Glade

To begin the build process, set the project options after launching Glade. Set the project directory, and enter the project name of ww_comm (for "worldwide commissions"). Disable Gnome and gettext support, as you did for the SESI project.

Create a new form and name it frm_login. For its Title property, enter Commissions Login. Drop in a four-row vbox named vbox_login, and then insert lbl_title and lbl_messages, as shown in Figure 8.2, setting the text for both as shown in Figure 8.1. Give lbl_title a bit of visual separation by setting its Y Pad property to 5. For the rest of the construction of frm_login, have Figures 8.1 and 8.2 available for quick reference.

Drop in frame_login and frame_change_password to their correct locations. Set their Label properties as shown in Figure 8.1. The frame widgets' appearance improves if they are given a bit of padding around the edges, so set their Border Width property to 5. Drop in tbl_login and tbl_change_password. Then drop in the four remaining label widgets for this form (lbl_name, lbl_password, lbl_new_password, and lbl_new_password_again) and set their properties. Do the same with the four respective entry widgets. For the entry widgets, the X Fill properties can be set to No. Set the Has Focus property for entry_name to Yes. Finally, drop in cmd_login and cmd_change_password to the bottom rows of their respective parent tables. Set their Col Span properties to 2 so they take up the entire bottom row of their table. Also, set their Y Expand properties to Yes so they will be centered vertically.

Set the Text Visible property to No for entry_password, entry_new_password, and entry_new_password_again so the user's password information will not be visible during entry. Set the Border Width property of cmd_login and cmd_change_password to 5 to separate them visually from the surrounding widgets.

At this point, if you Save and Build the project, frm_main will be the only form created and displayed when the project runs, which is the desired behavior. Figure 9.1 shows frm_login after compiling and launching the application as built so far.

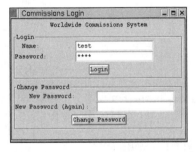

Figure 9.1   frm_login for the Worldwide Commissions Application.

Building frm_login

For frm_login, only three events should be taken into consideration: the `clicked` event for cmd_login, the `clicked` event for cmd_change_password, and the `delete` event of the form (in other words, the user presses the "X" or Close button in the upper-right corner). In this case, it has to be assumed that the user has decided not to log in to the commish database at all. So exit the application.

In the Signals tab of the properties window, select the `clicked` signal for the command buttons and the `delete` event for the window. (For detailed instructions, refer to the example in Chapter 7, "Construction of the SESI Order Entry Application.")

Create a new window named frm_table_display and for the Title property enter Commissions Database - Table View, as shown in Figure 8.3. Drop in the first vpaned widget, vpaned_table_top, and then drop another one, vpaned_table_bottom, into the bottom half of vpaned_table_top. Increase the Gutter Size property of both to 10 and deselect the Position check box for both vpaned widgets. Put vbox_commissions into the bottom half of vpaned_table_bottom. Place hbox_header and hbox_footer in place, with three and five columns, respectively; give their child widgets a bit of visual separation by setting their Border Width and Spacing properties to 5. Drop the status-bar into the bottom of vbox_commissions.

Into hbox_header, place lbl_table_list, cbo_tables, and cmd_process, and set their properties according to Figures 8.3 and 8.4. For cbo_tables, set the Value in List property to Yes, and the OK if Empty property to No. Set both the Expand and Fill properties for cbo_tables to No. For the entry child widget of cbo_tables, which is named combo-entry1 on my system, change the name to combo-entry_table. For cmd_process, set the Visible property to No because that widget will be available to only one of the application's users.

Select a CList widget from the palette and drop it into its proper place in frm_table_display. Because the CList widget is actually a CList widget contained in a Scrolledwindow widget (and it turns out the scrolledwindow widget is the one of interest later), name the widgets clist_table and scrolledwindow_table. Beyond that, accept the defaults for those widgets.

Into hbox_footer, drop the five widgets, as shown in Figure 8.4. Into the Items property of cbo_sort_type, add Ascending and Descending, set the Value in List property to Yes, and set the OK If Empty property to No.

Now set the signals for frm_display_table. Get the `changed` and `activate` events on combo-entry_table, and the `clicked` event for all of the command buttons. Also, get the `resize` event for the window widget: the `size_request` event. Select the `delete` event for the form also.

Building frm_commissions

Moving on to frm_commissions, create a new window widget from the Palette. Set its name to frm_commissions and its title according to Figure 8.5. Drop in vpaned_processing and vbox_processing, changing the names accordingly. Set the Gutter Size of vpaned_processing to 10. Put table_10_by_3 in the top part of vpaned_processing and set its Name property. Set both the Row Spacing and Column Spacing properties to 5. Create and set the three labels in the leftmost column of tbl_10_by_3, and then create the 10 command buttons in the center column. Set the names and visible text portions of these widgets according to Figures 8.5, 8.6, and 8.7. For the 10 command buttons in the middle column, set their X Fill properties to Yes. To finish table_10_by_3, create the label widgets that make up the third column, also according to Figure 8.7.

Add hbox_add_delete to the top row of vbox_processing. Set the Value In List property to Yes and the OK If Empty property to No for cbo_table; set both the Border Width and Spacing properties to 5. Create and place lbl_table and cbo_table. Here you will deviate slightly from the design in Figure 8.6. Before adding cmd_add, insert a frame widget and name it frame_add with its text set to "Add." Then add cmd_add_row as shown in Figure 8.6. The frame widget gives cmd_add the same vertical size as cmd_delete_row, rather than making cmd_add_row taller than cmd_delete_row, which would make the layout of the buttons look disjointed. Set the Fill and Expand properties of cbo_table to No. Get a frame object from the Palette and drop it into the right space of hbox_add_delete; this is frame_delete_group. Into it, place hbox_delete with two columns. As with the other hbox widgets, set its Border Width and Spacing to 5. Add cmd_delete and spinbutton_delete_row.

Add frame_update_group, as well as hbox_update. For hbox_update, set the Border Width and Spacing to 5. Add cmd_update, lbl_line_number, and spinbutton_update_line. For both spinbutton_delete_row and spinbutton_update_line, set the Numeric property to Yes, the Min to 1, and the Max to an arbitrarily high number. This example uses two million.

Add in lbl_column, entry_column_name, lbl_to, and entry_new_value to fill out hbox_update. Add statusbar_processing to the bottom, as shown in Figure 8.6.

Figure 9.2 shows Glade with all three of the forms open.

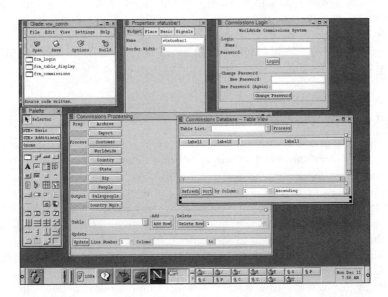

Figure 9.2   The Worldwide Commissions application you're builing with Glade.

Finally, specify the signals for the widgets in frm_commissions. Set the callbacks for all the `clicked` signals on the command button widgets, as well as the `delete` event of the form.

Rather than go into a lengthy discussion on building the interface with Glade as we did in Chapter 7, this discussion assumes the reader is familiar with the process of building the application in that manner. Download the code from the book's companion Web site (`www.newriders.com`) and review Figures 9.3, 9.4, and 9.5. Figure 9.3 shows the widget tree for frm_login, and Figure 9.4 shows the widget tree for frm_table_display. Figure 9.5 shows the widget tree for frm_commissions split over two windows. From that, you should be able to figure out the structure and build process for the Worldwide Commissions application in this chapter.

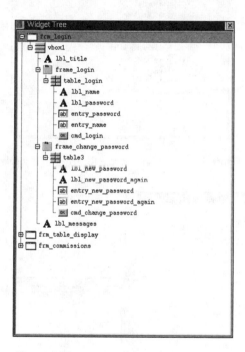

Figure 9.3 The widget tree for frm_login.

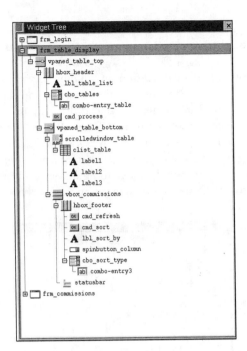

Figure 9.4 The widget tree for frm_table_display.

Figure 9.5 The widget tree for frm_commissions.

The Data Display Control (DDC)

This control will show one table at a time. When given an SQL "select" string, it dynamically generates a CList widget. It is not completely independent of the current project, but it could be with a little work. The code for the DDC is in a separate file, called ddc.c (and, of course, ddc.h). Listing 9.1 is ddc.c.

Listing 9.1 **Data Display Control (DDC) Code**

```
#ifdef HAVE_CONFIG_H
#  include <config.h>
#endif

#include <sys/types.h>
#include <sys/stat.h>
#include <unistd.h>
#include <string.h>

#include <gdk/gdkkeysyms.h>
#include <gtk/gtk.h>

#include <mysql.h>

#include "callbacks.h"
#include "interface.h"
#include "support.h"
#include "comm_utils.h"

GtkWidget *frm_table_display;

GtkWidget *create_ddc (gchar *table_name)
{
  /* This widget will create and return a scrolledwindow widget,
   * inside of which is the CList widget with the data. Obviously,
   * to make this more project-independent, such things as the
   * database connection would also need to be passed in as
   * parameters.
   */

    MYSQL     *conx;              //The connection to the database.
    GtkWidget *scrolledwindow1;   //Container for clist_table1.
    GtkWidget *clist_table;       //Table to display the data.
    GtkWidget *label;
    gint      counter;
    gint      cols = 3;           //Default value for number of columns.
    gchar     *sql;               //Generic value for sql string.
    MYSQL_RES *result_set;        //Holds data returned from MySQL.
    MYSQL_ROW db_row;             //A single row from result_set.
    MYSQL_FIELD *field;           //A single field from db_row.
```

continues

Listing 9.1 **Continued**

```c
/* row[20] is a placeholder, but the subscript needs to
 * be larger than the maximum number of columns in any
 * of the possible tables this could select from. In this
 * case, because the structure of the commish database is
 * known and controlled, 20 has a reasonable chance of
 * working for the foreseeable future.
 */
gchar     *row[20] = {"", "", "", "", "",
                      "", "", "", "", "",
                      "", "", "", "", "",
                      "", "", "", "", ""};

/* Create a new scrolled window, into which the CList
 * widget will be added.
 */

scrolledwindow1 = gtk_scrolled_window_new (NULL, NULL);
gtk_widget_show (scrolledwindow1);

conx = mysql_init(0L);
if (conx == 0L)
  {
     g_print("mysql_init failure...\n");
     return 0L;
  }

mysql_real_connect (conx, "einstein", "com_user",
                    "syL0U812", "commish", 0, 0L, 0);
if (conx == 0L)
  {
     g_print("mysql_real_connect failure...\n");
     return 0L;
  }

sql = g_strconcat("select * from ", table_name, 0L);

g_print("sql is:  %s\n", sql);

if (mysql_query (conx, sql) != 0)
  {
     g_print("query failure...\n");
     return 0L;
  }

result_set = mysql_store_result (conx);

/* Find out how many columns were in the returned result set.
 * This will be the number of columns in the CList widget.
 */

cols = mysql_num_fields(result_set);
```

```
/* Create a new CList widget and make it accessible from
 * frm_table_display.
 */

clist_table = gtk_clist_new (cols);
gtk_object_set_data_full(GTK_OBJECT(frm_table_display),
            "clist_table", clist_table,
            0L);

gtk_widget_show (clist_table);
gtk_container_add (GTK_CONTAINER (scrolledwindow1), clist_table);

gtk_clist_column_titles_show (GTK_CLIST (clist_table));

/* Now iterate through the columns, setting the column header
 * label for each column.
 */

for (counter = 0; counter < cols; counter++)
  {
     mysql_field_seek(result_set, counter);
     field = mysql_fetch_field(result_set);

     label = gtk_label_new (field->name);
     gtk_widget_show (label);
     gtk_clist_set_column_widget (GTK_CLIST (clist_table),
                                  counter, label);
     gtk_clist_set_column_width (GTK_CLIST (clist_table),
                                 counter, 80);
  }

/* Next iterate through the rows. With each row, add a row
 * to the CList widget clist_table. */

while ((db_row = mysql_fetch_row (result_set)) != 0L)
   {
      for (counter = 0; counter < cols; counter++)
        {
           row[counter] = db_row[counter];
        }

      gtk_clist_append(GTK_CLIST(clist_table), row);

   }

mysql_close(conx);

/* Send back the scrolledwindow widget that contains
 * the CList widget.
 */

return scrolledwindow1;
}
```

Utility Functions of the Application

This section lists and describes the code found in `comm_utils.c` (you can download the code from the www.newriders.com Web site). These are the "workhorse" functions of the application, much like `sesi_utils.c` was in Chapter 7.

Header, Logging, and Message Communication Functions

Listing 9.2 is the header section of `comm_utils.c` after the code has been written and compiled. It contains the `#include` statements, macro definitions, and such that will be used throughout the code.

Listing 9.2 **Header Section from** *comm_utils.c*

```
#include <gtk/gtk.h>
#include <mysql.h>

/* string.h is needed for the strlen() function.
 * time.h is needed for the date/time functions.
 * stdio.h is needed for the write-to-file operations. */

#include <string.h>
#include <time.h>
#include <stdio.h>

#include "support.h"
#include "ddc.h"

#define SERVER "einstein"
#define LOGIN  "com_user"
#define PASS   "syL0U812"
#define DB     "commish"

GtkWidget *frm_login;
GtkWidget *frm_table_display;
GtkWidget *frm_commissions;

/* The following generic variables are used in
 * many of the functions below. There is no reason they
 * HAVE to be global; however, if they aren't global, they
 * would have to be declared in each individual function and
 * passed in and out of functions repeatedly.
 */

MYSQL       *conx;        //Connection to the database.
MYSQL_RES   *result_set;  //The results from the sql query.
MYSQL_ROW   row;          //A single row from result_set.
gchar       *sql;         //Generic variable for a sql string.
gchar       *user_login;  //The name of the user logged in.
```

Listing 9.3 is the `log_event()` function. Recall that part of the project specification in Chapter 8 was some sort of simple logging procedure that would enable the database and application administrator to know if and when someone had hacked into the system via the application. Obviously, the hacker would have to have a compiled version of the application to attempt to hack in that way, but it still is important to check.

Listing 9.3   **log_event( ) Function from** *comm_utils.c*

```
void log_event(gchar *event_msg)
{
    /* This routine will quietly log who attempts to log in,
     * as well as other potential security flags.
     *
     * The one thing that would be important is the machine name
     * of the attempting login. However, because that has
     * been taken care of with a GRANT statement for each
     * machine that can potentially log in, it won't be
     * included here.
     *
     * The g_get_user_name() function gets the login
     * of the user at the operating system level.
     * In this case, the application maintains a separate list
     * of logins and passwords; the g_get_user_name() function
     * is used as a double check on the attempted login
     * and may be useful if someone who shouldn't have access
     * attempts to log in. Obviously, it could
     * also be used to "pass through" the machine login
     * to the application, avoiding the need for a separate
     * login and password per application.
     */

    sql = g_strconcat("insert into tbl_logged_events ",
                      "(user_login, event) ",
                      "values ('", user_login, "', '", event_msg,
                      " local login: ", g_get_user_name(), "')",
                      0L
                      );

    /* The following g_print() statements have been commented out;
     * because this is a very commonly used function, during debugging,
     * it might be helpful to comment them back in.
     */

    // g_print ("log_event init of mysql...\n");
    conx = mysql_init(0L);
    if (conx == 0L) g_print("init problem...\n");

    // g_print("real connecting...\n");
    conx = mysql_real_connect(conx, SERVER, LOGIN,
                              PASS, DB, 0, 0L, 0);
```

continues

Listing 9.3 **Continued**

```
// g_print("real connect done...\n");
if (conx == 0L) g_print("real connect problem...\n");

// g_print("querying...\n");
mysql_query (conx, sql);

// g_print("closing...\n");
mysql_close (conx);



}
```

Listing 9.4 is the `set_message()` function from `comm_utils.c`. To make things easy, it pushes messages to one widget in each of the three forms. That way it doesn't have to determine which form is currently "active."

Listing 9.4 **The *set_message()* Function from *comm_utils.c***

```
void set_message(gchar *msg)
{
  /* The application to offers three places
   * to communicate with the user:
   * the label widget at the bottom of frm_login and the statusbar
   * widgets at the bottom of each of the other two forms. To make
   * it easy, just push the message to all three.
   */

  g_print("set_message: %s\n", msg);

  gtk_label_set_text(GTK_LABEL(lookup_widget(frm_login,
                      "lbl_messages")), msg);

  gtk_statusbar_push(GTK_STATUSBAR(lookup_widget(frm_table_display,
                                  "statusbar")), 1, msg);

  gtk_statusbar_push(GTK_STATUSBAR(lookup_widget(frm_commissions,
                                  "statusbar_processing")), 1, msg);

  /* Of course, this could also send msg to log_event for
   * really detailed logging.
   */

  g_print("Exiting set_message...\n");
};
```

Login and Password Functions

This section contains the login and password functions from the application. Recall that "the application" (that is, the compiled executable) has a login to the MySQL server that it uses to connect and pass information to and from the database. The user login, however, is a set of tables within the database that checks the login and password of the user and maintains the permissions pertaining to what data the logged in user has access to.

Listing 9.5 is the code for the login and password functions from `comm_utils.c`. The function `check_login_and_password()` determines if the login and passwords given are correct, and `set_new_password()` works with `check_login_password()` to set a new password for the user. Note that both are called from `callbacks.c`.

Listing 9.5   **Login and Password Functions from *comm_utils.c***

```
gboolean check_login_and_password()
{
    g_print("inside check_login_and_password.\n");

    /* Take the user login ID and password from the entry
     * widgets on frm_login.
     */

    user_login = gtk_editable_get_chars(GTK_EDITABLE(
                            lookup_widget(frm_login, "entry_name")),
                            0, -1);

    g_print("user_login is %s\n", user_login);

    /* Create a SQL string that will return a row if the
     * user login and password are valid.
     */

    sql = g_strconcat("select * from ",
                    "tbl_security where user_login = '",
                    user_login,
                    "' and pass_word = password('",
                    gtk_editable_get_chars(GTK_EDITABLE(
                        lookup_widget(frm_login,
                        "entry_password")),
                        0, -1),
                    "')", 0L);

    /* This application takes a bit of a different approach
     * with the database connection mechanism. It will connect
     * and close the connection for each database operation
     * rather than attempt to maintain an open connection.
     *
     * Because the following code is the first attempt to connect,
```

continues

Listing 9.5   **Continued**

```
 * the error messages will be returned to the user if
 * something goes wrong. For later connections in this
 * application, it will be assumed that if the application
 * gets past these initial checks, the connection is
 * available and reliable.
 */

g_print("attemtpting init...\n");
if ((conx = mysql_init(0L)) == 0L)
    {
        set_message("Unable to initialize mysql.");
        return FALSE;
    }
g_print("init done...\n");

conx = mysql_real_connect(conx, SERVER, LOGIN,
                          PASS, DB, 0, 0L, 0);

if (conx == 0L)
    {
        mysql_close(conx);
        set_message("Unable to initialize database connection.");
        return FALSE;
    }
g_print("real_connect done...\n");

if (mysql_query (conx, sql) != 0)
    {
        g_print("query failed...\n");
        mysql_close(conx);
        set_message("Unable to query database.");
        return FALSE;
    }

set_message("Connected to commissions database...");

result_set = mysql_store_result(conx);

/* If the user login and password are correct, the result set
 * should contain exactly one row.
 */

if (mysql_num_rows (result_set) == 1)
    {
        mysql_free_result (result_set);
        mysql_close(conx);
        set_message("Logged in");
```

```
        /* As part of the audit trail, you must report who logged in.
         * Because the table that holds the logged events has a
         * timestamp column, the date and time of the login or
         * attempted login is captured.
         */

        log_event(g_strconcat("Login of ",
                              user_login, 0L));
        return TRUE;
    }
    else
    {
        mysql_free_result (result_set);
        mysql_close(conx);
        set_message("Unable to log in.  See Administrator.");

        log_event(g_strconcat("Failed Login attempt by ",
                              user_login, 0L));
        return FALSE;
    }

}

gboolean set_new_password()
{
    gchar    *str_new_pwd;
    gchar    *str_new_again;

    /* First, some basic checking. Make sure that the
     * new passwords have some length. Are the two
     * new passwords the same, and so on?
     * Generally, logins are
     * not case sensitive but passwords are.
     */

    g_print("starting set_new_password...\n");
    log_event(g_strconcat(user_login, " attempting to set "
                          "new password. ", 0L));

    /* Get the text the user has entered (twice) as the
     * value for the new password.
     */

    str_new_pwd =  gtk_editable_get_chars(GTK_EDITABLE(
                              lookup_widget(frm_login,
                              "entry_new_password")),
                              0, -1);
    str_new_again =  gtk_editable_get_chars(GTK_EDITABLE(
                              lookup_widget(frm_login,
                              "entry_new_password_again")),
                              0, -1);
```

continues

Listing 9.5 **Continued**

```c
/* Note that the next function sets the minimum length
 * of the password to one. Obviously, change the "0"
 * below to alter the minimum length of the password.
 */

if (strlen(str_new_pwd) == 0)
  {
    set_message("New password(s) not of sufficient length.");
    return FALSE;
  }

/* Here the strcmp() function is used instead of the
 * g_strcasecmp() function. The g_strcasecmp() function ignores
 * case in its comparison, which is not the desired behavior.
 */

if (strcmp(str_new_pwd, str_new_again) == 0)
    {
      set_message("New passwords matched...\n");
      sql = g_strconcat("update tbl_security ",
                        "set pass_word = password('",
                        str_new_pwd, "') ",
                        "where user_login = '", user_login, "'",
                        0L);

      g_print("sql is %s\n", sql);

      /* Because the new password has been typed the same
       * twice, consider it "validated" and connect to
       * the database to set the new password.
       */

      conx = mysql_init(0L);
      conx = mysql_real_connect(conx, SERVER, LOGIN,
                        PASS, DB, 0, 0L, 0);
      if (mysql_query (conx, sql) != 0)
        {
          set_message("Unable to change password.  "
                        "Database query failure.\n"
                        "Press Login to connect with "
                        "current name and password.");
          mysql_close(conx);
          return FALSE;
        }
      else
        {
          set_message("New password set.");
          mysql_close(conx);
```

```
        log_event(g_strconcat(user_login,
                    " changed password. ", 0L));
        return TRUE;


    }


    }
    else
    {
        set_message("New password(s) not matched.\n");
        return FALSE;
    }

    return FALSE;


}
```

Listing 9.6 is a couple of utility functions for filling in and correctly displaying the tables the user has access to while in this application. get_table_names() queries the database for a list of tables the user is authorized to see, and it returns those values in a Glist. The function(s) in callbacks.c then call fill_table_combos() to fill the drop-down lists of the combo boxes that list authorized table views.

Listing 9.6   **Authorized Table View Functions from** *comm_utils.c*

```
GList *get_table_names()
{
    /* Query the database and return a list of tables the
     * currently logged in user has authorization to view.
     */

    GList *list_of_tables = 0L;

    conx = mysql_init(0L);
    conx = mysql_real_connect(conx, SERVER, LOGIN,
                        PASS, DB, 0, 0L, 0);

    /* tbl_permissions lists database object permissions
     * by login.
     */

    sql = g_strconcat("select * from tbl_permissions ",
                    "where login = '", user_login, "'",
                    0L);

    if (mysql_query (conx, sql) != 0)
        {
            set_message("Unable to retrieve list of tables.");
            log_event(g_strconcat("Unable to retrieve list of tables",
                        " for user ", user_login, 0L));
```

continues

Listing 9.6 **Continued**

```c
            }
        else
            {
                result_set = mysql_store_result (conx);

                /* Now that the database has returned a result set,
                 * fetch each row and append the value of the second
                 * column to the GList.
                 */

                while (( row = mysql_fetch_row (result_set)) != 0L)
                    {
                        if (strcmp(row[1], "process") != 0)
                            list_of_tables = g_list_append(list_of_tables,
                                            row[1]);
                        else
                            gtk_widget_show(lookup_widget(frm_table_display,
                                        "cmd_process"));
                    }
            }

    mysql_close(conx);

    /* Finally, return the list of tables to the calling function,
     * fill_table_combos(), below.
     */

    return list_of_tables;

}

void fill_table_combos()
{
    /* This function fills the two combo boxes that list
     * the tables the user has access to.
     */

    gtk_combo_set_popdown_strings(GTK_COMBO(lookup_widget(
                    frm_table_display, "cbo_tables")),
                    get_table_names());

    gtk_combo_set_popdown_strings(GTK_COMBO(lookup_widget
                    (frm_commissions, "cbo_table")),
                    get_table_names());
}
```

Primary Data Processing Functions

The next three sections break the complexity of the application down into "preparation" (where old data is archived and other preparations are made for the incoming data) and the "main data processing" steps (as defined in Chapter 8). Finally, the application must produce the desired output. In this case, the text file reports for each salesperson and "country manager."

"Preparation" Functions

Listing 9.7 is the "pre" processing of the data; it prepares the database for the incoming data. frm_commissions has 10 buttons down the left side; Listing 9.7 shows the functions behind the first two of those buttons, as called from `callbacks.c` of course. The functions in Listing 9.7 occur in the same order as the command buttons on frm_commissions.

Listing 9.7   **Data Processing Functions Used by frm_commissions**

```
void archive_tbl_commissions()
{
    gchar       *str_table_name;
    time_t      now;
    gchar       *rows_before, *rows_after;

    /* This function will archive the existing tbl_commissions
     * and prepare it for a new round of processing.
     *
     * The function follows these steps:
     *      1. Get a count of the number of records currently
     *         in the table.
     *      2. Create a new table with a make table query that
     *         transfers the contents of tbl_commissions to the
     *         new table. This new table will be the date and
     *         time of its creation for archival purposes.
     *      3. Get a count of records in the newly created table
     *         and compare it to the original table.
     *      4. If the table record counts match, delete all rows
     *         from tbl_commissions and indicate success to the
     *         user.
     */

    log_event("Archiving tbl_commissions. ");

    conx = mysql_init(0L);
    conx = mysql_real_connect(conx, SERVER, LOGIN,
                              PASS, DB, 0, 0L, 0);

    sql = "select count(*) from tbl_commissions";
```

continues

Listing 9.7   **Continued**

```
if (mysql_query (conx, sql) != 0)
    {
        /* Query failure... */
        set_message("Query Failure in record "
                    "count on tbl_commissions.");
        gtk_label_set_text(GTK_LABEL(lookup_widget(frm_commissions,
                            "lbl_archive")), "Query Failure in "
                            "record count on "
                            "tbl_commissions.\n  Contact "
                            "administrator.");

        /* Nothing to do but abort. */
        mysql_close(conx);
        return;
    }
else
    {
        /* Query Success... */
        result_set = mysql_store_result (conx);
        row = mysql_fetch_row (result_set);
        g_print("tbl_commissions row count is %s...\n", row[0]);

        rows_before = row[0];

    }
/* Now to create the new table. */

time(&now);
str_table_name = g_strstrip((gchar *) ctime(&now));
str_table_name = g_strdelimit(str_table_name, " :,", '_');

g_print("new table name is %s\n", str_table_name);

/* The command used below is the CREATE TABLE command. Although
 * there are various ways to use this command, in this case the
 * syntax that will give the desired result is
 *
 *    create table tbl select-statement
 *
 * where tbl is the new table name and select-statement is a
 * valid sql select statement. This creates a new table from
 * the results of a valid select statement, rather than specifying
 * the columns explicitly.
 */

sql = g_strconcat("create table ", str_table_name,
                  " select * from tbl_commissions", 0L);

if (mysql_query (conx, sql) != 0)
    {
```

```
        /* Query failure… */
        set_message(g_strconcat("Query Failure in ",
                   "create table on ",
                   str_table_name, 0L));

        gtk_label_set_text(GTK_LABEL(lookup_widget(frm_commissions,
                           "lbl_archive")), "Query Failure "
                           "in create table statement.\n "
                           "Note the date and time "
                           "and contact administrator.");

        /* Nothing to do but abort. */
        mysql_close(conx);
        return;
    }
        /* Query Success… */

/* Now to count the rows in the new table and make sure it
 * compares to the number from the original.
 */

sql = g_strconcat("select count(*) from ", str_table_name, 0L);

if (mysql_query (conx, sql) != 0)
    {
        /* Query failure… */
        set_message(g_strconcat("Query Failure: count of table ",
                   str_table_name, 0L));
        gtk_label_set_text(GTK_LABEL(lookup_widget(frm_commissions,
                           "lbl_archive")), "Query Failure "
                           "in count of new table.\n"
                           "Note the date and time "
                           "and contact administrator.");

        mysql_close(conx);
        return;
    }
        /* Query Success… */

result_set = mysql_store_result (conx);
row = mysql_fetch_row (result_set);
g_print("new table row count is %s...\n", row[0]);

rows_after = row[0];

/* Compare the answers of the two count queries.
 * Whether integer or string, the answers should
 * be identical. In this case, because of the way
 * mysql queries are returned, the results are
 * strings.
 */
```

continues

Listing 9.7   **Continued**

```
if (g_strcasecmp(rows_after, rows_before) != 0)
    {
        /* Difference in query results; something
         * is wrong.
         */

        set_message("Failure comparing archived table "
                    "to current table.");
        gtk_label_set_text(GTK_LABEL(lookup_widget(frm_commissions,
                    "lbl_archive")), "Query Failure in comparison "
                    "of archived and new tables.\n"
                    "Note the date and time "
                    "and contact administrator.");

        mysql_close(conx);
        return;
    }
        /* The number of rows matches up
         * At this point, all indications are that
         * tbl_commissions has been correctly archived
         * and that the program can continue with
         * the processing operation.
         */

sql = "Delete from tbl_commissions";
if (mysql_query (conx, sql) != 0)
    {
        /* Query failure… */
        set_message("Failure deleting from tbl_commissions");
        gtk_label_set_text(GTK_LABEL(lookup_widget(frm_commissions,
                    "lbl_archive")), "Query Failure in delete "
                    "of records from tbl_commissions.\n  "
                    "Note the date and time "
                    "and contact administrator.");

        mysql_close(conx);
        return;
    }
        /* Query Success.
         * Remember, the mysql_query() function
         * returns an answer that indicates whether or not
         * it was given a properly formed SQL statement
         * that could be executed—not whether or not the
         * query actually deleted anything (in this
         * case). Therefore, the software needs to
         * check the count of rows in the table.
         *
         * Continue processing…
         */
```

```
        sql = "select count(*) from tbl_commissions";
        if (mysql_query (conx, sql) != 0)
            {
                /* Query failure… */
                set_message("Failure getting count from tbl_commissions");
                gtk_label_set_text(GTK_LABEL(lookup_widget(frm_commissions,
                            "lbl_archive")), "Query Failure in count "
                            "of records from tbl_commissions.\n  "
                            "Note the date and time "
                            "and contact administrator.");

                mysql_close(conx);
                return;
            }
                /* Query executed okay… */

        result_set = mysql_store_result (conx);
        row = mysql_fetch_row (result_set);
        g_print("old table row count is %s...\n", row[0]);

        if (g_strcasecmp(row[0], "0") != 0)
            {
                /* Difference in query results; something
                 * is wrong. */

                set_message("Not 0 rows in tbl_commissions");
                gtk_label_set_text(GTK_LABEL(lookup_widget(frm_commissions,
                            "lbl_archive")), "Query Failure: not 0 "
                            "rows in tbl_commissions.\n  "
                            "Note the date and time "
                            "and contact administrator.");

                mysql_close(conx);
                return;
            }
        else
            {
                /* All has gone correctly. */
                mysql_close(conx);
                gtk_label_set_text(GTK_LABEL(lookup_widget(frm_commissions,
                                "lbl_archive")), "Archive succeeded."
                                );
                log_event("Successfully archived tbl_commissions. ");
            }

}

void load_tbl_revenue()
{
    /* This function will load the text file into tbl_revenue.
     * It does the same thing as Listing 8.1 without the drop table
```

continues

Listing 9.7   **Continued**

```
 * and select count(*) statements. In fact, the LOAD
 * DATA statement is identical except for the escape characters
 * before the double-quotation marks in the first line.
 */

log_event("Improrting to tbl_revenue. ");

conx = mysql_init(0L);
conx = mysql_real_connect(conx, SERVER, LOGIN,
                          PASS, DB, 0, 0L, 0);

g_print("Starting import...\n");

/* First, empty tbl_revenue and verify that it is
 * empty before you import the text file.
 */
sql = "delete from tbl_revenue";

if (mysql_query (conx, sql) != 0)
    {
        /* Query failure… */
        mysql_close(conx);
        set_message("Query failure: delete from tbl_revenue");
        gtk_label_set_text(GTK_LABEL(lookup_widget(frm_commissions,
                "lbl_import")), "Query Failure deleteing from "
                "tbl_revenue.\n   "
                "Note the date and time "
                "and contact administrator.");
        return;
    }
else
    {
        g_print("Query success, delete from tbl_revenue.\n");
    }

/* Check to see that there are, in fact, 0 rows in tbl_revenue. */

sql = "select count(*) from tbl_revenue";

if (mysql_query (conx, sql) != 0)
    {
        /* Query failure… */
        mysql_close(conx);
        set_message("Query failure: count of rows from tbl_revenue");
        gtk_label_set_text(GTK_LABEL(lookup_widget(frm_commissions,
                "lbl_import")), "Query Failure counting rows from "
                "tbl_revenue.\n   "
                "Note the date and time "
                "and contact administrator.");
```

```
            return;
        }
            /* Query success. */

    result_set = mysql_store_result (conx);
    row = mysql_fetch_row (result_set);
    g_print("tbl_revenue row count is %s...\n", row[0]);

    if (g_strcasecmp(row[0], "0") != 0)
        {
            /* Not 0 rows in tbl_revenue. Importing now would
             * result in incorrect data processing, so exit.
             */

            set_message("Not ZERO rows in tbl_revenue");
            gtk_label_set_text(GTK_LABEL(lookup_widget(frm_commissions,
                            "lbl_import")), "Query Failure: not ZERO "
                            "rows in tbl_revenue.\n "
                            "Note the date and time "
                            "and contact administrator.");

            mysql_close(conx);
            return;
        }
            /* Query okay, so continue… */

    sql = "LOAD DATA INFILE "
        " \"/mnt/DOS_hda2/newriders/book/ch8/tbl_revenue.txt\" "
        "INTO TABLE tbl_revenue "
        "FIELDS TERMINATED BY \',\' "
        "IGNORE 1 LINES "
        "(customer_number,"
        " customer_name,"
        " salesperson,"
        " country,"
        " city,"
        " state,"
        " zip,"
        " ship_date,"
        " item_number,"
        " order_quantity,"
        " unit_price,"
        " net_value,"
        " invoice_number,"
        " invoice_date,"
        " invoice_quantity,"
        " invoice_value)";

    g_print("sql is: %s\n", sql);
```

continues

Listing 9.7 **Continued**

```
/* Note that in order for this application to
 * execute the query currently
 * in sql, the following permission must be set. In the mysql
 * database (which is actually a database within the mysql server),
 * in table 'user', the File_priv must be set to Y for the
 * specified user on the specified machine. In this
 * case, the user is com_user, and the machine name will be whatever
 * machine the user "processor" is on.
 *
 * Don't forget to give the flush privileges
 * command from the mysql> prompt
 * to reload the privileges to the database
 * (or reboot the machine, which also works).
 */

if (mysql_query (conx, sql) != 0)
    {
        /* Query failure… */
        g_print("Error number is %i...\n", mysql_errno(conx) );
        g_print("Error description is %s...\n",
                mysql_error(conx) );

        mysql_close(conx);
        set_message("Query failure in LOAD DATA statement");
        gtk_label_set_text(GTK_LABEL(lookup_widget(frm_commissions,
                "lbl_import")), "Query Failure in "
                "LOAD DATA statement.\n  "
                "Note the date and time "
                "and contact administrator.");
        return;
    }
        /* Query success… */

sql = "select count(*) from tbl_revenue";
if (mysql_query (conx, sql) != 0)
    {
        /* Query failure… */
        mysql_close(conx);
        set_message("Query failure in select count "
                "from tbl_revenue");
        gtk_label_set_text(GTK_LABEL(lookup_widget(frm_commissions,
                "lbl_import")), "Query Failure in "
                "select count from tbl_reveue..\n  "
                "Note the date and time "
                "and contact administrator.");
        return;
    }
        /* Query success… */
```

```
result_set = mysql_store_result (conx);
row = mysql_fetch_row (result_set);
g_print("tbl_revenue row count is %s...\n", row[0]);

if (g_strcasecmp(row[0], "0") != 0)
    {
        /* tbl_revenue should be populated now. So
         * report "success" back to the user.
         */
        gtk_label_set_text(GTK_LABEL(lookup_widget(frm_commissions,
                    "lbl_import")), g_strconcat("Import succeeded. ",
                    row[0], " rows imported.", 0L));

    }
else
    {
        /* There are 0 rows in the table after the import operation,
         * which is incorrect; the table should be populated now.
         */
        gtk_label_set_text(GTK_LABEL(lookup_widget(frm_commissions,
                    "lbl_import")), "0 rows in tbl_revenue after "
                    "import operation...\n  "
                    "Note the date and time "
                    "and contact administrator.");

    }

    mysql_close(conx);

}
```

Six Main Data Processing Steps

The application being built has six primary processing steps, which are the center six command buttons on frm_commissions of the ten down the left side of the form. Listing 9.8 lists the functions that perform those steps.

Listing 9.8 **Main Data Processing Functions**

```
void process_customer_commissions()
{

    /* If a row in tbl_revenue has a salesperson number in it,
     * that salesperson gets commission on the invoice. There may
     * be others that do also, and the salesperson in question may
     * also get other commissions, but the salesperson will always
     * get commissions for those rows in tbl_revenue where his or her
     * salesperson number shows up.
     */
```

continues

Listing 9.8 **Continued**

```c
log_event("Processing commissions on salepeople in tbl_revenue. ");

conx = mysql_init(0L);
conx = mysql_real_connect(conx, SERVER, LOGIN,
                          PASS, DB, 0, 0L, 0);

g_print("Starting customer processing...\n");

sql = "insert into tbl_commissions "
      "(salesperson, invoice_num, commission) "
      "select tbl_revenue.salesperson, "
      "tbl_revenue.invoice_number, "
      "tbl_people.commission * tbl_revenue.invoice_value "
      "from tbl_revenue, tbl_people "
      "where tbl_revenue.salesperson = tbl_people.salesperson";

if (mysql_query (conx, sql) != 0)
    {
        /* Query failure… */
        mysql_close(conx);
        set_message("Query failure in "
                    "process_customer_commissions.");
        gtk_label_set_text(GTK_LABEL(lookup_widget(frm_commissions,
                    "lbl_customers")), "Query Failure "
                    "procssing by saleperson in tbl_revenue. \n  "
                    "Could not execute Insert query. \n"
                    "Note the date and time "
                    "and contact administrator.");
        return;
    }
else
    {
        gtk_label_set_text(GTK_LABEL(lookup_widget(frm_commissions,
            "lbl_customer")), g_strconcat("Customer Succeeded. ",
            g_strdup_printf("%d",(gint) mysql_affected_rows(conx)),
            " rows inserted.", 0L));

        mysql_close(conx);
        set_message("process_customer_commissions succeeded.");
    }

}

void process_worldwide()
{
    /* In this step, the software should process commissions for those
     * salespeople who are paid a commission based on every invoice
     * issued worldwide. This will be a simple operation because there
     * are only two people in tbl_people_paid_on_worldwide.
     */
```

```
    log_event("Processing worldwide commissions.");

    conx = mysql_init(0L);
    conx = mysql_real_connect(conx, SERVER, LOGIN,
                              PASS, DB, 0, 0L, 0);

    g_print("Starting worldwide processing...\n");

    sql = "insert into tbl_commissions "
          "(salesperson, invoice_num, commission) "
          "select tbl_people_paid_on_worldwide.salesperson, "
          "       tbl_revenue.invoice_number, "
          "       tbl_people.commission * tbl_revenue.invoice_value "
          "from tbl_people_paid_on_worldwide, tbl_revenue, tbl_people "
          "where tbl_people.salesperson = "
          "       tbl_people_paid_on_worldwide.salesperson ";

    if (mysql_query (conx, sql) != 0)
        {
            /* Query failure… */
            mysql_close(conx);
            set_message("Query failure in process_worldwide.");
            gtk_label_set_text(GTK_LABEL(lookup_widget(frm_commissions,
                    "lbl_worldwide")), "Query Failure "
                    "procssing worldwide  \n  "
                    "Could not execute Insert query. \n"
                    "Note the date and time "
                    "and contact administrator.");
            return;
        }
    else
        {
            gtk_label_set_text(GTK_LABEL(lookup_widget(frm_commissions,
                "lbl_worldwide")), g_strconcat("Worldwide Succeeded. ",
                g_strdup_printf("%d",(gint) mysql_affected_rows(conx)),
                " rows inserted.", 0L));

            mysql_close(conx);
            set_message("process_worldwide succeeded.");
        }

}

void process_area(gchar *area)
{
    /* This function allows processing of the country and state
     * steps. This is due to the similar names of the label
     * widgets and MySQL tables. Unfortunately, because cmd_zip and
     * lbl_zip are not named cmd_zipcode and lbl_zipcode,
```

continues

Listing 9.8 **Continued**

```
 * this proceedure will not work for the zipcode
 * processing.
 */

log_event(g_strconcat("Processing ", area, " commissions.", 0L));

conx = mysql_init(0L);
conx = mysql_real_connect(conx, SERVER, LOGIN,
                          PASS, DB, 0, 0L, 0);

g_print("Starting %s processing...\n", area);

sql = g_strconcat(
    "insert into tbl_commissions "
    "(salesperson, invoice_num, commission) "
    "select tbl_people_paid_on_", area, ".salesperson, "
    "       tbl_revenue.invoice_number, "
    "       tbl_people.commission * tbl_revenue.invoice_value "
    "from tbl_people_paid_on_", area, ", tbl_revenue, tbl_people "
    "where tbl_people.salesperson=tbl_people_paid_on_",
        area, ".salesperson"
    "  and tbl_people_paid_on_", area, ".", area,
    "          =tbl_revenue.", area,
    0L);

if (mysql_query (conx, sql) != 0)
    {
        /* Query failure… */
        mysql_close(conx);
        set_message(g_strconcat("Query failure in process_",
                                area, ".", 0L));
        gtk_label_set_text(GTK_LABEL(lookup_widget(frm_commissions,
                g_strconcat("lbl_", area, 0L))),
                g_strconcat( "Query Failure "
                "procssing ", area, ". \n  "
                "Could not execute Insert query. \n"
                "Note the date and time "
                "and contact administrator.", 0L));
        return;
    }
else
    {
        gtk_label_set_text(GTK_LABEL(lookup_widget(frm_commissions,
            g_strconcat("lbl_", area, 0L))),
            g_strconcat(area, " Succeeded. ",
            g_strdup_printf("%d",(gint) mysql_affected_rows(conx)),
            " rows inserted.", 0L));

        mysql_close(conx);
```

```
                set_message(g_strconcat("process ", area,
                                   " succeeded.", 0L));
        }

}

void process_zipcode()
{

    /* Certain people are paid based on the zipcode that is in tbl_revenue
     * for that invoice. This function will add those lines to
     * tbl_commisisons.
     */

    log_event("Processing zipcodes.");

    conx = mysql_init(0L);
    conx = mysql_real_connect(conx, SERVER, LOGIN,
                              PASS, DB, 0, 0L, 0);

    g_print("Starting zipcode processing...\n");

    sql = "insert into tbl_commissions "
          "(salesperson, invoice_num, commission) "
          "select tbl_people_paid_on_zipcode.salesperson, "
          "       tbl_revenue.invoice_number, "
          "       tbl_people.commission * tbl_revenue.invoice_value "
          "from tbl_people_paid_on_zipcode, tbl_revenue, tbl_people "
          "where tbl_people.salesperson="
          "                   tbl_people_paid_on_zipcode.salesperson"
          "  and tbl_people_paid_on_zipcode.zipcode=tbl_revenue.zip";

    if (mysql_query (conx, sql) != 0)
        {
            /* Query failure... */
            mysql_close(conx);
            set_message("Query failure in process_zipcode");
            gtk_label_set_text(GTK_LABEL(lookup_widget(frm_commissions,
                    "lbl_zip")), "Query Failure "
                    "procssing zipcodes. \n  "
                    "Could not execute Insert query. \n"
                    "Note the date and time "
                    "and contact administrator.");
            return;
        }
    else
        {
            gtk_label_set_text(GTK_LABEL(lookup_widget(frm_commissions,
                "lbl_zip")), g_strconcat("Zipcodes Succeeded. ",
                g_strdup_printf("%d",(gint) mysql_affected_rows(conx)),
                " rows inserted.", 0L));
```

continues

Listing 9.8   **Continued**

```
            mysql_close(conx);
            set_message("process zipcodes succeeded.");
        }

}

void process_paid_on_people()
{

    /* Some people are paid based on the revenue generated by others; for
     * example, a regional manager may get a commission on his
     * salespersons' activity. This function inserts those
     * rows into tbl_commissions.
     */

    log_event("Processing people paid on other people.");

    conx = mysql_init(0L);
    conx = mysql_real_connect(conx, SERVER, LOGIN,
                              PASS, DB, 0, 0L, 0);

    g_print("Starting paid-on-others processing...\n");

    sql = "insert into tbl_commissions "
        "(salesperson, invoice_num, commission) "
        "select tbl_people_paid_on_other_people.person_paid, "
        "tbl_revenue.invoice_number, "
        "tbl_people.commission * tbl_revenue.invoice_value "
        "from tbl_revenue, tbl_people, "
        "    tbl_people_paid_on_other_people "
        "where tbl_revenue.salesperson = "
        "    tbl_people_paid_on_other_people.paid_on "
        " and tbl_people.salesperson = "
        "    tbl_people_paid_on_other_people.person_paid";

    if (mysql_query (conx, sql) != 0)
        {
            /* Query failure… */
            mysql_close(conx);
            set_message("Query failure in process_paid_on_people");
            gtk_label_set_text(GTK_LABEL(lookup_widget(frm_commissions,
                    "lbl_people")), "Query Failure "
                    "procssing those paid on others. \n  "
                    "Could not execute Insert query. \n"
                    "Note the date and time "
                    "and contact administrator.");
            return;
        }
    else
```

```
        {
            gtk_label_set_text(GTK_LABEL(lookup_widget(frm_commissions,
                "lbl_people")),
                g_strconcat("People paid on other",
                " People Succeeded. ",
                g_strdup_printf("%d",(gint) mysql_affected_rows(conx)),
                " rows inserted.", 0L));

            mysql_close(conx);
            set_message("process paid-on-others succeeded.");
        }

    }
```

Output Functions

Finally, this application must produce output for it to be useful. As outlined in Chapter 8, it produces two types of output: a text file for each salesperson, and a text file for each "country manager." The salesperson's text file summarizes his or her activity for the past month, and the country manager gets a report as to who was paid and how much, converted to the local currency. Listing 9.9 is the code that produces these files.

Listing 9.9 **Output Functions from _comm_utils.c_**

```
void write_salespeople_statements()
{
    gchar *file_name;
    FILE  *fp;
    gchar *current_salesperson = "nobody";

    log_event("Writing salespeople statements.");

    conx = mysql_init(0L);
    conx = mysql_real_connect(conx, SERVER, LOGIN,
                              PASS, DB, 0, 0L, 0);

    g_print("Starting write of salespeople statments.\n");
    gtk_label_set_text(GTK_LABEL(lookup_widget(frm_commissions,
                    "lbl_salespeople")), "Retrieving records "
                    "from the database...\n "
                    "This may take a few minutes..."
                    );

    gtk_widget_show(lookup_widget(frm_commissions, "lbl_salespeople"));

    sql = "select tbl_commissions.salesperson, "
        "        tbl_commissions.invoice_num, "
        "        tbl_commissions.commission, "
```

continues

Listing 9.9   **Continued**

```
             "       tbl_people.first_name, "
             "       tbl_people.last_name, "
             "       tbl_revenue.customer_name, "
             "       tbl_revenue.item_number, "
             "       tbl_revenue.order_quantity "
             "from tbl_commissions, tbl_people, tbl_revenue "
             "where tbl_commissions.salesperson = tbl_people.salesperson "
             "  and tbl_commissions.invoice_num ="
             "                          tbl_revenue.invoice_number "
             "order by tbl_commissions.salesperson, "
             "       tbl_commissions.invoice_num";

    if (mysql_query (conx, sql) != 0)
        {
            /* Query failure… */
            mysql_close(conx);
            set_message("Query failure: writing "
                    "salespeople statements");
            gtk_label_set_text(GTK_LABEL(lookup_widget(frm_commissions,
                    "lbl_salespeople")), "Query Failure "
                    "writing salespeople statements. \n  "
                    "Note the date and time "
                    "and contact administrator.");
            return;
        }
    else
        {

            result_set = mysql_store_result (conx);

            gtk_label_set_text(GTK_LABEL(lookup_widget(frm_commissions,
                    "lbl_salespeople")),
                    g_strconcat("Writing salespeople ",
                    "statements to disk...\n ",
                    "Total Records: ",
                    g_strdup_printf("%d",(gint)
                    mysql_num_rows(result_set)),
                    0L));

            set_message("Retrieved records for salesman statements.");

            /* The query executed okay, and result_set has returned
             * the total number of rows. So it is okay to continue…
             */
        }

    /* Now to move on to writing to the file. Because each
     * salesperson will have his or her own file, and because
     * result_set is organized by salesperson, the software will
     * iterate through the rows and create a new file each time
```

```
 * the value for salesperson changes.
 *
 * To start, you need a filename.
 *
 * Fetch the first row to get things started.
 */

if ((row = mysql_fetch_row (result_set)) == 0L)
   {
      /* Unable to get first row. */
      set_message("Unable to retrieve first row from result_set.");

      return;
   }
     /* Okay to continue. */

/* To avoid a core dump when the fclose() operation
 * is encountered, set up for the first salesperson.
 */

current_salesperson = row[0];
file_name = g_strconcat(current_salesperson, "-",
                   row[4], ".xls", 0L);

g_print("Current file is %s.\n", file_name);

/* Open the new file. */

if ((fp = fopen (file_name, "w")) == 0L)
    {
            set_message(g_strconcat("Unable to open first file ",
                       file_name,
                       " for write operation.", 0L));
            return;
    }
else
    {
            /* Write the header information. */
            fprintf(fp, "Commissions detail file for ");
            fprintf(fp, current_salesperson);
            fprintf(fp, ", ");
            fprintf(fp, row[3]);   /* The person's first name. */
            fprintf(fp, "\n");

            fprintf(fp, "All currency amounts are "
                       "in US Dollars.\n\n");

            fprintf(fp, "Invoice Number\t");
            fprintf(fp, "Commission Amt\t");
            fprintf(fp, "Customer Name\t");
            fprintf(fp, "Item Number\t");
```

continues

Listing 9.9 **Continued**

```
                fprintf(fp, "Order Quantity\n");
    }

/* The file will be the salesperson number plus the
 * person's last name. Because the salespersons are used
 * to getting files that work in Excel, this function
 * will write a tab-delimited file.
 */

do {
    if (g_strcasecmp(row[0], current_salesperson) == 0)
      {
        /* Still on the same salesperson. */

        fprintf(fp, row[1]); fprintf(fp, "\t");
        fprintf(fp, row[2]); fprintf(fp, "\t");
        fprintf(fp, row[5]); fprintf(fp, "\t");
        fprintf(fp, row[6]); fprintf(fp, "\t");
        fprintf(fp, row[7]); fprintf(fp, "\n");

      }
    else
      {
        /* row now contains a new salesperson.
         * Close the file currently open.
         */

        fclose(fp);

        /* Create a new filename. */

        current_salesperson = row[0];
        file_name = g_strconcat(current_salesperson, "-",
                        row[4], ".xls", 0L);

        g_print("Current file is %s.\n", file_name);

        /* Open the new file. */

        if ((fp = fopen (file_name, "w")) == 0L)
          {
            /* Unable to open the file for write operation
             * for some reason.
             */

            set_message(g_strconcat("Unable to open file ",
                        file_name,
                        " for write operation.", 0L));
```

```c
                    return;
            }
                /* File opened and ready for write operation. */

            /* Write the header information. */
            fprintf(fp, "Commissions detail file for ");
            fprintf(fp, current_salesperson);
            fprintf(fp, " - ");
            fprintf(fp, row[4]);   /* The person's last name. */
            fprintf(fp, ", ");
            fprintf(fp, row[3]);   /* The person's first name. */
            fprintf(fp, "\n");

            fprintf(fp, "All currency amounts are "
                        "in US Dollars.\n\n");

            fprintf(fp, "Invoice Number\t");
            fprintf(fp, "Commission Amt\t");
            fprintf(fp, "Customer Name\t");
            fprintf(fp, "Item Number\t");
            fprintf(fp, "Order Quantity\n");

        }

    } while ((row = mysql_fetch_row (result_set)) != 0L);

    g_print("Exiting write_salesperson_statements.\n");
    mysql_close(conx);

}

void write_country_manager_statements()
{
    /* This function produces the statements for the "country
     * managers." Each country gets its own statement, which is
     * then emailed to the "country manager."
     */

    gchar *file_name;
    FILE  *fp;
    gchar *current_country = "none";

    log_event("Writing country manager statements.");

    conx = mysql_init(0L);
    conx = mysql_real_connect(conx, SERVER, LOGIN,
                        PASS, DB, 0, 0L, 0);

    g_print("Starting write of country manager statments.\n");
    gtk_label_set_text(GTK_LABEL(lookup_widget(frm_commissions,
                    "lbl_country_managers")), "Retrieving records "
```

continues

Listing 9.9 **Continued**

```
                        "from the database...\n "
                        "This may take a few minutes..."
                        );

    sql = "select tbl_people.country, tbl_commissions.salesperson, "
            "       tbl_commissions.commission, "
            "       tbl_commissions.commission * tbl_exchange_rates.rate "
          "from tbl_commissions, tbl_people, tbl_exchange_rates "
          "where tbl_commissions.salesperson = tbl_people.salesperson "
          "  and tbl_people.country = tbl_exchange_rates.country "
          "group by tbl_commissions.salesperson "
          "order by tbl_people.country ";

    if (mysql_query (conx, sql) != 0)
        {
            /* Query failure… */
            mysql_close(conx);
            set_message("Query failure: "
                        "writing country manager's statements");
            gtk_label_set_text(GTK_LABEL(lookup_widget(frm_commissions,
                        "lbl_country_managers")), "Query Failure "
                        "writing country manager's statements. \n  "
                        "Note the date and time "
                        "and contact administrator.");
            return;
        }
    else
        {
            result_set = mysql_store_result (conx);

            gtk_label_set_text(GTK_LABEL(lookup_widget(frm_commissions,
                        "lbl_country_managers")),
                        g_strconcat("Writing country ",
                        "manager's statements to disk...\n ",
                        "Total Records: ",
                        g_strdup_printf("%d",(gint)
                        mysql_num_rows(result_set)),
                        0L));

            set_message("Retrieved records for country "
                        "manager's statements.");

            /* The query executed okay, and result_set has returned
             * the total number of rows. So it is okay to continue.
             */
        }

    /* Fetch the first row to get things started. */
```

```
if ((row = mysql_fetch_row (result_set)) == 0L)
    {
        /* Unable to get first row. */
        set_message("Unable to retrieve first row from result_set "
                    "for country manager's statements.");

        return;
    }
        /* Okay to continue. */

current_country = row[0];
file_name = g_strconcat(current_country, ".xls", 0L);

g_print("Current file is %s.\n", file_name);

/* Open the new file. */

if ((fp = fopen (file_name, "w")) == 0L)
    {
            set_message(g_strconcat("Unable to open first ",
                        "country file: ",
                        file_name,
                        ", for write operation.", 0L));
            return;
    }
else
    {
            /* Write the header information. */
            fprintf(fp, "Commissions detail file for country: ");
            fprintf(fp, current_country);
            fprintf(fp, "\n");

            fprintf(fp, "Salesperson\t");
            fprintf(fp, "US Dollars\t");
            fprintf(fp, "Local Currency\n");
    }

do {

    if (g_strcasecmp(row[0], current_country) == 0)
      {
        /* Still on the same country. */

        fprintf(fp, row[1]); fprintf(fp, "\t");
        fprintf(fp, row[2]); fprintf(fp, "\t");
        fprintf(fp, row[3]); fprintf(fp, "\n");

      }
    else
      {
```

continues

Listing 9.9 **Continued**

```c
                        /* row now contains a new country.
                         * Close the file currently open.
                         */

                        fclose(fp);

                        /* Create a new filename. */

                        current_country = row[0];
                        file_name = g_strconcat(current_country, ".xls", 0L);

                        g_print("Current file is %s.\n", file_name);

                        /* Open the new file. */

                        if ((fp = fopen (file_name, "w")) == 0L)
                            {
                                /* Unable to open the file for write operation
                                 * for some reason.
                                 */

                                set_message(g_strconcat("Unable to open ",
                                            "country file ",
                                            file_name,
                                            " for write operation.", 0L));

                                return;
                            }
                        else
                            {
                                /* File opened and ready for write operation. */
                            }

                        /* Write the header information. */
                        fprintf(fp, "Commissions detail file for country: ");
                        fprintf(fp, current_country);
                        fprintf(fp, "\n");

                        fprintf(fp, "Salesperson\t");
                        fprintf(fp, "US Dollars\t");
                        fprintf(fp, "Local Currency\n");

                    }

            } while ((row = mysql_fetch_row (result_set)) != 0L);

        g_print("Exiting write_country_manager_statements.\n");
        mysql_close(conx);


    }
```

Action Query Functions

Listing 9.10 contains the data insert, update, and delete functions that are used by "processor" (the person authorized to make changes to the database). These functions are called using the widgets at the bottom of frm_commissions.

Listing 9.10 **Action Query Functions from *comm_utils.c***

```
void insert_row()
{
    /* This function inserts a single row into a table in the
     * database. Along with the update and delete functions (below),
     * it allows the user to modify the data in the database rather
     * than having to make requests of the database administrator (dba).
     */

    gchar *str_table_name;

    str_table_name = gtk_entry_get_text(GTK_ENTRY(GTK_COMBO
                        (lookup_widget(
                        frm_commissions, "cbo_table"))->entry));

    sql = g_strconcat("insert into ", str_table_name,
                        "() values()", 0L);


    conx = mysql_init(0L);
    conx = mysql_real_connect(conx, SERVER, LOGIN,
                            PASS, DB, 0, 0L, 0);

    g_print("sql is %s\n", sql);

    if (mysql_query (conx, sql) != 0)
        {
            /* Query failure… */
            g_print("sql not ok in insert_row().\n");
            mysql_close(conx);
            g_print("connection closed.\n");
            set_message(g_strconcat("Query failure: "
                        "inserting to table",
                        str_table_name, 0L));
        }
    else
        {
            g_print("sql formatted ok.\n");
            set_message(g_strconcat("New row number is: ",
                    g_strdup_printf("%d",(gint) mysql_insert_id(conx)),
                    " in table ", str_table_name,
                    0L));

        }
```

continues

Listing 9.10 **Continued**

```c
    log_event(g_strconcat("insert query on ", str_table_name, 0L));
}

void update_row()
{
    gchar *str_table_name;

    str_table_name = gtk_entry_get_text(GTK_ENTRY(GTK_COMBO
                        (lookup_widget(
                        frm_commissions, "cbo_table"))->entry));

    /* The following sql statement is built assuming that it
     * will modify a character column, not a numeric column. Note,
     * however, that MySQL will do explicit type conversion
     * from char to numeric in this case,
     * and it will update numeric columns
     * if the conversion succeeds. However, if the user
     * attempts to incorrectly update a numeric column type
     * to a character value, the value being updated will
     * be set to 0.
     */

    sql = g_strconcat("update ", str_table_name, " set ",
                gtk_editable_get_chars(GTK_EDITABLE(
                            lookup_widget(frm_commissions,
                            "entry_column_name")), 0, -1),
                " = '",
                gtk_editable_get_chars(GTK_EDITABLE(
                            lookup_widget(frm_commissions,
                            "entry_new_value")), 0, -1),
                "'  where line_number = ",
                g_strdup_printf("%d",
                gtk_spin_button_get_value_as_int(GTK_SPIN_BUTTON(
                        lookup_widget(frm_commissions,
                        "spinbutton_update_line")))),
                0L);

    g_print("sql is: %s\n", sql);

    conx = mysql_init(0L);
    conx = mysql_real_connect(conx, SERVER, LOGIN,
                            PASS, DB, 0, 0L, 0);

    if (mysql_query (conx, sql) != 0)
        {
            /* Query failure… */
            g_print("sql not ok in update_row().\n");
            mysql_close(conx);
            g_print("connection closed.\n");
```

```
            set_message(g_strconcat("Query failure: updating row in ",
                        str_table_name, 0L));
        }
    else
        {
            g_print("sql formatted ok.\n");
            set_message(g_strconcat("Updated row in table ",
                    str_table_name, 0L));

        }

    mysql_close (conx);

    log_event(g_strconcat(user_login, " update query: ",
                        g_strdelimit(g_strstrip(sql), "*'\"", '^'),
                        0L));

}

void delete_row()
{
    /* This function deletes a row from the table specified in
     * cbo_table.
     */

    gchar *str_table_name;

    str_table_name = gtk_entry_get_text(GTK_ENTRY(GTK_COMBO
                    (lookup_widget(
                    frm_commissions, "cbo_table"))->entry));

    sql = g_strconcat("delete from ", str_table_name, " where ",
                "line_number = ",
                g_strdup_printf("%d",
                gtk_spin_button_get_value_as_int(GTK_SPIN_BUTTON(
                        lookup_widget(frm_commissions,
                        "spinbutton_delete_row")))),
                0L);
    g_print("sql is: %s\n", sql);

    conx = mysql_init(0L);
    conx = mysql_real_connect(conx, SERVER, LOGIN,
                        PASS, DB, 0, 0L, 0);

    if (mysql_query (conx, sql) != 0)
        {
            /* Query failure... */
            g_print("sql not ok in delete_row().\n");
            mysql_close(conx);
            g_print("connection closed.\n");
            set_message(g_strconcat("Query failure: ",
```

continues

Listing 9.10 **Continued**

```
                        "deleting row from ",
                        str_table_name, 0L));
        }
    else
        {
            g_print("sql formatted ok.\n");
            set_message(g_strconcat("Deleted row  from table ",
                    str_table_name, 0L));

        }

    log_event(g_strconcat(user_login, " delete query: ",
                    g_strdelimit(g_strstrip(sql), "*'\"", '^'),
                    0L));


}
```

The "Glue": *callbacks.c*

Listing 9.11 is `callbacks.c` for this project. In general, the aim has been to call functions here that are in `comm_utils.c` and keep the bulk of the code in that file (`comm_utils.c`).

Listing 9.11 *callbacks.c* **from the Worldwide Commissions Applications**

```
#ifdef HAVE_CONFIG_H
#  include <config.h>
#endif

#include <gtk/gtk.h>

#include "callbacks.h"
#include "interface.h"
#include "support.h"
#include "comm_utils.h"
#include "ddc.h"

GtkWidget *frm_login;
GtkWidget *frm_table_display;
GtkWidget *frm_commissions;

gboolean
on_frm_login_delete_event              (GtkWidget       *widget,
                                        GdkEvent        *event,
                                        gpointer         user_data)

    {
```

```
    /* This is the event to shut down the application. */

    gtk_main_quit();
    return FALSE;
}


void
on_cmd_login_clicked                        (GtkButton       *button,
                                             gpointer         user_data)
{
    /* This function is called when the user clicks
     * the "login" button.
     *
     * First, the function checks the login and password; then it shows
     * frm_table_display and hides frm_login.
     */

    g_print("on_cmd_login_clicked event...\n");

    if (check_login_and_password())
      {
        g_print("Login and password succeeded...\n");

        gtk_widget_show_all(frm_table_display);
        gtk_widget_hide(frm_login);

        /* After successful login, set the tables the user
         * can display.
         */

        gtk_widget_hide(lookup_widget(frm_table_display,
                        "cmd_process"));

        fill_table_combos();

      }
    else
      {
        g_print("Login and password failure...\n");
      }

    g_print("exit on_cmd_login_clicked event...\n");

}


void
on_cmd_change_password_clicked              (GtkButton       *button,
                                             gpointer         user_data)
{
```

continues

Listing 9.11 **Continued**

```
/* This is the function that attempts to change the user's
 * login and password.
 *
 * First, it must verify that a valid user is attempting
 * to log in; then it can change that user's password.
 */

g_print("on_cmd_change_password_clicked event...\n");

if (check_login_and_password())
  {
    if (set_new_password())
      {
          /* If the code reaches this point, the user has
           * successfully logged in, and his or her password
           * has successfully been changed. Therefore,
           * proceed to show frm_tbl_display and hide
           * frm_login.
           */
          gtk_widget_show_all(frm_table_display);
          gtk_widget_hide(frm_login);

          gtk_widget_hide(lookup_widget(frm_table_display,
                    "cmd_process"));

          fill_table_combos();
      }
    else
      {
          g_print("Unable to set new password.\n");
      }
  }
else
  {
    set_message("Unable to Login to set new Password.");
  }

}


void
on_frm_table_display_size_request      (GtkWidget      *widget,
                                        GtkRequisition *requisition,
                                        gpointer        user_data)
{
  g_print("on_frm_table_display_size_request event...\n");

}
```

```
void
on_frm_table_display_state_changed      (GtkWidget       *widget,
                                         GtkStateType    state,
                                         gpointer        user_data)
{
    g_print("on_frm_table_display_state_changed event...\n");

}


void
on_combo_entry_table_changed            (GtkEditable     *editable,
                                         gpointer        user_data)
{
    /* This callback is triggered whenever the user changes
     * cbo_tables in frm_display_table.
     */
    GtkWidget *scrolledwindow_table;
    gchar     *table_name;

    g_print("on_combo_entry_table_changed event...\n");


    gtk_widget_destroy(GTK_WIDGET(lookup_widget(frm_table_display,
            "scrolledwindow_table")));

    table_name = gtk_entry_get_text (GTK_ENTRY(GTK_COMBO(lookup_widget(
                frm_table_display,"cbo_tables"))->entry));

    g_print("table name is %s...\n", table_name);

    /* Having just destroyed the main table widget with the
     * gtk_widget_destroy() call, now create a new
     * GTK+ table widget showing the data from the table
     * named "table_name."
     */

    scrolledwindow_table = create_ddc(table_name);
    gtk_widget_ref(scrolledwindow_table);
    gtk_object_set_data_full (GTK_OBJECT(frm_table_display),
                    "scrolledwindow_table", scrolledwindow_table,
                    (GtkDestroyNotify) gtk_widget_unref);

    gtk_container_add (GTK_CONTAINER(lookup_widget(frm_table_display,
                    "vpaned_table_bottom")), scrolledwindow_table);

    gtk_widget_show(scrolledwindow_table);

    g_print("Exiting on_combo_entry_table_changed event...\n");

}
```

continues

Listing 9.11   **Continued**

```
void
on_cmd_process_clicked                    (GtkButton    *button,
                                           gpointer      user_data)
{
   g_print("on_cmd_process_clicked event...\n");
   gtk_widget_show_all(frm_commissions);

}


void
on_cmd_refresh_clicked                    (GtkButton    *button,
                                           gpointer      user_data)
{
   g_print("on_cmd_refresh_clicked event...\n");
   on_combo_entry_table_changed (0L, 0L);

}


void
on_cmd_sort_clicked                       (GtkButton    *button,
                                           gpointer      user_data)
{
   /* This function is called when the user pushes cmd_sort.
    *
    * It sets the sort on clist_table according to the choices
    * set by the user on frm_table_display.
    */

   gchar *sort_type;

   g_print("on_cmd_sort_clicked event...\n");

   gtk_clist_set_sort_column(GTK_CLIST(lookup_widget(
            frm_table_display, "clist_table")),
            gtk_spin_button_get_value_as_int(GTK_SPIN_BUTTON
              (lookup_widget(
              frm_table_display,
              "spinbutton_column")))-1
   );
   sort_type = gtk_entry_get_text(GTK_ENTRY(
            GTK_COMBO(lookup_widget(frm_table_display,
                    "cbo_sort_type"))->entry));

   if (g_strcasecmp(sort_type, "Ascending") == 0)
      gtk_clist_set_sort_type(GTK_CLIST(lookup_widget(
            frm_table_display, "clist_table")),
            GTK_SORT_ASCENDING);
```

```
        else
            gtk_clist_set_sort_type(GTK_CLIST(lookup_widget(
                    frm_table_display, "clist_table")),
                    GTK_SORT_DESCENDING);

        /* Now set the sort on the CList widget. */

        g_print("sort type is %s...\n", sort_type);

        gtk_clist_sort(GTK_CLIST(lookup_widget
                    (frm_table_display, "clist_table")));

        /* "Refresh" the form. */

        gtk_widget_show_all(frm_table_display);
}



gboolean
on_frm_table_display_delete_event        (GtkWidget         *widget,
                                          GdkEvent          *event,
                                          gpointer           user_data)
{
    /* After the user is logged in, closing frm_table_display will
     * be the signal to quit the application.
     */

    g_print("on_frm_table_display_delete_event...\n");
    gtk_main_quit();
    return FALSE;
}



gboolean
on_frm_commissions_delete_event          (GtkWidget         *widget,
                                          GdkEvent          *event,
                                          gpointer           user_data)
{
    /* If the user closes frm_commissions, it should still
     * be available; however, it will be hidden as
     * opposed to deleted or destroyed.
     */

    g_print("on_frm_commissions_delete_event...\n");


    /* When the user closes this form, the form should just
     * be hidden, not deleted. That is the function of the
     * return TRUE call below.
     */
```

continues

Listing 9.11 **Continued**

```
    gtk_widget_hide(GTK_WIDGET(widget));
    return TRUE;
}


void
on_cmd_country_managers_clicked         (GtkButton       *button,
                                         gpointer        user_data)
{
  g_print("on_cmd_country_managers_clicked event...\n");

  write_country_manager_statements();

}


void
on_cmd_import_clicked                    (GtkButton       *button,
                                         gpointer        user_data)
{
  g_print("on_cmd_import_clicked event...\n");

  load_tbl_revenue();
}


void
on_cmd_customer_clicked                  (GtkButton       *button,
                                         gpointer        user_data)
{
  g_print("on_cmd_customer_clicked event...\n");

  process_customer_commissions();
}


void
on_cmd_archive_clicked                   (GtkButton       *button,
                                         gpointer        user_data)
{
  g_print("on_cmd_archive_clicked event...\n");

  archive_tbl_commissions();
}


void
on_cmd_worldwide_clicked                 (GtkButton       *button,
                                         gpointer        user_data)
```

```c
{
    g_print("on_cmd_worldwide_clicked event...\n");

    process_worldwide();
}


void
on_cmd_country_clicked                  (GtkButton       *button,
                                         gpointer         user_data)
{
    g_print("on_cmd_country_clicked event...\n");

    process_area("country");
}


void
on_cmd_zip_clicked                      (GtkButton       *button,
                                         gpointer         user_data)
{
    g_print("on_cmd_zip_clicked event...\n");

    process_zipcode();
}


void
on_cmd_people_clicked                   (GtkButton       *button,
                                         gpointer         user_data)
{
    g_print("on_cmd_people_clicked event...\n");

    process_paid_on_people();
}


void
on_cmd_salespeople_clicked              (GtkButton       *button,
                                         gpointer         user_data)
{
    g_print("on_cmd_salespeople_clicked event...\n");

    write_salespeople_statements();
}


void
on_cmd_add_clicked                      (GtkButton       *button,
                                         gpointer         user_data)
{
```

continues

Listing 9.11 **Continued**

```
    g_print("on_cmd_add_clicked event...\n");

    insert_row();

}


void
on_cmd_delete_row_clicked               (GtkButton       *button,
                                         gpointer        user_data)
{
    g_print("on_cmd_delete_row_clicked event...\n");

    delete_row();
}


void
on_cmd_update_clicked                   (GtkButton       *button,
                                         gpointer        user_data)
{
    g_print("on_cmd_update_clicked event...\n");

    update_row();
}


void
on_cmd_state_clicked                    (GtkButton       *button,
                                         gpointer        user_data)
{
    g_print("on_cmd_state_clicked event...\n");

    process_area("state");
}
```

Project Post-Mortem

Figure 9.6 shows the application after it has been run as it normally would at the end of the month. It takes about 30 seconds to process from start to finish, which is not bad.

What could have been done better? Well, for starters, the Data Display Control probably could have been made more generic and less application-dependent. For that matter, on a larger project, it might be worthwhile to create a MySQL-specific data display widget from scratch. One that would let the user edit cells "in place" would be ideal and could probably be implemented using a table widget instead of a CList widget, putting entry widgets in the table's cells so the user could edit them directly. Oh well, that is why there is a "version 2" of the product.

Figure 9.6   The Worldwide Commissions application in action.

frm_table_display doesn't automatically expand its child widgets when the form is resized; it would be better if the table display area in the center of the form would automatically get the maximum allowable space.

Although the tables are sufficiently indexed, and the entire application runs completely in about 30 seconds, this metric is for a final dataset in tbl_commissions of about 100,000 rows. This has two implications: Will the dataset ever approach one million rows? And if it does, will response time be adequate? Also, a back-and-forth progress bar (the type that shows action-in-progress, not percent completed) would be a nice feature in case the user has to wait for the software. As it is now, if the user types the executable name from the command line, the terminal window will show some progress. However, if the user double-clicks an application icon, that terminal window is not displayed.

10

Commission Calculations Deployment

THIS CHAPTER COVERS HOW TO COMPILE AND DISTRIBUTE the Worldwide Commissions Application (WCA) specified in Chapter 8, "Admission Calculations Abstract and Design" and coded in Chapter 9, "Constructing the Commissions Application." It also covers more advanced topics, such as building an RPM and cross-compiling for Win32.

Compiling from the Command Line

This is the most basic option. It is almost identical to the compile command that was shown in Chapter 6, "Order Entry Abstract and Design." Listing 10.1 is the compile command for the WCA. If you download the files from the companion Web site for this book, you will find it in the "src" directory as a file named "build.sh" under Chapter 9.

Listing 10.1 **Compile Command for WCA**

```
gcc -Wall -g -o WCA callbacks.c interface.c \
          support.c   main.c \
          comm_utils.c   ddc.c \
      `gtk-config --cflags --libs` \
      -I/usr/include/mysql \
      -L/usr/lib/mysql -lmysqlclient -lm -lz
```

Recall that:

- `gcc` is the compiler being used.
- `-Wall` tells the compiler to output all warning messages.
- `-g` tells the compiler to compile debugger information into the executable for use with gdb. gdb allows you to step through a compiled program and examine variables as an aid to debugging. It's not absolutely necessary for a clean compile.
- `-o WCA` tells the compiler to create an executable named "WCA."
- the various `*.c` files are the code source files.
- `` `gtk-config --cflags --libs` `` is a program call that in this context acts as a macro because it is called and expands to produce other command line flags for the compiler (and again, don't forget that those are *backtick* characters, not single quotation marks!).
- `-I` and the path tells the compiler to include the mysql files.
- `-L` is the path to the library files that need to be included.
- `-l` tells the compiler to include the library files that follow; in this case, `mysqlclient`, `m` (math), and `z` (zip).
- The `\` is the line continuation character.

Also remember that:

- The path variables on your machine might be different.
- You might or might not need all the library files (`m`, `z`, and so on), or you might need others not listed here.
- In order for this to compile this way, you have to comment out the "...PIXMAP..." lines from `main.c` that Glade inserts. These are normally around line 23 or 24 in `main.c`.
- You have to edit `main.c` to move your form or window widgets up to global level, and you have to include them in the headers for any `*.c` files that reference them.

The Benefits of Using *Make*

`Make` is a command line utility for rebuilding project files. In this case, it will be applied to the WCA project, but you should find it relatively simple to port it to your own project.

`Make` provides the following benefits:

- It minimizes rebuilds by not recompiling or relinking more than is necessary; it does this by examining the file timestamps and deciding what has changed since the last build.

- It breaks the compile and link process down into discrete steps so that problems can be isolated.
- It becomes easier to change the compile and link process when the source code structure of the project changes, such as when a new *.c file needs to be included in the project.
- It examines and checks dependencies among the various project files.

Listing 10.2 is a simple makefile. From within its directory, type make at the command line; make will automatically find Makefile.

Listing 10.2 Simple *makefile* for the Worldwide Commissions Application

```
INCLUDES = -I/usr/include/mysql
LIBS = -L/usr/include/mysql -L/usr/lib/mysql -lmysqlclient -lz
GTK-CONFIG = `gtk-config --cflags --libs`


# For the second line, below, it is ABSOLUTELY ESSENTIAL
# that it begin with a Tab character. Executed commands
# like that are indicated to make by a tab character as
# the first character on the line.

WCA : main.o interface.o support.o callbacks.o comm_utils.o ddc.o
        gcc -o WCA *.o $(GTK-CONFIG) $(INCLUDES) $(LIBS)

main.o : main.c
        gcc -c main.c $(GTK CONFIG)

interface.o : interface.c
        gcc -c interface.c $(GTK-CONFIG)

support.o : support.c
        gcc -c support.c $(GTK-CONFIG)

callbacks.o : callbacks.c
        gcc -c callbacks.c $(GTK-CONFIG)

comm_utils.o : comm_utils.c
        gcc -c comm_utils.c $(GTK-CONFIG) $(INCLUDES)

ddc.o : ddc.c
        gcc -c ddc.c $(GTK-CONFIG) $(INCLUDES)

clean::
        rm -f $(PROG).o $(PROG)
```

Recall that:

- A pound sign (#) designates a comment.
- The equals signs (=) mark lines that create variables.
- The $() notation expands the variables.
- The makefile breaks demonstrate the dependencies among the program; that is, each .o file is dependent on its .c file, and the WCA executable is dependent on all the .o files.

Deploying the Application

This section covers several methods of integrating custom applications with the user's desktop; a very simple method of getting the application onto the user's desktop workspace has already been covered (in the last part of Chapter 6, "Order Entry Abstracts and Design). That method will not be covered here, but you might want to review it if you haven't already. The methods covered here will focus on the Linux version of the ubiquitous "Start Bar," specifically the GNOME Start Bar.

As you read this section, keep in mind that all this takes place on Red Hat version 6.2 with the GNOME desktop selected as the default. (At the time this is being written, that is the leading distribution and its default setup. So it is assumed that will also be true for the largest number of readers. Sorry, but there just isn't time or space to cover all the combinations and permutations.) By the time this gets into your hands, you may have a different distribution and desktop; if so, you're on your own to figure out its menuing system.

Manually Setting Up the GNOME "Start Bar"

The following steps walk you through putting an entry in the GNOME Start Menu.

1. Open the GNOME Menu Editor application. Look in Start | Settings. Figure 10.1 shows where to find it, along with a running instance.

   As you can see, the choices in the left pane of the GNOME Menu Editor window mirror those available on the GNOME Start Bar, from the lower-left corner of the screen.

2. Create a subdirectory and call it "In House Applications." In the Menu Editor, select System Menus and then New Submenu. For the Name and Comment, enter In House Applications. Change the icon to whatever you would like and click the Save button. Figure 10.2 shows the Menu Editor after this operation. Notice the statusbar at the bottom of the screen: It says "/usr/share/gnome/ apps/In House Applications." This is the directory tree from which the GNOME Start Bar structure is taken.

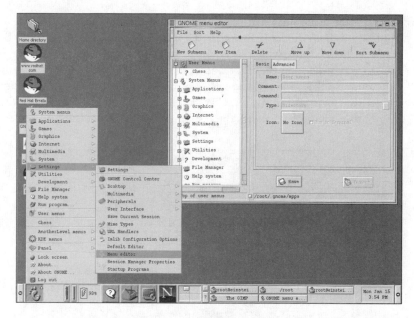

Figure 10.1   The GNOME Menu Editor: where to find it and what it looks like.

Figure 10.2   The Menu Editor after a new submenu is added.

3. To create the menu item that will launch the application, select In House Applications from the left pane of the GNOME Menu Editor, and then click the New Item button, which should give you an item called "untitled." In the Name entry widget on the right side of the GNOME Menu Editor as well as the Comment field, enter Worldwide Commissions. Set the Command entry widget to /usr/local/bin/WCA. Change the icon if you like. Then click the Save button. Figure 10.3 shows the resulting GNOME Menu Editor screen.

Figure 10.3   The Menu Editor after a new item is added.

4. Copy the compiled executable (in this instance, called "WCA") to the /usr/local/bin directory.

5. From the GNOME Start Bar, select In House Applications and then select Worldwide Commissions. Figure 10.4 shows the GNOME Start Bar menu and the WCA in action.

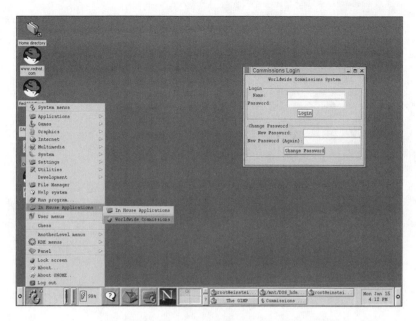

Figure 10.4   The application works (not running from a terminal window).
WCA has been launched from the GNOME Start Bar.

Now examine what the Menu Editor did. First, of course, it created a subdirectory
called In House Applications. Second, it created a file called Worldwide
Commissions.desktop that tells the operating system what to do when the user selects
the item. Going to the /usr/share/gnome/apps/ directory, you will find the In House
Applications directory. In that directory, you find the Worldwide Commissions.desktop
file. Listing 10.3 shows the contents of the file.

Listing 10.3   **Worldwide Commissions.desktop File Contents**

```
[Desktop Entry]
Name[en_US.ISO8859-1]=Worldwide Commissions
Comment[en_US.ISO8859-1]=Worldwide Commissions
Exec=/usr/local/bin/WCA
Icon=/usr/share/pixmaps/gnome-lockscreen.png
Terminal=false
MultipleArgs=false
Type=Application
```

The file is self-explanatory. Next, return to the GNOME Menu Editor and select the
Worldwide Commissions menu item. Note that there is a check box for running the
application from a terminal window; it is labeled "Run in Terminal." Click it, click
Save, close the GNOME Menu Editor, and then rerun the Worldwide Commissions
Application. Figure 10.5 shows the result.

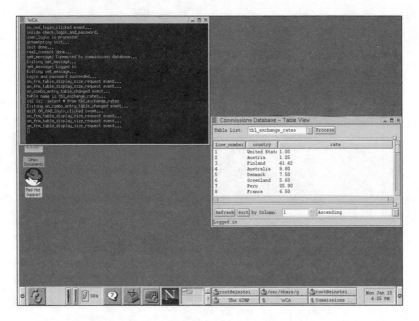

Figure 10.5   The Worldwide Commissions Application with an
attendant terminal window. Compare this figure with Figure 10.4.

In the case of this application, it makes sense to have a terminal window running with
the application because of the overuse of g_print() statements. My personal opinion is
that this is a reasonably good method of communicating with the user, and it doesn't
require the user to respond by clicking OK buttons in message boxes (when the user
can't do anything about the message anyway). This has to be a design consideration
because it is a possible method of communicating with the user, and (IMHO) it is a
better option than the typical "message boxes" that pop up when something goes
wrong. If you open the Worldwide Commissions.desktop file, you will find that the line
that previously read "Terminal=false" now reads "Terminal=true".

That is all it takes to integrate your own applications into the GNOME Desktop.
Obviously, if you have a large number of installed users, going to each user's desk and
performing these steps could get to be a hassle after a while. So the next obvious step
is to write a shell script that will do it for you. Then all you have to do is provide the
users with the shell script (for instance by email) and tell them how to run it. This
shell script will be covered in the next section.

Using a Shell Script to Set Up the GNOME "Start Bar"

This section contains a small shell script that will set up the user's machine with the
right files in the right places. This text makes the assumption that the system administrator has gathered the necessary files and somehow sent them to the user. You could
provide those files as an email attachment or perhaps by sending the user a floppy. Of

course, you would then have to assume that the user knows how to save files from email to a specific place in the directory structure, or how to mount a floppy, and so on. The shell script uses the default shell for Linux: bash. If you are running a different shell, you will need to make changes appropriate to your environment.

Listing 10.4 is the sample shell script. There could, of course, be more to this file. It could assume the files were either on a floppy or on a server that all the workstations have similarly mounted. (Of course, if you're going to do that, you could just as easily keep the executable on the server and only push the menu item file down to the desktop.) Also, it assumes that the .png file (the icon) is on the user's machine. Obviously, if the icon isn't on a particular user's machine, it would need to be included and moved to the location specified in Listing 10.3.

Listing 10.4 **Shell Script for Installing the Worldwide Commissions Application**

```
# This file is a shell script for moving the Worldwide
# Commissions Application into place on a user's machine.

# This file makes the following assumptions:
#    1.  This shell script is being called from the same
#        directory where the application files have been stored.
#    2. The user has placed the following files here:
#            WCA
#            Worldwide Commissions.desktop

# First, create the necessary directories.

mkdir "/usr/share/gnome/apps/In House Applications/"

# Next, copy the target files into place.

cp "Worldwide Commissions.desktop" "/usr/share/gnome/apps/In House Applications"
cp WCA /usr/local/bin

# Now set the permissions.

chmod 755 /usr/local/bin/WCA

echo Finished.
```

Adding the "Install" Target to *Makefile*

At this point, the `Makefile` you looked at in the previous section needs to be updated just a bit in preparation for RPM (as will become obvious in the next section). Specifically, `Makefile` needs to have an "install target" added to it. This lists the actions necessary to install the software to the user's machine, according to the shell script you just created (Listing 10.4).

Listing 10.5 **Changes to *Makefile* to Add an Install Target**

```
# Makefile for the Worldwide Commissions Application.
# Chapters 8, 9, and 10.

INCLUDES = -I/usr/include/mysql
LIBS = -L/usr/include/mysql -L/usr/lib/mysql -lmysqlclient -lz
GTK-CONFIG = `gtk-config --cflags --libs`

WCA : main.o interface.o support.o callbacks.o comm_utils.o ddc.o
      gcc -o WCA *.o $(GTK-CONFIG) $(INCLUDES) $(LIBS)

main.o : main.c
      gcc -c main.c $(GTK-CONFIG)

interface.o : interface.c
      gcc -c interface.c $(GTK-CONFIG)

support.o : support.c
      gcc -c support.c $(GTK-CONFIG)

callbacks.o : callbacks.c
      gcc -c callbacks.c $(GTK-CONFIG)

comm_utils.o : comm_utils.c
      gcc -c comm_utils.c $(GTK-CONFIG) $(INCLUDES)

ddc.o : ddc.c
      gcc -c ddc.c $(GTK-CONFIG) $(INCLUDES)

clean::
      rm -f $(PROG).o $(PROG)


EXE_LOCATION = /usr/local/bin/
MENU_LOCATION = "/usr/share/gnome/apps/In House Applications/"

# In the commands below...
#     The -p after mkdir tells mkdir not to return an error if the
#         directory already exists.
#     The -f after cp tells cp to overwrite an existing file of
#         the same name in the target location if the file
#         already exists.

install : WCA
      echo $(MENU_LOCATION)
      mkdir -p $(MENU_LOCATION)
      cp -f "Worldwide Commissions.desktop" $(MENU_LOCATION)
      cp -f WCA $(EXE_LOCATION)WCA
      chmod 755 $(EXE_LOCATION)WCA
      echo Worldwide Commissions Application Installed.
```

As you can see, the last third of the file is new; a couple of new macro variables were added, but it was essentially the same as Listing 10.4 after the `install : WCA` line. That line tells `make` that the "install target" is dependent on `WCA`, and that if it is up to date, to execute the following commands to install the software.

The normal way to use `Makefile` is for the user to type

```
% make
```

at the command line, followed by

```
% make install
```

These commands build and install the software; `make install` tells the `make` to go directly to the install target.

Creating an RPM File

Red Hat Package Manager (RPM) is the best and closest thing the Linux community has to an installer. Refer to Chapter 1, "MySQL for Access and SQL Server Developers and DBAs," for a brief overview of RPM.

This section covers the creation of a very simple "spec" file, which is used with the `rpm` command to build a *.rpm file. The rpm file provides a quick and easy way for a user to get an application installed or upgraded on his or her machine. I want to add here that *Maximum RPM* by Edward C. Bailey (RedHat Press/SAMS Publishing, 1997) was absolutely fundamental to completing this section. It is the only work I know of on the topic. Note that it is available online at `http://rpmdp.org/rpmbook/`. Other RPM information can be found at `http://rpm.redhat.com/RPM-HOWTO/`.

Listing 10.6 is the file that was used to create the RPM file for the WCA.

Listing 10.6   **WCA_comm.spec: The "spec" File that rpm Uses to Build a *.rpm File**

```
# The spec file for building the rpm to distribute the
# Worldwide Commissions Application built in Chapters
# 8 and 9.

# The Preamble Section

Summary:  Worldwide Commissions Applications
Name: WCA
Version: 0.1
Release: 1
Copyright: Proprietary
Group: Applications/Databases
Packager:  Matt Stucky <stuckym@prodigy.net>

%description
In house application for computing Worldwide Commissions
each month.

# Preparation Section
```

continues

Listing 10.6 **Continued**

```
%prep

# Clean out the rpm build and source directories in preparation for
# the build.

rm -rf $RPM_BUILD_DIR/*
rm -rf $RPM_SOURCE_DIR/*

# Copy the source files to the rpm BUILD and SOURCES directory.

cp /mnt/DOS_hda2/newriders/book/ch09/src/Makefile
/usr/src/redhat/SOURCES/Makefile
cp /mnt/DOS_hda2/newriders/book/ch09/src/*.c        /usr/src/redhat/SOURCES/
cp /mnt/DOS_hda2/newriders/book/ch09/src/*.h        /usr/src/redhat/SOURCES/
cp /mnt/DOS_hda2/newriders/book/ch09/src/*.desktop /usr/src/redhat/SOURCES/

cp /mnt/DOS_hda2/newriders/book/ch09/src/Makefile  /usr/src/redhat/BUILD/Makefile
cp /mnt/DOS_hda2/newriders/book/ch09/src/*.c        /usr/src/redhat/BUILD/
cp /mnt/DOS_hda2/newriders/book/ch09/src/*.h        /usr/src/redhat/BUILD/
cp /mnt/DOS_hda2/newriders/book/ch09/src/*.desktop /usr/src/redhat/BUILD/

# These next two sections are simple if you have already created the
# make file with a make install included.

%build
make

%install
make install

# Finally, here's a list of the files needed for the application to install.

%files
/usr/local/bin/WCA
"/usr/share/gnome/apps/In House Applications/Worldwide Commissions.desktop"
```

To build the rpm file, type this at the command prompt:

```
% rpm -ba WCA_comm.spec
```

This will force a rebuild (the -b option) of all files (the a after the -b) and will output two files: WCA-0.1–1.i386.rpm and WCA-0.1–1.src.rpm. The first is the install of the compiled application (the WCA executable), and the second is the Worldwide Commissions.desktop file, along with instructions as to how install the application. Listing 10.7 is the output of the rpm build command.

Listing 10.7   **The Output of rpm During the WCA Build Process**

```
Executing(%prep): /bin/sh -e /var/tmp/rpm-tmp.78223
Executing(%build): /bin/sh -e /var/tmp/rpm-tmp.85210
gcc -c main.c `gtk-config --cflags --libs`
gcc -c interface.c `gtk-config --cflags --libs`
gcc -c support.c `gtk-config --cflags --libs`
gcc -c callbacks.c `gtk-config --cflags --libs`
gcc -c comm_utils.c `gtk-config --cflags --libs` -I/usr/include/mysql
gcc -c ddc.c `gtk-config --cflags --libs` -I/usr/include/mysql
gcc -o WCA *.o `gtk-config --cflags --libs` -I/usr/include/mysql -
L/usr/include/mysql -L/usr/lib/mysql -lmysqlclient -lz
Executing(%install): /bin/sh -e /var/tmp/rpm-tmp.51916
echo "/usr/share/gnome/apps/In House Applications/"
/usr/share/gnome/apps/In House Applications/
mkdir -p "/usr/share/gnome/apps/In House Applications/"
cp -f "Worldwide Commissions.desktop" "/usr/share/gnome/apps/In House
Applications/"
cp -f WCA /usr/local/bin/WCA
chmod 755 /usr/local/bin/WCA
echo Worldwide Commissions Application Installed.
Worldwide Commissions Application Installed.
Processing files: WCA-0.1-1
Finding  Provides: (using /usr/lib/rpm/find-provides)...
Finding  Requires: (using /usr/lib/rpm/find-requires)...
Requires: ld-linux.so.2 libX11.so.6 libXext.so.6 libXi.so.6 libo.oo.0 libdl.so.2
libgdk-1.2.so.0 libglib-1.2.so.0 libgmodule-1.2.so.0 libgtk-1.2.so.0 libm.so.6
libz.so.1 libc.so.6(GLIBC_2.0) libc.so.6(GLIBC_2.1)
Wrote: /usr/src/redhat/SRPMS/WCA-0.1-1.src.rpm
Wrote: /usr/src/redhat/RPMS/i386/WCA-0.1-1.i386.rpm
```

If you have followed the make and make install portions of this chapter to this point, most of this should be self-explanatory. The only thing I am going to point out quickly is the line that is third from the bottom—the line that begins with Requires:. The last two lines show the packages that were output. This tells you which packages must be installed on the user's machine.

Figure 10.6 shows the package installed under KDE. Figure 10.7 shows the installed application from the KDE RPM manager. Figure 10.8 shows the application running on a client machine under KDE, and Figure 10.9 shows the application running on a client GNOME desktop.

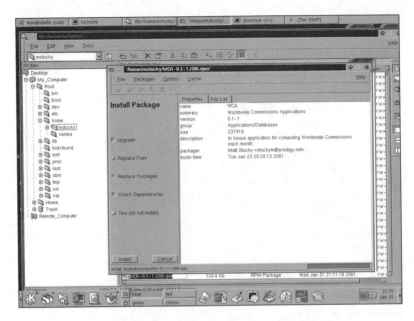

Figure 10.6 Installing the package under KDE.

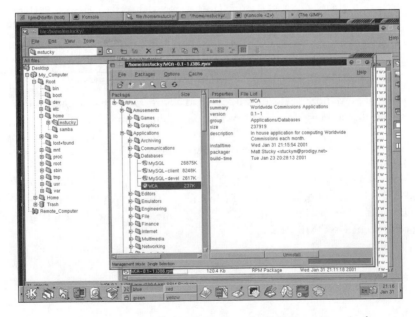

Figure 10.7 The installed package from the RPM manager—in the "Applications/Databases" category.

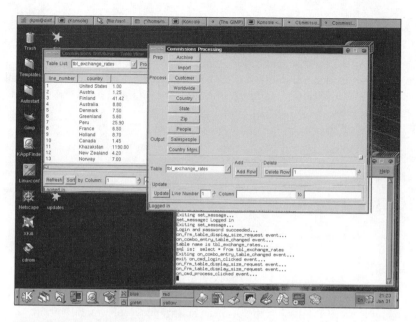

Figure 10.8   The application running on a KDE. Notice the funky window manager.

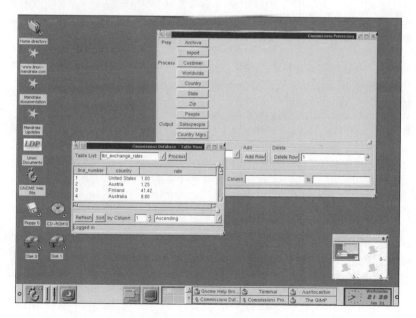

Figure 10.9   WCA running on a GNOME desktop client.

A Quick Tour of the RPM "Spec" File

In order for RPM to build an *.rpm file, it must have a spec file to build from. Listing 10.6 is the spec file for this application—and a very simple one at that. RPM is a topic by itself, and an in-depth discussion is far beyond the scope of this book. The following sections give a quick description of the various sections of an RPM file and the possibilities of each.

An RPM spec file can be divided into eight sections:

- the preamble
- prep
- build
- install
- scripts
- verify
- clean
- files

The preamble section describes the package and provides information about the package. In Listing 10.6, this is the entire section before %prep. The Group: line tells RPM what category the application in question should fall into; this is the categorization RPM keeps for itself, not a directory tree or other external path.

The prep section is used to prepare for the build. In other cases, this would be the place to unpack the sources if they had been sent to you in a tar ball (a *.tar or *.tar.gz file). In this case, it is the place where you clean out the build directories and copy the source files to /usr/source/redhat/.

The %build section (in Listing 10.6) is very simple because of the previous work in building a make file for this application. In this case, it consists of a shell script (make, which uses Makefile), but it could also be more complex if the situation required.

The %install section is equally easy, again because of the previous work to create an install target in Makefile. Without this, the package author would need to put the necessary commands in this section in order to perform the install.

The scripts, verify, and clean sections are not present in Listing 10.6. If needed, shell scripts to be run before and/or after an install and/or uninstall can be included (in the scripts section), a verify script can be used to verify a working package beyond the capabilities of RPM, and the clean section can perform any necessary cleanup actions.

Last is the file list to be included in the binary rpm (the *86.rpm file). In this case, only two files are necessary: the executable and the "shortcut" or *.desktop file. Both point to the "installed" location on the development machine, but because those files also exist in the development subdirectory, they could have also pointed to that path.

Building a simple *.rpm file is not terribly difficult; for example, I found out in this example that the "Copyright:" line is required, even though I doubt that "Proprietary" is a recognized copyright value.

Compiling for Win32 Using MS VC++

This section covers how to use the same (or nearly the same) code used to create the Linux application to compile and run the same application under MS Windows.

Before we get started here, let me take a moment to say that I don't intend in any way to be an expert on MS Visual C++, and that if you have any pointers for me on how to improve its usage in cases like this, feel absolutely free to send them to me. The compile and link below using VC++ is an admitted hack; however, the focus of this book is that Linux is the primary client platform, and Windows is viewed in a somewhat lesser status. Therefore, this section assumes that the target audience consists primarily of Linux clients, but that there might be a few Windows holdouts to be taken care of.

Also, note that the code for this application was developed on a dual-boot Red Hat 6.2 / Windows 98 machine, which made it simple to keep track of the code and the application. As with all things software, "Your mileage may vary." Visual C++ 6.0 Standard was used (less than $100 cost).

Gathering the Necessary Files

First you will need to download a number of files. You will need the MySQL for Windows files. At the time of this writing, the current file was:

```
mysql-3.23.32-win.zip
```

That file, or its current release at the time you read this, is the file you'll need. When you install it, be sure to select a custom install and to include libraries and include files. This will install not only a MySQL server on your machine (which is actually not needed here), but also the header files, libraries, and dll files.

Next, you will need the GTK+ files for Windows. These can be downloaded from `http://user.sgic.fi/~tml/gimp/win32/`.

The files you will need are

```
glib-dev-20001226.zip or newer (glib files)
libiconv-dev-20001007.zip or newer (Libiconv, used by Glib)
gtk+-dev-20001226.zip or newer (GTK+ headers, dll files, and import libraries)
```

After you have downloaded them, extract to a directory of your choosing.

Next, you will need a file from mingw; mingw is a gcc port to Win32. Fetch the latest version of gcc for mingw and the msvcrt runtime, which are currently available from:

```
ftp://ftp.nanotech.wisc.edu/pub/khan/gnu-win32/mingw32/snapshots/gcc-2.95.2-1/
```

Then download the following file:

```
mingw-msvcrt-19991107.zip (or newest release)
```

In this case, you don't necessarily need to unzip the file; you will only need one file from it, and that will be covered shortly.

Configuring the Project and Compiling

Before diving into this section, you should read the sidebar "Using Visual C++" for information on how and why Visual C++ is used here and other options you need to be aware of.

> **Using Visual C++**
>
> In this section, I commit a bit of Visual C++ heresy. The way I use Visual C++ for the include files and libraries is "incorrect," or rather, it's not the way Visual C++ is meant to be used.
>
> Specifically, instead of adding the /I and /libpath paths in this section as shown, do the following. From the Tools menu, select Options. In the Options dialog, select the Directories tab and make the directory entries here for the include files, library files, executable, files, and source files.
>
> I do it this way primarily because I prefer the visibility provided by adding the /I and /libflags the way I have done in this chapter. That is, the *.dsw, or workspace, file (the one presented at the end of this chapter) is a plain text file, and from my experience, that is helpful. Let me give an example.
>
> At a client site, a failure in controlling the development environment lead to two different versions of the same include file being on the primary build machine. I decided the more recent of the two was the desired file. However, more than a dozen different applications were regularly compiled on the target machine, and I didn't know which applications compiled with which include file. Having the /I and /libpath in a plain text *.dsw file made it easy to parse the *.dsw files on the development machine to find all the files and line numbers for a specific text string. A person could manually examine a few applications, or even a dozen, in a reasonable amount of time, but if you have a few extremely complicated applications or even dozens of simple ones, being able to quickly and easily parse, sort, and examine the files used in the build process can aid the development process significantly.
>
> Such are my reasons for doing this project in Visual C++ as I did; you will have to judge which approach works best for you. As one of my professors at UWF was fond of saying, this is a point on which "men of goodwill could disagree."

Open `main.c` in Visual C++ and try to compile. It will ask you if you want to create a "default workspace." Answer Yes and save to the directory of your choice.

In Project | Settings | C/C++ | Project Options, add

```
/I "Drive:\path\to\gtk+"
/I "Drive:\path\to\glib"
/I "Drive:\path\to\gtk"
/I "Drive:\path\to\gdk"
/I "Drive:\path\to\mysql\include"
/I "Drive:\path\to\mysql\debug"
```

where /I is the compiler "include" directive, and `Drive` is C: or D: (or whatever), and path is wherever you put `gtk.h`, `gdk.h`, `mysql.h`, and so on. Don't put trailing backslashes on.

Go to Project | Add to Project | Files and add all *.c and *.h files for this project. Those files should now show in the "file view" pane (see Figure 10.10).

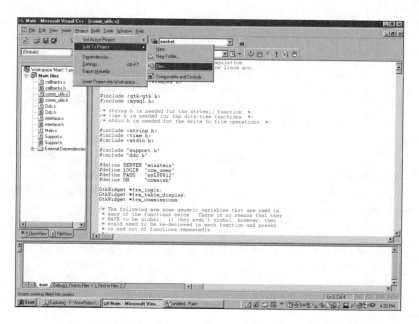

Figure 10.10 Adding the project files to this workspace.

Try to compile, but not to link. At this point, you should get a clean compile—that is, no errors and no warnings. If you do not, review your steps and take any new steps necessary to get a clean compile on the project.

Copy all dll files and libs to a single place. Add that path to Project | Settings | Link | Project Options as follows:

```
/libpath:"Drive:\path\to\files"
```

Again, don't put a trailing backslash on. In my project, I included several libpaths:

```
/libpath:"d:\GLIB\src\glib"
/libpath:"d:\GTK\src\gtk+\gtk"
/libpath:"d:\GTK\src\gtk+\gdk"
/libpath:"D:\MySQL\win32\lib\debug"
```

In Project | Settings | Link | Object/Library Modules, add:

```
gtk-1.3.lib  (or newest equivalent)
glib-1.3.lib
gdk-1.3.lib
libmysql.lib
zlib.lib
```

Do *not* add mysqlclient.lib.

From mingw.zip, extract the file unistd.h and put it in the gtk\ directory (where gtk.h is). Actually, you could put it any number of places, just as long as the compiler finds it.

In `ddc.c` and `comm_utils.c`, add the following line:

```
#include <windows.h>
```

You might also want to comment that the above line is for "Windows only" and will need to be commented back out in order to compile under Linux. This line is necessary because these are the only two files in the project that access the MySQL library, and the MySQL library on Win32 makes use of `windows.h`.

Edit `support.c` as outlined here:

- Change "`..\pixmpaps`" to "`../pixmpaps,`" or else the compiler will think it is an escape character.
- remove "` && S_ISREF(s.st_mode).`" This is a macro defined in `stat.h`, and the MS version of `stat.h` is different from the mingw version.

It is important to note here that we are violating one of the rules-of-thumb that will help us at a later date if we stick to it: That is, we are editing `support.c`, which GLADE will overwrite the next time it is used to modify the UI for this project. This is just something to keep in mind; obviously two changes are not a terribly big deal.

At this point, you should be able to link the compiled files without errors or warnings.

Finally, to run the application, copy the following files to your Windows system directory (in my case, I just used C:\Windows\), or to somewhere in your PATH, or in the same directory as the executable:

```
gtk-1.3.dll
glib-1.3.dll
gdk-1.3.dll
iconv.dll
gmodule.1.3.dll
gnu-intl.dll
libmysql.dll
```

Now you should be able to run the compiled application on your local (development) machine. (Of course you could also have altered your target machines' PATH variables to look in the directory where dll files are stored rather than copying them.) Figure 10.11 shows the Windows version of the application. Note the default GTK icon. Nice touch, guys.

Listing 10.8 at the end of this chapter displays the workspace file for this project under Visual C++; you can see the above settings reflected there for further reference.

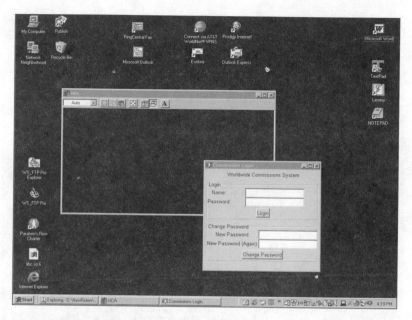

Figure 10.11   The same source code compiled and running under Windows. Note that this is on the same machine that did the development, so it can't actually connect to the MySQL server on "einstein."

Deploying the Windows Executable

Now that you have the executable, you need to get it up and running on the target client.

Copy the seven dll files from above to a location target machine's PATH, and copy the executable to the desired location. (On the machine in Figure 10.11, it was C:\Win95.) Figure 10.12 shows the Windows executable operating on a Windows machine. The MySQL database that it is using is running on a Linux server, and the network is TCP/IP. Note that in Figure 10.12, "einstein" is a Samba share on my network (see the sidebar titled "About Samba").

About Samba

In order to run Windows client/Linux server, the Linux server has to have a simple Samba share available and must broadcast so that the Windows machine can resolve the server name in the database connectivity code of the application to an IP address. This is neither the time nor the place to cover Samba; just let me say that it makes your Linux box look like a Windows box to all the other Windows machines on the network. Also, I set up my first (very simple) Samba share in five minutes by reading the /etc/smb.conf file, commenting in, and changing a few lines to conform to my network. Then it was off and running! I was amazed. In Figure 10.12, you can see the "einstein" server in the Network Neighborhood; einstein is the Linux server.

Note that, of course, you could overcome this by substituting the IP address for the server name in the code.

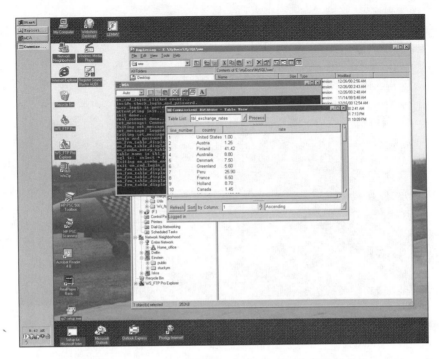

Figure 10.12 The WCA deployed to a Windows PC; this instance of the application is connected to the Linux server "einstein."

The Project Workspace File

Listing 10.8 is the ★.dsw file for the Worldwide Commissions compile and build on Windows. The dsw file is the file MS Visual C++ uses to set the workspace for the project. I have included it so you can see the final results of the previous section.

Listing 10.8 **Workspace File for WCA.exe When You Compile Under MS VC++**

```
# Microsoft Developer Studio Project File - Name="Main" - Package Owner=<4>
# Microsoft Developer Studio Generated Build File, Format Version 6.00
# ** DO NOT EDIT **/

# TARGTYPE "Win32 (x86) Console Application" 0x0103

CFG=Main - Win32 Debug
!MESSAGE This is not a valid makefile. To build this project using NMAKE,
!MESSAGE use the Export Makefile command and run
!MESSAGE
!MESSAGE NMAKE /f "Main.mak".
!MESSAGE
```

```
!MESSAGE You can specify a csconfiguration when running NMAKE
!MESSAGE by defining the macro CFG on the command line:
!MESSAGE
!MESSAGE NMAKE /f "Main.mak" CFG="Main - Win32 Debug"
!MESSAGE
!MESSAGE Possible choices for configuration are:
!MESSAGE
!MESSAGE "Main - Win32 Release" (based on "Win32 (x86) Console Application")
!MESSAGE "Main - Win32 Debug" (based on "Win32 (x86) Console Application")
!MESSAGE

# Begin Project
# PROP AllowPerConfigDependencies 0
# PROP Scc_ProjName ""
# PROP Scc_LocalPath ""
CPP=cl.exe
RSC=rc.exe

!IF  "$(CFG)" == "Main - Win32 Release"
# PROP BASE Use_MFC 0
# PROP BASE Use_Debug_Libraries 0
# PROP BASE Output_Dir "Release"
# PROP BASE Intermediate_Dir "Release"
# PROP BASE Target_Dir ""
# PROP Use_MFC 0
# PROP Use_Debug_Libraries 0
# PROP Output_Dir "Release"
# PROP Intermediate_Dir "Release"
# PROP Target_Dir ""
# ADD BASE CPP /nologo /W3 /GX /O2 /D "WIN32" /D "NDEBUG" /D "_CONSOLE" /D "_MBCS"
/YX /FD /c
# ADD CPP /nologo /W3 /GX /O2 /D "WIN32" /D "NDEBUG" /D "_CONSOLE" /D "_MBCS" /YX
/FD /c
# ADD BASE RSC /l 0x409 /d "NDEBUG"
# ADD RSC /l 0x409 /d "NDEBUG"
BSC32=bscmake.exe
# ADD BASE BSC32 /nologo
# ADD BSC32 /nologo
LINK32=link.exe
# ADD BASE LINK32 kernel32.lib user32.lib gdi32.lib winspool.lib comdlg32.lib
advapi32.lib shell32.lib ole32.lib oleaut32.lib uuid.lib odbc32.lib odbccp32.lib
/nologo /subsystem:console /machine:I386
# ADD LINK32 kernel32.lib user32.lib gdi32.lib winspool.lib comdlg32.lib
advapi32.lib shell32.lib ole32.lib oleaut32.lib uuid.lib odbc32.lib odbccp32.lib
/nologo /subsystem:console /machine:I386

!ELSEIF  "$(CFG)" == "Main - Win32 Debug"

# PROP BASE Use_MFC 0
# PROP BASE Use_Debug_Libraries 1
# PROP BASE Output_Dir "Debug"
```

continues

Listing 10.8 **Continued**

```
# PROP BASE Intermediate_Dir "Debug"
# PROP BASE Target_Dir ""
# PROP Use_MFC 0
# PROP Use_Debug_Libraries 1
# PROP Output_Dir "Debug"
# PROP Intermediate_Dir "Debug"
# PROP Ignore_Export_Lib 0
# PROP Target_Dir ""
# ADD BASE CPP /nologo /W3 /Gm /GX /ZI /Od /D "WIN32" /D "_DEBUG" /D "_CONSOLE" /D
"_MBCS" /YX /FD /GZ /c
# ADD CPP /nologo /W3 /Gm /GX /ZI /Od /I "D:\GTK\src\gtk+" /I "D:\GLIB\src\glib"
/I "D:\GTK\src\gtk+\gdk" /I "D:\GTK\src\gtk+\gtk" /I "D:\MySQL\Win32\include" /I
"D:\MySQL\Win32\lib\debug" /D "_DEBUG" /D "_CONSOLE" /D "_MBCS" /FR /YX /FD /GZ /c
# ADD BASE RSC /l 0x409 /d "_DEBUG"
# ADD RSC /l 0x409 /d "_DEBUG"
BSC32=bscmake.exe
# ADD BASE BSC32 /nologo
# ADD BSC32 /nologo
LINK32=link.exe
# ADD BASE LINK32 kernel32.lib user32.lib gdi32.lib winspool.lib comdlg32.lib
advapi32.lib shell32.lib ole32.lib oleaut32.lib uuid.lib odbc32.lib odbccp32.lib
/nologo /subsystem:console /debug /machine:I386 /pdbtype:sept
# ADD LINK32 glib-1.3.lib gtk-1.3.lib gdk-1.3.lib libmysql.lib zlib.lib
kernel32.lib user32.lib gdi32.lib winspool.lib comdlg32.lib advapi32.lib
shell32.lib ole32.lib oleaut32.lib uuid.lib odbc32.lib odbccp32.lib /nologo
/subsystem:console /debug /machine:I386 /nodefaultlib:"library" /out:"WCA.exe"
/pdbtype:sept /libpath:"d:\GLIB\src\glib" /libpath:"d:\GTK\src\gtk+\gtk"
/libpath:"d:\GTK\src\gtk+\gdk" /libpath:"D:\MySQL\win32\lib\debug"
# SUBTRACT LINK32 /pdb:none /nodefaultlib

!ENDIF

# Begin Target

# Name "Main - Win32 Release"
# Name "Main - Win32 Debug"
# Begin Source File

SOURCE=.\callbacks.c
# End Source File
# Begin Source File

SOURCE=.\callbacks.h
# End Source File
# Begin Source File

SOURCE=.\comm_utils.c
# End Source File
# Begin Source File
```

```
SOURCE=.\comm_utils.h
# End Source File
# Begin Source File

SOURCE=.\Ddc.c
# End Source File
# Begin Source File

SOURCE=.\Ddc.h
# End Source File
# Begin Source File

SOURCE=.\interface.c
# End Source File
# Begin Source File

SOURCE=.\interface.h
# End Source File
# Begin Source File

SOURCE=.\Main.c
# End Source File
# Begin Source File

SOURCE=.\Support.c
# End Source File
# Begin Source File

SOURCE=.\Support.h
# End Source File
# End Target
# End Project
```

11

Management Reporting Abstract and Design

THIS FINAL PROJECT IS CALLED "KEY BUSINESS INDICATORS" or "KBI" for short. It covers a problem that's common to in-house information departments in companies of all sizes.

Problem Definition

A business captures data in a database. Soon after that happens, people within the business start asking questions about the data, and the Information Systems/Information Technology (IS/IT) department is tasked with creating reports for the business. These reports can take any number of forms, from email to printed reports and any number of distribution methods.

This project will create a framework into which new reports can be added, and it will produce a few initial reports. The "real" problem is that a never-ending queue of new reports needs to be produced. Therefore, the real trick is to create an application that only requires the new addition to be compiled, not the entire application.

To that end, this "application" will actually be a series of smaller applications. There will be a main form that will present to the user a list of "reports" from which he or she can choose. Each of these reports will be its own executable, which can be launched from the main window.

Security Concerns

Although there are security concerns with this application, they are not as extensive as with the Worldwide Commissions application of Chapters 8 "Commissions Calculations Abstract and Design," 9 "Constructing the Commissions Applications," and 10 "Commission Calculations Deployment." In this case, the application will query the local machine for the login of the current user and will then authenticate that against the database of authorized users. (This is the same configuration as the Worldwide Commissions application, but it does not require a separate login and password.)

This security presents the following questions:

1. If the user is logged in as "root," what should the software display?
2. The user could create a local account with the same login as the CEO, and the application would pass that login through to the database and show the CEO's reports. Is the data sensitive enough to warrant more security?

In this case, the answers are

1. Show all reports.
2. No. But anybody who figures that out and does it should be either (a) fired or (b) moved to the IS/IT department.

In either case, the reports displayed by this application are not deemed sensitive enough to warrant heavier security.

Existing Data Information

The canned reports defined in the next section will use data from the existing SESI and Worldwide Commissions databases, as well as new data, but any given dataset could be used.

User Interface

The user interface will consist of an initial form to display when the user launches the application: frm_reports. From there, each of the other separate reports is launched.

Login Screen—frm_reports.

This form will be the "control point" for all the reports available in this application. Figure 11.1 shows the UI design.

Figure 11.1 frm_reports—the main control of the application.

Figure 11.1 is the window that will initially come up for the user. He or she will pick one of the available reports and click Open to view the report in its own window. Each report will be its own executable stored on the local machine in order to add new reports without having to recompile everything in this project. Also, the list of available reports will be kept in a table so that when new reports come online, a new line will be added and the KBI application will automatically bring it up.

Report 1: Tabular Report—Salesperson Ranking

This one shouldn't be too tough. In fact, the "data display control" from the Worldwide Commissions project can be modified slightly for use here. See Figure 11.2 for an example.

Remember that the window shown in Figure 11.2 will be running in its own process space. When opened, the software will do the following:

```
drop table tbl_top_salespeople;

create table tbl_top_salespeople
    select distinct last-name & salesperson as salesperson,
           /* (to sort and view by name not just number) */
           sum(commission) as commission,
           count(*) as row_count
    from tbl_commissions
    group by salesperson;

select * from tbl_top_salespeople order by commission DESC;
```

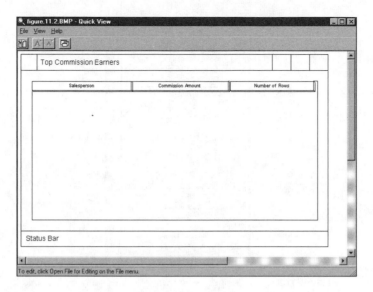

Figure 11.2 Tabular report example.

Then the software will create the tabular display using the "data display control" from Chapters 8 and 9 (modified for this project). It will be a simple display, sorted down by the sum of commissions paid by salesperson.

Report 2: Pie Chart—Sales by Division

This report will show you how to build a pie chart from a dataset. The data will show sales by division (the data is in Listing 11.2).

The following are the five divisions for the Sales by Division report:

- Widgets
- Components
- Connections
- Peripherals
- Hardware

The report will show data for the most recently completed month. In other words, the software will find out the current month by getting the current date, and then it will retrieve the data for the previous month. Also, the definition of this report is to show sales by division; if a new division appears in the data, the software should take that into account and produce a chart with six pie slices instead of five. Figure 11.3 shows an example report; note that in the final on-screen version, the pie wedges will be color-coded with matching colors in the Legend.

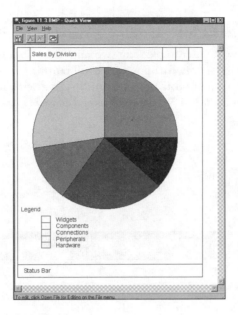

Figure 11.3 Pie chart report example.

Report 3: Bar Chart—Year-to-Date Sales Trend Versus Quota

This report will show sales year-to-date as a bar chart with the months running along the horizontal axis and the numbers along the vertical. Overlayed on that bar chart will be a line showing the sales goal or "quota." By definition, this report will always show 12 calendar months, so it can make the assumption that the horizontal will always show 12 values. Figure 11.4 shows the desired result.

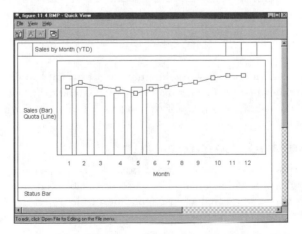

Figure 11.4 In the example bar chart, the bars represent sales for the current year, and the line shows the sales goal.

Report 4: Scatter Plot—Finding Correlations in Numeric Data

This view will allow the user to plot any two numeric columns from tbl_revenue; this will allow the user to identify data points that fall outside the "norm." The norm will usually be a bisecting line of data points from the lower-left corner to the upper-right corner, as shown in Figure 11.5. There are several candidate columns to choose from:

- order_quantity
- unit_price
- net_value
- invoice_quantity
- invioce_value

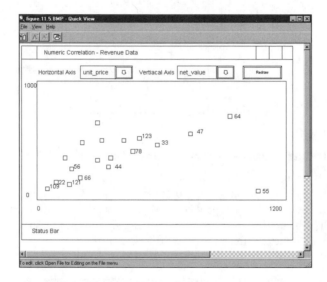

Figure 11.5   Correlating two numeric variables: Who is data point (line number) "55," and why is he out there all by himself?

The numbers in parentheses show the line number of the data point. This is to allow the user to identify a line for further analysis (which would make a good follow-up for this graph; after all, what's the use if the user can't investigate further?).

Database and Login Setup

As did the Worldwide Commissions Application (WCA) presented in Chapters 8, 9, and 10, this application will maintain its own security tables. The login and password the user enters will be compared against application tables to set the user interface correctly for the given user. The application login and password will be

Login: kbi_user

Password: dengissa

Also like WCA, the MySQL server on the server machine needs to know which machines on the network will be logging in via the application login (kbi_user). In the following, "einstein" is the server machine, and for an example, "delfin" will be one of the desktop machines. Launch mysql as administrator, and from the mysql> prompt, send the following command:

```
mysql> Grant All on kbi.* to kbi_user@delfin Identified by "dengissa";
```

"kbi" is the name of the database (see the next section, "Creating the Database"). Also, to test the application and develop it on the server, the same command needs to be sent regarding the server, as was explained in more detail in Chapter 8. Remember that you will need to issue this command for every client machine that intends to run this application.

Creating the Database

The KBI database has to be created (see Listing 11.1). It keeps its own user-login permissions, as well as the data for Reports 2 and 3. (Reports 1 and 4 will use existing data from the WCA application's commish database.)

First, create the database by launching mysql and issuing the following command at the mysql> prompt:

```
create database kbi;
```

Listing 11.1 **Creating the KBI Database**

```
use kbi;

/* The first thing to do is to create the table of authorized users.
 * This table is just the user name; no password is required
 * for the KBI application.
 *
 * usage:
 *
 * % mysql -t < listing.11.1
 */

drop table if exists tbl_authorized_users;

create table tbl_authorized_users
(
    user_name    varchar(20)
);

insert into tbl_authorized_users
    values('root'), ('jsmith'),('mstucky');
```

The data for Report 1—Salesperson Ranking, is already in the commish database. Because this new application is a "user" of the commish database, a new user login will be created that will have access to only those tables that are required for this report. For Report 2—Pie Chart/Sales by Division and Report 3—Bar Chart/Year Trend Versus Quota, the data will have to be entered into the KBI database (see Listing 11.2).

Listing 11.2 **Entering the Data for Report 2 (Pie Chart) and Report 3 (Bar/Line Chart).**

```
use kbi;

/* This set of commands will create the tables necessary for Report 2 - Pie
 * Chart and Report 3 - Bar/Line Chart. It also fills each with the
 * required data.
 *
 * usage:
 *
 * % mysql -t < listing.11.2
 *
 * The first table is tbl_sales_by_division. It is the data for
 * Report 2 - Pie Chart. Note that if you want to run the application
 * as built in Chapter 12, you need to either insert five
 * rows of your own data or change the month number on one of the
 * months inserted below. The month number must be the previous
 * completed month; for example, in July there must be some rows in the
 * data with a sales_month of 6 (June). The following update query will
 * work; substitute your most recently completed month for 13. 13 is a
 * dummy value here. If you insert 13 into the target rows, your
 * application will never work!
 *
 * update sales_by_division set sales_month = 13 where sales_month = 2
 */

drop table if exists tbl_sales_by_division;

create table tbl_sales_by_division
(
    sales_year          smallint,
    sales_month         tinyint,
    sales_division      varchar(35),
    sales_amount        decimal(9,2)
);

insert into tbl_sales_by_division
    values (2001, 1, 'Widgets',      4098.56),
           (2001, 1, 'Components',   5099.37),
           (2001, 1, 'Peripherals', 10358.69),
           (2001, 1, 'Hardware',     3045.21),
           (2001, 1, 'Connections',   998.04),
           (2001, 2, 'Widgets',      4378.21),
```

```
        (2001, 2, 'Components',   4875.32),
        (2001, 2, 'Peripherals', 12875.34),
        (2001, 2, 'Hardware',     3007.98),
        (2001, 2, 'Connections',  1093.88);

/* The next table is tbl_sales_vs_quota. It is the data source
 * for Report 3 - Bar/Line Chart. The reason for the zeros in months 8
 * through 12 is that this chart shows year-to-date sales information,
 * and those month's sales haven't occurred yet.
 */

drop table if exists tbl_sales_vs_quota;

create table tbl_sales_vs_quota
(
    sales_year      smallint,
    sales_month     tinyint,
    sales_amount    int,
    sales_quota     int
);

insert into tbl_sales_vs_quota
    values (2001, 1, 304567, 300000),
           (2001, 2, 300234, 300900),
           (2001, 3, 299345, 300900),
           (2001, 4, 010430, 300900),
           (2001, 5, 309234, 303000),
           (2001, 6, 315098, 320000),
           (2001, 7, 303870, 325000),
           (2001, 8,      0, 325000),
           (2001, 9,      0, 350000),
           (2001, 10,     0, 360000),
           (2001, 11,     0, 390000),
           (2001, 12,     0, 400000);
```

Lastly, Report 4—Scatter Plot/Finding Correlations in Numeric Data will use tbl_revenue in the WCA database. It will also be able to use the login set up in Report 1.

12

Management Reporting Construction

AKEY FUNCTION IN THE INFORMATION SYSTEMS (IS) department of many businesses is the generation of reports. In this project, you will use Glade, GTK+, and MySQL to generate a series of reports in different formats. This application will be called KBI for "Key Business Indicators."

Support files for these applications can be found in Appendix C, "Glade-Generated Files from the Key Business Indicators Application."

Problem Definition

The trick with this application will be to make it scalable so that every time a new report is added, it can be easily integrated to the existing application. In the case of this application, the "controlling application" (the KBI executable) will be a separate executable from the reports, each of which will also have a separate executable. This will allow the administrator to add new reports without recompiling the entire application. The KBI executable will query a table in the KBI database (created in Chapter 11, "Management Reporting Abstract adn Design") that will list the reports and the names of the executables that create the individual reports. The KBI executable will then launch each of the reports as separate executables. Remember that the system administrator will place only the KBI executable in the user's "Start bar" or on the desktop. So to the user, it appears to be one single application.

The Controlling Application: KBI

Here are some notes regarding building the KBI application as it is shown in
Figure 12.1.

- Remember to deselect the Enable GNOME Support option and the Gettext
Support option from the project options.

- Set the name (frm_kbi) and the title, and then insert a three-row vertical
packing box. Place a List widget in the top, a horizontal packing box with two
columns in the middle, and a status bar in the bottom row of the vertical packing box. Place a button in each of the cells of the horizontal packing box.

- Call the List widget lst_reports. For the name of the horizontal packing box,
use hbox_buttons. The button on the left is cmd_close, and the one on the right
is cmd_open. Their labels should be Close and Open, respectively.

- For hbox_buttons, Homogenous should be set to No, Expand should be No, and
both Fill and Pack Start should be Yes. For both command buttons, set Expand
and Pack Start to Yes, as well as Fill.

- Finally, set the clicked signal for each of the two command buttons, as well as
the show event for the form. Set the delete_event on the form as the place for
the gtk_main_quit() call (and you might as well put it there at this time).

If you want to do a quick compile at this point, don't forget to comment out lines 23
and 24 in main.c (the lines with PACKAGE_DATA_DIR and PACKAGE_SRC_DIR). Also, move
frm_kbi to be global in scope in main.c.

Figure 12.1 shows the KBI application being built via Glade.

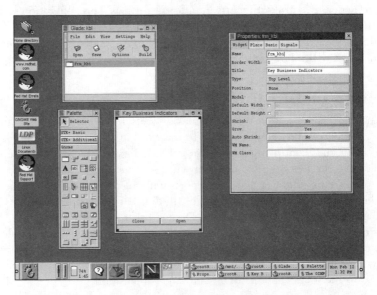

Figure 12.1 The KBI application launches other
applications under development with Glade.

Listing 12.1 is the `kbi_utils.c` file. It contains the code for functions that authenticate the user, provide him/her with a pick-list of available reports, and launch the selected report.

Listing 12.1 *kbi_utils.c*

```
#include <gtk/gtk.h>
#include <mysql.h>

#include "support.h"

/* stdio.h is needed for the file read operation. */

#include <stdio.h>

#define     SERVER   "einstein"
#define     LOGIN    "kbi_user"
#define PASS  "dengissa"
#define DB    "kbi"

GtkWidget *frm_kbi;

/* The following generic variables have worked fine in the past.
 * So, to keep things simple, use them again.
 */

MYSQL       *conx;
MYSQL_RES   *result_set;
MYSQL_ROW   row;
gchar       *sql;
gchar       *user_login;

/* Begin Function Code... */

gboolean authenticate_user()
{
    /* This function will query the operating system for the currently
     * logged in user and then query the database for that user.
     * This is primitive security that's completely hidden from the user,
     * and it is a simple form of authentication.
     */

    g_print("Starting authenticate_user.\n");

    conx = mysql_init((MYSQL *)0L);

    if (conx == 0L)
      {
        gtk_statusbar_push(GTK_STATUSBAR(lookup_widget(frm_kbi,
                    "statusbar1")), 1,"mysql_init problem");
```

continues

Listing 12.1 **Continued**

```
        return FALSE;
    }

gtk_statusbar_push(GTK_STATUSBAR(lookup_widget(frm_kbi,
                    "statusbar1")), 1, "mysql_init ok");

conx = mysql_real_connect(conx, SERVER, LOGIN, PASS, DB, 0, 0L, 0);

if (conx == 0L)
    {
        gtk_statusbar_push(GTK_STATUSBAR(lookup_widget(frm_kbi,
                    "statusbar1")), 1,"mysql_real_connect problem");
        return FALSE;
    }

gtk_statusbar_push(GTK_STATUSBAR(lookup_widget(frm_kbi,
                    "statusbar1")), 1, "mysql_real_connect ok");

/* Create the sql string to query the database for the
 * current user.
 */

sql = g_strconcat("select * from tbl_authorized_users ",
                    "where user_name = '",
                    g_get_user_name(), "'", 0L);

g_print("sql is %s\n", sql);

/* Next, query tbl_authorized_users to see if the currently
 * logged-in person is on the list.
 */

if (mysql_query (conx, sql) != 0)
    {
        gtk_statusbar_push(GTK_STATUSBAR(lookup_widget(frm_kbi,
                    "statusbar1")), 1,"mysql_query problem");
        return FALSE;
    }

gtk_statusbar_push(GTK_STATUSBAR(lookup_widget(frm_kbi,
                    "statusbar1")), 1, "mysql_query ok");

result_set = mysql_store_result(conx);

if (mysql_num_rows(result_set) != 1)
    {
        /* Something is wrong here... */
        gtk_statusbar_push(GTK_STATUSBAR(lookup_widget(frm_kbi,
                    "statusbar1")), 1,"mysql_num_rows problem");
```

```
        return FALSE;
      }

  gtk_statusbar_push(GTK_STATUSBAR(lookup_widget(frm_kbi,
                   "statusbar1")), 1, "mysql_num_rows ok");

  /* If the code reaches this point, the user
   * is authorized to run this application.
   */

  gtk_statusbar_push(GTK_STATUSBAR(lookup_widget(frm_kbi,
                   "statusbar1")), 1, "user authenticated");

  mysql_free_result (result_set);
  mysql_close (conx);

  return TRUE;
}

void fill_lst_reports()
{
  /* This routine will fill the list box of the KBI application
   * with the reports that are authorized for the currently
   * logged-in user.
   */

  GList *list_of_reports = 0L;

  conx = mysql_init((MYSQL *)0L);

  if (conx == 0L)
    {
      gtk_statusbar_push(GTK_STATUSBAR(lookup_widget(frm_kbi,
                   "statusbar1")), 1,"mysql_init problem");
      return;
    }

  gtk_statusbar_push(GTK_STATUSBAR(lookup_widget(frm_kbi,
                   "statusbar1")), 1, "mysql_init ok");

  conx = mysql_real_connect(conx, SERVER, LOGIN, PASS, DB, 0, 0L, 0);

  if (conx == 0L)
    {
      gtk_statusbar_push(GTK_STATUSBAR(lookup_widget(frm_kbi,
                   "statusbar1")), 1,"mysql_real_connect problem");
      return;
    }
```

continues

Listing 12.1 **Continued**

```
gtk_statusbar_push(GTK_STATUSBAR(lookup_widget(frm_kbi,
                   "statusbar1")), 1, "mysql_real_connect ok");

sql = "select * from tbl_reports";

if (mysql_query (conx, sql) != 0)
   {
     gtk_statusbar_push(GTK_STATUSBAR(lookup_widget(frm_kbi,
                   "statusbar1")), 1,"mysql_query problem");
     mysql_close(conx);
     return;
   }

gtk_statusbar_push(GTK_STATUSBAR(lookup_widget(frm_kbi,
                   "statusbar1")), 1, "mysql_query ok");

result_set = mysql_store_result(conx);

/* At this point, result_set holds a list of the reports that
 * are available to be viewed. Create a GList structure to
 * hold that list.
 */

while (( row = mysql_fetch_row (result_set)) != 0)
  {
      GtkWidget *list_item;

      //g_print("Report name is %s\n", row[0]);

      list_item = gtk_list_item_new_with_label(row[0]);

      /* This next call is used to associate the
       * name of the report with the list item in the GtkList
       * widget lst_reports. The three parameters are the
       * list item, the "key," and the data to be retrieved
       * when this object is queried for the key. This is
       * done so the user will be able to retrieve the text of the item
       * selected in lst_reports. See get_report_name() below
       * for the retrieval procedures.
       */

      gtk_object_set_data(GTK_OBJECT(list_item), "rept_name", row[0]);

      list_of_reports = g_list_append(list_of_reports,
            list_item);

  }

/* Now a GList object called list_of_reports contains all the
```

```
     * report names returned by the sql statement. Insert that
     * list into lst_reports.
     */

    gtk_list_append_items(GTK_LIST(lookup_widget(frm_kbi, "lst_reports")),
              list_of_reports);

    mysql_close(conx);

    /* Refresh the form. */
    gtk_widget_show_all(frm_kbi);

}

gchar *get_report_name()
{
    /* When the user clicks the Open command button on frm_kbi,
     * this routine is called to determine which value was selected
     * in the list widget at the time.
     */

    GtkWidget *target_list;
    GList     *target_GList;
    GtkObject *list_item;

    g_print("starting get_report_name.\n");

    target_list = lookup_widget(frm_kbi, "lst_reports");
    target_GList = GTK_LIST(target_list)->selection;

    if (target_GList)
      {
        g_print("target_GList populated.\n");
      }
    else
      {
        g_print("target_GList not populated.\n");
        return "";
      }

    g_print("target_label identified.\n");

    list_item = GTK_OBJECT(target_GList->data);

    g_print("data item identified.\n");

    /* Now that there is a pointer to the selected list item,
     * query that object for the data associated with the
     * object – in this case the report name. In the following
     * call, rept_data acts as a key that allows the user to retrieve
     * a specific piece of data from list_item. See fill_list_reports()
```

continues

Listing 12.1   **Continued**

```c
    * above for the specifics of attaching data to an object.
    */

    return gtk_object_get_data(list_item, "rept_name");
}

gchar *get_exe_name(gchar *rept_name)
{
    /* When the application knows the name of the target report,
     * the database can be queried for the name of the
     * executable.
     */

    g_print("Starting get_exe_name\n");

    sql = g_strconcat("select exe_name "
                      "from tbl_reports "
                      "where report_name = '", rept_name, "'", 0L);

    conx = mysql_init((MYSQL *)0L);
    conx = mysql_real_connect(conx, SERVER, LOGIN, PASS, DB, 0, 0L, 0);
    if (mysql_query (conx, sql) != 0)
        {
            /* Error, malformed sql... */
            gtk_statusbar_push(GTK_STATUSBAR(lookup_widget(frm_kbi,
                    "statusbar1")), 1,
                    "mysql_query problem in get_exe_name");
        mysql_close(conx);
        return "";
        }

    result_set = mysql_store_result(conx);

    row = mysql_fetch_row (result_set);

    mysql_free_result(result_set);
    mysql_close(conx);
    return row[0];
}

gboolean check_file_exists(target_file)
{
    /* This function checks to see if a file exists on the
     * user's machine; there is not much point in
     * trying to open the report selected by the user if the
     * executable has not been loaded onto the user's machine.
     *
     * If a file does not exist, the fopen call returns
     * Null (0L). The r parameter stands for "read only."
     */
```

```
    g_print("Starting check_file_exists.\n");

    if ( fopen((char*) target_file, "r") == 0L )
        {
            g_print("File does not exist.\n");
            return FALSE;
        }
    else
        /* File does exist. */
        g_print("File does exist.\n");

    return TRUE;
}
```

Listing 12.2 lists the callbacks as they're filled in after Glade has created them.

Listing 12.2   *callbacks.c* **from KBI**

```
#ifdef HAVE_CONFIG_H
#   include <config.h>
#endif

#include <gtk/gtk.h>

/* unistd.h is needed for the execl() command in
 * on_cmd_open_click().
 */

#include <unistd.h>

/* stdlib.h is needed for the pid_t type (process
 * identifier) in on_cmd_open_click().
 */

#include <stdlib.h>

#include "callbacks.h"
#include "interface.h"
#include "support.h"
#include "kbi_utils.h"

void
on_cmd_close_clicked                      (GtkButton        *button,
                                           gpointer          user_data)
{
    g_print("on_cmd_close_clicked\n");
    gtk_main_quit();
}
```

continues

Listing 12.2 **Continued**

```
void
on_cmd_open_clicked                    (GtkButton      *button,
                                        gpointer        user_data)
{
   pid_t pid;
   gchar *exe_name = "./kbi";
   gchar *report_name = "another kbi";

   /* This function creates a separate executable for the
    * target application, as selected in the list box on
    * frm_kbi.
    */

   g_print("on_cmd_open_clicked\n");

   /* Get the exe name and the
    * report name for the execl() call below.
    */

   report_name = get_report_name();
   g_print("report_name is %s\n", report_name);

   if (g_strcasecmp(report_name, "") == 0)
     {
        g_print("No report selected.");
        return;
     }

   exe_name = get_exe_name(report_name);

   g_print("exe_name is %s\n", exe_name);

   if (g_strcasecmp(exe_name, "") == 0)
     {
        g_print("No executable returned.\n");
        return;
     }

   /* The following function call assumes that the executables
    * have been installed to the /usr/local/bin/ directory.
    * Obviously, they could be in a different location, or
    * it might be necessary to include the path information
    * in the database table that lists the executable name.
    */

   exe_name = g_strconcat("/usr/local/bin/", exe_name, 0L);

   /* Confirm that the target executable is on this machine
    * in the place that it should be: /usr/local/bin/.
    */
```

```
        g_print("Check that file exists.\n");

        if (check_file_exists(exe_name) == FALSE)
            {
                /* The target executable doesn't exist... */
                g_print("Target exe not found.\n");

                return;
            }

        /* This section requires a bit of an explanation. The fork() call
         * creates a copy of the running program in a separate process
         * space. That is, it - the "child" process - has its own
         * copy of the program, including variables, memory, and so on.
         *
         * Following that is the execl() call inside the if statement.
         * This changes the existing program by replacing it with the
         * program called in the first parameter.
         */

        g_print("Fork off a new process.\n");
        pid = fork();

        if (pid == 0)
            {
                /* If you have entered this if statement, then this must
                 * be the child process that was fork()-ed off in the
                 * previous statements. Therefore, this (child) process
                 * should change itself to become the "target" process,
                 * that is, the program that needs to be run.
                 */

                g_print("initiating child process.\n");
                execl (exe_name, report_name);
                g_print("child process launched.\n");
            }

}


gboolean
on_frm_kbi_delete_event                 (GtkWidget       *widget,
                                         GdkEvent        *event,
                                         gpointer         user_data)
{
    g_print("on_frm_kbi_delete_event\n");
    gtk_main_quit();
    return FALSE;
}
```

continues

Listing 12.2 **Continued**

```
void
on_frm_kbi_show                        (GtkWidget      *widget,
                                        gpointer        user_data)
{
  g_print("on_frm_kbi_show\n");

  if (authenticate_user())
    {
        fill_lst_reports();
    }

}


void
on_frm_kbi_realize                     (GtkWidget      *widget,
                                        gpointer        user_data)
{
   g_print("on_frm_kbi_realize\n");
}
```

Listing 12.3 is `main.c` for KBI. All the following reports in this chapter will have very similar `main.c` files, so those will not be listed. (They are, of course, posted at this book's companion Web site.)

Listing 12.3 *main.c* **from KBI**

```
/*
 * Initial main.c file generated by Glade. Edit as required.
 * Glade will not overwrite this file.
 */

#ifdef HAVE_CONFIG_H
#  include <config.h>
#endif

#include <gtk/gtk.h>

#include "interface.h"
#include "support.h"

GtkWidget *frm_kbi;

int
main (int argc, char *argv[])
{

  gtk_set_locale ();
```

```
    gtk_init (&argc, &argv);

//  add_pixmap_directory (PACKAGE_DATA_DIR "/pixmaps");
//  add_pixmap_directory (PACKAGE_SOURCE_DIR "/pixmaps");

   /*
    * The following code was added by Glade to create one of each component
    * (except popup menus), just so that you can see something after building
    * the project. Delete any components that you don't want shown initially.
    */
   frm_kbi = create_frm_kbi ();
   gtk_widget_show (frm_kbi);

   gtk_main ();
   return 0;
}
```

Report 1: Tabular

This report in Listing 12.4 is a simple tabular report that uses a modified version of
the "data display control" from Chapters 8, "Commission Calculations Abstract and
Design," 9, "Constructing the Commissions Application," and 10, "Commission
Calculations Deployment." In this incarnation, it will not be dynamically created and
destroyed as it was in the WCA application, but instead it will query and display the
data once as stated by the report definition ("show top salespeople").

Listing 12.4   *ddc.c* **for the Tabular Report; Updated from the ddc In Chapter 9**

```
/* The following line is needed for compilation
 * on Windows - comment the line out for Linux gcc.
 */

//#include        <windows.h>

#ifdef HAVE_CONFIG_H
#  include <config.h>
#endif

#include <gdk/gdkkeysyms.h>
#include <gtk/gtk.h>

#include <mysql.h>

#include "callbacks.h"
#include "interface.h"
#include "support.h"

/* The following is the updated version of the ddc. The
 * added parameters allow it to be much more flexible and
```

continues

Listing 12.4 **Continued**

```
 * portable to other applications.
 */

GtkWidget *create_ddc (gchar *table_name, gchar *server_name,
                       gchar *user_name,  gchar *user_pwd,
                       gchar *db_name, GtkWidget *frm_target)
{
  MYSQL     *conx;
  GtkWidget *scrolledwindow1;
  GtkWidget *clist_table;
  GtkWidget *label;
  gint      counter;
  gint      cols = 3;
  gchar     *sql;
  MYSQL_RES *result_set;
  MYSQL_ROW db_row;
  MYSQL_FIELD *field;
  gchar     *row[20] = {"", "", "", "", "",
                        "", "", "", "", "",
                        "", "", "", "", "",
                        "", "", "", "", ""};

  scrolledwindow1 = gtk_scrolled_window_new (NULL, NULL);
  gtk_widget_show (scrolledwindow1);

  conx = mysql_init((MYSQL *)0L);
  if (conx == 0L)
    {
       g_print("mysql_init failure...\n");
       return 0L;
    }

  mysql_real_connect (conx, server_name, user_name,
                      user_pwd, db_name, 0, 0L, 0);
  if (conx == 0L)
    {
       g_print("mysql_real_connect failure...\n");
       return 0L;
    }

  sql = g_strconcat("select * from ", table_name, 0L);

  g_print("sql is:  %s\n", sql);

  if (mysql_query (conx, sql) != 0)
    {
       g_print("query failure...\n");
       return 0L;
    }
```

```
    result_set = mysql_store_result (conx);

    cols = mysql_num_fields (result_set);

    clist_table = gtk_clist_new (cols);
    gtk_object_set_data_full(GTK_OBJECT(frm_target), "clist_table",
            clist_table, 0L);

    gtk_widget_show (clist_table);
    gtk_container_add (GTK_CONTAINER (scrolledwindow1), clist_table);

    gtk_clist_column_titles_show (GTK_CLIST (clist_table));

    /* First iterate through the columns. */

    for (counter = 0; counter < cols; counter++)
      {
        mysql_field_seek(result_set, counter);
        field = mysql_fetch_field(result_set);

        label = gtk_label_new (field->name);
        gtk_widget_show (label);
        gtk_clist_set_column_widget (GTK_CLIST (clist_table), counter, label);
        gtk_clist_set_column_width (GTK_CLIST (clist_table), counter, 80);
      }

    /* Then iterate through the rows.  */

    while ((db_row = mysql_fetch_row (result_set)) != 0L)
      {
        for (counter = 0; counter < cols; counter++)
          {
            row[counter] = db_row[counter];
          }

        gtk_clist_append(GTK_CLIST(clist_table), row);

      }

  mysql_close(conx);

  return scrolledwindow1;

}
```

Listing 12.5 contains the callbacks for the tabular form. Listings 12.4 and 12.5 are the most important parts of the "tabular" report for the KBI application (although other support files are listed in Appendix C).

Listing 12.5 *callbacks.c* **for the Tabular Report**

```c
#ifdef HAVE_CONFIG_H
#  include <config.h>
#endif

#include <gtk/gtk.h>
#include <mysql.h>

#include "callbacks.h"
#include "interface.h"
#include "support.h"
#include "ddc.h"

GtkWidget *frm_tabular;

void
on_frm_tabular_show                      (GtkWidget      *widget,
                                          gpointer       user_data)
{
  gchar      *sql;
  MYSQL      *conx;
  GtkWidget *scrolledwindow1;
  GtkWidget *statusbar1;

  /* When frm_tabular opens, it needs to show the top salespeople
   * in descending order of commissions paid.
   * For it to do that, this routine must do the following things
   * in this order:
   *
   * In the "commish" database:
   * 1.  Drop table tbl_top_salespeople if it exists.
   * 2.  Create tbl_top_salespeople by drawing data from tbl_commissions.
   * 3.  Select from the recently created tbl_top_salespeople.
   *
   * Of course, the first two steps could be added to
   * the WCA application of Chapters 8, 9, and 10 as a final
   * step, and then it wouldn't be needed here.
   */

  g_print("on_frm_tabular_show.\n");

  /* First, connect to the database. */

  conx = mysql_init((MYSQL *)0L);

  /* The same connection parameters  that
   * were used for the WCA application in Chapter 9 can be used here.
   */
  conx = mysql_real_connect(conx, "einstein", "com_user",
                            "syL0U812", "commish", 0, 0L, 0);
```

```
if (conx == 0L)
    {
        g_print("Unable to connect to database.\n");
        gtk_statusbar_push(GTK_STATUSBAR(lookup_widget(frm_tabular,
                     "statusbar1")), 1, "Unable to Connect to database.");
        return;
    }

g_print("connected to commish db.\n");

sql = "drop table if exists tbl_top_salespeople";

if (mysql_query (conx, sql) != 0)
  {
     g_print("Error dropping table.\n");
     g_print("Error number is %i\n", mysql_errno (conx));
     g_print("Error msg is %s\n", mysql_error (conx));
     gtk_statusbar_push(GTK_STATUSBAR(lookup_widget(frm_tabular,
                  "statusbar1")), 1, "Error dropping table.");
     mysql_close (conx);
     return;

  }

g_print("table dropped.\n");

sql = g_strconcat("create table tbl_top_salespeople ",
                 "select distinct salesperson, ",
                     "sum(commission) as commission, "
                     "count(*) as Count_rows "
                 "from tbl_commissions "
                 "group by salesperson", 0L);

if (mysql_query (conx, sql) != 0)
  {
     g_print("Error creating table.\n");
     g_print("Error number is %i\n", mysql_errno (conx));
     g_print("Error msg is %s\n", mysql_error (conx));
     gtk_statusbar_push(GTK_STATUSBAR(lookup_widget(frm_tabular,
                  "statusbar1")), 1, "Error creating table.");
     mysql_close (conx);
     return;

  }

g_print("table created.\n");

mysql_close (conx);
```

continues

Listing 12.5 **Continued**

```
g_print("First connection closed.\n");

sql = "tbl_top_salespeople order by commission DESC";

gtk_widget_destroy(GTK_WIDGET(lookup_widget(frm_tabular,
            "scrolledwindow1")));

g_print("Calling create_ddc.\n");
scrolledwindow1 = create_ddc(sql, "einstein", "com_user",
                            "syL0U812", "commish", frm_tabular);
g_print("Returned from create_ddc.\n");

gtk_widget_ref(scrolledwindow1);
gtk_object_set_data_full(GTK_OBJECT(frm_tabular),
            "scrolledwindow1", scrolledwindow1,
            0L);

gtk_box_pack_start(GTK_BOX(lookup_widget(frm_tabular,
            "vbox1")), scrolledwindow1, TRUE, TRUE, 0);

gtk_widget_show(scrolledwindow1);

/* Unfortunately, the packing box widgets don't have any
 * way to insert a child widget at a certain position - only
 * at the start and end. Therefore, destroy the statusbar widget
 * created in Glade and create a new one.
 *
 * Remember, however, that the statusbar was needed prior
 * to this point to communicate with the user.
 */

gtk_widget_destroy(GTK_WIDGET(lookup_widget(frm_tabular,
        "statusbar1")));

statusbar1 = gtk_statusbar_new();

gtk_box_pack_start(GTK_BOX(lookup_widget(frm_tabular,
            "vbox1")), statusbar1, FALSE, FALSE, 0);
gtk_widget_show(statusbar1);

gtk_statusbar_push(GTK_STATUSBAR(lookup_widget(frm_tabular,
                    "statusbar1")), 1, "Done.");
}


gboolean
on_frm_tabular_delete_event             (GtkWidget       *widget,
                                         GdkEvent        *event,
                                         gpointer         user_data)
```

```
    {

    g_print("on_frm_delete_event.\n");

    gtk_main_quit();
    return FALSE;

    }
```

Figure 12.2 shows the finished tabular report. It is running in its own process space. The KBI controlling form can be closed before the tabular form.

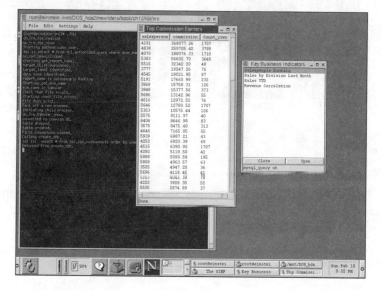

Figure 12.2   The "tabular report" as launched from KBI.

Report 2: Pie Chart

This second report will be a pie chart display of sales by division. Obviously, this type of display best lends itself to displaying a limited number of values, normally between 2 and 15. A pie chart that attempts to show more than that becomes too fragmented to show anything but the largest slices, if the data breaks out as such.

Figure 12.3 shows Glade highlighting the DrawingArea widget, which will be used extensively in the next three reports. Listing 12.6 is the code for the pie chart report.

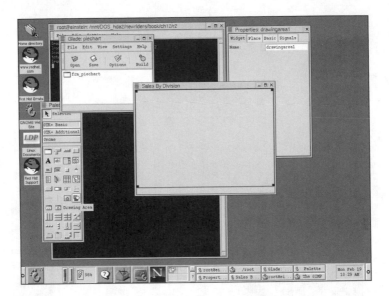

Figure 12.3 The pie chart project is under construction with Glade; the DrawingArea widget is highlighted in the palette.

Listing 12.6 *piechart_utils.c*

```c
#include <gtk/gtk.h>
#include <mysql.h>

/* time.h is needed for the calls to find the current
 * month and year.
 */

#include <time.h>

/* stdlib.h is needed for the atoi/atof call. */

#include <stdlib.h>

#include "support.h"

#define SERVER  "einstein"
#define LOGIN   "kbi_user"
#define PASS    "dengissa"
#define DB      "kbi"
#define max_div 10          /* The maximum number of business
                             * divisions, or "departments,"
                             * this application can handle.
                             */
```

```
GtkWidget *frm_piechart;

MYSQL          *conx;
MYSQL_RES      *result_set;
MYSQL_ROW      row;
gchar          *sql;

gint           number_of_divisions = 0;
gint           total_sales = 0;

/* This assumes there will never be more than 10 divisions. */

gchar      *division_names[max_div];
gint        division_sales[max_div];
GdkColor    color[max_div];

gchar  *color_choices[max_div] = {"Yellow", "Blue", "Red", "Gray", "Black",
                       "White", "Green", "Purple", "Orange", "Gold"};
void draw_legend(gint posit_x, gint posit_y,
                 gchar* legend_text, GdkColor my_color);

void draw_pie_wedge(gint start_deg, gint end_deg, GdkColor my_color)
{
   /* This function will draw one pie wedge. It is called repeatedly with a
    * different value each time until the entire pie shape is drawn.
    */

   GdkGC  *gc;

   gc = gdk_gc_new(GTK_WIDGET(lookup_widget(frm_piechart,
                   "drawingarea1"))->window);

   if (!gdk_colormap_alloc_color(gdk_colormap_get_system(),
         &my_color, FALSE, TRUE))
     {
       g_print("unable to allocate colormap\n");
       gtk_statusbar_push(GTK_STATUSBAR(lookup_widget(frm_piechart,
           "statusbar1")), 1, "Unable to allocate colormap.");
     }

   gdk_gc_set_foreground(gc, &my_color);

   //g_print("Drawing Arc.\n");
   gdk_draw_arc( GTK_WIDGET(lookup_widget(frm_piechart,
         "drawingarea1"))->window,
         gc, TRUE, 10, 10, 350, 350, start_deg*64, end_deg*64);

   //g_print("exiting draw_pie_wedge\n");
   gtk_statusbar_push(GTK_STATUSBAR(lookup_widget(frm_piechart,
         "statusbar1")), 1, "Done with draw_pie_wedge");
```

continues

Listing 12.6 **Continued**

```
}

void parse_colors()
{
   /* As part of the startup procedure for this application,
    * you need to parse each of the colors in color_choices[].
    */

   gint     i;

   for (i=0; i<10; i++)
      {

         if (!gdk_color_parse(color_choices[i], &color[i]))
            {
              g_print("unable to parse color %d.\n", i);
              gtk_statusbar_push(GTK_STATUSBAR(
                  lookup_widget(frm_piechart,
                  "statusbar1")), 1, "Unable to parse colors.");
            }
      }
}

void draw_pie_chart()
{
    /* This function draws the entire pie shape by calculating the
     * values for each wedge and calling draw_pie_wedge().
     */

    gint   i;
    gint   current_pct;
    gint   current_degree = 0;  // The degree for starting, for GTK+
                                // it is the "3 o'clock" position.

    gint   legend_vertical = 405;  // An arbitrary number of pixels
                                   // down from the top to start drawing
                                   // the legend.

    //g_print("Number of divisions is %d\n", number_of_divisions);

    for (i=1; i<=number_of_divisions; i++)
      {

        /* First calculate what percentage the current pie
         * slice is compared to the total.
         */

        //g_print("div sales i - 1 is %d\n", division_sales[i-1]);
        //g_print("total sales is %d\n", total_sales);
```

```
/* This is truncating. So it is necessary to compensate.
 * In the following call, the "+ .5" compensates
 * for the fact that current_pct is an integer,
 * and so the division calculation is truncated.
 * One half is a good "fudge factor" because the
 * truncation will always be between .001 and .999,
 * and .5 is right in the middle of those two.
 * On a pie graph, +/-.5 of a percent does not
 * show to the human eye.
 */

current_pct = ((gdouble) division_sales[i - 1] /
            (gdouble) total_sales) * 100 + .5;


//g_print("current percentage is %d\n", current_pct);


/* If this is the final pie wedge, you might as well
 * close the circle rather than leave a sliver of open
 * space that may be caused by rounding.
 */


/* In the draw_pie_wedge() function, the second
 * parameter is degrees of arc, not ending degrees. */


if (i == number_of_divisions)
    {
      /* This is the final pie wedge; you might as well
       * go ahead and close the circle, rather than
       * showing a small slice that's left because of rounding
       * errors.
       */
      draw_pie_wedge(current_degree,
            360 - current_degree, color[i - 1]);
    }
else
    {
      /* The 3.6 conversion factor is due to the
       * ratio of percentage to degrees - that is,
       * 100:360.
       */

      draw_pie_wedge(current_degree,
            current_pct * 3.6, color[i - 1]);
    }

current_degree += current_pct * 3.6;

draw_legend(legend_vertical, 0,
          g_strconcat(division_names[i - 1], " - ",
          g_strdup_printf("%d", division_sales[i - 1]),
          " (", g_strdup_printf("%d", current_pct),
          "%)", 0L),
          color[i - 1]);
```

continues

Listing 12.6 **Continued**

```
        /* Put 20 pixels between the legend line that was just
         * drawn and the next one that will be drawn.
         */

        legend_vertical += 20;

        gtk_statusbar_push(GTK_STATUSBAR(lookup_widget(frm_piechart,
                "statusbar1")), 1, "Done drawing pie chart.");
    }
}

void draw_legend(gint posit_x, gint posit_y,
                gchar* legend_text, GdkColor my_color)
{
    /* This function draws one line in the legend. Thus, the
     * legend is created by repeated calls to this function,
     * once for each line in the legend.
     */

    GdkGC    *gc;
    GdkColor black;

    gc = gdk_gc_new(GTK_WIDGET(lookup_widget(frm_piechart,
                "drawingarea1"))->window);

    if (!gdk_colormap_alloc_color(gdk_colormap_get_system(),
            &my_color, FALSE, TRUE))
        {
            gtk_statusbar_push(GTK_STATUSBAR(
                lookup_widget(frm_piechart,
                "statusbar1")), 1, "Unable to allocate colormap.");
        }

    gdk_gc_set_foreground(gc, &my_color);

    gdk_draw_rectangle(GTK_WIDGET(lookup_widget(frm_piechart,
        "drawingarea1"))->window, gc, TRUE, 20, posit_x, 10, 10);

    if (!gdk_color_parse("Black", &black))
        {
            g_print("unable to parse black.\n");
            gtk_statusbar_push(GTK_STATUSBAR(
                lookup_widget(frm_piechart,
                "statusbar1")), 1, "Unable to parse Black.");
        }

    if (!gdk_colormap_alloc_color(gdk_colormap_get_system(),
            &black, FALSE, TRUE))
```

```
        {
            g_print("unable to allocate colormap\n");
            gtk_statusbar_push(GTK_STATUSBAR(lookup_widget(frm_piechart,
                    "statusbar1")), 1, "Unable to allocate colormap.");
        }

    gdk_gc_set_foreground(gc, &black);

    gdk_draw_string(
        GTK_WIDGET(lookup_widget(frm_piechart, "drawingarea1"))->window,
        GTK_WIDGET(lookup_widget(frm_piechart, "drawingarea1"))->style->font,
        gc, 35, posit_x + 10, legend_text);

}

gboolean load_data()
{
    /* Connect to the database and return the data to be used
     * for the pie chart.
     */

    gchar *str_year, *str_month;
    struct tm *ptr;
    time_t now;

    conx = mysql_init((MYSQL *)0l );

    if (conx == 0L)
      {
        gtk_statusbar_push(GTK_STATUSBAR(lookup_widget(frm_piechart,
                    "statusbar1")), 1,"mysql_init problem");
        return FALSE;
      }

    gtk_statusbar_push(GTK_STATUSBAR(lookup_widget(frm_piechart,
                    "statusbar1")), 1, "mysql_init ok");

    conx = mysql_real_connect(conx, SERVER, LOGIN, PASS, DB, 0, 0L, 0);

    if (conx == 0L)
      {
        gtk_statusbar_push(GTK_STATUSBAR(lookup_widget(frm_piechart,
                    "statusbar1")), 1,"mysql_real_connect problem");
        return FALSE;
      }

    gtk_statusbar_push(GTK_STATUSBAR(lookup_widget(frm_piechart,
                    "statusbar1")), 1, "mysql_real_connect ok");

    /* Figure out the current month and year. Then extract the
     * previous month's data.
     */
```

continues

Listing 12.6   **Continued**

```c
time(&now);
ptr = localtime(&now);

/* tm_year is the number of years since 1900. So add 1900
 * to get the current year as an integer.
 */

str_year = g_strdup_printf("%d", ptr->tm_year + 1900);

/* tm_mon returns a number between 0 and 11 for the month.
 * So adding 1 would make it more understandable - so that
 * 1 = January instead of 0 and so on. However, because the desired
 * data is for the last completed calendar month, in effect,
 * you let the tm_mon call return the current month as a
 * zero-based array, which translates to the current
 * month minus one.
 */

str_month = g_strdup_printf("%d", ptr->tm_mon);

/* What if it is January? In that case, the month/year information
 * needs to reflect the last month of the previous year.
 */

if (g_strcasecmp(str_month, "0") == 0)
    {
        /* For clarity, use the same function call as before,
         * subtracting one "year."
         */

        str_year = g_strdup_printf("%d", ptr->tm_year + 1900 - 1);
        str_month = "12";
    }

g_print("Year and month for query are %s and %s\n",
        str_year, str_month);

sql = g_strconcat("select * from tbl_sales_by_division ",
            "where sales_month = ", str_month,
            " and sales_year  = ", str_year, 0L);

g_print("sql is %s\n", sql);

if (mysql_query (conx, sql) != 0)
    {
        gtk_statusbar_push(GTK_STATUSBAR(lookup_widget(frm_piechart,
                    "statusbar1")), 1,"mysql_query problem");
        g_print("mysql_query problem in load_data.\n");
        mysql_close(conx);
```

```
        return FALSE;
    }

gtk_statusbar_push(GTK_STATUSBAR(lookup_widget(frm_piechart,
                    "statusbar1")), 1, "mysql_query ok");

result_set = mysql_store_result(conx);
/* The result set with the data has been returned and is
 * contained in the variable result_set. Next, take
 * that data and fill in the arrays that will be used
 * to present the pie chart.
 */

while (( row = mysql_fetch_row (result_set)) != 0)
  {
      static gint i = 0;

      division_names[i] = row[2];
      division_sales[i] = atoi(row[3]);

      //g_print("data is %s and %d\n",
      //            division_names[i], division_sales[i]);

      total_sales += division_sales[i];
      //g_print("Total sales is %d.\n", total_sales);

      i++;

      //g_print("Number of divisions is %d\n", i);
      number_of_divisions = i;
  }

mysql_close(conx);

return TRUE;

}
```

Listing 12.7 is the callbacks.c listing for the pie chart report. Most of the calls in it are simple and make use of the functions in piechart_utils.c (refer to Listing 12.6).

Listing 12.7   *callbacks.c* **for the Pie Chart Application**

```
#ifdef HAVE_CONFIG_H
#  include <config.h>
#endif

#include <gtk/gtk.h>

#include "callbacks.h"
```

continues

Listing 12.7 **Continued**

```c
#include "interface.h"
#include "support.h"
#include "piechart_utils.h"

void
on_frm_piechart_show                    (GtkWidget      *widget,
                                         gpointer       user_data)
{
  if (load_data() == FALSE)
     {
         g_print("Unable to load data for pie chart.\n");
         return;
     }

  parse_colors();

  draw_pie_chart();
  g_print("on_frm_piechart_show\n");
}



gboolean
on_frm_piechart_delete_event            (GtkWidget      *widget,
                                         GdkEvent       *event,
                                         gpointer       user_data)
{
  g_print("on_frm_piechart_delete_event\n");
  gtk_main_quit();
  return FALSE;
}
/* The following functions are included so the reader can see the
 * event sequence for the DrawingArea widget. Strictly speaking,
 * they are not absolutely needed for the application.
 */

gboolean
on_drawingarea1_delete_event            (GtkWidget      *widget,
                                         GdkEvent       *event,
                                         gpointer        user_data)
{

  //g_print("on_drawingarea1_delete_event\n");
  return FALSE;
}
```

```
void
on_drawingarea1_show                        (GtkWidget         *widget,
                                             gpointer          user_data)
{

    //g_print("on_drawingarea1_show\n");

}


void
on_drawingarea1_draw                        (GtkWidget         *widget,
                                             GdkRectangle      *area,
                                             gpointer          user_data)
{

    //g_print("on_drawingarea1_draw\n");
}


gboolean
on_drawingarea1_event                       (GtkWidget         *widget,
                                             GdkEvent          *event,
                                             gpointer          user_data)
{
    /* Putting the draw_pie_chart() function call in the event event
     * of the GTK+ DrawingArea widget ensures that the pie graph
     * redraws itself when something happens to it, for example, if another
     * window or tooltip was drawn over the pie chart.
     *
     * This works fine for simple graphics like this one, but it can
     * measurably affect performance in a complicated application,
     * such as the scatter plot later in this chapter, which plots
     * nearly 4,000 points (vice ~6 for the pie chart).
     */

    draw_pie_chart();
    //g_print("on_drawingarea1_event\n");
    return FALSE;
}
```

Figure 12.4 shows the Pie Chart Report running. Note that it will not redraw itself to a different size if its parent window is resized.

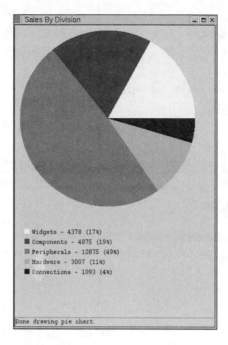

Figure 12.4   The pie chart applications.

Report 3: Bar/Line Chart

Listing 12.8 is the source for `barline_utils.c`, the code functions that are called from `callbacks.c` (for the third report) to create the bar/line chart.

Listing 12.8   *barline_utils.c*

```
#include <gtk/gtk.h>
#include <mysql.h>

/* stdlib.h is needed for the atoi/atof call. */

#include <stdlib.h>

#include "support.h"

#define SERVER  "einstein"
#define LOGIN   "kbi_user"
#define PASS    "dengissa"
#define DB      "kbi"
```

```
#define BASELINE_CHART      350     //the number of pixels from the top
                                    //of the drawingarea to the "baseline"
                                    //of the bars in the bar graph
#define BASELINE_MONTHS     370     //the number of pixels down to draw
                                    //the month names
#define SCALE_DENOMINATOR 1235      //the division factor to scale the bars
                                    //and lines to the drawingarea
#define BAR_WIDTH           25      //width in pixels of the bars

GtkWidget *frm_barline;

MYSQL           *conx;
MYSQL_RES       *result_set;
MYSQL_ROW       row;
gchar           *sql;

gchar *month_names[12] = {"Jan", "Feb", "Mar", "Apr", "May", "Jun",
                          "Jul", "Aug", "Sep", "Oct", "Nov", "Dec"};

gint month_bar_amounts[12];     //the values the bar chart should show
gint month_line_amounts[12];    //the values for the line chart
gint month_indents[12];         //number of pixels from the left to
                                //print the month names


void draw_bar(gint bar_left, gint bar_width, gint bar_height, gchar *bar_color);

GdkGC *get_gc(gchar *in_color)
{
    /* This function will return a graphics context in the
     * color as specified by the in_color parameter.
     */

    GdkGC    *gc;
    GdkColor my_color;

    gc = gdk_gc_new(GTK_WIDGET(lookup_widget(frm_barline,
            "drawingarea1"))->window);

    if (!gdk_color_parse(in_color, &my_color))
        {
            g_print("Unable to parse %s.\n", in_color);
            gtk_statusbar_push(GTK_STATUSBAR(lookup_widget(frm_barline,
                "statusbar1")), 1, "Unable to parse color.\n");
            return 0L;
        }

    if (!gdk_colormap_alloc_color(gdk_colormap_get_system(),
        &my_color, FALSE, TRUE))
        {
            g_print("Unable to allocate colormap for %s.\n", in_color);
            gtk_statusbar_push(GTK_STATUSBAR(lookup_widget(frm_barline,
```

continues

Listing 12.8 **Continued**

```
                        "statusbar1")), 1, "Unable to allocate colormap.\n");
            return 0L;
        }

    gdk_gc_set_foreground(gc, &my_color);

    return gc;

}

void draw_axis_and_scales()
{
    /* This function will draw the axis and scales for the graph.
     */

    GdkGC    *gc;
    gint     i;
    gint     from_left = 90;

    gc = get_gc("Black");

    gdk_draw_string(
        GTK_WIDGET(lookup_widget(frm_barline, "drawingarea1"))->window,
        GTK_WIDGET(lookup_widget(frm_barline, "drawingarea1"))->style->font,
        gc, 5, 100, "Sales (Bar)");

    gdk_draw_string(
        GTK_WIDGET(lookup_widget(frm_barline, "drawingarea1"))->window,
        GTK_WIDGET(lookup_widget(frm_barline, "drawingarea1"))->style->font,
        gc, 5, 130, "Quota (Line)");

    gdk_draw_line(
            GTK_WIDGET(lookup_widget(frm_barline, "drawingarea1"))->window,
            gc, from_left -1, 10, from_left -1, BASELINE_MONTHS - 20);

    gdk_draw_line(
            GTK_WIDGET(lookup_widget(frm_barline, "drawingarea1"))->window,
            gc, from_left, BASELINE_MONTHS - 20, 550, BASELINE_MONTHS - 20);


    /* Establish the spacing for the months, both the names along
     * the horizontal axis and the bars as well.
     */

    for (i=0; i<=11; i++)
      {
          month_indents[i] = from_left;
```

```
        gdk_draw_string(
          GTK_WIDGET(lookup_widget(frm_barline, "drawingarea1"))->window,
          GTK_WIDGET(lookup_widget(frm_barline, "drawingarea1"))->style->font,
          gc, from_left, BASELINE_MONTHS, month_names[i]);

        from_left += 40;

    }

}

void draw_bar_chart()
{
    gint i;

    /* The first thing that is necessary here is to figure out scale.
     * In this case, the largest value in the data is 400,000. In the
     * "drawingarea," the left line is drawn between vertical pixel
     * 10 at the top and 350 at the bottom, leaving a vertical distance
     * of 340 pixels in which to represent values from 0 to
     * 400,000.
     *
     * So to calculate the scale for that area, take the maximum value
     * plus a bit of padding. For this exercise, the value will be
     * 420,000. When you divide that by 340, it gives a value of
     * (approximately) 1,235. If you then turn the calculation around
     * and divide the 400,000 value by 1,235, you should never get more
     * than 340. Thus, the software can take all the values given to
     * it in the 300,000 to 400,000 range and divide them by 1,235 in
     * order to draw the bars to scale correctly.
     *
     * Note that the software could, of course, query the data
     * with an SQL max() statement to determine what this program
     * sets with a #define statement. In other words, the 1,235 value
     * used here could be calculated from the data itself.
     *
     * It is from this discussion that MAX_VALUE is defined in the
     * header section of this file.
     */

    /* Make repeat calls to draw_bar() for each month. */

    for (i=0;  i<=11; i++)
       {
         draw_bar(month_indents[i], BAR_WIDTH,
                 month_bar_amounts[i]/SCALE_DENOMINATOR, "Red");

       }
}
```

continues

Listing 12.8   **Continued**

```
void draw_bar(gint bar_left, gint bar_width, gint bar_height, gchar *bar_color)
{
   gdk_draw_rectangle(GTK_WIDGET(lookup_widget(frm_barline,
           "drawingarea1"))->window, get_gc(bar_color), TRUE, bar_left,
           BASELINE_CHART - bar_height,
           bar_width, bar_height);

}

void draw_line(gint from_left_1, gint from_top_1,
           gint from_left_2, gint from_top_2)

{
   gdk_draw_line(
           GTK_WIDGET(lookup_widget(frm_barline, "drawingarea1"))->window,
           get_gc("Blue"), from_left_1, from_top_1, from_left_2, from_top_2);


}

void draw_line_chart()
{
   /* This function will draw the line chart by repeated calls to
    * draw_line().
    */

   gint i;
   gint from_left, from_top;

   /* The first thing necessary is to calculate the starting point
    * for the first line. In this case, that is the middle of the
    * "January" bar for the measurement from the left of the window,
    * and the vertical will be month_line_amounts[0].
    */

   from_left = month_indents[0] + BAR_WIDTH/2;
   from_top  = BASELINE_CHART - month_line_amounts[0]/SCALE_DENOMINATOR;

   for (i=1;  i<=11; i++)
      {
         draw_line(from_left, from_top,
                 month_indents[i] + BAR_WIDTH/2,
                 BASELINE_CHART - month_line_amounts[i]/SCALE_DENOMINATOR);

         gdk_draw_rectangle(GTK_WIDGET(lookup_widget(frm_barline,
             "drawingarea1"))->window, get_gc("RoyalBlue"),
             TRUE, from_left - 2, from_top - 2, 3, 3);
```

```
            from_left = month_indents[i] + BAR_WIDTH/2;
            from_top  = BASELINE_CHART - month_line_amounts[i]/SCALE_DENOMINATOR;

      }

   /* You need to plot a point at the December quota data point as
    * the finishing touch.
    */

   gdk_draw_rectangle(GTK_WIDGET(lookup_widget(frm_barline,
            "drawingarea1"))->window, get_gc("RoyalBlue"),
            TRUE, from_left - 2, from_top - 2, 3, 3);

}

gboolean load_data()
{
   /* Connect to the database and retrieve the values for
    * the bar/line chart.
    */

   conx = mysql_init((MYSQL *)0L);

   if (conx == 0L)
     {
        gtk_statusbar_push(GTK_STATUSBAR(lookup_widget(frm_barline,
                     "statusbar1")), 1,"mysql_init problem");
        return FALSE;
     }

   gtk_statusbar_push(GTK_STATUSBAR(lookup_widget(frm_barline,
                  "statusbar1")), 1, "mysql_init ok");

   conx = mysql_real_connect(conx, SERVER, LOGIN, PASS, DB, 0, 0L, 0);

   if (conx == 0L)
     {
        gtk_statusbar_push(GTK_STATUSBAR(lookup_widget(frm_barline,
                     "statusbar1")), 1,"mysql_real_connect problem");
        return FALSE;
     }

   gtk_statusbar_push(GTK_STATUSBAR(lookup_widget(frm_barline,
                  "statusbar1")), 1, "mysql_real_connect ok");

   sql = g_strconcat("select * from tbl_sales_vs_quota ",
                  " order by sales_month", 0L);

   g_print("sql is %s\n", sql);
```

continues

Listing 12.8 **Continued**

```c
if (mysql_query (conx, sql) != 0)
  {
    gtk_statusbar_push(GTK_STATUSBAR(lookup_widget(frm_barline,
                   "statusbar1")), 1, "mysql_query problem");
    g_print("mysql_query problem in load_data.\n");
    mysql_close(conx);
    return FALSE;
  }

gtk_statusbar_push(GTK_STATUSBAR(lookup_widget(frm_barline,
               "statusbar1")), 1, "mysql_query ok");

result_set = mysql_store_result(conx);

while (( row = mysql_fetch_row (result_set)) != 0)
  {
    static gint i = 0;

    /* Convert the values returned by MySQL to integers
     * and fill the arrays to hold the data values.
     */

    month_bar_amounts[i] = atoi(row[2]);
    month_line_amounts[i] = atoi(row[3]);

    g_print("data is %d and %d\n", month_bar_amounts[i],
                               month_line_amounts[i]);

    i++;
  }

mysql_close(conx);

return TRUE;


}
```

For completeness, Listing 12.9 is `callbacks.c` for the bar/line chart. It is rather straightforward, and it makes a series of simple calls to the functions defined in `barline_utils.c` (Listing 12.8).

Listing 12.9   *callbacks.c* **for the Bar/Line Chart**

```
#ifdef HAVE_CONFIG_H
#   include <config.h>
#endif

#include <gtk/gtk.h>

#include "callbacks.h"
#include "interface.h"
#include "support.h"
#include "barline_utils.h"

void
on_frm_barline_show                    (GtkWidget      *widget,
                                        gpointer       user_data)

{
    load_data();
    draw_axis_and_scales();
    draw_bar_chart();
    draw_line_chart();
}


gboolean
on_frm_barline_delete_event            (GtkWidget      *widget,
                                        GdkEvent       *event,
                                        gpointer        user_data)

{
    gtk_main_quit();
    return FALSE;
}


gboolean
on_drawingarea1_event                  (GtkWidget      *widget,
                                        GdkEvent       *event,
                                        gpointer        user_data)

{
    draw_axis_and_scales();
    draw_bar_chart();
    draw_line_chart();

    return FALSE;
}
```

Figure 12.5 shows the bar/line chart application running.

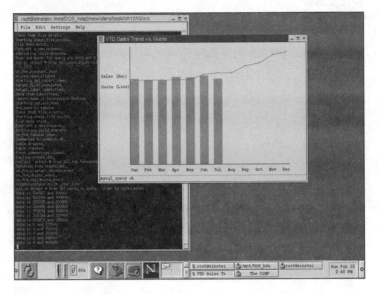

Figure 12.5   A bar/line chart program.

Report 4: Scatter Plot

The fourth and final report for this project is a scatter plot. A scatter plot shows the relationship between two sets of numbers as a series of points. Plotting two datasets is relatively straightforward; the difficult part of this application is making it dynamic so that the user has a choice of multiple values, any of which can be plotted along either axis. Also, the axes are dynamic because each value has a different maximum value. Listing 12.10 is the C code that creates the scatter plot application.

Listing 12.10   *scatter_utils.c*

```c
#include <gtk/gtk.h>
#include <mysql.h>

/* stdlib.h is needed for the atoi/atof call. */

#include <stdlib.h>

#include "support.h"

#define SERVER   "einstein"
#define LOGIN    "com_user"
#define PASS     "syL0U812"
```

```
#define DB        "commish"

#define HORIZONTAL_LINE 550   //The locations of the horizontal and
#define VERTICAL_LINE    40   //vertical axis lines, in pixels from
                              //the top and left, respectively.

GtkWidget *frm_scatter;

MYSQL          *conx;
MYSQL_RES      *result_set;
MYSQL_ROW      row;
gchar          *sql;

gint    vertical_index;       //An integer representing which column
gint    horizontal_index;     //in the mysql result set to plot along
                              //each axis.

gint max_vertical = 0;        //Variables to hold the max and min values
gint max_horizontal = 0;      //for each axis.

/* The next two variables are the scale multipliers for plotting the
 * various points. For example, if the maximum value in a dataset
 * is 600 and the graph has a distance of 540 pixels in which to
 * represent the value of 600, the multiplier in that case would be .9.
 * That is, 600 x .9 = 540.
 */

gdouble vertical_scale_multiplier = 1.0;
gdouble horizontal_scale_multiplier = 1.0;

void set_indices();
gboolean load_data();

GdkGC *get_gc(gchar *in_color)
{
    /* This is the same get_gc() from the bar/line report.
     * It returns a graphics context in the color specified
     * by the parameter in_color.
     */

    GdkGC     *gc;
    GdkColor my_color;

    gc = gdk_gc_new(GTK_WIDGET(lookup_widget(frm_scatter,
            "drawingarea1"))->window);

    if (!gdk_color_parse(in_color, &my_color))
        {
            g_print("Unable to parse %s.\n", in_color);
            gtk_statusbar_push(GTK_STATUSBAR(lookup_widget(frm_scatter,
                "statusbar1")), 1, "Unable to parse color.\n");
```

continues

Listing 12.10   **Continued**

```
        return 0L;
    }

    if (!gdk_colormap_alloc_color(gdk_colormap_get_system(),
        &my_color, FALSE, TRUE))

    {
        g_print("Unable to allocate colormap for %s.\n", in_color);
        gtk_statusbar_push(GTK_STATUSBAR(lookup_widget(frm_scatter,
            "statusbar1")), 1, "Unable to allocate colormap.\n");
        return 0L;
    }

    gdk_gc_set_foreground(gc, &my_color);

    return gc;

}

void draw_axis_and_scales()
{
    /* Also similar to the previous examples, this function
     * plots the horizontal and vertical axis and maximum
     * values.
     */

    GdkGC    *gc;

    gc = get_gc("Black");

    gdk_draw_string(
        GTK_WIDGET(lookup_widget(frm_scatter, "drawingarea1"))->window,
        GTK_WIDGET(lookup_widget(frm_scatter, "drawingarea1"))->style->font,
        gc, 25, HORIZONTAL_LINE, "0");

    gdk_draw_string(
        GTK_WIDGET(lookup_widget(frm_scatter, "drawingarea1"))->window,
        GTK_WIDGET(lookup_widget(frm_scatter, "drawingarea1"))->style->font,
        gc, 45, HORIZONTAL_LINE + 15, "0");


    gdk_draw_line(
        GTK_WIDGET(lookup_widget(frm_scatter, "drawingarea1"))->window,
        gc, VERTICAL_LINE, 10, VERTICAL_LINE, HORIZONTAL_LINE);

    gdk_draw_line(
        GTK_WIDGET(lookup_widget(frm_scatter, "drawingarea1"))->window,
        gc, VERTICAL_LINE, HORIZONTAL_LINE, 875, HORIZONTAL_LINE);
```

```
}

void plot_point(gint from_left, gint from_bottom, gchar *legend)
{
    /* This function plots a single point and the data point
     * identifier contained in the "legend" parameter.
     */

    gdk_draw_rectangle(
        GTK_WIDGET(lookup_widget(frm_scatter, "drawingarea1"))->window,
        get_gc("Black"), FALSE, from_left, from_bottom - 3, 3, 3);

    gdk_draw_string(
        GTK_WIDGET(lookup_widget(frm_scatter, "drawingarea1"))->window,
        GTK_WIDGET(lookup_widget(frm_scatter, "drawingarea1"))->style->font,
        get_gc("Black"), from_left + 4, from_bottom + 2, legend);
}

void set_maximums()
{
    /* This function will scan the result set returned by
     * mysql for the maximum values. These values will then
     * be used to determine the maximums for the graph axis and
     * the multiplication factors used to plot the points.
     *
     * Reset result_set to point to the first row of the data;
     * 0 is the first row in a zero-based structure.
     */

    mysql_data_seek(result_set, 0);
    /* Iterate through the values to find the maximum; that
     * value will be used to set the vertical axis scale.
     */

    while (( row = mysql_fetch_row (result_set)) != 0)
        {
            if (atoi (row[vertical_index]) > max_vertical)
                {
                    max_vertical = atoi(row[vertical_index]);
                    g_print("max_vertical is now %d\n", max_vertical);
                }
        }
    vertical_scale_multiplier = (gdouble) 540/max_vertical;
    g_print("vertical_scale_multiplier is %f\n",
            vertical_scale_multiplier);

    mysql_data_seek(result_set, 0);
    /* Now do the same thing with the horizontal axis. */

    while (( row = mysql_fetch_row (result_set)) != 0)
        {
```

continues

Listing 12.10 **Continued**

```
                if (atoi (row[horizontal_index]) > max_horizontal)
                    {
                        max_horizontal = atoi(row[horizontal_index]);
                        g_print("max_horizontal is now %d\n",
                                max_horizontal);
                    }
            }
        horizontal_scale_multiplier = (gdouble) 835/max_horizontal;
        g_print("horizontal_scale_multiplier is %f\n",
                horizontal_scale_multiplier);
}

void plot_maximums()
{
    /* This function will draw the maximum value strings that are
     * placed in the top left (for the vertical axis) and the bottom
     * right (for the horizontal axis).
     */

    GdkGC    *gc;
    gc = get_gc("Black");

    gdk_draw_string(
        GTK_WIDGET(lookup_widget(frm_scatter, "drawingarea1"))->window,
        GTK_WIDGET(lookup_widget(frm_scatter, "drawingarea1"))->style->font,
        gc, 0, 10, g_strdup_printf("%d", max_vertical));

    gdk_draw_string(
        GTK_WIDGET(lookup_widget(frm_scatter, "drawingarea1"))->window,
        GTK_WIDGET(lookup_widget(frm_scatter, "drawingarea1"))->style->font,
        gc, 845, HORIZONTAL_LINE + 15, g_strdup_printf("%d",
        max_horizontal));

}

void plot_graph()
{
    /* This function is the workhorse that calls other functions to
     * redraw and plot the graph.
     */

    gint i = 0;

    gdk_draw_rectangle(
        GTK_WIDGET(lookup_widget(frm_scatter, "drawingarea1"))->window,
        get_gc("Gray"), TRUE, 0, 0, 900, 575);

    load_data();
    draw_axis_and_scales();
    set_indices();
```

```
    set_maximums();
    plot_maximums();

    mysql_data_seek(result_set, 0);

    while (( row = mysql_fetch_row (result_set)) != 0)
      {

        plot_point(
          VERTICAL_LINE +
          atoi(row[horizontal_index])*horizontal_scale_multiplier,
          HORIZONTAL_LINE -
          atoi(row[vertical_index])*vertical_scale_multiplier,
          row[0]);

        i++;
      }

void set_indices()
{
    /* Set the variables horizontal_index and vertical_index
     * so that the software knows which columns in result_set to
     * plot. This is done by reading the combo boxes on frm_scatter.
     */

    GtkCombo   *cbo;
    gchar      *cbo_text;

    cbo = GTK_COMBO(lookup_widget(frm_scatter, "cbo_vertical"));
    cbo_text = gtk_entry_get_text(GTK_ENTRY(cbo->entry));
    g_print("vertical axis is %s\n", cbo_text);

    if (g_strcasecmp(cbo_text, "Order Quantity") == 0)
        vertical_index = 1;
    else if (g_strcasecmp(cbo_text, "Unit Price") == 0)
        vertical_index = 2;
    else if (g_strcasecmp(cbo_text, "Net Value") == 0)
        vertical_index = 3;
    else if (g_strcasecmp(cbo_text, "Invoice Quantity") == 0)
        vertical_index = 4;
    else if (g_strcasecmp(cbo_text, "Invoice Value") == 0)
        vertical_index = 5;
    else vertical_index = -1;

    g_print("vertical_index is %d\n", vertical_index);

    cbo = GTK_COMBO(lookup_widget(frm_scatter, "cbo_horizontal"));
    cbo_text = gtk_entry_get_text(GTK_ENTRY(cbo->entry));
    g_print("horizontal axis is %s\n", cbo_text);
```

continues

Listing 12.10 **Continued**

```
    if (g_strcasecmp(cbo_text, "Order Quantity") == 0)
        horizontal_index = 1;
    else if (g_strcasecmp(cbo_text, "Unit Price") == 0)
        horizontal_index = 2;
    else if (g_strcasecmp(cbo_text, "Net Value") == 0)
        horizontal_index = 3;
    else if (g_strcasecmp(cbo_text, "Invoice Quantity") == 0)
        horizontal_index = 4;
    else if (g_strcasecmp(cbo_text, "Invoice Value") == 0)
        horizontal_index = 5;
    else horizontal_index = -1;

    g_print("horizontal_index is %d\n", horizontal_index);

}

gboolean load_data()
{
    /* This function connects to the database and retrieves the
     * data to plot. In this case, the data is about 4,000 rows.
     * So once the data has been successfully pulled from the
     * database, there is no need to pull it again.
     *
     * To that end, the first thing the function does is check
     * to see if it has run successfully before (by setting the
     * already-loaded variable to TRUE at the end of the function).
     *
     * The function returns TRUE if the data has previously been
     * retrieved or if it can successfully do so this time.
     */

    static gboolean already_loaded = FALSE;

    if (already_loaded)
      {
        g_print("Data has been previously loaded.\n");
        return TRUE;
      }

    conx = mysql_init((MYSQL *)0L);

    if (conx == 0L)
      {
        gtk_statusbar_push(GTK_STATUSBAR(lookup_widget(frm_scatter,
                    "statusbar1")), 1, "mysql_init problem");
        return FALSE;
      }
    gtk_statusbar_push(GTK_STATUSBAR(lookup_widget(frm_scatter,
                    "statusbar1")), 1, "mysql_init ok");
```

```
        conx = mysql_real_connect(conx, SERVER, LOGIN, PASS, DB, 0, 0L, 0);

        if (conx == 0L)
          {
            gtk_statusbar_push(GTK_STATUSBAR(lookup_widget(frm_scatter,
                         "statusbar1")), 1,"mysql_real_connect problem");
            return FALSE;
          }

        gtk_statusbar_push(GTK_STATUSBAR(lookup_widget(frm_scatter,
                     "statusbar1")), 1, "mysql_real_connect ok");

        sql = g_strconcat("select line_number, order_quantity, ",
                     "       unit_price, net_value, ",
                     "       invoice_quantity, invoice_value ",
                     " from tbl_revenue ",
                     " order by line_number", 0L);

        g_print("sql is %s\n", sql);

        if (mysql_query (conx, sql) != 0)
          {
            gtk_statusbar_push(GTK_STATUSBAR(lookup_widget(frm_scatter,
                         "statusbar1")), 1, "mysql_query problem");
            g_print("mysql_query problem in load data.\n");
            mysql_close(conx);
            return FALSE;
          }
        gtk_statusbar_push(GTK_STATUSBAR(lookup_widget(frm_scatter,
                     "statusbar1")), 1, "mysql_query ok");

        result_set = mysql_store_result(conx);

        mysql_close(conx);

        already_loaded = TRUE;
        return TRUE;


}
```

Listing 12.11 is the callbacks.c file for the scatter plot program. It makes a series of
calls to the functions in scatter_utils.c (Listing 12.10).

Listing 12.11   *callbacks.c* **for the Scatter Plot Program**

```
#ifdef HAVE_CONFIG_H
#  include <config.h>
#endif

#include <gtk/gtk.h>
```

continues

Listing 12.11   **Continued**

```
#include "callbacks.h"
#include "interface.h"
#include "support.h"
#include "scatter_utils.h"

gboolean
on_frm_scatter_delete_event             (GtkWidget       *widget,
                                         GdkEvent        *event,
                                         gpointer        user_data)

{
  gtk_main_quit();
  return FALSE;
}


void
on_frm_scatter_show                     (GtkWidget       *widget,
                                         gpointer        user_data)
{
  g_print("starting on_frm_scatter_show.\n");
  load_data();
  draw_axis_and_scales();
  plot_graph();

}


void
on_cmd_redraw_clicked                   (GtkButton       *button,
                                         gpointer        user_data)
{
  load_data();
  draw_axis_and_scales();
  plot_graph();
}


gboolean
on_drawingarea1_event                   (GtkWidget       *widget,
                                         GdkEvent        *event,
                                         gpointer        user_data)
{
  g_print("starting on_drawingarea1_event.\n");
  draw_axis_and_scales();
  plot_graph();
  return FALSE;

}
```

```
gboolean
on_frm_scatter_event                    (GtkWidget      *widget,
                                         GdkEvent       *event,
                                         gpointer       user_data)
{
  g_print("on_frm_scatter_event\n");
  return FALSE;
}
```

Finally, Figure 12.6 shows the scatter plot program. Are points 2244, 2086, 2317, and 2560 profitable or not? Why are they out to the right all by themselves? Does the fact that they have a high invoice value and a low order quantity mean the overhead in filling those orders was lower? Or that those customers are more profitable than others? Or that those products are more profitable?

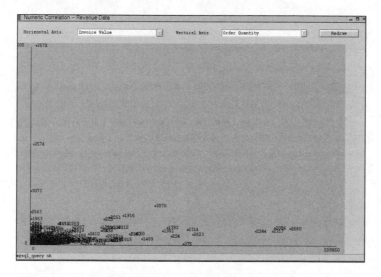

Figure 12.6 The scatter plot program.

The type of "executive reporting" presented in this chapter is a very common requirement in many corporations around the world. If you are considering embarking on this path, however, you should know that "there is always one more question." When one set of data is given some visibility, there will always be someone who will want to know more, faster. Don't say you weren't warned!

13

Compiling the Key Business Indicators Application

THIS CHAPTER COVERS COMPILING AND DISTRIBUTING THE APPLICATION as an RPM file, first covering the makefiles that are used to create the separate executables.

Compiling and Distributing Via an RPM

The makefiles for the application are covered first, followed by the RPM spec file. The makefiles for the KBI and tabular executables are given in Listings 13.1 and 13.2; the other makefiles (those for the pie chart, the bar/line chart, and the scatter plot chart) are the same as that in Listing 13.2, except that the name of the executable is different for each one.

The *Makefiles*

Listing 13.1 is the makefile for the KBI executable. It is the controlling application that calls the other executables, which is why it has a slightly more complicated install section than those in Listings 13.2 and 13.3.

Listing 13.1   *Makefile* **for the KBI Executable**

```
# Makefile for the KBI Application.
# Chapters 11, 12, and 13. */

CC = gcc -Wall
MYSQL-INCLUDES = -I/usr/include/mysql
MYSQL-LIBS = -L/usr/include/mysql -L/usr/lib/mysql -lmysqlclient -lz
GTK-CONFIG = `gtk-config --cflags --libs`
GTK-INCLUDES = `gtk-config --cflags`
GTK-LINKS = `gtk-config --libs`

kbi : main.o interface.o support.o callbacks.o kbi_utils.o
        $(CC) -o kbi *.o $(GTK-CONFIG) $(MYSQL-INCLUDES) $(MYSQL-LIBS)
        cp -f kbi /usr/local/bin/kbi

main.o : main.c
        $(CC) -c main.c $(GTK-INCLUDES)

interface.o : interface.c
        $(CC) -c interface.c $(GTK-INCLUDES)

support.o : support.c
        $(CC) -c support.c $(GTK-INCLUDES)

callbacks.o : callbacks.c
        $(CC) -c callbacks.c $(GTK-INCLUDES)

kbi_utils.o : kbi_utils.c
        $(CC) -c kbi_utils.c $(GTK-INCLUDES) $(MYSQL-INCLUDES)

# Note that you can force a full rebuild by calling
# make clean before calling make or make install. By removing
# all the intermediate object files, you force a full
# rebuild of the KBI executable. When make goes to compare
# the time of the KBI exe to that of the *.o files and finds
# no *.o files, it re-runs all the rules to make the object
# files. Then, of course, the *.o files are newer than the
# last KBI executable, so the exe is rebuilt. */

clean::
        rm -f *.o


EXE_LOCATION = /usr/local/bin/
MENU_LOCATION = "/usr/share/gnome/apps/In House Applications/"

# In the commands below...
#       The -f after cp tells cp to overwrite an existing file of
#               the same name in the target location if such a file
#               already exists. */
```

```
install : kbi
        cp -f "Key Business Indicators.desktop" $(MENU_LOCATION)
        cp -f kbi $(EXE_LOCATION)kbi
        chmod 755 $(EXE_LOCATION)kbi
        echo Key Business Indicators Application Installed.
```

Listings 13.2 and 13.3 are the makefiles for the tabular and pie executables, respectively. The fundamental difference between them is that the makefile for tabular (Listing 13.2) includes ddc.c, whereas the pie program makefile compiles piechart_utils.c.

Listing 13.2   *Makefile* **for the Tabular Executable**

```
# Makefile for the KBI Application.
# Chapters 11, 12, and 13. */

CC = gcc -Wall
MYSQL-INCLUDES = -I/usr/include/mysql
MYSQL-LIBS = -L/usr/include/mysql -L/usr/lib/mysql -lmysqlclient -lz
GTK-CONFIG = `gtk-config --cflags --libs`
GTK-INCLUDES = `gtk-config --cflags`
GTK-LINKS = `gtk-config --libs`

tabular : main.o interface.o support.o callbacks.o ddc.o
        $(CC) -o tabular *.o $(GTK-CONFIG) $(MYSQL-INCLUDES) $(MYSQL-LIBS)
        cp -f tabular /usr/local/bin/tabular

main.o : main.c
        $(CC) -c main.c $(GTK-INCLUDES)

interface.o : interface.c
        $(CC) -c interface.c $(GTK-INCLUDES)

support.o : support.c
        $(CC) -c support.c $(GTK-INCLUDES)

callbacks.o : callbacks.c
        $(CC) -c callbacks.c $(GTK-INCLUDES) $(MYSQL-INCLUDES)

ddc.o : ddc.c
        $(CC) -c ddc.c $(GTK-INCLUDES) $(MYSQL-INCLUDES)

clean::
        rm -f *.o


EXE_LOCATION = /usr/local/bin/
```

continues

Listing 13.2 **Continued**

```
# In the commands below...
#     The -f after cp tells cp to overwrite an existing file of
#           the same name in the target location if such a file
#           already exists. */

install : tabular
        cp -f tabular $(EXE_LOCATION)tabular
        chmod 755 $(EXE_LOCATION)tabular
        echo Tabular Graph Installed.
```

Listing 13.3 is the makefile for the pie chart executable. It is the same basic structure as the tabular and KBI makefiles in Listings 13.1 and 13.2. The makefiles for bar_line and scatter will be the same as Listing 13.3, except the name of the executable will be different, of course.

Listing 13.3 *Makefile* **for the "Pie" Program**

```
# Makefile for the KBI Application.
# Chapters 11, 12, and 13. */

CC = gcc -Wall
MYSQL-INCLUDES = -I/usr/include/mysql
MYSQL-LIBS = -L/usr/include/mysql -L/usr/lib/mysql -lmysqlclient -lz
GTK-CONFIG = `gtk-config --cflags --libs`
GTK-INCLUDES = `gtk-config --cflags`
GTK-LINKS = `gtk-config --libs`

pie : main.o interface.o support.o callbacks.o piechart_utils.o
        $(CC) -o pie *.o $(GTK-CONFIG) $(MYSQL-INCLUDES) $(MYSQL-LIBS)
        cp -f pie /usr/local/bin/pie

main.o : main.c
        $(CC) -c main.c $(GTK-INCLUDES)

interface.o : interface.c
        $(CC) -c interface.c $(GTK-INCLUDES)

support.o : support.c
        $(CC) -c support.c $(GTK-INCLUDES)

callbacks.o : callbacks.c
        $(CC) -c callbacks.c $(GTK-INCLUDES)

piechart_utils.o : piechart_utils.c
        $(CC) -c piechart_utils.c $(GTK-INCLUDES) $(MYSQL-INCLUDES)

clean::
        rm -f *.o
```

```
EXE_LOCATION = /usr/local/bin/

# In the commands below…
#     The -f after cp tells cp to overwrite an existing file of
#           the same name in the target location if such a file
#           already exists.

install : pie
      cp -f pie $(EXE_LOCATION)pie
      chmod 755 $(EXE_LOCATION)pie
      echo Pie Chart Installed.
```

The RPM Spec File

Listing 13.4 is the `kbi.spec` file used to create the RPM. This spec file differs in several fundamental ways from that of the Worldwide Commissions Application in Chapter 9, "Constructing the Commissions Application," and Chapter 10, "Commission Calculations Deployment."

The Preamble, description, and prep sections are essentially the same. The build section is empty, however, because each of the executables is built separately using its own `makefile`. The install section consists of copying the executables to /usr/local/bin where the KBI executable can find them. The %files section includes the files from the development machine's /usr/local/bin directory; the `makefiles` copy them to that location as part of the `make` process to ensure that /usr/local/bin always contains the latest executables.

Listing 13.4 kbi.spec: The RPM Spec File for the KBI (group of) Applications

```
# The spec file for building the RPM to distribute the
# KBI Application built in Chapters 11 and 12.

# The Preamble Section

Summary:  Key Business Applications
Name: kbi
Version: 0.1
Release: 1
Copyright: Proprietary
Group:  Applications/Databases
Packager:  Matt Stucky <stuckym@prodigy.net>

%description
In house application for executive reporting on "key business
indicators"

# Preparation Section
```

continues

Listing 13.4 **Continued**

```
%prep

# Clean out the RPM build and source directories in preparation for
# the build.

rm -rf $RPM_BUILD_DIR/*
rm -rf $RPM_SOURCE_DIR/*

cd /mnt/DOS_hda2/newriders/book/ch12/
cp kbi/src/kbi        $RPM_BUILD_DIR
cp r1/src/tabular          $RPM_BUILD_DIR
cp r2/src/pie              $RPM_BUILD_DIR
cp r3/src/bar_line         $RPM_BUILD_DIR
cp r4/src/scatter          $RPM_BUILD_DIR
cp "kbi/src/Key Business Indicators.desktop" $RPM_BUILD_DIR

# These next two sections are simple because the
# makefile has already been created with a make install included.

%build

# This application will not distribute the source.
# Therefore, there is no source to build.

%install
# Unlike the previous RPM spec file, this one has no "make install"
# because it distributes several packages in binary only.

cp -f kbi        /usr/local/bin
cp -f tabular    /usr/local/bin
cp -f pie        /usr/local/bin
cp -f bar_line   /usr/local/bin
cp -f scatter    /usr/local/bin
cp -f "Key Business Indicators.desktop" "/usr/share/gnome/apps/In House
Applications"

# Finally, a list of the files needed for the application to install.

%files
/usr/local/bin/kbi
/usr/local/bin/tabular
/usr/local/bin/pie
/usr/local/bin/bar_line
/usr/local/bin/scatter
"/mnt/DOS_hda2/newriders/book/ch12/kbi/src/Key Business Indicators.desktop"
```

Figure 13.1 shows the KBI application installed using the RPM. The appropriate menu choice has been added to the GNOME menu, and the GNOMERPM displays the installed package.

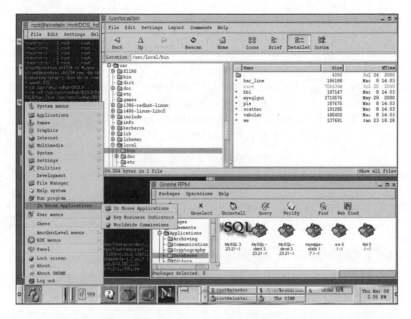

Figure 13.1   The KBI group of applications is installed. The menu bar shows the "In House Application" start menu, the file manager shows the contents of /usr/local/bin, and the GNOMERPM window shows the installed package.

To build the RPM file, enter the following command:

```
% rpm -bb kbi.spec
```

The -bb switch tells RPM to build only the binary .rpm file, not the source .rpm file.

Compiling with MinGW for Win32

This section covers the MinGW gcc compiler for the Win32 platform. This is a port of the GNU gcc compiler, and with a bit of effort, it can be used to compile and run GTK+ and MySQL client applications. You will have to download and install several *.zip or *.tar.gz files. The gcc command line has to be structured correctly, but it is possible.

What Is MinGW?

For our purposes, MinGW is "gcc for Windows." That is all that will be used of it in this context, but in truth, that is selling it short. In a larger context, it is a full set of GNU tools that have been ported to the Win32 environment.

MinGW is the "Minimalist GNU for Windows" port of the gcc compiler. Its biggest selling point is that it allows the developer to compile programs on Windows that don't rely on any third-party dll files. (Cygwin is a prime example.) In addition to the gcc compiler, the MinGW project also provides a Windows port of GNU `make` and GNU Debugger (gdb), all under the GNU General License. At the time this book was written, the MinGW Web site directed browsers to `http://www.gnu.org/copyleft/gpl.html` for further explanation of the GPL.

The MinGW Web site is `http://www.mingw.org./`.

Files and URLs Needed

In addition to the Glade, GTK+, Glib, and MySQL client files needed for the section on building for Windows with MS Visual C++ in Chapter 10, what follows is a list of files needed to build a MySQL/GTK+ application with the gcc compiler from MinGW.

You will need the MinGW distribution from `http://www.mingw.org/`. Specifically, you may need some or all of the following files (or their newest equivalents):

- `binutils-2.10.91-20010114.zip`
- `binutils-19990818-1-msvcrt.zip`
- `gcc-2.95.2-1-msvcrt.zip`
- `ld-2.10.91-20010126.zip`
- `mingw-msvcrt-19991107.zip`
- `mingw-runtime-0.5-20010221.tar.gz`
- `w32api-0.5-20010301.tar.gz`

Some files that are needed are included in multiple files, and some may not be needed unless you want to access the C Windows API. At the very minimum, you will need the `gcc-version-msvcrt`, `mingw-msvcrt-datetime`, and `binutils-datetime-msvcrt` files.

You will, of course, need the GTK+, GDK, Glib, and other files from Tor Lilquist's Web site at `http://user.sgic.fi/~tml/gimp/win32/`. Refer to Chapter 10 for specifics.

You will also need some of the MySQL client for windows files. The URL for those is `http://www.mysql.com/`. You can refer to Chapter 10 for specifics.

You will also need a very special set of files from Jan Dvorak's "JohnyDog's MinGW ports" Web site at `http://doga.go.cz/ports.html`. (You can also download this file from this book's companion Web site.) Specifically, you will need `3.23.32-mingw32-binary.tar.gz` (or its most recent equivalent). These are the MySQL client files modified for MinGW, but the most important is the libmysqlclient.a file, which gcc will need in order to properly compile the application.

There will also be copies of most of the above—to the extent possible—at the book's companion Web site on http//www.newriders.com.

Setup and Compile Instructions

For purposes of this demonstration, I have chosen the bar_line executable to compile and run as a demonstration rather than all the executables in the KBI application. In other words, change all instances that call to the "bar/line" code or executable to "scatter" (or whatever your target is) in the call to gcc.exe at the end of Listing 13.5, and you should be able to compile and link. If you understand the mechanics of the gcc command line in Listing 13.5, you should be able to use this to produce any Windows executable.

Listing 13.5 is the batch file that was put together to compile the bar_line.exe file. It uses the same source code as its Linux version with the following exceptions:

- The addition of #include <windows.h> to the top of barline_utils.c
- A recursive call to "limits.h" from limits.h was commented out at the end of the limits.h file

Also, I had to do the following in order to get a clean compile and link:

- Put libbfd-2.10.91 in the same directory location as as.exe; from MinGW.
- Put crt2.o in the same subdirectory as the source code; also from MinGW.
- Put libmingw32.a, libmoldname.a, libuser32.a, libkernel32.a, libadvapi32.a, and libshell32.a in the same subdirectory as the MinGw "specs" file (the name of the file is "specs", nothing more).

Listing 13.5 **Windows Batch File for Compiling** *bar_line.exe*, **the Windows Version of the Bar/Line Chart from the KBI Application**

```
@echo off

rem . This is the gcc command line compile for the Win32 platform.
rem . Having WinZip will make all this MUCH easier because
rem . most of the target files listed here are downloaded as
rem . *.zip files.
rem . www.winzip.com.
rem .
rem . Get the newest file when you run this batch file, not
rem . necessarily the files listed here; they are just the ones
rem . current at the time the book was written.

rem . ============================================================
rem . URLs and files needed at various places.
rem . ============================================================
```

continues

Listing 13.5 **Continued**

```
rem . gcc for Windows
rem . URL:        http://www.mingw.org./
rem . File:       mingw-runtime-0.5-200102
rem .
rem . MySQL for MinGW files, including libmysqlclient.a
rem . URL:        http://doga.go.cz/ports.html
rem . File:       MySQL-3.23.32-mingw32-binary.tar.gz
rem .
rem . GTK+, GDK, GLib, etc, for Windows
rem . URL:        http://user.sgic.fi/~tml/gimp/win32/
rem . Files:      glib-dev-20001226.zip, glib-src-2001226.zip,
rem .             gtk+-dev-20001226.zip, gtk+-src-20001226.zip
rem .
rem . zlib library, needed by the MySQL for MinGW files
rem . URL:        http://penguin.at0.net/~fredo/files/
rem . File:       zlib-1.1.3-mingw.zip


rem . ============================================================
rem . Set the system path to search for the executables. The
rem . examples below are for the book's development system; you
rem . will need to change the paths.
rem . ============================================================

rem . Path Variable:   d:\mingw\bin
rem . Location of:     gcc.exe
rem . File (mingw):    gcc-2.95.2-1.msvcrt.zip

rem . Path Variable:   d:\mingw\binutils\bin
rem . Location of:     as.exe, ld.exe
rem . Files (mingw):   binuitls-2.10.91-20010114.zip,
rem .                  ld-2.10.91-20010126.zip

PATH=d:\mingw\bin\;d:\mingw\binutils\bin\;

rem . Set the current directory to the location of this batch file.
D:
cd \NewRiders\book\ch12\r3\src\

rem . ============================================================
echo  Starting compile...
rem . ============================================================

rem . The order of the *.c files is important.
rem .
rem . -Wall               show all warnings
rem . -o bar_line.exe     the executable name
rem . *.c                 the source files
rem . -I                  "Include" directories for *.h files
```

```
rem . -l                 link the following library; the file
rem .                      gcc will search for is actually called
rem .                      libwhatever.a, but on the command line
rem .                      the link command is -lwhatever
rem . -L                 Look in these directories for the
rem .                      library files indicated by the -l flags

rem . Option:  -ID:\mingw\bin\mingwbinary\include\mysql\
rem . What:    mysql header files for mingw

rem . Option:  -ID:\MySQL\Win32\include\
rem . What:    mysql header files from mysql, any not covered previously

rem . Option:  -ID:\gtk\src\gtk+\
rem .          -ID:\GLIB\src\glib\
rem .          -ID:\GTK\src\gtk+\gdk\
rem .          -ID:\gtk\src\gtk+\gtk\
rem . What:    gtk\gtk.h, glib.h and other header files and
rem .          any other gtk+ and gdk files not already covered.

rem . Options:  -ID:\MySQL\Win32\lib\opt\
rem .           -ID:\mingw\lib\gcc-lib\i386-mingw32msvc\2.95.2\include\
rem .           -ID:\mingw\msvcrt\i386-mingw32msvc\include\
rem . What:    assorted *.h files
rem . Option:  -ID:\mingw\msvcrt\i386-mingw32msvc\lib\
rem .          assorted *.a files

rem . Option:   -mno-cygwin
rem . Purpose:  don't compile with the cygwin dll if it is present

rem . Option:   -fnative-struct
rem . Purpose:  the "struct" layout is the same as that used by MS VC++

rem . Option:   -lgdk-1.3
rem .           -lgtk-1.3
rem .           -lgmodule-1.3
rem .           -lglib-1.3
rem . What:    gtk and gdk libraries

rem . Option:   -lmysqlclient
rem . What:    link in file libmysqlclient.a

rem . Option:   -lwsock32
rem . Purpose:  needed with the libmysqlclient.a file used

rem . Option:   -lzlib
rem . What:    link file libzlib.a
rem . Purpose:  compression and decompression

rem . Option:   -LD:\mingw\bin\mingwbinary\lib
rem . What:    location of file libmysqlclient.a; this one has
```

continues

Listing 13.5 **Continued**

```
rem .               been put first so that any files found in this
rem .               directory get used, even if duplicates or different
rem .               versions are found in any of the directories below.

rem . Option:   -LD:\mingw\msvcrt\i386-mingw32msvc\lib\
rem .           -LD:\MySQL\win32\lib\opt
rem .           Other directories to search in case libmysqlclient.a
rem .               is not found in the previous directory.

rem . Option:   -Ld:\GLIB\src\glib
rem .           -Ld:\GTK\src\gtk+\gtk
rem .           -Ld:\GTK\src\gtk+\gdk
rem .           -LD:\GLib\src\glib\gmodule
rem . What:     libgtk-1.3.a, libgdk-1.3a, etc.  Same as Chapter 10.

rem . Option:   -LD:\mingw\lib\zlib
rem . What:     location of libzlib.a


rem . ===============================================================
rem . Here is the actual call to gcc…
rem ================================================================

gcc -Wall -o bar_line.exe main.c support.c interface.c callbacks.c barline_utils.c
➥ID:\mingw\bin\mingwbinary\include\mysql\ -ID:\MySQL\Win32\include\ -
➥ID:\gtk\src\gtk+\ -ID:\GLIB\src\glib\ -ID:\GTK\src\gtk+\gdk\ -
➥ID:\gtk\src\gtk+\gtk -ID:\MySQL\Win32\lib\opt\
➥ -ID:\mingw\lib\gcc-lib\i386-mingw32msvc\2.95.2\include\ -ID:\mingw\msvcrt\i386-
➥mingw32msvc\include\ -ID:\mingw\msvcrt\i386-mingw32msvc\lib\  -mno-cygwin -
➥fnative-struct -lgdk-1.3 -lgtk-1.3 -lgmodule-1.3 -lglib-1.3 -lmysqlclient
➥-lwsock32 -lzlib -LD:\mingw\bin\mingwbinary\lib -LD:\mingw\msvcrt\i386-
➥mingw32msvc\lib\ -Ld:\GLIB\src\glib -Ld:\GTK\src\gtk+\gtk -Ld:\GTK\src\gtk+\gdk
➥-LD:\MySQL\win32\lib\opt -LD:\GLib\src\glib\gmodule -LD:\mingw\lib\zlib

echo Done.

rem . You may need to include the math library, -lm.
rem . The Win32 version of -lz is the -lzlib above.

rem . Good Luck!
```

Figure 13.2 shows the compiled executable running on a Windows 95 machine. Remember (from Chapter 10) that the server name as called from within the MySQL client code is "einstein" and that "einstein" is a Samba share on this network, which allows the Windows machines to resolve the server name.

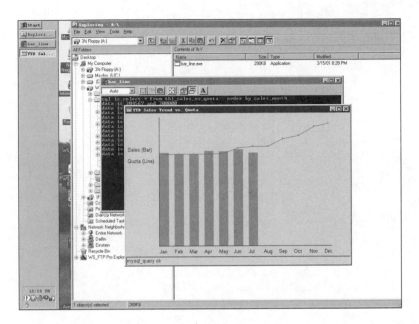

Figure 13.2   `bar_line.exe` running on Windows95. Notice the stock icon in the upper-left corner of the application window; contrast that with Figure 10.11.

III

Example

Dynamic User Interface Control with XML

T HIS CHAPTER PRESENTS A FEW QUICK AND SIMPLE LESSONS ON how to do dynamic user interface generation with `glade.h`; that is, the widgets and windows will be built at runtime, not compiled as part of the application. This allows the application developer to distribute an XML file that describes the user interface and to compile only the signals needed to perform the desired actions.

As a developer, it is inviting to only have to distribute a new XML file to add a button (or other) widget to a form. However, you should note that the code to perform when the button is pushed is still compiled C code. Therefore, you have to plan to modify your *.c files, and distribute the executable.

HelloWorld!...One More Time

This section provides a quick tutorial on how to use `glade.h` to build the user interface at runtime.

1. First, open Glade and build the window (form) widget shown in Figure 14.1.

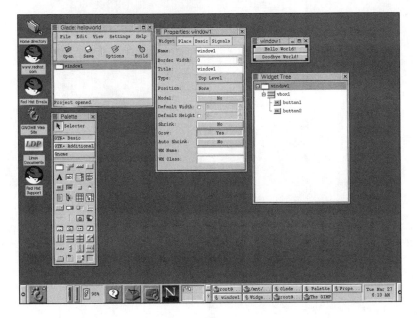

Figure 14.1 The main form of `HelloWorld.glade` in design view.

2. In the Project Options dialog, deselect the Enable GNOME Support check box; and on the second tab, deselect the check boxes labeled Output Support Functions and Output Build Files, as shown in Figure 14.2.

Figure 14.2 `HelloWorld.glade` with the appropriate options set.

3. Save the file, but in this case, you do not need to click the "Build" button. (There is nothing to build; the `HelloWorld.glade` file is what is required of this process, and it is created by clicking the Save button.)

4. Return to the main form for HelloWorld, select the "HelloWorld!" command button, and then click the Signals tab in the Properties dialog box. Note that in Figure 14.3, the signal for this command button is `button1_clicked`. In this case, that signal handler was typed in by hand as opposed to being generated by Glade. `button1_clicked` is the function that should fire when button1 ("Hello World!") is clicked. Click the Add button to bring the project to the point shown in Figure 14.3

Figure 14.3   Manually setting the callback for button1.

5. Repeat these steps for button2 ("Goodbye World!"), but for the signal handler for button2's `clicked` event, specify `button2_clicked`.

Next, an examination of the `HelloWorld.glade` file is in order. Listing 14.1 is that file. For a review of XML as it relates to *.glade files, refer to Chapter 5, "Glade for VB Developers."

Listing 14.1   *HelloWorld.glade*

```
<?xml version="1.0"?>
<GTK-Interface>

<project>
  <name>helloworld</name>
  <program_name>helloworld</program_name>
  <directory></directory>
  <source_directory>src</source_directory>
  <pixmaps_directory>pixmaps</pixmaps_directory>
  <language>C</language>
  <gnome_support>False</gnome_support>
  <gettext_support>False</gettext_support>
  <use_widget_names>False</use_widget_names>
  <output_main_file>True</output_main_file>
  <output_support_files>False</output_support_files>
  <output_build_files>False</output_build_files>
  <backup_source_files>True</backup_source_files>
```

continues

Listing 14.1 **Continued**

```xml
    <main_source_file>interface.c</main_source_file>
    <main_header_file>interface.h</main_header_file>
    <handler_source_file>callbacks.c</handler_source_file>
    <handler_header_file>callbacks.h</handler_header_file>
    <support_source_file>support.c</support_source_file>
    <support_header_file>support.h</support_header_file>
    <translatable_strings_file></translatable_strings_file>
</project>

<widget>
  <class>GtkWindow</class>
  <name>window1</name>
  <title>window1</title>
  <type>GTK_WINDOW_TOPLEVEL</type>
  <position>GTK_WIN_POS_NONE</position>
  <modal>False</modal>
  <allow_shrink>False</allow_shrink>
  <allow_grow>True</allow_grow>
  <auto_shrink>False</auto_shrink>

  <widget>
    <class>GtkVBox</class>
    <name>vbox1</name>
    <homogeneous>False</homogeneous>
    <spacing>0</spacing>

    <widget>
      <class>GtkButton</class>
      <name>button1</name>
      <can_focus>True</can_focus>
      <signal>
      <name>clicked</name>
      <handler>button1_clicked</handler>
      <last_modification_time>Wed, 21 Mar 2001 10:46:25
GMT</last_modification_time>
      </signal>
      <label>Hello World!</label>
      <child>
      <padding>0</padding>
      <expand>False</expand>
      <fill>False</fill>
      </child>
    </widget>

    <widget>
      <class>GtkButton</class>
      <name>button2</name>
      <can_focus>True</can_focus>
      <signal>
```

```
        <name>clicked</name>
        <handler>button2_clicked</handler>
        <last_modification_time>Wed, 21 Mar 2001 10:46:13
GMT</last_modification_time>
        </signal>
        <label>Goodbye World!</label>
        <child>
        <padding>0</padding>
        <expand>False</expand>
        <fill>False</fill>
        </child>
      </widget>
    </widget>
  </widget>

</GTK-Interface>
```

So far nothing too complicated has been done. An examination of Listing 14.1 provides some important points for future reference. There are two command buttons, button1 ("Hello World!") and button2 ("Goodbye World!"); and they will call functions `button1_clicked()` and `button2_clicked()`, respectively.

Now move on to `helloworld.c`, which is Listing 14.2. Note that Glade output it as `main.c`, and I have changed the name for clarity. (This listing, like all the listings in this book, is available from the companion Web site.)

Listing 14.2   *helloworld.c*

```
/* Initial main.c file generated by Glade. Edit as required.
 * Glade will not overwrite this file.
 */

#ifdef HAVE_CONFIG_H
#  include <config.h>
#endif

#include <gtk/gtk.h>
#include <glade/glade.h>

GtkWidget *window1;

void button1_clicked()
{
    g_print("Hello World...\n");
}

void button2_clicked()
{
    gtk_main_quit();
}
```

continues

Listing 14.2 **Continued**

```
int
main (int argc, char *argv[])
{

  GladeXML  *xml;

  gtk_init (&argc, &argv);
  glade_init();

  xml = glade_xml_new("../helloworld.glade", "window1");

  if (!xml)
     {
       g_print("unable to load interface...\n");
       return 1;
     }

  window1 = glade_xml_get_widget(xml, "window1");

  glade_xml_signal_autoconnect(xml);

  /* The following code was added by Glade to create one of each component
   * (except popup menus), just so that you see something after building
   * the project. Delete any components you don't want shown initially.
   */

  gtk_widget_show (window1);

  gtk_main ();
  return 0;
}
```

Following is a list of things to note about Listing 14.2:

- #include <glade.h> is in the header. It is needed for the *_xml_* calls in the file.
- GtkWidget *window1 is the main window of the application, and it has been made global in scope.
- button1_clicked() and button2_clicked() are simple and self-explanatory. They are the functions executed by the "Hello World" and "Goodbye World" buttons, respectively.
- There is a GladeXML variable type, and glade_init() appears at the start of function main(). These are needed by glade.h and for assigning a value to the *xml variable.

- The `glade_xml_new()` call opens the *.glade file assigned and looks for the specification of a widget named "window1".
- The `glade_xml_get_widget()` call builds window1.

The rest is the same as with any Glade/GTK+ project. Figure 14.4 shows the application running.

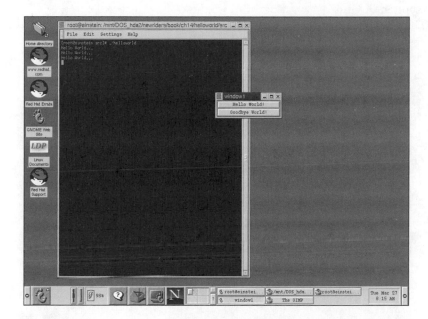

Figure 14.4 `HelloWorld` running.

Finally, one small change is required when you compile the application. You must add the `libglade.a` library as shown at the following gcc command line:

```
% gcc -Wall `gtk-config —cflags —libs` helloworld.c -o helloworld -lglade
```

Cross-Window Communication

This next example will revisit the method of the "Getting Cross-Window Widgets to Communicate" example from Chapter 5. The fundamental problem is this: In a given window widget, or form, the child widgets do not know about the existence of other child widgets in other forms. Therefore, what is needed is a way to get the child widgets in one form to be able to send information to and receive information from the child widgets in other forms. Recall from Chapter 5 that the way to do this is to first make the forms global in scope and then use Glade's `lookup_widget()` function to find the child widget when you're given the form widget. (Again, refer to the section

"Getting Cross-Window Widgets to Communicate," in Chapter 5.) At this point, however, there is one thing that needs to be mentioned: The Glade interface builder, that is, the part that writes the `interface.c` file, connects the child widgets to the parent widgets automatically. So it is already done for you in the example from Chapter 5. In this example, however, because `interface.c` is not going to be used, those connections have to be put into the code manually. `cross-window.glade` is created by the Save button in Glade.

The example below is called "cross-window" and can be downloaded from the companion Web site (`www.newriders.com`).

First, open Glade and create two identical windows, as shown in Figure 14.5. The widget tree shows the structure of the two windows.

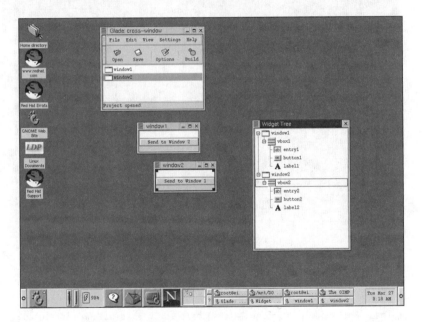

Figure 14.5   `cross-window.glade` as built with Glade.

Listing 14.3 contains the `cross-window.glade` file. Again, this is to show the structure displayed in Figure 14.5.

Listing 14.3   ***cross-window.glade***

```
<?xml version="1.0"?>
<GTK-Interface>

<project>
  <name>cross-window</name>
  <program_name>cross-window</program_name>
```

```
    <directory></directory>
    <source_directory>src</source_directory>
    <pixmaps_directory>pixmaps</pixmaps_directory>
    <language>C</language>
    <gnome_support>False</gnome_support>
    <gettext_support>False</gettext_support>
    <use_widget_names>False</use_widget_names>
    <output_main_file>False</output_main_file>
    <output_support_files>False</output_support_files>
    <output_build_files>False</output_build_files>
    <backup_source_files>True</backup_source_files>
    <main_source_file>interface.c</main_source_file>
    <main_header_file>interface.h</main_header_file>
    <handler_source_file>callbacks.c</handler_source_file>
    <handler_header_file>callbacks.h</handler_header_file>
    <support_source_file>support.c</support_source_file>
    <support_header_file>support.h</support_header_file>
    <translatable_strings_file></translatable_strings_file>
</project>

<widget>
  <class>GtkWindow</class>
  <name>window1</name>
  <signal>
    <name>delete_event</name>
    <handler>quit_application</handler>
    <last_modification_time>Wed, 21 Mar 2001 11:14:55 GMT</last_modification_time>
  </signal>
  <title>window1</title>
  <type>GTK_WINDOW_TOPLEVEL</type>
  <position>GTK_WIN_POS_NONE</position>
  <modal>False</modal>
  <allow_shrink>False</allow_shrink>
  <allow_grow>True</allow_grow>
  <auto_shrink>False</auto_shrink>

  <widget>
    <class>GtkVBox</class>
    <name>vbox1</name>
    <homogeneous>False</homogeneous>
    <spacing>0</spacing>

    <widget>
      <class>GtkEntry</class>
      <name>entry1</name>
      <can_focus>True</can_focus>
      <editable>True</editable>
      <text_visible>True</text_visible>
      <text_max_length>0</text_max_length>
      <text></text>
      <child>
```

continues

Listing 14.3 **Continued**

```
        <padding>0</padding>
        <expand>False</expand>
        <fill>False</fill>
        </child>
      </widget>

      <widget>
        <class>GtkButton</class>
        <name>button1</name>
        <can_focus>True</can_focus>
        <signal>
        <name>clicked</name>
        <handler>button1_clicked</handler>
        <last_modification_time>Wed, 21 Mar 2001 11:08:25 GMT</last_modification_time>
        </signal>
        <label>Send to Window 2</label>
        <child>
        <padding>0</padding>
        <expand>False</expand>
        <fill>False</fill>
        </child>
      </widget>

      <widget>
        <class>GtkLabel</class>
        <name>label1</name>
        <label></label>
        <justify>GTK_JUSTIFY_CENTER</justify>
        <wrap>False</wrap>
        <xalign>0.5</xalign>
        <yalign>0.5</yalign>
        <xpad>0</xpad>
        <ypad>0</ypad>
        <child>
        <padding>0</padding>
        <expand>False</expand>
        <fill>False</fill>
        </child>
      </widget>
    </widget>
  </widget>

<widget>
  <class>GtkWindow</class>
  <name>window2</name>
  <signal>
    <name>delete_event</name>
    <handler>quit_application</handler>
```

```
    <last_modification_time>Wed, 21 Mar 2001 11:15:07 GMT</last_modification_time>
  </signal>
  <title>window2</title>
  <type>GTK_WINDOW_TOPLEVEL</type>
  <position>GTK_WIN_POS_NONE</position>
  <modal>False</modal>
  <allow_shrink>False</allow_shrink>
  <allow_grow>True</allow_grow>
  <auto_shrink>False</auto_shrink>

  <widget>
    <class>GtkVBox</class>
    <name>vbox2</name>
    <homogeneous>False</homogeneous>
    <spacing>0</spacing>

    <widget>
      <class>GtkEntry</class>
      <name>entry2</name>
      <can_focus>True</can_focus>
      <editable>True</editable>
      <text_visible>True</text_visible>
      <text_max_length>0</text_max_length>
      <text></text>
      <child>
      <padding>0</padding>
      <expand>False</expand>
      <fill>False</fill>
      </child>
    </widget>

    <widget>
      <class>GtkButton</class>
      <name>button2</name>
      <can_focus>True</can_focus>
      <signal>
      <name>clicked</name>
      <handler>button2_clicked</handler>
      <last_modification_time>Wed, 21 Mar 2001 11:08:11 GMT</last_modification_time>
      </signal>
      <label>Send to Window 1</label>
      <child>
      <padding>0</padding>
      <expand>False</expand>
      <fill>False</fill>
      </child>
    </widget>

    <widget>
      <class>GtkLabel</class>
```

continues

Listing 14.3 **Continued**

```
            <name>label2</name>
            <label></label>
            <justify>GTK_JUSTIFY_CENTER</justify>
            <wrap>False</wrap>
            <xalign>0.5</xalign>
            <yalign>0.5</yalign>
            <xpad>0</xpad>
            <ypad>0</ypad>
            <child>
            <padding>0</padding>
            <expand>False</expand>
            <fill>False</fill>
            </child>
        </widget>
      </widget>
  </widget>

</GTK-Interface>
```

Cross-window has two forms, each of which has a three-row vertical packing box containing an entry widget, a command button, and a label widget.

The application should work in such a way that if the user types something in the entry box of window1 and clicks the Send to Window 2 command button also in window1, the text in window1 will be displayed in the label widget in window2. Figure 14.6 shows cross-window running.

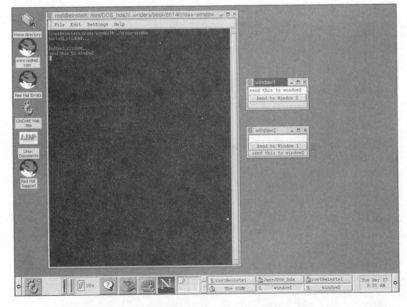

Figure 14.6 Cross-window communication.

Next, examine the code for cross-window.c in Listing 14.4.

Listing 14.4 *cross-window.c*

```
#ifdef HAVE_CONFIG_H
#  include <config.h>
#endif

#include <gtk/gtk.h>
#include <glade/glade.h>

#include "support.h"

GtkWidget *window1;
GtkWidget *window2;

void button1_clicked()
{
    GtkWidget *txt;
    gchar *txt1;

    g_print("button1_clicked...\n");

    /* Retrieve the text in the entry widget of the form
     * that holds the button that was clicked.
     */

    txt = lookup_widget(window1, "entry1");
    txt1 = gtk_editable_get_chars(GTK_EDITABLE(txt), 0, -1);

    g_print("%s\n", txt1);

    /* Push the retrieved text from above to the label widget of
     * the other window.
     */

    gtk_label_set_text(GTK_LABEL(lookup_widget(window2, "label2")), txt1);
}

void button2_clicked()
{
    GtkWidget *txt;
    gchar *txt2;

    /* button2_clicked has the same structure as button1_clicked.
     * However, the target widgets are different.
     */

    g_print("button2_clicked...\n");

    txt = lookup_widget(window2, "entry2");
```

continues

Listing 14.4 **Continued**

```
    txt2 = gtk_editable_get_chars(GTK_EDITABLE(txt), 0, -1);

    g_print("%s\n", txt2);

    gtk_label_set_text(GTK_LABEL(lookup_widget(window1, "label1")), txt2);
}

void quit_application()
{
    /* The glade XML file identifies this function with the delete-event
     * for both window1 and window2.
     */

    gtk_main_quit();
}

int main (int argc, char *argv[])
{

    GladeXML   *xml;

    gtk_init (&argc, &argv);
    glade_init();

    /* window1 */

    xml = glade_xml_new("cross-window.glade", "window1");

    if (!xml)
        {
            g_print("unable to load interface window1...\n");
            return 1;
        }

    window1 = glade_xml_get_widget(xml, "window1");

    /* Link the called widgets to the window widget so that
     * the called widgets can be retrieved with a lookup_widget()
     * call.
     */

    gtk_object_set_data_full(GTK_OBJECT(window1), "entry1",
                             glade_xml_get_widget(xml, "entry1"), 0L);
    gtk_object_set_data_full(GTK_OBJECT(window1), "label1",
                             glade_xml_get_widget(xml, "label1"), 0L);
    /* Connect the signals to their handlers, as defined in the
     * .glade file.
     */
```

```
glade_xml_signal_autoconnect(xml);

/* In window2, the code structure is the same as that above,
 * except that the widgets in question are different.
 */

xml = glade_xml_new("cross-window.glade", "window2");

if (!xml)
    {
        g_print("unable to load interface window2...\n");
        return 1;
    }

window2 = glade_xml_get_widget(xml, "window2");
gtk_object_set_data_full(GTK_OBJECT(window2), "entry2",
                            glade_xml_get_widget(xml, "entry2"), 0L);
gtk_object_set_data_full(GTK_OBJECT(window2), "label2",
                            glade_xml_get_widget(xml, "label2"), 0L);
glade_xml_signal_autoconnect(xml);

/* Finally, show the two window widgets. */

gtk_widget_show (window1);
gtk_widget_show (window2);

gtk_main ();
return 0;
}
```

The button1_clicked(), button2_clicked(), and quit_application() functions come before main()—each of which is simple enough. main() is not fundamentally different from the previous example, except that now there are two form widgets to set up and the gtk_object_set_data_full() calls. The purpose of these calls is to connect the child label and entry widgets with their parent window widgets in such a way that the lookup_widget() function in support.c can find all the widgets correctly. The lookup_widget() function used here is the same as that shown in Chapter 5, Listing 5.5, in lines 25 through 47.

Finally, to compile the application, enter the following command from the project subdirectory:

```
% gcc -Wall `gtk-config —cflags —libs` *.c -o cross-window -lglade
```

Changing the Application Without Recompiling

Now so you can see how this capability could be used, open up `cross-window.glade` in Glade and select window2. Select vbox2 (the child widget of window2) and view its properties in the Glade property editor. Change its number of rows from 3 to 4 and drop a command button in the newly created space at the bottom of vbox2. Figure 14.7 shows the resulting screen.

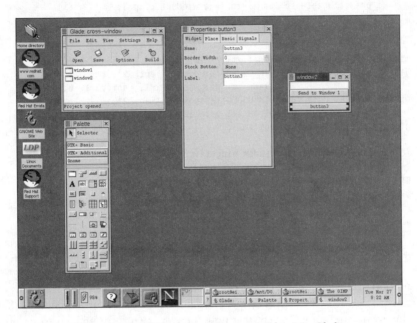

Figure 14.7   Add a row and button to vbox2 in Glade.

Now select the button that was just added and change its text to "Quit" or "Quit Application," as shown in Figure 14.7. In the Properties dialog, select the Signals tab, enter "clicked" for the signal, and enter "quit_application" in the handler space, as shown in Figure 14.8.

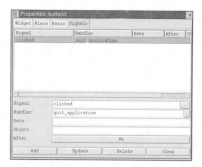

Figure 14.8 Connect a new button `clicked` signal to the `quit_application` function.

Remember that `quit_application()` has already been defined in `cross-window.c`. The primary limitation of this method is that you have to already have the function compiled into the executable (or you have to code it and recompile).

Now run the cross-windows application without recompiling the *.c files. Figure 14.9 shows the results. Without recompiling, the Quit button has been added and can now be used to close the application.

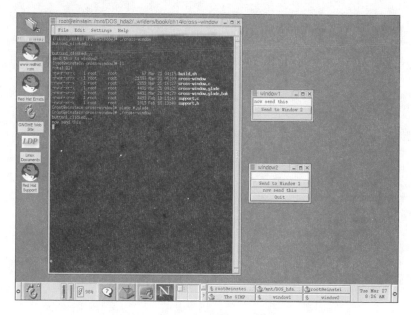

Figure 14.9 You changed the cross-windows application
user interface and added new functionality without recompiling.

IV

Appendixes

A

Glade-Generated Files from the SESI Order Application

THIS APPENDIX COVERS TWO FILES THAT ARE VERY IMPORTANT to the SESI Order application built in Chapter 6, "Order Entry Abstract and Design," and Chapter 7, "Construction of the SESI Order Entry Application." The two files are `interface.c` and `sesi.glade`. `interface.c` is the Glade-generated file that builds the forms for the application. In it you will see a function called `create_frm_main()`, which returns a GtkWidget; this is the function called by `main.c` to create form frm_main. `sesi.glade` is the SESI Order project file; it stores the application interface in an XML format for use by Glade. Both are generated by Glade and are overwritten each time the "Build" button is pressed.

It is important to note that—as tempting as it may be—you should not alter these functions unless you really, really have to. Remember that if you do, your changes will be lost the next time you open Glade and "build" the project. If you do find it necessary to change these functions after Glade has created them, I strongly suggest that you make very detailed notes of precisely what changes you've made, where, and why.

interface.c

This file contains the various functions for creating the forms that make up the user interface (see Listing A.1). The functions are create_frm_main(), create_frm_items_ordered(), create_frm_find_item(), and create_frm_find_customer(). Each of these functions returns a pointer to a GtkWidget (review main.c) to see how these functions are implemented.

Listing A.1   *interface.c* **from the SESI Order Application**

```c
/* DO NOT EDIT THIS FILE. It is generated by Glade.
 */

#ifdef HAVE_CONFIG_H
#  include <config.h>
#endif

#include <sys/types.h>
#include <sys/stat.h>
#include <unistd.h>
#include <string.h>

#include <gdk/gdkkeysyms.h>
#include <gtk/gtk.h>

#include "callbacks.h"
#include "interface.h"
#include "support.h"

GtkWidget*
create_frm_main (void)
{
  GtkWidget *frm_main;
  GtkWidget *vbox_main;
  GtkWidget *table_2_by_2;
  GtkWidget *vbox_customer_number;
  GtkWidget *lbl_customer_number;
  GtkWidget *cbo_customer_number;
  GtkWidget *combo_entry_customer_number;
  GtkWidget *vbox_customer_name;
  GtkWidget *cmd_customer_name;
  GtkWidget *entry_customer_name;
  GtkWidget *vbuttonbox;
  guint cmd_search_key;
  GtkWidget *cmd_search;
  guint cmd_save_edits_key;
  GtkWidget *cmd_save_edits;
  guint cmd_select_items_key;
  GtkWidget *cmd_select_items;
  guint cmd_print_order_key;
```

```
GtkWidget *cmd_print_order;
guint cmd_exit_key;
GtkWidget *cmd_exit;
GtkWidget *vbox_data;
GtkWidget *table_3_by_3;
GtkWidget *lbl_primary_contact;
GtkWidget *lbl_name_last_first;
GtkWidget *lbl_title_and_phone;
GtkWidget *entry_last;
GtkWidget *entry_first;
GtkWidget *entry_title;
GtkWidget *entry_phone;
GtkWidget *table_4_by_2;
GtkWidget *lbl_ship_to;
GtkWidget *lbl_bill_to;
GtkWidget *entry_ship_to_addr1;
GtkWidget *entry_bill_to_addr1;
GtkWidget *entry_ship_to_addr2;
GtkWidget *entry_bill_to_addr2;
GtkWidget *hbox1;
GtkWidget *entry_ship_to_city;
GtkWidget *entry_ship_to_st;
GtkWidget *entry_ship_to_zip;
GtkWidget *hbox2;
GtkWidget *entry_bill_to_city;
GtkWidget *entry_bill_to_st;
GtkWidget *entry_bill_to_zip;
GtkWidget *lbl_order_comments;
GtkWidget *scrolledwindow1;
GtkWidget *txt_order_comments;
GtkWidget *lbl_customer_comments;
GtkWidget *scrolledwindow2;
GtkWidget *txt_customer_comments;
GtkWidget *statusbar;
GtkAccelGroup *accel_group;

accel_group = gtk_accel_group_new ();

frm_main = gtk_window_new (GTK_WINDOW_TOPLEVEL);
gtk_object_set_data (GTK_OBJECT (frm_main), "frm_main", frm_main);
gtk_window_set_title (GTK_WINDOW (frm_main), "SESI Customer Order");

vbox_main = gtk_vbox_new (FALSE, 0);
gtk_widget_ref (vbox_main);
gtk_object_set_data_full (GTK_OBJECT (frm_main), "vbox_main", vbox_main,
                          (GtkDestroyNotify) gtk_widget_unref);
gtk_widget_show (vbox_main);
gtk_container_add (GTK_CONTAINER (frm_main), vbox_main);

table_2_by_2 = gtk_table_new (2, 2, FALSE);
gtk_widget_ref (table_2_by_2);
```

continues

Listing A.1 **Continued**

```
gtk_object_set_data_full (GTK_OBJECT (frm_main), "table_2_by_2", table_2_by_2,
                          (GtkDestroyNotify) gtk_widget_unref);
gtk_widget_show (table_2_by_2);
gtk_box_pack_start (GTK_BOX (vbox_main), table_2_by_2, TRUE, TRUE, 0);

vbox_customer_number = gtk_vbox_new (FALSE, 0);
gtk_widget_ref (vbox_customer_number);
gtk_object_set_data_full (GTK_OBJECT (frm_main), "vbox_customer_number",
➥vbox_customer_number,
                          (GtkDestroyNotify) gtk_widget_unref);
gtk_widget_show (vbox_customer_number);
gtk_table_attach (GTK_TABLE (table_2_by_2), vbox_customer_number, 0, 1, 0, 1,
                  (GtkAttachOptions) (GTK_EXPAND ¦ GTK_FILL),
                  (GtkAttachOptions) (GTK_EXPAND ¦ GTK_FILL), 0, 0);

lbl_customer_number = gtk_label_new ("Customer Number");
gtk_widget_ref (lbl_customer_number);
gtk_object_set_data_full (GTK_OBJECT (frm_main), "lbl_customer_number",
➥lbl_customer_number
                          (GtkDestroyNotify) gtk_widget_unref);
gtk_widget_show (lbl_customer_number);
gtk_box_pack_start (GTK_BOX (vbox_customer_number), lbl_customer_number, FALSE,
➥FALSE, 0);
gtk_label_set_justify (GTK_LABEL (lbl_customer_number), GTK_JUSTIFY_LEFT);

cbo_customer_number = gtk_combo_new ();
gtk_widget_ref (cbo_customer_number);
gtk_object_set_data_full (GTK_OBJECT (frm_main), "cbo_customer_number",
➥cbo_customer_number,
                          (GtkDestroyNotify) gtk_widget_unref);
gtk_widget_show (cbo_customer_number);
gtk_box_pack_start (GTK_BOX (vbox_customer_number), cbo_customer_number, FALSE,
➥FALSE, 0);

combo_entry_customer_number = GTK_COMBO (cbo_customer_number)->entry;
gtk_widget_ref (combo_entry_customer_number);
gtk_object_set_data_full (GTK_OBJECT (frm_main), "combo_entry_customer_number",
➥combo_entry_customer_number,
                          (GtkDestroyNotify) gtk_widget_unref);
gtk_widget_show (combo_entry_customer_number);

vbox_customer_name = gtk_vbox_new (FALSE, 0);
gtk_widget_ref (vbox_customer_name);
gtk_object_set_data_full (GTK_OBJECT (frm_main), "vbox_customer_name",
➥vbox_customer_name,
                          (GtkDestroyNotify) gtk_widget_unref);
gtk_widget_show (vbox_customer_name);
```

```
gtk_table_attach (GTK_TABLE (table_2_by_2), vbox_customer_name, 1, 2, 0, 1,
                  (GtkAttachOptions) (GTK_EXPAND ¦ GTK_FILL),
                  (GtkAttachOptions) (GTK_FILL), 0, 0);

cmd_customer_name = gtk_label_new ("Customer Name");
gtk_widget_ref (cmd_customer_name);
gtk_object_set_data_full (GTK_OBJECT (frm_main), "cmd_customer_name",
➥cmd_customer_name,
                          (GtkDestroyNotify) gtk_widget_unref);
gtk_widget_show (cmd_customer_name);
gtk_box_pack_start (GTK_BOX (vbox_customer_name), cmd_customer_name, FALSE,
➥FALSE, 0);
gtk_label_set_justify (GTK_LABEL (cmd_customer_name), GTK_JUSTIFY_LEFT);

entry_customer_name = gtk_entry_new ();
gtk_widget_ref (entry_customer_name);
gtk_object_set_data_full (GTK_OBJECT (frm_main), "entry_customer_name",
➥entry_customer_name,
                          (GtkDestroyNotify) gtk_widget_unref);
gtk_widget_show (entry_customer_name);
gtk_box_pack_start (GTK_BOX (vbox_customer_name), entry_customer_name, FALSE,
➥FALSE, 0);

vbuttonbox = gtk_vbutton_box_new ();
gtk_widget_ref (vbuttonbox);
gtk_object_set_data_full (GTK_OBJECT (frm_main), "vbuttonbox", vbuttonbox,
                          (GtkDestroyNotify) gtk_widget_unref);
gtk_widget_show (vbuttonbox);
gtk_table_attach (GTK_TABLE (table_2_by_2), vbuttonbox, 0, 1, 1, 2,
                  (GtkAttachOptions) (GTK_FILL),
                  (GtkAttachOptions) (GTK_EXPAND ¦ GTK_FILL), 0, 0);

cmd_search = gtk_button_new_with_label ("");
cmd_search_key = gtk_label_parse_uline (GTK_LABEL (GTK_BIN (cmd_search)->child),
                                "_Search...");
gtk_widget_add_accelerator (cmd_search, "clicked", accel_group,
                            cmd_search_key, GDK_MOD1_MASK, 0);
gtk_widget_ref (cmd_search);
gtk_object_set_data_full (GTK_OBJECT (frm_main), "cmd_search", cmd_search,
                          (GtkDestroyNotify) gtk_widget_unref);
gtk_widget_show (cmd_search);
gtk_container_add (GTK_CONTAINER (vbuttonbox), cmd_search);
GTK_WIDGET_SET_FLAGS (cmd_search, GTK_CAN_DEFAULT);
gtk_widget_add_accelerator (cmd_search, "clicked", accel_group,
                            GDK_S, GDK_MOD1_MASK,
                            GTK_ACCEL_VISIBLE);

cmd_save_edits = gtk_button_new_with_label ("");
cmd_save_edits_key = gtk_label_parse_uline (GTK_LABEL (GTK_BIN (cmd_save_edits)-
➥>child),
                                "Save  Edits");
```

continues

Listing A.1 **Continued**

```
gtk_widget_add_accelerator (cmd_save_edits, "clicked", accel_group,
                            cmd_save_edits_key, GDK_MOD1_MASK, 0);
gtk_widget_ref (cmd_save_edits);
gtk_object_set_data_full (GTK_OBJECT (frm_main), "cmd_save_edits",
➥cmd_save_edits,
                            (GtkDestroyNotify) gtk_widget_unref);
gtk_widget_show (cmd_save_edits);
gtk_container_add (GTK_CONTAINER (vbuttonbox), cmd_save_edits);
gtk_widget_set_sensitive (cmd_save_edits, FALSE);
GTK_WIDGET_SET_FLAGS (cmd_save_edits, GTK_CAN_DEFAULT);
gtk_widget_add_accelerator (cmd_save_edits, "clicked", accel_group,
                            GDK_E, GDK_MOD1_MASK,
                            GTK_ACCEL_VISIBLE);

cmd_select_items = gtk_button_new_with_label ("");
cmd_select_items_key = gtk_label_parse_uline (GTK_LABEL (GTK_BIN
➥(cmd_select_items)->child),
                                "Select _Items");
gtk_widget_add_accelerator (cmd_select_items, "clicked", accel_group,
                            cmd_select_items_key, GDK_MOD1_MASK, 0);
gtk_widget_ref (cmd_select_items);
gtk_object_set_data_full (GTK_OBJECT (frm_main), "cmd_select_items",
➥cmd_select_items,
                            (GtkDestroyNotify) gtk_widget_unref);
gtk_widget_show (cmd_select_items);
gtk_container_add (GTK_CONTAINER (vbuttonbox), cmd_select_items);
GTK_WIDGET_SET_FLAGS (cmd_select_items, GTK_CAN_DEFAULT);
gtk_widget_add_accelerator (cmd_select_items, "clicked", accel_group,
                            GDK_I, GDK_MOD1_MASK,
                            GTK_ACCEL_VISIBLE);

cmd_print_order = gtk_button_new_with_label ("");
cmd_print_order_key = gtk_label_parse_uline (GTK_LABEL (GTK_BIN
➥(cmd_print_order)->child),
                                "_Print Order");
gtk_widget_add_accelerator (cmd_print_order, "clicked", accel_group,
                            cmd_print_order_key, GDK_MOD1_MASK, 0);
gtk_widget_ref (cmd_print_order);
gtk_object_set_data_full (GTK_OBJECT (frm_main), "cmd_print_order",
➥cmd_print_order,
                            (GtkDestroyNotify) gtk_widget_unref);
gtk_widget_show (cmd_print_order);
gtk_container_add (GTK_CONTAINER (vbuttonbox), cmd_print_order);
GTK_WIDGET_SET_FLAGS (cmd_print_order, GTK_CAN_DEFAULT);
gtk_widget_add_accelerator (cmd_print_order, "clicked", accel_group,
                            GDK_P, GDK_MOD1_MASK,
                            GTK_ACCEL_VISIBLE);

cmd_exit = gtk_button_new_with_label ("");
```

```
cmd_exit_key = gtk_label_parse_uline (GTK_LABEL (GTK_BIN (cmd_exit)->child),
                             "E_xit");
gtk_widget_add_accelerator (cmd_exit, "clicked", accel_group,
                            cmd_exit_key, GDK_MOD1_MASK, 0);
gtk_widget_ref (cmd_exit);
gtk_object_set_data_full (GTK_OBJECT (frm_main), "cmd_exit", cmd_exit,
                          (GtkDestroyNotify) gtk_widget_unref);
gtk_widget_show (cmd_exit);
gtk_container_add (GTK_CONTAINER (vbuttonbox), cmd_exit);
GTK_WIDGET_SET_FLAGS (cmd_exit, GTK_CAN_DEFAULT);
gtk_widget_add_accelerator (cmd_exit, "clicked", accel_group,
                            GDK_x, GDK_MOD1_MASK,
                            GTK_ACCEL_VISIBLE);


vbox_data = gtk_vbox_new (FALSE, 0);
gtk_widget_ref (vbox_data);
gtk_object_set_data_full (GTK_OBJECT (frm_main), "vbox_data", vbox_data,
                          (GtkDestroyNotify) gtk_widget_unref);
gtk_widget_show (vbox_data);
gtk_table_attach (GTK_TABLE (table_2_by_2), vbox_data, 1, 2, 1, 2,
                  (GtkAttachOptions) (GTK_FILL),
                  (GtkAttachOptions) (GTK_FILL), 0, 0);


table_3_by_3 = gtk_table_new (3, 3, FALSE);
gtk_widget_ref (table_3_by_3);
gtk_object_set_data_full (GTK_OBJECT (frm_main), "table_3_by_3", table_3_by_3,
                          (GtkDestroyNotify) gtk_widget_unref);
gtk_widget_show (table_3_by_3);
gtk_box_pack_start (GTK_BOX (vbox_data), table_3_by_3, TRUE, TRUE, 0);


lbl_primary_contact = gtk_label_new ("Primary Contact:");
gtk_widget_ref (lbl_primary_contact);
gtk_object_set_data_full (GTK_OBJECT (frm_main), "lbl_primary_contact",
➥lbl_primary_contact,
                          (GtkDestroyNotify) gtk_widget_unref);
gtk_widget_show (lbl_primary_contact);
gtk_table_attach (GTK_TABLE (table_3_by_3), lbl_primary_contact, 0, 3, 0, 1,
                  (GtkAttachOptions) (0),
                  (GtkAttachOptions) (0), 0, 0);
gtk_label_set_justify (GTK_LABEL (lbl_primary_contact), GTK_JUSTIFY_LEFT);


lbl_name_last_first = gtk_label_new ("Name (Last, First):");
gtk_widget_ref (lbl_name_last_first);
gtk_object_set_data_full (GTK_OBJECT (frm_main), "lbl_name_last_first",
➥lbl_name_last_first,
                          (GtkDestroyNotify) gtk_widget_unref);
gtk_widget_show (lbl_name_last_first);
gtk_table_attach (GTK_TABLE (table_3_by_3), lbl_name_last_first, 0, 1, 1, 2,
                  (GtkAttachOptions) (0),
                  (GtkAttachOptions) (0), 0, 0);
```

continues

Listing A.1 **Continued**

```
gtk_label_set_justify (GTK_LABEL (lbl_name_last_first), GTK_JUSTIFY_LEFT);

lbl_title_and_phone = gtk_label_new ("Title and Phone");
gtk_widget_ref (lbl_title_and_phone);
gtk_object_set_data_full (GTK_OBJECT (frm_main), "lbl_title_and_phone",
➥lbl_title_and_phone,
                          (GtkDestroyNotify) gtk_widget_unref);
gtk_widget_show (lbl_title_and_phone);
gtk_table_attach (GTK_TABLE (table_3_by_3), lbl_title_and_phone, 0, 1, 2, 3,
                  (GtkAttachOptions) (0),
                  (GtkAttachOptions) (0), 0, 0);
gtk_label_set_justify (GTK_LABEL (lbl_title_and_phone), GTK_JUSTIFY_LEFT);

entry_last = gtk_entry_new ();
gtk_widget_ref (entry_last);
gtk_object_set_data_full (GTK_OBJECT (frm_main), "entry_last", entry_last,
                          (GtkDestroyNotify) gtk_widget_unref);
gtk_widget_show (entry_last);
gtk_table_attach (GTK_TABLE (table_3_by_3), entry_last, 1, 2, 1, 2,
                  (GtkAttachOptions) (GTK_FILL),
                  (GtkAttachOptions) (0), 0, 0);
gtk_widget_set_usize (entry_last, 100, -2);

entry_first = gtk_entry_new ();
gtk_widget_ref (entry_first);
gtk_object_set_data_full (GTK_OBJECT (frm_main), "entry_first", entry_first,
                          (GtkDestroyNotify) gtk_widget_unref);
gtk_widget_show (entry_first);
gtk_table_attach (GTK_TABLE (table_3_by_3), entry_first, 2, 3, 1, 2,
                  (GtkAttachOptions) (GTK_FILL),
                  (GtkAttachOptions) (0), 0, 0);
gtk_widget_set_usize (entry_first, 100, -2);

entry_title = gtk_entry_new ();
gtk_widget_ref (entry_title);
gtk_object_set_data_full (GTK_OBJECT (frm_main), "entry_title", entry_title,
                          (GtkDestroyNotify) gtk_widget_unref);
gtk_widget_show (entry_title);
gtk_table_attach (GTK_TABLE (table_3_by_3), entry_title, 1, 2, 2, 3,
                  (GtkAttachOptions) (GTK_FILL),
                  (GtkAttachOptions) (0), 0, 0);
gtk_widget_set_usize (entry_title, 100, -2);

entry_phone = gtk_entry_new ();
gtk_widget_ref (entry_phone);
gtk_object_set_data_full (GTK_OBJECT (frm_main), "entry_phone", entry_phone,
                          (GtkDestroyNotify) gtk_widget_unref);
gtk_widget_show (entry_phone);
```

```
gtk_table_attach (GTK_TABLE (table_3_by_3), entry_phone, 2, 3, 2, 3,
                  (GtkAttachOptions) (GTK_FILL),
                  (GtkAttachOptions) (0), 0, 0);
gtk_widget_set_usize (entry_phone, 100, -2);

table_4_by_2 = gtk_table_new (4, 2, FALSE);
gtk_widget_ref (table_4_by_2);
gtk_object_set_data_full (GTK_OBJECT (frm_main), "table_4_by_2", table_4_by_2,
                          (GtkDestroyNotify) gtk_widget_unref);
gtk_widget_show (table_4_by_2);
gtk_box_pack_start (GTK_BOX (vbox_data), table_4_by_2, TRUE, TRUE, 0);

lbl_ship_to = gtk_label_new ("Ship To:");
gtk_widget_ref (lbl_ship_to);
gtk_object_set_data_full (GTK_OBJECT (frm_main), "lbl_ship_to", lbl_ship_to,
                          (GtkDestroyNotify) gtk_widget_unref);
gtk_widget_show (lbl_ship_to);
gtk_table_attach (GTK_TABLE (table_4_by_2), lbl_ship_to, 0, 1, 0, 1,
                  (GtkAttachOptions) (0),
                  (GtkAttachOptions) (0), 0, 0);
gtk_label_set_justify (GTK_LABEL (lbl_ship_to), GTK_JUSTIFY_LEFT);

lbl_bill_to = gtk_label_new ("Bill To:");
gtk_widget_ref (lbl_bill_to);
gtk_object_set_data_full (GTK_OBJECT (frm_main), "lbl_bill_to", lbl_bill_to,
                          (GtkDestroyNotify) gtk_widget_unref),
gtk_widget_show (lbl_bill_to);
gtk_table_attach (GTK_TABLE (table_4_by_2), lbl_bill_to, 1, 2, 0, 1,
                  (GtkAttachOptions) (0),
                  (GtkAttachOptions) (0), 0, 0);
gtk_label_set_justify (GTK_LABEL (lbl_bill_to), GTK_JUSTIFY_LEFT);

entry_ship_to_addr1 = gtk_entry_new ();
gtk_widget_ref (entry_ship_to_addr1);
gtk_object_set_data_full (GTK_OBJECT (frm_main), "entry_ship_to_addr1",
➥entry_ship_to_addr1,
                          (GtkDestroyNotify) gtk_widget_unref);
gtk_widget_show (entry_ship_to_addr1);
gtk_table_attach (GTK_TABLE (table_4_by_2), entry_ship_to_addr1, 0, 1, 1, 2,
                  (GtkAttachOptions) (GTK_FILL),
                  (GtkAttachOptions) (0), 0, 0);
gtk_widget_set_usize (entry_ship_to_addr1, 160, -2);

entry_bill_to_addr1 = gtk_entry_new ();
gtk_widget_ref (entry_bill_to_addr1);
gtk_object_set_data_full (GTK_OBJECT (frm_main), "entry_bill_to_addr1",
➥entry_bill_to_addr1,
                          (GtkDestroyNotify) gtk_widget_unref);
gtk_widget_show (entry_bill_to_addr1);
gtk_table_attach (GTK_TABLE (table_4_by_2), entry_bill_to_addr1, 1, 2, 1, 2,
                  (GtkAttachOptions) (GTK_FILL),
                  (GtkAttachOptions) (0), 0, 0);
```

continues

Listing A.1 **Continued**

```
entry_ship_to_addr2 = gtk_entry_new ();
gtk_widget_ref (entry_ship_to_addr2);
gtk_object_set_data_full (GTK_OBJECT (frm_main), "entry_ship_to_addr2",
➥entry_ship_to_addr2,
                            (GtkDestroyNotify) gtk_widget_unref);
gtk_widget_show (entry_ship_to_addr2);
gtk_table_attach (GTK_TABLE (table_4_by_2), entry_ship_to_addr2, 0, 1, 2, 3,
                  (GtkAttachOptions) (GTK_FILL),
                  (GtkAttachOptions) (0), 0, 0);

entry_bill_to_addr2 = gtk_entry_new ();
gtk_widget_ref (entry_bill_to_addr2);
gtk_object_set_data_full (GTK_OBJECT (frm_main), "entry_bill_to_addr2",
➥entry_bill_to_addr2,
                            (GtkDestroyNotify) gtk_widget_unref);
gtk_widget_show (entry_bill_to_addr2);
gtk_table_attach (GTK_TABLE (table_4_by_2), entry_bill_to_addr2, 1, 2, 2, 3,
                  (GtkAttachOptions) (GTK_FILL),
                  (GtkAttachOptions) (0), 0, 0);

hbox1 = gtk_hbox_new (FALSE, 0);
gtk_widget_ref (hbox1);
gtk_object_set_data_full (GTK_OBJECT (frm_main), "hbox1", hbox1,
                            (GtkDestroyNotify) gtk_widget_unref);
gtk_widget_show (hbox1);
gtk_table_attach (GTK_TABLE (table_4_by_2), hbox1, 0, 1, 3, 4,
                  (GtkAttachOptions) (GTK_FILL),
                  (GtkAttachOptions) (GTK_EXPAND | GTK_FILL), 0, 0);

entry_ship_to_city = gtk_entry_new ();
gtk_widget_ref (entry_ship_to_city);
gtk_object_set_data_full (GTK_OBJECT (frm_main), "entry_ship_to_city",
➥entry_ship_to_city,
                            (GtkDestroyNotify) gtk_widget_unref);
gtk_widget_show (entry_ship_to_city);
gtk_box_pack_start (GTK_BOX (hbox1), entry_ship_to_city, FALSE, TRUE, 0);
gtk_widget_set_usize (entry_ship_to_city, 100, -2);

entry_ship_to_st = gtk_entry_new ();
gtk_widget_ref (entry_ship_to_st);
gtk_object_set_data_full (GTK_OBJECT (frm_main), "entry_ship_to_st",
➥entry_ship_to_st,
                            (GtkDestroyNotify) gtk_widget_unref);
gtk_widget_show (entry_ship_to_st);
gtk_box_pack_start (GTK_BOX (hbox1), entry_ship_to_st, FALSE, TRUE, 0);
gtk_widget_set_usize (entry_ship_to_st, 35, -2);

entry_ship_to_zip = gtk_entry_new ();
gtk_widget_ref (entry_ship_to_zip);
```

```
gtk_object_set_data_full (GTK_OBJECT (frm_main), "entry_ship_to_zip",
→entry_ship_to_zip,
                          (GtkDestroyNotify) gtk_widget_unref);
gtk_widget_show (entry_ship_to_zip);
gtk_box_pack_start (GTK_BOX (hbox1), entry_ship_to_zip, FALSE, TRUE, 0);
gtk_widget_set_usize (entry_ship_to_zip, 70, -2);

hbox2 = gtk_hbox_new (FALSE, 0);
gtk_widget_ref (hbox2);
gtk_object_set_data_full (GTK_OBJECT (frm_main), "hbox2", hbox2,
                          (GtkDestroyNotify) gtk_widget_unref);
gtk_widget_show (hbox2);
gtk_table_attach (GTK_TABLE (table_4_by_2), hbox2, 1, 2, 3, 4,
                  (GtkAttachOptions) (GTK_FILL),
                  (GtkAttachOptions) (GTK_FILL), 0, 0);

entry_bill_to_city = gtk_entry_new ();
gtk_widget_ref (entry_bill_to_city);
gtk_object_set_data_full (GTK_OBJECT (frm_main), "entry_bill_to_city",
→entry_bill_to_city,
                          (GtkDestroyNotify) gtk_widget_unref);
gtk_widget_show (entry_bill_to_city);
gtk_box_pack_start (GTK_BOX (hbox2), entry_bill_to_city, FALSE, TRUE, 0);
gtk_widget_set_usize (entry_bill_to_city, 100, -2);

entry_bill_to_st = gtk_entry_new ();
gtk_widget_ref (entry_bill_to_st);
gtk_object_set_data_full (GTK_OBJECT (frm_main), "entry_bill_to_st",
→entry_bill_to_st,
                          (GtkDestroyNotify) gtk_widget_unref);
gtk_widget_show (entry_bill_to_st);
gtk_box_pack_start (GTK_BOX (hbox2), entry_bill_to_st, FALSE, TRUE, 0);
gtk_widget_set_usize (entry_bill_to_st, 35, -2);

entry_bill_to_zip = gtk_entry_new ();
gtk_widget_ref (entry_bill_to_zip);
gtk_object_set_data_full (GTK_OBJECT (frm_main), "entry_bill_to_zip",
→entry_bill_to_zip,
                          (GtkDestroyNotify) gtk_widget_unref);
gtk_widget_show (entry_bill_to_zip);
gtk_box_pack_start (GTK_BOX (hbox2), entry_bill_to_zip, FALSE, TRUE, 0);
gtk_widget_set_usize (entry_bill_to_zip, 70, -2);

lbl_order_comments = gtk_label_new ("Order Comments");
gtk_widget_ref (lbl_order_comments);
gtk_object_set_data_full (GTK_OBJECT (frm_main), "lbl_order_comments",
→lbl_order_comments,
                          (GtkDestroyNotify) gtk_widget_unref);
gtk_widget_show (lbl_order_comments);
gtk_box_pack_start (GTK_BOX (vbox_data), lbl_order_comments, FALSE, FALSE, 0);
gtk_label_set_justify (GTK_LABEL (lbl_order_comments), GTK_JUSTIFY_LEFT);
```

continues

Listing A.1 **Continued**

```
scrolledwindow1 = gtk_scrolled_window_new (NULL, NULL);
gtk_widget_ref (scrolledwindow1);
gtk_object_set_data_full (GTK_OBJECT (frm_main), "scrolledwindow1",
➥scrolledwindow1,
                          (GtkDestroyNotify) gtk_widget_unref);
gtk_widget_show (scrolledwindow1);
gtk_box_pack_start (GTK_BOX (vbox_data), scrolledwindow1, TRUE, TRUE, 0);
gtk_scrolled_window_set_policy (GTK_SCROLLED_WINDOW (scrolledwindow1),
➥GTK_POLICY_NEVER, GTK_POLICY_ALWAYS);

txt_order_comments = gtk_text_new (NULL, NULL);
gtk_widget_ref (txt_order_comments);
gtk_object_set_data_full (GTK_OBJECT (frm_main), "txt_order_comments",
➥txt_order_comments,
                          (GtkDestroyNotify) gtk_widget_unref);
gtk_widget_show (txt_order_comments);
gtk_container_add (GTK_CONTAINER (scrolledwindow1), txt_order_comments);
gtk_text_set_editable (GTK_TEXT (txt_order_comments), TRUE);

lbl_customer_comments = gtk_label_new ("Customer Comments");
gtk_widget_ref (lbl_customer_comments);
gtk_object_set_data_full (GTK_OBJECT (frm_main), "lbl_customer_comments",
➥lbl_customer_comments,
                          (GtkDestroyNotify) gtk_widget_unref);
gtk_widget_show (lbl_customer_comments);
gtk_box_pack_start (GTK_BOX (vbox_data), lbl_customer_comments, FALSE, FALSE, 0);
gtk_label_set_justify (GTK_LABEL (lbl_customer_comments), GTK_JUSTIFY_LEFT);

scrolledwindow2 = gtk_scrolled_window_new (NULL, NULL);
gtk_widget_ref (scrolledwindow2);
gtk_object_set_data_full (GTK_OBJECT (frm_main), "scrolledwindow2",
➥scrolledwindow2,
                          (GtkDestroyNotify) gtk_widget_unref);
gtk_widget_show (scrolledwindow2);
gtk_box_pack_start (GTK_BOX (vbox_data), scrolledwindow2, TRUE, TRUE, 0);
gtk_scrolled_window_set_policy (GTK_SCROLLED_WINDOW (scrolledwindow2),
➥GTK_POLICY_NEVER, GTK_POLICY_ALWAYS);

txt_customer_comments = gtk_text_new (NULL, NULL);
gtk_widget_ref (txt_customer_comments);
gtk_object_set_data_full (GTK_OBJECT (frm_main), "txt_customer_comments",
➥txt_customer_comments,
                          (GtkDestroyNotify) gtk_widget_unref);
gtk_widget_show (txt_customer_comments);
gtk_container_add (GTK_CONTAINER (scrolledwindow2), txt_customer_comments);
gtk_text_set_editable (GTK_TEXT (txt_customer_comments), TRUE);

statusbar = gtk_statusbar_new ();
gtk_widget_ref (statusbar);
gtk_object_set_data_full (GTK_OBJECT (frm_main), "statusbar", statusbar,
                          (GtkDestroyNotify) gtk_widget_unref);
```

```
gtk_widget_show (statusbar);
gtk_box_pack_start (GTK_BOX (vbox_main), statusbar, FALSE, FALSE, 0);

gtk_signal_connect (GTK_OBJECT (frm_main), "set_focus",
                    GTK_SIGNAL_FUNC (on_frm_main_set_focus),
                    NULL);
gtk_signal_connect (GTK_OBJECT (frm_main), "button_press_event",
                    GTK_SIGNAL_FUNC (on_frm_main_button_press_event),
                    NULL);
gtk_signal_connect (GTK_OBJECT (frm_main), "button_release_event",
                    GTK_SIGNAL_FUNC (on_frm_main_button_release_event),
                    NULL);
gtk_signal_connect (GTK_OBJECT (frm_main), "delete_event",
                    GTK_SIGNAL_FUNC (on_frm_main_delete_event),
                    NULL);
gtk_signal_connect (GTK_OBJECT (frm_main), "hide",
                    GTK_SIGNAL_FUNC (on_frm_main_hide),
                    NULL);
gtk_signal_connect (GTK_OBJECT (frm_main), "key_release_event",
                    GTK_SIGNAL_FUNC (on_frm_main_key_press_event),
                    NULL);
gtk_signal_connect (GTK_OBJECT (frm_main), "key_press_event",
                    GTK_SIGNAL_FUNC (on_frm_main_key_press_event),
                    NULL);
gtk_signal_connect (GTK_OBJECT (frm_main), "realize",
                    GTK_SIGNAL_FUNC (on_frm_main_realize),
                    NULL);
gtk_signal_connect (GTK_OBJECT (frm_main), "destroy_event",
                    GTK_SIGNAL_FUNC (on_frm_main_destroy_event),
                    NULL);
gtk_signal_connect (GTK_OBJECT (frm_main), "event",
                    GTK_SIGNAL_FUNC (on_frm_main_event),
                    NULL);
gtk_signal_connect (GTK_OBJECT (frm_main), "show",
                    GTK_SIGNAL_FUNC (on_frm_main_show),
                    NULL);
gtk_signal_connect (GTK_OBJECT (combo_entry_customer_number), "activate",
                    GTK_SIGNAL_FUNC (on_combo_entry_customer_number_activate),
                    NULL);
gtk_signal_connect (GTK_OBJECT (combo_entry_customer_number), "changed",
                    GTK_SIGNAL_FUNC (on_combo_entry_customer_number_changed),
                    NULL);
gtk_signal_connect (GTK_OBJECT (combo_entry_customer_number), "delete_text",
                    GTK_SIGNAL_FUNC (on_combo_entry_customer_number_delete_text),
                    NULL);
gtk_signal_connect (GTK_OBJECT (combo_entry_customer_number), "insert_text",
                    GTK_SIGNAL_FUNC (on_combo_entry_customer_number_insert_text),
                    NULL);
```

continues

Listing A.1 **Continued**

```
gtk_signal_connect (GTK_OBJECT (entry_customer_name), "changed",
                    GTK_SIGNAL_FUNC (on_entry_customer_name_changed),
                    NULL);
gtk_signal_connect (GTK_OBJECT (cmd_search), "clicked",
                    GTK_SIGNAL_FUNC (on_cmd_search_clicked),
                    NULL);
gtk_signal_connect (GTK_OBJECT (cmd_save_edits), "clicked",
                    GTK_SIGNAL_FUNC (on_cmd_save_edits_clicked),
                    NULL);
gtk_signal_connect (GTK_OBJECT (cmd_select_items), "clicked",
                    GTK_SIGNAL_FUNC (on_cmd_select_items_clicked),
                    NULL);
gtk_signal_connect (GTK_OBJECT (cmd_print_order), "clicked",
                    GTK_SIGNAL_FUNC (on_cmd_print_order_clicked),
                    NULL);
gtk_signal_connect (GTK_OBJECT (cmd_exit), "clicked",
                    GTK_SIGNAL_FUNC (on_cmd_exit_clicked),
                    NULL);
gtk_signal_connect (GTK_OBJECT (entry_last), "changed",
                    GTK_SIGNAL_FUNC (on_entry_last_changed),
                    NULL);
gtk_signal_connect (GTK_OBJECT (entry_first), "changed",
                    GTK_SIGNAL_FUNC (on_entry_first_changed),
                    NULL);
gtk_signal_connect (GTK_OBJECT (entry_title), "changed",
                    GTK_SIGNAL_FUNC (on_entry_title_changed),
                    NULL);
gtk_signal_connect (GTK_OBJECT (entry_phone), "changed",
                    GTK_SIGNAL_FUNC (on_entry_phone_changed),
                    NULL);
gtk_signal_connect (GTK_OBJECT (entry_ship_to_addr1), "changed",
                    GTK_SIGNAL_FUNC (on_entry_ship_to_addr1_changed),
                    NULL);
gtk_signal_connect (GTK_OBJECT (entry_ship_to_addr2), "changed",
                    GTK_SIGNAL_FUNC (on_entry_ship_to_addr2_changed),
                    NULL);
gtk_signal_connect (GTK_OBJECT (entry_bill_to_addr2), "changed",
                    GTK_SIGNAL_FUNC (on_entry_bill_to_addr2_changed),
                    NULL);
gtk_signal_connect (GTK_OBJECT (entry_ship_to_city), "changed",
                    GTK_SIGNAL_FUNC (on_entry_ship_to_city_changed),
                    NULL);
gtk_signal_connect (GTK_OBJECT (entry_ship_to_st), "changed",
                    GTK_SIGNAL_FUNC (on_entry_ship_to_st_changed),
                    NULL);
gtk_signal_connect (GTK_OBJECT (entry_ship_to_zip), "changed",
                    GTK_SIGNAL_FUNC (on_entry_ship_to_zip_changed),
                    NULL);
```

```
    gtk_signal_connect (GTK_OBJECT (entry_bill_to_city), "changed",
                        GTK_SIGNAL_FUNC (on_entry_bill_to_city_changed),
                        NULL);
    gtk_signal_connect (GTK_OBJECT (entry_bill_to_st), "changed",
                        GTK_SIGNAL_FUNC (on_entry_bill_to_st_changed),
                        NULL);
    gtk_signal_connect (GTK_OBJECT (entry_bill_to_zip), "changed",
                        GTK_SIGNAL_FUNC (on_entry_bill_to_zip_changed),
                        NULL);
    gtk_signal_connect (GTK_OBJECT (txt_customer_comments), "changed",
                        GTK_SIGNAL_FUNC (on_txt_customer_comments_changed),
                        NULL);

    gtk_window_add_accel_group (GTK_WINDOW (frm_main), accel_group);

    return frm_main;
}

GtkWidget*
create_frm_items_ordered (void)
{
  GtkWidget *frm_items_ordered;
  GtkWidget *hpaned1;
  GtkWidget *vbox3;
  GtkWidget *lbl_item_number;
  GtkWidget *entry_item_number;
  GtkWidget *lbl_quantity;
  GtkObject *spinbutton_quantity_adj;
  GtkWidget *spinbutton_quantity;
  guint cmd_Add_key;
  GtkWidget *cmd_Add;
  guint cmd_search_for_item_key;
  GtkWidget *cmd_search_for_item;
  GtkWidget *lbl_order_total;
  GtkWidget *frame1;
  GtkWidget *lbl_order_total_numeric;
  guint cmd_done_key;
  GtkWidget *cmd_done;
  GtkWidget *vpaned1;
  GtkWidget *scrolledwindow3;
  GtkWidget *clist_items;
  GtkWidget *clist_items_lbl_item_number;
  GtkWidget *clist_items_lbl_description;
  GtkWidget *clist_items_lbl_price;
  GtkWidget *vpaned2;
  GtkWidget *hbox3;
  GtkWidget *cmd_add_down;
  GtkObject *spinbutton1_adj;
  GtkWidget *spinbutton1;
  GtkWidget *cmd_remove;
```

continues

Listing A.1 **Continued**

```
GtkWidget *scrolledwindow4;
GtkWidget *clist_items_ordered;
GtkWidget *clist_items_ordered_lbl_item_number;
GtkWidget *clist_items_ordered_lbl_description;
GtkWidget *clist_items_ordered_lbl_quantity;
GtkWidget *clist_items_ordered_lbl_total_price;
GtkAccelGroup *accel_group;

accel_group = gtk_accel_group_new ();

frm_items_ordered = gtk_window_new (GTK_WINDOW_TOPLEVEL);
gtk_object_set_data (GTK_OBJECT (frm_items_ordered), "frm_items_ordered",
➥frm_items_ordered);
gtk_window_set_title (GTK_WINDOW (frm_items_ordered), "Items Ordered");

hpaned1 = gtk_hpaned_new ();
gtk_widget_ref (hpaned1);
gtk_object_set_data_full (GTK_OBJECT (frm_items_ordered), "hpaned1", hpaned1,
                          (GtkDestroyNotify) gtk_widget_unref);
gtk_widget_show (hpaned1);
gtk_container_add (GTK_CONTAINER (frm_items_ordered), hpaned1);
gtk_paned_set_gutter_size (GTK_PANED (hpaned1), 10);

vbox3 = gtk_vbox_new (FALSE, 0);
gtk_widget_ref (vbox3);
gtk_object_set_data_full (GTK_OBJECT (frm_items_ordered), "vbox3", vbox3,
                          (GtkDestroyNotify) gtk_widget_unref);
gtk_widget_show (vbox3);
gtk_container_add (GTK_CONTAINER (hpaned1), vbox3);

lbl_item_number = gtk_label_new ("Item Number:");
gtk_widget_ref (lbl_item_number);
gtk_object_set_data_full (GTK_OBJECT (frm_items_ordered), "lbl_item_number",
➥lbl_item_number,
                          (GtkDestroyNotify) gtk_widget_unref);
gtk_widget_show (lbl_item_number);
gtk_box_pack_start (GTK_BOX (vbox3), lbl_item_number, FALSE, FALSE, 0);

entry_item_number = gtk_entry_new ();
gtk_widget_ref (entry_item_number);
gtk_object_set_data_full (GTK_OBJECT (frm_items_ordered), "entry_item_number",
➥entry_item_number,
                          (GtkDestroyNotify) gtk_widget_unref);
gtk_widget_show (entry_item_number);
gtk_box_pack_start (GTK_BOX (vbox3), entry_item_number, FALSE, FALSE, 0);

lbl_quantity = gtk_label_new ("Quantity");
gtk_widget_ref (lbl_quantity);
gtk_object_set_data_full (GTK_OBJECT (frm_items_ordered), "lbl_quantity",
➥lbl_quantity,
                          (GtkDestroyNotify) gtk_widget_unref);
```

```
gtk_widget_show (lbl_quantity);
gtk_box_pack_start (GTK_BOX (vbox3), lbl_quantity, FALSE, FALSE, 0);


spinbutton_quantity_adj = gtk_adjustment_new (1, 0, 100, 1, 10, 10);
spinbutton_quantity = gtk_spin_button_new (GTK_ADJUSTMENT
➥(spinbutton_quantity_adj), 1, 0);
gtk_widget_ref (spinbutton_quantity);
gtk_object_set_data_full (GTK_OBJECT (frm_items_ordered), "spinbutton_quantity",
➥spinbutton_quantity,
                          (GtkDestroyNotify) gtk_widget_unref);
gtk_widget_show (spinbutton_quantity);
gtk_box_pack_start (GTK_BOX (vbox3), spinbutton_quantity, FALSE, FALSE, 0);


cmd_Add = gtk_button_new_with_label ("");
cmd_Add_key = gtk_label_parse_uline (GTK_LABEL (GTK_BIN (cmd_Add)->child),
                                "_Add");
gtk_widget_add_accelerator (cmd_Add, "clicked", accel_group,
                            cmd_Add_key, GDK_MOD1_MASK, 0);
gtk_widget_ref (cmd_Add);
gtk_object_set_data_full (GTK_OBJECT (frm_items_ordered), "cmd_Add", cmd_Add,
                          (GtkDestroyNotify) gtk_widget_unref);
gtk_widget_show (cmd_Add);
gtk_box_pack_start (GTK_BOX (vbox3), cmd_Add, FALSE, FALSE, 0);
gtk_container_set_border_width (GTK_CONTAINER (cmd_Add), 5);
gtk_widget_add_accelerator (cmd_Add, "clicked", accel_group,
                            GDK_A, GDK_MOD1_MASK,
                            GTK_ACCEL_VISIBLE);


cmd_search_for_item = gtk_button_new_with_label ("");
cmd_search_for_item_key = gtk_label_parse_uline (GTK_LABEL (GTK_BIN
➥(cmd_search_for_item)->child),
                                "Search _For Item");
gtk_widget_add_accelerator (cmd_search_for_item, "clicked", accel_group,
                            cmd_search_for_item_key, GDK_MOD1_MASK, 0);
gtk_widget_ref (cmd_search_for_item);
gtk_object_set_data_full (GTK_OBJECT (frm_items_ordered), "cmd_search_for_item",
➥cmd_search_for_item,
                          (GtkDestroyNotify) gtk_widget_unref);
gtk_widget_show (cmd_search_for_item);
gtk_box_pack_start (GTK_BOX (vbox3), cmd_search_for_item, FALSE, FALSE, 0);
gtk_container_set_border_width (GTK_CONTAINER (cmd_search_for_item), 5);
gtk_widget_add_accelerator (cmd_search_for_item, "clicked", accel_group,
                            GDK_f, GDK_MOD1_MASK,
                            GTK_ACCEL_VISIBLE);


lbl_order_total = gtk_label_new ("Order Total:");
gtk_widget_ref (lbl_order_total);
gtk_object_set_data_full (GTK_OBJECT (frm_items_ordered), "lbl_order_total",
➥lbl_order_total,
                          (GtkDestroyNotify) gtk_widget_unref);
gtk_widget_show (lbl_order_total);
gtk_box_pack_start (GTK_BOX (vbox3), lbl_order_total, FALSE, FALSE, 0);
```

continues

Listing A.1 **Continued**

```
frame1 = gtk_frame_new (NULL);
gtk_widget_ref (frame1);
gtk_object_set_data_full (GTK_OBJECT (frm_items_ordered), "frame1", frame1,
                          (GtkDestroyNotify) gtk_widget_unref);
gtk_widget_show (frame1);
gtk_box_pack_start (GTK_BOX (vbox3), frame1, FALSE, FALSE, 0);

lbl_order_total_numeric = gtk_label_new ("0.00");
gtk_widget_ref (lbl_order_total_numeric);
gtk_object_set_data_full (GTK_OBJECT (frm_items_ordered),
➥"lbl_order_total_numeric", lbl_order_total_numeric,
                          (GtkDestroyNotify) gtk_widget_unref);
gtk_widget_show (lbl_order_total_numeric);
gtk_container_add (GTK_CONTAINER (frame1), lbl_order_total_numeric);

cmd_done = gtk_button_new_with_label ("");
cmd_done_key = gtk_label_parse_uline (GTK_LABEL (GTK_BIN (cmd_done)->child),
                              "_Done");
gtk_widget_add_accelerator (cmd_done, "clicked", accel_group,
                            cmd_done_key, GDK_MOD1_MASK, 0);
gtk_widget_ref (cmd_done);
gtk_object_set_data_full (GTK_OBJECT (frm_items_ordered), "cmd_done", cmd_done,
                          (GtkDestroyNotify) gtk_widget_unref);
gtk_widget_show (cmd_done);
gtk_box_pack_start (GTK_BOX (vbox3), cmd_done, FALSE, FALSE, 0);
gtk_container_set_border_width (GTK_CONTAINER (cmd_done), 5);
gtk_widget_add_accelerator (cmd_done, "clicked", accel_group,
                            GDK_d, GDK_MOD1_MASK,
                            GTK_ACCEL_VISIBLE);

vpaned1 = gtk_vpaned_new ();
gtk_widget_ref (vpaned1);
gtk_object_set_data_full (GTK_OBJECT (frm_items_ordered), "vpaned1", vpaned1,
                          (GtkDestroyNotify) gtk_widget_unref);
gtk_widget_show (vpaned1);
gtk_container_add (GTK_CONTAINER (hpaned1), vpaned1);
gtk_paned_set_gutter_size (GTK_PANED (vpaned1), 10);

scrolledwindow3 = gtk_scrolled_window_new (NULL, NULL);
gtk_widget_ref (scrolledwindow3);
gtk_object_set_data_full (GTK_OBJECT (frm_items_ordered), "scrolledwindow3",
➥scrolledwindow3,
                          (GtkDestroyNotify) gtk_widget_unref);
gtk_widget_show (scrolledwindow3);
gtk_container_add (GTK_CONTAINER (vpaned1), scrolledwindow3);

clist_items = gtk_clist_new (3);
gtk_widget_ref (clist_items);
gtk_object_set_data_full (GTK_OBJECT (frm_items_ordered), "clist_items",
➥clist_items,
                          (GtkDestroyNotify) gtk_widget_unref);
```

```
gtk_widget_show (clist_items);
gtk_container_add (GTK_CONTAINER (scrolledwindow3), clist_items);
gtk_widget_set_usize (clist_items, 266, 150);
gtk_clist_set_column_width (GTK_CLIST (clist_items), 0, 80);
gtk_clist_set_column_width (GTK_CLIST (clist_items), 1, 154);
gtk_clist_set_column_width (GTK_CLIST (clist_items), 2, 80);
gtk_clist_column_titles_show (GTK_CLIST (clist_items));

clist_items_lbl_item_number = gtk_label_new ("Item Number");
gtk_widget_ref (clist_items_lbl_item_number);
gtk_object_set_data_full (GTK_OBJECT (frm_items_ordered),
➥"clist_items_lbl_item_number", clist_items_lbl_item_number,
                          (GtkDestroyNotify) gtk_widget_unref);
gtk_widget_show (clist_items_lbl_item_number);
gtk_clist_set_column_widget (GTK_CLIST (clist_items), 0,
➥clist_items_lbl_item_number);

clist_items_lbl_description = gtk_label_new ("Description");
gtk_widget_ref (clist_items_lbl_description);
gtk_object_set_data_full (GTK_OBJECT (frm_items_ordered),
➥"clist_items_lbl_description", clist_items_lbl_description,
                          (GtkDestroyNotify) gtk_widget_unref);
gtk_widget_show (clist_items_lbl_description);
gtk_clist_set_column_widget (GTK_CLIST (clist_items), 1,
➥clist_items_lbl_description);

clist_items_lbl_price = gtk_label_new ("Price");
gtk_widget_ref (clist_items_lbl_price);
gtk_object_set_data_full (GTK_OBJECT (frm_items_ordered),
➥"clist_items_lbl_price", clist_items_lbl_price,
                          (GtkDestroyNotify) gtk_widget_unref);
gtk_widget_show (clist_items_lbl_price);
gtk_clist_set_column_widget (GTK_CLIST (clist_items), 2, clist_items_lbl_price);

vpaned2 = gtk_vpaned_new ();
gtk_widget_ref (vpaned2);
gtk_object_set_data_full (GTK_OBJECT (frm_items_ordered), "vpaned2", vpaned2,
                          (GtkDestroyNotify) gtk_widget_unref);
gtk_widget_show (vpaned2);
gtk_container_add (GTK_CONTAINER (vpaned1), vpaned2);
gtk_paned_set_gutter_size (GTK_PANED (vpaned2), 10);

hbox3 = gtk_hbox_new (TRUE, 12);
gtk_widget_ref (hbox3);
gtk_object_set_data_full (GTK_OBJECT (frm_items_ordered), "hbox3", hbox3,
                          (GtkDestroyNotify) gtk_widget_unref);
gtk_widget_show (hbox3);
gtk_container_add (GTK_CONTAINER (vpaned2), hbox3);
gtk_container_set_border_width (GTK_CONTAINER (hbox3), 10);
```

continues

Listing A.1 **Continued**

```
cmd_add_down = gtk_button_new_with_label ("Add");
gtk_widget_ref (cmd_add_down);
gtk_object_set_data_full (GTK_OBJECT (frm_items_ordered), "cmd_add_down",
➥cmd_add_down,
                          (GtkDestroyNotify) gtk_widget_unref);
gtk_widget_show (cmd_add_down);
gtk_box_pack_start (GTK_BOX (hbox3), cmd_add_down, FALSE, FALSE, 0);

spinbutton1_adj = gtk_adjustment_new (1, 0, 100, 1, 10, 10);
spinbutton1 = gtk_spin_button_new (GTK_ADJUSTMENT (spinbutton1_adj), 1, 0);
gtk_widget_ref (spinbutton1);
gtk_object_set_data_full (GTK_OBJECT (frm_items_ordered), "spinbutton1",
➥spinbutton1,
                          (GtkDestroyNotify) gtk_widget_unref);
gtk_widget_show (spinbutton1);
gtk_box_pack_start (GTK_BOX (hbox3), spinbutton1, FALSE, FALSE, 0);

cmd_remove = gtk_button_new_with_label ("Remove");
gtk_widget_ref (cmd_remove);
gtk_object_set_data_full (GTK_OBJECT (frm_items_ordered), "cmd_remove",
➥cmd_remove,
                          (GtkDestroyNotify) gtk_widget_unref);
gtk_widget_show (cmd_remove);
gtk_box_pack_start (GTK_BOX (hbox3), cmd_remove, FALSE, FALSE, 0);

scrolledwindow4 = gtk_scrolled_window_new (NULL, NULL);
gtk_widget_ref (scrolledwindow4);
gtk_object_set_data_full (GTK_OBJECT (frm_items_ordered), "scrolledwindow4",
➥scrolledwindow4,
                          (GtkDestroyNotify) gtk_widget_unref);
gtk_widget_show (scrolledwindow4);
gtk_container_add (GTK_CONTAINER (vpaned2), scrolledwindow4);

clist_items_ordered = gtk_clist_new (4);
gtk_widget_ref (clist_items_ordered);
gtk_object_set_data_full (GTK_OBJECT (frm_items_ordered), "clist_items_ordered",
➥clist_items_ordered,
                          (GtkDestroyNotify) gtk_widget_unref);
gtk_widget_show (clist_items_ordered);
gtk_container_add (GTK_CONTAINER (scrolledwindow4), clist_items_ordered);
gtk_widget_set_usize (clist_items_ordered, 353, 100);
gtk_clist_set_column_width (GTK_CLIST (clist_items_ordered), 0, 80);
gtk_clist_set_column_width (GTK_CLIST (clist_items_ordered), 1, 80);
gtk_clist_set_column_width (GTK_CLIST (clist_items_ordered), 2, 80);
gtk_clist_set_column_width (GTK_CLIST (clist_items_ordered), 3, 80);
gtk_clist_column_titles_show (GTK_CLIST (clist_items_ordered));

clist_items_ordered_lbl_item_number = gtk_label_new ("Item Number");
gtk_widget_ref (clist_items_ordered_lbl_item_number);
```

```
gtk_object_set_data_full (GTK_OBJECT (frm_items_ordered),
↪"clist_items_ordered_lbl_item_number", clist_items_ordered_lbl_item_number,
                        (GtkDestroyNotify) gtk_widget_unref);
gtk_widget_show (clist_items_ordered_lbl_item_number);
gtk_clist_set_column_widget (GTK_CLIST (clist_items_ordered), 0,
↪clist_items_ordered_lbl_item_number);

clist_items_ordered_lbl_description = gtk_label_new ("Description");
gtk_widget_ref (clist_items_ordered_lbl_description);
gtk_object_set_data_full (GTK_OBJECT (frm_items_ordered),
↪"clist_items_ordered_lbl_description", clist_items_ordered_lbl_description,
                        (GtkDestroyNotify) gtk_widget_unref);
gtk_widget_show (clist_items_ordered_lbl_description);
gtk_clist_set_column_widget (GTK_CLIST (clist_items_ordered), 1,
↪clist_items_ordered_lbl_description);

clist_items_ordered_lbl_quantity = gtk_label_new ("Quantity");
gtk_widget_ref (clist_items_ordered_lbl_quantity);
gtk_object_set_data_full (GTK_OBJECT (frm_items_ordered),
↪"clist_items_ordered_lbl_quantity", clist_items_ordered_lbl_quantity,
                        (GtkDestroyNotify) gtk_widget_unref);
gtk_widget_show (clist_items_ordered_lbl_quantity);
gtk_clist_set_column_widget (GTK_CLIST (clist_items_ordered), 2,
↪clist_items_ordered_lbl_quantity);

clist_itoms_ordered_lbl_total_price = gtk_label_new ("Total Price");
gtk_widget_ref (clist_items_ordered_lbl_total_price);
gtk_object_set_data_full (GTK_OBJECT (frm_items_ordered),
↪"clist_items_ordered_lbl_total_price", clist_items_ordered_lbl_total_price,
                        (GtkDestroyNotify) gtk_widget_unref);
gtk_widget_show (clist_items_ordered_lbl_total_price);
gtk_clist_set_column_widget (GTK_CLIST (clist_items_ordered), 3,
↪clist_items_ordered_lbl_total_price);

gtk_signal_connect (GTK_OBJECT (frm_items_ordered), "set_focus",
                    GTK_SIGNAL_FUNC (on_frm_items_ordered_set_focus),
                    NULL);
gtk_signal_connect (GTK_OBJECT (frm_items_ordered), "button_press_event",
                    GTK_SIGNAL_FUNC (on_frm_items_ordered_button_press_event),
                    NULL);
gtk_signal_connect (GTK_OBJECT (frm_items_ordered), "button_release_event",
                    GTK_SIGNAL_FUNC (on_frm_items_ordered_button_release_event),
                    NULL);
gtk_signal_connect (GTK_OBJECT (frm_items_ordered), "delete_event",
                    GTK_SIGNAL_FUNC (on_frm_items_ordered_delete_event),
                    NULL);
gtk_signal_connect (GTK_OBJECT (frm_items_ordered), "destroy_event",
                    GTK_SIGNAL_FUNC (on_frm_items_ordered_destroy_event),
                    NULL);
gtk_signal_connect (GTK_OBJECT (frm_items_ordered), "event",
                    GTK_SIGNAL_FUNC (on_frm_items_ordered_event),
                    NULL);
```

continues

Listing A.1 **Continued**

```
gtk_signal_connect (GTK_OBJECT (frm_items_ordered), "hide",
                    GTK_SIGNAL_FUNC (on_frm_items_ordered_hide),
                    NULL);
gtk_signal_connect (GTK_OBJECT (frm_items_ordered), "key_press_event",
                    GTK_SIGNAL_FUNC (on_frm_items_ordered_key_press_event),
                    NULL);
gtk_signal_connect (GTK_OBJECT (frm_items_ordered), "key_release_event",
                    GTK_SIGNAL_FUNC (on_frm_items_ordered_key_release_event),
                    NULL);
gtk_signal_connect (GTK_OBJECT (frm_items_ordered), "realize",
                    GTK_SIGNAL_FUNC (on_frm_items_ordered_realize),
                    NULL);
gtk_signal_connect (GTK_OBJECT (frm_items_ordered), "show",
                    GTK_SIGNAL_FUNC (on_frm_items_ordered_show),
                    NULL);
gtk_signal_connect (GTK_OBJECT (frm_items_ordered), "unrealize",
                    GTK_SIGNAL_FUNC (on_frm_items_ordered_unrealize),
                    NULL);
gtk_signal_connect (GTK_OBJECT (frm_items_ordered), "destroy",
                    GTK_SIGNAL_FUNC (on_frm_items_ordered_destroy),
                    NULL);
gtk_signal_connect (GTK_OBJECT (entry_item_number), "activate",
                    GTK_SIGNAL_FUNC (on_entry_item_number_activate),
                    NULL);
gtk_signal_connect (GTK_OBJECT (entry_item_number), "changed",
                    GTK_SIGNAL_FUNC (on_entry_item_number_changed),
                    NULL);
gtk_signal_connect (GTK_OBJECT (entry_item_number), "delete_text",
                    GTK_SIGNAL_FUNC (on_entry_item_number_delete_text),
                    NULL);
gtk_signal_connect (GTK_OBJECT (entry_item_number), "insert_text",
                    GTK_SIGNAL_FUNC (on_entry_item_number_insert_text),
                    NULL);
gtk_signal_connect (GTK_OBJECT (spinbutton_quantity), "activate",
                    GTK_SIGNAL_FUNC (on_spinbutton_quantity_activate),
                    NULL);
gtk_signal_connect (GTK_OBJECT (spinbutton_quantity), "changed",
                    GTK_SIGNAL_FUNC (on_spinbutton_quantity_changed),
                    NULL);
gtk_signal_connect (GTK_OBJECT (cmd_Add), "clicked",
                    GTK_SIGNAL_FUNC (on_cmd_Add_clicked),
                    NULL);
gtk_signal_connect (GTK_OBJECT (cmd_search_for_item), "clicked",
                    GTK_SIGNAL_FUNC (on_cmd_search_for_item_clicked),
                    NULL);
gtk_signal_connect (GTK_OBJECT (cmd_done), "clicked",
                    GTK_SIGNAL_FUNC (on_cmd_done_clicked),
                    NULL);
```

```
  gtk_signal_connect (GTK_OBJECT (clist_items), "select_row",
                      GTK_SIGNAL_FUNC (on_clist_items_select_row),
                      NULL);
  gtk_signal_connect (GTK_OBJECT (clist_items), "unselect_row",
                      GTK_SIGNAL_FUNC (on_clist_items_unselect_row),
                      NULL);
  gtk_signal_connect (GTK_OBJECT (clist_items), "button_press_event",
                      GTK_SIGNAL_FUNC (on_clist_items_button_press_event),
                      NULL);
  gtk_signal_connect (GTK_OBJECT (clist_items), "button_release_event",
                      GTK_SIGNAL_FUNC (on_clist_items_button_release_event),
                      NULL);
  gtk_signal_connect (GTK_OBJECT (cmd_add_down), "clicked",
                      GTK_SIGNAL_FUNC (on_cmd_add_down_clicked),
                      NULL);
  gtk_signal_connect (GTK_OBJECT (cmd_remove), "clicked",
                      GTK_SIGNAL_FUNC (on_cmd_remove_clicked),
                      NULL);
  gtk_signal_connect (GTK_OBJECT (clist_items_ordered), "select_row",
                      GTK_SIGNAL_FUNC (on_clist_items_ordered_select_row),
                      NULL);
  gtk_signal_connect (GTK_OBJECT (clist_items_ordered), "unselect_row",
                      GTK_SIGNAL_FUNC (on_clist_items_ordered_unselect_row),
                      NULL);
  gtk_signal_connect (GTK_OBJECT (clist_items_ordered), "button_press_event",
                      GTK_SIGNAL_FUNC (on_clist_items_ordered_button_press_event),
                      NULL);
  gtk_signal_connect (GTK_OBJECT (clist_items_ordered), "button_release_event",
                      GTK_SIGNAL_FUNC (on_clist_items_ordered_button_release_event),
                      NULL);

  gtk_window_add_accel_group (GTK_WINDOW (frm_items_ordered), accel_group);

  return frm_items_ordered;
}

GtkWidget*
create_frm_find_customer (void)
{
  GtkWidget *frm_find_customer;
  GtkWidget *hbox4;
  GtkWidget *vbox4;
  GtkWidget *lbl_search_for_customer;
  GtkWidget *entry_find_customer;
  GtkWidget *cmd_find_customer;
  GtkWidget *cmd_find_customer_done;
  GtkWidget *scrolledwindow7;
  GtkWidget *clist_found_customer;
  GtkWidget *label7;
  GtkWidget *label8;
```

continues

Listing A.1 **Continued**

```
GtkWidget *label9;
GtkWidget *label10;
GtkWidget *label11;
GtkWidget *label12;
GtkWidget *label13;
GtkWidget *label14;
GtkWidget *label15;
GtkWidget *label16;
GtkWidget *label17;
GtkWidget *label18;
GtkWidget *label19;
GtkWidget *label20;
GtkWidget *label21;
GtkWidget *label22;
GtkWidget *label23;

frm_find_customer = gtk_window_new (GTK_WINDOW_TOPLEVEL);
gtk_object_set_data (GTK_OBJECT (frm_find_customer), "frm_find_customer",
➥frm_find_customer);
gtk_window_set_title (GTK_WINDOW (frm_find_customer), "Find Customer");
gtk_window_set_modal (GTK_WINDOW (frm_find_customer), TRUE);

hbox4 = gtk_hbox_new (FALSE, 0);
gtk_widget_ref (hbox4);
gtk_object_set_data_full (GTK_OBJECT (frm_find_customer), "hbox4", hbox4,
                          (GtkDestroyNotify) gtk_widget_unref);
gtk_widget_show (hbox4);
gtk_container_add (GTK_CONTAINER (frm_find_customer), hbox4);

vbox4 = gtk_vbox_new (FALSE, 11);
gtk_widget_ref (vbox4);
gtk_object_set_data_full (GTK_OBJECT (frm_find_customer), "vbox4", vbox4,
                          (GtkDestroyNotify) gtk_widget_unref);
gtk_widget_show (vbox4);
gtk_box_pack_start (GTK_BOX (hbox4), vbox4, FALSE, FALSE, 0);
gtk_container_set_border_width (GTK_CONTAINER (vbox4), 11);

lbl_search_for_customer = gtk_label_new ("Search for Customer...");
gtk_widget_ref (lbl_search_for_customer);
gtk_object_set_data_full (GTK_OBJECT (frm_find_customer),
➥"lbl_search_for_customer", lbl_search_for_customer,
                          (GtkDestroyNotify) gtk_widget_unref);
gtk_widget_show (lbl_search_for_customer);
gtk_box_pack_start (GTK_BOX (vbox4), lbl_search_for_customer, FALSE, FALSE, 0);

entry_find_customer = gtk_entry_new ();
gtk_widget_ref (entry_find_customer);
gtk_object_set_data_full (GTK_OBJECT (frm_find_customer), "entry_find_customer",
➥entry_find_customer,
                          (GtkDestroyNotify) gtk_widget_unref);
```

```
gtk_widget_show (entry_find_customer);
gtk_box_pack_start (GTK_BOX (vbox4), entry_find_customer, FALSE, FALSE, 0);

cmd_find_customer = gtk_button_new_with_label ("Find...");
gtk_widget_ref (cmd_find_customer);
gtk_object_set_data_full (GTK_OBJECT (frm_find_customer), "cmd_find_customer",
⇒cmd_find_customer,
                         (GtkDestroyNotify) gtk_widget_unref);
gtk_widget_show (cmd_find_customer);
gtk_box_pack_start (GTK_BOX (vbox4), cmd_find_customer, FALSE, FALSE, 0);

cmd_find_customer_done = gtk_button_new_with_label ("Done");
gtk_widget_ref (cmd_find_customer_done);
gtk_object_set_data_full (GTK_OBJECT (frm_find_customer),
⇒"cmd_find_customer_done", cmd_find_customer_done,
                         (GtkDestroyNotify) gtk_widget_unref);
gtk_widget_show (cmd_find_customer_done);
gtk_box_pack_start (GTK_BOX (vbox4), cmd_find_customer_done, FALSE, FALSE, 0);

scrolledwindow7 = gtk_scrolled_window_new (NULL, NULL);
gtk_widget_ref (scrolledwindow7);
gtk_object_set_data_full (GTK_OBJECT (frm_find_customer), "scrolledwindow7",
⇒scrolledwindow7,
                         (GtkDestroyNotify) gtk_widget_unref);
gtk_widget_show (scrolledwindow7);
gtk_box_pack_start (GTK_BOX (hbox4), scrolledwindow7, TRUE, TRUE, 0);

clist_found_customer = gtk_clist_new (17);
gtk_widget_ref (clist_found_customer);
gtk_object_set_data_full (GTK_OBJECT (frm_find_customer),
⇒"clist_found_customer", clist_found_customer,
                         (GtkDestroyNotify) gtk_widget_unref);
gtk_widget_show (clist_found_customer);
gtk_container_add (GTK_CONTAINER (scrolledwindow7), clist_found_customer);
gtk_clist_set_column_width (GTK_CLIST (clist_found_customer), 0, 80);
gtk_clist_set_column_width (GTK_CLIST (clist_found_customer), 1, 80);
gtk_clist_set_column_width (GTK_CLIST (clist_found_customer), 2, 80);
gtk_clist_set_column_width (GTK_CLIST (clist_found_customer), 3, 80);
gtk_clist_set_column_width (GTK_CLIST (clist_found_customer), 4, 80);
gtk_clist_set_column_width (GTK_CLIST (clist_found_customer), 5, 80);
gtk_clist_set_column_width (GTK_CLIST (clist_found_customer), 6, 80);
gtk_clist_set_column_width (GTK_CLIST (clist_found_customer), 7, 80);
gtk_clist_set_column_width (GTK_CLIST (clist_found_customer), 8, 80);
gtk_clist_set_column_width (GTK_CLIST (clist_found_customer), 9, 80);
gtk_clist_set_column_width (GTK_CLIST (clist_found_customer), 10, 80);
gtk_clist_set_column_width (GTK_CLIST (clist_found_customer), 11, 80);
gtk_clist_set_column_width (GTK_CLIST (clist_found_customer), 12, 80);
gtk_clist_set_column_width (GTK_CLIST (clist_found_customer), 13, 80);
gtk_clist_set_column_width (GTK_CLIST (clist_found_customer), 14, 80);
gtk_clist_set_column_width (GTK_CLIST (clist_found_customer), 15, 80);
gtk_clist_set_column_width (GTK_CLIST (clist_found_customer), 16, 80);
```

continues

Listing A.1 **Continued**

```
gtk_clist_column_titles_show (GTK_CLIST (clist_found_customer)));

label7 = gtk_label_new ("Customer");
gtk_widget_ref (label7);
gtk_object_set_data_full (GTK_OBJECT (frm_find_customer), "label7", label7,
                          (GtkDestroyNotify) gtk_widget_unref);
gtk_widget_show (label7);
gtk_clist_set_column_widget (GTK_CLIST (clist_found_customer), 0, label7);

label8 = gtk_label_new ("Name");
gtk_widget_ref (label8);
gtk_object_set_data_full (GTK_OBJECT (frm_find_customer), "label8", label8,
                          (GtkDestroyNotify) gtk_widget_unref);
gtk_widget_show (label8);
gtk_clist_set_column_widget (GTK_CLIST (clist_found_customer), 1, label8);

label9 = gtk_label_new ("Ship Addr");
gtk_widget_ref (label9);
gtk_object_set_data_full (GTK_OBJECT (frm_find_customer), "label9", label9,
                          (GtkDestroyNotify) gtk_widget_unref);
gtk_widget_show (label9);
gtk_clist_set_column_widget (GTK_CLIST (clist_found_customer), 2, label9);

label10 = gtk_label_new ("Ship Addr");
gtk_widget_ref (label10);
gtk_object_set_data_full (GTK_OBJECT (frm_find_customer), "label10", label10,
                          (GtkDestroyNotify) gtk_widget_unref);
gtk_widget_show (label10);
gtk_clist_set_column_widget (GTK_CLIST (clist_found_customer), 3, label10);

label11 = gtk_label_new ("Ship City");
gtk_widget_ref (label11);
gtk_object_set_data_full (GTK_OBJECT (frm_find_customer), "label11", label11,
                          (GtkDestroyNotify) gtk_widget_unref);
gtk_widget_show (label11);
gtk_clist_set_column_widget (GTK_CLIST (clist_found_customer), 4, label11);

label12 = gtk_label_new ("Ship St");
gtk_widget_ref (label12);
gtk_object_set_data_full (GTK_OBJECT (frm_find_customer), "label12", label12,
                          (GtkDestroyNotify) gtk_widget_unref);
gtk_widget_show (label12);
gtk_clist_set_column_widget (GTK_CLIST (clist_found_customer), 5, label12);

label13 = gtk_label_new ("Ship Zip");
gtk_widget_ref (label13);
gtk_object_set_data_full (GTK_OBJECT (frm_find_customer), "label13", label13,
                          (GtkDestroyNotify) gtk_widget_unref);
gtk_widget_show (label13);
```

```
gtk_clist_set_column_widget (GTK_CLIST (clist_found_customer), 6, label13);

label14 = gtk_label_new ("Bill Addr");
gtk_widget_ref (label14);
gtk_object_set_data_full (GTK_OBJECT (frm_find_customer), "label14", label14,
                          (GtkDestroyNotify) gtk_widget_unref);
gtk_widget_show (label14);
gtk_clist_set_column_widget (GTK_CLIST (clist_found_customer), 7, label14);

label15 = gtk_label_new ("Bill Addr");
gtk_widget_ref (label15);
gtk_object_set_data_full (GTK_OBJECT (frm_find_customer), "label15", label15,
                          (GtkDestroyNotify) gtk_widget_unref);
gtk_widget_show (label15);
gtk_clist_set_column_widget (GTK_CLIST (clist_found_customer), 8, label15);

label16 = gtk_label_new ("Bill City");
gtk_widget_ref (label16);
gtk_object_set_data_full (GTK_OBJECT (frm_find_customer), "label16", label16,
                          (GtkDestroyNotify) gtk_widget_unref);
gtk_widget_show (label16);
gtk_clist_set_column_widget (GTK_CLIST (clist_found_customer), 9, label16);

label17 = gtk_label_new ("Bill St");
gtk_widget_ref (label17);
gtk_object_set_data_full (GTK_OBJECT (frm_find_customer), "label17", label17,
                          (GtkDestroyNotify) gtk_widget_unref);
gtk_widget_show (label17);
gtk_clist_set_column_widget (GTK_CLIST (clist_found_customer), 10, label17);

label18 = gtk_label_new ("Bill Zip");
gtk_widget_ref (label18);
gtk_object_set_data_full (GTK_OBJECT (frm_find_customer), "label18", label18,
                          (GtkDestroyNotify) gtk_widget_unref);
gtk_widget_show (label18);
gtk_clist_set_column_widget (GTK_CLIST (clist_found_customer), 11, label18);

label19 = gtk_label_new ("First");
gtk_widget_ref (label19);
gtk_object_set_data_full (GTK_OBJECT (frm_find_customer), "label19", label19,
                          (GtkDestroyNotify) gtk_widget_unref);
gtk_widget_show (label19);
gtk_clist_set_column_widget (GTK_CLIST (clist_found_customer), 12, label19);

label20 = gtk_label_new ("Last");
gtk_widget_ref (label20);
gtk_object_set_data_full (GTK_OBJECT (frm_find_customer), "label20", label20,
                          (GtkDestroyNotify) gtk_widget_unref);
gtk_widget_show (label20);
gtk_clist_set_column_widget (GTK_CLIST (clist_found_customer), 13, label20);
```

continues

Listing A.1 **Continued**

```
    label21 = gtk_label_new ("Phone");
    gtk_widget_ref (label21);
    gtk_object_set_data_full (GTK_OBJECT (frm_find_customer), "label21", label21,
                              (GtkDestroyNotify) gtk_widget_unref);
    gtk_widget_show (label21);
    gtk_clist_set_column_widget (GTK_CLIST (clist_found_customer), 14, label21);

    label22 = gtk_label_new ("Title");
    gtk_widget_ref (label22);
    gtk_object_set_data_full (GTK_OBJECT (frm_find_customer), "label22", label22,
                              (GtkDestroyNotify) gtk_widget_unref);
    gtk_widget_show (label22);
    gtk_clist_set_column_widget (GTK_CLIST (clist_found_customer), 15, label22);

    label23 = gtk_label_new ("Comments");
    gtk_widget_ref (label23);
    gtk_object_set_data_full (GTK_OBJECT (frm_find_customer), "label23", label23,
                              (GtkDestroyNotify) gtk_widget_unref);
    gtk_widget_show (label23);
    gtk_clist_set_column_widget (GTK_CLIST (clist_found_customer), 16, label23);

    gtk_signal_connect (GTK_OBJECT (frm_find_customer), "delete_event",
                        GTK_SIGNAL_FUNC (on_frm_find_customer_delete_event),
                        NULL);
    gtk_signal_connect (GTK_OBJECT (cmd_find_customer), "clicked",
                        GTK_SIGNAL_FUNC (on_cmd_find_customer_clicked),
                        NULL);
    gtk_signal_connect (GTK_OBJECT (cmd_find_customer_done), "clicked",
                        GTK_SIGNAL_FUNC (on_cmd_find_customer_done_clicked),
                        NULL);

    return frm_find_customer;
}

GtkWidget*
create_frm_find_item (void)
{
  GtkWidget *frm_find_item;
  GtkWidget *hbox5;
  GtkWidget *vbox5;
  GtkWidget *lbl_search_for_item;
  GtkWidget *entry_find_item;
  GtkWidget *cmd_find_item;
  GtkWidget *cmd_find_item_done;
  GtkWidget *scrolledwindow6;
  GtkWidget *clist_found_items;
  GtkWidget *label4;
  GtkWidget *label5;
  GtkWidget *label6;
```

```
frm_find_item = gtk_window_new (GTK_WINDOW_TOPLEVEL);
gtk_object_set_data (GTK_OBJECT (frm_find_item), "frm_find_item",
➥frm_find_item);
gtk_window_set_title (GTK_WINDOW (frm_find_item), "Find Item");
gtk_window_set_modal (GTK_WINDOW (frm_find_item), TRUE);

hbox5 = gtk_hbox_new (FALSE, 0);
gtk_widget_ref (hbox5);
gtk_object_set_data_full (GTK_OBJECT (frm_find_item), "hbox5", hbox5,
                          (GtkDestroyNotify) gtk_widget_unref);
gtk_widget_show (hbox5);
gtk_container_add (GTK_CONTAINER (frm_find_item), hbox5);

vbox5 = gtk_vbox_new (FALSE, 10);
gtk_widget_ref (vbox5);
gtk_object_set_data_full (GTK_OBJECT (frm_find_item), "vbox5", vbox5,
                          (GtkDestroyNotify) gtk_widget_unref);
gtk_widget_show (vbox5);
gtk_box_pack_start (GTK_BOX (hbox5), vbox5, FALSE, FALSE, 0);
gtk_container_set_border_width (GTK_CONTAINER (vbox5), 15);

lbl_search_for_item = gtk_label_new ("Search for Item...");
gtk_widget_ref (lbl_search_for_item);
gtk_object_set_data_full (GTK_OBJECT (frm_find_item), "lbl_search_for_item",
➥lbl_search_for_item,
                          (GtkDestroyNotify) gtk_widget_unref);
gtk_widget_show (lbl_search_for_item);
gtk_box_pack_start (GTK_BOX (vbox5), lbl_search_for_item, FALSE, FALSE, 0);

entry_find_item = gtk_entry_new ();
gtk_widget_ref (entry_find_item);
gtk_object_set_data_full (GTK_OBJECT (frm_find_item), "entry_find_item",
➥entry_find_item,
                          (GtkDestroyNotify) gtk_widget_unref);
gtk_widget_show (entry_find_item);
gtk_box_pack_start (GTK_BOX (vbox5), entry_find_item, FALSE, FALSE, 0);

cmd_find_item = gtk_button_new_with_label ("Find...");
gtk_widget_ref (cmd_find_item);
gtk_object_set_data_full (GTK_OBJECT (frm_find_item), "cmd_find_item",
➥cmd_find_item,
                          (GtkDestroyNotify) gtk_widget_unref);
gtk_widget_show (cmd_find_item);
gtk_box_pack_start (GTK_BOX (vbox5), cmd_find_item, FALSE, FALSE, 0);

cmd_find_item_done = gtk_button_new_with_label ("Done");
gtk_widget_ref (cmd_find_item_done);
gtk_object_set_data_full (GTK_OBJECT (frm_find_item), "cmd_find_item_done",
➥cmd_find_item_done,
                          (GtkDestroyNotify) gtk_widget_unref);
gtk_widget_show (cmd_find_item_done);
gtk_box_pack_start (GTK_BOX (vbox5), cmd_find_item_done, FALSE, FALSE, 0);
```

continues

Listing A.1   **Continued**

```
scrolledwindow6 = gtk_scrolled_window_new (NULL, NULL);
gtk_widget_ref (scrolledwindow6);
gtk_object_set_data_full (GTK_OBJECT (frm_find_item), "scrolledwindow6",
↪scrolledwindow6,
                           (GtkDestroyNotify) gtk_widget_unref);
gtk_widget_show (scrolledwindow6);
gtk_box_pack_start (GTK_BOX (hbox5), scrolledwindow6, TRUE, TRUE, 0);

clist_found_items = gtk_clist_new (3);
gtk_widget_ref (clist_found_items);
gtk_object_set_data_full (GTK_OBJECT (frm_find_item), "clist_found_items",
↪clist_found_items,
                           (GtkDestroyNotify) gtk_widget_unref);
gtk_widget_show (clist_found_items);
gtk_container_add (GTK_CONTAINER (scrolledwindow6), clist_found_items);
gtk_clist_set_column_width (GTK_CLIST (clist_found_items), 0, 80);
gtk_clist_set_column_width (GTK_CLIST (clist_found_items), 1, 80);
gtk_clist_set_column_width (GTK_CLIST (clist_found_items), 2, 80);
gtk_clist_column_titles_show (GTK_CLIST (clist_found_items));

label4 = gtk_label_new ("Item Num.");
gtk_widget_ref (label4);
gtk_object_set_data_full (GTK_OBJECT (frm_find_item), "label4", label4,
                           (GtkDestroyNotify) gtk_widget_unref);
gtk_widget_show (label4);
gtk_clist_set_column_widget (GTK_CLIST (clist_found_items), 0, label4);

label5 = gtk_label_new ("Description");
gtk_widget_ref (label5);
gtk_object_set_data_full (GTK_OBJECT (frm_find_item), "label5", label5,
                           (GtkDestroyNotify) gtk_widget_unref);
gtk_widget_show (label5);
gtk_clist_set_column_widget (GTK_CLIST (clist_found_items), 1, label5);

label6 = gtk_label_new ("Price");
gtk_widget_ref (label6);
gtk_object_set_data_full (GTK_OBJECT (frm_find_item), "label6", label6,
                           (GtkDestroyNotify) gtk_widget_unref);
gtk_widget_show (label6);
gtk_clist_set_column_widget (GTK_CLIST (clist_found_items), 2, label6);

gtk_signal_connect (GTK_OBJECT (frm_find_item), "delete_event",
                     GTK_SIGNAL_FUNC (on_frm_find_item_delete_event),
                     NULL);
gtk_signal_connect (GTK_OBJECT (cmd_find_item), "clicked",
                     GTK_SIGNAL_FUNC (on_cmd_find_item_clicked),
                     NULL);
gtk_signal_connect (GTK_OBJECT (cmd_find_item_done), "clicked",
                     GTK_SIGNAL_FUNC (on_cmd_find_item_done_clicked),
```

```
                    NULL);

    return frm_find_item;
  }
```

sesi.glade

The file sesi.glade is the project file where Glade keeps the specifications you create when you point-and-click the user interface into existence (see Listing A.2). Like interface.c, it is not something you want to tweak manually unless you really, really need to. Remember, unlike interface.c, it is read into as well as written out of Glade. However, it does provide instructive insight into the way Glade organizes and handles the various GTK+ widgets.

Listing A.2 *sesi.glade:* **The Glade Project File for the SESI Order Application**

```
<?xml version="1.0"?>
<GTK-Interface>         *

<project>
  <name>sesi</name>
  <program_name>sesi</program_name>
  <directory></directory>
  <source_directory>src</source_directory>
  <pixmaps_directory>pixmaps</pixmaps_directory>
  <language>C</language>
  <gnome_support>False</gnome_support>
  <gettext_support>False</gettext_support>
  <use_widget_names>False</use_widget_names>
  <output_main_file>True</output_main_file>
  <output_support_files>True</output_support_files>
  <output_build_files>True</output_build_files>
  <backup_source_files>True</backup_source_files>
  <main_source_file>interface.c</main_source_file>
  <main_header_file>interface.h</main_header_file>
  <handler_source_file>callbacks.c</handler_source_file>
  <handler_header_file>callbacks.h</handler_header_file>
  <support_source_file>support.c</support_source_file>
  <support_header_file>support.h</support_header_file>
  <translatable_strings_file></translatable_strings_file>
</project>

<widget>
  <class>GtkWindow</class>
  <name>frm_main</name>
  <signal>
    <name>set_focus</name>
```

continues

Listing A.2 **Continued**

```
  <handler>on_frm_main_set_focus</handler>
  <last_modification_time>Thu, 16 Nov 2000 01:56:53 GMT</last_modification_time>
</signal>
<signal>
  <name>button_press_event</name>
  <handler>on_frm_main_button_press_event</handler>
  <last_modification_time>Thu, 16 Nov 2000 01:58:11 GMT</last_modification_time>
</signal>
<signal>
  <name>button_release_event</name>
  <handler>on_frm_main_button_release_event</handler>
  <last_modification_time>Thu, 16 Nov 2000 01:58:15 GMT</last_modification_time>
</signal>
<signal>
  <name>delete_event</name>
  <handler>on_frm_main_delete_event</handler>
  <last_modification_time>Thu, 16 Nov 2000 01:58:24 GMT</last_modification_time>
</signal>
<signal>
  <name>hide</name>
  <handler>on_frm_main_hide</handler>
  <last_modification_time>Thu, 16 Nov 2000 01:58:54 GMT</last_modification_time>
</signal>
<signal>
  <name>key_release_event</name>
  <handler>on_frm_main_key_press_event</handler>
  <last_modification_time>Thu, 16 Nov 2000 01:59:17 GMT</last_modification_time>
</signal>
<signal>
  <name>key_press_event</name>
  <handler>on_frm_main_key_press_event</handler>
  <last_modification_time>Thu, 16 Nov 2000 01:59:27 GMT</last_modification_time>
</signal>
<signal>
  <name>realize</name>
  <handler>on_frm_main_realize</handler>
  <last_modification_time>Thu, 16 Nov 2000 01:59:43 GMT</last_modification_time>
</signal>
<signal>
  <name>destroy_event</name>
  <handler>on_frm_main_destroy_event</handler>
  <last_modification_time>Fri, 17 Nov 2000 02:45:55 GMT</last_modification_time>
</signal>
<signal>
  <name>event</name>
  <handler>on_frm_main_event</handler>
  <last_modification_time>Fri, 17 Nov 2000 02:46:34 GMT</last_modification_time>
</signal>
<signal>
```

```
  <name>show</name>
  <handler>on_frm_main_show</handler>
  <last_modification_time>Tue, 21 Nov 2000 13:26:03 GMT</last_modification_time>
</signal>
<title>SESI Customer Order</title>
<type>GTK_WINDOW_TOPLEVEL</type>
<position>GTK_WIN_POS_NONE</position>
<modal>False</modal>
<allow_shrink>False</allow_shrink>
<allow_grow>True</allow_grow>
<auto_shrink>False</auto_shrink>

<widget>
  <class>GtkVBox</class>
  <name>vbox_main</name>
  <homogeneous>False</homogeneous>
  <spacing>0</spacing>

  <widget>
    <class>GtkTable</class>
    <name>table_2_by_2</name>
    <rows>2</rows>
    <columns>2</columns>
    <homogeneous>False</homogeneous>
    <row_spacing>0</row_spacing>
    <column_spacing>0</column_spacing>
    <child>
    <padding>0</padding>
    <expand>True</expand>
    <fill>True</fill>
    </child>

    <widget>
    <class>GtkVBox</class>
    <name>vbox_customer_number</name>
    <homogeneous>False</homogeneous>
    <spacing>0</spacing>
    <child>
      <left_attach>0</left_attach>
      <right_attach>1</right_attach>
      <top_attach>0</top_attach>
      <bottom_attach>1</bottom_attach>
      <xpad>0</xpad>
      <ypad>0</ypad>
      <xexpand>True</xexpand>
      <yexpand>True</yexpand>
      <xshrink>False</xshrink>
      <yshrink>False</yshrink>
      <xfill>True</xfill>
      <yfill>True</yfill>
    </child>
```

continues

Listing A.2 **Continued**

```
<widget>
  <class>GtkLabel</class>
  <name>lbl_customer_number</name>
  <label>Customer Number</label>
  <justify>GTK_JUSTIFY_LEFT</justify>
  <wrap>False</wrap>
  <xalign>0.5</xalign>
  <yalign>0.5</yalign>
  <xpad>0</xpad>
  <ypad>0</ypad>
  <child>
    <padding>0</padding>
    <expand>False</expand>
    <fill>False</fill>
  </child>
</widget>

<widget>
  <class>GtkCombo</class>
  <name>cbo_customer_number</name>
  <value_in_list>False</value_in_list>
  <ok_if_empty>True</ok_if_empty>
  <case_sensitive>False</case_sensitive>
  <use_arrows>True</use_arrows>
  <use_arrows_always>False</use_arrows_always>
  <items></items>
  <child>
    <padding>0</padding>
    <expand>False</expand>
    <fill>False</fill>
  </child>

  <widget>
    <class>GtkEntry</class>
    <child_name>GtkCombo:entry</child_name>
    <name>combo-entry_customer_number</name>
    <can_focus>True</can_focus>
    <signal>
      <name>activate</name>
      <handler>on_combo-entry_customer_number_activate</handler>
      <last_modification_time>Mon, 20 Nov 2000 13:31:03
      ➥GMT</last_modification_time>
    </signal>
    <signal>
      <name>changed</name>
      <handler>on_combo-entry_customer_number_changed</handler>
      <last_modification_time>Mon, 20 Nov 2000 13:31:10
      ➥GMT</last_modification_time>
    </signal>
```

```
      <signal>
        <name>delete_text</name>
        <handler>on_combo-entry_customer_number_delete_text</handler>
        <last_modification_time>Mon, 20 Nov 2000 13:32:26
        ➥GMT</last_modification_time>
      </signal>
      <signal>
        <name>insert_text</name>
        <handler>on_combo-entry_customer_number_insert_text</handler>
        <last_modification_time>Mon, 20 Nov 2000 13:32:33
        ➥GMT</last_modification_time>
      </signal>
      <editable>True</editable>
      <text_visible>True</text_visible>
      <text_max_length>0</text_max_length>
      <text></text>
    </widget>
  </widget>
  </widget>

<widget>
<class>GtkVBox</class>
<name>vbox_customer_name</name>
<homogeneous>False</homogeneous>
<spacing>0</spacing>
<child>
  <left_attach>1</left_attach>
  <right_attach>2</right_attach>
  <top_attach>0</top_attach>
  <bottom_attach>1</bottom_attach>
  <xpad>0</xpad>
  <ypad>0</ypad>
  <xexpand>True</xexpand>
  <yexpand>False</yexpand>
  <xshrink>False</xshrink>
  <yshrink>False</yshrink>
  <xfill>True</xfill>
  <yfill>True</yfill>
</child>

<widget>
  <class>GtkLabel</class>
  <name>cmd_customer_name</name>
  <label>Customer Name</label>
  <justify>GTK_JUSTIFY_LEFT</justify>
  <wrap>False</wrap>
  <xalign>0.5</xalign>
  <yalign>0.5</yalign>
  <xpad>0</xpad>
  <ypad>0</ypad>
  <child>
```

continues

Listing A.2 **Continued**

```
          <padding>0</padding>
          <expand>False</expand>
          <fill>False</fill>
        </child>
      </widget>

      <widget>
        <class>GtkEntry</class>
        <name>entry_customer_name</name>
        <can_focus>True</can_focus>
        <signal>
          <name>changed</name>
          <handler>on_entry_customer_name_changed</handler>
          <last_modification_time>Tue, 28 Nov 2000 02:05:23
          ➥GMT</last_modification_time>
        </signal>
        <editable>True</editable>
        <text_visible>True</text_visible>
        <text_max_length>0</text_max_length>
        <text></text>
        <child>
          <padding>0</padding>
          <expand>False</expand>
          <fill>False</fill>
        </child>
      </widget>
      </widget>

      <widget>
      <class>GtkVButtonBox</class>
      <name>vbuttonbox</name>
      <layout_style>GTK_BUTTONBOX_DEFAULT_STYLE</layout_style>
      <spacing>10</spacing>
      <child_min_width>85</child_min_width>
      <child_min_height>27</child_min_height>
      <child_ipad_x>7</child_ipad_x>
      <child_ipad_y>0</child_ipad_y>
      <child>
        <left_attach>0</left_attach>
        <right_attach>1</right_attach>
        <top_attach>1</top_attach>
        <bottom_attach>2</bottom_attach>
        <xpad>0</xpad>
        <ypad>0</ypad>
        <xexpand>False</xexpand>
        <yexpand>True</yexpand>
        <xshrink>False</xshrink>
        <yshrink>False</yshrink>
        <xfill>True</xfill>
```

```
    <yfill>True</yfill>
  </child>

  <widget>
    <class>GtkButton</class>
    <name>cmd_search</name>
    <can_default>True</can_default>
    <can_focus>True</can_focus>
    <accelerator>
      <modifiers>GDK_MOD1_MASK</modifiers>
      <key>GDK_S</key>
      <signal>clicked</signal>
    </accelerator>
    <signal>
      <name>clicked</name>
      <handler>on_cmd_search_clicked</handler>
      <last_modification_time>Fri, 17 Nov 2000 02:33:45
      ➥GMT</last_modification_time>
    </signal>
    <label>_Search...</label>
  </widget>

  <widget>
    <class>GtkButton</class>
    <name>cmd_save_edits</name>
    <sensitive>False</sensitive>
    <can_default>True</can_default>
    <can_focus>True</can_focus>
    <accelerator>
      <modifiers>GDK_MOD1_MASK</modifiers>
      <key>GDK_E</key>
      <signal>clicked</signal>
    </accelerator>
    <signal>
      <name>clicked</name>
      <handler>on_cmd_save_edits_clicked</handler>
      <last_modification_time>Fri, 17 Nov 2000 02:43:10
      ➥GMT</last_modification_time>
    </signal>
    <label>Save _Edits</label>
  </widget>

  <widget>
    <class>GtkButton</class>
    <name>cmd_select_items</name>
    <can_default>True</can_default>
    <can_focus>True</can_focus>
    <accelerator>
      <modifiers>GDK_MOD1_MASK</modifiers>
      <key>GDK_I</key>
      <signal>clicked</signal>
```

continues

Listing A.2 **Continued**

```
    </accelerator>
    <signal>
      <name>clicked</name>
      <handler>on_cmd_select_items_clicked</handler>
      <last_modification_time>Fri, 17 Nov 2000 02:43:15
      ➥GMT</last_modification_time>
    </signal>
    <label>Select _Items</label>
  </widget>

  <widget>
    <class>GtkButton</class>
    <name>cmd_print_order</name>
    <can_default>True</can_default>
    <can_focus>True</can_focus>
    <accelerator>
      <modifiers>GDK_MOD1_MASK</modifiers>
      <key>GDK_P</key>
      <signal>clicked</signal>
    </accelerator>
    <signal>
      <name>clicked</name>
      <handler>on_cmd_print_order_clicked</handler>
      <last_modification_time>Fri, 17 Nov 2000 02:43:23
      ➥GMT</last_modification_time>
    </signal>
    <label>_Print Order</label>
  </widget>

  <widget>
    <class>GtkButton</class>
    <name>cmd_exit</name>
    <can_default>True</can_default>
    <can_focus>True</can_focus>
    <accelerator>
      <modifiers>GDK_MOD1_MASK</modifiers>
      <key>GDK_x</key>
      <signal>clicked</signal>
    </accelerator>
    <signal>
      <name>clicked</name>
      <handler>on_cmd_exit_clicked</handler>
      <last_modification_time>Fri, 17 Nov 2000 02:43:29
      ➥GMT</last_modification_time>
    </signal>
    <label>E_xit</label>
  </widget>
  </widget>
```

```
<widget>
<class>GtkVBox</class>
<name>vbox_data</name>
<homogeneous>False</homogeneous>
<spacing>0</spacing>
<child>
  <left_attach>1</left_attach>
  <right_attach>2</right_attach>
  <top_attach>1</top_attach>
  <bottom_attach>2</bottom_attach>
  <xpad>0</xpad>
  <ypad>0</ypad>
  <xexpand>False</xexpand>
  <yexpand>False</yexpand>
  <xshrink>False</xshrink>
  <yshrink>False</yshrink>
  <xfill>True</xfill>
  <yfill>True</yfill>
</child>

<widget>
  <class>GtkTable</class>
  <name>table_3_by_3</name>
  <rows>3</rows>
  <columns>3</columns>
  <homogeneous>False</homogeneous>
  <row_spacing>0</row_spacing>
  <column_spacing>0</column_spacing>
  <child>
    <padding>0</padding>
    <expand>True</expand>
    <fill>True</fill>
  </child>

  <widget>
    <class>GtkLabel</class>
    <name>lbl_primary_contact</name>
    <label>Primary Contact:</label>
    <justify>GTK_JUSTIFY_LEFT</justify>
    <wrap>False</wrap>
    <xalign>0.5</xalign>
    <yalign>0.5</yalign>
    <xpad>0</xpad>
    <ypad>0</ypad>
    <child>
      <left_attach>0</left_attach>
      <right_attach>3</right_attach>
      <top_attach>0</top_attach>
      <bottom_attach>1</bottom_attach>
      <xpad>0</xpad>
      <ypad>0</ypad>
```

continues

Listing A.2 **Continued**

```
        <xexpand>False</xexpand>
        <yexpand>False</yexpand>
        <xshrink>False</xshrink>
        <yshrink>False</yshrink>
        <xfill>False</xfill>
        <yfill>False</yfill>
      </child>
    </widget>

    <widget>
      <class>GtkLabel</class>
      <name>lbl_name_last_first</name>
      <label>Name (Last, First):</label>
      <justify>GTK_JUSTIFY_LEFT</justify>
      <wrap>False</wrap>
      <xalign>0.5</xalign>
      <yalign>0.5</yalign>
      <xpad>0</xpad>
      <ypad>0</ypad>
      <child>
        <left_attach>0</left_attach>
        <right_attach>1</right_attach>
        <top_attach>1</top_attach>
        <bottom_attach>2</bottom_attach>
        <xpad>0</xpad>
        <ypad>0</ypad>
        <xexpand>False</xexpand>
        <yexpand>False</yexpand>
        <xshrink>False</xshrink>
        <yshrink>False</yshrink>
        <xfill>False</xfill>
        <yfill>False</yfill>
      </child>
    </widget>

    <widget>
      <class>GtkLabel</class>
      <name>lbl_title_and_phone</name>
      <label>Title and Phone</label>
      <justify>GTK_JUSTIFY_LEFT</justify>
      <wrap>False</wrap>
      <xalign>0.5</xalign>
      <yalign>0.5</yalign>
      <xpad>0</xpad>
      <ypad>0</ypad>
      <child>
        <left_attach>0</left_attach>
        <right_attach>1</right_attach>
        <top_attach>2</top_attach>
```

```
            <bottom_attach>3</bottom_attach>
            <xpad>0</xpad>
            <ypad>0</ypad>
            <xexpand>False</xexpand>
            <yexpand>False</yexpand>
            <xshrink>False</xshrink>
            <yshrink>False</yshrink>
            <xfill>False</xfill>
            <yfill>False</yfill>
        </child>
    </widget>

    <widget>
        <class>GtkEntry</class>
        <name>entry_last</name>
        <width>100</width>
        <can_focus>True</can_focus>
        <signal>
            <name>changed</name>
            <handler>on_entry_last_changed</handler>
            <last_modification_time>Tue, 28 Nov 2000 02:05:36
            ↪GMT</last_modification_time>
        </signal>
        <editable>True</editable>
        <text_visible>True</text_visible>
        <text_max_length>0</text_max_length>
        <text></text>
        <child>
            <left_attach>1</left_attach>
            <right_attach>2</right_attach>
            <top_attach>1</top_attach>
            <bottom_attach>2</bottom_attach>
            <xpad>0</xpad>
            <ypad>0</ypad>
            <xexpand>False</xexpand>
            <yexpand>False</yexpand>
            <xshrink>False</xshrink>
            <yshrink>False</yshrink>
            <xfill>True</xfill>
            <yfill>False</yfill>
        </child>
    </widget>

    <widget>
        <class>GtkEntry</class>
        <name>entry_first</name>
        <width>100</width>
        <can_focus>True</can_focus>
        <signal>
            <name>changed</name>
            <handler>on_entry_first_changed</handler>
```

continues

Listing A.2 **Continued**

```
      <last_modification_time>Tue, 28 Nov 2000 02:05:43
      ➥GMT</last_modification_time>
    </signal>
    <editable>True</editable>
    <text_visible>True</text_visible>
    <text_max_length>0</text_max_length>
    <text></text>
    <child>
      <left_attach>2</left_attach>
      <right_attach>3</right_attach>
      <top_attach>1</top_attach>
      <bottom_attach>2</bottom_attach>
      <xpad>0</xpad>
      <ypad>0</ypad>
      <xexpand>False</xexpand>
      <yexpand>False</yexpand>
      <xshrink>False</xshrink>
      <yshrink>False</yshrink>
      <xfill>True</xfill>
      <yfill>False</yfill>
    </child>
  </widget>

  <widget>
    <class>GtkEntry</class>
    <name>entry_title</name>
    <width>100</width>
    <can_focus>True</can_focus>
    <signal>
      <name>changed</name>
      <handler>on_entry_title_changed</handler>
      <last_modification_time>Tue, 28 Nov 2000 02:06:02
      ➥GMT</last_modification_time>
    </signal>
    <editable>True</editable>
    <text_visible>True</text_visible>
    <text_max_length>0</text_max_length>
    <text></text>
    <child>
      <left_attach>1</left_attach>
      <right_attach>2</right_attach>
      <top_attach>2</top_attach>
      <bottom_attach>3</bottom_attach>
      <xpad>0</xpad>
      <ypad>0</ypad>
      <xexpand>False</xexpand>
      <yexpand>False</yexpand>
      <xshrink>False</xshrink>
      <yshrink>False</yshrink>
      <xfill>True</xfill>
```

```
        <yfill>False</yfill>
      </child>
    </widget>

    <widget>
      <class>GtkEntry</class>
      <name>entry_phone</name>
      <width>100</width>
      <can_focus>True</can_focus>
      <signal>
        <name>changed</name>
        <handler>on_entry_phone_changed</handler>
        <last_modification_time>Tue, 28 Nov 2000 02:06:08
        ↪GMT</last_modification_time>
      </signal>
      <editable>True</editable>
      <text_visible>True</text_visible>
      <text_max_length>0</text_max_length>
      <text></text>
      <child>
        <left_attach>2</left_attach>
        <right_attach>3</right_attach>
        <top_attach>2</top_attach>
        <bottom_attach>3</bottom_attach>
        <xpad>0</xpad>
        <ypad>0</ypad>
        <xexpand>False</xexpand>
        <yexpand>False</yexpand>
        <xshrink>False</xshrink>
        <yshrink>False</yshrink>
        <xfill>True</xfill>
        <yfill>False</yfill>
      </child>
    </widget>
  </widget>

  <widget>
    <class>GtkTable</class>
    <name>table_4_by_2</name>
    <rows>4</rows>
    <columns>2</columns>
    <homogeneous>False</homogeneous>
    <row_spacing>0</row_spacing>
    <column_spacing>0</column_spacing>
    <child>
      <padding>0</padding>
      <expand>True</expand>
      <fill>True</fill>
    </child>
```

continues

Listing A.2 **Continued**

```
<widget>
  <class>GtkLabel</class>
  <name>lbl_ship_to</name>
  <label>Ship To:</label>
  <justify>GTK_JUSTIFY_LEFT</justify>
  <wrap>False</wrap>
  <xalign>0.5</xalign>
  <yalign>0.5</yalign>
  <xpad>0</xpad>
  <ypad>0</ypad>
  <child>
    <left_attach>0</left_attach>
    <right_attach>1</right_attach>
    <top_attach>0</top_attach>
    <bottom_attach>1</bottom_attach>
    <xpad>0</xpad>
    <ypad>0</ypad>
    <xexpand>False</xexpand>
    <yexpand>False</yexpand>
    <xshrink>False</xshrink>
    <yshrink>False</yshrink>
    <xfill>False</xfill>
    <yfill>False</yfill>
  </child>
</widget>

<widget>
  <class>GtkLabel</class>
  <name>lbl_bill_to</name>
  <label>Bill To:</label>
  <justify>GTK_JUSTIFY_LEFT</justify>
  <wrap>False</wrap>
  <xalign>0.5</xalign>
  <yalign>0.5</yalign>
  <xpad>0</xpad>
  <ypad>0</ypad>
  <child>
    <left_attach>1</left_attach>
    <right_attach>2</right_attach>
    <top_attach>0</top_attach>
    <bottom_attach>1</bottom_attach>
    <xpad>0</xpad>
    <ypad>0</ypad>
    <xexpand>False</xexpand>
    <yexpand>False</yexpand>
    <xshrink>False</xshrink>
    <yshrink>False</yshrink>
    <xfill>False</xfill>
    <yfill>False</yfill>
```

```
      </child>
    </widget>

    <widget>
      <class>GtkEntry</class>
      <name>entry_ship_to_addr1</name>
      <width>160</width>
      <can_focus>True</can_focus>
      <signal>
        <name>changed</name>
        <handler>on_entry_ship_to_addr1_changed</handler>
        <last_modification_time>Tue, 28 Nov 2000 02:05:51
        ↳GMT</last_modification_time>
      </signal>
      <editable>True</editable>
      <text_visible>True</text_visible>
      <text_max_length>0</text_max_length>
      <text></text>
      <child>
        <left_attach>0</left_attach>
        <right_attach>1</right_attach>
        <top_attach>1</top_attach>
        <bottom_attach>2</bottom_attach>
        <xpad>0</xpad>
        <ypad>0</ypad>
        <xexpand>False</xexpand>
        <yexpand>False</yexpand>
        <xshrink>False</xshrink>
        <yshrink>False</yshrink>
        <xfill>True</xfill>
        <yfill>False</yfill>
      </child>
    </widget>

    <widget>
      <class>GtkEntry</class>
      <name>entry_bill_to_addr1</name>
      <can_focus>True</can_focus>
      <editable>True</editable>
      <text_visible>True</text_visible>
      <text_max_length>0</text_max_length>
      <text></text>
      <child>
        <left_attach>1</left_attach>
        <right_attach>2</right_attach>
        <top_attach>1</top_attach>
        <bottom_attach>2</bottom_attach>
        <xpad>0</xpad>
        <ypad>0</ypad>
        <xexpand>False</xexpand>
        <yexpand>False</yexpand>
```

continues

Listing A.2 **Continued**

```
          <xshrink>False</xshrink>
          <yshrink>False</yshrink>
          <xfill>True</xfill>
          <yfill>False</yfill>
        </child>
      </widget>

      <widget>
        <class>GtkEntry</class>
        <name>entry_ship_to_addr2</name>
        <can_focus>True</can_focus>
        <signal>
          <name>changed</name>
          <handler>on_entry_ship_to_addr2_changed</handler>
          <last_modification_time>Tue, 28 Nov 2000 02:06:19
          ⇒GMT</last_modification_time>
        </signal>
        <editable>True</editable>
        <text_visible>True</text_visible>
        <text_max_length>0</text_max_length>
        <text></text>
        <child>
          <left_attach>0</left_attach>
          <right_attach>1</right_attach>
          <top_attach>2</top_attach>
          <bottom_attach>3</bottom_attach>
          <xpad>0</xpad>
          <ypad>0</ypad>
          <xexpand>False</xexpand>
          <yexpand>False</yexpand>
          <xshrink>False</xshrink>
          <yshrink>False</yshrink>
          <xfill>True</xfill>
          <yfill>False</yfill>
        </child>
      </widget>

      <widget>
        <class>GtkEntry</class>
        <name>entry_bill_to_addr2</name>
        <can_focus>True</can_focus>
        <signal>
          <name>changed</name>
          <handler>on_entry_bill_to_addr2_changed</handler>
          <last_modification_time>Tue, 28 Nov 2000 02:06:25
          ⇒GMT</last_modification_time>
        </signal>
        <editable>True</editable>
        <text_visible>True</text_visible>
```

```
    <text_max_length>0</text_max_length>
    <text></text>
    <child>
      <left_attach>1</left_attach>
      <right_attach>2</right_attach>
      <top_attach>2</top_attach>
      <bottom_attach>3</bottom_attach>
      <xpad>0</xpad>
      <ypad>0</ypad>
      <xexpand>False</xexpand>
      <yexpand>False</yexpand>
      <xshrink>False</xshrink>
      <yshrink>False</yshrink>
      <xfill>True</xfill>
      <yfill>False</yfill>
    </child>
  </widget>

  <widget>
    <class>GtkHBox</class>
    <name>hbox1</name>
    <homogeneous>False</homogeneous>
    <spacing>0</spacing>
    <child>
      <left_attach>0</left_attach>
      <right_attach>1</right_attach>
      <top_attach>3</top_attach>
      <bottom_attach>4</bottom_attach>
      <xpad>0</xpad>
      <ypad>0</ypad>
      <xexpand>False</xexpand>
      <yexpand>True</yexpand>
      <xshrink>False</xshrink>
      <yshrink>False</yshrink>
      <xfill>True</xfill>
      <yfill>True</yfill>
    </child>

    <widget>
      <class>GtkEntry</class>
      <name>entry_ship_to_city</name>
      <width>100</width>
      <can_focus>True</can_focus>
      <signal>
        <name>changed</name>
        <handler>on_entry_ship_to_city_changed</handler>
        <last_modification_time>Tue, 28 Nov 2000 02:06:32
        ↪GMT</last_modification_time>
      </signal>
      <editable>True</editable>
      <text_visible>True</text_visible>
```

continues

Listing A.2 **Continued**

```
<text_max_length>0</text_max_length>
<text></text>
<child>
    <padding>0</padding>
    <expand>False</expand>
    <fill>True</fill>
</child>
</widget>

<widget>
  <class>GtkEntry</class>
  <name>entry_ship_to_st</name>
  <width>35</width>
  <can_focus>True</can_focus>
  <signal>
    <name>changed</name>
    <handler>on_entry_ship_to_st_changed</handler>
    <last_modification_time>Tue, 28 Nov 2000 02:06:38
    ↩GMT</last_modification_time>
  </signal>
  <editable>True</editable>
  <text_visible>True</text_visible>
  <text_max_length>0</text_max_length>
  <text></text>
  <child>
      <padding>0</padding>
      <expand>False</expand>
      <fill>True</fill>
  </child>
</widget>

<widget>
  <class>GtkEntry</class>
  <name>entry_ship_to_zip</name>
  <width>70</width>
  <can_focus>True</can_focus>
  <signal>
    <name>changed</name>
    <handler>on_entry_ship_to_zip_changed</handler>
    <last_modification_time>Tue, 28 Nov 2000 02:06:45
    ↩GMT</last_modification_time>
  </signal>
  <editable>True</editable>
  <text_visible>True</text_visible>
  <text_max_length>0</text_max_length>
  <text></text>
  <child>
      <padding>0</padding>
      <expand>False</expand>
```

```
        <fill>True</fill>
      </child>
    </widget>
  </widget>
</widget>

<widget>
  <class>GtkHBox</class>
  <name>hbox2</name>
  <homogeneous>False</homogeneous>
  <spacing>0</spacing>
  <child>
    <left_attach>1</left_attach>
    <right_attach>2</right_attach>
    <top_attach>3</top_attach>
    <bottom_attach>4</bottom_attach>
    <xpad>0</xpad>
    <ypad>0</ypad>
    <xexpand>False</xexpand>
    <yexpand>False</yexpand>
    <xshrink>False</xshrink>
    <yshrink>False</yshrink>
    <xfill>True</xfill>
    <yfill>True</yfill>
  </child>

  <widget>
    <class>GtkEntry</class>
    <name>entry_bill_to_city</name>
    <width>100</width>
    <can_focus>True</can_focus>
    <signal>
      <name>changed</name>
      <handler>on_entry_bill_to_city_changed</handler>
      <last_modification_time>Tue, 28 Nov 2000 02:07:06
      ➥GMT</last_modification_time>
    </signal>
    <editable>True</editable>
    <text_visible>True</text_visible>
    <text_max_length>0</text_max_length>
    <text></text>
    <child>
      <padding>0</padding>
      <expand>False</expand>
      <fill>True</fill>
    </child>
  </widget>

  <widget>
    <class>GtkEntry</class>
    <name>entry_bill_to_st</name>
    <width>35</width>
```

continues

Listing A.2 **Continued**

```
            <can_focus>True</can_focus>
            <signal>
              <name>changed</name>
              <handler>on_entry_bill_to_st_changed</handler>
              <last_modification_time>Tue, 28 Nov 2000 02:07:16
              ↪GMT</last_modification_time>
            </signal>
            <editable>True</editable>
            <text_visible>True</text_visible>
            <text_max_length>0</text_max_length>
            <text></text>
            <child>
              <padding>0</padding>
              <expand>False</expand>
              <fill>True</fill>
            </child>
          </widget>

          <widget>
            <class>GtkEntry</class>
            <name>entry_bill_to_zip</name>
            <width>70</width>
            <can_focus>True</can_focus>
            <signal>
              <name>changed</name>
              <handler>on_entry_bill_to_zip_changed</handler>
              <last_modification_time>Tue, 28 Nov 2000 02:07:22
              ↪GMT</last_modification_time>
            </signal>
            <editable>True</editable>
            <text_visible>True</text_visible>
            <text_max_length>0</text_max_length>
            <text></text>
            <child>
              <padding>0</padding>
              <expand>False</expand>
              <fill>True</fill>
            </child>
          </widget>
        </widget>
      </widget>

      <widget>
        <class>GtkLabel</class>
        <name>lbl_order_comments</name>
        <label>Order Comments</label>
        <justify>GTK_JUSTIFY_LEFT</justify>
        <wrap>False</wrap>
        <xalign>0.5</xalign>
```

```
        <yalign>0.5</yalign>
        <xpad>0</xpad>
        <ypad>0</ypad>
        <child>
          <padding>0</padding>
          <expand>False</expand>
          <fill>False</fill>
        </child>
      </widget>

      <widget>
        <class>GtkScrolledWindow</class>
        <name>scrolledwindow1</name>
        <hscrollbar_policy>GTK_POLICY_NEVER</hscrollbar_policy>
        <vscrollbar_policy>GTK_POLICY_ALWAYS</vscrollbar_policy>
        <hupdate_policy>GTK_UPDATE_CONTINUOUS</hupdate_policy>
        <vupdate_policy>GTK_UPDATE_CONTINUOUS</vupdate_policy>
        <child>
          <padding>0</padding>
          <expand>True</expand>
          <fill>True</fill>
        </child>

        <widget>
          <class>GtkText</class>
          <name>txt_order_comments</name>
          <can_focus>True</can_focus>
          <editable>True</editable>
          <text></text>
        </widget>
      </widget>

      <widget>
        <class>GtkLabel</class>
        <name>lbl_customer_comments</name>
        <label>Customer Comments</label>
        <justify>GTK_JUSTIFY_LEFT</justify>
        <wrap>False</wrap>
        <xalign>0.5</xalign>
        <yalign>0.5</yalign>
        <xpad>0</xpad>
        <ypad>0</ypad>
        <child>
          <padding>0</padding>
          <expand>False</expand>
          <fill>False</fill>
        </child>
      </widget>

      <widget>
        <class>GtkScrolledWindow</class>
```

continues

Listing A.2   **Continued**

```
      <name>scrolledwindow2</name>
      <hscrollbar_policy>GTK_POLICY_NEVER</hscrollbar_policy>
      <vscrollbar_policy>GTK_POLICY_ALWAYS</vscrollbar_policy>
      <hupdate_policy>GTK_UPDATE_CONTINUOUS</hupdate_policy>
      <vupdate_policy>GTK_UPDATE_CONTINUOUS</vupdate_policy>
      <child>
        <padding>0</padding>
        <expand>True</expand>
        <fill>True</fill>
      </child>

      <widget>
        <class>GtkText</class>
        <name>txt_customer_comments</name>
        <can_focus>True</can_focus>
        <signal>
          <name>changed</name>
          <handler>on_txt_customer_comments_changed</handler>
          <last_modification_time>Tue, 28 Nov 2000 02:07:29
          ↪GMT</last_modification_time>
        </signal>
        <editable>True</editable>
        <text></text>
      </widget>
      </widget>
      </widget>
    </widget>

    <widget>
      <class>GtkStatusbar</class>
      <name>statusbar</name>
      <child>
      <padding>0</padding>
      <expand>False</expand>
      <fill>False</fill>
      </child>
    </widget>
  </widget>
</widget>

<widget>
  <class>GtkWindow</class>
  <name>frm_items_ordered</name>
  <signal>
    <name>set_focus</name>
    <handler>on_frm_items_ordered_set_focus</handler>
    <last_modification_time>Mon, 20 Nov 2000 23:07:30 GMT</last_modification_time>
  </signal>
  <signal>
```

```
    <name>button_press_event</name>
    <handler>on_frm_items_ordered_button_press_event</handler>
    <last_modification_time>Mon, 20 Nov 2000 23:07:40 GMT</last_modification_time>
  </signal>
  <signal>
    <name>button_release_event</name>
    <handler>on_frm_items_ordered_button_release_event</handler>
    <last_modification_time>Mon, 20 Nov 2000 23:07:45 GMT</last_modification_time>
  </signal>
  <signal>
    <name>delete_event</name>
    <handler>on_frm_items_ordered_delete_event</handler>
    <last_modification_time>Mon, 20 Nov 2000 23:07:56 GMT</last_modification_time>
  </signal>
  <signal>
    <name>destroy_event</name>
    <handler>on_frm_items_ordered_destroy_event</handler>
    <last_modification_time>Mon, 20 Nov 2000 23:08:05 GMT</last_modification_time>
  </signal>
  <signal>
    <name>event</name>
    <handler>on_frm_items_ordered_event</handler>
    <last_modification_time>Mon, 20 Nov 2000 23:08:22 GMT</last_modification_time>
  </signal>
  <signal>
    <name>hide</name>
    <handler>on_frm_items_ordered_hide</handler>
    <last_modification_time>Mon, 20 Nov 2000 23:08:40 GMT</last_modification_time>
  </signal>
  <signal>
    <name>key_press_event</name>
    <handler>on_frm_items_ordered_key_press_event</handler>
    <last_modification_time>Mon, 20 Nov 2000 23:08:50 GMT</last_modification_time>
  </signal>
  <signal>
    <name>key_release_event</name>
    <handler>on_frm_items_ordered_key_release_event</handler>
    <last_modification_time>Mon, 20 Nov 2000 23:08:58 GMT</last_modification_time>
  </signal>
  <signal>
    <name>realize</name>
    <handler>on_frm_items_ordered_realize</handler>
    <last_modification_time>Mon, 20 Nov 2000 23:09:09 GMT</last_modification_time>
  </signal>
  <signal>
    <name>show</name>
    <handler>on_frm_items_ordered_show</handler>
    <last_modification_time>Mon, 20 Nov 2000 23:09:18 GMT</last_modification_time>
  </signal>
  <signal>
    <name>unrealize</name>
```

continues

Listing A.2 **Continued**

```
  <handler>on_frm_items_ordered_unrealize</handler>
  <last_modification_time>Mon, 20 Nov 2000 23:09:38 GMT</last_modification_time>
</signal>
<signal>
  <name>destroy</name>
  <handler>on_frm_items_ordered_destroy</handler>
  <last_modification_time>Mon, 20 Nov 2000 23:09:45 GMT</last_modification_time>
</signal>
<title>Items Ordered</title>
<type>GTK_WINDOW_TOPLEVEL</type>
<position>GTK_WIN_POS_NONE</position>
<modal>False</modal>
<allow_shrink>False</allow_shrink>
<allow_grow>True</allow_grow>
<auto_shrink>False</auto_shrink>

<widget>
  <class>GtkHPaned</class>
  <name>hpaned1</name>
  <handle_size>10</handle_size>
  <gutter_size>10</gutter_size>

  <widget>
    <class>GtkVBox</class>
    <name>vbox3</name>
    <homogeneous>False</homogeneous>
    <spacing>0</spacing>
    <child>
    <shrink>True</shrink>
    <resize>False</resize>
    </child>

    <widget>
    <class>GtkLabel</class>
    <name>lbl_item_number</name>
    <label>Item Number:</label>
    <justify>GTK_JUSTIFY_CENTER</justify>
    <wrap>False</wrap>
    <xalign>0.5</xalign>
    <yalign>0.5</yalign>
    <xpad>0</xpad>
    <ypad>0</ypad>
    <child>
      <padding>0</padding>
      <expand>False</expand>
      <fill>False</fill>
    </child>
    </widget>
```

```
<widget>
<class>GtkEntry</class>
<name>entry_item_number</name>
<can_focus>True</can_focus>
<signal>
  <name>activate</name>
  <handler>on_entry_item_number_activate</handler>
  <last_modification_time>Mon, 20 Nov 2000 23:21:16
  ➥GMT</last_modification_time>
</signal>
<signal>
  <name>changed</name>
  <handler>on_entry_item_number_changed</handler>
  <last_modification_time>Mon, 20 Nov 2000 23:21:20
  ➥GMT</last_modification_time>
</signal>
<signal>
  <name>delete_text</name>
  <handler>on_entry_item_number_delete_text</handler>
  <last_modification_time>Mon, 20 Nov 2000 23:21:31
  ➥GMT</last_modification_time>
</signal>
<signal>
  <name>insert_text</name>
  <handler>on_entry_item_number_insert_text</handler>
  <last_modification_time>Mon, 20 Nov 2000 23:21:36
  ➥GMT</last_modification_time>
</signal>
<editable>True</editable>
<text_visible>True</text_visible>
<text_max_length>0</text_max_length>
<text></text>
<child>
  <padding>0</padding>
  <expand>False</expand>
  <fill>False</fill>
</child>
</widget>

<widget>
<class>GtkLabel</class>
<name>lbl_quantity</name>
<label>Quantity</label>
<justify>GTK_JUSTIFY_CENTER</justify>
<wrap>False</wrap>
<xalign>0.5</xalign>
<yalign>0.5</yalign>
<xpad>0</xpad>
<ypad>0</ypad>
<child>
  <padding>0</padding>
```

continues

Listing A.2   **Continued**

```
<expand>False</expand>
<fill>False</fill>
</child>
</widget>

<widget>
<class>GtkSpinButton</class>
<name>spinbutton_quantity</name>
<can_focus>True</can_focus>
<signal>
  <name>activate</name>
  <handler>on_spinbutton_quantity_activate</handler>
  <last_modification_time>Mon, 20 Nov 2000 23:21:59
  ⮌GMT</last_modification_time>
</signal>
<signal>
  <name>changed</name>
  <handler>on_spinbutton_quantity_changed</handler>
  <last_modification_time>Mon, 20 Nov 2000 23:22:11
  ⮌GMT</last_modification_time>
</signal>
<climb_rate>1</climb_rate>
<digits>0</digits>
<numeric>False</numeric>
<update_policy>GTK_UPDATE_ALWAYS</update_policy>
<snap>False</snap>
<wrap>False</wrap>
<value>1</value>
<lower>0</lower>
<upper>100</upper>
<step>1</step>
<page>10</page>
<page_size>10</page_size>
<child>
  <padding>0</padding>
  <expand>False</expand>
  <fill>False</fill>
</child>
</widget>

<widget>
<class>GtkButton</class>
<name>cmd_Add</name>
<border_width>5</border_width>
<can_focus>True</can_focus>
<accelerator>
  <modifiers>GDK_MOD1_MASK</modifiers>
  <key>GDK_A</key>
  <signal>clicked</signal>
```

```
  </accelerator>
  <signal>
    <name>clicked</name>
    <handler>on_cmd_Add_clicked</handler>
    <last_modification_time>Mon, 20 Nov 2000 23:10:00
    ↪GMT</last_modification_time>
  </signal>
  <label>_Add</label>
  <child>
    <padding>0</padding>
    <expand>False</expand>
    <fill>False</fill>
  </child>
  </widget>

  <widget>
  <class>GtkButton</class>
  <name>cmd_search_for_item</name>
  <border_width>5</border_width>
  <can_focus>True</can_focus>
  <accelerator>
    <modifiers>GDK_MOD1_MASK</modifiers>
    <key>GDK_f</key>
    <signal>clicked</signal>
  </accelerator>
  <signal>
    <name>clicked</name>
    <handler>on_cmd_search_for_item_clicked</handler>
    <last_modification_time>Mon, 20 Nov 2000 23:10:07
    ↪GMT</last_modification_time>
  </signal>
  <label>Search _For Item</label>
  <child>
    <padding>0</padding>
    <expand>False</expand>
    <fill>False</fill>
  </child>
  </widget>

  <widget>
  <class>GtkLabel</class>
  <name>lbl_order_total</name>
  <label>Order Total:</label>
  <justify>GTK_JUSTIFY_CENTER</justify>
  <wrap>False</wrap>
  <xalign>0.5</xalign>
  <yalign>0.5</yalign>
  <xpad>0</xpad>
  <ypad>0</ypad>
  <child>
    <padding>0</padding>
```

continues

Listing A.2 **Continued**

```
      <expand>False</expand>
      <fill>False</fill>
   </child>
   </widget>

   <widget>
   <class>GtkFrame</class>
   <name>frame1</name>
   <label_xalign>0</label_xalign>
   <shadow_type>GTK_SHADOW_ETCHED_IN</shadow_type>
   <child>
      <padding>0</padding>
      <expand>False</expand>
      <fill>False</fill>
   </child>

   <widget>
      <class>GtkLabel</class>
      <name>lbl_order_total_numeric</name>
      <label>0.00</label>
      <justify>GTK_JUSTIFY_CENTER</justify>
      <wrap>False</wrap>
      <xalign>0.5</xalign>
      <yalign>0.5</yalign>
      <xpad>0</xpad>
      <ypad>0</ypad>
   </widget>
   </widget>

   <widget>
   <class>GtkButton</class>
   <name>cmd_done</name>
   <border_width>5</border_width>
   <can_focus>True</can_focus>
   <accelerator>
      <modifiers>GDK_MOD1_MASK</modifiers>
      <key>GDK_d</key>
      <signal>clicked</signal>
   </accelerator>
   <signal>
      <name>clicked</name>
      <handler>on_cmd_done_clicked</handler>
      <last_modification_time>Mon, 20 Nov 2000 23:10:15
      ↪GMT</last_modification_time>
   </signal>
   <label>_Done</label>
   <child>
      <padding>0</padding>
      <expand>False</expand>
```

```
    <fill>False</fill>
  </child>
  </widget>
</widget>

<widget>
  <class>GtkVPaned</class>
  <name>vpaned1</name>
  <handle_size>10</handle_size>
  <gutter_size>10</gutter_size>
  <child>
  <shrink>True</shrink>
  <resize>True</resize>
  </child>

  <widget>
  <class>GtkScrolledWindow</class>
  <name>scrolledwindow3</name>
  <hscrollbar_policy>GTK_POLICY_ALWAYS</hscrollbar_policy>
  <vscrollbar_policy>GTK_POLICY_ALWAYS</vscrollbar_policy>
  <hupdate_policy>GTK_UPDATE_CONTINUOUS</hupdate_policy>
  <vupdate_policy>GTK_UPDATE_CONTINUOUS</vupdate_policy>
  <child>
    <shrink>True</shrink>
    <resize>False</resize>
  </child>

  <widget>
    <class>GtkCList</class>
    <name>clist_items</name>
    <width>266</width>
    <height>150</height>
    <can_focus>True</can_focus>
    <signal>
      <name>select_row</name>
      <handler>on_clist_items_select_row</handler>
      <last_modification_time>Mon, 20 Nov 2000 23:27:05
      ➥GMT</last_modification_time>
    </signal>
    <signal>
      <name>unselect_row</name>
      <handler>on_clist_items_unselect_row</handler>
      <last_modification_time>Mon, 20 Nov 2000 23:27:15
      ➥GMT</last_modification_time>
    </signal>
    <signal>
      <name>button_press_event</name>
      <handler>on_clist_items_button_press_event</handler>
      <last_modification_time>Mon, 20 Nov 2000 23:27:23
      ➥GMT</last_modification_time>
    </signal>
```

continues

Listing A.2   **Continued**

```
<signal>
  <name>button_release_event</name>
  <handler>on_clist_items_button_release_event</handler>
  <last_modification_time>Mon, 20 Nov 2000 23:27:31
  ↪GMT</last_modification_time>
</signal>
<columns>3</columns>
<column_widths>80,154,80</column_widths>
<selection_mode>GTK_SELECTION_SINGLE</selection_mode>
<show_titles>True</show_titles>
<shadow_type>GTK_SHADOW_IN</shadow_type>

<widget>
  <class>GtkLabel</class>
  <child_name>CList:title</child_name>
  <name>clist_items_lbl_item_number</name>
  <label>Item Number</label>
  <justify>GTK_JUSTIFY_CENTER</justify>
  <wrap>False</wrap>
  <xalign>0.5</xalign>
  <yalign>0.5</yalign>
  <xpad>0</xpad>
  <ypad>0</ypad>
</widget>

<widget>
  <class>GtkLabel</class>
  <child_name>CList:title</child_name>
  <name>clist_items_lbl_description</name>
  <label>Description</label>
  <justify>GTK_JUSTIFY_CENTER</justify>
  <wrap>False</wrap>
  <xalign>0.5</xalign>
  <yalign>0.5</yalign>
  <xpad>0</xpad>
  <ypad>0</ypad>
</widget>

<widget>
  <class>GtkLabel</class>
  <child_name>CList:title</child_name>
  <name>clist_items_lbl_price</name>
  <label>Price</label>
  <justify>GTK_JUSTIFY_CENTER</justify>
  <wrap>False</wrap>
  <xalign>0.5</xalign>
  <yalign>0.5</yalign>
  <xpad>0</xpad>
  <ypad>0</ypad>
```

```
      </widget>
    </widget>
  </widget>

<widget>
<class>GtkVPaned</class>
<name>vpaned2</name>
<handle_size>10</handle_size>
<gutter_size>10</gutter_size>
<child>
  <shrink>True</shrink>
  <resize>True</resize>
</child>

<widget>
  <class>GtkHBox</class>
  <name>hbox3</name>
  <border_width>10</border_width>
  <homogeneous>True</homogeneous>
  <spacing>12</spacing>
  <child>
    <shrink>True</shrink>
    <resize>False</resize>
  </child>

  <widget>
    <class>GtkButton</class>
    <name>cmd_add_down</name>
    <can_focus>True</can_focus>
    <signal>
      <name>clicked</name>
      <handler>on_cmd_add_down_clicked</handler>
      <last_modification_time>Mon, 20 Nov 2000 23:10:22
      ↦GMT</last_modification_time>
    </signal>
    <label>Add</label>
    <child>
      <padding>0</padding>
      <expand>False</expand>
      <fill>False</fill>
    </child>
  </widget>

  <widget>
    <class>GtkSpinButton</class>
    <name>spinbutton1</name>
    <can_focus>True</can_focus>
    <climb_rate>1</climb_rate>
    <digits>0</digits>
    <numeric>False</numeric>
    <update_policy>GTK_UPDATE_ALWAYS</update_policy>
```

continues

Listing A.2 **Continued**

```
      <snap>False</snap>
      <wrap>False</wrap>
      <value>1</value>
      <lower>0</lower>
      <upper>100</upper>
      <step>1</step>
      <page>10</page>
      <page_size>10</page_size>
      <child>
        <padding>0</padding>
        <expand>False</expand>
        <fill>False</fill>
      </child>
    </widget>

    <widget>
      <class>GtkButton</class>
      <name>cmd_remove</name>
      <can_focus>True</can_focus>
      <signal>
        <name>clicked</name>
        <handler>on_cmd_remove_clicked</handler>
        <last_modification_time>Mon, 20 Nov 2000 23:10:29
        ⇒GMT</last_modification_time>
      </signal>
      <label>Remove</label>
      <child>
        <padding>0</padding>
        <expand>False</expand>
        <fill>False</fill>
      </child>
    </widget>
  </widget>

  <widget>
    <class>GtkScrolledWindow</class>
    <name>scrolledwindow4</name>
    <hscrollbar_policy>GTK_POLICY_ALWAYS</hscrollbar_policy>
    <vscrollbar_policy>GTK_POLICY_ALWAYS</vscrollbar_policy>
    <hupdate_policy>GTK_UPDATE_CONTINUOUS</hupdate_policy>
    <vupdate_policy>GTK_UPDATE_CONTINUOUS</vupdate_policy>
    <child>
      <shrink>True</shrink>
      <resize>True</resize>
    </child>

    <widget>
      <class>GtkCList</class>
      <name>clist_items_ordered</name>
```

```
<width>353</width>
<height>100</height>
<can_focus>True</can_focus>
<signal>
  <name>select_row</name>
  <handler>on_clist_items_ordered_select_row</handler>
  <last_modification_time>Mon, 20 Nov 2000 23:28:50
  ➥GMT</last_modification_time>
</signal>
<signal>
  <name>unselect_row</name>
  <handler>on_clist_items_ordered_unselect_row</handler>
  <last_modification_time>Mon, 20 Nov 2000 23:29:04
  ➥GMT</last_modification_time>
</signal>
<signal>
  <name>button_press_event</name>
  <handler>on_clist_items_ordered_button_press_event</handler>
  <last_modification_time>Mon, 20 Nov 2000 23:29:09
  ➥GMT</last_modification_time>
</signal>
<signal>
  <name>button_release_event</name>
  <handler>on_clist_items_ordered_button_release_event</handler>
  <last_modification_time>Mon, 20 Nov 2000 23:29:16
  ➥GMT</last_modification_time>
</signal>
<columns>4</columns>
<column_widths>80,80,80,80</column_widths>
<selection_mode>GTK_SELECTION_SINGLE</selection_mode>
<show_titles>True</show_titles>
<shadow_type>GTK_SHADOW_IN</shadow_type>

<widget>
  <class>GtkLabel</class>
  <child_name>CList:title</child_name>
  <name>clist_items_ordered_lbl_item_number</name>
  <label>Item Number</label>
  <justify>GTK_JUSTIFY_CENTER</justify>
  <wrap>False</wrap>
  <xalign>0.5</xalign>
  <yalign>0.5</yalign>
  <xpad>0</xpad>
  <ypad>0</ypad>
</widget>

<widget>
  <class>GtkLabel</class>
  <child_name>CList:title</child_name>
  <name>clist_items_ordered_lbl_description</name>
  <label>Description</label>
```

continues

Listing A.2 **Continued**

```
                    <justify>GTK_JUSTIFY_CENTER</justify>
                    <wrap>False</wrap>
                    <xalign>0.5</xalign>
                    <yalign>0.5</yalign>
                    <xpad>0</xpad>
                    <ypad>0</ypad>
                  </widget>

                  <widget>
                    <class>GtkLabel</class>
                    <child_name>CList:title</child_name>
                    <name>clist_items_ordered_lbl_quantity</name>
                    <label>Quantity</label>
                    <justify>GTK_JUSTIFY_CENTER</justify>
                    <wrap>False</wrap>
                    <xalign>0.5</xalign>
                    <yalign>0.5</yalign>
                    <xpad>0</xpad>
                    <ypad>0</ypad>
                  </widget>

                  <widget>
                    <class>GtkLabel</class>
                    <child_name>CList:title</child_name>
                    <name>clist_items_ordered_lbl_total_price</name>
                    <label>Total Price</label>
                    <justify>GTK_JUSTIFY_CENTER</justify>
                    <wrap>False</wrap>
                    <xalign>0.5</xalign>
                    <yalign>0.5</yalign>
                    <xpad>0</xpad>
                    <ypad>0</ypad>
                  </widget>
                </widget>
              </widget>
            </widget>
          </widget>
        </widget>
      </widget>

<widget>
  <class>GtkWindow</class>
  <name>frm_find_customer</name>
  <signal>
    <name>delete_event</name>
    <handler>on_frm_find_customer_delete_event</handler>
    <last_modification_time>Tue, 21 Nov 2000 15:31:24 GMT</last_modification_time>
  </signal>
  <title>Find Customer</title>
```

```
<type>GTK_WINDOW_TOPLEVEL</type>
<position>GTK_WIN_POS_NONE</position>
<modal>True</modal>
<allow_shrink>False</allow_shrink>
<allow_grow>True</allow_grow>
<auto_shrink>False</auto_shrink>

<widget>
  <class>GtkHBox</class>
  <name>hbox4</name>
  <homogeneous>False</homogeneous>
  <spacing>0</spacing>

  <widget>
    <class>GtkVBox</class>
    <name>vbox4</name>
    <border_width>11</border_width>
    <homogeneous>False</homogeneous>
    <spacing>11</spacing>
    <child>
    <padding>0</padding>
    <expand>False</expand>
    <fill>False</fill>
    </child>

    <widget>
    <class>GtkLabel</class>
    <name>lbl_search_for_customer</name>
    <label>Search for Customer...</label>
    <justify>GTK_JUSTIFY_CENTER</justify>
    <wrap>False</wrap>
    <xalign>0.5</xalign>
    <yalign>0.5</yalign>
    <xpad>0</xpad>
    <ypad>0</ypad>
    <child>
      <padding>0</padding>
      <expand>False</expand>
      <fill>False</fill>
    </child>
    </widget>

    <widget>
    <class>GtkEntry</class>
    <name>entry_find_customer</name>
    <can_focus>True</can_focus>
    <editable>True</editable>
    <text_visible>True</text_visible>
    <text_max_length>0</text_max_length>
    <text></text>
    <child>
```

continues

Listing A.2 **Continued**

```
        <padding>0</padding>
        <expand>False</expand>
        <fill>False</fill>
      </child>
      </widget>

      <widget>
      <class>GtkButton</class>
      <name>cmd_find_customer</name>
      <can_focus>True</can_focus>
      <signal>
        <name>clicked</name>
        <handler>on_cmd_find_customer_clicked</handler>
        <last_modification_time>Tue, 21 Nov 2000 15:31:02
        ↪GMT</last_modification_time>
      </signal>
      <label>Find...</label>
      <child>
        <padding>0</padding>
        <expand>False</expand>
        <fill>False</fill>
      </child>
      </widget>

      <widget>
      <class>GtkButton</class>
      <name>cmd_find_customer_done</name>
      <can_focus>True</can_focus>
      <signal>
        <name>clicked</name>
        <handler>on_cmd_find_customer_done_clicked</handler>
        <last_modification_time>Tue, 21 Nov 2000 15:31:06
        ↪GMT</last_modification_time>
      </signal>
      <label>Done</label>
      <child>
        <padding>0</padding>
        <expand>False</expand>
        <fill>False</fill>
      </child>
      </widget>
    </widget>

    <widget>
      <class>GtkScrolledWindow</class>
      <name>scrolledwindow7</name>
      <hscrollbar_policy>GTK_POLICY_ALWAYS</hscrollbar_policy>
      <vscrollbar_policy>GTK_POLICY_ALWAYS</vscrollbar_policy>
      <hupdate_policy>GTK_UPDATE_CONTINUOUS</hupdate_policy>
```

```
      <vupdate_policy>GTK_UPDATE_CONTINUOUS</vupdate_policy>
      <child>
      <padding>0</padding>
      <expand>True</expand>
      <fill>True</fill>
      </child>

      <widget>
      <class>GtkCList</class>
      <name>clist_found_customer</name>
      <can_focus>True</can_focus>
      <columns>17</columns>
<column_widths>80,80,80,80,80,80,80,80,80,80,80,80,80,80,80,80,80</column_widths>
      <selection_mode>GTK_SELECTION_SINGLE</selection_mode>
      <show_titles>True</show_titles>
      <shadow_type>GTK_SHADOW_IN</shadow_type>

      <widget>
        <class>GtkLabel</class>
        <child_name>CList:title</child_name>
        <name>label7</name>
        <label>Customer</label>
        <justify>GTK_JUSTIFY_CENTER</justify>
        <wrap>False</wrap>
        <xalign>0.5</xalign>
        <yalign>0.5</yalign>
        <xpad>0</xpad>
        <ypad>0</ypad>
      </widget>

      <widget>
        <class>GtkLabel</class>
        <child_name>CList:title</child_name>
        <name>label8</name>
        <label>Name</label>
        <justify>GTK_JUSTIFY_CENTER</justify>
        <wrap>False</wrap>
        <xalign>0.5</xalign>
        <yalign>0.5</yalign>
        <xpad>0</xpad>
        <ypad>0</ypad>
      </widget>

      <widget>
        <class>GtkLabel</class>
        <child_name>CList:title</child_name>
        <name>label9</name>
        <label>Ship Addr</label>
        <justify>GTK_JUSTIFY_CENTER</justify>
        <wrap>False</wrap>
```

continues

Listing A.2 **Continued**

```
      <xalign>0.5</xalign>
      <yalign>0.5</yalign>
      <xpad>0</xpad>
      <ypad>0</ypad>
    </widget>

    <widget>
      <class>GtkLabel</class>
      <child_name>CList:title</child_name>
      <name>label10</name>
      <label>Ship Addr</label>
      <justify>GTK_JUSTIFY_CENTER</justify>
      <wrap>False</wrap>
      <xalign>0.5</xalign>
      <yalign>0.5</yalign>
      <xpad>0</xpad>
      <ypad>0</ypad>
    </widget>

    <widget>
      <class>GtkLabel</class>
      <child_name>CList:title</child_name>
      <name>label11</name>
      <label>Ship City</label>
      <justify>GTK_JUSTIFY_CENTER</justify>
      <wrap>False</wrap>
      <xalign>0.5</xalign>
      <yalign>0.5</yalign>
      <xpad>0</xpad>
      <ypad>0</ypad>
    </widget>

    <widget>
      <class>GtkLabel</class>
      <child_name>CList:title</child_name>
      <name>label12</name>
      <label>Ship St</label>
      <justify>GTK_JUSTIFY_CENTER</justify>
      <wrap>False</wrap>
      <xalign>0.5</xalign>
      <yalign>0.5</yalign>
      <xpad>0</xpad>
      <ypad>0</ypad>
    </widget>

    <widget>
      <class>GtkLabel</class>
      <child_name>CList:title</child_name>
      <name>label13</name>
```

```
  <label>Ship Zip</label>
  <justify>GTK_JUSTIFY_CENTER</justify>
  <wrap>False</wrap>
  <xalign>0.5</xalign>
  <yalign>0.5</yalign>
  <xpad>0</xpad>
  <ypad>0</ypad>
</widget>

<widget>
  <class>GtkLabel</class>
  <child_name>CList:title</child_name>
  <name>label14</name>
  <label>Bill Addr</label>
  <justify>GTK_JUSTIFY_CENTER</justify>
  <wrap>False</wrap>
  <xalign>0.5</xalign>
  <yalign>0.5</yalign>
  <xpad>0</xpad>
  <ypad>0</ypad>
</widget>

<widget>
  <class>GtkLabel</class>
  <child_name>CList:title</child_name>
  <name>label15</name>
  <label>Bill Addr</label>
  <justify>GTK_JUSTIFY_CENTER</justify>
  <wrap>False</wrap>
  <xalign>0.5</xalign>
  <yalign>0.5</yalign>
  <xpad>0</xpad>
  <ypad>0</ypad>
</widget>

<widget>
  <class>GtkLabel</class>
  <child_name>CList:title</child_name>
  <name>label16</name>
  <label>Bill City</label>
  <justify>GTK_JUSTIFY_CENTER</justify>
  <wrap>False</wrap>
  <xalign>0.5</xalign>
  <yalign>0.5</yalign>
  <xpad>0</xpad>
  <ypad>0</ypad>
</widget>

<widget>
  <class>GtkLabel</class>
  <child_name>CList:title</child_name>
```

continues

Listing A.2 **Continued**

```
    <name>label17</name>
    <label>Bill St</label>
    <justify>GTK_JUSTIFY_CENTER</justify>
    <wrap>False</wrap>
    <xalign>0.5</xalign>
    <yalign>0.5</yalign>
    <xpad>0</xpad>
    <ypad>0</ypad>
  </widget>

  <widget>
    <class>GtkLabel</class>
    <child_name>CList:title</child_name>
    <name>label18</name>
    <label>Bill Zip</label>
    <justify>GTK_JUSTIFY_CENTER</justify>
    <wrap>False</wrap>
    <xalign>0.5</xalign>
    <yalign>0.5</yalign>
    <xpad>0</xpad>
    <ypad>0</ypad>
  </widget>

  <widget>
    <class>GtkLabel</class>
    <child_name>CList:title</child_name>
    <name>label19</name>
    <label>First</label>
    <justify>GTK_JUSTIFY_CENTER</justify>
    <wrap>False</wrap>
    <xalign>0.5</xalign>
    <yalign>0.5</yalign>
    <xpad>0</xpad>
    <ypad>0</ypad>
  </widget>

  <widget>
    <class>GtkLabel</class>
    <child_name>CList:title</child_name>
    <name>label20</name>
    <label>Last</label>
    <justify>GTK_JUSTIFY_CENTER</justify>
    <wrap>False</wrap>
    <xalign>0.5</xalign>
    <yalign>0.5</yalign>
    <xpad>0</xpad>
    <ypad>0</ypad>
  </widget>
```

```
      <widget>
        <class>GtkLabel</class>
        <child_name>CList:title</child_name>
        <name>label21</name>
        <label>Phone</label>
        <justify>GTK_JUSTIFY_CENTER</justify>
        <wrap>False</wrap>
        <xalign>0.5</xalign>
        <yalign>0.5</yalign>
        <xpad>0</xpad>
        <ypad>0</ypad>
      </widget>

      <widget>
        <class>GtkLabel</class>
        <child_name>CList:title</child_name>
        <name>label22</name>
        <label>Title</label>
        <justify>GTK_JUSTIFY_CENTER</justify>
        <wrap>False</wrap>
        <xalign>0.5</xalign>
        <yalign>0.5</yalign>
        <xpad>0</xpad>
        <ypad>0</ypad>
      </widget>

      <widget>
        <class>GtkLabel</class>
        <child_name>CList:title</child_name>
        <name>label23</name>
        <label>Comments</label>
        <justify>GTK_JUSTIFY_CENTER</justify>
        <wrap>False</wrap>
        <xalign>0.5</xalign>
        <yalign>0.5</yalign>
        <xpad>0</xpad>
        <ypad>0</ypad>
      </widget>
      </widget>
    </widget>
  </widget>
</widget>

<widget>
  <class>GtkWindow</class>
  <name>frm_find_item</name>
  <signal>
    <name>delete_event</name>
    <handler>on_frm_find_item_delete_event</handler>
    <last_modification_time>Tue, 21 Nov 2000 15:31:32 GMT</last_modification_time>
  </signal>
```

continues

Listing A.2 **Continued**

```
<title>Find Item</title>
<type>GTK_WINDOW_TOPLEVEL</type>
<position>GTK_WIN_POS_NONE</position>
<modal>True</modal>
<allow_shrink>False</allow_shrink>
<allow_grow>True</allow_grow>
<auto_shrink>False</auto_shrink>

<widget>
  <class>GtkHBox</class>
  <name>hbox5</name>
  <homogeneous>False</homogeneous>
  <spacing>0</spacing>

  <widget>
    <class>GtkVBox</class>
    <name>vbox5</name>
    <border_width>15</border_width>
    <homogeneous>False</homogeneous>
    <spacing>10</spacing>
    <child>
    <padding>0</padding>
    <expand>False</expand>
    <fill>False</fill>
    </child>

    <widget>
    <class>GtkLabel</class>
    <name>lbl_search_for_item</name>
    <label>Search for Item...</label>
    <justify>GTK_JUSTIFY_CENTER</justify>
    <wrap>False</wrap>
    <xalign>0.5</xalign>
    <yalign>0.5</yalign>
    <xpad>0</xpad>
    <ypad>0</ypad>
    <child>
      <padding>0</padding>
      <expand>False</expand>
      <fill>False</fill>
    </child>
    </widget>

    <widget>
    <class>GtkEntry</class>
    <name>entry_find_item</name>
    <can_focus>True</can_focus>
    <editable>True</editable>
    <text_visible>True</text_visible>
```

```
      <text_max_length>0</text_max_length>
      <text></text>
      <child>
        <padding>0</padding>
        <expand>False</expand>
        <fill>False</fill>
      </child>
      </widget>

      <widget>
      <class>GtkButton</class>
      <name>cmd_find_item</name>
      <can_focus>True</can_focus>
      <signal>
        <name>clicked</name>
        <handler>on_cmd_find_item_clicked</handler>
        <last_modification_time>Tue, 21 Nov 2000 15:30:45
        ➥GMT</last_modification_time>
      </signal>
      <label>Find...</label>
      <child>
        <padding>0</padding>
        <expand>False</expand>
        <fill>False</fill>
      </child>
      </widget>

      <widget>
      <class>GtkButton</class>
      <name>cmd_find_item_done</name>
      <can_focus>True</can_focus>
      <signal>
        <name>clicked</name>
        <handler>on_cmd_find_item_done_clicked</handler>
        <last_modification_time>Mon, 27 Nov 2000 01:52:37
        ➥GMT</last_modification_time>
      </signal>
      <label>Done</label>
      <child>
        <padding>0</padding>
        <expand>False</expand>
        <fill>False</fill>
      </child>
      </widget>
    </widget>

    <widget>
      <class>GtkScrolledWindow</class>
      <name>scrolledwindow6</name>
      <hscrollbar_policy>GTK_POLICY_ALWAYS</hscrollbar_policy>
      <vscrollbar_policy>GTK_POLICY_ALWAYS</vscrollbar_policy>
```

continues

Listing A.2   **Continued**

```
<hupdate_policy>GTK_UPDATE_CONTINUOUS</hupdate_policy>
<vupdate_policy>GTK_UPDATE_CONTINUOUS</vupdate_policy>
<child>
<padding>0</padding>
<expand>True</expand>
<fill>True</fill>
</child>

<widget>
<class>GtkCList</class>
<name>clist_found_items</name>
<can_focus>True</can_focus>
<columns>3</columns>
<column_widths>80,80,80</column_widths>
<selection_mode>GTK_SELECTION_SINGLE</selection_mode>
<show_titles>True</show_titles>
<shadow_type>GTK_SHADOW_IN</shadow_type>

<widget>
  <class>GtkLabel</class>
  <child_name>CList:title</child_name>
  <name>label4</name>
  <label>Item Num.</label>
  <justify>GTK_JUSTIFY_CENTER</justify>
  <wrap>False</wrap>
  <xalign>0.5</xalign>
  <yalign>0.5</yalign>
  <xpad>0</xpad>
  <ypad>0</ypad>
</widget>

<widget>
  <class>GtkLabel</class>
  <child_name>CList:title</child_name>
  <name>label5</name>
  <label>Description</label>
  <justify>GTK_JUSTIFY_CENTER</justify>
  <wrap>False</wrap>
  <xalign>0.5</xalign>
  <yalign>0.5</yalign>
  <xpad>0</xpad>
  <ypad>0</ypad>
</widget>

<widget>
  <class>GtkLabel</class>
  <child_name>CList:title</child_name>
  <name>label6</name>
  <label>Price</label>
```

```
        <justify>GTK_JUSTIFY_CENTER</justify>
        <wrap>False</wrap>
        <xalign>0.5</xalign>
        <yalign>0.5</yalign>
        <xpad>0</xpad>
        <ypad>0</ypad>
      </widget>
      </widget>
    </widget>
  </widget>
</widget>

</GTK-Interface>
```

B

Glade-Generated Files from the Worldwide Commissions Application

THIS APPENDIX CONTAINS SUPPORTING CODE FOR THE Worldwide Commissions Application (Chapters 8, "Commission Calculations Abstract and Design," 9, "Constructing the Commissions Application," and 10, "Commission Calculations Deployment"). The following are Glade-generated files; the same warnings apply here as with Appendix A, "Glade Generated Files from the SESI Order Application." If you hand-edit these files, Glade may overwrite your changes.

interface.c

Listing B.1 is `interface.c` for the Worldwide Commissions application. Its use and implementation is the same as described for Appendix A.

Listing B.1 contains three functions: `create_frm_login()`, `create_frm_table_display()`, and `create_frm_commissions()`. Each creates the form widget and child widgets for the forms and then connects the signals with the callbacks (found in `callbacks.c`, see Chapter 9, or download from the book's companion Web site).

Listing B.1 *interface.c* **for the Worldwide Commissions Application**

```
/* DO NOT EDIT THIS FILE. It is generated by Glade.
 */

#ifdef HAVE_CONFIG_H
#  include <config.h>
#endif

#include <sys/types.h>
#include <sys/stat.h>
#include <unistd.h>
#include <string.h>

#include <gdk/gdkkeysyms.h>
#include <gtk/gtk.h>

#include "callbacks.h"
#include "interface.h"
#include "support.h"

GtkWidget*
create_frm_login (void)
{
  GtkWidget *frm_login;
  GtkWidget *vbox1;
  GtkWidget *lbl_title;
  GtkWidget *frame_login;
  GtkWidget *table_login;
  GtkWidget *lbl_name;
  GtkWidget *lbl_password;
  GtkWidget *entry_password;
  GtkWidget *entry_name;
  GtkWidget *cmd_login;
  GtkWidget *frame_change_password;
  GtkWidget *table3;
  GtkWidget *lbl_new_password;
  GtkWidget *lbl_new_password_again;
  GtkWidget *entry_new_password;
  GtkWidget *entry_new_password_again;
  GtkWidget *cmd_change_password;
  GtkWidget *lbl_messages;

  frm_login = gtk_window_new (GTK_WINDOW_TOPLEVEL);
  gtk_object_set_data (GTK_OBJECT (frm_login), "frm_login", frm_login);
  gtk_window_set_title (GTK_WINDOW (frm_login), "Commissions Login");

  vbox1 = gtk_vbox_new (FALSE, 0);
  gtk_widget_ref (vbox1);
  gtk_object_set_data_full (GTK_OBJECT (frm_login), "vbox1", vbox1,
                            (GtkDestroyNotify) gtk_widget_unref);
```

```
gtk_widget_show (vbox1);
gtk_container_add (GTK_CONTAINER (frm_login), vbox1);

lbl_title = gtk_label_new ("Worldwide Commissions System");
gtk_widget_ref (lbl_title);
gtk_object_set_data_full (GTK_OBJECT (frm_login), "lbl_title", lbl_title,
                          (GtkDestroyNotify) gtk_widget_unref);
gtk_widget_show (lbl_title);
gtk_box_pack_start (GTK_BOX (vbox1), lbl_title, FALSE, FALSE, 0);
gtk_misc_set_padding (GTK_MISC (lbl_title), 0, 5);

frame_login = gtk_frame_new ("Login");
gtk_widget_ref (frame_login);
gtk_object_set_data_full (GTK_OBJECT (frm_login), "frame_login", frame_login,
                          (GtkDestroyNotify) gtk_widget_unref);
gtk_widget_show (frame_login);
gtk_box_pack_start (GTK_BOX (vbox1), frame_login, TRUE, TRUE, 0);
gtk_container_set_border_width (GTK_CONTAINER (frame_login), 5);

table_login = gtk_table_new (3, 2, FALSE);
gtk_widget_ref (table_login);
gtk_object_set_data_full (GTK_OBJECT (frm_login), "table_login", table_login,
                          (GtkDestroyNotify) gtk_widget_unref);
gtk_widget_show (table_login);
gtk_container_add (GTK_CONTAINER (frame_login), table_login);

lbl_name = gtk_label_new ("Name:");
gtk_widget_ref (lbl_name);
gtk_object_set_data_full (GTK_OBJECT (frm_login), "lbl_name", lbl_name,
                          (GtkDestroyNotify) gtk_widget_unref);
gtk_widget_show (lbl_name);
gtk_table_attach (GTK_TABLE (table_login), lbl_name, 0, 1, 0, 1,
                  (GtkAttachOptions) (0),
                  (GtkAttachOptions) (0), 0, 0);

lbl_password = gtk_label_new ("Password:");
gtk_widget_ref (lbl_password);
gtk_object_set_data_full (GTK_OBJECT (frm_login), "lbl_password", lbl_password,
                          (GtkDestroyNotify) gtk_widget_unref);
gtk_widget_show (lbl_password);
gtk_table_attach (GTK_TABLE (table_login), lbl_password, 0, 1, 1, 2,
                  (GtkAttachOptions) (0),
                  (GtkAttachOptions) (0), 0, 0);

entry_password = gtk_entry_new ();
gtk_widget_ref (entry_password);
gtk_object_set_data_full (GTK_OBJECT (frm_login), "entry_password", entry_password,
                          (GtkDestroyNotify) gtk_widget_unref);
gtk_widget_show (entry_password);
gtk_table_attach (GTK_TABLE (table_login), entry_password, 1, 2, 1, 2,
```

continues

Listing B.1 **Continued**

```
                         (GtkAttachOptions) (GTK_EXPAND),
                         (GtkAttachOptions) (0), 0, 0);
    gtk_entry_set_visibility (GTK_ENTRY (entry_password), FALSE);

    entry_name = gtk_entry_new ();
    gtk_widget_ref (entry_name);
    gtk_object_set_data_full (GTK_OBJECT (frm_login), "entry_name", entry_name,
                         (GtkDestroyNotify) gtk_widget_unref);
    gtk_widget_show (entry_name);
    gtk_table_attach (GTK_TABLE (table_login), entry_name, 1, 2, 0, 1,
                         (GtkAttachOptions) (GTK_EXPAND),
                         (GtkAttachOptions) (0), 0, 0);


    cmd_login = gtk_button_new_with_label ("Login");
    gtk_widget_ref (cmd_login);
    gtk_object_set_data_full (GTK_OBJECT (frm_login), "cmd_login", cmd_login,
                         (GtkDestroyNotify) gtk_widget_unref);
    gtk_widget_show (cmd_login);
    gtk_table_attach (GTK_TABLE (table_login), cmd_login, 0, 2, 2, 3,
                         (GtkAttachOptions) (0),
                         (GtkAttachOptions) (GTK_EXPAND), 0, 0);
    gtk_container_set_border_width (GTK_CONTAINER (cmd_login), 5);

    frame_change_password = gtk_frame_new ("Change Password");
    gtk_widget_ref (frame_change_password);
    gtk_object_set_data_full (GTK_OBJECT (frm_login), "frame_change_password",
    ➥frame_change_password,
                         (GtkDestroyNotify) gtk_widget_unref);
    gtk_widget_show (frame_change_password);
    gtk_box_pack_start (GTK_BOX (vbox1), frame_change_password, TRUE, TRUE, 0);
    gtk_container_set_border_width (GTK_CONTAINER (frame_change_password), 5);

    table3 = gtk_table_new (3, 2, FALSE);
    gtk_widget_ref (table3);
    gtk_object_set_data_full (GTK_OBJECT (frm_login), "table3", table3,
                         (GtkDestroyNotify) gtk_widget_unref);
    gtk_widget_show (table3);
    gtk_container_add (GTK_CONTAINER (frame_change_password), table3);

    lbl_new_password = gtk_label_new ("New Password:");
    gtk_widget_ref (lbl_new_password);
    gtk_object_set_data_full (GTK_OBJECT (frm_login), "lbl_new_password",
    ➥lbl_new_password,
                         (GtkDestroyNotify) gtk_widget_unref);
    gtk_widget_show (lbl_new_password);
    gtk_table_attach (GTK_TABLE (table3), lbl_new_password, 0, 1, 0, 1,
                         (GtkAttachOptions) (0),
                         (GtkAttachOptions) (0), 0, 0);
```

```
lbl_new_password_again = gtk_label_new ("New Password (Again):");
gtk_widget_ref (lbl_new_password_again);
gtk_object_set_data_full (GTK_OBJECT (frm_login), "lbl_new_password_again",
➥lbl_new_password_again,
                            (GtkDestroyNotify) gtk_widget_unref);
gtk_widget_show (lbl_new_password_again);
gtk_table_attach (GTK_TABLE (table3), lbl_new_password_again, 0, 1, 1, 2,
                  (GtkAttachOptions) (0),
                  (GtkAttachOptions) (0), 0, 0);

entry_new_password = gtk_entry_new ();
gtk_widget_ref (entry_new_password);
gtk_object_set_data_full (GTK_OBJECT (frm_login), "entry_new_password",
➥entry_new_password,
                            (GtkDestroyNotify) gtk_widget_unref);
gtk_widget_show (entry_new_password);
gtk_table_attach (GTK_TABLE (table3), entry_new_password, 1, 2, 0, 1,
                  (GtkAttachOptions) (GTK_EXPAND),
                  (GtkAttachOptions) (0), 0, 0);
gtk_entry_set_visibility (GTK_ENTRY (entry_new_password), FALSE);

entry_new_password_again = gtk_entry_new ();
gtk_widget_ref (entry_new_password_again);
gtk_object_set_data_full (GTK_OBJECT (frm_login), "entry_new_password_again",
➥entry_new_password_again,
                            (GtkDestroyNotify) gtk_widget_unref);
gtk_widget_show (entry_new_password_again);
gtk_table_attach (GTK_TABLE (table3), entry_new_password_again, 1, 2, 1, 2,
                  (GtkAttachOptions) (GTK_EXPAND),
                  (GtkAttachOptions) (0), 0, 0);
gtk_entry_set_visibility (GTK_ENTRY (entry_new_password_again), FALSE);

cmd_change_password = gtk_button_new_with_label ("Change Password");
gtk_widget_ref (cmd_change_password);
gtk_object_set_data_full (GTK_OBJECT (frm_login), "cmd_change_password",
➥cmd_change_password,
                            (GtkDestroyNotify) gtk_widget_unref);
gtk_widget_show (cmd_change_password);
gtk_table_attach (GTK_TABLE (table3), cmd_change_password, 0, 2, 2, 3,
                  (GtkAttachOptions) (0),
                  (GtkAttachOptions) (GTK_EXPAND), 0, 0);
gtk_container_set_border_width (GTK_CONTAINER (cmd_change_password), 5);

lbl_messages = gtk_label_new ("");
gtk_widget_ref (lbl_messages);
gtk_object_set_data_full (GTK_OBJECT (frm_login), "lbl_messages", lbl_messages,
                            (GtkDestroyNotify) gtk_widget_unref);
gtk_widget_show (lbl_messages);
gtk_box_pack_start (GTK_BOX (vbox1), lbl_messages, FALSE, FALSE, 0);
```

continues

Listing B.1 **Continued**

```
    gtk_signal_connect (GTK_OBJECT (frm_login), "delete_event",
                        GTK_SIGNAL_FUNC (on_frm_login_delete_event),
                        NULL);
    gtk_signal_connect (GTK_OBJECT (cmd_login), "clicked",
                        GTK_SIGNAL_FUNC (on_cmd_login_clicked),
                        NULL);
    gtk_signal_connect (GTK_OBJECT (cmd_change_password), "clicked",
                        GTK_SIGNAL_FUNC (on_cmd_change_password_clicked),
                        NULL);

  gtk_widget_grab_focus (entry_name);
  return frm_login;
}

GtkWidget*
create_frm_table_display (void)
{
  GtkWidget *frm_table_display;
  GtkWidget *vpaned_table_top;
  GtkWidget *hbox_header;
  GtkWidget *lbl_table_list;
  GtkWidget *cbo_tables;
  GtkWidget *combo_entry_table;
  GtkWidget *cmd_process;
  GtkWidget *vpaned_table_bottom;
  GtkWidget *scrolledwindow_table;
  GtkWidget *clist_table;
  GtkWidget *label1;
  GtkWidget *label2;
  GtkWidget *label3;
  GtkWidget *vbox_commissions;
  GtkWidget *hbox_footer;
  GtkWidget *cmd_refresh;
  GtkWidget *cmd_sort;
  GtkWidget *lbl_sort_by;
  GtkObject *spinbutton_column_adj;
  GtkWidget *spinbutton_column;
  GtkWidget *cbo_sort_type;
  GList *cbo_sort_type_items = NULL;
  GtkWidget *combo_entry3;
  GtkWidget *statusbar;

  frm_table_display = gtk_window_new (GTK_WINDOW_TOPLEVEL);
  gtk_object_set_data (GTK_OBJECT (frm_table_display), "frm_table_display",
  ↪frm_table_display);
  gtk_window_set_title (GTK_WINDOW (frm_table_display), "Commissions Database -
  ↪Table View");

  vpaned_table_top = gtk_vpaned_new ();
```

```
gtk_widget_ref (vpaned_table_top);
gtk_object_set_data_full (GTK_OBJECT (frm_table_display), "vpaned_table_top",
➥vpaned_table_top,
                        (GtkDestroyNotify) gtk_widget_unref);
gtk_widget_show (vpaned_table_top);
gtk_container_add (GTK_CONTAINER (frm_table_display), vpaned_table_top);
gtk_paned_set_gutter_size (GTK_PANED (vpaned_table_top), 10);

hbox_header = gtk_hbox_new (FALSE, 5);
gtk_widget_ref (hbox_header);
gtk_object_set_data_full (GTK_OBJECT (frm_table_display), "hbox_header",
➥hbox_header,
                        (GtkDestroyNotify) gtk_widget_unref);
gtk_widget_show (hbox_header);
gtk_container_add (GTK_CONTAINER (vpaned_table_top), hbox_header);
gtk_container_set_border_width (GTK_CONTAINER (hbox_header), 5);

lbl_table_list = gtk_label_new ("Table List: ");
gtk_widget_ref (lbl_table_list);
gtk_object_set_data_full (GTK_OBJECT (frm_table_display), "lbl_table_list",
➥lbl_table_list,
                        (GtkDestroyNotify) gtk_widget_unref);
gtk_widget_show (lbl_table_list);
gtk_box_pack_start (GTK_BOX (hbox_header), lbl_table_list, FALSE, FALSE, 0);

cbo_tables = gtk_combo_new ();
gtk_widget_ref (cbo_tables);
gtk_object_set_data_full (GTK_OBJECT (frm_table_display), "cbo_tables",
➥cbo_tables,
                        (GtkDestroyNotify) gtk_widget_unref);
gtk_widget_show (cbo_tables);
gtk_box_pack_start (GTK_BOX (hbox_header), cbo_tables, FALSE, FALSE, 0);
gtk_combo_set_value_in_list (GTK_COMBO (cbo_tables), TRUE, FALSE);

combo_entry_table = GTK_COMBO (cbo_tables)->entry;
gtk_widget_ref (combo_entry_table);
gtk_object_set_data_full (GTK_OBJECT (frm_table_display), "combo_entry_table",
➥combo_entry_table,
                        (GtkDestroyNotify) gtk_widget_unref);
gtk_widget_show (combo_entry_table);

cmd_process = gtk_button_new_with_label ("Process");
gtk_widget_ref (cmd_process);
gtk_object_set_data_full (GTK_OBJECT (frm_table_display), "cmd_process",
➥cmd_process,
                        (GtkDestroyNotify) gtk_widget_unref);
gtk_box_pack_start (GTK_BOX (hbox_header), cmd_process, FALSE, FALSE, 0);

vpaned_table_bottom = gtk_vpaned_new ();
gtk_widget_ref (vpaned_table_bottom);
```

continues

Listing B.1 **Continued**

```
gtk_object_set_data_full (GTK_OBJECT (frm_table_display), "vpaned_table_bottom",
➥vpaned_table_bottom,
                          (GtkDestroyNotify) gtk_widget_unref);
gtk_widget_show (vpaned_table_bottom);
gtk_container_add (GTK_CONTAINER (vpaned_table_top), vpaned_table_bottom);
gtk_paned_set_gutter_size (GTK_PANED (vpaned_table_bottom), 10);
gtk_paned_set_position (GTK_PANED (vpaned_table_bottom), 251);

scrolledwindow_table = gtk_scrolled_window_new (NULL, NULL);
gtk_widget_ref (scrolledwindow_table);
gtk_object_set_data_full (GTK_OBJECT (frm_table_display),
➥"scrolledwindow_table", scrolledwindow_table,
                          (GtkDestroyNotify) gtk_widget_unref);
gtk_widget_show (scrolledwindow_table);
gtk_container_add (GTK_CONTAINER (vpaned_table_bottom), scrolledwindow_table);

clist_table = gtk_clist_new (3);
gtk_widget_ref (clist_table);
gtk_object_set_data_full (GTK_OBJECT (frm_table_display), "clist_table",
➥clist_table,
                          (GtkDestroyNotify) gtk_widget_unref);
gtk_widget_show (clist_table);
gtk_container_add (GTK_CONTAINER (scrolledwindow_table), clist_table);
gtk_clist_set_column_width (GTK_CLIST (clist_table), 0, 80);
gtk_clist_set_column_width (GTK_CLIST (clist_table), 1, 80);
gtk_clist_set_column_width (GTK_CLIST (clist_table), 2, 80);
gtk_clist_column_titles_show (GTK_CLIST (clist_table));

label1 = gtk_label_new ("label1");
gtk_widget_ref (label1);
gtk_object_set_data_full (GTK_OBJECT (frm_table_display), "label1", label1,
                          (GtkDestroyNotify) gtk_widget_unref);
gtk_widget_show (label1);
gtk_clist_set_column_widget (GTK_CLIST (clist_table), 0, label1);

label2 = gtk_label_new ("label2");
gtk_widget_ref (label2);
gtk_object_set_data_full (GTK_OBJECT (frm_table_display), "label2", label2,
                          (GtkDestroyNotify) gtk_widget_unref);
gtk_widget_show (label2);
gtk_clist_set_column_widget (GTK_CLIST (clist_table), 1, label2);

label3 = gtk_label_new ("label3");
gtk_widget_ref (label3);
gtk_object_set_data_full (GTK_OBJECT (frm_table_display), "label3", label3,
                          (GtkDestroyNotify) gtk_widget_unref);
gtk_widget_show (label3);
gtk_clist_set_column_widget (GTK_CLIST (clist_table), 2, label3);
```

```
vbox_commissions = gtk_vbox_new (FALSE, 0);
gtk_widget_ref (vbox_commissions);
gtk_object_set_data_full (GTK_OBJECT (frm_table_display), "vbox_commissions",
➥vbox_commissions,
                          (GtkDestroyNotify) gtk_widget_unref);
gtk_widget_show (vbox_commissions);
gtk_container_add (GTK_CONTAINER (vpaned_table_bottom), vbox_commissions);

hbox_footer = gtk_hbox_new (FALSE, 5);
gtk_widget_ref (hbox_footer);
gtk_object_set_data_full (GTK_OBJECT (frm_table_display), "hbox_footer",
➥hbox_footer,
                          (GtkDestroyNotify) gtk_widget_unref);
gtk_widget_show (hbox_footer);
gtk_box_pack_start (GTK_BOX (vbox_commissions), hbox_footer, FALSE, FALSE, 0);
gtk_container_set_border_width (GTK_CONTAINER (hbox_footer), 5);

cmd_refresh = gtk_button_new_with_label ("Refresh");
gtk_widget_ref (cmd_refresh);
gtk_object_set_data_full (GTK_OBJECT (frm_table_display), "cmd_refresh",
➥cmd_refresh,
                          (GtkDestroyNotify) gtk_widget_unref);
gtk_widget_show (cmd_refresh);
gtk_box_pack_start (GTK_BOX (hbox_footer), cmd_refresh, FALSE, FALSE, 0);

cmd_sort = gtk_button_new_with_label ("Sort");
gtk_widget_ref (cmd_sort);
gtk_object_set_data_full (GTK_OBJECT (frm_table_display), "cmd_sort", cmd_sort,
                          (GtkDestroyNotify) gtk_widget_unref);
gtk_widget_show (cmd_sort);
gtk_box_pack_start (GTK_BOX (hbox_footer), cmd_sort, FALSE, FALSE, 0);

lbl_sort_by = gtk_label_new ("by Column: ");
gtk_widget_ref (lbl_sort_by);
gtk_object_set_data_full (GTK_OBJECT (frm_table_display), "lbl_sort_by",
➥lbl_sort_by,
                          (GtkDestroyNotify) gtk_widget_unref);
gtk_widget_show (lbl_sort_by);
gtk_box_pack_start (GTK_BOX (hbox_footer), lbl_sort_by, FALSE, FALSE, 0);

spinbutton_column_adj = gtk_adjustment_new (1, 0, 100, 1, 10, 10);
spinbutton_column = gtk_spin_button_new (GTK_ADJUSTMENT (spinbutton_column_adj),
➥1, 0);
gtk_widget_ref (spinbutton_column);
gtk_object_set_data_full (GTK_OBJECT (frm_table_display), "spinbutton_column",
➥spinbutton_column,
                          (GtkDestroyNotify) gtk_widget_unref);
gtk_widget_show (spinbutton_column);
gtk_box_pack_start (GTK_BOX (hbox_footer), spinbutton_column, TRUE, TRUE, 0);
```

continues

Listing B.1 **Continued**

```
cbo_sort_type = gtk_combo_new ();
gtk_widget_ref (cbo_sort_type);
gtk_object_set_data_full (GTK_OBJECT (frm_table_display), "cbo_sort_type",
➥cbo_sort_type,
                            (GtkDestroyNotify) gtk_widget_unref);
gtk_widget_show (cbo_sort_type);
gtk_box_pack_start (GTK_BOX (hbox_footer), cbo_sort_type, TRUE, TRUE, 0);
gtk_combo_set_value_in_list (GTK_COMBO (cbo_sort_type), TRUE, FALSE);
cbo_sort_type_items = g_list_append (cbo_sort_type_items, "Ascending");
cbo_sort_type_items = g_list_append (cbo_sort_type_items, "Descending");
gtk_combo_set_popdown_strings (GTK_COMBO (cbo_sort_type), cbo_sort_type_items);
g_list_free (cbo_sort_type_items);

combo_entry3 = GTK_COMBO (cbo_sort_type)->entry;
gtk_widget_ref (combo_entry3);
gtk_object_set_data_full (GTK_OBJECT (frm_table_display), "combo_entry3",
➥combo_entry3,
                            (GtkDestroyNotify) gtk_widget_unref);
gtk_widget_show (combo_entry3);
gtk_entry_set_text (GTK_ENTRY (combo_entry3), "Ascending");

statusbar = gtk_statusbar_new ();
gtk_widget_ref (statusbar);
gtk_object_set_data_full (GTK_OBJECT (frm_table_display), "statusbar",
➥statusbar,
                            (GtkDestroyNotify) gtk_widget_unref);
gtk_widget_show (statusbar);
gtk_box_pack_start (GTK_BOX (vbox_commissions), statusbar, FALSE, FALSE, 0);

gtk_signal_connect (GTK_OBJECT (frm_table_display), "size_request",
                    GTK_SIGNAL_FUNC (on_frm_table_display_size_request),
                    NULL);
gtk_signal_connect (GTK_OBJECT (frm_table_display), "state_changed",
                    GTK_SIGNAL_FUNC (on_frm_table_display_state_changed),
                    NULL);
gtk_signal_connect (GTK_OBJECT (frm_table_display), "delete_event",
                    GTK_SIGNAL_FUNC (on_frm_table_display_delete_event),
                    NULL);
gtk_signal_connect (GTK_OBJECT (combo_entry_table), "changed",
                    GTK_SIGNAL_FUNC (on_combo_entry_table_changed),
                    NULL);
gtk_signal_connect (GTK_OBJECT (combo_entry_table), "activate",
                    GTK_SIGNAL_FUNC (on_combo_entry_table_activate),
                    NULL);
gtk_signal_connect (GTK_OBJECT (cmd_process), "clicked",
                    GTK_SIGNAL_FUNC (on_cmd_process_clicked),
                    NULL);
gtk_signal_connect (GTK_OBJECT (cmd_refresh), "clicked",
                    GTK_SIGNAL_FUNC (on_cmd_refresh_clicked),
                    NULL);
```

```c
  gtk_signal_connect (GTK_OBJECT (cmd_sort), "clicked",
                      GTK_SIGNAL_FUNC (on_cmd_sort_clicked),
                      NULL);

  return frm_table_display;
}

GtkWidget*
create_frm_commissions (void)
{
  GtkWidget *frm_commissions;
  GtkWidget *vpaned_processing;
  GtkWidget *table4;
  GtkWidget *lbl_prep;
  GtkWidget *lbl_process;
  GtkWidget *lbl_output;
  GtkWidget *cmd_country_managers;
  GtkWidget *lbl_archive;
  GtkWidget *cmd_import;
  GtkWidget *cmd_customer;
  GtkWidget *cmd_archive;
  GtkWidget *cmd_worldwide;
  GtkWidget *cmd_country;
  GtkWidget *cmd_state;
  GtkWidget *cmd_zip;
  GtkWidget *cmd_people;
  GtkWidget *cmd_salespeople;
  GtkWidget *lbl_import;
  GtkWidget *lbl_customer;
  GtkWidget *lbl_worldwide;
  GtkWidget *lbl_country;
  GtkWidget *lbl_state;
  GtkWidget *lbl_zip;
  GtkWidget *lbl_people;
  GtkWidget *lbl_salespeople;
  GtkWidget *lbl_country_managers;
  GtkWidget *vbox_processing;
  GtkWidget *hbox_add_delete;
  GtkWidget *lbl_table;
  GtkWidget *cbo_table;
  GtkWidget *combo_entry4;
  GtkWidget *frame_add;
  GtkWidget *cmd_add;
  GtkWidget *frame_delete_group;
  GtkWidget *hbox_delete;
  GtkWidget *cmd_delete_row;
  GtkObject *spinbutton_delete_row_adj;
  GtkWidget *spinbutton_delete_row;
  GtkWidget *frame_update_group;
  GtkWidget *hbox_update;
  GtkWidget *cmd_update;
```

continues

Listing B.1 **Continued**

```
GtkWidget *lbl_line_number;
GtkObject *spinbutton_update_line_adj;
GtkWidget *spinbutton_update_line;
GtkWidget *lbl_column;
GtkWidget *entry_column_name;
GtkWidget *lbl_to;
GtkWidget *entry_new_value;
GtkWidget *statusbar_processing;

frm_commissions = gtk_window_new (GTK_WINDOW_TOPLEVEL);
gtk_object_set_data (GTK_OBJECT (frm_commissions), "frm_commissions",
➥frm_commissions);
gtk_window_set_title (GTK_WINDOW (frm_commissions), "Commissions Processing");

vpaned_processing = gtk_vpaned_new ();
gtk_widget_ref (vpaned_processing);
gtk_object_set_data_full (GTK_OBJECT (frm_commissions), "vpaned_processing",
➥vpaned_processing,
                          (GtkDestroyNotify) gtk_widget_unref);
gtk_widget_show (vpaned_processing);
gtk_container_add (GTK_CONTAINER (frm_commissions), vpaned_processing);
gtk_paned_set_gutter_size (GTK_PANED (vpaned_processing), 10);

table4 = gtk_table_new (10, 3, FALSE);
gtk_widget_ref (table4);
gtk_object_set_data_full (GTK_OBJECT (frm_commissions), "table4", table4,
                          (GtkDestroyNotify) gtk_widget_unref);
gtk_widget_show (table4);
gtk_container_add (GTK_CONTAINER (vpaned_processing), table4);
gtk_table_set_row_spacings (GTK_TABLE (table4), 5);
gtk_table_set_col_spacings (GTK_TABLE (table4), 5);

lbl_prep = gtk_label_new ("Prep");
gtk_widget_ref (lbl_prep);
gtk_object_set_data_full (GTK_OBJECT (frm_commissions), "lbl_prep", lbl_prep,
                          (GtkDestroyNotify) gtk_widget_unref);
gtk_widget_show (lbl_prep);
gtk_table_attach (GTK_TABLE (table4), lbl_prep, 0, 1, 0, 1,
                  (GtkAttachOptions) (0),
                  (GtkAttachOptions) (0), 0, 0);

lbl_process = gtk_label_new ("Process");
gtk_widget_ref (lbl_process);
gtk_object_set_data_full (GTK_OBJECT (frm_commissions), "lbl_process",
➥lbl_process,
                          (GtkDestroyNotify) gtk_widget_unref);
gtk_widget_show (lbl_process);
gtk_table_attach (GTK_TABLE (table4), lbl_process, 0, 1, 2, 3,
                  (GtkAttachOptions) (0),
                  (GtkAttachOptions) (0), 0, 0);
```

```
lbl_output = gtk_label_new ("Output");
gtk_widget_ref (lbl_output);
gtk_object_set_data_full (GTK_OBJECT (frm_commissions), "lbl_output",
➡lbl_output,
                          (GtkDestroyNotify) gtk_widget_unref);
gtk_widget_show (lbl_output);
gtk_table_attach (GTK_TABLE (table4), lbl_output, 0, 1, 8, 9,
                  (GtkAttachOptions) (0),
                  (GtkAttachOptions) (0), 0, 0);


cmd_country_managers = gtk_button_new_with_label ("Country Mgrs.");
gtk_widget_ref (cmd_country_managers);
gtk_object_set_data_full (GTK_OBJECT (frm_commissions), "cmd_country_managers",
➡cmd_country_managers,
                          (GtkDestroyNotify) gtk_widget_unref);
gtk_widget_show (cmd_country_managers);
gtk_table_attach (GTK_TABLE (table4), cmd_country_managers, 1, 2, 9, 10,
                  (GtkAttachOptions) (0),
                  (GtkAttachOptions) (0), 0, 0);


lbl_archive = gtk_label_new ("");
gtk_widget_ref (lbl_archive);
gtk_object_set_data_full (GTK_OBJECT (frm_commissions), "lbl_archive",
➡lbl_archive,
                          (GtkDestroyNotify) gtk_widget_unref);
gtk_widget_show (lbl_archive);
gtk_table_attach (GTK_TABLE (table4), lbl_archive, 2, 3, 0, 1,
                  (GtkAttachOptions) (0),
                  (GtkAttachOptions) (0), 0, 0);


cmd_import = gtk_button_new_with_label ("Import");
gtk_widget_ref (cmd_import);
gtk_object_set_data_full (GTK_OBJECT (frm_commissions), "cmd_import",
➡cmd_import,
                          (GtkDestroyNotify) gtk_widget_unref);
gtk_widget_show (cmd_import);
gtk_table_attach (GTK_TABLE (table4), cmd_import, 1, 2, 1, 2,
                  (GtkAttachOptions) (GTK_FILL),
                  (GtkAttachOptions) (0), 0, 0);


cmd_customer = gtk_button_new_with_label ("Customer");
gtk_widget_ref (cmd_customer);
gtk_object_set_data_full (GTK_OBJECT (frm_commissions), "cmd_customer",
➡cmd_customer,
                          (GtkDestroyNotify) gtk_widget_unref);
gtk_widget_show (cmd_customer);
gtk_table_attach (GTK_TABLE (table4), cmd_customer, 1, 2, 2, 3,
                  (GtkAttachOptions) (GTK_FILL),
                  (GtkAttachOptions) (0), 0, 0);
```

continues

Listing B.1 **Continued**

```
cmd_archive = gtk_button_new_with_label ("Archive");
gtk_widget_ref (cmd_archive);
gtk_object_set_data_full (GTK_OBJECT (frm_commissions), "cmd_archive",
➥cmd_archive,
                          (GtkDestroyNotify) gtk_widget_unref);
gtk_widget_show (cmd_archive);
gtk_table_attach (GTK_TABLE (table4), cmd_archive, 1, 2, 0, 1,
                  (GtkAttachOptions) (GTK_FILL),
                  (GtkAttachOptions) (0), 0, 0);

cmd_worldwide = gtk_button_new_with_label ("Worldwide");
gtk_widget_ref (cmd_worldwide);
gtk_object_set_data_full (GTK_OBJECT (frm_commissions), "cmd_worldwide",
➥cmd_worldwide,
                          (GtkDestroyNotify) gtk_widget_unref);
gtk_widget_show (cmd_worldwide);
gtk_table_attach (GTK_TABLE (table4), cmd_worldwide, 1, 2, 3, 4,
                  (GtkAttachOptions) (GTK_FILL),
                  (GtkAttachOptions) (0), 0, 0);

cmd_country = gtk_button_new_with_label ("Country");
gtk_widget_ref (cmd_country);
gtk_object_set_data_full (GTK_OBJECT (frm_commissions), "cmd_country",
➥cmd_country,
                          (GtkDestroyNotify) gtk_widget_unref);
gtk_widget_show (cmd_country);
gtk_table_attach (GTK_TABLE (table4), cmd_country, 1, 2, 4, 5,
                  (GtkAttachOptions) (GTK_FILL),
                  (GtkAttachOptions) (0), 0, 0);

cmd_state = gtk_button_new_with_label ("State");
gtk_widget_ref (cmd_state);
gtk_object_set_data_full (GTK_OBJECT (frm_commissions), "cmd_state", cmd_state,
                          (GtkDestroyNotify) gtk_widget_unref);
gtk_widget_show (cmd_state);
gtk_table_attach (GTK_TABLE (table4), cmd_state, 1, 2, 5, 6,
                  (GtkAttachOptions) (GTK_FILL),
                  (GtkAttachOptions) (0), 0, 0);

cmd_zip = gtk_button_new_with_label ("Zip");
gtk_widget_ref (cmd_zip);
gtk_object_set_data_full (GTK_OBJECT (frm_commissions), "cmd_zip", cmd_zip,
                          (GtkDestroyNotify) gtk_widget_unref);
gtk_widget_show (cmd_zip);
gtk_table_attach (GTK_TABLE (table4), cmd_zip, 1, 2, 6, 7,
                  (GtkAttachOptions) (GTK_FILL),
                  (GtkAttachOptions) (0), 0, 0);

cmd_people = gtk_button_new_with_label ("People");
gtk_widget_ref (cmd_people);
```

```
gtk_object_set_data_full (GTK_OBJECT (frm_commissions), "cmd_people",
➥cmd_people,
                             (GtkDestroyNotify) gtk_widget_unref);
gtk_widget_show (cmd_people);
gtk_table_attach (GTK_TABLE (table4), cmd_people, 1, 2, 7, 8,
                  (GtkAttachOptions) (GTK_FILL),
                  (GtkAttachOptions) (0), 0, 0);

cmd_salespeople = gtk_button_new_with_label ("Salespeople");
gtk_widget_ref (cmd_salespeople);
gtk_object_set_data_full (GTK_OBJECT (frm_commissions), "cmd_salespeople",
➥cmd_salespeople,
                             (GtkDestroyNotify) gtk_widget_unref);
gtk_widget_show (cmd_salespeople);
gtk_table_attach (GTK_TABLE (table4), cmd_salespeople, 1, 2, 8, 9,
                  (GtkAttachOptions) (GTK_FILL),
                  (GtkAttachOptions) (0), 0, 0);

lbl_import = gtk_label_new ("");
gtk_widget_ref (lbl_import);
gtk_object_set_data_full (GTK_OBJECT (frm_commissions), "lbl_import",
➥lbl_import,
                             (GtkDestroyNotify) gtk_widget_unref);
gtk_widget_show (lbl_import);
gtk_table_attach (GTK_TABLE (table4), lbl_import, 2, 3, 1, 2,
                  (GtkAttachOptions) (0),
                  (GtkAttachOptions) (0), 0, 0);

lbl_customer = gtk_label_new ("");
gtk_widget_ref (lbl_customer);
gtk_object_set_data_full (GTK_OBJECT (frm_commissions), "lbl_customer",
➥lbl_customer,
                             (GtkDestroyNotify) gtk_widget_unref);
gtk_widget_show (lbl_customer);
gtk_table_attach (GTK_TABLE (table4), lbl_customer, 2, 3, 2, 3,
                  (GtkAttachOptions) (0),
                  (GtkAttachOptions) (0), 0, 0);

lbl_worldwide = gtk_label_new ("");
gtk_widget_ref (lbl_worldwide);
gtk_object_set_data_full (GTK_OBJECT (frm_commissions), "lbl_worldwide",
➥lbl_worldwide,
                             (GtkDestroyNotify) gtk_widget_unref);
gtk_widget_show (lbl_worldwide);
gtk_table_attach (GTK_TABLE (table4), lbl_worldwide, 2, 3, 3, 4,
                  (GtkAttachOptions) (0),
                  (GtkAttachOptions) (0), 0, 0);

lbl_country = gtk_label_new ("");
gtk_widget_ref (lbl_country);
gtk_object_set_data_full (GTK_OBJECT (frm_commissions), "lbl_country",
➥lbl_country,
                             (GtkDestroyNotify) gtk_widget_unref);
```

continues

Listing B.1   **Continued**

```
gtk_widget_show (lbl_country);
gtk_table_attach (GTK_TABLE (table4), lbl_country, 2, 3, 4, 5,
                    (GtkAttachOptions) (0),
                    (GtkAttachOptions) (0), 0, 0);

lbl_state = gtk_label_new ("");
gtk_widget_ref (lbl_state);
gtk_object_set_data_full (GTK_OBJECT (frm_commissions), "lbl_state", lbl_state,
                    (GtkDestroyNotify) gtk_widget_unref);
gtk_widget_show (lbl_state);
gtk_table_attach (GTK_TABLE (table4), lbl_state, 2, 3, 5, 6,
                    (GtkAttachOptions) (0),
                    (GtkAttachOptions) (0), 0, 0);

lbl_zip = gtk_label_new ("");
gtk_widget_ref (lbl_zip);
gtk_object_set_data_full (GTK_OBJECT (frm_commissions), "lbl_zip", lbl_zip,
                    (GtkDestroyNotify) gtk_widget_unref);
gtk_widget_show (lbl_zip);
gtk_table_attach (GTK_TABLE (table4), lbl_zip, 2, 3, 6, 7,
                    (GtkAttachOptions) (0),
                    (GtkAttachOptions) (0), 0, 0);

lbl_people = gtk_label_new ("");
gtk_widget_ref (lbl_people);
gtk_object_set_data_full (GTK_OBJECT (frm_commissions), "lbl_people", lbl_people,
                    (GtkDestroyNotify) gtk_widget_unref);
gtk_widget_show (lbl_people);
gtk_table_attach (GTK_TABLE (table4), lbl_people, 2, 3, 7, 8,
                    (GtkAttachOptions) (0),
                    (GtkAttachOptions) (0), 0, 0);

lbl_salespeople = gtk_label_new ("");
gtk_widget_ref (lbl_salespeople);
gtk_object_set_data_full (GTK_OBJECT (frm_commissions), "lbl_salespeople",
➥lbl_salespeople,
                    (GtkDestroyNotify) gtk_widget_unref);
gtk_widget_show (lbl_salespeople);
gtk_table_attach (GTK_TABLE (table4), lbl_salespeople, 2, 3, 8, 9,
                    (GtkAttachOptions) (0),
                    (GtkAttachOptions) (0), 0, 0);

lbl_country_managers = gtk_label_new ("");
gtk_widget_ref (lbl_country_managers);
gtk_object_set_data_full (GTK_OBJECT (frm_commissions), "lbl_country_managers",
➥lbl_country_managers,
                    (GtkDestroyNotify) gtk_widget_unref);
gtk_widget_show (lbl_country_managers);
```

```
gtk_table_attach (GTK_TABLE (table4), lbl_country_managers, 2, 3, 9, 10,
                   (GtkAttachOptions) (0),
                   (GtkAttachOptions) (0), 0, 0);

vbox_processing = gtk_vbox_new (FALSE, 0);
gtk_widget_ref (vbox_processing);
gtk_object_set_data_full (GTK_OBJECT (frm_commissions), "vbox_processing",
➡vbox_processing,
                          (GtkDestroyNotify) gtk_widget_unref);
gtk_widget_show (vbox_processing);
gtk_container_add (GTK_CONTAINER (vpaned_processing), vbox_processing);

hbox_add_delete = gtk_hbox_new (FALSE, 5);
gtk_widget_ref (hbox_add_delete);
gtk_object_set_data_full (GTK_OBJECT (frm_commissions), "hbox_add_delete",
➡hbox_add_delete,
                          (GtkDestroyNotify) gtk_widget_unref);
gtk_widget_show (hbox_add_delete);
gtk_box_pack_start (GTK_BOX (vbox_processing), hbox_add_delete, TRUE, TRUE, 0);
gtk_container_set_border_width (GTK_CONTAINER (hbox_add_delete), 5);

lbl_table = gtk_label_new ("Table ");
gtk_widget_ref (lbl_table);
gtk_object_set_data_full (GTK_OBJECT (frm_commissions), "lbl_table", lbl_table,
                          (GtkDestroyNotify) gtk_widget_unref);
gtk_widget_show (lbl_table),
gtk_box_pack_start (GTK_BOX (hbox_add_delete), lbl_table, FALSE, FALSE, 0);

cbo_table = gtk_combo_new ();
gtk_widget_ref (cbo_table);
gtk_object_set_data_full (GTK_OBJECT (frm_commissions), "cbo_table", cbo_table,
                          (GtkDestroyNotify) gtk_widget_unref);
gtk_widget_show (cbo_table);
gtk_box_pack_start (GTK_BOX (hbox_add_delete), cbo_table, FALSE, FALSE, 0);
gtk_combo_set_value_in_list (GTK_COMBO (cbo_table), TRUE, FALSE);

combo_entry4 = GTK_COMBO (cbo_table)->entry;
gtk_widget_ref (combo_entry4);
gtk_object_set_data_full (GTK_OBJECT (frm_commissions), "combo_entry4",
➡combo_entry4,
                          (GtkDestroyNotify) gtk_widget_unref);
gtk_widget_show (combo_entry4);

frame_add = gtk_frame_new ("Add");
gtk_widget_ref (frame_add);
gtk_object_set_data_full (GTK_OBJECT (frm_commissions), "frame_add", frame_add,
                          (GtkDestroyNotify) gtk_widget_unref);
gtk_widget_show (frame_add);
gtk_box_pack_start (GTK_BOX (hbox_add_delete), frame_add, FALSE, FALSE, 0);
```

continues

Listing B.1 **Continued**

```
cmd_add = gtk_button_new_with_label ("Add Row");
gtk_widget_ref (cmd_add);
gtk_object_set_data_full (GTK_OBJECT (frm_commissions), "cmd_add", cmd_add,
                          (GtkDestroyNotify) gtk_widget_unref);
gtk_widget_show (cmd_add);
gtk_container_add (GTK_CONTAINER (frame_add), cmd_add);
gtk_container_set_border_width (GTK_CONTAINER (cmd_add), 5);

frame_delete_group = gtk_frame_new ("Delete");
gtk_widget_ref (frame_delete_group);
gtk_object_set_data_full (GTK_OBJECT (frm_commissions), "frame_delete_group",
➥frame_delete_group,
                          (GtkDestroyNotify) gtk_widget_unref);
gtk_widget_show (frame_delete_group);
gtk_box_pack_start (GTK_BOX (hbox_add_delete), frame_delete_group, TRUE, TRUE, 0);

hbox_delete = gtk_hbox_new (FALSE, 5);
gtk_widget_ref (hbox_delete);
gtk_object_set_data_full (GTK_OBJECT (frm_commissions), "hbox_delete",
➥hbox_delete,
                          (GtkDestroyNotify) gtk_widget_unref);
gtk_widget_show (hbox_delete);
gtk_container_add (GTK_CONTAINER (frame_delete_group), hbox_delete);
gtk_container_set_border_width (GTK_CONTAINER (hbox_delete), 5);

cmd_delete_row = gtk_button_new_with_label ("Delete Row");
gtk_widget_ref (cmd_delete_row);
gtk_object_set_data_full (GTK_OBJECT (frm_commissions), "cmd_delete_row",
➥cmd_delete_row,
                          (GtkDestroyNotify) gtk_widget_unref);
gtk_widget_show (cmd_delete_row);
gtk_box_pack_start (GTK_BOX (hbox_delete), cmd_delete_row, FALSE, FALSE, 0);

spinbutton_delete_row_adj = gtk_adjustment_new (1, 1, 2e+06, 1, 10, 10);
spinbutton_delete_row = gtk_spin_button_new (GTK_ADJUSTMENT
➥(spinbutton_delete_row_adj), 1, 0);
gtk_widget_ref (spinbutton_delete_row);
gtk_object_set_data_full (GTK_OBJECT (frm_commissions), "spinbutton_delete_row",
➥spinbutton_delete_row,
                          (GtkDestroyNotify) gtk_widget_unref);
gtk_widget_show (spinbutton_delete_row);
gtk_box_pack_start (GTK_BOX (hbox_delete), spinbutton_delete_row, TRUE, TRUE, 0);
gtk_spin_button_set_numeric (GTK_SPIN_BUTTON (spinbutton_delete_row), TRUE);

frame_update_group = gtk_frame_new ("Update");
gtk_widget_ref (frame_update_group);
gtk_object_set_data_full (GTK_OBJECT (frm_commissions), "frame_update_group",
➥frame_update_group,
                          (GtkDestroyNotify) gtk_widget_unref);
```

```
gtk_widget_show (frame_update_group);
gtk_box_pack_start (GTK_BOX (vbox_processing), frame_update_group, TRUE, TRUE, 0);
gtk_container_set_border_width (GTK_CONTAINER (frame_update_group), 5);

hbox_update = gtk_hbox_new (FALSE, 5);
gtk_widget_ref (hbox_update);
gtk_object_set_data_full (GTK_OBJECT (frm_commissions), "hbox_update",
➥hbox_update,
                          (GtkDestroyNotify) gtk_widget_unref);
gtk_widget_show (hbox_update);
gtk_container_add (GTK_CONTAINER (frame_update_group), hbox_update);
gtk_container_set_border_width (GTK_CONTAINER (hbox_update), 5);

cmd_update = gtk_button_new_with_label ("Update");
gtk_widget_ref (cmd_update);
gtk_object_set_data_full (GTK_OBJECT (frm_commissions), "cmd_update", cmd_update,
                          (GtkDestroyNotify) gtk_widget_unref);
gtk_widget_show (cmd_update);
gtk_box_pack_start (GTK_BOX (hbox_update), cmd_update, FALSE, FALSE, 0);

lbl_line_number = gtk_label_new ("Line Number");
gtk_widget_ref (lbl_line_number);
gtk_object_set_data_full (GTK_OBJECT (frm_commissions), "lbl_line_number",
➥lbl_line_number,
                          (GtkDestroyNotify) gtk_widget_unref);
gtk_widget_show (lbl_line_number);
gtk_box_pack_start (GTK_BOX (hbox_update), lbl_line_number, FALSE, FALSE, 0);

spinbutton_update_line_adj = gtk_adjustment_new (1, 1, 2e+06, 1, 10, 10);
spinbutton_update_line = gtk_spin_button_new (GTK_ADJUSTMENT
➥(spinbutton_update_line_adj), 1, 0);
gtk_widget_ref (spinbutton_update_line);
gtk_object_set_data_full (GTK_OBJECT (frm_commissions), "spinbutton_update_line",
➥spinbutton_update_line,
                          (GtkDestroyNotify) gtk_widget_unref);
gtk_widget_show (spinbutton_update_line);
gtk_box_pack_start (GTK_BOX (hbox_update), spinbutton_update_line, TRUE, TRUE, 0);
gtk_spin_button_set_numeric (GTK_SPIN_BUTTON (spinbutton_update_line), TRUE);

lbl_column = gtk_label_new ("Column");
gtk_widget_ref (lbl_column);
gtk_object_set_data_full (GTK_OBJECT (frm_commissions), "lbl_column", lbl_column,
                          (GtkDestroyNotify) gtk_widget_unref);
gtk_widget_show (lbl_column);
gtk_box_pack_start (GTK_BOX (hbox_update), lbl_column, FALSE, FALSE, 0);

entry_column_name = gtk_entry_new ();
gtk_widget_ref (entry_column_name);
gtk_object_set_data_full (GTK_OBJECT (frm_commissions), "entry_column_name",
➥entry_column_name,
                          (GtkDestroyNotify) gtk_widget_unref);
```

continues

Listing B.1 **Continued**

```
gtk_widget_show (entry_column_name);
gtk_box_pack_start (GTK_BOX (hbox_update), entry_column_name, TRUE, TRUE, 0);

lbl_to = gtk_label_new ("to");
gtk_widget_ref (lbl_to);
gtk_object_set_data_full (GTK_OBJECT (frm_commissions), "lbl_to", lbl_to,
                          (GtkDestroyNotify) gtk_widget_unref);
gtk_widget_show (lbl_to);
gtk_box_pack_start (GTK_BOX (hbox_update), lbl_to, FALSE, FALSE, 0);

entry_new_value = gtk_entry_new ();
gtk_widget_ref (entry_new_value);
gtk_object_set_data_full (GTK_OBJECT (frm_commissions), "entry_new_value",
➥entry_new_value,
                          (GtkDestroyNotify) gtk_widget_unref);
gtk_widget_show (entry_new_value);
gtk_box_pack_start (GTK_BOX (hbox_update), entry_new_value, TRUE, TRUE, 0);

statusbar_processing = gtk_statusbar_new ();
gtk_widget_ref (statusbar_processing);
gtk_object_set_data_full (GTK_OBJECT (frm_commissions), "statusbar_processing",
➥statusbar_processing,
                          (GtkDestroyNotify) gtk_widget_unref);
gtk_widget_show (statusbar_processing);
gtk_box_pack_start (GTK_BOX (vbox_processing), statusbar_processing, FALSE,
➥FALSE, 0);

gtk_signal_connect (GTK_OBJECT (frm_commissions), "delete_event",
                    GTK_SIGNAL_FUNC (on_frm_commissions_delete_event),
                    NULL);
gtk_signal_connect (GTK_OBJECT (cmd_country_managers), "clicked",
                    GTK_SIGNAL_FUNC (on_cmd_country_managers_clicked),
                    NULL);
gtk_signal_connect (GTK_OBJECT (cmd_import), "clicked",
                    GTK_SIGNAL_FUNC (on_cmd_import_clicked),
                    NULL);
gtk_signal_connect (GTK_OBJECT (cmd_customer), "clicked",
                    GTK_SIGNAL_FUNC (on_cmd_customer_clicked),
                    NULL);
gtk_signal_connect (GTK_OBJECT (cmd_archive), "clicked",
                    GTK_SIGNAL_FUNC (on_cmd_archive_clicked),
                    NULL);
gtk_signal_connect (GTK_OBJECT (cmd_worldwide), "clicked",
                    GTK_SIGNAL_FUNC (on_cmd_worldwide_clicked),
                    NULL);
gtk_signal_connect (GTK_OBJECT (cmd_country), "clicked",
                    GTK_SIGNAL_FUNC (on_cmd_country_clicked),
                    NULL);
gtk_signal_connect (GTK_OBJECT (cmd_state), "clicked",
                    GTK_SIGNAL_FUNC (on_cmd_state_clicked),
                    NULL);
```

```
    gtk_signal_connect (GTK_OBJECT (cmd_zip), "clicked",
                        GTK_SIGNAL_FUNC (on_cmd_zip_clicked),
                        NULL);
    gtk_signal_connect (GTK_OBJECT (cmd_people), "clicked",
                        GTK_SIGNAL_FUNC (on_cmd_people_clicked),
                        NULL);
    gtk_signal_connect (GTK_OBJECT (cmd_salespeople), "clicked",
                        GTK_SIGNAL_FUNC (on_cmd_salespeople_clicked),
                        NULL);
    gtk_signal_connect (GTK_OBJECT (cmd_add), "clicked",
                        GTK_SIGNAL_FUNC (on_cmd_add_clicked),
                        NULL);
    gtk_signal_connect (GTK_OBJECT (cmd_delete_row), "clicked",
                        GTK_SIGNAL_FUNC (on_cmd_delete_row_clicked),
                        NULL);
    gtk_signal_connect (GTK_OBJECT (cmd_update), "clicked",
                        GTK_SIGNAL_FUNC (on_cmd_update_clicked),
                        NULL);

    return frm_commissions;
}
```

sesi.glade

Listing B.2 is the XML file that Glade uses to save the user interface you create while using Glade.

Listing B.2 *ww_comm.glade:* **The Glade Project File for the Worldwide Commissions Application**

```
<?xml version="1.0"?>
<GTK-Interface>

<project>
  <name>ww_comm</name>
  <program_name>ww_comm</program_name>
  <directory></directory>
  <source_directory>src</source_directory>
  <pixmaps_directory>pixmaps</pixmaps_directory>
  <language>C</language>
  <gnome_support>False</gnome_support>
  <gettext_support>False</gettext_support>
  <use_widget_names>False</use_widget_names>
  <output_main_file>True</output_main_file>
  <output_support_files>True</output_support_files>
  <output_build_files>True</output_build_files>
  <backup_source_files>True</backup_source_files>
  <main_source_file>interface.c</main_source_file>
```

continues

Listing B.2 **Continued**

```
  <main_header_file>interface.h</main_header_file>
  <handler_source_file>callbacks.c</handler_source_file>
  <handler_header_file>callbacks.h</handler_header_file>
  <support_source_file>support.c</support_source_file>
  <support_header_file>support.h</support_header_file>
  <translatable_strings_file></translatable_strings_file>
</project>

<widget>
  <class>GtkWindow</class>
  <name>frm_login</name>
  <signal>
    <name>delete_event</name>
    <handler>on_frm_login_delete_event</handler>
    <last_modification_time>Sun, 10 Dec 2000 17:45:47 GMT</last_modification_time>
  </signal>
  <title>Commissions Login</title>
  <type>GTK_WINDOW_TOPLEVEL</type>
  <position>GTK_WIN_POS_NONE</position>
  <modal>False</modal>
  <allow_shrink>False</allow_shrink>
  <allow_grow>True</allow_grow>
  <auto_shrink>False</auto_shrink>

  <widget>
    <class>GtkVBox</class>
    <name>vbox1</name>
    <homogeneous>False</homogeneous>
    <spacing>0</spacing>

    <widget>
      <class>GtkLabel</class>
      <name>lbl_title</name>
      <label>Worldwide Commissions System</label>
      <justify>GTK_JUSTIFY_CENTER</justify>
      <wrap>False</wrap>
      <xalign>0.5</xalign>
      <yalign>0.5</yalign>
      <xpad>0</xpad>
      <ypad>5</ypad>
      <child>
      <padding>0</padding>
      <expand>False</expand>
      <fill>False</fill>
      </child>
    </widget>
```

```
<widget>
  <class>GtkFrame</class>
  <name>frame_login</name>
  <border_width>5</border_width>
  <label>Login</label>
  <label_xalign>0</label_xalign>
  <shadow_type>GTK_SHADOW_ETCHED_IN</shadow_type>
  <child>
  <padding>0</padding>
  <expand>True</expand>
  <fill>True</fill>
  </child>

  <widget>
  <class>GtkTable</class>
  <name>table_login</name>
  <rows>3</rows>
  <columns>2</columns>
  <homogeneous>False</homogeneous>
  <row_spacing>0</row_spacing>
  <column_spacing>0</column_spacing>

  <widget>
    <class>GtkLabel</class>
    <name>lbl_name</name>
    <label>Name:</label>
    <justify>GTK_JUSTIFY_CENTER</justify>
    <wrap>False</wrap>
    <xalign>0.5</xalign>
    <yalign>0.5</yalign>
    <xpad>0</xpad>
    <ypad>0</ypad>
    <child>
      <left_attach>0</left_attach>
      <right_attach>1</right_attach>
      <top_attach>0</top_attach>
      <bottom_attach>1</bottom_attach>
      <xpad>0</xpad>
      <ypad>0</ypad>
      <xexpand>False</xexpand>
      <yexpand>False</yexpand>
      <xshrink>False</xshrink>
      <yshrink>False</yshrink>
      <xfill>False</xfill>
      <yfill>False</yfill>
    </child>
  </widget>
```

continues

Listing B.2 **Continued**

```
<widget>
  <class>GtkLabel</class>
  <name>lbl_password</name>
  <label>Password:</label>
  <justify>GTK_JUSTIFY_CENTER</justify>
  <wrap>False</wrap>
  <xalign>0.5</xalign>
  <yalign>0.5</yalign>
  <xpad>0</xpad>
  <ypad>0</ypad>
  <child>
    <left_attach>0</left_attach>
    <right_attach>1</right_attach>
    <top_attach>1</top_attach>
    <bottom_attach>2</bottom_attach>
    <xpad>0</xpad>
    <ypad>0</ypad>
    <xexpand>False</xexpand>
    <yexpand>False</yexpand>
    <xshrink>False</xshrink>
    <yshrink>False</yshrink>
    <xfill>False</xfill>
    <yfill>False</yfill>
  </child>
</widget>

<widget>
  <class>GtkEntry</class>
  <name>entry_password</name>
  <can_focus>True</can_focus>
  <editable>True</editable>
  <text_visible>False</text_visible>
  <text_max_length>0</text_max_length>
  <text></text>
  <child>
    <left_attach>1</left_attach>
    <right_attach>2</right_attach>
    <top_attach>1</top_attach>
    <bottom_attach>2</bottom_attach>
    <xpad>0</xpad>
    <ypad>0</ypad>
    <xexpand>True</xexpand>
    <yexpand>False</yexpand>
    <xshrink>False</xshrink>
    <yshrink>False</yshrink>
    <xfill>False</xfill>
    <yfill>False</yfill>
  </child>
</widget>
```

```
<widget>
  <class>GtkEntry</class>
  <name>entry_name</name>
  <can_focus>True</can_focus>
  <has_focus>True</has_focus>
  <editable>True</editable>
  <text_visible>True</text_visible>
  <text_max_length>0</text_max_length>
  <text></text>
  <child>
    <left_attach>1</left_attach>
    <right_attach>2</right_attach>
    <top_attach>0</top_attach>
    <bottom_attach>1</bottom_attach>
    <xpad>0</xpad>
    <ypad>0</ypad>
    <xexpand>True</xexpand>
    <yexpand>False</yexpand>
    <xshrink>False</xshrink>
    <yshrink>False</yshrink>
    <xfill>False</xfill>
    <yfill>False</yfill>
  </child>
</widget>

<widget>
  <class>GtkButton</class>
  <name>cmd_login</name>
  <border_width>5</border_width>
  <can_focus>True</can_focus>
  <signal>
    <name>clicked</name>
    <handler>on_cmd_login_clicked</handler>
    <last_modification_time>Sun, 10 Dec 2000 17:45:17
    ➥GMT</last_modification_time>
  </signal>
  <label>Login</label>
  <child>
    <left_attach>0</left_attach>
    <right_attach>2</right_attach>
    <top_attach>2</top_attach>
    <bottom_attach>3</bottom_attach>
    <xpad>0</xpad>
    <ypad>0</ypad>
    <xexpand>False</xexpand>
    <yexpand>True</yexpand>
    <xshrink>False</xshrink>
    <yshrink>False</yshrink>
    <xfill>False</xfill>
    <yfill>False</yfill>
```

continues

Listing B.2 **Continued**

```
      </child>
    </widget>
    </widget>
  </widget>

  <widget>
    <class>GtkFrame</class>
    <name>frame_change_password</name>
    <border_width>5</border_width>
    <label>Change Password</label>
    <label_xalign>0</label_xalign>
    <shadow_type>GTK_SHADOW_ETCHED_IN</shadow_type>
    <child>
    <padding>0</padding>
    <expand>True</expand>
    <fill>True</fill>
    </child>

    <widget>
    <class>GtkTable</class>
    <name>table3</name>
    <rows>3</rows>
    <columns>2</columns>
    <homogeneous>False</homogeneous>
    <row_spacing>0</row_spacing>
    <column_spacing>0</column_spacing>

    <widget>
      <class>GtkLabel</class>
      <name>lbl_new_password</name>
      <label>New Password:</label>
      <justify>GTK_JUSTIFY_CENTER</justify>
      <wrap>False</wrap>
      <xalign>0.5</xalign>
      <yalign>0.5</yalign>
      <xpad>0</xpad>
      <ypad>0</ypad>
      <child>
        <left_attach>0</left_attach>
        <right_attach>1</right_attach>
        <top_attach>0</top_attach>
        <bottom_attach>1</bottom_attach>
        <xpad>0</xpad>
        <ypad>0</ypad>
        <xexpand>False</xexpand>
        <yexpand>False</yexpand>
        <xshrink>False</xshrink>
        <yshrink>False</yshrink>
        <xfill>False</xfill>
```

```
      <yfill>False</yfill>
    </child>
</widget>

<widget>
  <class>GtkLabel</class>
  <name>lbl_new_password_again</name>
  <label>New Password (Again):</label>
  <justify>GTK_JUSTIFY_CENTER</justify>
  <wrap>False</wrap>
  <xalign>0.5</xalign>
  <yalign>0.5</yalign>
  <xpad>0</xpad>
  <ypad>0</ypad>
  <child>
    <left_attach>0</left_attach>
    <right_attach>1</right_attach>
    <top_attach>1</top_attach>
    <bottom_attach>2</bottom_attach>
    <xpad>0</xpad>
    <ypad>0</ypad>
    <xexpand>False</xexpand>
    <yexpand>False</yexpand>
    <xshrink>False</xshrink>
    <yshrink>False</yshrink>
    <xfill>False</xfill>
    <yfill>False</yfill>
  </child>
</widget>

<widget>
  <class>GtkEntry</class>
  <name>entry_new_password</name>
  <can_focus>True</can_focus>
  <editable>True</editable>
  <text_visible>False</text_visible>
  <text_max_length>0</text_max_length>
  <text></text>
  <child>
    <left_attach>1</left_attach>
    <right_attach>2</right_attach>
    <top_attach>0</top_attach>
    <bottom_attach>1</bottom_attach>
    <xpad>0</xpad>
    <ypad>0</ypad>
    <xexpand>True</xexpand>
    <yexpand>False</yexpand>
    <xshrink>False</xshrink>
    <yshrink>False</yshrink>
    <xfill>False</xfill>
    <yfill>False</yfill>
```

continues

Listing B.2 **Continued**

```
    </child>
  </widget>

  <widget>
    <class>GtkEntry</class>
    <name>entry_new_password_again</name>
    <can_focus>True</can_focus>
    <editable>True</editable>
    <text_visible>False</text_visible>
    <text_max_length>0</text_max_length>
    <text></text>
    <child>
      <left_attach>1</left_attach>
      <right_attach>2</right_attach>
      <top_attach>1</top_attach>
      <bottom_attach>2</bottom_attach>
      <xpad>0</xpad>
      <ypad>0</ypad>
      <xexpand>True</xexpand>
      <yexpand>False</yexpand>
      <xshrink>False</xshrink>
      <yshrink>False</yshrink>
      <xfill>False</xfill>
      <yfill>False</yfill>
    </child>
  </widget>

  <widget>
    <class>GtkButton</class>
    <name>cmd_change_password</name>
    <border_width>5</border_width>
    <can_focus>True</can_focus>
    <signal>
      <name>clicked</name>
      <handler>on_cmd_change_password_clicked</handler>
      <last_modification_time>Sun, 10 Dec 2000 17:45:25
      ➥GMT</last_modification_time>
    </signal>
    <label>Change Password</label>
    <child>
      <left_attach>0</left_attach>
      <right_attach>2</right_attach>
      <top_attach>2</top_attach>
      <bottom_attach>3</bottom_attach>
      <xpad>0</xpad>
      <ypad>0</ypad>
      <xexpand>False</xexpand>
      <yexpand>True</yexpand>
      <xshrink>False</xshrink>
```

```
          <yshrink>False</yshrink>
          <xfill>False</xfill>
          <yfill>False</yfill>
        </child>
      </widget>
      </widget>
    </widget>

    <widget>
      <class>GtkLabel</class>
      <name>lbl_messages</name>
      <label></label>
      <justify>GTK_JUSTIFY_CENTER</justify>
      <wrap>False</wrap>
      <xalign>0.5</xalign>
      <yalign>0.5</yalign>
      <xpad>0</xpad>
      <ypad>0</ypad>
      <child>
      <padding>0</padding>
      <expand>False</expand>
      <fill>False</fill>
      </child>
    </widget>
  </widget>
</widget>

<widget>
  <class>GtkWindow</class>
  <name>frm_table_display</name>
  <signal>
    <name>size_request</name>
    <handler>on_frm_table_display_size_request</handler>
    <last_modification_time>Mon, 11 Dec 2000 12:21:31 GMT</last_modification_time>
  </signal>
  <signal>
    <name>state_changed</name>
    <handler>on_frm_table_display_state_changed</handler>
    <last_modification_time>Mon, 11 Dec 2000 12:21:43 GMT</last_modification_time>
  </signal>
  <signal>
    <name>delete_event</name>
    <handler>on_frm_table_display_delete_event</handler>
    <last_modification_time>Mon, 11 Dec 2000 15:00:24 GMT</last_modification_time>
  </signal>
  <title>Commissions Database - Table View</title>
  <type>GTK_WINDOW_TOPLEVEL</type>
  <position>GTK_WIN_POS_NONE</position>
  <modal>False</modal>
  <allow_shrink>False</allow_shrink>
  <allow_grow>True</allow_grow>
  <auto_shrink>False</auto_shrink>
```

continues

Listing B.2 **Continued**

```
<widget>
  <class>GtkVPaned</class>
  <name>vpaned_table_top</name>
  <handle_size>10</handle_size>
  <gutter_size>10</gutter_size>

  <widget>
    <class>GtkHBox</class>
    <name>hbox_header</name>
    <border_width>5</border_width>
    <homogeneous>False</homogeneous>
    <spacing>5</spacing>
    <child>
    <shrink>True</shrink>
    <resize>False</resize>
    </child>

    <widget>
    <class>GtkLabel</class>
    <name>lbl_table_list</name>
    <label>Table List: </label>
    <justify>GTK_JUSTIFY_CENTER</justify>
    <wrap>False</wrap>
    <xalign>0.5</xalign>
    <yalign>0.5</yalign>
    <xpad>0</xpad>
    <ypad>0</ypad>
    <child>
      <padding>0</padding>
      <expand>False</expand>
      <fill>False</fill>
    </child>
    </widget>

    <widget>
    <class>GtkCombo</class>
    <name>cbo_tables</name>
    <value_in_list>True</value_in_list>
    <ok_if_empty>False</ok_if_empty>
    <case_sensitive>False</case_sensitive>
    <use_arrows>True</use_arrows>
    <use_arrows_always>False</use_arrows_always>
    <items></items>
    <child>
      <padding>0</padding>
      <expand>False</expand>
      <fill>False</fill>
    </child>
```

```
  <widget>
    <class>GtkEntry</class>
    <child_name>GtkCombo:entry</child_name>
    <name>combo-entry_table</name>
    <can_focus>True</can_focus>
    <signal>
      <name>changed</name>
      <handler>on_combo-entry_table_changed</handler>
      <last_modification_time>Mon, 11 Dec 2000 12:18:39
      ↪GMT</last_modification_time>
    </signal>
    <signal>
      <name>activate</name>
      <handler>on_combo-entry_table_activate</handler>
      <last_modification_time>Mon, 11 Dec 2000 12:18:43
      ↪GMT</last_modification_time>
    </signal>
    <editable>True</editable>
    <text_visible>True</text_visible>
    <text_max_length>0</text_max_length>
    <text></text>
  </widget>
  </widget>

  <widget>
  <class>GtkButton</class>
  <name>cmd_process</name>
  <visible>False</visible>
  <can_focus>True</can_focus>
  <signal>
    <name>clicked</name>
    <handler>on_cmd_process_clicked</handler>
    <last_modification_time>Mon, 11 Dec 2000 12:19:36
    ↪GMT</last_modification_time>
  </signal>
  <label>Process</label>
  <child>
    <padding>0</padding>
    <expand>False</expand>
    <fill>False</fill>
  </child>
  </widget>
</widget>

<widget>
  <class>GtkVPaned</class>
  <name>vpaned_table_bottom</name>
  <handle_size>10</handle_size>
  <gutter_size>10</gutter_size>
  <position>251</position>
```

continues

Listing B.2 **Continued**

```
<child>
<shrink>True</shrink>
<resize>True</resize>
</child>

<widget>
<class>GtkScrolledWindow</class>
<name>scrolledwindow_table</name>
<hscrollbar_policy>GTK_POLICY_ALWAYS</hscrollbar_policy>
<vscrollbar_policy>GTK_POLICY_ALWAYS</vscrollbar_policy>
<hupdate_policy>GTK_UPDATE_CONTINUOUS</hupdate_policy>
<vupdate_policy>GTK_UPDATE_CONTINUOUS</vupdate_policy>
<child>
  <shrink>True</shrink>
  <resize>False</resize>
</child>

<widget>
  <class>GtkCList</class>
  <name>clist_table</name>
  <can_focus>True</can_focus>
  <columns>3</columns>
  <column_widths>80,80,80</column_widths>
  <selection_mode>GTK_SELECTION_SINGLE</selection_mode>
  <show_titles>True</show_titles>
  <shadow_type>GTK_SHADOW_IN</shadow_type>

  <widget>
    <class>GtkLabel</class>
    <child_name>CList:title</child_name>
    <name>label1</name>
    <label>label1</label>
    <justify>GTK_JUSTIFY_CENTER</justify>
    <wrap>False</wrap>
    <xalign>0.5</xalign>
    <yalign>0.5</yalign>
    <xpad>0</xpad>
    <ypad>0</ypad>
  </widget>

  <widget>
    <class>GtkLabel</class>
    <child_name>CList:title</child_name>
    <name>label2</name>
    <label>label2</label>
    <justify>GTK_JUSTIFY_CENTER</justify>
    <wrap>False</wrap>
    <xalign>0.5</xalign>
    <yalign>0.5</yalign>
```

```
      <xpad>0</xpad>
      <ypad>0</ypad>
    </widget>

  <widget>
    <class>GtkLabel</class>
    <child_name>CList:title</child_name>
    <name>label3</name>
    <label>label3</label>
    <justify>GTK_JUSTIFY_CENTER</justify>
    <wrap>False</wrap>
    <xalign>0.5</xalign>
    <yalign>0.5</yalign>
    <xpad>0</xpad>
    <ypad>0</ypad>
  </widget>
</widget>
</widget>

<widget>
<class>GtkVBox</class>
<name>vbox_commissions</name>
<homogeneous>False</homogeneous>
<spacing>0</spacing>
<child>
  <shrink>False</shrink>
  <resize>False</resize>
</child>

<widget>
  <class>GtkHBox</class>
  <name>hbox_footer</name>
  <border_width>5</border_width>
  <homogeneous>False</homogeneous>
  <spacing>5</spacing>
  <child>
    <padding>0</padding>
    <expand>False</expand>
    <fill>False</fill>
  </child>

  <widget>
    <class>GtkButton</class>
    <name>cmd_refresh</name>
    <can_focus>True</can_focus>
    <signal>
      <name>clicked</name>
      <handler>on_cmd_refresh_clicked</handler>
      <last_modification_time>Mon, 11 Dec 2000 12:19:32
      ➥GMT</last_modification_time>
    </signal>
```

continues

Listing B.2 **Continued**

```
        <label>Refresh</label>
        <child>
          <padding>0</padding>
          <expand>False</expand>
          <fill>False</fill>
        </child>
      </widget>

      <widget>
        <class>GtkButton</class>
        <name>cmd_sort</name>
        <can_focus>True</can_focus>
        <signal>
          <name>clicked</name>
          <handler>on_cmd_sort_clicked</handler>
          <last_modification_time>Mon, 11 Dec 2000 12:19:48
          ⇒GMT</last_modification_time>
        </signal>
        <label>Sort</label>
        <child>
          <padding>0</padding>
          <expand>False</expand>
          <fill>False</fill>
        </child>
      </widget>

      <widget>
        <class>GtkLabel</class>
        <name>lbl_sort_by</name>
        <label>by Column: </label>
        <justify>GTK_JUSTIFY_CENTER</justify>
        <wrap>False</wrap>
        <xalign>0.5</xalign>
        <yalign>0.5</yalign>
        <xpad>0</xpad>
        <ypad>0</ypad>
        <child>
          <padding>0</padding>
          <expand>False</expand>
          <fill>False</fill>
        </child>
      </widget>

      <widget>
        <class>GtkSpinButton</class>
        <name>spinbutton_column</name>
        <can_focus>True</can_focus>
        <climb_rate>1</climb_rate>
        <digits>0</digits>
```

```
          <numeric>False</numeric>
          <update_policy>GTK_UPDATE_ALWAYS</update_policy>
          <snap>False</snap>
          <wrap>False</wrap>
          <value>1</value>
          <lower>0</lower>
          <upper>100</upper>
          <step>1</step>
          <page>10</page>
          <page_size>10</page_size>
          <child>
            <padding>0</padding>
            <expand>True</expand>
            <fill>True</fill>
          </child>
        </widget>

        <widget>
          <class>GtkCombo</class>
          <name>cbo_sort_type</name>
          <value_in_list>True</value_in_list>
          <ok_if_empty>False</ok_if_empty>
          <case_sensitive>False</case_sensitive>
          <use_arrows>True</use_arrows>
          <use_arrows_always>False</use arrows always>
          <items>Ascending
Descending
</items>
          <child>
            <padding>0</padding>
            <expand>True</expand>
            <fill>True</fill>
          </child>

          <widget>
            <class>GtkEntry</class>
            <child_name>GtkCombo:entry</child_name>
            <name>combo-entry3</name>
            <can_focus>True</can_focus>
            <editable>True</editable>
            <text_visible>True</text_visible>
            <text_max_length>0</text_max_length>
            <text>Ascending</text>
          </widget>
        </widget>
      </widget>

      <widget>
        <class>GtkStatusbar</class>
        <name>statusbar</name>
        <child>
```

continues

Listing B.2 **Continued**

```
            <padding>0</padding>
            <expand>False</expand>
            <fill>False</fill>
          </child>
        </widget>
        </widget>
      </widget>
    </widget>
</widget>

<widget>
  <class>GtkWindow</class>
  <name>frm_commissions</name>
  <signal>
    <name>delete_event</name>
    <handler>on_frm_commissions_delete_event</handler>
    <last_modification_time>Mon, 11 Dec 2000 15:00:35 GMT</last_modification_time>
  </signal>
  <title>Commissions Processing</title>
  <type>GTK_WINDOW_TOPLEVEL</type>
  <position>GTK_WIN_POS_NONE</position>
  <modal>False</modal>
  <allow_shrink>False</allow_shrink>
  <allow_grow>True</allow_grow>
  <auto_shrink>False</auto_shrink>

  <widget>
    <class>GtkVPaned</class>
    <name>vpaned_processing</name>
    <handle_size>10</handle_size>
    <gutter_size>10</gutter_size>

    <widget>
      <class>GtkTable</class>
      <name>table4</name>
      <rows>10</rows>
      <columns>3</columns>
      <homogeneous>False</homogeneous>
      <row_spacing>5</row_spacing>
      <column_spacing>5</column_spacing>
      <child>
      <shrink>True</shrink>
      <resize>False</resize>
      </child>

      <widget>
      <class>GtkLabel</class>
      <name>lbl_prep</name>
      <label>Prep</label>
```

```
<justify>GTK_JUSTIFY_CENTER</justify>
<wrap>False</wrap>
<xalign>0.5</xalign>
<yalign>0.5</yalign>
<xpad>0</xpad>
<ypad>0</ypad>
<child>
  <left_attach>0</left_attach>
  <right_attach>1</right_attach>
  <top_attach>0</top_attach>
  <bottom_attach>1</bottom_attach>
  <xpad>0</xpad>
  <ypad>0</ypad>
  <xexpand>False</xexpand>
  <yexpand>False</yexpand>
  <xshrink>False</xshrink>
  <yshrink>False</yshrink>
  <xfill>False</xfill>
  <yfill>False</yfill>
</child>
</widget>

<widget>
<class>GtkLabel</class>
<name>lbl_process</name>
<label>Process</label>
<justify>GTK_JUSTIFY_CENTER</justify>
<wrap>False</wrap>
<xalign>0.5</xalign>
<yalign>0.5</yalign>
<xpad>0</xpad>
<ypad>0</ypad>
<child>
  <left_attach>0</left_attach>
  <right_attach>1</right_attach>
  <top_attach>2</top_attach>
  <bottom_attach>3</bottom_attach>
  <xpad>0</xpad>
  <ypad>0</ypad>
  <xexpand>False</xexpand>
  <yexpand>False</yexpand>
  <xshrink>False</xshrink>
  <yshrink>False</yshrink>
  <xfill>False</xfill>
  <yfill>False</yfill>
</child>
</widget>

<widget>
<class>GtkLabel</class>
<name>lbl_output</name>
```

continues

Listing B.2 **Continued**

```
<label>Output</label>
<justify>GTK_JUSTIFY_CENTER</justify>
<wrap>False</wrap>
<xalign>0.5</xalign>
<yalign>0.5</yalign>
<xpad>0</xpad>
<ypad>0</ypad>
<child>
  <left_attach>0</left_attach>
  <right_attach>1</right_attach>
  <top_attach>8</top_attach>
  <bottom_attach>9</bottom_attach>
  <xpad>0</xpad>
  <ypad>0</ypad>
  <xexpand>False</xexpand>
  <yexpand>False</yexpand>
  <xshrink>False</xshrink>
  <yshrink>False</yshrink>
  <xfill>False</xfill>
  <yfill>False</yfill>
</child>
</widget>

<widget>
<class>GtkButton</class>
<name>cmd_country_managers</name>
<can_focus>True</can_focus>
<signal>
  <name>clicked</name>
  <handler>on_cmd_country_managers_clicked</handler>
  <last_modification_time>Mon, 11 Dec 2000 15:01:46
  ➥GMT</last_modification_time>
</signal>
<label>Country Mgrs.</label>
<child>
  <left_attach>1</left_attach>
  <right_attach>2</right_attach>
  <top_attach>9</top_attach>
  <bottom_attach>10</bottom_attach>
  <xpad>0</xpad>
  <ypad>0</ypad>
  <xexpand>False</xexpand>
  <yexpand>False</yexpand>
  <xshrink>False</xshrink>
  <yshrink>False</yshrink>
  <xfill>False</xfill>
  <yfill>False</yfill>
</child>
</widget>
```

```
<widget>
<class>GtkLabel</class>
<name>lbl_archive</name>
<label></label>
<justify>GTK_JUSTIFY_CENTER</justify>
<wrap>False</wrap>
<xalign>0.5</xalign>
<yalign>0.5</yalign>
<xpad>0</xpad>
<ypad>0</ypad>
<child>
  <left_attach>2</left_attach>
  <right_attach>3</right_attach>
  <top_attach>0</top_attach>
  <bottom_attach>1</bottom_attach>
  <xpad>0</xpad>
  <ypad>0</ypad>
  <xexpand>False</xexpand>
  <yexpand>False</yexpand>
  <xshrink>False</xshrink>
  <yshrink>False</yshrink>
  <xfill>False</xfill>
  <yfill>False</yfill>
</child>
</widget>

<widget>
<class>GtkButton</class>
<name>cmd_import</name>
<can_focus>True</can_focus>
<signal>
  <name>clicked</name>
  <handler>on_cmd_import_clicked</handler>
  <last_modification_time>Mon, 11 Dec 2000 15:00:55
  ➥GMT</last_modification_time>
</signal>
<label>Import</label>
<child>
  <left_attach>1</left_attach>
  <right_attach>2</right_attach>
  <top_attach>1</top_attach>
  <bottom_attach>2</bottom_attach>
  <xpad>0</xpad>
  <ypad>0</ypad>
  <xexpand>False</xexpand>
  <yexpand>False</yexpand>
  <xshrink>False</xshrink>
  <yshrink>False</yshrink>
  <xfill>True</xfill>
  <yfill>False</yfill>
```

continues

Listing B.2 **Continued**

```
    </child>
  </widget>

  <widget>
    <class>GtkButton</class>
    <name>cmd_customer</name>
    <can_focus>True</can_focus>
    <signal>
      <name>clicked</name>
      <handler>on_cmd_customer_clicked</handler>
      <last_modification_time>Mon, 11 Dec 2000 15:01:00
      ↪GMT</last_modification_time>
    </signal>
    <label>Customer</label>
    <child>
      <left_attach>1</left_attach>
      <right_attach>2</right_attach>
      <top_attach>2</top_attach>
      <bottom_attach>3</bottom_attach>
      <xpad>0</xpad>
      <ypad>0</ypad>
      <xexpand>False</xexpand>
      <yexpand>False</yexpand>
      <xshrink>False</xshrink>
      <yshrink>False</yshrink>
      <xfill>True</xfill>
      <yfill>False</yfill>
    </child>
  </widget>

  <widget>
    <class>GtkButton</class>
    <name>cmd_archive</name>
    <can_focus>True</can_focus>
    <signal>
      <name>clicked</name>
      <handler>on_cmd_archive_clicked</handler>
      <last_modification_time>Mon, 11 Dec 2000 15:00:51
      ↪GMT</last_modification_time>
    </signal>
    <label>Archive</label>
    <child>
      <left_attach>1</left_attach>
      <right_attach>2</right_attach>
      <top_attach>0</top_attach>
      <bottom_attach>1</bottom_attach>
      <xpad>0</xpad>
      <ypad>0</ypad>
      <xexpand>False</xexpand>
```

```
  <yexpand>False</yexpand>
  <xshrink>False</xshrink>
  <yshrink>False</yshrink>
  <xfill>True</xfill>
  <yfill>False</yfill>
</child>
</widget>

<widget>
<class>GtkButton</class>
<name>cmd_worldwide</name>
<can_focus>True</can_focus>
<signal>
  <name>clicked</name>
  <handler>on_cmd_worldwide_clicked</handler>
  <last_modification_time>Mon, 11 Dec 2000 15:01:05
  ➥GMT</last_modification_time>
</signal>
<label>Worldwide</label>
<child>
  <left_attach>1</left_attach>
  <right_attach>2</right_attach>
  <top_attach>3</top_attach>
  <bottom_attach>4</bottom_attach>
  <xpad>0</xpad>
  <ypad>0</ypad>
  <xexpand>False</xexpand>
  <yexpand>False</yexpand>
  <xshrink>False</xshrink>
  <yshrink>False</yshrink>
  <xfill>True</xfill>
  <yfill>False</yfill>
</child>
</widget>

<widget>
<class>GtkButton</class>
<name>cmd_country</name>
<can_focus>True</can_focus>
<signal>
  <name>clicked</name>
  <handler>on_cmd_country_clicked</handler>
  <last_modification_time>Mon, 11 Dec 2000 15:01:11
  ➥GMT</last_modification_time>
</signal>
<label>Country</label>
<child>
  <left_attach>1</left_attach>
  <right_attach>2</right_attach>
  <top_attach>4</top_attach>
  <bottom_attach>5</bottom_attach>
```

continues

Listing B.2 **Continued**

```
    <xpad>0</xpad>
    <ypad>0</ypad>
    <xexpand>False</xexpand>
    <yexpand>False</yexpand>
    <xshrink>False</xshrink>
    <yshrink>False</yshrink>
    <xfill>True</xfill>
    <yfill>False</yfill>
</child>
</widget>

<widget>
<class>GtkButton</class>
<name>cmd_state</name>
<can_focus>True</can_focus>
<signal>
  <name>clicked</name>
  <handler>on_cmd_state_clicked</handler>
  <last_modification_time>Mon, 11 Dec 2000 15:14:10
  ➥GMT</last_modification_time>
</signal>
<label>State</label>
<child>
  <left_attach>1</left_attach>
  <right_attach>2</right_attach>
  <top_attach>5</top_attach>
  <bottom_attach>6</bottom_attach>
  <xpad>0</xpad>
  <ypad>0</ypad>
  <xexpand>False</xexpand>
  <yexpand>False</yexpand>
  <xshrink>False</xshrink>
  <yshrink>False</yshrink>
  <xfill>True</xfill>
  <yfill>False</yfill>
</child>
</widget>

<widget>
<class>GtkButton</class>
<name>cmd_zip</name>
<can_focus>True</can_focus>
<signal>
  <name>clicked</name>
  <handler>on_cmd_zip_clicked</handler>
  <last_modification_time>Mon, 11 Dec 2000 15:01:25
  ➥GMT</last_modification_time>
</signal>
<label>Zip</label>
```

```
<child>
  <left_attach>1</left_attach>
  <right_attach>2</right_attach>
  <top_attach>6</top_attach>
  <bottom_attach>7</bottom_attach>
  <xpad>0</xpad>
  <ypad>0</ypad>
  <xexpand>False</xexpand>
  <yexpand>False</yexpand>
  <xshrink>False</xshrink>
  <yshrink>False</yshrink>
  <xfill>True</xfill>
  <yfill>False</yfill>
</child>
</widget>

<widget>
<class>GtkButton</class>
<name>cmd_people</name>
<can_focus>True</can_focus>
<signal>
  <name>clicked</name>
  <handler>on_cmd_people_clicked</handler>
  <last_modification_time>Mon, 11 Dec 2000 15:01:30
  ➥GMT</last_modification_time>
</signal>
<label>People</label>
<child>
  <left_attach>1</left_attach>
  <right_attach>2</right_attach>
  <top_attach>7</top_attach>
  <bottom_attach>8</bottom_attach>
  <xpad>0</xpad>
  <ypad>0</ypad>
  <xexpand>False</xexpand>
  <yexpand>False</yexpand>
  <xshrink>False</xshrink>
  <yshrink>False</yshrink>
  <xfill>True</xfill>
  <yfill>False</yfill>
</child>
</widget>

<widget>
<class>GtkButton</class>
<name>cmd_salespeople</name>
<can_focus>True</can_focus>
<signal>
  <name>clicked</name>
  <handler>on_cmd_salespeople_clicked</handler>
  <last_modification_time>Mon, 11 Dec 2000 15:01:40
```

continues

Listing B.2   **Continued**

```
↩GMT</last_modification_time>
</signal>
<label>Salespeople</label>
<child>
  <left_attach>1</left_attach>
  <right_attach>2</right_attach>
  <top_attach>8</top_attach>
  <bottom_attach>9</bottom_attach>
  <xpad>0</xpad>
  <ypad>0</ypad>
  <xexpand>False</xexpand>
  <yexpand>False</yexpand>
  <xshrink>False</xshrink>
  <yshrink>False</yshrink>
  <xfill>True</xfill>
  <yfill>False</yfill>
</child>
</widget>

<widget>
<class>GtkLabel</class>
<name>lbl_import</name>
<label></label>
<justify>GTK_JUSTIFY_CENTER</justify>
<wrap>False</wrap>
<xalign>0.5</xalign>
<yalign>0.5</yalign>
<xpad>0</xpad>
<ypad>0</ypad>
<child>
  <left_attach>2</left_attach>
  <right_attach>3</right_attach>
  <top_attach>1</top_attach>
  <bottom_attach>2</bottom_attach>
  <xpad>0</xpad>
  <ypad>0</ypad>
  <xexpand>False</xexpand>
  <yexpand>False</yexpand>
  <xshrink>False</xshrink>
  <yshrink>False</yshrink>
  <xfill>False</xfill>
  <yfill>False</yfill>
</child>
</widget>

<widget>
<class>GtkLabel</class>
<name>lbl_customer</name>
```

```
<label></label>
<justify>GTK_JUSTIFY_CENTER</justify>
<wrap>False</wrap>
<xalign>0.5</xalign>
<yalign>0.5</yalign>
<xpad>0</xpad>
<ypad>0</ypad>
<child>
  <left_attach>2</left_attach>
  <right_attach>3</right_attach>
  <top_attach>2</top_attach>
  <bottom_attach>3</bottom_attach>
  <xpad>0</xpad>
  <ypad>0</ypad>
  <xexpand>False</xexpand>
  <yexpand>False</yexpand>
  <xshrink>False</xshrink>
  <yshrink>False</yshrink>
  <xfill>False</xfill>
  <yfill>False</yfill>
</child>
</widget>

<widget>
<class>GtkLabel</class>
<name>lbl_worldwide</name>
<label></label>
<justify>GTK_JUSTIFY_CENTER</justify>
<wrap>False</wrap>
<xalign>0.5</xalign>
<yalign>0.5</yalign>
<xpad>0</xpad>
<ypad>0</ypad>
<child>
  <left_attach>2</left_attach>
  <right_attach>3</right_attach>
  <top_attach>3</top_attach>
  <bottom_attach>4</bottom_attach>
  <xpad>0</xpad>
  <ypad>0</ypad>
  <xexpand>False</xexpand>
  <yexpand>False</yexpand>
  <xshrink>False</xshrink>
  <yshrink>False</yshrink>
  <xfill>False</xfill>
  <yfill>False</yfill>
</child>
</widget>

<widget>
<class>GtkLabel</class>
```

continues

Listing B.2   **Continued**

```
<name>lbl_country</name>
<label></label>
<justify>GTK_JUSTIFY_CENTER</justify>
<wrap>False</wrap>
<xalign>0.5</xalign>
<yalign>0.5</yalign>
<xpad>0</xpad>
<ypad>0</ypad>
<child>
  <left_attach>2</left_attach>
  <right_attach>3</right_attach>
  <top_attach>4</top_attach>
  <bottom_attach>5</bottom_attach>
  <xpad>0</xpad>
  <ypad>0</ypad>
  <xexpand>False</xexpand>
  <yexpand>False</yexpand>
  <xshrink>False</xshrink>
  <yshrink>False</yshrink>
  <xfill>False</xfill>
  <yfill>False</yfill>
</child>
</widget>

<widget>
<class>GtkLabel</class>
<name>lbl_state</name>
<label></label>
<justify>GTK_JUSTIFY_CENTER</justify>
<wrap>False</wrap>
<xalign>0.5</xalign>
<yalign>0.5</yalign>
<xpad>0</xpad>
<ypad>0</ypad>
<child>
  <left_attach>2</left_attach>
  <right_attach>3</right_attach>
  <top_attach>5</top_attach>
  <bottom_attach>6</bottom_attach>
  <xpad>0</xpad>
  <ypad>0</ypad>
  <xexpand>False</xexpand>
  <yexpand>False</yexpand>
  <xshrink>False</xshrink>
  <yshrink>False</yshrink>
  <xfill>False</xfill>
  <yfill>False</yfill>
</child>
</widget>
```

```
<widget>
<class>GtkLabel</class>
<name>lbl_zip</name>
<label></label>
<justify>GTK_JUSTIFY_CENTER</justify>
<wrap>False</wrap>
<xalign>0.5</xalign>
<yalign>0.5</yalign>
<xpad>0</xpad>
<ypad>0</ypad>
<child>
  <left_attach>2</left_attach>
  <right_attach>3</right_attach>
  <top_attach>6</top_attach>
  <bottom_attach>7</bottom_attach>
  <xpad>0</xpad>
  <ypad>0</ypad>
  <xexpand>False</xexpand>
  <yexpand>False</yexpand>
  <xshrink>False</xshrink>
  <yshrink>False</yshrink>
  <xfill>False</xfill>
  <yfill>False</yfill>
</child>
</widget>

<widget>
<class>GtkLabel</class>
<name>lbl_people</name>
<label></label>
<justify>GTK_JUSTIFY_CENTER</justify>
<wrap>False</wrap>
<xalign>0.5</xalign>
<yalign>0.5</yalign>
<xpad>0</xpad>
<ypad>0</ypad>
<child>
  <left_attach>2</left_attach>
  <right_attach>3</right_attach>
  <top_attach>7</top_attach>
  <bottom_attach>8</bottom_attach>
  <xpad>0</xpad>
  <ypad>0</ypad>
  <xexpand>False</xexpand>
  <yexpand>False</yexpand>
  <xshrink>False</xshrink>
  <yshrink>False</yshrink>
  <xfill>False</xfill>
  <yfill>False</yfill>
</child>
```

continues

Listing B.2 **Continued**

```
</widget>

<widget>
<class>GtkLabel</class>
<name>lbl_salespeople</name>
<label></label>
<justify>GTK_JUSTIFY_CENTER</justify>
<wrap>False</wrap>
<xalign>0.5</xalign>
<yalign>0.5</yalign>
<xpad>0</xpad>
<ypad>0</ypad>
<child>
  <left_attach>2</left_attach>
  <right_attach>3</right_attach>
  <top_attach>8</top_attach>
  <bottom_attach>9</bottom_attach>
  <xpad>0</xpad>
  <ypad>0</ypad>
  <xexpand>False</xexpand>
  <yexpand>False</yexpand>
  <xshrink>False</xshrink>
  <yshrink>False</yshrink>
  <xfill>False</xfill>
  <yfill>False</yfill>
</child>
</widget>

<widget>
<class>GtkLabel</class>
<name>lbl_country_managers</name>
<label></label>
<justify>GTK_JUSTIFY_CENTER</justify>
<wrap>False</wrap>
<xalign>0.5</xalign>
<yalign>0.5</yalign>
<xpad>0</xpad>
<ypad>0</ypad>
<child>
  <left_attach>2</left_attach>
  <right_attach>3</right_attach>
  <top_attach>9</top_attach>
  <bottom_attach>10</bottom_attach>
  <xpad>0</xpad>
  <ypad>0</ypad>
  <xexpand>False</xexpand>
  <yexpand>False</yexpand>
  <xshrink>False</xshrink>
  <yshrink>False</yshrink>
  <xfill>False</xfill>
```

```
        <yfill>False</yfill>
      </child>
    </widget>
</widget>

<widget>
  <class>GtkVBox</class>
  <name>vbox_processing</name>
  <homogeneous>False</homogeneous>
  <spacing>0</spacing>
  <child>
  <shrink>True</shrink>
  <resize>True</resize>
  </child>

  <widget>
  <class>GtkHBox</class>
  <name>hbox_add_delete</name>
  <border_width>5</border_width>
  <homogeneous>False</homogeneous>
  <spacing>5</spacing>
  <child>
    <padding>0</padding>
    <expand>True</expand>
    <fill>True</fill>
  </child>

  <widget>
    <class>GtkLabel</class>
    <name>lbl_table</name>
    <label>Table </label>
    <justify>GTK_JUSTIFY_CENTER</justify>
    <wrap>False</wrap>
    <xalign>0.5</xalign>
    <yalign>0.5</yalign>
    <xpad>0</xpad>
    <ypad>0</ypad>
    <child>
      <padding>0</padding>
      <expand>False</expand>
      <fill>False</fill>
    </child>
  </widget>

  <widget>
    <class>GtkCombo</class>
    <name>cbo_table</name>
    <value_in_list>True</value_in_list>
    <ok_if_empty>False</ok_if_empty>
    <case_sensitive>False</case_sensitive>
    <use_arrows>True</use_arrows>
```

continues

Listing B.2   **Continued**

```
<use_arrows_always>False</use_arrows_always>
<items></items>
<child>
  <padding>0</padding>
  <expand>False</expand>
  <fill>False</fill>
</child>

<widget>
  <class>GtkEntry</class>
  <child_name>GtkCombo:entry</child_name>
  <name>combo-entry4</name>
  <can_focus>True</can_focus>
  <editable>True</editable>
  <text_visible>True</text_visible>
  <text_max_length>0</text_max_length>
  <text></text>
</widget>
</widget>

<widget>
  <class>GtkFrame</class>
  <name>frame_add</name>
  <label>Add</label>
  <label_xalign>0</label_xalign>
  <shadow_type>GTK_SHADOW_ETCHED_IN</shadow_type>
  <child>
    <padding>0</padding>
    <expand>False</expand>
    <fill>False</fill>
  </child>

  <widget>
    <class>GtkButton</class>
    <name>cmd_add</name>
    <border_width>5</border_width>
    <can_focus>True</can_focus>
    <signal>
      <name>clicked</name>
      <handler>on_cmd_add_clicked</handler>
      <last_modification_time>Mon, 11 Dec 2000 15:01:52
      ↜GMT</last_modification_time>
    </signal>
    <label>Add Row</label>
  </widget>
</widget>

<widget>
  <class>GtkFrame</class>
```

```
<name>frame_delete_group</name>
<label>Delete</label>
<label_xalign>0</label_xalign>
<shadow_type>GTK_SHADOW_ETCHED_IN</shadow_type>
<child>
  <padding>0</padding>
  <expand>True</expand>
  <fill>True</fill>
</child>

<widget>
  <class>GtkHBox</class>
  <name>hbox_delete</name>
  <border_width>5</border_width>
  <homogeneous>False</homogeneous>
  <spacing>5</spacing>

  <widget>
    <class>GtkButton</class>
    <name>cmd_delete_row</name>
    <can_focus>True</can_focus>
    <signal>
      <name>clicked</name>
      <handler>on_cmd_delete_row_clicked</handler>
      <last_modification_time>Mon, 11 Dec 2000 15:02:07
      -GMT</last_modification_time>
    </signal>
    <label>Delete Row</label>
    <child>
      <padding>0</padding>
      <expand>False</expand>
      <fill>False</fill>
    </child>
  </widget>

  <widget>
    <class>GtkSpinButton</class>
    <name>spinbutton_delete_row</name>
    <can_focus>True</can_focus>
    <climb_rate>1</climb_rate>
    <digits>0</digits>
    <numeric>True</numeric>
    <update_policy>GTK_UPDATE_ALWAYS</update_policy>
    <snap>False</snap>
    <wrap>False</wrap>
    <value>1</value>
    <lower>1</lower>
    <upper>2e+06</upper>
    <step>1</step>
    <page>10</page>
    <page_size>10</page_size>
```

continues

Listing B.2   **Continued**

```
            <child>
                <padding>0</padding>
                <expand>True</expand>
                <fill>True</fill>
            </child>
        </widget>
    </widget>
</widget>
</widget>

<widget>
<class>GtkFrame</class>
<name>frame_update_group</name>
<border_width>5</border_width>
<label>Update</label>
<label_xalign>0</label_xalign>
<shadow_type>GTK_SHADOW_ETCHED_IN</shadow_type>
<child>
    <padding>0</padding>
    <expand>True</expand>
    <fill>True</fill>
</child>

<widget>
    <class>GtkHBox</class>
    <name>hbox_update</name>
    <border_width>5</border_width>
    <homogeneous>False</homogeneous>
    <spacing>5</spacing>

    <widget>
        <class>GtkButton</class>
        <name>cmd_update</name>
        <can_focus>True</can_focus>
        <signal>
            <name>clicked</name>
            <handler>on_cmd_update_clicked</handler>
            <last_modification_time>Mon, 11 Dec 2000 15:02:12
            ↩GMT</last_modification_time>
        </signal>
        <label>Update</label>
        <child>
            <padding>0</padding>
            <expand>False</expand>
            <fill>False</fill>
        </child>
    </widget>

    <widget>
```

```
    <class>GtkLabel</class>
    <name>lbl_line_number</name>
    <label>Line Number</label>
    <justify>GTK_JUSTIFY_CENTER</justify>
    <wrap>False</wrap>
    <xalign>0.5</xalign>
    <yalign>0.5</yalign>
    <xpad>0</xpad>
    <ypad>0</ypad>
    <child>
      <padding>0</padding>
      <expand>False</expand>
      <fill>False</fill>
    </child>
  </widget>

  <widget>
    <class>GtkSpinButton</class>
    <name>spinbutton_update_line</name>
    <can_focus>True</can_focus>
    <climb_rate>1</climb_rate>
    <digits>0</digits>
    <numeric>True</numeric>
    <update_policy>GTK_UPDATE_ALWAYS</update_policy>
    <snap>False</snap>
    <wrap>False</wrap>
    <value>1</value>
    <lower>1</lower>
    <upper>2e+06</upper>
    <step>1</step>
    <page>10</page>
    <page_size>10</page_size>
    <child>
      <padding>0</padding>
      <expand>True</expand>
      <fill>True</fill>
    </child>
  </widget>

  <widget>
    <class>GtkLabel</class>
    <name>lbl_column</name>
    <label>Column</label>
    <justify>GTK_JUSTIFY_CENTER</justify>
    <wrap>False</wrap>
    <xalign>0.5</xalign>
    <yalign>0.5</yalign>
    <xpad>0</xpad>
    <ypad>0</ypad>
    <child>
      <padding>0</padding>
```

continues

Listing B.2 **Continued**

```
          <expand>False</expand>
          <fill>False</fill>
        </child>
      </widget>

      <widget>
        <class>GtkEntry</class>
        <name>entry_column_name</name>
        <can_focus>True</can_focus>
        <editable>True</editable>
        <text_visible>True</text_visible>
        <text_max_length>0</text_max_length>
        <text></text>
        <child>
          <padding>0</padding>
          <expand>True</expand>
          <fill>True</fill>
        </child>
      </widget>

      <widget>
        <class>GtkLabel</class>
        <name>lbl_to</name>
        <label>to</label>
        <justify>GTK_JUSTIFY_CENTER</justify>
        <wrap>False</wrap>
        <xalign>0.5</xalign>
        <yalign>0.5</yalign>
        <xpad>0</xpad>
        <ypad>0</ypad>
        <child>
          <padding>0</padding>
          <expand>False</expand>
          <fill>False</fill>
        </child>
      </widget>

      <widget>
        <class>GtkEntry</class>
        <name>entry_new_value</name>
        <can_focus>True</can_focus>
        <editable>True</editable>
        <text_visible>True</text_visible>
        <text_max_length>0</text_max_length>
        <text></text>
        <child>
          <padding>0</padding>
          <expand>True</expand>
          <fill>True</fill>
```

```
          </child>
        </widget>
      </widget>
      </widget>

      <widget>
      <class>GtkStatusbar</class>
      <name>statusbar_processing</name>
      <child>
        <padding>0</padding>
        <expand>False</expand>
        <fill>False</fill>
      </child>
      </widget>
    </widget>
  </widget>
</widget>

</GTK-Interface>
```

C

Glade-Generated Files from the Key Business Indicators Application

This is the appendix for the applications in Chapters 11,"Management Reporting Abstract and Design," 12,"Management Reporting Construction" and 13, "Management Reporting Deployment and Upgrades," ("the KBI application"). For each of the executables that make up the KBI application (kbi, tabular, pie, bar/line, and scatter),the `interface.c` and glade configuration files are presented.

KBI Files

The next two listings are the `interface.c` and `kbi.glade` files for the KBI executable created in Chapter 12.

interface.c for KBI

Listing C.1 is the Glade-generated file for creating the interface to KBI (the executable). It creates the form and returns a pointer to the newly created "frm_kbi."

Listing C.1   *interface.c* for the KBI executable

```
/* DO NOT EDIT THIS FILE - it is generated by Glade.
 */

#ifdef HAVE_CONFIG_H
#  include <config.h>
#endif
```

continues

Listing C.1 **Continued**

```
#include <sys/types.h>
#include <sys/stat.h>
#include <unistd.h>
#include <string.h>

#include <gdk/gdkkeysyms.h>
#include <gtk/gtk.h>

#include "callbacks.h"
#include "interface.h"
#include "support.h"

GtkWidget*
create_frm_kbi (void)
{
  GtkWidget *frm_kbi;
  GtkWidget *vbox1;
  GtkWidget *lst_reports;
  GtkWidget *hbox_buttons;
  GtkWidget *cmd_close;
  GtkWidget *cmd_open;
  GtkWidget *statusbar1;

  frm_kbi = gtk_window_new (GTK_WINDOW_TOPLEVEL);
  gtk_object_set_data (GTK_OBJECT (frm_kbi), "frm_kbi", frm_kbi);
  gtk_window_set_title (GTK_WINDOW (frm_kbi), "Key Business Indicators");
  gtk_window_set_default_size (GTK_WINDOW (frm_kbi), 240, 300);

  vbox1 = gtk_vbox_new (FALSE, 0);
  gtk_widget_ref (vbox1);
  gtk_object_set_data_full (GTK_OBJECT (frm_kbi), "vbox1", vbox1,
                            (GtkDestroyNotify) gtk_widget_unref);
  gtk_widget_show (vbox1);
  gtk_container_add (GTK_CONTAINER (frm_kbi), vbox1);

  lst_reports = gtk_list_new ();
  gtk_widget_ref (lst_reports);
  gtk_object_set_data_full (GTK_OBJECT (frm_kbi), "lst_reports", lst_reports,
                            (GtkDestroyNotify) gtk_widget_unref);
  gtk_widget_show (lst_reports);
  gtk_box_pack_start (GTK_BOX (vbox1), lst_reports, TRUE, TRUE, 0);

  hbox_buttons = gtk_hbox_new (FALSE, 0);
  gtk_widget_ref (hbox_buttons);
  gtk_object_set_data_full (GTK_OBJECT (frm_kbi), "hbox_buttons", hbox_buttons,
                            (GtkDestroyNotify) gtk_widget_unref);
  gtk_widget_show (hbox_buttons);
  gtk_box_pack_start (GTK_BOX (vbox1), hbox_buttons, FALSE, TRUE, 0);
```

```
cmd_close = gtk_button_new_with_label ("Close");
gtk_widget_ref (cmd_close);
gtk_object_set_data_full (GTK_OBJECT (frm_kbi), "cmd_close", cmd_close,
                          (GtkDestroyNotify) gtk_widget_unref);
gtk_widget_show (cmd_close);
gtk_box_pack_start (GTK_BOX (hbox_buttons), cmd_close, TRUE, TRUE, 0);

cmd_open = gtk_button_new_with_label ("Open");
gtk_widget_ref (cmd_open);
gtk_object_set_data_full (GTK_OBJECT (frm_kbi), "cmd_open", cmd_open,
                          (GtkDestroyNotify) gtk_widget_unref);
gtk_widget_show (cmd_open);
gtk_box_pack_start (GTK_BOX (hbox_buttons), cmd_open, TRUE, TRUE, 0);

statusbar1 = gtk_statusbar_new ();
gtk_widget_ref (statusbar1);
gtk_object_set_data_full (GTK_OBJECT (frm_kbi), "statusbar1", statusbar1,
                          (GtkDestroyNotify) gtk_widget_unref);
gtk_widget_show (statusbar1);
gtk_box_pack_start (GTK_BOX (vbox1), statusbar1, FALSE, FALSE, 0);

gtk_signal_connect (GTK_OBJECT (frm_kbi), "realize",
                    GTK_SIGNAL_FUNC (on_frm_kbi_realize),
                    NULL);
gtk_signal_connect (GTK_OBJECT (frm_kbi), "show",
                    GTK_SIGNAL_FUNC (on_frm_kbi_show),
                    NULL);
gtk_signal_connect (GTK_OBJECT (frm_kbi), "delete_event",
                    GTK_SIGNAL_FUNC (on_frm_kbi_delete_event),
                    NULL);
gtk_signal_connect (GTK_OBJECT (cmd_close), "clicked",
                    GTK_SIGNAL_FUNC (on_cmd_close_clicked),
                    NULL);
gtk_signal_connect (GTK_OBJECT (cmd_open), "clicked",
                    GTK_SIGNAL_FUNC (on_cmd_open_clicked),
                    NULL);

return frm_kbi;
}
```

kbi.glade

Listing C.2 is the Glade project file for the KBI executable; it is generated by Glade in

XML format.

Listing C.2 **Glade XML File For the KBI Executable**

```xml
<?xml version="1.0"?>
<GTK-Interface>

<project>
  <name>kbi</name>
  <program_name>kbi</program_name>
  <directory></directory>
  <source_directory>src</source_directory>
  <pixmaps_directory>pixmaps</pixmaps_directory>
  <language>C</language>
  <gnome_support>False</gnome_support>
  <gettext_support>False</gettext_support>
  <use_widget_names>False</use_widget_names>
  <output_main_file>True</output_main_file>
  <output_support_files>True</output_support_files>
  <output_build_files>True</output_build_files>
  <backup_source_files>True</backup_source_files>
  <main_source_file>interface.c</main_source_file>
  <main_header_file>interface.h</main_header_file>
  <handler_source_file>callbacks.c</handler_source_file>
  <handler_header_file>callbacks.h</handler_header_file>
  <support_source_file>support.c</support_source_file>
  <support_header_file>support.h</support_header_file>
  <translatable_strings_file></translatable_strings_file>
</project>

<widget>
  <class>GtkWindow</class>
  <name>frm_kbi</name>
  <signal>
    <name>realize</name>
    <handler>on_frm_kbi_realize</handler>
    <last_modification_time>Wed, 14 Feb 2001 12:01:32 GMT</last_modification_time>
  </signal>
  <signal>
    <name>show</name>
    <handler>on_frm_kbi_show</handler>
    <last_modification_time>Wed, 14 Feb 2001 12:24:29 GMT</last_modification_time>
  </signal>
  <signal>
    <name>delete_event</name>
    <handler>on_frm_kbi_delete_event</handler>
    <last_modification_time>Wed, 14 Feb 2001 12:30:44 GMT</last_modification_time>
  </signal>
  <title>Key Business Indicators</title>
  <type>GTK_WINDOW_TOPLEVEL</type>
  <position>GTK_WIN_POS_NONE</position>
```

```
<modal>False</modal>
<default_width>240</default_width>
<default_height>300</default_height>
<allow_shrink>False</allow_shrink>
<allow_grow>True</allow_grow>
<auto_shrink>False</auto_shrink>

<widget>
  <class>GtkVBox</class>
  <name>vbox1</name>
  <homogeneous>False</homogeneous>
  <spacing>0</spacing>

  <widget>
    <class>GtkList</class>
    <name>lst_reports</name>
    <selection_mode>GTK_SELECTION_SINGLE</selection_mode>
    <child>
    <padding>0</padding>
    <expand>True</expand>
    <fill>True</fill>
    </child>
  </widget>

  <widget>
    <class>GtkHBox</class>
    <name>hbox_buttons</name>
    <homogeneous>False</homogeneous>
    <spacing>0</spacing>
    <child>
    <padding>0</padding>
    <expand>False</expand>
    <fill>True</fill>
    </child>

    <widget>
    <class>GtkButton</class>
    <name>cmd_close</name>
    <can_focus>True</can_focus>
    <signal>
      <name>clicked</name>
      <handler>on_cmd_close_clicked</handler>
      <last_modification_time>Mon, 12 Feb 2001 20:34:11
      ↪GMT</last_modification_time>
    </signal>
    <label>Close</label>
    <child>
      <padding>0</padding>
      <expand>True</expand>
      <fill>True</fill>
    </child>
```

continues

Listing C.2   **Continued**

```
        </widget>

        <widget>
        <class>GtkButton</class>
        <name>cmd_open</name>
        <can_focus>True</can_focus>
        <signal>
          <name>clicked</name>
          <handler>on_cmd_open_clicked</handler>
          <last_modification_time>Mon, 12 Feb 2001 20:34:22
          ➥GMT</last_modification_time>
        </signal>
        <label>Open</label>
        <child>
          <padding>0</padding>
          <expand>True</expand>
          <fill>True</fill>
        </child>
        </widget>
      </widget>

      <widget>
        <class>GtkStatusbar</class>
        <name>statusbar1</name>
        <child>
        <padding>0</padding>
        <expand>False</expand>
        <fill>False</fill>
        </child>
      </widget>
    </widget>
</widget>

</GTK-Interface>
```

Tabular Files

The interface.c and tabular.glade files are included in this section.

interface.c for the Tabular Executable

Listing C.3 is the Glade-generated file for the tabular executable window widget. It creates a single form (frm_tabular) and returns a pointer to the newly created form.

Listing C.3 *interface.c* **for the Tabular Executable**

```c
/*
 * DO NOT EDIT THIS FILE - it is generated by Glade.
 */

#ifdef HAVE_CONFIG_H
#  include <config.h>
#endif

#include <sys/types.h>
#include <sys/stat.h>
#include <unistd.h>
#include <string.h>

#include <gdk/gdkkeysyms.h>
#include <gtk/gtk.h>

#include "callbacks.h"
#include "interface.h"
#include "support.h"

GtkWidget*
create_frm_tabular (void)
{
  GtkWidget *frm_tabular;
  GtkWidget *vbox1;
  GtkWidget *scrolledwindow1;
  GtkWidget *clist1;
  GtkWidget *label1;
  GtkWidget *label2;
  GtkWidget *label3;
  GtkWidget *statusbar1;

  frm_tabular = gtk_window_new (GTK_WINDOW_TOPLEVEL);
  gtk_object_set_data (GTK_OBJECT (frm_tabular), "frm_tabular", frm_tabular);
  gtk_window_set_title (GTK_WINDOW (frm_tabular), "Top Commission Earners");
  gtk_window_set_default_size (GTK_WINDOW (frm_tabular), 280, 500);

  vbox1 = gtk_vbox_new (FALSE, 0);
  gtk_widget_ref (vbox1);
  gtk_object_set_data_full (GTK_OBJECT (frm_tabular), "vbox1", vbox1,
                            (GtkDestroyNotify) gtk_widget_unref);
  gtk_widget_show (vbox1);
  gtk_container_add (GTK_CONTAINER (frm_tabular), vbox1);

  scrolledwindow1 = gtk_scrolled_window_new (NULL, NULL);
  gtk_widget_ref (scrolledwindow1);
  gtk_object_set_data_full (GTK_OBJECT (frm_tabular), "scrolledwindow1",
➥scrolledwindow1,
                            (GtkDestroyNotify) gtk_widget_unref);
```

continues

Listing C.3 **Continued**

```
gtk_widget_show (scrolledwindow1);
gtk_box_pack_start (GTK_BOX (vbox1), scrolledwindow1, TRUE, TRUE, 0);

clist1 = gtk_clist_new (3);
gtk_widget_ref (clist1);
gtk_object_set_data_full (GTK_OBJECT (frm_tabular), "clist1", clist1,
                          (GtkDestroyNotify) gtk_widget_unref);
gtk_widget_show (clist1);
gtk_container_add (GTK_CONTAINER (scrolledwindow1), clist1);
gtk_clist_set_column_width (GTK_CLIST (clist1), 0, 80);
gtk_clist_set_column_width (GTK_CLIST (clist1), 1, 80);
gtk_clist_set_column_width (GTK_CLIST (clist1), 2, 80);
gtk_clist_column_titles_show (GTK_CLIST (clist1));

label1 = gtk_label_new ("label1");
gtk_widget_ref (label1);
gtk_object_set_data_full (GTK_OBJECT (frm_tabular), "label1", label1,
                          (GtkDestroyNotify) gtk_widget_unref);
gtk_widget_show (label1);
gtk_clist_set_column_widget (GTK_CLIST (clist1), 0, label1);

label2 = gtk_label_new ("label2");
gtk_widget_ref (label2);
gtk_object_set_data_full (GTK_OBJECT (frm_tabular), "label2", label2,
                          (GtkDestroyNotify) gtk_widget_unref);
gtk_widget_show (label2);
gtk_clist_set_column_widget (GTK_CLIST (clist1), 1, label2);

label3 = gtk_label_new ("label3");
gtk_widget_ref (label3);
gtk_object_set_data_full (GTK_OBJECT (frm_tabular), "label3", label3,
                          (GtkDestroyNotify) gtk_widget_unref);
gtk_widget_show (label3);
gtk_clist_set_column_widget (GTK_CLIST (clist1), 2, label3);

statusbar1 = gtk_statusbar_new ();
gtk_widget_ref (statusbar1);
gtk_object_set_data_full (GTK_OBJECT (frm_tabular), "statusbar1", statusbar1,
                          (GtkDestroyNotify) gtk_widget_unref);
gtk_widget_show (statusbar1);
gtk_box_pack_start (GTK_BOX (vbox1), statusbar1, FALSE, FALSE, 0);

gtk_signal_connect (GTK_OBJECT (frm_tabular), "show",
                    GTK_SIGNAL_FUNC (on_frm_tabular_show),
                    NULL);
gtk_signal_connect (GTK_OBJECT (frm_tabular), "delete_event",
                    GTK_SIGNAL_FUNC (on_frm_tabular_delete_event),
                    NULL);

return frm_tabular;
}
```

tabular.glade

Listing C.4 is the Glade project file for the tabular executable. It is in XML format and is created by Glade.

Listing C.4 **Glade XML File for the Tabular Executable**

```
<?xml version="1.0"?>
<GTK-Interface>

<project>
  <name>tabular</name>
  <program_name>tabular</program_name>
  <directory></directory>
  <source_directory>src</source_directory>
  <pixmaps_directory>pixmaps</pixmaps_directory>
  <language>C</language>
  <gnome_support>False</gnome_support>
  <gettext_support>False</gettext_support>
  <use_widget_names>False</use_widget_names>
  <output_main_file>True</output_main_file>
  <output_support_files>True</output_support_files>
  <output_build_files>True</output_build_files>
  <backup_source_files>True</backup_source_files>
  <main_source_file>interface.c</main_source_file>
  <main_header_file>interface.h</main_header_file>
  <handler_source_file>callbacks.c</handler_source_file>
  <handler_header_file>callbacks.h</handler_header_file>
  <support_source_file>support.c</support_source_file>
  <support_header_file>support.h</support_header_file>
  <translatable_strings_file></translatable_strings_file>
</project>

<widget>
  <class>GtkWindow</class>
  <name>frm_tabular</name>
  <signal>
    <name>show</name>
    <handler>on_frm_tabular_show</handler>
    <last_modification_time>Sun, 18 Feb 2001 21:58:53 GMT</last_modification_time>
  </signal>
  <signal>
    <name>delete_event</name>
    <handler>on_frm_tabular_delete_event</handler>
    <last_modification_time>Sun, 18 Feb 2001 22:10:58 GMT</last_modification_time>
  </signal>
  <title>Top Commission Earners</title>
  <type>GTK_WINDOW_TOPLEVEL</type>
  <position>GTK_WIN_POS_NONE</position>
  <modal>False</modal>
  <default_width>280</default_width>
```

continues

Listing C.4 **Continued**

```
<default_height>500</default_height>
<allow_shrink>False</allow_shrink>
<allow_grow>True</allow_grow>
<auto_shrink>False</auto_shrink>

<widget>
  <class>GtkVBox</class>
  <name>vbox1</name>
  <homogeneous>False</homogeneous>
  <spacing>0</spacing>

  <widget>
    <class>GtkScrolledWindow</class>
    <name>scrolledwindow1</name>
    <hscrollbar_policy>GTK_POLICY_ALWAYS</hscrollbar_policy>
    <vscrollbar_policy>GTK_POLICY_ALWAYS</vscrollbar_policy>
    <hupdate_policy>GTK_UPDATE_CONTINUOUS</hupdate_policy>
    <vupdate_policy>GTK_UPDATE_CONTINUOUS</vupdate_policy>
    <child>
    <padding>0</padding>
    <expand>True</expand>
    <fill>True</fill>
    </child>

    <widget>
    <class>GtkCList</class>
    <name>clist1</name>
    <can_focus>True</can_focus>
    <columns>3</columns>
    <column_widths>80,80,80</column_widths>
    <selection_mode>GTK_SELECTION_SINGLE</selection_mode>
    <show_titles>True</show_titles>
    <shadow_type>GTK_SHADOW_IN</shadow_type>

    <widget>
      <class>GtkLabel</class>
      <child_name>CList:title</child_name>
      <name>label1</name>
      <label>label1</label>
      <justify>GTK_JUSTIFY_CENTER</justify>
      <wrap>False</wrap>
      <xalign>0.5</xalign>
      <yalign>0.5</yalign>
      <xpad>0</xpad>
      <ypad>0</ypad>
    </widget>

    <widget>
      <class>GtkLabel</class>
```

```
        <child_name>CList:title</child_name>
        <name>label2</name>
        <label>label2</label>
        <justify>GTK_JUSTIFY_CENTER</justify>
        <wrap>False</wrap>
        <xalign>0.5</xalign>
        <yalign>0.5</yalign>
        <xpad>0</xpad>
        <ypad>0</ypad>
      </widget>

      <widget>
        <class>GtkLabel</class>
        <child_name>CList:title</child_name>
        <name>label3</name>
        <label>label3</label>
        <justify>GTK_JUSTIFY_CENTER</justify>
        <wrap>False</wrap>
        <xalign>0.5</xalign>
        <yalign>0.5</yalign>
        <xpad>0</xpad>
        <ypad>0</ypad>
      </widget>
      </widget>
    </widget>

    <widget>
      <class>GtkStatusbar</class>
      <name>statusbar1</name>
      <child>
      <padding>0</padding>
      <expand>False</expand>
      <fill>False</fill>
      </child>
    </widget>
   </widget>
 </widget>

 </GTK-Interface>
```

Pie Chart Files

Listing C.5 is the `interface.c` file for the pie chart executable, and Listing C.6 is the Glade project file.

interface.c for the Pie Chart Executable

Listing C.5 is the Glade-generated file for creating the interface for the pie chart executable. As with the previous two examples in this appendix, it creates a single window widget and returns that widget to the calling program.

Listing C.5 *interface.c* **for the Pie Chart Executable**

```c
/* DO NOT EDIT THIS FILE - it is generated by Glade.
 */

#ifdef HAVE_CONFIG_H
#  include <config.h>
#endif

#include <sys/types.h>
#include <sys/stat.h>
#include <unistd.h>
#include <string.h>

#include <gdk/gdkkeysyms.h>
#include <gtk/gtk.h>

#include "callbacks.h"
#include "interface.h"
#include "support.h"

GtkWidget*
create_frm_piechart (void)
{
  GtkWidget *frm_piechart;
  GtkWidget *vbox1;
  GtkWidget *drawingarea1;
  GtkWidget *statusbar1;

  frm_piechart = gtk_window_new (GTK_WINDOW_TOPLEVEL);
  gtk_object_set_data (GTK_OBJECT (frm_piechart), "frm_piechart", frm_piechart);
  gtk_window_set_title (GTK_WINDOW (frm_piechart), "Sales By Division");
  gtk_window_set_default_size (GTK_WINDOW (frm_piechart), 400, 600);

  vbox1 = gtk_vbox_new (FALSE, 0);
  gtk_widget_ref (vbox1);
  gtk_object_set_data_full (GTK_OBJECT (frm_piechart), "vbox1", vbox1,
                            (GtkDestroyNotify) gtk_widget_unref);
  gtk_widget_show (vbox1);
  gtk_container_add (GTK_CONTAINER (frm_piechart), vbox1);

  drawingarea1 = gtk_drawing_area_new ();
  gtk_widget_ref (drawingarea1);
  gtk_object_set_data_full (GTK_OBJECT (frm_piechart), "drawingarea1",
  drawingarea1,
                            (GtkDestroyNotify) gtk_widget_unref);
  gtk_widget_show (drawingarea1);
  gtk_box_pack_start (GTK_BOX (vbox1), drawingarea1, TRUE, TRUE, 0);

  statusbar1 = gtk_statusbar_new ();
```

```
    gtk_widget_ref (statusbar1);
    gtk_object_set_data_full (GTK_OBJECT (frm_piechart), "statusbar1", statusbar1,
                              (GtkDestroyNotify) gtk_widget_unref);
    gtk_widget_show (statusbar1);
    gtk_box_pack_start (GTK_BOX (vbox1), statusbar1, FALSE, FALSE, 0);

    gtk_signal_connect (GTK_OBJECT (frm_piechart), "show",
                        GTK_SIGNAL_FUNC (on_frm_piechart_show),
                        NULL);
    gtk_signal_connect (GTK_OBJECT (frm_piechart), "delete_event",
                        GTK_SIGNAL_FUNC (on_frm_piechart_delete_event),
                        NULL);
    gtk_signal_connect (GTK_OBJECT (frm_piechart), "realize",
                        GTK_SIGNAL_FUNC (on_frm_piechart_realize),
                        NULL);
    gtk_signal_connect (GTK_OBJECT (frm_piechart), "event",
                        GTK_SIGNAL_FUNC (on_frm_piechart_event),
                        NULL);
    gtk_signal_connect (GTK_OBJECT (drawingarea1), "delete_event",
                        GTK_SIGNAL_FUNC (on_drawingarea1_delete_event),
                        NULL);
    gtk_signal_connect (GTK_OBJECT (drawingarea1), "show",
                        GTK_SIGNAL_FUNC (on_drawingarea1_show),
                        NULL);
    gtk_signal_connect (GTK_OBJECT (drawingarea1), "draw",
                        GTK_SIGNAL_FUNC (on_drawingarea1_draw),
                        NULL);
    gtk_signal_connect (GTK_OBJECT (drawingarea1), "event",
                        GTK_SIGNAL_FUNC (on_drawingarea1_event),
                        NULL);
    gtk_signal_connect (GTK_OBJECT (drawingarea1), "realize",
                        GTK_SIGNAL_FUNC (on_drawingarea1_realize),
                        NULL);

    return frm_piechart;
}
```

piechart.glade

Listing C.6 is the Glade XML File for the Pie Chart Executable.

Listing C.6 **Glade XML file for the pie chart executable**

```
<?xml version="1.0"?>
<GTK-Interface>

<project>
  <name>piechart</name>
  <program_name>piechart</program_name>
```

continues

Listing C.6 **Continued**

```
  <directory></directory>
  <source_directory>src</source_directory>
  <pixmaps_directory>pixmaps</pixmaps_directory>
  <language>C</language>
  <gnome_support>False</gnome_support>
  <gettext_support>False</gettext_support>
  <use_widget_names>False</use_widget_names>
  <output_main_file>True</output_main_file>
  <output_support_files>True</output_support_files>
  <output_build_files>True</output_build_files>
  <backup_source_files>True</backup_source_files>
  <main_source_file>interface.c</main_source_file>
  <main_header_file>interface.h</main_header_file>
  <handler_source_file>callbacks.c</handler_source_file>
  <handler_header_file>callbacks.h</handler_header_file>
  <support_source_file>support.c</support_source_file>
  <support_header_file>support.h</support_header_file>
  <translatable_strings_file></translatable_strings_file>
</project>

<widget>
  <class>GtkWindow</class>
  <name>frm_piechart</name>
  <signal>
    <name>show</name>
    <handler>on_frm_piechart_show</handler>
    <last_modification_time>Mon, 19 Feb 2001 17:34:16 GMT</last_modification_time>
  </signal>
  <signal>
    <name>delete_event</name>
    <handler>on_frm_piechart_delete_event</handler>
    <last_modification_time>Mon, 19 Feb 2001 17:34:26 GMT</last_modification_time>
  </signal>
  <signal>
    <name>realize</name>
    <handler>on_frm_piechart_realize</handler>
    <last_modification_time>Mon, 19 Feb 2001 21:25:59 GMT</last_modification_time>
  </signal>
  <signal>
    <name>event</name>
    <handler>on_frm_piechart_event</handler>
    <last_modification_time>Mon, 19 Feb 2001 21:26:12 GMT</last_modification_time>
  </signal>
  <title>Sales By Division</title>
  <type>GTK_WINDOW_TOPLEVEL</type>
  <position>GTK_WIN_POS_NONE</position>
  <modal>False</modal>
  <default_width>400</default_width>
  <default_height>600</default_height>
```

```
<allow_shrink>False</allow_shrink>
<allow_grow>True</allow_grow>
<auto_shrink>False</auto_shrink>

<widget>
  <class>GtkVBox</class>
  <name>vbox1</name>
  <homogeneous>False</homogeneous>
  <spacing>0</spacing>

  <widget>
    <class>GtkDrawingArea</class>
    <name>drawingarea1</name>
    <signal>
    <name>delete_event</name>
    <handler>on_drawingarea1_delete_event</handler>
    <last_modification_time>Mon, 19 Feb 2001 17:32:26
    ⮩GMT</last_modification_time>
    </signal>
    <signal>
    <name>show</name>
    <handler>on_drawingarea1_show</handler>
    <last_modification_time>Mon, 19 Feb 2001 17:32:34
    ⮩GMT</last_modification_time>
    </signal>
    <signal>
    <name>draw</name>
    <handler>on_drawingarea1_draw</handler>
    <last_modification_time>Mon, 19 Feb 2001 19:53:13
    ⮩GMT</last_modification_time>
    </signal>
    <signal>
    <name>event</name>
    <handler>on_drawingarea1_event</handler>
    <last_modification_time>Mon, 19 Feb 2001 19:53:29
    ⮩GMT</last_modification_time>
    </signal>
    <signal>
    <name>realize</name>
    <handler>on_drawingarea1_realize</handler>
    <last_modification_time>Mon, 19 Feb 2001 21:18:25
    ⮩GMT</last_modification_time>
    </signal>
    <child>
    <padding>0</padding>
    <expand>True</expand>
    <fill>True</fill>
    </child>
  </widget>
```

continues

Listing C.6 **Continued**

```
    <widget>
      <class>GtkStatusbar</class>
      <name>statusbar1</name>
      <child>
      <padding>0</padding>
      <expand>False</expand>
      <fill>False</fill>
      </child>
    </widget>
  </widget>
</widget>

</GTK-Interface>
```

bar_line Files

Below are the `interface.c` file and `barline.glade` files for the bar_line executable.
Listing C.7 is `interface.c` and Listing C.8 is `barline.glade`.

interface.c **for the bar_line Executable**

Listing C.7 is the interface generation file for the bar_line executable. It is generated
by Glade and creates frm_barline, the main form for the bar/line graph example.

Listing C.7 *interface.c* **for the bar_line executable**

```c
/* DO NOT EDIT THIS FILE - it is generated by Glade.
 */

#ifdef HAVE_CONFIG_H
#  include <config.h>
#endif

#include <sys/types.h>
#include <sys/stat.h>
#include <unistd.h>
#include <string.h>

#include <gdk/gdkkeysyms.h>
#include <gtk/gtk.h>

#include "callbacks.h"
#include "interface.h"
#include "support.h"

GtkWidget*
```

```
create_frm_barline (void)
{
  GtkWidget *frm_barline;
  GtkWidget *vbox1;
  GtkWidget *drawingarea1;
  GtkWidget *statusbar1;

  frm_barline = gtk_window_new (GTK_WINDOW_TOPLEVEL);
  gtk_object_set_data (GTK_OBJECT (frm_barline), "frm_barline", frm_barline);
  gtk_window_set_title (GTK_WINDOW (frm_barline), "YTD Sales Trend vs. Quota");
  gtk_window_set_default_size (GTK_WINDOW (frm_barline), 600, 400);

  vbox1 = gtk_vbox_new (FALSE, 0);
  gtk_widget_ref (vbox1);
  gtk_object_set_data_full (GTK_OBJECT (frm_barline), "vbox1", vbox1,
                            (GtkDestroyNotify) gtk_widget_unref);
  gtk_widget_show (vbox1);
  gtk_container_add (GTK_CONTAINER (frm_barline), vbox1);

  drawingarea1 = gtk_drawing_area_new ();
  gtk_widget_ref (drawingarea1);
  gtk_object_set_data_full (GTK_OBJECT (frm_barline), "drawingarea1",
  drawingarea1,
                            (GtkDestroyNotify) gtk_widget_unref);
  gtk_widget_show (drawingarea1);
  gtk_box_pack_start (GTK_BOX (vbox1), drawingarea1, TRUE, TRUE, 0);

  statusbar1 = gtk_statusbar_new ();
  gtk_widget_ref (statusbar1);
  gtk_object_set_data_full (GTK_OBJECT (frm_barline), "statusbar1", statusbar1,
                            (GtkDestroyNotify) gtk_widget_unref);
  gtk_widget_show (statusbar1);
  gtk_box_pack_start (GTK_BOX (vbox1), statusbar1, FALSE, FALSE, 0);

  gtk_signal_connect (GTK_OBJECT (frm_barline), "show",
                      GTK_SIGNAL_FUNC (on_frm_barline_show),
                      NULL);
  gtk_signal_connect (GTK_OBJECT (frm_barline), "delete_event",
                      GTK_SIGNAL_FUNC (on_frm_barline_delete_event),
                      NULL);
  gtk_signal_connect (GTK_OBJECT (drawingarea1), "event",
                      GTK_SIGNAL_FUNC (on_drawingarea1_event),
                      NULL);

  return frm_barline;
}
```

barline.glade

Listing C.8 is the Glade project file for the bar_line executable, in XML format.

Listing C.8 **Glade XML file for the bar_line executable**

```xml
<?xml version="1.0"?>
<GTK-Interface>

<project>
  <name>barline</name>
  <program_name>barline</program_name>
  <directory></directory>
  <source_directory>src</source_directory>
  <pixmaps_directory>pixmaps</pixmaps_directory>
  <language>C</language>
  <gnome_support>False</gnome_support>
  <gettext_support>False</gettext_support>
  <use_widget_names>False</use_widget_names>
  <output_main_file>True</output_main_file>
  <output_support_files>True</output_support_files>
  <output_build_files>True</output_build_files>
  <backup_source_files>True</backup_source_files>
  <main_source_file>interface.c</main_source_file>
  <main_header_file>interface.h</main_header_file>
  <handler_source_file>callbacks.c</handler_source_file>
  <handler_header_file>callbacks.h</handler_header_file>
  <support_source_file>support.c</support_source_file>
  <support_header_file>support.h</support_header_file>
  <translatable_strings_file></translatable_strings_file>
</project>

<widget>
  <class>GtkWindow</class>
  <name>frm_barline</name>
  <signal>
    <name>show</name>
    <handler>on_frm_barline_show</handler>
    <last_modification_time>Fri, 23 Feb 2001 12:25:31 GMT</last_modification_time>
  </signal>
  <signal>
    <name>delete_event</name>
    <handler>on_frm_barline_delete_event</handler>
    <last_modification_time>Fri, 23 Feb 2001 12:25:37 GMT</last_modification_time>
  </signal>
  <title>YTD Sales Trend vs. Quota</title>
  <type>GTK_WINDOW_TOPLEVEL</type>
  <position>GTK_WIN_POS_NONE</position>
  <modal>False</modal>
  <default_width>600</default_width>
  <default_height>400</default_height>
```

```
<allow_shrink>False</allow_shrink>
<allow_grow>True</allow_grow>
<auto_shrink>False</auto_shrink>

<widget>
  <class>GtkVBox</class>
  <name>vbox1</name>
  <homogeneous>False</homogeneous>
  <spacing>0</spacing>

  <widget>
    <class>GtkDrawingArea</class>
    <name>drawingarea1</name>
    <signal>
    <name>event</name>
    <handler>on_drawingarea1_event</handler>
    <last_modification_time>Fri, 23 Feb 2001 12:25:48
    ⇒GMT</last_modification_time>
    </signal>
    <child>
    <padding>0</padding>
    <expand>True</expand>
    <fill>True</fill>
    </child>
  </widget>

  <widget>
    <class>GtkStatusbar</class>
    <name>statusbar1</name>
    <child>
    <padding>0</padding>
    <expand>False</expand>
    <fill>False</fill>
    </child>
  </widget>
  </widget>
</widget>

</GTK-Interface>
```

Scatter Plot Files

Listing C.9 is the interface.c for the scatter plot example program, and Listing C.10 is the corresponding Glade XML file.

interface.c for the Scatter Plot Example

Listing C.9 is the Glade-generated file for building the interface for the "scatter plot" program.

Listing C.9 *interface.c* **for the Scatter Plot Executable**

```c
/* DO NOT EDIT THIS FILE - it is generated by Glade.
 */

#ifdef HAVE_CONFIG_H
#  include <config.h>
#endif

#include <sys/types.h>
#include <sys/stat.h>
#include <unistd.h>
#include <string.h>

#include <gdk/gdkkeysyms.h>
#include <gtk/gtk.h>

#include "callbacks.h"
#include "interface.h"
#include "support.h"

GtkWidget*
create_frm_scatter (void)
{
  GtkWidget *frm_scatter;
  GtkWidget *vbox1;
  GtkWidget *hbox1;
  GtkWidget *label1;
  GtkWidget *cbo_horizontal;
  GList *cbo_horizontal_items = NULL;
  GtkWidget *combo_entry1;
  GtkWidget *label2;
  GtkWidget *cbo_vertical;
  GList *cbo_vertical_items = NULL;
  GtkWidget *combo_entry2;
  GtkWidget *cmd_redraw;
  GtkWidget *drawingarea1;
  GtkWidget *statusbar1;

  frm_scatter = gtk_window_new (GTK_WINDOW_TOPLEVEL);
  gtk_object_set_data (GTK_OBJECT (frm_scatter), "frm_scatter", frm_scatter);
  gtk_window_set_title (GTK_WINDOW (frm_scatter), "Numeric Correlation - Revenue
⮞Data");
  gtk_window_set_default_size (GTK_WINDOW (frm_scatter), 900, 650);

  vbox1 = gtk_vbox_new (FALSE, 0);
  gtk_widget_ref (vbox1);
  gtk_object_set_data_full (GTK_OBJECT (frm_scatter), "vbox1", vbox1,
                            (GtkDestroyNotify) gtk_widget_unref);
  gtk_widget_show (vbox1);
```

```
gtk_container_add (GTK_CONTAINER (frm_scatter), vbox1);

hbox1 = gtk_hbox_new (FALSE, 35);
gtk_widget_ref (hbox1);
gtk_object_set_data_full (GTK_OBJECT (frm_scatter), "hbox1", hbox1,
                          (GtkDestroyNotify) gtk_widget_unref);
gtk_widget_show (hbox1);
gtk_box_pack_start (GTK_BOX (vbox1), hbox1, FALSE, TRUE, 0);
gtk_container_set_border_width (GTK_CONTAINER (hbox1), 19);

label1 = gtk_label_new ("Horizontal Axis:");
gtk_widget_ref (label1);
gtk_object_set_data_full (GTK_OBJECT (frm_scatter), "label1", label1,
                          (GtkDestroyNotify) gtk_widget_unref);
gtk_widget_show (label1);
gtk_box_pack_start (GTK_BOX (hbox1), label1, FALSE, FALSE, 0);

cbo_horizontal = gtk_combo_new ();
gtk_widget_ref (cbo_horizontal);
gtk_object_set_data_full (GTK_OBJECT (frm_scatter), "cbo_horizontal",
➥cbo_horizontal,
                          (GtkDestroyNotify) gtk_widget_unref);
gtk_widget_show (cbo_horizontal);
gtk_box_pack_start (GTK_BOX (hbox1), cbo_horizontal, TRUE, TRUE, 0);
cbo_horizontal_items = g_list_append (cbo_horizontal_items, "Unit Price");
cbo_horizontal_items = g_list_append (cbo_horizontal_items, "Net Value");
cbo_horizontal_items = g_list_append (cbo_horizontal_items, "Invoice Quantity");
cbo_horizontal_items = g_list_append (cbo_horizontal_items, "Invoice Value");
cbo_horizontal_items = g_list_append (cbo_horizontal_items, "Order Quantity");
gtk_combo_set_popdown_strings (GTK_COMBO (cbo_horizontal),
➥cbo_horizontal_items);
g_list_free (cbo_horizontal_items);

combo_entry1 = GTK_COMBO (cbo_horizontal)->entry;
gtk_widget_ref (combo_entry1);
gtk_object_set_data_full (GTK_OBJECT (frm_scatter), "combo_entry1",
➥combo_entry1,
                          (GtkDestroyNotify) gtk_widget_unref);
gtk_widget_show (combo_entry1);
gtk_entry_set_text (GTK_ENTRY (combo_entry1), "Unit Price");

label2 = gtk_label_new ("Vertical Axis");
gtk_widget_ref (label2);
gtk_object_set_data_full (GTK_OBJECT (frm_scatter), "label2", label2,
                          (GtkDestroyNotify) gtk_widget_unref);
gtk_widget_show (label2);
gtk_box_pack_start (GTK_BOX (hbox1), label2, FALSE, FALSE, 0);

cbo_vertical = gtk_combo_new ();
gtk_widget_ref (cbo_vertical);
gtk_object_set_data_full (GTK_OBJECT (frm_scatter), "cbo_vertical", cbo_vertical,
```

continues

Listing C.9 **Continued**

```
                              (GtkDestroyNotify) gtk_widget_unref);
gtk_widget_show (cbo_vertical);
gtk_box_pack_start (GTK_BOX (hbox1), cbo_vertical, TRUE, TRUE, 0);
cbo_vertical_items = g_list_append (cbo_vertical_items, "Order Quantity");
cbo_vertical_items = g_list_append (cbo_vertical_items, "Unit Price");
cbo_vertical_items = g_list_append (cbo_vertical_items, "Net Value");
cbo_vertical_items = g_list_append (cbo_vertical_items, "Invoice Quantity");
cbo_vertical_items = g_list_append (cbo_vertical_items, "Invoice Value");
gtk_combo_set_popdown_strings (GTK_COMBO (cbo_vertical), cbo_vertical_items);
g_list_free (cbo_vertical_items);

combo_entry2 = GTK_COMBO (cbo_vertical)->entry;
gtk_widget_ref (combo_entry2);
gtk_object_set_data_full (GTK_OBJECT (frm_scatter), "combo_entry2",
➥combo_entry2,
                              (GtkDestroyNotify) gtk_widget_unref);
gtk_widget_show (combo_entry2);
gtk_entry_set_text (GTK_ENTRY (combo_entry2), "Order Quantity");

cmd_redraw = gtk_button_new_with_label ("Redraw");
gtk_widget_ref (cmd_redraw);
gtk_object_set_data_full (GTK_OBJECT (frm_scatter), "cmd_redraw", cmd_redraw,
                              (GtkDestroyNotify) gtk_widget_unref);
gtk_widget_show (cmd_redraw);
gtk_box_pack_start (GTK_BOX (hbox1), cmd_redraw, TRUE, TRUE, 0);

drawingarea1 = gtk_drawing_area_new ();
gtk_widget_ref (drawingarea1);
gtk_object_set_data_full (GTK_OBJECT (frm_scatter), "drawingarea1",
➥drawingarea1,
                              (GtkDestroyNotify) gtk_widget_unref);
gtk_widget_show (drawingarea1);
gtk_box_pack_start (GTK_BOX (vbox1), drawingarea1, TRUE, TRUE, 0);

statusbar1 = gtk_statusbar_new ();
gtk_widget_ref (statusbar1);
gtk_object_set_data_full (GTK_OBJECT (frm_scatter), "statusbar1", statusbar1,
                              (GtkDestroyNotify) gtk_widget_unref);
gtk_widget_show (statusbar1);
gtk_box_pack_start (GTK_BOX (vbox1), statusbar1, FALSE, FALSE, 0);

gtk_signal_connect (GTK_OBJECT (frm_scatter), "delete_event",
                       GTK_SIGNAL_FUNC (on_frm_scatter_delete_event),
                       NULL);
gtk_signal_connect (GTK_OBJECT (frm_scatter), "show",
                       GTK_SIGNAL_FUNC (on_frm_scatter_show),
                       NULL);
gtk_signal_connect (GTK_OBJECT (frm_scatter), "event",
                       GTK_SIGNAL_FUNC (on_frm_scatter_event),
```

```
                            NULL);
    gtk_signal_connect (GTK_OBJECT (cmd_redraw), "clicked",
                        GTK_SIGNAL_FUNC (on_cmd_redraw_clicked),
                        NULL);
    gtk_signal_connect (GTK_OBJECT (drawingarea1), "event",
                        GTK_SIGNAL_FUNC (on_drawingarea1_event),
                        NULL);

    return frm_scatter;
}
```

scatter.glade

Listing C.10 is the Glade project file for the scatter program in XML format.

Listing C.10 Glade XML File for the Scatter Executable

```
<?xml version="1.0"?>
<GTK-Interface>

<project>
  <name>scatter</name>
  <program_name>scatter</program_name>
  <directory></directory>
  <source_directory>src</source_directory>
  <pixmaps_directory>pixmaps</pixmaps_directory>
  <language>C</language>
  <gnome_support>False</gnome_support>
  <gettext_support>False</gettext_support>
  <use_widget_names>False</use_widget_names>
  <output_main_file>True</output_main_file>
  <output_support_files>True</output_support_files>
  <output_build_files>True</output_build_files>
  <backup_source_files>True</backup_source_files>
  <main_source_file>interface.c</main_source_file>
  <main_header_file>interface.h</main_header_file>
  <handler_source_file>callbacks.c</handler_source_file>
  <handler_header_file>callbacks.h</handler_header_file>
  <support_source_file>support.c</support_source_file>
  <support_header_file>support.h</support_header_file>
  <translatable_strings_file></translatable_strings_file>
</project>

<widget>
  <class>GtkWindow</class>
  <name>frm_scatter</name>
  <signal>
    <name>delete_event</name>
    <handler>on_frm_scatter_delete_event</handler>
```

continues

Listing C.10 **Continued**

```
    <last_modification_time>Sun, 25 Feb 2001 22:05:08 GMT</last_modification_time>
  </signal>
  <signal>
    <name>show</name>
    <handler>on_frm_scatter_show</handler>
    <last_modification_time>Sun, 25 Feb 2001 22:05:18 GMT</last_modification_time>
  </signal>
  <signal>
    <name>event</name>
    <handler>on_frm_scatter_event</handler>
    <last_modification_time>Tue, 27 Feb 2001 20:34:23 GMT</last_modification_time>
  </signal>
  <title>Numeric Correlation - Revenue Data</title>
  <type>GTK_WINDOW_TOPLEVEL</type>
  <position>GTK_WIN_POS_NONE</position>
  <modal>False</modal>
  <default_width>900</default_width>
  <default_height>650</default_height>
  <allow_shrink>False</allow_shrink>
  <allow_grow>True</allow_grow>
  <auto_shrink>False</auto_shrink>

  <widget>
    <class>GtkVBox</class>
    <name>vbox1</name>
    <homogeneous>False</homogeneous>
    <spacing>0</spacing>

    <widget>
      <class>GtkHBox</class>
      <name>hbox1</name>
      <border_width>19</border_width>
      <homogeneous>False</homogeneous>
      <spacing>35</spacing>
      <child>
      <padding>0</padding>
      <expand>False</expand>
      <fill>True</fill>
      </child>

      <widget>
      <class>GtkLabel</class>
      <name>label1</name>
      <label>Horizontal Axis:</label>
      <justify>GTK_JUSTIFY_CENTER</justify>
      <wrap>False</wrap>
      <xalign>0.5</xalign>
      <yalign>0.5</yalign>
      <xpad>0</xpad>
```

```xml
<ypad>0</ypad>
<child>
  <padding>0</padding>
  <expand>False</expand>
  <fill>False</fill>
</child>
</widget>

<widget>
<class>GtkCombo</class>
<name>cbo_horizontal</name>
<value_in_list>False</value_in_list>
<ok_if_empty>True</ok_if_empty>
<case_sensitive>False</case_sensitive>
<use_arrows>True</use_arrows>
<use_arrows_always>False</use_arrows_always>
<items>Unit Price
Net Value
Invoice Quantity
Invoice Value
Order Quantity
</items>
<child>
  <padding>0</padding>
  <expand>True</expand>
  <fill>True</fill>
</child>

<widget>
  <class>GtkEntry</class>
  <child_name>GtkCombo:entry</child_name>
  <name>combo-entry1</name>
  <can_focus>True</can_focus>
  <editable>True</editable>
  <text_visible>True</text_visible>
  <text_max_length>0</text_max_length>
  <text>Unit Price</text>
</widget>
</widget>

<widget>
<class>GtkLabel</class>
<name>label2</name>
<label>Vertical Axis</label>
<justify>GTK_JUSTIFY_CENTER</justify>
<wrap>False</wrap>
<xalign>0.5</xalign>
<yalign>0.5</yalign>
<xpad>0</xpad>
<ypad>0</ypad>
<child>
```

continues

Listing C.10 **Continued**

```
    <padding>0</padding>
    <expand>False</expand>
    <fill>False</fill>
</child>
</widget>

<widget>
<class>GtkCombo</class>
<name>cbo_vertical</name>
<value_in_list>False</value_in_list>
<ok_if_empty>True</ok_if_empty>
<case_sensitive>False</case_sensitive>
<use_arrows>True</use_arrows>
<use_arrows_always>False</use_arrows_always>
<items>Order Quantity
Unit Price
Net Value
Invoice Quantity
Invoice Value
</items>
    <child>
        <padding>0</padding>
        <expand>True</expand>
        <fill>True</fill>
    </child>

    <widget>
      <class>GtkEntry</class>
      <child_name>GtkCombo:entry</child_name>
      <name>combo-entry2</name>
      <can_focus>True</can_focus>
      <editable>True</editable>
      <text_visible>True</text_visible>
      <text_max_length>0</text_max_length>
      <text>Order Quantity</text>
    </widget>
    </widget>

    <widget>
    <class>GtkButton</class>
    <name>cmd_redraw</name>
    <can_focus>True</can_focus>
    <signal>
      <name>clicked</name>
      <handler>on_cmd_redraw_clicked</handler>
      <last_modification_time>Sun, 25 Feb 2001 22:05:39
      ➥GMT</last_modification_time>
    </signal>
    <label>Redraw</label>
```

```
      <child>
        <padding>0</padding>
        <expand>True</expand>
        <fill>True</fill>
      </child>
      </widget>
    </widget>

    <widget>
      <class>GtkDrawingArea</class>
      <name>drawingarea1</name>
      <signal>
      <name>event</name>
      <handler>on_drawingarea1_event</handler>
      <last_modification_time>Sun, 25 Feb 2001 22:05:53
      ↪GMT</last_modification_time>
      </signal>
      <child>
      <padding>0</padding>
      <expand>True</expand>
      <fill>True</fill>
      </child>
    </widget>

    <widget>
      <class>GtkStatusbar</class>
      <name>statusbar1</name>
      <child>
      <padding>0</padding>
      <expand>False</expand>
      <fill>False</fill>
      </child>
    </widget>
  </widget>
</widget>

</GTK-Interface>
```

Index

Symbols

A

B

C

H

I

U

V

W

X-Z

HOW TO CONTACT US

VOICES THAT MATTER

VISIT OUR WEB SITE

WWW.NEWRIDERS.COM

On our web site, you'll find information about our other books, authors, tables of contents, and book errata. You will also find information about book registration and how to purchase our books, both domestically and internationally.

EMAIL US

Contact us at: **nrfeedback@newriders.com**

- If you have comments or questions about this book
- To report errors that you have found in this book
- If you have a book proposal to submit or are interested in writing for New Riders
- If you are an expert in a computer topic or technology and are interested in being a technical editor who reviews manuscripts for technical accuracy

Contact us at: **nreducation@newriders.com**

- If you are an instructor from an educational institution who wants to preview New Riders books for classroom use. Email should include your name, title, school, department, address, phone number, office days/hours, text in use, and enrollment, along with your request for desk/examination copies and/or additional information.

Contact us at: **nrmedia@newriders.com**

- If you are a member of the media who is interested in reviewing copies of New Riders books. Send your name, mailing address, and email address, along with the name of the publication or web site you work for.

BULK PURCHASES/CORPORATE SALES

If you are interested in buying 10 or more copies of a title or want to set up an account for your company to purchase directly from the publisher at a substantial discount, contact us at 800-382-3419 or email your contact information to corpsales@pearsontechgroup.com. A sales representative will contact you with more information.

WRITE TO US

New Riders Publishing
201 W. 103rd St.
Indianapolis, IN 46290-1097

CALL/FAX US

Toll-free (800) 571-5840
If outside U.S. (317) 581-3500
Ask for New Riders
FAX: (317) 581-4663

New Riders

RELATED NEW RIDERS TITLES

ISBN: 0735709211
800 pages
US $49.99

MySQL

Paul DuBois

MySQL teaches readers how to use the tools provided by the MySQL distribution, by covering installation, setup, daily use, security, optimization, maintenance, and troubleshooting. It also discusses important third-party tools, such as the Perl DBI and Apache/PHP interfaces that provide access to MySQL.

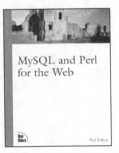

ISBN: 0735710546
500 pages
US $44.99

MySQL and Perl for the Web

Paul DuBois

This book teaches readers the best method for providing information services through the use of Perl, MySQL, and the web; a powerful system when combined.

MySQL and Perl for the Web focuses on Perl scripting combined with the MySQL database because the combination is an important one that has not been adequately documented even though it is one of the more robust systems available today. This book covers how to put a database on the web, related performance issues, form processing, searching abilities, security, common e-commerce tasks, XML, and more.

ISBN 073570970X
500 pages
US $44.99

PHP Functions Essential Reference

The *PHP Functions Essential Reference* is a simple, clear and authoritative function reference that clarifies and expands upon PHP's existing documentation. This book will help the reader write effective code that makes full use of the rich variety of functions available in PHP.

ISBN 0735710910
416 pages
US $34.99

ISBN: 0735710430
368 pages
US $45.00

Python Essential Reference, Second Edition

David Beazley

Python Essential Reference, Second Edition, concisely describes the Python programming language and its large library of standard modules—collectively known as the Python programming environment. It is arranged into four major parts. First, a brief tutorial and introduction is presented, then an informal language reference covers lexical conventions, functions, statements, control flow, datatypes, classes, and execution models. The third section covers the Python library, and the final section covers the Python C API that is used to write Python extensions. This book is highly focused and clearly provides the things a reader needs to know to best utilize Python.

Advanced Linux Programming

CodeSourcery, LLC

An in-depth guide to programming Linux from the most recognized leaders in the Open Source community, this book is the ideal reference for Linux programmers who are reasonably skilled in the C programming language and who are in need of a book that covers the Linux C library (glibc).

Solutions from experts you know and trust.

www.informit.com

New Riders has partnered with **InformIT.com** to bring technical information to your desktop. Drawing on New Riders authors and reviewers to provide additional information on topics you're interested in, **InformIT.com** has free, in-depth information you won't find anywhere else.

- **Master the skills you need, when you need them**

- **Call on resources from some of the best minds in the industry**

- **Get answers when you need them, using InformIT's comprehensive library or live experts online**

- **Go above and beyond what you find in New Riders books, extending your knowledge**

As an **InformIT** partner, **New Riders** has shared the wisdom and knowledge of our authors with you online. Visit **InformIT.com** to see what you're missing.

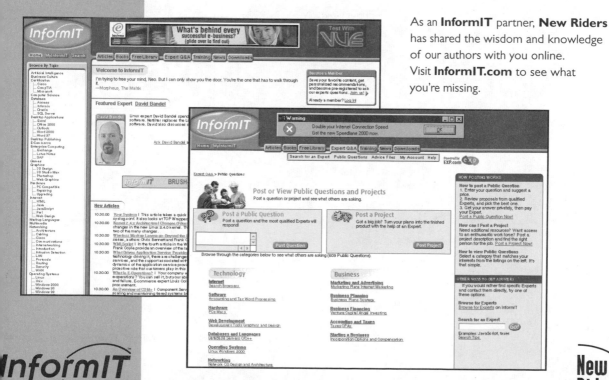

www.informit.com ■ www.newriders.com

New Riders

Colophon

The image on the cover of this book, captured by photographer Kim Steele, is that of the Propylea Gate of the Acropolis in Athens, Greece. Designed by the renowned architect, Mnesicles, between 437 BC and 432 BC, this roofed structure was the entrance to the sacred areas of the Acropolis.

This book was written and edited in Microsoft Word, and laid out in QuarkXPress. The fonts used for the body text are Bembo and MCPdigital. It was printed on 50# Husky Offset Smooth paper at R.R. Donnelley & Sons in Crawfordsville, Indiana. Prepress consisted of PostScript computer-to-plate technology (filmless process). The cover was printed at Moore Langen Printing in Terre Haute, Indiana, on Carolina, coated on one side.